Development of the Child

Development of the Child

DAVID ELKIND
University of Rochester

IRVING B. WEINER
Case Western Reserve University

JOHN WILEY & SONS, INC.
New York   Santa Barbara   Chichester   Brisbane   Toronto

Library of Congress Cataloging in Publication Data

Elkind, David, 1931
Development of the child.

Includes bibliographies and index.
1. Child development. I. Weiner, Irving B., joint author. II. Title.

HQ767.9.E37   301.43′1   77-14214
ISBN 0-471-23785-X

Printed in the United States of America

10 9 8 7 6 5 4 3

Preface

This book presents a comprehensive survey of how children grow and develop. It is comprehensive in three respects: first, it covers the development of the child from the prenatal period through adolescence; second, it deals not only with typical patterns of development but also with variations related to individual and group differences and with abnormal development; third, it addresses both the known facts about child development, as indicated by available research, and important theoretical, methodological, and practical issues in child study.

We begin with a chapter on history and methods in the study of child development followed by a chapter on the prenatal period. The remainder of the text is organized into units on infancy, the preschool years, middle childhood, and adolescence, and each of these units contains chapters on physical and mental growth, personality and social development, individual and group variations, and abnormal development.

This organization combines sequential and topical approaches to the study of child development and allows considerable flexibility in how the book can be used. Those who want to begin with a comprehensive, integrated understanding of infancy before moving on to the preschool years, for example, would read Chapter 3, 4, 5, and 6 in sequence; those wishing to learn about physical and mental growth from infancy through adolescence before turning to other topics would start with Chapters 3, 7, 11, and 15. We have tried to prepare the individual chapters so that they flow smoothly whether used sequentially or topically.

In our coverage we have given considerably more weight to individual and group variations (particularly as these are revealed in cross-cultural studies) than is usual in introductory texts on child development. This emphasis reflects our belief that such variations are an essential part of child development theory and research and a necessary if not indispensable counterpart to purely normative studies of the "average" child. The study of individual and group variations is a useful safeguard against facile generalizations about the "nature" of children.

We have also devoted more space than is customary to abnormal development. This coverage is warranted by the amount of research on abnormal development being conducted by child specialists. In addition, we attach great importance to placing childrens' abnormalities in the general context of human development rather than considering them in isolation. For example, we feel strongly that the growth and significance of intelligence cannot be fully understood without some knowledge of mental retardation and, conversely, that the nature and implications of mental retardation cannot be fully grasped except in the light of general knowledge about intellectual functioning. We have accordingly attempted to give students an integrated perspective from which to view both normal and abnormal development. This effort seems particularly appropriate today, when the educational and training needs of exceptional and handicapped children are finally receiving the national attention and support they deserve.

Within each of the individual chapters we have tried to reflect as accurately as possible the breadth of both investigation and theory in the study of child development. The field includes experimental studies of how children grow, learn, think, feel, and act; and it also includes applied studies of how children respond to various child-rearing, educational, social, and psychotherapeutic practices. As for theory, some child specialists are sympathetic to a behavioral or social learning point of view that stresses environmental control of behavior; others are more comfortable with a cognitive or ethological orientation that emphasizes the relatively spontaneous emergence of self-regulating potentials in children; and many others hold positions either in between or more extreme than these two.

To reflect this empirical and theoretical diversity, we have included up-to-date accounts of basic and applied research in all aspects of child development. Our special attention to language, memory, attachment, prosocial behavior, sex differences, mental retardation, and juvenile delinquency is in keeping with the attention currently being paid these topics by workers in the field. In addition, to go beyond the concepts and research results discussed in Chapters 3 through 18, we have added to each of these chapters a topical essay on practical application. We believe students should get some sense of how knowledge about children is translated into prescriptions for social action. The topics we have chosen for these essays—such as day care, early childhood education, the impact of television on aggressive behavior, the use of stimulant drugs with hyperactive children, the feminized classroom, and learning to read—are of interest in their own right and will also make students sensitive to current political and social controversies that affect children.

With respect to theoretical orientation, our primary concern has been to present the facts and issues rather than to attempt to fit them within any single frame of reference. The studies of researchers and writers of many different persuasions are drawn on for their contribution to knowledge; as a result we feel that students and instructors with a wide range of theoretical preferences will find the text compatible with their needs. When we do pay special attention to a particular conceptual approach—as we do in considering Piaget-related research on cognitive development and Erikson-related research on identity formation—our decision simply acknowledges the very great impact these people have had on the particular area of investigation.

In this vein, we have included eight brief biographies. In reading about a psychologist's theories or research, students often wonder about the kind of person who did the work. From the leading child development workers of today and of the past, we have tried to select individuals who have made major contributions in the different areas we have touched on in the book. We hope that these brief biographies will give students a sense of the people behind the references.

The last, but by no means the least, thing that needs to be said about the contents of the book concerns the matter of sexist language and sex-role stereotyping. We believe strongly that it is important to avoid sexist language even at the risk of awkward writing at times. On the other hand, now that we have become sensitive to the issue we find in our own reading that we are distracted by the exclusive use of male pronouns. Apparently, the use of certain pronouns is simply a habit that can easily be overcome. In addition, we have tried, throughout the book, to present sex differences along with a discussion of possible causation. To avoid discussion of causation leaves the impression that differences are genetic. We hope, therefore, in our own small way to contribute to the discarding of sexist language and to the elimination of false and/or misleading sex-role stereotyping.

The accompanying *Study Guide,* by Jerome S. Meyer, offers a wide variety of aids for comprehending the materials of the text: overviews of each chapter; chapter objectives; lists of key concepts and names; a diverse array of review questions (fill-in sentences, multiple-choice questions, problem questions, on key concepts, content review questions) — all cross referenced to the text; and a distinctive set of case studies with direct applications to the chapters.

Writing a textbook such as this one requires the help and cooperation of a good many people. We are particularly indebted to our secretaries, Nancy Popoff and Marilyn Hogle, for patience, good humor, and genuine help in the writing. Our wives and children, too, were most patient and understanding when we had to forego some of the usual joint family activities in favor of working on the manuscript. Charlotte Allstrom, the depth editor, worked hard to smooth our writing and eliminate jargon. Stella Kupferberg and Ron Nelson helped select and clarify tables, figures, and illustrations, and we are most thankful to them for the very fine visual materials in the book. And Debbie Wiley, who saw the book through, from the time when it was hardly more than fingerprints on cold beer glasses at a convention to its present finished state, is especially deserving of our thanks for her continued support and encouragement.

It seems fitting to end this list of acknowledgements with the names of the child development professionals who reviewed the book at many different points along the way. Their thoughtful suggestions and concerns helped us to better adapt the material to the needs of students. We are most grateful to the following people: Dr. Irvin J. Badin; Dr. L. DeMoyne

Bekker; Dr. Thomas Berndt; Dr. Larry Fenson; Dr. Norejane J. Hendrickson; Dr. Richard La Barba; Dr. John McKinney; Dr. Pat Miller; Dr. Victoria Moltese; Dr. Marion H. Typpo; Dr. Frances Whaley; and Dr. Gerald Winer.

DAVID ELKIND
IRVING B. WEINER

Contents

PART 1
INTRODUCTION

1   History and Methods   3
   Antecedents   4
   History: Origins of the Cognition and Language Study; Tradition in
      Child Psychology; Origins of the Clinical, Social, and Personality;
      Study Tradition in Child Psychology; Child Development between
      the Two World Wars and after; Current Research Areas in Develop-
      mental Psychology   9
   Methods: Correlative Methods; Causative Methods; Differential
      Methods   18
   Summary   30
   References   31

2   Prenatal Growth and Pregnancy   35
   Prenatal Growth: Gametes and Genes; Embryonic Development   36
   Pregnancy: Pregnancy as a Life Crisis; Maternal-Fetal Interactions;
      Labor and Delivery   49
   Summary   61
   References   62

PART 2
INFANCY

3   Physical and Mental Growth   67
   Principles of Physical Growth: Direction of Growth; Differentiation
      and Integration; The Sequence of Development   68
   Physical Development During the First Two Years of Life: Infancy: The
      First Year; Infancy: The Second Year   71
   Mental Growth: Quantitative Aspects of Mental Growth; Qualitative
      Aspects of Mental Growth; Perception; Language; Cognitive
      Processes   77
   Essay: Parent Education and Infant Stimulation   101
   Biography: Jean Piaget   102
   Summary   104
   References   106

4   Personality and Social Development   113
   Signaling and Orienting Behaviors: Crying; Gazing; Smiling; Babbling;
      Imitation; Factors That Affect Signaling and Orienting
      Behaviors   114
   Attachments to People: Behaviors That Foster Attachment; Stranger
      Anxiety; Separation Anxiety   121
   Theories of the Origins of Interpersonal Attachments   127

Detachment and Individuation: The Beginnings of Individuation; Maternal Responses to Individuation   129
Attitudes toward the World: Infants' Influences on the Care They Receive; Implications for Child Rearing; Short-Term and Long-Term Effects of Infant-Care Practices   131
Essay: On the Care and Spoiling of Infants   136
Biography: John Bowlby   136
Summary   137
References   139

5   Infant Variations   147
Genetic Endowment   148
The Genetic Contribution of IQ and Temperamental Traits   150
Nutrition: Malnutrition; Obesity   155
Sex Differences   159
Social Class   161
Family Constellation and Home Environment: Birth Order; Home Environment; Intervention Program; Reversibility of Early Deprivation   162
Cultural Differences: Latin America and the Caribbean; Europe; Africa; Japan; India; Israel   169
Essay: Daycare   174
Summary   177
References   178

6   Abnormal Development   183
Identifying and Classifying Abnormal Behavior   184
Mental Retardation: Categories of Mental Retardation; Causes of Mental Retardation   185
Infantile Autism: Characteristics of Infantile Autism; Origins of Infantile Autism; Outcome and Treatment   193
Social Isolation Syndromes: The Nature of Social Isolation Syndromes; Recovery from Social Isolation Syndromes   196
Essay: Special or Regular Classes for the Mildly Retarded?   199
Summary   201
References   202

PART 3
PRESCHOOL
YEARS

7   Physical and Mental Growth   211
Physical Growth   212
Mental Growth: Assessment of Intelligence; Perceptual Development; Memory; Discrimination Learning; Conservation Behavior; Language Development; Theories of Attainment; Referential Communication   219
The Conceptual World of the Young Child   242
Essay: Early Childhood Education   245
Biography: Maria Montessori   246

Summary   247
References   248

8   Personality and Social Development   255
Self-Awareness and Self-Attitudes: Awareness of the Body; Feelings of
  Mastery   256
Expanding Family and Social Relationships: Role of the Father; Rela-
  tionships with Siblings; Contacts with Peers   262
Socialization: Discipline; Identification   271
Essay: The Impact of Television on Aggressive and Altruistic Behavior
  in Children   284
Biography: Erik Erikson   287
Summary   290
References   292

9   Preschool Variations   299
Intelligence: The Contributions of Heredity and Environment: Group
  Differences in IQ; Patterns of Ability within Racial/Ethnic
  Groups   300
Sex Differences: Birth Order; Father Absence   307
Social and Cultural Differences: Social Class Differences in Language;
  Social and Cultural Variations in Reinforcement Styles; Child-Rear-
  ing Practices in Three Countries   314
Interventions at the Preschool Level   324
Essay: Life and Death: The Feelings and Concepts of Children   329
Summary   331
References   332

10   Abnormal Development   339
Minimal Brain Dysfunction (MBD): Manifestations of MBD; Maladap-
  tive Consequences of MBD; Causes of MBD; Treatment
  of MBD   340
Childhood Schizophrenia: Symptoms and Childhood Schizophrenia;
  The Origin of Schizophrenia; Prognosis and Treatment   347
Phobias and Rituals: Fears and Phobias; The Disposition to Early Child-
  hood Phobias; The Focus of Phobic Reactions; Routines and Rituals;
  Treatment   354
Essay: Stimulant Drugs for Hyperactive Children: A Blessing or a
  Curse?   359
Summary   362
References   363

PART 4
MIDDLE
CHILDHOOD
11   Physical and Mental Growth   373
Physical Growth: Motor Skills; Body Image   374
Mental Development: Academic Testing; Perceptual Development;
  Language Development; Memory; Conservation Behavior; Moral

Development 380
The Conceptual World of Childhood 401
Essay: Learning to Read 402
Biography: Alfred Binet 404
Summary 406
References 407

12 Personality and Social Development 413

Entry into School: Attitudes toward School; The Sense of Industry or Inferiority 414
Increasing Importance of the Peer Group: Self-Perceptions and Popularity; Individualism; Conformity, and Other Ways of Dealing with People; Feelings of Belonging or Alienation; Changes in the Structure of Peer-Group Relationships 427
Sex-Role Identity: Psychosexual "Latency" 434
Family Relations: Parental Adjustment to a School-Age Child; Reassessment of Parents by School-Age Children 438
Essay: The Feminized Classroom 441
Biography: Sigmund Freud 443
Summary 445
References 447

13 Child Variations 453

Cognitive Processes: School Achievement; Creativity; Cognitive Styles 454
Sex Differences: Sex Differences in Academic Achievement; Sex Differences in Cognitive Styles; Sex-Role Stereotyping 463
Family Configuration: Family Size, Intelligence, and Achievement; Maternal Employment 471
Ethnic-Group Differences: Academic Achievement in American Indian Children; Self-Esteem 474
Cultural Differences: Conservation Behavior; Cognitive Style; Pictorial Depth Perception 476
Essay: Curriculum-Disabled Children 479
Summary 481
References 482

14 Abnormal Development 489

Learning Disabilities: Effects of MBD on School Learning; Psychological Impact of Learning Disabilities; Treatment 490
School Phobia: Origins of School Phobia; Recognizing the Seriousness of School Phobia; Treatment 496
Other Neuroses: Conversion and Hypochondriasis; Depression; Habit Disturbances; Conduct Disorders; Treatment 502
Essay: Priorities in Mental Health Services for Children 512

Summary   514
References   516

PART 5
ADOLESCENCE

15   Physical and Mental Growth   525
Physical and Physiological Changes: Changes in Body Size and Con-
figuration; Development of Primary and Secondary Sex Character-
istics; The Secular Trend; Body Image and Self-Satisfaction   526
Mental Development: Test Intelligence; Formal Operational Thought
and Its Manifestations; Issues in Formal Operational Thought;
Affective Consequences of Formal Operational Thought   535
Essay: Implications of the Secular Trend   553
Biography: G. Stanley Hall   554
Summary   556
References   557

16   Personality and Social Development   563
Striving for Independence: Origins of Adolescent Independence-
Striving; Ambivalent Feelings about Adolescent Independence;
Patterns of Parental Authority   564
Progress toward Mature Social Relationships: Peer-Group Belonging-
ness; Heterosexual Interest and Dating; Sexuality, Security, and
Intimacy; Attitudes toward Parents   571
Integration of a Personal Identity: Identity Achievement and Identity
Crisis; Continuity in Personality Development   582
Sex Behavior: Incidence of Premarital Intercourse; Permissiveness and
Affection   588
Drug Use: Incidence of Drug Use; Reasons for Using Drugs; Differ-
ences between Groups of Drug Users and Nonusers   591
Essay: Two Myths: Adolescent Rebellion and the Generation Gap   597
Biography: Harry Stack Sullivan   599
Summary   601
References   603

17   Adolescent Variations   613
Physical Differences: Early and Late Maturation; Physique, Tempera-
ment, and Interpersonal Attractiveness   614
School-related Differences: Sex-Role Stereotyping in Secondary School;
Creativity in High School; The High-School Dropout   623
Sex Differences: Varying Patterns of Adolescent Development; Father
Absence and Adolescent Girls   629
Racial and Cultural Differences: Self-Concept among Black and White
Adolescents; Self-Concept Development in Other Cultures   639
Essay: From Ghetto School to College Campus; Discontinuities;
Continuities   642

Summary   644
References   645

18   Abnormal Development   651

Schizophrenia: Indications of Adolescent Schizophrenia; Outcome of
   Adolescent Schizophrenia   654
Depression and Suicidal Behavior: Basic Facts about Adolescent
   Suicidal Behavior; Origins of Adolescent Suicidal Behavior   656
Academic Underachievement: Sociocultural Reasons for Academic
   Underachievement; Psychological Reasons for Academic Under-
   achievement; Treatment   660
Delinquent Behavior: Incidence of Delinquency; Causes of Delin-
   quency; Intervention   666
Essay: On the Continuity of Normal and Abnormal Behavior   671
Summary   672
References   675

Glossary   681

Photo Credits   701

Name Index   703

Subject Index   721

1 History and Methods

ANTECEDENTS

HISTORY

Origins of the Cognition and Language Study
Tradition in Child Psychology

Origins of the Clinical, Social, and Personality
Study Tradition in Child Psychology

Child Development between the Two World Wars and after

Current Research Areas in Developmental Psychology

METHODS

Correlative Methods

Causative Methods

Differential Methods

SUMMARY

REFERENCES

The scientific study of children has a relatively short history—it is hardly more than a century old. But interest in how children are to be reared and educated dates back at least as far as the start of recorded history. In an Egyptian book written some 3500 years ago boys were instructed:

Be industrious, let your eyes be open lest you become a beggar; for the man that is idle cometh not to honor . . . before all things guard your speech, for a man's ruin lies in his tongue. (1)

And, in the Old Testament, parents were instructed:

Withhold not correction from the child for though thou beat him with the rod, he will not die. Thou beatest him with the rod, and wilt deliver his soul from the nether world. [Proverbs 23: 13–14]

Before turning to the history of child psychology itself, we need to look at some of its antecedents. Here the views of the moral and secular educators loom large because it was they, more than any other group, who formulated for their times the conception of childhood and who enunciated the principles of child rearing and of education.

ANTECEDENTS

Contemporary ideas regarding liberal or general education probably date back to Graeco-Roman times. In ancient Greece the concept of **liberal education** evolved gradually. It was liberal in the sense that it focused on the development of mind and body—on the development of the whole person, as we would say today. For the Greeks, the major aim of education was to train future citizens of the state while at the same time adapting educational measures to the nature of man. The basic organization of Greek education was described by Aristotle (2). Schooling was to last from birth to the age of 21. Formal education, however, was not commenced until the age of puberty. At that time reading, writing, and arithmetic were introduced as preparation for later studies, which included science, philosophy, and literature. Aristotle also put great store in the study of political science and psychology. Like Plato, Aristotle believed that engaging in these studies sharpened a young man's faculties. The belief that the study of certain subjects, such as Latin, would strengthen the mind (a doctrine called **formal discipline**) persists today.

Roman educational practice also evolved during the period of Rome's ascendance and decline but never fully incorporated the concept of liberal education as known in Greece. There was, for example, little concern with physical education such as gymnastics and dancing, which were an important part of Greek educational practice. The major aim of Roman education was the perfection of an orator—in Roman times conceived broadly as a well-educated man who was familiar with philosophy, law, literature, and so on. There was general agreement that, in Cato's words, an orator was a "good man skilled in speaking." (1)

The organization of Roman education was somewhat like that of Greek education. From about 7 to 12 children attended the *ludus* or elementary school, where they learned reading, writing, and arithmetic and some aspects of Roman Law. Beginning close to the age of 12, boys attended a grammar school for about four years. During this period they were exposed to a broad survey of prose writing, poetry, and drama. There was also instruction in history, geography, and mythology. The curriculum of the Roman grammar school came closest to the Grecian concept of a liberal education.

After completion of the grammar school, a Roman youth entered the *rhetorical school* at about the age of sixteen. It was here that he studied the techniques of oratory; the major subjects were oratorical theory and declamation. Now the young men were encouraged to use all they had learned in the grammar school to good purpose in debates and declamations that were largely concerned with various facets of public life. Toward the end of the Roman empire, the rhetorical school became more formalized—there were rules for all aspects of oratory, including gestures and facial expressions. For the Romans, oratory was regarded as the principal skill required by a citizen living in a free society. (1)

With the decline of Graeco-Roman civilization and the rise of Christianity, new educational aims and methods came to the fore. Whereas in Greece and Rome the state was regarded as the most important social institution, in medieval times the Church came to vie with the state as the supreme social institution. The Church had its own courts, prisons, and property. Moreover, it controlled both secular and religious education. The Church generally prevailed over the state because it was widely believed that while the state was created by man, ecclesiastical power came from God. When, beginning in the twelfth century, city-states progressively increased their power, the Church gradually lost its hold on the citizenry, and this marked the beginning of the end of the medieval period.

When the Church was the major social institution, education had a very different aim than in Graeco-Roman times. Basically, the major purpose of education during this period in history was to prepare a man for the service of God, the Church, his fellows, and his soul. With few exceptions, the Greek concept of a liberal education found no place in medieval thinking. The Church aimed at neither the free citizen nor the orator. Rather it sought to produce a man of modest and meek character who would subordinate himself to the authority of the Church. Religious training to produce such men was the preparation for all positions and professions, both civil and ecclesiastical. (1)

The organization of schooling during medieval times was loose and diversified. The parallel to the *ludus* of Roman times was the *cathedral school* where children learned reading and writing, memorization of psalms, and some basic arithmetic. The language of instruction was Latin, and students often learned to read Latin without understanding it. At the secondary level, students learned the "seven liberal arts," but these were taught as preparation for the study and interpretation of the Holy Scripture. The seven liberal arts were: grammar, rhetoric, and dialectic (the so-called lower studies) and arithmetic, geometry, music, and astronomy (the so-called higher studies). The source of study for these subjects was one or another encyclopedia containing many Greek and Roman ideas regarding the liberal arts.

It should be said that the medieval concept of man as moral and religious being colored education in ways other than its basic organization. The physical body was regarded as sinful and the source of lustful wishes, hence its cultivation by exercise, dance, and gymnastics was to be shunned. Individual desires had to be curbed and disciplined, and obedience to divine authority had to be instilled. Many of the educational methods of these times were devised with the aim of teaching moral, mental, and religious discipline. Education was as much in the service of the life hereafter as it was for life in the immediate world. (1)

During the Age of Enlightenment and with the decline of Church authority, philosophers re-examined the human condition; they looked to nature, rather than to authority, for knowledge. The first great educator and child psychologist of the Enlightenment was Jan Amos Comenius (1592–1670). He was born in what is now Czechoslovakia, but traveled all over Europe and wrote prodigiously. He argued that the purpose of education was to prepare children for happiness in this life and not in the next, and he felt girls as well as boys should be educated. In his view, a mother was a child's first teacher and thus had the responsibility of teaching the concept of right and wrong.

Comenius believed that at the age of 6 the child should enter *vernacular school*—so called because the teaching was in the native tongue rather than in Greek or Latin, as had been the custom since ancient times. At the vernacular school, the child would learn the three Rs; basic religious concepts such as the creation and man's fall and redemption; and something about astronomy, geography, the trades, medicine, law and currency. Comenius advocated compulsory schooling until the age of 12. At that time the majority of children would find their place in the larger society, but a small number of boys would be selected to attend an institute of higher learning called the "Latin school." After that would come the university, with its broader academic offerings. In effect Comenius gave us our contemporary "ladder" of education from grammar school through high school (the expanded Latin school) to the university.

Although Comenius advocated universal education, much of the writing about education for the next two centuries focused on the children of the well-to-do. Both John Locke (1632–1704) and Jean-Jacques Rousseau (1712–1778) discussed the proper preparation of a boy for a "gentleman's calling." Locke believed that education should emphasize "a sound mind in a sound body" and suggested a Spartan regime for youngsters who were to be taught to be "obedient to discipline and pliable to reason." Locke believed that a child's mind was a *tabula rasa,* a blank tablet upon which experience writes, thereby determining the child's future. Clearly, exposure to beneficial experiences was extremely important.

A somewhat different approach to education was suggested by Rousseau. As a result of his experiences as a tutor, this famous philosopher came to some radical conclusions about education, which he presented in his well-known book *Émile* (3). Here Rousseau laid down the basic tenets of what has now come to be known as progressive (or child-centered) education. Rousseau felt that education should adapt itself to the needs and abilities of children and not simply reflect adult priorities. He argued for education based upon experience: "Never substitute the word for the thing itself, except when it is impossible to show the thing. . . . We give too much power to words. . . . Let all the lessons of young people take the form of doing rather than talking." These and other maxims of Rousseau have been urged by educators for several centuries, but they are not often heard (or listened to) even today.

In a sense, Rousseau was the first child psychologist. He observed children carefully, noted how they behaved and learned, and tried to adapt education to the child's level of development. Later, well-known educators followed this model and were child naturalists as much as educators. Unfortunately this combination of child psychologist–educator was lost when child psychology became a separate discipline. However, with the influence of famed Swiss psychologist Jean Piaget's work since the 1960s, closer links have become established between child development and education (see, for example, references 4–6).

The next noted educator, from Switzerland, was Johann Heinrich Pestalozzi (1746–1827); he founded several schools that were child-centered (his inspiration was Rousseau's *Émile*). Pestalozzi wrote a novel, *Leonard and Gertrude*, which told the romantic story of how a wife saved her husband from alcohol and her community from perdition. Interspersed throughout were a number of educational maxims that won Pestalozzi international acclaim. But his efforts to apply child-centered principles in his schools came to naught. He was a poor manager; that as well as bad luck made his schools, if not his ideas, short-lived.

In the school that he founded at Yverdon, Pestalozzi created the forerunner of modern elementary schools. Although it was a boarding school with a rigorous schedule, it also had flexibility and freedom. Since Pestalozzi believed that the school should be continuous with the home and community, the children had a scheduled rest period every afternoon. Pestalozzi also arranged for the children to have their more difficult subjects in the morning, when they were usually brighter and more alert, while keeping such lighter subjects as music, drawing, fencing, and handicrafts for the afternoon. The school at Yverdon received international attention and became a model for educational innovation.

Pestalozzi utilized Rousseau's idea that children should be taught by experience and not by rote. He would take specific objects and ask the children questions about them in order to help them to gain maximum benefit from what they had seen. Pestalozzi carried out these "object lessons" in a way that sparked the creative spirit of children. For example, he had children observe and classify plants. But in the hands of others who were less skilled the lessons became little more than a variant of the rote-learning procedures of old.

One of Pestalozzi's notable students was Friedrich Wilhelm Froebel (1782–1852), who was of German background. Because of a troubled childhood and youth, Froebel did not find his calling as a teacher and educator until he was close to 30. Like Pestalozzi, Froebel established a number of schools, several of which failed. The last one he founded, in Blankenburg, Germany, had a long name that was eventually shortened to *kindergarten,* and it is as the founder of the kindergarten movement that Froebel is best known.

Many of Froebel's ideas are quite contemporary more than a century after his death. For example, he believed that play was an important educational experience; he even wrote songs that mothers could sing and games that they could play with their children. This kind of parent–child interaction is being encouraged today by parent-education programs. A deeply religious man, Froebel believed in the essential goodness of children and the unity of the individual and the godhead. He believed that a very simple experience could lead to universal and abstract conceptions: for example, a ball provides an idea of the universe. He felt that young children should have a peaceful and harmonious environment and that kindergarten should provide opportunities for play, games, and stories, which are the natural mode of learning for this age group. This was in sharp contrast to the then-prevailing view of children as miniature adults who could be put to work at an early age. Froebel was moving to a naturalistic view of the child that was soon to be accelerated by the work of Charles Darwin.

One major event in the history of child psychology was Darwin's theory of evolution, which was published in 1859, just seven years after Froebel's death. This theory eventually led to a more naturalistic approach to child behavior and human development. If human beings were not a separate species but on a continuum with animals, children could be studied as natural phenomena; this was not possible as long as they were regarded solely as God's creation.

Other events were taking place that were accelerating the movement toward the scientific study of children. Partly as a result of Darwin's work and partly as a result of new medical knowledge, a new interest in child welfare emerged. The exploitation of children by parents and by unscrupulous entrepreneurs began to receive public attention, as did the use of young children to work in mines and factories. In England Charles Dickens wrote memorably in his novels about the deplorable treatment of children in the cities and in factories.

Thanks in part to these developments, there was a wave of child-welfare reforms in the second half of the nineteenth century. In America daycare centers for the children of working mothers were established, as were homes for delinquent, retarded, and emotionally troubled youngsters. Whereas before this time handicaps were often referred to as the "devil's work" or as punishment for the child's or the parent's evil deeds, these were now seen as natural phenomena and those who exhibited them were considered worthy of attention and humane care. In response to this humanistic attitude, several disciplines arose that eventually led to child psychology as we know it today.

HISTORY

Unlike many other disciplines, child psychology emerged from the demands of various fields for more systematic knowledge about children. There were demands for tests that would distinguish between normal and retarded children, and for methods and techniques to use in education and in child rearing. As the discipline has matured, however, it has become more "scientific" and thus more removed from the practical needs that stimulated its growth. We tend to agree with those who believe that child psychology must deal with practical as well as academic issues if it is to continue to enjoy the vitality it has shown in the last half century (7).

Origins of the Cognition and Language Study Tradition in Child Psychology

Baby Biographers. The first systematic investigations of children were made of their own offspring by parents. In one classic, *The Mind of the Child,* physiologist Wilhelm Preyer recorded his son's development during the first 4 years of life. Preyer was primarily interested in the development of reflexive behaviors and in the influence of experience and training in modifying these behaviors. Since he was a physiologist, his interest in reflexes was understandable. But Preyer observed many other things as well, such as the child's language and play. Although he did not always separate his observations from his inferences, his work is still highly regarded (8). Here is one of his observations regarding the development of reasoning in the child:

> *The adult is not in the habit of trying a door which he sees bolted and well closed. A child, on the contrary, will closely examine the edge of the door he wants to push to see if it really is closed. He does this because he does not understand the operation of bolts and locks. At 18 months, my son walked around the desk carrying a key that he liked very much. Apparently he thought walking around the desk with the key was the way to lock it.* [8, p. 301; author's translation].

Charles Darwin kept a diary about his infant son that he began in 1840 but did not publish until thirty years later. Darwin was particularly interested in the evolutionary aspects of child behavior; that is, in its relationship to animal behavior. Darwin's baby biography as well as his work on the evolution of emotions in animals and men (9, 10) were landmarks in what is known today as comparative psychology.

Other baby biographers include Bronson Alcott, the father of Louisa May Alcott (11), and Melissa Shinn, an American woman who attempted a more scientific biography by giving her baby little tests (12). Although he was not a baby biographer in the classic sense, James Sully used observations of his own and other children to write an early book on child psychology (13). And James Mark Baldwin observed children in order to construct a genetic epistemology, a forerunner of the more successful one created by Jean Piaget (14, 15). The best of the baby biographies and the ones that were most useful to and influential on later investigators dealt at length with language and with sensorimotor development.

Although baby biographies have obvious limitations since they are based on no more than a few children, the observations are generally not controlled, and the observers are not entirely objective, they have continued to be used as a viable scientific method. Piaget used observations of his own three infants in his classic books (16–18) that have stimulated much of the current work on infant behavior. Psycholinguists such as Roger Brown (19) have also studied a few small children to good advantage over an extended period of time.

The Child Study Movement. The baby biographies indicated a growing scientific interest in children during the nineteenth century. They were the forerunners of the developmental and experimental traditions in child psychology. The next step in this direction was taken by G. Stanley Hall, a prolific writer and investigator who became the first president of Clark University, an institution that has specialized in training psychologists. Hall was instrumental in helping to establish the American Psychological Association and several journals, including the *Journal of Genetic Psychology*.

Hall founded the short-lived "child study movement," which was intended to explore the evolution of children's ideas. He was intrigued with the doctrine of **recapitulation,** the idea that the child in his or her development recapitulates the history of the race. In the 1890s Hall sponsored a large number of questionnaire studies of children's views about everything from death to sex. Although some of the early studies were quite respectable in the sense that Hall trained the teachers and designed the questionnaires very carefully, these high standards were not maintained; many of the later studies were therefore invalid. Among the topics explored by Hall and his associates were children's sexual fantasies and play interests. While there were a few interesting results (e.g., that girls thought that they could become pregnant by kissing), the movement died when it came under attack by scientific methodologists. Hall lost interest in the movement and went on to other things.

If nothing else, the child study movement brought to public attention the need for scientific data on children. Hall had hoped that this knowledge would eventually form the basis for a new pedagogy, but this was not to be. What the child study movement did do, however, was pave the way for the establishment of child study institutes at major universities around the country. This was the next step in the development of a scientific study of the child in America.

The Institutes. Robert R. Sears (7) traces the establishment of these child study institutes and gives much of the initial credit to Mrs. Cora Bressey Hills. Although it is not clear how she was influenced by the child study movement, Mrs. Hills did believe that if research "could improve cows and hogs, it could also improve children" (7, p. 19). She worked diligently to establish a child research institute that would parallel the agricultural research institute at the University of Iowa. The institute would have three functions—research, teaching, and the dissemination of information. Although Mrs. Hills began her efforts in 1906 and 1907, it was not until a decade later, with the help of many organizations and the Iowa legislature, that the Iowa Child Welfare Research station was established.

After World War I, the public became much more aware of the problems of children. In addition to the concern that arose for children orphaned by the war, pre-draft testing of young men found that a substantial percentage was illiterate and in poor health. Therefore, it was felt that a more systematic study of children and their needs could help prevent adult ill health and illiteracy. Although the government provided some money, substantially more came from private foundations. In memory of Laura Spelman Rockefeller, $12 million was donated for research, teaching, and the dissemination of information in child development.

A crucial figure in the development of the institutes and of child psychology in America was Lawrence K. Frank. Trained as an economist, he early developed a lively and abiding interest in child welfare. Frank was instrumental in getting foundations to support child development institutes and research. But more than that, he brought together researchers of diverse training and interests and got them working together. He not only helped get the institutes started, he also helped find the psychologists to man them. Perhaps the best way to think of Frank's role in the development of child psychology is to think of him as analogous to a producer of a play or film. The producer gets together the resources and the talent and makes suggestions about the production but leaves most of the actual work to the director and actors. That in effect was the role of Lawrence K. Frank in expanding child psychology in America.

This was the start of the child development institute as we know it today. With support from the Rockefeller Memorial Fund, the Child Development Institute was founded at Teachers College of Columbia University (1924) and the Institute of Child Welfare at the University of Minnesota in 1925. At Yale—where Arnold Gesell (a student of G. Stanley Hall) had been studying children since 1911—the Institute for Child

Study was funded by the Rockefeller Memorial Fund in 1928. Another Child Development Institute at Berkeley was also begun at about the same time. Thanks to these institutes, by the 1930s research in child development was flourishing and there were graduate programs to train Ph.D.s in this field. These graduates went on to teach child development at most colleges and universities throughout the country. In the 1930s, child development finally emerged as a psychological discipline.

Origins of the Clinical, Social, and Personality Study Tradition in Child Psychology

As we have seen, the study of cognition and language tradition in child psychology had its origins in the baby biographies. Clinical, social, and personality study on the other hand had its origins in popular writings, often by physicians, regarding the care and rearing of children. In America at the beginning of the nineteenth century, socialization of children was heavily freighted by the concepts of evangelical Protestantism. When such Europeans as Rousseau and Froebel were arguing the basic goodness of children, such Americans as Jonathan Edwards proclaimed that unrepentant children were "young vipers and infinitely more hateful than vipers" (45). The Calvinists attacked permissive child rearing and argued that even little children "were not too young to go to hell for their misdeeds" (45).

Parents were thus urged to rear their children in the paths of righteousness by exposing them to moralistic literature and by frequent Bible readings and church attendance. But the piety of evangelical Protestantism clashed with some of the other values of frontier American society, particularly with the high esteem placed on financial and social success. Parents were caught between religious and secular values. Perhaps because of this conflict, the demand for piety on the part of children began to lessen by the middle of the nineteenth century. Some of the European ideas about childhood education may also have helped the process.

One reflection of this modification in attitude was the change in the professional advice given parents regarding corporal punishment. In the late eighteenth and early nineteenth centuries harsh discipline, including whipping, was advised to make children obedient. By the middle of the nineteenth century, professional opinion began to move away from the idea that corporal punishment was necessary and beneficial. It began to be recognized that "young children often do wrong merely from the immaturity of their reason or from mistaken principle" (45). Punishment, the new opinion held, should fit the crime, and was to be used only as a last resort. Rather than punishment, love and gentleness were said to be the best inducements for children to form good moral character (45).

After the Civil War, the more optimistic view of child nature—that children could be led to good character by gentle guidance—was reinforced by Darwinian arguments. Children could evolve for the better, much as animals have evolved to better adapt to the environments in

LESSON 26.

GENERAL WASHINGTON

Was once a little child like one of us,
But he would never tell a lie.
His father once gave him a hatchet,
And George went into the garden with it.
In the garden was a beautiful young tree,
And he cut the tree till he spoilt it.
When his father saw it, he was grieved,
And he called all his people before him,
And asked who had ruined his tree?
No one could tell any thing about it.
His son then came in, and his father said,
George, who killed my cherry tree?
And George was silent for a moment,
But he soon wiped the tear from his eye,
And looking at his father, he replied,
I can't tell a lie!....Pa, you know I can't!
It was I did cut it with my hatchet.

His father held out his hands, and said,
Run to my _____ my dear boy!
You have told the truth, and it is better
Than a thousand, thousand trees,
If all their fruits were silver and gold.

INFANT SCHOOL CARDS, PUBLISHED BY MUNROE AND FRANCIS, BOSTON.

A nineteenth-century school lesson reflecting the moral emphasis of pre Civil War educational practice.

which they lived. In 1871 Jacob Abbot published his book *Gentle Measures in the Management and Training of the Young* (46), in which the Darwinian conceptions were the background for positive measures of encouraging good moral character. Much less emphasis was placed on the "innate" badness of children and much more on the importance of experience and training in the formation of character. In contrast to Jonathan Edwards, who would stamp the bad out of children, Jacob Abbot would nudge the good in.

These enlightened views regarding child nature in the last quarter of the nineteenth century had many far-reaching effects, among them the re-evaluation of mental retardation and emotional disturbance in children. These problems gradually came to be seen not as the devil's work, or as punishments for evil deeds, but as illness or part of the human condition. These positive views of child nature paved the way for the child guidance and mental hygiene movements around the turn of the century. But the writings of professionals regarding the care and rearing of children were also the forerunners of the more systematic research into personality and social development that was undertaken by some of the child development institutes after World War I.

Child Guidance and Mental Hygiene. The development of the child guidance and mental hygiene movements around the turn of the century had a direct effect upon child psychology. The focus of the baby biographies, Hall, and the institutes had been essentially normative; that is, to discover general principles of development and learning that would hold true for all children. But the child guidance and mental hygiene movement focused on individuals and on individual variations—another important aspect of child development research.

The humanistic approach of the late nineteenth century, together with the Darwinian thesis that man was a direct descendent of animals, led to a re-evaluation of disturbed behavior. If it was no longer believed that man was divine, and if his disorders could not be attributed to such causes as the influence of the devil or original sin, one was obliged to look for more mundane causes such as his or her life experiences. Disturbed behavior of all kinds now came to be regarded as "illnesses" that, if properly diagnosed, might be cured.

Sigmund Freud (21) made a significant contribution to this movement. His demonstration that such physical symptoms as paralysis could be produced by mental conflicts was a vivid illustration of the "natural" causes of mental illness. Freud's work added to the momentum of the humanitarian reform movement in America as well as in Europe. In America, the first psychological clinic for children with school problems was opened by Lightner Witmer at the University of Pennsylvania in 1896. In France about the same time, Alfred Binet was working on an intelligence test to screen children who might need special training because of retardation. Binet's tests, published in 1906 and 1908, stimulated the whole mental testing movement. When Binet's test was translated into English by Lewis Terman (1916), it became an important tool in clinics such as Witmer's. Individual psychological testing is now regarded as primarily a clinical method.

As Sears (7) points out, another characteristic of clinics was their interdisciplinary nature. In 1915 William Healy opened a psychiatric clinic for delinquent youths who were being seen in a juvenile court in Chicago. In that clinic psychiatrists, psychologists, and social workers participated in the diagnosis and treatment of these young people. Often the psychologists handled the diagnosis because of their expertise with tests, the social workers counseled the families and did case histories, while the psychiatrists actually treated the youths.

Many child guidance clinics, modeled after the Healy clinic, opened in the 1920s and 1930s, and soon there were clinics in most of the major cities of the nation. This movement was helped enormously, as were child development institutes, by private philanthropy. The Commonwealth Fund began to support a number of demonstration clinics, which increased public awareness of the need for more such institutions. Today, most states have departments of mental hygiene which support hospitals and clinics for retarded and troubled children.

The child guidance movement, with its emphasis upon individual differences, had a beneficial, counterbalancing effect on the strong, normative approach of the institutes. Clinical workers were interested in the whole child, which came to be embodied in the term *personality,* and their writings dealt with theories of personality and of how particular events brought about certain effects. Because clinics were often associated with universities, students were exposed to the conflict between the professors who were oriented toward the normative and those who emphasized the whole child. Some of these differences and conflicts persist today.

Child Development between the Two World Wars and after

Between the two world wars the institutes and the students they sent to universities around the country turned out a prodigious amount of research. Longitudinal studies on physical, mental, and personality growth and cross-sectional studies of language, motivation, emotions, perception, learning, and moral development were carried out. It was the period during which Arnold Gesell carried out his careful and detailed studies of infant development with the aid of motion pictures. It was likewise the period during which Lewis Terman and his colleagues carried out their longitudinal studies of gifted children. It was a busy, active time for child development research that established a solid body of information about the growth and development of children.

Unfortunately, the growth of child development as a discipline was given a major setback as a consequence of World War II. Child development workers were dispersed among the various armed services and the remaining faculty took over the entire teacher load, which left them little time for research and writing. Publication of the journals lagged or was dropped and there was a discontinuance of meetings. Not until the early 1950s did child development research and training begin to regain the momentum it had built up before World War II.

Several different circumstances in the middle and late 1950s and early 1960s led to a resurgence of growth in the child development field. One of these was launching of the Russian Sputnik in 1957. This event caused the U.S. government great concern and convinced many members of Congress that American education was at fault in not emphasizing science and mathematics. This led to a re-examination of school curricula and the provision of research funds to study the processes of learning in children and government contracts to construct new and updated curricula in science, math, and social studies. These programs created a demand for child psychologists and were an incentive to train more young people in the discipline.

Another factor that contributed to the growth of child development in the 1960s was the civil rights movement. The revelation of the poor academic achievement of minority-group children in the schools again caused the government to act. It not only funded a number of educational programs, such as Head Start, but it also required that the effects of such programs should be evaluated. Again, child psychologists were called in to do the evaluations. In addition, the government also sponsored a number of "early intervention" programs to assess the long-range effects of enriching the lives of minority children early in life. Child psychologists directed or were involved in many of these early intervention programs.

A third factor in the resurgence of the child development field after World War II was the discovery and appreciation of the work of Swiss psychologist Jean Piaget. Although Piaget had been studying the development of intelligence in children since the 1920s, his work got little recognition in this country with the exception of a brief flurry of interest in the 1930s. But the curriculum-builders rediscovered Piaget, and the scope and breadth of his work began to have increasing impact upon American psychology and education. His work has been a major stimulus for the enormous amount of research undertaken on the cognitive development of infants and children since the early 1960s.

Another factor that stimulated the growth of child development as a field was government-sponsored training programs arranged through the National Institutes of Human Growth and Development. These programs provided for faculty salaries, student stipends, and the purchase of research equipment. Training grants made it possible for many more people to study child development; thus the field came of age, and almost every psychology department in the country had child development specialists on its staff.

In the late 1970s, child development as a discipline appears to be retrenching again as government support for research and training is being cut back. Fewer young men and women are being trained in the field and academic positions are more difficult to attain because colleges and universities are no longer expanding their faculties. But if child development as a discipline has lost some momentum it has nonetheless won a permanent place in the ranks of psychology departments in the universities and colleges of the United States. Whereas in the past no self-respecting psychology department would be without its learning theorist, by the late 1970s no major department of psychology can call itself that without a developmentalist on its faculty. Child development has come of age in the scientific community.

Current Research Areas in Developmental Psychology

Contemporary child development might be said to have six major trends (22). First, an increasing number of experimentally trained and technologically sophisticated researchers are coming into the field. One of the reasons for this is that child development has become a "prestige" area so that it is attracting researchers from less "glamorous" fields who have a solid background in experimental work. Another reason is that as psychology has matured as a discipline, its methods have become more exact and elaborate. Child development specialists have been trained in general psychology as well, and so they have a methodological sophistication in electronics, computers, and statistics.

Another contemporary trend in child psychology is the use of the methods and ideas of B. F. Skinner (23), who introduced the concept of "operant conditioning" and of reinforcing or "shaping" behavior. His reinforcement methods and ideas are sometimes used in schools and curriculum projects, and they have proved useful with infants. Skinnerian-oriented researchers have also shown how his methods could be applied in treating troubled children.

A third major trend is an interest in cognitive development. It is probably fair to say that this interest stems largely from Piaget's work for example (23–25). There have been numerous studies of conservation (the child's understanding that a given quantity remains the same despite a change in its appearance) in the journals during the past ten years. Studies of moral development and, more recently, of imagery, perception, and memory have also been stimulated by Piaget's work. This trend appears to be growing, and there are still a great many concepts explored by Piaget that so far have scarcely been touched by others.

A fourth trend in contemporary child development is an interest in children's grammar, which can be traced to Noam Chomsky (27) and also to Piaget (25). Although children's language has always been included in child study, interest has increased because of Chomsky's revolutionary view that even young children generate or construct their own grammars. Psychologists and linguists have combined their interests into a new field—psycholinguistics. Early psycholinguistic research dealt primarily with grammar; the present focus is on meanings as well (that is, semantics) and on the relationship between cognitive development and language growth.

The fifth trend is an interest in infancy, thanks in part to Piaget. His studies of his own three infants (16–18) raised a number of questions and problems that have been pursued by others. But many of the problems studied by researchers concerned with infants were first introduced by the baby biographers. Infants are of course more accessible to study than any other age group: they are confined to small areas for long periods of time and they have very little mobility. At the other extreme are adolescents, who are not studied very much, partly because it is so difficult to get their cooperation. The focus of psychological research is often determined by the availability of subjects—witness the number of studies done on college students.

The final trend is research in social learning, a field first pioneered by psychologist Kurt Lewin (29). During the past twenty years or so, this field has been expanded and now includes theoretical conceptions that are related to the learning theories of Skinner as well as the dynamic theories of Freud. Much of the research in social learning is an attempt to study complex interpersonal and social processes within a general, dynamic learning theory framework (for example, 28).

This brief survey indicates the rapidity with which the field of child psychology (or, as it is now known, child development) has grown since its formal inception with baby biographies and popular writings by physicians more than a century ago.

METHODS

In studying behavior, psychologists select the methods appropriate to the question or questions under consideration. Perhaps the most difficult task in scientific research is the formulation of a question in such a way that it can be answered by the collection of data. Once a question has been clearly formulated, the particular method chosen to answer it will depend upon a variety of practical considerations. For example, if the question was "Do 5-year-old boys and girls differ in the amount of fighting they engage in?" data pertinent to the question might be obtained by a number of different methods, ranging from controlled observation to experiment.

Although it is true that a given question can be answered with a variety of methods, it is also true that some methods are more appropriate than others for answering certain types of question. Accordingly we will organize our discussion of methods under the three major types of questions that are usually asked in developmental research—although it should be kept in mind that any given method or combination of methods can be and often is used to answer these questions. These three types of questions are the correlative, the causative, and the differential.

Correlative Methods

Correlative methods are employed whenever we ask the question "What goes with what?" For example, if we wanted to know how much vocabulary increased between 2 and 5 years of age we would be asking a correla-

Natural observation. This observer recording children's use of different play areas is an example of situation sampling, discussed on p. 20.

tive question in the sense that we wanted to know what number of words goes with what age. To answer this question we might use one of a number of correlative methods. Some of the most frequently used of these methods are described below.

Controlled Observation. A method for answering correlative questions is controlled observation. Such observation is most useful when the correlative question has to do with the frequency of occurrence of certain behaviors, such as attentiveness in particular situations or in particular groups of children. Frequency of occurrence might then be related to other variables such as home background.

One form of controlled observation has been called **situation sampling.** In situation sampling the investigator selects distinctive situations and records the reactions of children to these situations. Situation sampling is often used in the study of interpersonal relations, of play preference, and so on. For example, an investigator might set up both a "doll corner" and a workshop (with hammer, nails, wood, and so forth) in a nursery schoolroom. He or she would then record the frequency with which boys and girls went to the doll or workshop area and the amount of time children of either sex spent in one or the other area. Situation sampling thus provides a measure of how often children use a particular facility, toy, or the like.

Another form of systematic observation is **time sampling.** Time sampling involves recording the number of times a particular form of behavior occurs during a fixed time interval. To illustrate, in a recent study the investigators were interested in whether black children were less attentive to their schoolwork than were white children (47). The behaviors regarded as attentive and nonattentive are given in Table 1.1. Each child in the

Table 1.1   Types of Attending and Nonattending Behaviors Tallied by the Observers

Attending behavior
1. Attending by participating in the assigned activity. This includes
   (a) looking at the teacher while the teacher is addressing the class,
   (b) actively attending to an assigned task (reading, working on a notebook),
   (c) working at the blackboard,
   (d) working on supplementary materials,
   (e) helping another student with assigned material.

Nonattending behavior
2. Blank stare when a presentation is being made to the class (teacher is talking or television is on).
3. Blank stare when nothing is being presented to the class.
4. Attending to a classroom disturbance.
5. Attending to a nonassigned task (looking at the clock or calendar).
6. Sitting quietly after assigned task completion.
7. Ignoring individual teacher instruction (teacher is talking to individual being observed).
8. Working on nonassigned material.
9. Exhibiting finicky mannerisms indicating boredom (yawning, scratching, etc.).
10. Going to the bathroom or leaving the room.
11. Talking with another student about unassigned task (talking about the teacher, another student, etc.).
12. Physically interacting with other children (fighting, swearing, passing notes).
13. Exhibiting miscellaneous nonattending behaviors not otherwise covered.
14. Hand raising while waiting to be called on.

Source: Hall, V. C., Huppertz, J. W. & Levi, A. Attention and achievement exhibited by middle class and lower class black and white elementary school children. *Journal of Educational Psychology,* 1977, **69,** 115–120.

study was observed for 15 minutes. Several different observers were employed and each one recorded four behaviors per minute. This was done by having each observer watch the child for 5 seconds and record for 10 seconds. It was thus possible to record 60 attentive or nonattentive behaviors per 15-minute period. The investigators found no differences between black and white children in their attend-behaviors in relation to schoolwork (47).

Another method for dealing with correlative questions was introduced by Jean Piaget, the Swiss psychologist. This method has been called the **semi-clinical interview** (32). Piaget was interested in the correlative question of how children's thinking about a variety of subjects changed with age. He wanted to construct a method sufficiently uniform that responses from different children could be compared and sufficiently flexible that the interviewer could follow out the child's thought. The semi-clinical interview was the result and combines the uniformity of the mental test with the flexibility of the psychiatric interview. Because this is a method students can employ without special equipment and with younger siblings,

Famed Swiss psychologist Jean Piaget observing children at play.

relatives, or neighbors, it will be described in detail here. Trying the method out with children provides a useful practical exercise which may help to make the text material more meaningful.

In discussing his method, Piaget (32) suggests that it is best to start with children's own spontaneous remarks, which can lead to the standard questions that will be used to open the interview. For example, after the assassination of President John F. Kennedy, one of the authors heard a child say, "Are they going to shoot God next?"—which suggested that the child grouped all important people together. If one wanted to pursue this issue further, one might ask children of different ages, "Can God be president of the United States?" or "Who chooses the president?" or "Who chooses God?" or "How did God become God?" Which questions prove helpful in revealing hidden facets of a child's thinking can only be determined by pilot work with a few children, a process that Piaget calls **sondage** (soundings).

Interview Technique. Once a group of questions on a given topic has been assembled, the interviewing can begin. The child should be seen in a quiet place where there are few distractions and at a time he or she does not have any special wish to be somewhere else. As soon as the interviewer has established rapport with the child (this is done most easily by asking the youngster a few questions about himself or herself) the interview questions can begin. After the child has replied, it is usually necessary to ask a few more questions to clarify the meaning of the response. Much skill is required for this free-inquiry part of the interview because the examiner must direct the child's thought without at the same time suggesting an answer. The best preparation for this part of the examination is a course in Rorschach testing because this procedure has developed suggestive questioning to a fine art.

Interpretation of Results: Validity.* Both during the examination and afterward, it is important to know to what extent the child's responses truly reflect his or her own ideas. Therefore, Piaget has described five types of response that need to be distinguished. When the child is not interested in the question or is bored or tired, he or she may simply say anything that comes to mind just to satisfy the examiner; Piaget calls these responses **answers at random.** When a child makes up an answer without really thinking about the question, Piaget calls the process **romancing.** On the other hand, when the child does pay attention to the question but his or her answer stems from a desire to please the examiner or is suggested by the question, Piaget calls it **suggested conviction.**

These three types of reply are obviously of little value to the investigator. However, when the child thinks about a question that is new and answers it from the depths of his or her own mind, Piaget calls the result a

---

*Validity is a general problem of all psychological testing and involves procedures which insure that the test measures what is purports to measure.

liberated conviction. And when the child answers quickly, without reflection, because he or she already knows his or her feelings or inclinations, Piaget calls the response a **spontaneous conviction.**

Since the investigator is primarily interested in the liberated and spontaneous convictions, it is important to be able to separate them from answers at random, romancing, and suggested convictions. This can be done at two points during the investigation, one during and the other following the interview. If, during the interview itself, the examiner suspects that a reply is not a spontaneous or a liberated conviction, it can be checked in several ways. First, the examiner can offer countersuggestions to see how firmly rooted the idea is in the child's thought. A liberated or spontaneous conviction can easily withstand countersuggestions, whereas the others cannot. Second, one can ask about related issues. If the idea is truly the child's conviction, it will fit a pattern of ideas that Piaget calls a **schème.** If the child's response fits the general scheme of his or her thought, it is probably either a spontaneous or a liberated conviction.

The second point at which one can determine whether the replies represent genuine convictions is after the interview when the data have been collected. First, if most of the children of the same age give similar replies, their responses reflect a form of thought that is characteristic of that age. There would be no such uniformity if their answers were random, suggested, or romancing. Second, if the responses show a gradual change with age toward a closer approximation of the adult conception, the re-

A psychologist engaging a child in a semi-clinical interview discussion.

plies reflect a true developmental trend. Finally, a valid developmental sequence must show continuity in the sense that among the abstract conceptions of older children there would be traces of the concrete ideas they held at an earlier age (**adherences**) and that among the concrete expressions of young children there would be a foreshadowing of the abstract ideas they will hold when they are older (**anticipations**).

With these approaches one can check the validity of the data obtained by Piaget's semi-clinical interview.

Interpretation of Results: Reliability.* Although Piaget has always been concerned about the validity of his observations, he has virtually ignored the question of their **reliability;** that is, their repeatability. A possible reason for this gap is the fact that Piaget's training in biological science may have led him to assume that a characteristic found in one individual can be found throughout the species. Such a position is less defensible for human beings than it is for lesser organisms, however, and reliability measures probably should be made with Piaget's method. Two such measures are needed. One would measure the consistency with which individual children respond to interview questions at different times. This measure can be obtained by retesting each child, preferably neither sooner than 1 nor later than 6 months after the original examination. Correlating the initial and retest responses will provide an index of response reliability.

The second reliability measure that should be obtained is the categorization of responses into stages or sequences of development. That is to say, it is necessary to decide whether the responses are sufficiently distinctive for individual workers to classify them in similar ways. If several persons independently categorize the responses and a measure of their agreement is determined, this measure will serve as an index of the reliability of the categorization. These steps to ensure the reliability of the responses, together with the fulfillment of Piaget's criteria for determining validity, should suffice to make sure that investigations using the semi-clinical interview will be acceptable to even the most hard-headed experimentalist.

Causative Methods When we are interested in determining not what goes with what but what causes something else, a different methodology is required. Causative questions are best answered by experimentation. In the experimental method, there is generally an **independent variable** (the dimension under the control of the experimenter) and a **dependent variable** (the subject's response to the independent variable). Crucial to the experimental method are the **control variables**—those dimensions, situations, or events

*Reliability is a general problem of all psychological testing and is concerned with the issue of whether a given instrument will produce the same result on successive trials.

which are kept constant so as not to affect the action of the independent variable upon the dependent variable.

Although the basic pattern of an experiment is straightforward, it is an extraordinarily flexible method. The independent variable, to illustrate, might be anything from a set of different teaching techniques to a series of ambiguous pictures. Dependent variables can be anything from scores on a test to the intensity of a fear response measured electronically. And, thanks to modern statistical methods, it is now possible to assess the effects of multiple independent variables acting separately or together.

To make the use of the experimental method in child development research concrete a couple of examples will be given. In one study (48) investigators were concerned with the effects of the speed, with which lists of numbers were read, and upon the ability of children to recall them. The lists of digits were presented at five different speeds, which were the values of the independent variable. Children's recall scores were the dependent variable. Controls included presenting the lists by a tape-recorded voice, choosing the digits in any given list from a table of random numbers, and using only males as subjects. In addition, all of the subjects were attending the same school and all had IQs in the average range. By controlling these various factors, the investigators could be reasonably sure that any variations in children's recall scores were attributable to variation in the presentation rate.

Another type of experiment which is frequent in developmental psychology is the *training* experiment. In such experiments, the same or different groups of children are given different forms of training on a particular task to determine which mode of training was most efficacious. In the past decade many training studies have been undertaken to determine whether the appearance of certain concepts, usually associated with particular age levels, can be made to appear earlier as a consequence of training.

Piaget (49), for example, has suggested that most children attain a true concept of number (the understanding that the number of elements in a set remains the same no matter how they are arranged) between the ages of 5 and 6. Training studies have been undertaken to determine whether a true number concept could be induced in younger children over a short period of time as a result of training. The basic paradigm of such experiments is to test the children first (pretest), then train them, and then retest them (post-test). The difference in scores between the pre- and the post-tests then provides a measure of the effectiveness of the various training procedures.

An early study of this kind was undertaken by Wohlwill and Lowe in 1962 (50). They used 72 kindergarten children as subjects. First the subjects were tested for their understanding of whether the number of a set of six, seven, or eight elements (corks, wooden stars) changes as a result of a change in their spatial relation to one another. Spatial relation was changed by placing the elements closer or farther apart. The subjects were divided into four groups of 18 children. Each group was then given a different form of training. One group (the RP group) was trained with reinforced practice. In effect, they were asked to count the elements after they were rearranged. A second group, the addition and subtraction group (the A & S group), was shown the sets and asked whether they remained the same in number when some elements were taken away or were added. A third group (the Diss group) was given dissociated training in the sense that subjects were asked whether different numbers of elements changed as a result of physical proximity. A fourth (control) group was simply asked to count the number of elements in the sets but the sets were not changed in any way. Conservation was measured by verbal responses and by subjects' actions. The differential effects of the training are shown in Table 1.2.

In this study, the independent variable was the type of training and the dependent variable was the post-test score. Controls included using children of about the same age, IQ, and socioeconomic status. Additional controls were the pretests and the control group, which gave baselines for ensuring that the groups were roughly comparable in ability before the training and to ensure that the mere fact of pretesting did not serve as a form of training. These two examples of experiments in child development are but a couple of the many ways that experimental methodology is employed in child development research.

Differential Methods

When the question the investigator is interested in has to do with an individual child rather than with groups of children, differential methods are usually employed. Such methods include mental testing, self-report techniques, projective methods, and play observation. In the use of these methods, the individual is always compared to an implicit or explicit **norm group** to determine the extent to which the individual is like or different from the norm. One of the most difficult problems in the use of differential

Table 1.2   Performance on Number Conservation Tasks before and after Training

Condition of Training	Verbal Conservation[a]			Nonverbal Conservation[b]		
	Pretest	Post-test	Net Change	Pretest	Post-test	Net Change
A&S	1	3	+2	1.05	1.77	+.72
RP	2	3	+1	1.22	1.50	+.28
Diss.	4	2	−2	1.05	1.16	+.11
Control	2	4	+2	1.44	1.96	+.52

[a]Number of Ss giving correct responses to verbal conservation question.
[b]Mean correct responses out of three trials.

Source: Wohlwill, J. F., & Lowe, R. C. An experimental analysis of the development of the conservation of number. *Child Development,* 1962, **33,** 153–167.

methods is ensuring that the norm group is an appropriate one against which to compare the particular child.

Perhaps a concrete example will help to make the matter of an appropriate norm group more concrete. Although it deals with the comparison of one group of children with another rather than with a single child, the principle is the same. One of us (DE) once spent a week on an Indian reservation in the Southwest where he tested a group of Sioux children. The children were attending a missionary school that was run by Jesuits. At dinner one evening one of the teachers asked me if I would visit his sixth-grade language arts class. He knew that I was interested in reading and he was concerned that his students were not reading very well. I attended the class and listened to the children read. They seemed to be reading on a level comparable to what I had observed in city school children of about the same age. I wondered about the teacher's implicit norm group and asked him where he had taught before he came out to the reservation. It turned out that he had just arrived after teaching for years at an exclusive prep school in Connecticut. Clearly his implicit norm group was not an appropriate one against which to compare a Sioux child or children.

This is not to say that all norms need to be objective; even subjective norms can be valuable. Clinicians who do a great deal of testing, for example, will eventually establish personal norms that can be useful in making a diagnosis. One of us has noted (34) that slow or retarded children often laugh at the first items of an intelligence test. A possible explanation may be that the slow child is extremely apprehensive about the test and about revealing his or her slowness. The first items, which are easy, come as such a relief that the youngster laughs in a release of tension. Used with caution, the personal norms of the clinician can be a useful supplement to objective norms.

Intelligence Tests. In succeeding chapters we will talk a great deal about intelligence tests and testing. What needs to be said at this point is that intelligence tests always involve the use of rather large norm groups for the standardization of items. *Standardization* simply means that an item's difficulty is determined by the success or failure of large groups of children who have responded to that item.

The norm groups for the most widely used intelligence tests, such as the Stanford-Binet and the Wechsler Intelligence Scale for Children, are usually acquired by taking samples of children from all over the United States, from urban and rural areas, and from different socioeconomic strata. Even so, the norms may still not be appropriate for all children in our society, particularly if the children come from home backgrounds where a language other than English is spoken and where the culture is quite different than that of middle-class America. Results of standardized tests given to such children should be interpreted with great caution. To illustrate how culture can affect performance on an intelligence test, look

Figure 1.1 The Chitling Test. *(Source.* A Dove, "The Chitling Test." In "Taking the Chitling Test." *Newsweek,* July 15, 1968. © Copyright Newsweek, Inc., 1968, reprinted by permission.)

1. A "handkerchief head" is: (a) a cool cat, (b) a porter, (c) an Uncle Tom, (d) a hoddi, (e) a preacher.
2. Which word is most out of place here: (a) splib, (b) blood, (c) gray, (d) spook, (e) black.
3. A "gas head" is a person who has a: (a) fast moving car, (b) stable of "lace," (c) "process," (d) habit of stealing cars, (e) long jail record for arson.
4. "Hully Gully" came from: (a) East Oakland, (b) Fillmore, (c) Watts, (d) Harlem, (e) Motor City.
5. If you throw the dice and seven is showing on the top, what is facing down? (a) seven, (b) snake eyes, (c) boxcars, (d) little joes, (e) 11.
6. T-Bone Walker got famous for playing what? (a) a trombone, (b) piano, (c) "T-flute," (d) guitar, (e) "Hambone."

[The correct answers are 1,c; 2,c; 3,c; 4,c; 5,a; 6.d.].

at the "Chitling Test" depicted in Figure 1.1 If the reader is not black, taking this test may provide an idea of what it is like to take a test based on the norms of quite a different group.

Self-Report Techniques. This method comprises a wide range of instruments in which children are asked to answer questions about themselves or the world. For example, in a study of self-esteem (36), children might be asked to indicate which adjectives in a list applied or did not apply to them. A child who thought that there were more positive than negative adjectives that described him or her would be said to have a positive self-image, whereas one who found more negative than positive adjectives that were applicable would be said to have a negative self-image.

Self-report schedules have been used to determine attitudes toward school, test anxiety, interests and vocational aptitudes. Although self-report techniques are useful, they always pose the problem of **social desirability**; that is, to what extent is a child responding according to what he or she knows is socially desirable and to what extent is the response an honest reflection of feelings and attitudes? One way to deal with this problem is to include "lie scales." These are items that are so extreme (for example, "I am always good" or "I am always bad") that a child who agrees to them demonstrates a tendency either to "fake good" or to "fake bad." Having these items on the scale allows one to discount certain extreme scores and to identify children who are responding primarily according to social desirability or undesirability. That may be useful information by itself, but determining the honesty of the subject's replies is still a problem with the self-report techniques.

Projective Methods. In the self-report techniques, the subject generally has some idea about what he or she is revealing about himself or herself. But with the so-called projective techniques, this is not the case. These techniques, which include the well-known Rorschach Inkblot Test and the Thematic Apperception Test (TAT), were devised to reveal "hidden" aspects of the personality. A subject who is responding to an inkblot, for example, has no idea how his or her response will be scored or how it will be interpreted. Of course, as these tests become more widely known, prospective subjects may become more knowledgeable about them and so the hidden aims of the test may no longer be as hidden as the tester would like to believe. Especially with projective tests, the value of the findings is largely dependent upon the skill, experience, and talent of the person who interprets the test results.

There is a new variant of projective techniques that in some ways bypasses the interpretation problems. It is really an updating of one of the oldest psychological findings. Long ago astronomers discovered what has been called the "personal equation"—the fact that various observers have different reaction times, so they recorded different times for stellar events. That is to say that while people were performing a simple task, such as pressing a button when the stars and coordinates intersected, their individual differences were revealed. Similar procedures are now being used to assess **cognitive styles** (persistent patterns of performance that can be found in a variety of tasks). These procedures expose certain aspects of the personality that the individual is not aware of exposing because the trait is incidental to the task. On the children's Embedded Figure Test (51), for example, children have to find simple figures embedded in a more complex one. Children who succeed quickly are said to be **field independent,** capable of dealing with distracting external stimuli; children who have trouble with the task are said to be **field dependent,** more susceptible to the influence of environmental stimuli. While such methods avoid some of the problems of self-report techniques they introduce new problems of interpretation. For example, how general or how situation-limited are these styles?

Play Observations. One differential method that enjoys continued use is the observation of children's play. In some respects children's play is like a projective test because playing may enable children to reveal aspects of themselves of which they are totally unaware. In most play observations, children are in a room with a number of toys, dollhouses, dolls, blocks, and so forth, and they are allowed to play with them. In a *structured* play situation, children are asked to play with certain toys; in *unstructured* play situations, the child may play with whatever toys he or she chooses.

Play observation can be used for diagnostic purposes. To assess a boy's emotional problem, for example, he might be placed in a structured play situation where there is a miniature house, toy people, and furniture. If he puts his mother, father, and sister in one room and himself in another, it might mean that he feels rejected by his parents or isolated from the rest of the family. In most play observations used for diagnostic purposes, children are asked either to tell a story about their play activities or to respond to the examiner's interpretation of their arrangement of the play materials.

Although it is primarily a differential method, the play observation technique has been used by Erik Erikson to answer correlative questions (35). He asked boys and girls to build towers with blocks, and then observed and photographed their buildings. He found interesting sex differences. Boys tended to build tall buildings, whereas girls tended to build enclosed spaces and spaces that were difficult to enter. Erikson suggested that the obvious sexual symbolism was perhaps less important than the fact that boys and girls had totally different spatial orientations because of the physical differences in their sexual organs.

Observing children's free play on playgrounds, in the classroom, and elsewhere is another rich source of information. Play observations, like most other observations, are generally quite useful at the beginning of an investigation, but more specific information about individuals and about groups must be obtained by other techniques. For individual assessment, data from play observations can be combined with data from other assessment techniques. For correlative purposes, play observation can be a fruitful source of hypotheses that can then be rigorously tested with experimental procedures.

As we have suggested in the discussion of play observations, the connections between questions and methods is not hard and fast. In particular, differential methods are often employed to answer correlative questions, as in the Erikson example. On the other hand, the experimental method is the only one applicable to answering causal questions. In short, some questions require specific methods while others do not.

Summary

The antecedents of child psychology were the writings of philosophers and educators who were interested in the upbringing of children. The concept of a broad liberal education, geared to physical as well as mental development, was originated by the Greeks. The Romans had a somewhat narrower view of education and hoped to produce citizen orators. During the Middle Ages, preparation for life after death became the major aim of education and the concept of liberal education was, with a few exceptions, lost. With the Enlightenment, the concept of a broad liberal education preparing individuals for life in this world was resurrected by a series of writers including Comenius, Rousseau, Pestalozzi, and Froebel.

In America in the antebellum period, children were looked upon as sinners in need of redemption and education was aimed at "breaking the child's will" and at instilling piety. But the American values of social and financial success conflicted with and moderated the religious values. After the Civil War, attitudes toward children became more sympathetic and parents were counseled that love was more important than corporal punishment. The spread of Darwinian ideas also led to a more sympathetic view of deviations such as mental retardation and emotional disturbance. Deviant children came to be viewed as the result of natural rather than supernatural causes and as worthy of societal attention.

It was within this framework of a sympathetic and naturalistic view of childhood that child psychology as a discipline came into being during the last decades of the nineteenth century. The forerunners of contemporary studies of cognitive and language development were the baby biographies and the questionnaire research of G. Stanley Hall. The forerunners of studies of personality and social development were the writings of professionals, usually physicians, regarding the care and rearing of children.

Child psychology as we now know it originated in the research institutes established at various universities after World War I and funded primarily by private foundations. It can also be traced back to the child guidance clinics, family courts, and daycare centers that handled children with problems. Hence contemporary child development emphasizes both normative development and individual differences. The major trends in child development today are increased experimentation, an interest in behavior modification, an interest in cognitive development, sophisticated and extensive research in infancy, substantial work in psycholinguistics, and a continuing interest in social learning theory.

The methods used in child development research can be grouped according to the types of question they are usually employed to answer. Correlative questions ask what goes with what and are usually answered with controlled observation, or with semi-clinical interviews aimed at finding out how children's thought or behavior changes with age. Causative questions are answered with the aid of experimental methods aimed at systematic control of variables so that reasonable conclusions can be drawn as to what *leads to* what. Finally, differential questions are concerned with describing individuals, usually in relation to norms, and include mental tests, self-report schedules, projective techniques, and play observation. Some differential methods, such as tests and play observation, are sometimes used to answer correlative questions. And sometimes a combination of methods will be used to answer a specific question. Once the research question is formulated, the particular method or methods to be used will depend upon many different considerations.

References

1. Mulhern, J. *A history of education*. New York: Ronald Press, 1946.
2. McKeon, R. (Ed.) *The basic works of Aristotle*. New York: Random House, 1941.
3. Rousseau, J. J. *Émile*. New York: Dutton, 1955. (Translated by Barbara Foxley.)
4. Furth, H. *Piaget for teachers*. Englewood Cliffs, N.J.: Prentice-Hall, 1970.
5. Piaget, J. *Science of education and the psychology of the child*. New York: Orion Press, 1970.
6. Elkind, D. *Child development and education: A Piagetian perspective*. New York: Oxford University Press, 1976.

7. Sears, R. R. Our ancients revisited. In E. Mavis Hetheringon (Ed.), *Review of child development research*. Vol. 5. Chicago: University of Chicago Press, 1975.

8. Preyer, *The mind of a child*. Paris: Félix Alcan, 1887.

9. Darwin, C. A biographical sketch of an infant. *Mind,* 1877, **2**, 285–294.

10. Darwin, C. *The expression of emotions in animal and man*. London: Murray, 1872.

11. Alcott, A. B. *Observations on the principles and methods of infant instruction*. Boston: Carler & Hendee, 1830.

12. Shinn, M. W. *Biography of a baby*. Boston: Houghton Mifflin, 1900.

13. Sully, J. *Studies of childhood*. New York: Appleton, 1903.

14. Baldwin, J. M. *Thought and things*. Vol. 1. New York: Macmillan, 1906.

15. Baldwin, J. M. *Genetic logic*. Vol. 2. New York: Macmillan, 1908.

16. Piaget, J. *The origins of intelligence in children*. New York: Basic Books, 1952.

17. Piaget, J. *The construction of reality in the child*. New York: Basic Books, 1954.

18. Piaget, J. *Play dreams and imitation in childhood*. New York: Norton, 1952.

19. Brown, R. *A first language*. Cambridge, Mass.: Harvard University Press, 1973.

20. Hall, J. S. The contents of children's minds on entering school. *Pedagogical Seminary and Journal of Genetic Psychology,* 1891, **1**, 139–173.

21. Freud, S. *The basic writings of Sigmund Freud*. New York: Modern Library, 1938.

22. Wohlwill, J. *The study of behavioral development*. New York: Academic Press, 1973.

23. Skinner, B. F. *Science and human behavior*. New York: Macmillan, 1953.

24. Piaget, J. *The psychology of intelligence*. London: Routledge & Kegan Paul, 1951.

25. Piaget, J. *The language and thought of the child*. London: Routledge & Kegan Paul, 1926.

26. Piaget, J. *The moral judgment of the child*. Glencoe, Ill.: The Free Press, 1948.

27. Chomsky, N. *Syntactic structures*. The Hague: Mouton, 1957.

28. Bandura, A. Social learning theory of identification processes. In D. A. Goslin (Ed.), *Handbook of socialization theory and research*. Chicago: Rand-McNally, 1969.

29. Lewin, K. Behavior and development as a function of the total situation. In L. Carmichael (Ed.), *Manual of child psychology* (2nd ed.). New York: Wiley, 1954.

30. Cronbach, L. J. The two disciplines of scientific psychology. *American Psychologist,* 1957, **12**, 671–684.

31. Rosenthal, R. *Experimenter effects in behavioral research*. New York: Appleton, Century, Crofts, 1966.

32. Piaget, J. *The child's conception of the world*. London: Routledge & Kegan Paul, 1929, introduction.

33. Castaneda, A., Palermo, D. S., & McCandless, B. R. Complex learning and performance as a function of anxiety in children. *Child Development,* 1956, **27**, 327–332.

34. Elkind, D. Borderline retardation in low and middle income adolescents. In R. M. Allen, A. D. Cortazzo, & R. P. Toister (Eds.), *Theories of cognitive development*. Coral Gables, Fla.: University of Miami Press, 1973.

35. Erikson, E. H. Sex differences in the play configurations of American preadolescents. *American Journal of Orthopsychiatry,* 1951, **21**, 667–692.

36. Coopersmith, S. *The antecedents of self-esteem*. San Francisco: W. H. Freeman, 1967.

37. Goodnow, J. J. Problems in research on culture and thought. In D. Elkind and J. H. Flavell (Eds.), *Studies in cognitive development*. New York: Oxford University Press, 1969.

38. Vernon, P. E. *Intelligence and cultural environment*. New York: Barnes and Noble, 1969.

39. Piaget, J. *Reussir et comprendre*. Paris: Presses Universitaires de France, 1974.

40. Piaget, J. *Les explications causales*. Paris: Presses Universitaires de France, 1974.

41. Piaget, J. *La prise de conscience*. Paris: Presses Universitaires de France, 1974.

42. Wallach, M. A., & Kogan, N. *Modes of thinking in young children*. New York: Holt, 1965.

43. Getzels, J. W., & Jackson, P. W. *Creativity and intelligence*. New York: Wiley, 1962.

44. Senn, M. J. E. Insights on the child development movement in the United States. *Monographs of the Society for Research in Child Development,* No. 166, 1975.

45. Wishy, B. *The child and the republic*. Philadelphia: University of Pennsylvania Press, 1968.

46. Abbot, J. *Gentle measures in the management and training of the young*. New York: Harper, 1871.

47. Hall, V. C., Huppertz, J. W., & Levi, A. Attention and achievement exhibited by middle class and lower class black and white elementary school boys. *Journal of Educational Psychology,* 1977, **69,** 115–120.

48. Sarver, G. S., Howland, A., & McManus, T. Effects of age and stimulus presentation rate on immediate and delayed recall in children. *Child Development,* 1976, **47,** 452–458.

49. Piaget, J., & Szeminska, A. *The child's conception of number.* London: Routledge & Kegan Paul, 1952.

50. Wohlwill, J. F., & Lowe, R. C. An experimental analysis of the development of the conservation of number. *Child Development,* 1962, **33,** 153–167.

51. Karp, S. A. & Konstadt, L. *Children's embedded figures test.* Palo Alto, Calif.: Consulting Psychologists Press, 1963.

2 Prenatal Growth and Pregnancy

PRENATAL GROWTH

Gametes and Genes

Embryonic Development

PREGNANCY

Pregnancy as a Life Crisis

Maternal-Fetal Interactions

Labor and Delivery

SUMMARY

REFERENCES

The title of this chapter may sound a bit redundant inasmuch as prenatal growth and pregnancy encompass the same period of time and roughly the same events. But prenatal growth pertains to the development of the infant from inception to birth, while pregnancy deals with the experiences and behaviors of the woman who is carrying the fetus. Thus, although the events are about the same, the perspective is quite different.

PRENATAL
GROWTH

At the moment of conception, when a sperm fertilizes an ovum, both an evolutionary and an immediate event occur. Contained in the united sperm and in the ovum are blueprints for human development that have been revised and reworked over eons of time. How these blueprints are carried and then utilized in shaping the organism is a matter of human genetics.

Gametes and Genes

The male sperm and the female ova are generally called **gametes.** In order to reproduce a new individual, these gametes must have special properties that are actually quite extraordinary. First, they must carry enough nourishing material to reproduce cells and yet be mobile enough to unite with one another. Second, they must be able to switch from their usual inert role within the adult to a more active role in reproducing cells. They must also be so constructed that they do not start to reproduce until they meet with a complementary gamete; that is, until a sperm meets an ovum. Finally, the gametes must bring enough hereditary information from the parent to contribute exactly half—no more and no less—of the total information that will form the blueprint for the development of the new organism. How is all of this accomplished by these tiny bits of matter?

The Action of Gametes. The first requirement is that the gametes have enough nourishment to generate a new organism and yet be mobile enough to unite. This is accomplished by a division of labor. The female gamete, the ovum, is relatively large and immobile, while the male gamete is relatively small and very mobile. To get some idea of their relative size, the human ovum is 0.14 mm. in diameter (about the size of a period on this page) and, under good conditions, can barely be seen by the human eye. The sperm, in contrast, is only 0.06 mm. long and cannot be seen by the naked eye. While the ovum is egg-shaped, the sperm is somewhat like a tadpole in appearance and most of the genetic material is contained in the head (1).

The second requirement of the gametes is that they must switch from a passive to an active role once they unite. It is generally thought that the ovum is stimulated by material carried in the **acrosome,** something like a cap on the head of the sperm. The materials in the acrosome make it possible for the sperm to penetrate the ovum and, once there, to initiate reproduction. Human sperm may also contain some sort of guidance system that enables them to swim upstream (at about 3 mm. per hour) against a slow movement of female fluids to find the ovum and orient it in the direction necessary for fertilization.

Sperm are produced in much greater quantities than are ova. During their reproductive years, for example, most women will produce only 300 to 400 ova. In contrast, a normal male emits 200 to 300 million sperm in a single ejaculation. It would appear that this extraordinarily large number of sperm is required for fertility because males with a lower sperm count are often infertile. Of the millions of sperm ejaculated, only 100 or so reach the oviducts (partly through the pumping action of the vaginal, uterine, and oviduct walls and partly through their own swimming action) where the egg is located. Although only one sperm fertilizes the egg, the presence of other sperm, together with the vaginal fluid, facilitates the process (1).

When the ovum is discharged from the follicle and moves toward the oviducts where fertilization can take place, it is still surrounded by follicular cells. Evidence suggests that sperm release an enzyme that dissolves the cellular ''glue'' that holds the follicles together. The presence of many sperm in the vicinity of the ovum may thus be necessary to provide an opening for the one that will actually fertilize the ovum. Once a sperm reaches the membranes surrounding the ovum, the membranes themselves appear to swell and to engulf the successful sperm. After a sperm is inside the ovum, the ovum becomes resistant to penetration by other

The chromosome pairs of a human. Note that there are three chromosomes at the 21 locus, indicating an individual with Down's syndrome.

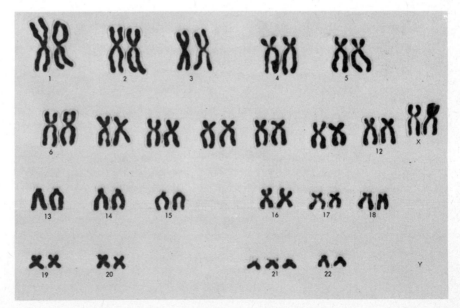

sperm. As soon as the sperm is inside the nucleus of the ovum, it disintegrates and the nuclei of the two unite to form a new single cell with a single nucleus; this is called a **zygote,** the beginning of a new organism (2).

Genes. Each gamete contains a large amount of genetic information that is carried in minute chemical substances called **genes.** The genes are arranged on larger bodies of material that are called **chromosomes.** Every species has a specific number of chromosomes, which helps to determine its unique identity. For decades it was believed that human beings had 48 chromosomes, but it is now recognized that this was an error. To the best of our knowledge, human cells contain 46 chromosomes. In general chromosomes are arranged in pairs; such pairs are *homologous* because the chromosomes are alike in size, shape, and general appearance (1).

Once the zygote is formed, cell division begins enabling all of the genetic information contained in the zygote to be transmitted to each of the new daughter cells. Cell division, which is called **mitosis,** means that there is longitudinal splitting of each of the 46 chromosomes. As each chromosome splits, it spontaneously reconstructs itself so that each half becomes identical to the original and contains its full complement of genes. Mitosis is more like cutting back on a plant than cutting an apple in half. Cutting back on a plant usually produces additional new shoots since the cutting generates new growth, and that is what happens in mitosis. An illustration of mitosis is shown in Figure 2.1.

Once the organism is fully formed, a second type of cell division occurs, resulting in the production of gametes. This is called **meiosis** and is somewhat the reverse of fertilization. That is to say, in fertilization two gametes, the ovum and sperm, join to make a new cell with a full complement of 46 chromosomes. But in meiosis complete cells split to produce gametes with only one-half the chromosomes of the parent cells. An illustration of meiotic cell division is given in Figure 2.2.

It is the process of meiosis, together with fertilization, that accounts for individual differences.

Figure 2.1 Mitotic cell division. (From: Saunders, J. W. *Animal Morphogenesis*, New York: The Macmillan Co., 1968.)

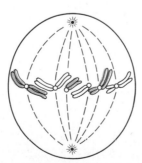
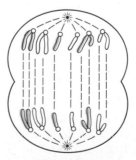
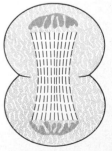

Chromosomes, having been duplicated, are arranged in joint pairs aligned in center of cell

Chromosomes separate and move to opposite ends of the cell

Cell divides, producing two new cells, each with the original number of chromosomes

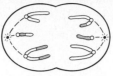

After one cell division, there are two cells, each with the original number of chromosomes

Chromosomes separate and move to opposite ends of the cell, which begins to divide

Cell division complete, with half the original number of chromosomes in each cell

Figure 2.2 Meiotic cell division. (From: Saunders, J. W. *Animal Morphogenesis* New York: Macmillan, 1968.)

It should be pointed out that the genes of any given chromosome occupy a specific place or **locus.** The genes that determine eye color, for example, have a particular locus on a particular chromosome. In homologous chromosomes the gene loci for particular traits are directly opposite one another and usually function together to produce a given trait. During meiosis the chromosomes first split as in mitosis, but the division is not complete and the split pair of homologous chromosomes is *synapsed* (joined) by a structure called a *centromere*. Thus, at this stage in meiosis there are 23 bundles of four chromosome strands, whereas in mitosis at this stage there were 46 bundles of two chromosome strands (3).

As meiosis continues, the homologous pairs of chromosomes appear to repel one another (as do the like poles of two magnets) so that the bundle of four strands splits into two, moving toward opposite "poles" in the cell. Which direction the chromosomes take seems to be random, and some maternal and some paternal chromosomes collect at each pole. During the remainder of meiosis the chromosomes separate into single strands, and as the cell divides each new cell contains only 23 chromosomes and is a gamete. Each gamete contains randomly determined chromosomes from the mother and father, and it is this random assortment of parental chromosomes that produces individual variability.

When gametes from a male and a female recombine during fertilization, a zygote or new organism is begun that has genetic contributions from both. Two siblings who are not identical twins will have different combinations of parental chromosomes, thanks to the random separation of chromosome pairs during meiosis and the formation of gametes. The fact that human beings have 46 chromosomes ensures that there will be a certain uniformity among the species, but the infinite number of chromosome combinations ensures variability.

Gene Action. As mentioned earlier, each chromosome is made up of a large number of genes, each of which has a specific locus on the chromosome strand. Each locus (or a combination of several) is responsible for a particular trait. Because chromosomes work together as pairs, each member of a homologous pair can provide instructions how that trait is to be realized. The genes or combinations of genes that function at a particular locus to produce a specific trait are called **alleles.** Two alleles are required for most traits, and homologous chromosomes are arranged so that the two alleles for a given trait act in unison.

When the allele from each of the two homologous loci give the same instructions, the individual is said to be **homozygous** for that trait. For example, if an individual has an allele for brown eyes from both paternal and maternal chromosomes, he or she would be homozygous for brown eyes. On the other hand, if the person has two different alleles for the same trait (say, one for blue eyes and one for brown eyes), then the person would be **heterozygous** for that trait. It should be noted that many complex traits, such as mating behavior, may be produced by a combination of alleles and not just by a single pair; this makes possible even greater diversity (2).

That which an individual inherits from his or her parents—the unique set of 46 chromosomes that was joined at the time of fertilization—is called the person's **genotype.** It constitutes the sum total of his or her genetic potential. How that potential is actually expressed, however, depends upon whether the subject is homozygous or heterozygous for a particular trait. For example, a person who is heterozygous for eye color may have an allele for blue eyes and one for brown eyes, but the person has brown eyes. The actual expression of the genotype in physical or behavioral traits is called the **phenotype.**

In the foregoing example, the person actually had brown eyes because in the matter of phenotypic **expression,** some alleles are **dominant** and others are **recessive.** When this occurs for an allele pair where one is dominant and one is recessive, only the dominant allele appears in the phenotype. To have blue eyes an individual must be homozygous for blue eyes. If both parents have blue eyes, all of their children will have blue eyes. But if both parents have brown eyes and both parents are heterozygous with respect to eye color, some of their children might have blue eyes. In such a case, the probability of a blue-eyed child is about one in four.

This discussion of the inheritance of eye color has been oversimplified for the purpose of introducing basic concepts. In actuality, eye color is probably determined by more than one pair of alleles functioning at several different loci. And not all alleles are dominant or recessive with respect to one another—sometimes there is a **blending** of the given trait. The existence of gray, green, and various shades of blue and brown eyes indicates that blending is another phenotypic byproduct of heterozygous allele pairs (2).

There is one exception to the rule of homologous chromosomes; it occurs with the chromosome pair that is associated with sexual differentiation. Females have a pair of chromosomes, known as X chromosomes, that are medium-sized. Males have one X chromosome and a smaller one—the Y chromosome. When the male produces sperm or gametes, meiosis results in gametes with either the X or the Y chromosome. Females, on the other hand, produce gametes with only X chromosomes. It is the male gametes, therefore, that determine the sex of the offspring.

Since the sex chromosomes have been extensively studied, we probably know more about them than about most of the other human chromosomes. It is known that the X chromosome has many loci that have little to do with sexual differentiation but, because they are found in the X chromosome, are called *sex-linked*. One example is color blindness, which occurs more often among males than among females. Color blindness is a recessive trait for which there is no complementary allele on the Y chromosome. Hence, if a boy receives the allele for color blindness from his mother, he will be color-blind. For a girl to be color-blind, both parents must have at least one allele for the recessive trait. Since there is less likelihood that both parents will have the allele than that the mother will, more boys than girls are color-blind. Because the X and Y chromosomes are not homologous, the mechanisms of dominance and recessiveness operate in somewhat unusual ways.

Since the 1960s we have learned a great deal about the chemical activity that underlies hereditary transmission. Chromosomes can be viewed as carriers of information, or codes that serve to tell cells how to act. Actually the genes do not code for cells but rather for much smaller units—protein molecules—the building blocks of cells. These molecules are themselves quite complex and are made up of chains of amino acids. There are only about 20 different amino acids but, because they can be ordered in many ways, they give rise to at least 1000 different protein molecules.

Genes themselves are complex molecules of **deoxyribonucleic acid** (DNA) that are strung together in a double helix arrangement. Nucleic acids are special substances that do not fit into the usual classification of carbohydrates, fats, and proteins. While nucleic acids resemble proteins somewhat, they are not proteins. It is now believed that genetic coding is accomplished by information that is stored in DNA and that there are four basic characters in the DNA code. Since the total length of a coiled DNA molecule is about 4000 times the length of the coil, each molecule contains a tremendous amount of information (2).

The genes, or DNA strands, in effect tell the protein molecules how to construct various types of cells. For example, some genes are concerned with the manufacture of the protein coloring matter in red blood cells (hemoglobin). In this case the genes provide a code or blueprint that instructs the cells how to produce the correct amino acid chain for hemoglobin. The cell receives the necessary materials for translating the code

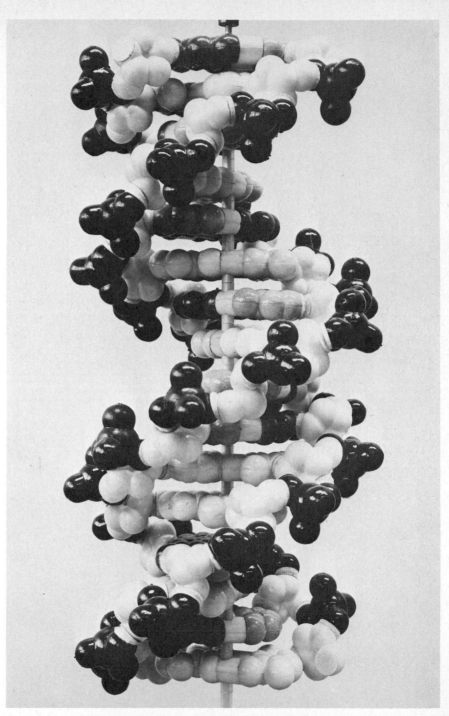

A model of the DNA molecule showing its double helix structure.

provided by the genes and for producing the prescribed material. Genetic processes are extremely intricate, and there is still much more to be learned about the mechanisms of genetic transmission.

We have now covered some of the basic physiology and genetics of the reproductive system. Let us now turn from physiology and genetics to embryology—the way in which a fully functioning organism is formed from a zygote.

Embryonic Development

The development of a human being from a single cell is a truly miraculous process. During the embryonic period the zygote becomes an extraordinarily complex organism consisting of millions of cells, with at least 100 different cell types and a system of interrelated organs including the brain, heart, lungs, stomach, kidneys, and so forth. Although the zygote has none of the life-sustaining and -perpetuating systems of the adult organism, it gives rise to this organism. We know today that this comes about not because the zygote is simply an adult in miniature, but rather because it contains the information—the blueprints—for constructing an organism.

Although the development of the **embryo** is continuous, the process can be divided into a series of stages, according to the major changes that are taking place at that time. While it is appropriate to call the developing organism an embryo throughout the prenatal period, there are specific terms for the embryo during the various stages of prenatal development. As we shall see, it is useful to understand these stages, for at certain times the embryo is more susceptible to environmental influences—such as the mother's illness or ingestion of drugs—than at other times.

The Blastocyst Period. The time from fertilization until about the fifteenth day of development is usually called the period of the **blastocyst.** As the zygote begins to produce daughter cells, it forms a rather shapeless mass that moves down the fallopian tubes and then attaches itself to the uterine wall, after which it begins to produce structures that will provide nourishment for additional growth. The first such structure, called the **trophoblast** (or **chorion**), consists of several layers of cells whose function is to absorb nutriments from its surroundings, specifically the tissues of the uterine wall. Eventually the trophoblast will develop into the **placenta,** a combination of embryonic and uterine tissues that serves as the major conduit for oxygen, nutriments, and waste products between the embryo and the mother.

The cell mass changes in several other ways during this early period. Cells that are close to the inner cavity of the blastocyst become distinguishable from those on the outer surface. This is an initial differentiation of cell types that will become much more prominent later. Cells near to or making up the outer surfaces of the blastocyst are called **ectoderm** ("outer

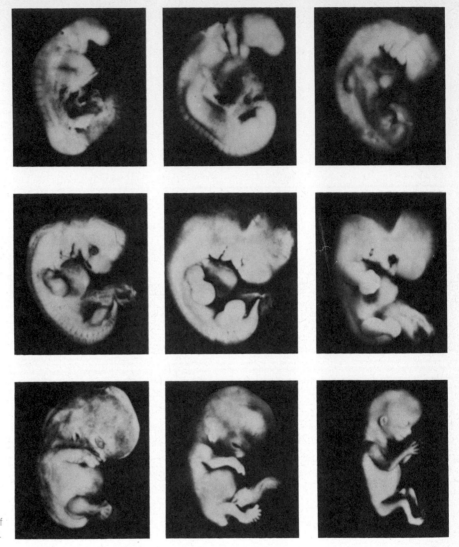

Stages in the evolution of
the human embryo.

layer''). Later on the **endoderm** (inner layer) cells will constitute most
body organs and inner body surfaces, while the ectoderm cells will make
up the outer skin.

During the blastocyst period the cells of the ectoderm expand and move
apart in order to create a new inner cavity called the **amniotic cavity.** The
surrounding membrane of the cavity—made of ectoderm cells—is called
the **amnion.** As development progresses the amniotic cavity will fill with
fluid, forming a protective shield about the developing embryo. Mean-
while, another cavity made of endoderm cells begins to develop; it, to-

gether with its surrounding cells, is called the **yolk sac.** A rough analogy might be the hen's egg. The shell would be the amnion, the white would be the amniotic fluid, and the yolk would correspond to yolk sac. But the large yolk of the hen's egg is a sort of throwback to the evolutionary stage when most of the nutriments for growth were contained in the yolk. In humans the development of the placenta as a means of nourishing the embryo from the mother eliminated the need for large yolks; the human yolk sac has other purposes (2).

Between the amnion and the yolk sac are layers of ectoderm and endoderm cells that comprise the embryo proper. As these cells multiply, a third type appears that is known as **mesoderm** cells; they will make up the bulk of the body, including bones, muscles, and circulatory system. These three types of cells—ectoderm, endoderm, and mesoderm—which lie between the amniotic cavity and the yolk sac are called the *primary germ layers.* As development proceeds the embryo changes in shape; also, where it is attached to the placenta disc there grows a ropelike *umbilical cord* that carries fetal blood to and from the placenta.

During the blastocyst period, therefore, nourishment and protection are provided for the embryo, which begins to become differentiated into the primary germ layers. During this initial period more than 90 percent of the embryonic tissue is made up of temporary support structures—the chorion, amnion, and yolk sac—which are necessary for later development.

The Embryonic Period. During this period, which lasts from about the third through the eighth week, various body organs are constructed. At any time during this 6-week period, different organs will be in the process of being formed, and each one usually requires a couple of weeks.

The first system to develop during this period is the circulatory system. Cords of cells in various parts of the embryo—the amnion, chorion, and yolk sac—develop hollow inner spaces that are capable of transmitting fluids. These primitive tubes then join with one another to form a system that brings together structures from different parts of the embryo. Eventually one of the larger vessels will become the heart, while the others will become veins, arteries, and capillaries. On about the twenty-second day after conception the heart begins to beat, and a day or two later blood is being pumped into the chorion, where it distributes both food and oxygen. It should be pointed out that there is no direct transfer of blood between the mother and the embryo. As the chorion invades the uterine wall and becomes the placenta, it is constantly immersed in uterine blood. The nutriments that pass from the maternal blood to the embryo are filtered by the cell masses of the chorion. Likewise, the waste products that are produced by the embryo are not transmitted directly to the mother but are diffused through the walls of the chorion (2).

On or about the thirty-fifth day of embryonic development the organs of digestion begin to become differentiated, and the cell structures that will eventually become the esophagus, stomach, and intestines can be distin-

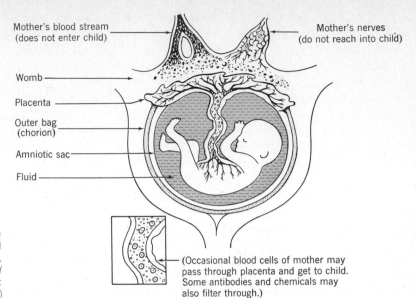

Mother's blood stream
(does not enter child)

Mother's nerves
(do not reach into child)

Womb

Placenta

Outer bag
(chorion)

Amniotic sac

Fluid

Figure 2.3 The
relationship of mother and
fetus. (*Source.* Scheinfeld,
A. *Your heredity and
environment.* Philadelphia:
Lippincott, 1965.)

(Occasional blood cells of mother may
pass through placenta and get to child.
Some antibodies and chemicals may
also filter through.)

guished. Other organs such as the pancreas and liver will develop as a ballooning out of the cell walls of the intestines. By the thirty-fifth day, the trachea has been formed and the lungs are small folded buds that will not become functional until birth.

During this period the physical features of the body also take shape. Probably one of the most complex processes is the creation of the face, which is formed when extensions of various other body parts grow together. It is not dissimilar to the process of sculpting a bust out of clay by pushing inward from the sides, down from the top, and up from the bottom to produce the facial features. Other parts of the body are also developing rapidly: the limb buds appear at the twenty-eighth day and by the forty-seventh day not only are the upper and lower arms and legs discernible, but so too are the hands and feet, fingers, and toes.

The nervous system develops from an early structure of the mesoderm and ectoderm that by the twenty-second day forms a **neural tube.** Cellular outgrowths from the neural tube to all parts of the body begin to make up the neural network that will convey information back and forth from the central nervous system and body. The brain develops at one end of the neural tube by successive layers of cells folding and refolding; as this takes place, connections form with the limbs and various body organs so that each part of the body is represented in some part of the brain. By the end of 3 months, different parts of the brain are clearly distinguishable, and the cerebrum, cerebellum, and medula are all well demarcated (2).

This is only a brief and incomplete description of a few of the structures that are formed during the embryonic period; it should be emphasized, however, that these structures are all extremely small and that by the end of this period the embryo itself is only about *1 inch* long. During the next period the embryo attains the size it will have at birth.

The Fetal Period. During this period—from the end of the second month until delivery—many refinements take place in the basic structures. For example, the various organs of the body need such further elaboration as the formation of connecting vessels before they can be fully functional. The brain, as well as many other organs, increases rapidly in size during the fetal period, but its specific "human" foldings do not occur until later.

Many of the fetal organs, such as the heart, digestive system, and excretory systems, are not yet self-sufficient; they must still rely upon the placenta. That is why a fetus with a defective organ system may survive until birth, but not thereafter. The time of birth is not accidental; it is usually triggered by internal mechanisms indicating that the fetus is large enough and that its organ systems have a good chance of making it on their own. Before we turn to the psychological aspects of embryological growth—pregnancy—let us examine some of the ways in which normal prenatal development can go wrong (2).

Abnormalities in Embryological Development. As we have indicated above, embryological development is something of a miracle because of the delicate interaction of many different chemical and physiological processes; it is amazing that things do not go wrong more often. When they do, the pregnant woman may have a spontaneous abortion. But sometimes the abnormalities are not serious enough to interrupt the pregnancy; thus, the infant will be born with a defect that may be immediately apparent or one that will manifest itself only later on. Two of the most common types of abnormalities pertain to chromosomes or to enzymes.

One type of chromosome abnormality consists of their translocation so that instead of a pair of chromosomes, the subject has three. The first such anomaly was discovered for chromosome 21, one of the smallest of the pairs. It was observed that in children who appeared to have **Down's syndrome** (mongolism) there were 47 chromosomes, with the extra one of the 21 type. We now know that there are other syndromes associated with having 47 chromosomes, and these are called **trisomies.** Since a particular syndrome is usually designated by the identification number of the extra chromosome, Down's syndrome is also known as 21-trisomy.

It appears that the extra chromosome impairs the genetic coding that is associated with that particular chromosome. In the case of Down's syndrome, for example, the subjects have characteristic physical features such as "mongoloid" eyefold, stubby fingers, light hair, and limited intellectual ability. It is not known exactly what causes 21-trisomy, but it is known that such trisomes tend to be associated with the mother's age; that is, a woman over 40 years of age is 20 times more likely than a woman of 20 to give birth to an infant with 21-trisomy (4).

Trisomies associated with the sex chromosomes have also been studied. One sex chromosome combination, XXY, is called **Klinefelter's syndrome.** So long as a person has at least one Y chromosome, he is a male. But in Klinefelter's syndrome the extra X chromosome produces such characteristics as small testicles, tallness, thinness, long arms and legs, sterility, low IQ, and personality instability (5). But this syndrome has not been associated with criminality. Again, the cause of this particular trisomy is not known.

Another sex chromosome trisomy, XYY, has been much discussed in the popular press. Since the Y chromosome determines maleness, one might expect that men with an extra Y chromosome would have exaggerated male traits. This indeed does occur. Some people have argued that XYY men nearly always tend to be criminals, and they claim that there is an unusually large number of them—relative to their numbers in the population—in prison. But one should be cautious about generalizing from a trisomy to behavioral traits. Not all XYY males are criminals, and those who do get into trouble with the law probably do so as a result of complex interactions between their genetic endowment and life experiences.

In some cases, genetic abnormalities are not related to whole chromosomes but rather to alleles for specific traits. During the course of human evolution most alleles for defective traits have been eliminated because those who are afflicted with the trait usually do not have offspring. But some alleles for harmful traits persist because of spontaneous mutations (aberrations of genes produced by such factors as radiation and drugs) and because some traits are recessive and appear only in those rare instances when an individual inherits the recessive gene from both parents. In the case of genetic enzyme deficiency, an abnormality is produced when a defective gene does not code for the appropriate enzyme.

Perhaps the most well-known condition caused by a genetically linked enzyme deficiency is **phenylketonuria** (PKU). In most individuals an enzyme is produced that breaks down phenylalanine, an amino acid that is found in most protein foods. When this amino acid is not broken down for use in building body tissue, it is retained in excessive amounts in the body. Furthermore, the surplus phenylalanine is transformed by other enzymes in the body into substances that are not usually produced by the body. Since these substances are excreted in the urine, PKU can be detected by urinalysis (the word "phenylketonuria" is derived in part from this fact).

Tests for PKU are now normally conducted on all newborn infants. If the condition is detected, the infant can be placed on a special diet that is low in proteins containing phenylalanine. Such diets are expensive and often rather restricted so that it may be a burden for the older child who wants to eat what his or her peers are eating. There is some controversy as to how long a child should remain on the low-phenylalanine diet. Without this diet in early life children show varying degrees of mental retardation. Children with PKU tend to be blond and blue-eyed and to have sensitive skin (6).

Another condition caused by a specific enzyme deficiency is **albinism.** The person with this condition, usually called an *albino,* lacks the pigment melanin, which produces variations in skin color. Melanin is created by the breakdown of several amino acids, but the albino does not have the enzyme for producing this chemical breakdown. Albinism is a recessive trait and it does not occur very often. The condition is mildly disabling inasmuch as the person must avoid the sun (because of the lack of melanin, the tanning pigment, in the skin) and is sensitive to bright light (because of the lack of pigment in the eyes which ordinarily absorbs stray light).

Since the 1960s another enzyme deficiency has been discussed often in the popular press—*sickle cell anemia*. In this case the defective gene is responsible for the production of hemoglobin, the iron-containing protein pigment that is found in the red blood cells. Actually the deficiency is minute—only one of the 287 amino acids that make up the hemoglobin molecule is affected. Nevertheless the defect results in red cells that are sickle-shaped and that clump and break apart easily. Individuals who are afflicted with this condition have chronic anemia and occasionally suffer sharp pains from the stretching of blood vessels that have been clogged by the defective sickle cells.

A method for detecting genetic abnormalities before birth has now been developed. It is called **amniocentesis.** Since the amniotic fluid contains embryonic cells, these can be examined when some of the amniotic fluid is removed by inserting a slender needle either into the vagina or through the abdominal wall. Those genetic abnormalities that appear in single random cells, such as Down's syndrome, can be detected with this technique. Although amniocentesis is still fairly new, it can reveal certain genetic defects early in pregnancy. Whether or not the mother should seek an abortion for a defective fetus is social, moral, religious, and political issue that is beyond the scope of this book.

PREGNANCY

Prenatal development can also be viewed from the psychological and sociological perspective of the woman in whom these events are happening. Some psychologists have claimed that pregnancy is a major life crisis comparable to that of adolescence (7–9), and they have focused on the psychological significance of this event to the mother and father as well. We will look at some of the psychological aspects first.

Over the years there has been a wide divergence of opinion about the relationship between the mother's actions and emotions and the well-being of the fetus. At one time it was believed that even the slightest emotional stress or overindulgence in eating, drinking, sexual activity, and so forth, could affect the embryo. But at another time, opinion had it that the embryo was so well protected that overindulgence by the mother would not affect the developing organism. At present physicians and psychologists take a middle-of-the-road approach (10).

We will also discuss the act of birth itself. At present there is a lot of controversy about the best and most healthy way to deliver babies—about whether drugs should be used, about the delivery-room environment, and about whether the father should be present in the delivery room.

Pregnancy as a Life Crisis

How any given couple will react to pregnancy will depend upon a number of factors. Probably the most important are whether the baby is wanted, whether the parents are relatively mature, whether they have a good relationship with one another and with their own parents, whether they have a sense of their own identity in relation to the baby, and much more. Above all, the reaction to pregnancy is emotional, not rational. Some couples who planned for and tried to maximize the possibility of pregnancy may find that they are disappointed when it actually occurs. Other couples, for whom the pregnancy was an unwanted surprise, may discover that they are actually thrilled by the idea (11).

In general parenthood constitutes a new stage of development that encompasses, paradoxically, a further growing away from as well as a further growing toward the couple's own parents. By becoming parents young people assume new responsibilities and move even further from their previous dependency upon their parents. Yet they are also fulfilling the desire of their own parents for grandchildren and are thus re-establishing bonds that may have been broken during adolescence and young adulthood. Many young mothers-to-be, for example, often want their own mothers nearby during the final months of pregnancy. For the expectant woman, pregnancy is both a sign of her mature womanhood and an opportunity to re-establish emotional bonds with her parents that were broken or weakened by marriage.

For the male, parenthood may be a reflection of potency and virility. But it may also be viewed as a sign of permanent bondage—of an end to adventure and freedom. For some men the aura of domesticity signaled by a baby may be very welcome, but for others it may seem a threat. Whereas the impregnation of a woman is seen as a sign of virility, caring for an infant and child is viewed as a feminine activity. Although these attitudes still exist, they are changing with the contemporary movement toward equalization of rights for men and women and with the breakdown of rigid sex-role stereotypes (12).

For the pregnant woman, particularly during her first pregnancy, one can usually observe three successive transformations of attitudes and feelings that are associated with the trimesters of pregnancy (11). During the first trimester, the woman tends to focus on changes in her body. She will wonder and/or worry about whether she "shows." Such changes as a swelling of the breasts, morning sickness and nausea, and unusual food cravings bring about a certain self-centeredness. And feelings of weakness, fatigue, irritability, and mood swings tend to make the woman feel that she is changing in ways over which she has no control. Her heightened egocentrism and physical discomfort may make her unhappy with her husband, whom she may feel to be insufficiently attentive.

Psychologically, this is the period when childhood fantasies about childbearing become a reality. There is a sense of her creative potential, of being an important, indeed essential, part in the whole scheme of things. As in adolescence, when the young woman becomes sexually mature and has to develop a new self-concept, so, too, when she becomes pregnant she must modify her conception of herself and her relation to the world (13).

With the onset of the second trimester (after the fetus's organs have been formed), the pregnant woman begins to think less about herself and more about the embryo that is beginning to stir. At first the movements are slight and delicate "like holding a butterfly in your hand and it was fluttering" or "gentle strokings from a soft glove" (11). The husband can now share in the experience by feeling the movements and by listening for the heartbeats. At this stage the pregnant woman may feel that she is inhabited by a stranger. During the second trimester the pregnancy usually becomes apparent, and the woman switches from her usual clothes to maternity clothes. Those women who have taken great pride in their appearance and sexual attractiveness may see their new clumsiness and heaviness as ugly and distressing. Such women may have fantasies that their husbands find them unattractive and are dating other women. Yet other women become radiant during this period and take great pleasure in this new expression of womanhood.

The realization that there is another life within her can produce a different kind of conflict in the contemporary woman. Once the pregnant woman begins to feel the fetus within, she also must decide how much of her own individuality and career to sacrifice for her child. Thankfully, for most women today, this need not be a problem. Many professional women work almost until the day of birth. Then, after a brief recuperation following delivery, they return to work. Of course, they are able to find excellent persons to care for their babies when they are away from home, but were also competent women who are able to reconcile a career with motherhood.

During the last trimester, the prospective mother's orientation changes once again. Although she is rather large now and has to be careful about her balance, she is really less concerned about her appearance and is simply eager to get the whole thing over with. According to Abigail Lewis:

In the early months I was very self-conscious about myself. There are about three stages of self-consciousness. The first is when you wonder if you are noticeable or not and don't know if it is better to have people realize you are pregnant or just let them think you are getting fat. The second covers all the middle months when you are quite obviously pregnant; then it is a queer feeling to walk along the street and feel no longer anonymous, realizing that there is one secret of your life that everyone who looks can know—that at least one private incident of your past has become almost incredibly public and that you can bear, as it were, the stigma of post passion wherever you go. The third stage, which I have mercifully entered now, is when you don't care very much; the event is so close you are living more in the future than in the present [14].

There are certain negative aspects about this last phase of pregnancy. Because of their size and certain other physiological considerations, many women who may have continued to be active in one or another sport up until this time may now find that they have to curtail their physical activities seriously. The subtle flutterings of butterfly wings now become heavy thumps that are sometimes painful and may even keep the prospective mother awake at night. Morning sickness and nausea give way to constipation, hemorrhoids, and an urgency to urinate and in some women the appearance of varicose veins. Women occasionally get angry at the other within and feel "I'll get even with you" when the kicks become rather sharp.

The saving grace, of course, is that there is a terminal date—the day when the baby will be born at last. Again, however, the mother-to-be may have conflicted feelings. On the one hand she is probably tired of being clumsy, of not being able to wear her usual clothes, of having her usual activities restricted, and so she is probably eager to have the whole thing over with. On the other hand, she may be afraid because of what she has read and heard about the pains and dangers of childbirth. The expectant mother may even feel sad about giving up the unique union that exists between her and the fetus. But the overriding feeling among most women is to have the pregnancy over and to return to their normal selves (11).

Obviously, the reactions of the fathers-to-be have no relationship to the trimesters of pregnancy; their reactions pertain to how they view the birth in relation to themselves, their marriage, their work, and so forth.

In one study (15) a sociologist interviewed 29 university-student husbands whose wives were expecting their first child. Among these men he found three prevailing attitudes about parenthood and marriage. One group had a *romantic* orientation toward their forthcoming role; another group had a *family* orientation, while the third group had what might be called a *career* orientation toward parenthood. While these orientations are relatively distinct, there is always some overlapping, and of course these orientations can change as the father matures (15).

Those men with a *romantic* orientation were somewhat overawed at the thought of becoming a father. Many of these young men had enjoyed being the son and they felt somewhat overwhelmed at the thought of taking on the new responsibilities of a family. Many of these young men had been supported by their parents or by their wives, and now their wives' forthcoming dependency made them aware of their new role as provider. Thus, the pregnancy produced a maturational crisis in which these men had to shift from carefree adolescence to responsible adulthood. For some of them, the process entailed considerable conflict with both their parents and their wives.

Those men with a *family* orientation had already accepted the responsibility of providing for their wives and had often helped their parents as well. For these men the paternal role was an easy one to adopt; it entailed a closer relationship with their wives and a great deal of planning for and about the forthcoming child. Such men began to notice other children and to look forward to having children of their own to enjoy and provide for.

The third, or *career*-oriented group, often saw the expected baby as a burden and as a threat. For these men the costs and responsibilities of parenthood meant giving up some of their freedom and certain material things. Many saw the baby as an intrusion on their career plans and feared that the baby might interfere with their study and research. More than anything else, they did not want the pattern of their lives to be disturbed and they did not want anything to be asked of them, in terms of responsibility and time, that had not been asked before. The career-oriented men denied that prospective fatherhood changed their self-conception in any way.

We can thus see that the prenatal period is not only a time of growth for the new individual but for his or her parents as well. Pregnancy is a life crisis for parents that is just as significant as adolescence. But whereas adolescence entails primarily a breaking away, parenthood reunites young people with their own parents. By assuming parental roles, young people are also preparing themselves for the possibility of caring for their own parents when they become elderly. In a very real sense, therefore, parenthood brings the generations together.

Maternal-Fetal Interactions

When the attitudes of the expectant mother are negative, she may be emotionally upset; a fair amount of contemporary research has been done to understand the effect of the mother's emotional state on the developing fetus. Other research has focused on the effects of maternal smoking, drug use, and illness upon the fetus during pregnancy.

Effects of Maternal Emotions. According to folklore, if a pregnant woman was frightened by a rabbit she would have a timid child, or if she read a great deal during pregnancy the child would be intelligent. These folk myths all assume that what happens to a woman during pregnancy can affect the fetus. Modern science, however, has determined more exactly what factors do and do not have an effect. Certain evidence has been found that emotional stress during pregnancy may affect fetal development (16–19). Several physical defects such as misshapen ears and toes, wide gaps between the first and second toe, and a curved fifth finger seem to be associated with maternal stress during the embryonic period—the time when the body structure is being formed. Although these defects are genetically determined, they are not inherited; that is, they are due to damaged chromosomal materials rather than to defective information contained in the alleles. But it is not clear just how emotional stress during the early weeks of pregnancy creates these abnormalities.

Emotional stress has also been associated with spontaneous abortions. Several studies have found that women who repeatedly abort tend to have more psychic conflicts, to be more dependent, and to be less interested in having children than women who carry their babies to full term (20–22). Of course, it is possible that for these women their first spontaneous abortion may have led to anxiety about subsequent pregnancies.

The tendency to deliver babies prematurely has also been associated with the mother's emotional state. In one study it was found that the mothers of premature infants were more emotionally troubled, were more dependent, and had more negative attitudes toward pregnancy than a comparable group of women who had carried to full term (23–25). Of course, it should be noted that these studies were retrospective in the sense that they were conducted after the babies had been born. Although it is possible that the mother's condition and attitudes after delivery are approximately what they had been before, this needs to be demonstrated directly.

Expectant mothers with more severe emotional problems, such as schizophrenia, appear to have a higher incidence of prenatal complications (spontaneous abortion, premature delivery, delivery complications) than do nonschizophrenic women. Some research suggests, however, that it is the length of time the woman has been emotionally ill rather than the severity of the illness as such that leads to prenatal difficulties (26).

Maternal Habits. The habit that has been researched the most during the past 10 or 15 years is smoking, and much of this research was done by Yerushalmy (27, 28). He found that there was a consistent relationship between maternal smoking during pregnancy and the infant's low birth weight. Low birth weight is generally associated with a variety of physical defects and higher-than-average rates of infant mortality. But, as in all of these studies, the chain of causation is not clear-cut. In another study, Yerushalmy found that even those women who stopped smoking during pregnancy had babies with low birth weight. Apparently there is some factor about women who normally smoke, rather than smoking per se, that leads to this condition.

Another controversial issue is what constitutes an adequate diet during pregnancy. In this area as well, there is as much folklore as there is fact. For example, it was once believed that eating certain "brain foods" would make the baby intelligent. What needs to be remembered in any discussion on diet is that the developing fetus takes top priority when essential nutrients are in short supply; that is, a poor diet during pregnancy may cause more serious harm to the mother than to the fetus. If the mother does not consume enough calcium, for example, calcium will be removed from her own bones and teeth to meet the needs of the fetus. In the case of extreme protein deficiency, however, it has been found that this can lead to infants with lower intelligence (31, 32). In such cases protein deficiency may be associated with other aspects of extreme poverty that could result in a lower intelligence.

For the woman of average means, however, it is suggested that she eat a well-balanced diet, supplemented with certain vitamins and minerals (especially calcium and iron) to meet the requirements of the developing fetus. As to the expectant mother's total weight gain during pregnancy, physicians are not in agreement on this issue. It was once advised that the woman gain 2 pounds a month for a maximum total increase of 18 pounds; now this advice seems to be too rigid in view of wide individual differences. Probably the expectant mother should confine her total weight gain to between 18 and 24 pounds.

Apparently a moderate use of alcohol (such as a cocktail before dinner) does not harm the fetus. Women who have a drinking problem, however, may eat poorly during pregnancy, and this may affect their own health as well as that of the fetus. With respect to alcohol as well as diet, moderation would seem to be advisable.

Drug Use. For a time, European physicians were prescribing certain tranquilizers for pregnant women. However, one of them—Thalidomide (introduced in 1958)—produced disastrous effects upon thousands of children (mostly in Europe) whose mothers had taken the drug during the embryonic period. Many of these children were born with short fins instead of arms and legs. Thalidomide was never approved by the Food and Drug Administration for use in the United States. Since the Thalidomide tragedy, physicians have been reluctant to prescribe drugs for pregnant women. It is now advised that a pregnant woman should not use drugs unless the potential benefits to her and the fetus are greater than the potential risks.

Illness during Pregnancy. Perhaps the illness whose detrimental effects are best known is rubella (German measles). In the case of adults this is usually a mild disease that produces a slight rash and fever and lasts for a few days. For a pregnant woman, however, contracting rubella during first trimester greatly increases the probability that the fetus will be harmed. The estimates of risk vary according to many factors, including the particular strain of rubella virus. However, it is reasonable to estimate that if a woman contracts rubella during the fourth week of pregnancy, there is a 50 percent chance that the baby will be born with a defect. The risk decreases steadily after the fourth week, and women who contract the illness after 18 weeks run little risk of bearing a child with a defect that is the result of rubella (29).

Although most of our knowledge about the detrimental effects of viruses on the embryo come from studies of rubella, there are other viruses that cause or are suspected of causing defects. Mumps is known to increase the risk of fetal death and defects when it is contracted by a pregnant woman. Hepatitis (liver inflammation caused by a virus) and even some common "cold" and "flu" viruses may also increase the risk of defects. In general the danger tends to be greatest during the earliest weeks and months of pregnancy when the fetus's body and organs are being formed.

Rh Incompatibility. The Rh blood type, as well as the ABO blood type, is related to chemical substances that rest upon the surface of the red blood cells. The Rh factor, which is associated with the immune system, can be viewed as being inherited according to rules of dominance and recession. Inasmuch as Rh is dominant, a person with one or both alleles for the trait will show the factor and be Rh positive; a person with two recessive alleles for the trait will not show it and will be Rh negative.

Complications occur when Rh negative and Rh positive blood are mixed. A person with Rh negative blood who receives some Rh positive blood will build up antibodies against it; in effect, the one blood type rejects the other. This is a unilateral rejection, however, because a person with Rh positive blood can receive Rh negative blood without rejecting it. Now the only situation in which there is an incompatibility between the mother and fetus occurs when the mother is Rh negative and fetus is Rh positive.

The situation is dangerous because, although there is no direct blood exchange between the mother and fetus, fetal blood can sometimes enter the maternal circulation. When this happens, the mother's blood builds up antibodies against the Rh positive blood. If this happens several times (as in the case of repeated pregnancies), some of the antibodies may enter the fetus's blood and begin to attack the Rh positive cells. If not arrested, this process can cause serious damage or death to the fetus. Since this problem was diagnosed in 1940, it has been possible to anticipate the difficulty in individual cases and counsel the parents accordingly. In some cases of Rh incompatibility, the baby may be given a complete transfusion at birth to get rid of the antibodies. Since the 1960s, however, a new procedure is being used that eliminates the need for complete transfusions. This method involves injecting specific anti-Rh gamma globulins into the mother after the birth of a heterozygous child. These gamma globulins destroy the Rh positive cells circulating in the mother and prevent the buildup of antibodies that would otherwise affect subsequent children (33).

Labor and Delivery

Finally, between the thirty-fifth and forty-third week after the expectant mother's last menstrual period, the baby is ready to be born; the average gestation time is about 40 weeks. We will describe the birth process, some of the hazards of delivery, adjustments made by the newborn infant, and some of the points of view regarding delivery-room procedures.

The Process of Birth. The onset of labor which leads to birth is caused by a variety of factors, including hormone signals from the fetus, stress signals from the aging placenta, and perhaps mechanical stimulation from the fully developed fetus. These factors, and perhaps others as well, give rise to mild uterine contractions that are not always noticeable. These usually begin about a week or two before delivery.

As the time of birth approaches, the uterine contractions become stronger, more frequent, and much more noticeable. What are usually

Hospital delivery of an infant provides many safeguards against infection and birth complications.

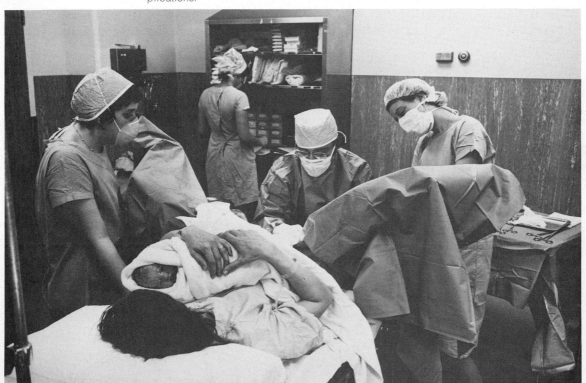

called "labor pains" are contractions that occur about every minute; some women compare the intensity of these contractions to menstrual cramps. About 7 to 10 hours elapse between the beginning of labor and delivery. For women who are giving birth for the first time, the interval of time tends to be longer than for women who have previously given birth; for the latter group no more than several hours may pass between labor and delivery.

In the later stages of labor the contractions last longer (about a minute) and are more frequent. As a result of these contractions, the baby is pushed into a new position with its head toward the cervix (the narrow outer end of the uterus). Partly due to this mechanical pressure, the cervix begins to widen or *dilate,* and it continues to do so as the baby's head presses against it. Fortunately, the baby's head, which is the largest part of the body (the shoulders are wider but more flexible), is still relatively soft and so it can be squeezed somewhat out of shape in order to pass through the cervix. Thus, newborn babies usually have funny-looking heads for a few days after birth.

Sometime after labor begins, the amniotic sac ruptures and the amniotic fluids come out. These fluids act as a kind of lubricant to help the baby pass through the cervix and into the birth canal (the vagina). As the baby is ready to move out of the vagina, the obstetrician may make a small incision (called an **episiotomy**) to prevent any uncontrolled tearing of the external membranes. This incision is then sewed up immediately after birth. Shortly after delivery, placenta is dislodged from the uterine wall and expelled; it is sometimes called the *afterbirth*.

Hazards of Delivery. Not all babies are delivered quite so easily. For example, sometimes the infant's buttocks, rather than the head, press against the cervix. In effect the baby is in a bent-over position, which makes it larger and more difficult to deliver. This is called a **breech delivery,** and if the baby cannot be turned around, birth is more difficult and dangerous than normal. There can be other complications if the placenta blocks the cervix. Fortunately modern medical practice is usually able to cope with these once-dangerous and often fatal risks of pregnancy and birth.

Another problem arises when it is judged that the mother's pelvic bones are too small for delivery or that other conditions such as a twisted umbilical cord are present. In these cases the obstetrician makes an incision in the abdomen and removes the baby directly from the uterus. This operation, called a *cesarean section,* is now a well-established, routine, and safe procedure. The availability of antibiotics and blood transfusions today has removed much of the danger from this operation.

A rather pervasive risk of pregnancy is oxygen deprivation; because the brain requires oxygen, even a slight deprivation may cause the brain cells to die. Oxygen may be in short supply for a number of reasons. During labor undue pressure on the umbilical cord may curtail the blood flow and oxygen supply; the same thing may happen if there is a premature separation of the placenta from the uterine wall. Sometimes drugs that are used to alleviate maternal pain can anesthetize the infant and delay its breathing. Permanent injuries, from minimal brain injury to the cerebral palsies, have been associated with oxygen deprivation at birth, but awareness of these problems has also helped to prevent them.

The hazards of childbirth for the mother have been greatly reduced since the 1920s. Fifty years ago in the United States the maternal death rate at delivery was 67 per 10,000 live births, while in the mid-1970s it was less than 4 per 10,000 live births. Better medical practice, improved health, more informed knowledge about pregnancy, and better prenatal care have all helped to reduce the dangers of pregnancy and childbirth.

Care of the Newborn Infant. After delivery, a number of procedures are followed to ensure the baby's well-being. First its mouth and nostrils are cleared of mucus with the aid of a syringe. Then the baby is held upside down to drain any remaining fluids from its windpipe. Usually the baby starts breathing immediately, partly in response to the influx of air, but sometimes this initial breathing is helped along by the obstetrician. This can be done by splashing the infant with cold water or by slapping its buttocks. The newborn infant can function for several minutes after birth without breathing and without damage; beyond this, though, oxygen deprivation can cause serious injury.

Once the baby is breathing—and the first intake of air usually produces a loud cry—the umbilical cord is cut and tied. The baby is then washed and wrapped up warmly. Newborns do not need much food for the first few days, but they can be helped by ingesting *colostrum,* a watery secretion of the mother's breast that precedes the production of milk. Colostrum contains many antibodies that provide the newborn with initial immunity to infection. The baby's sucking at the breast also helps the mother because this action stimulates the production of a hormone, *oxytocin,* that speeds coagulation of the blood (and hence reduces postpartum bleeding) and helps the uterus return to its normal size.

There are differences of opinion as to whether or not the baby should continue to be breast-fed after the first few days. Many physicians believe that the mother should do whatever feels most comfortable and right for her. Infant formulas are rather similar to mother's milk from the point of view of basic nutriments. What is most important is the affective bond between mother and child. Since some women suffer from depression after delivery, it may not be a good idea for their babies to nurse. Most mothers are pleased and proud of their new babies and they convey their positive feelings whether they decide to breast-feed or bottle-feed.

Controversies about Childbirth Procedures. As we have indicated, there is a great deal of folklore about pregnancy and childbirth. For example, it was once thought necessary for a new mother to remain in bed for several weeks after delivery. But that idea emerged from the fact that

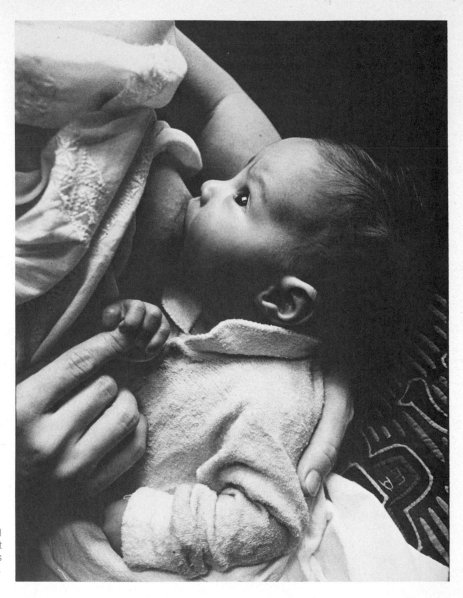

Breast feeding is healthful for both mother and infant in the first few days after delivery.

childbirth once entailed a considerable loss of blood, and the prolonged bed rest gave the mother enough time to replenish her lost blood. With modern medical procedures, however, not much blood is lost, and even if it is, it can be replenished with transfusions. Because of the new procedures, new mothers are encouraged to get out of bed within hours after delivery and usually to leave the hospital within a few days.

There is a difference of opinion as to whether drugs should be used to ease the mother's pain at delivery and to facilitate delivery. Since the

Thalidomide tragedy, however, parents as well as obstetricians have been wary of drugs. Many women have enrolled in "natural childbirth" classes to learn appropriate breathing and muscle contraction; one purpose here is "childbirth without pain" and another is to obviate the need for potentially dangerous drugs and forceps. The fathers-to-be also attend these classes and are encouraged to be present during the delivery. This participation of the father in the delivery process (not condoned by all physicians or by all fathers!) can make the parents feel that the delivery as well as the conception is a joint effort. In the past decade there has also been a return to the use of trained midwives and to having babies at home.

Perhaps the greatest current controversy about childbirth procedures stems from the writings of a French physician, Frederick Leboyer (30). He argues that the well-lighted, relatively cold, and noisy delivery room is such a contrast to the dark, warm, and quiet womb that it produces an unnecessary shock. He prefers a delivery room that is dimly lighted, warm, and quiet; he prefers to bathe the baby in warm water and generally provide an environment that is as much like the womb as possible. Other physicians contend that they will not practice medicine in the dark and that the infant's sensory mechanisms are not assaulted by conditions in the delivery room. There is probably some truth on both sides; Leboyer's views may serve a useful purpose if certain delivery-room practices can be modified to produce a smoother transition from the environment of the womb to the environment of the outside world.

Summary

The prenatal period can be viewed from at least two different perspectives: the genetic and embryological, which looks at the development of the embryo within the womb, and the pregnancy experience as viewed by the mother and father and what it means in their lives.

The male sperm and the female ova are called gametes. Each gamete carries one half of the to be formed individual's genetic endowment. This endowment is carried in chemical substances called genes that carry blueprints for organismic development. The genes are arranged in chains called chromosomes that occur in pairs. For each species, there is a specific number of chromosome pairs, and for the human species this number is twenty-three. Development occurs primarily through cell division of which there are two types. Mitosis is that type of cell division in which each daughter cell contains a full complement of parental chromosomes. The cell division that results in gametes, each of which contains only half of the parental complement of chromosones is called meiosis. The process of development is extraordinarily complex and many abnormalities of a physical and/or mental type can be traced to defective genes or to the processes that are regulated by them.

Once the sperm has fertilized the ovum, there is a period of rapid growth and differentiation that takes place in three phases. During the first 2 weeks, the blastocyst period, certain structures are established for the protection and nourishment of the developing embryo. During the second, or embryonic, period (which extends from the third to eighth week), the body structures and organ systems are formed. During the remaining prenatal period—the fetal period—the structures and organ systems that were formed during the embryonic period are enlarged and filled out. The total prenatal period lasts, on the average, about 40 weeks.

Looked at from the viewpoint of the mother and father, pregnancy can be seen as a life crisis comparable to that of adolescence. By presenting their own parents with grandchildren, the mother and father are able to re-establish the bonds of caring and affection that may have been broken or strained during adolescence and young adulthood. During pregnancy the woman goes through several stages. During the first stage she may experience nausea, have unusual food cravings, and wonder about whether or not she ''shows.'' During the second stage she may think more about the ''other'' within her and be awed by the miracle of creation. Toward the end of pregnancy, what with all of the imposed restrictions and its discomforts, the expectant mother may be eager to have the whole matter over with. The reaction of the father to the pregnancy will depend upon whether he is romantically, family-, or career-oriented.

The process of childbirth itself has become less of a hazard to both mother and child than it was formerly. Even so, emotional stress on the part of the mother-to-be has been associated with deformities, spontaneous abortions, and prematurity. Maternal habits such as diet and nutrition, smoking, and drinking may be related (although probably indirectly) to the size and health of the baby. With respect to delivery, obstetricians today try to avoid the use of drugs and forceps in order not to run the risk of prolonged oxygen deprivation. Opinions differ as to how much light, heat, and noise there should be in the delivery room; it is not known what the short-term or long-term effects of such stimulation at birth will be on the infant.

References

1. Levitan, M., & Montagu, A. *Textbook of human genetics.* New York: Oxford University Press, 1971.
2. Swanson, H. D. *Human reproduction.* New York: Oxford University Press, 1974.
3. Cavalli-Sforza, L. L. *Elements of human genetics.* Reading, Mass.: Addison-Wesley, 1973.
4. Achenbach, T. M. *Developmental psychopathology.* New York: Ronald Press, 1974.
5. Money, J. Behavior genetics: Principles, methods and examples from XO, XXY, and XYY syndromes. *Seminars in Psychiatry,* 1970, **2,** 11–29.
6. Robinson, H. B., & Robinson, N. M. *The mentally retarded child.* New York: McGraw-Hill, 1965.

7. Bibring, G. L., Dwyer, T. F., Huntington, D. S., & Valenstein, A. F. A study of the psychological processes in pregnancy and of the earliest mother-child relationship: I. Some propositions and comments. *Psychoanalytic Study of the Child,* 1961, **16,** 9–24.

8. Benedek, T. Parenthood as a developmental phase: A contribution to the libido theory. *Journal of American Psychoanalytic Association,* 1959, **7,** 389–417.

9. Erikson, E. H. Identity and the life cycle. Selected papers. *Psychological Issues,* 1959, **1,** 1–171.

10. Sameroff, A. J., & Chandler, M. J. Reproductive risk and the continuum of caretaking causality. In F. D. Horowitz (Ed.), *Review of child development research.* Vol. 4. Chicago: University of Chicago Press, 1975.

11. Jessner, T., Weigert, E., & Foy, J. L. The development of parental attitudes during pregnancy. In E. James Anthony & T. Benedek (Eds.), *Parenthood: Its psychology and psychopathology.* Boston: Little, Brown, 1970.

12. Schaefer, G. The expectant father: His care and management. *Postgraduate Medicine,* 1965, **38,** 658–663.

13. Rheingold, J. C. *The fear of being a woman.* New York: Grune & Stratton, 1964.

14. Lewis, A. *An interesting condition.* New York: Doubleday, 1950.

15. McCorkel, R. J., Jr. Husbands and pregnancy: An exploratory study. Unpublished master's thesis. University of North Carolina, 1964.

16. Stott, D. H. The child's hazards in utero. In J. G. Howells (Ed.), *Modern perspectives in international child psychiatry.* New York: Bruner/Mazel, 1971.

17. Niswander, K. R., & Gordon, M. (Eds.), *The collaborative perinatal study of the national institute of neurological diseases and stroke.* Philadelphia: Saunders, 1972.

18. Drillien, C. M., & Wilkinson, E. M. Emotional stress and mongoloid birth. *Developmental Medicine and Child Neurology,* 1964, **6,** 140–143.

19. Drillien, C. M., Ingram, T. T. S., & Wilkinson, E. M. *The causes and natural history of cleft lip and palate.* Edinburgh: Livingstone, 1966.

20. Ferreira, A. J. Emotional factors in prenatal environment: A review. *Journal of Nervous and Mental Disease,* 1965, **141,** 108–118.

21. Joffe, J. M. *Prenatal detriments of behavior.* Oxford, Eng.: Pergamon, 1969.

22. Javert, C. T. Further follow-up on habitual abortion patients. *American Journal of Obstetrics and Gynecology,* 1962, **84,** 1149–1159.

23. Blau, A., Slaff, B., Easton, E., Walkowitz, J., & Cohen, J. The psychogenic etiology of premature births: A preliminary report. *Psychosomatic Medicine,* 1963, **25,** 201–211.

24. Gunter, L. Psychopathology and stress in the life experience of mothers of premature infants. *American Journal of Obstetrics & Gynecology,* 1963, **86,** 333–340.

25. McDonald, R. I. The role of emotional factors in obstetric complications: A review. *Psychosomatic Medicine,* 1968, **30,** 222–237.

26. Sameroff, A. J., & Zax, M. Perinatal characteristics of the offspring of schizophrenic women. *Journal of Nervous and Mental Diseases,* 1973, **157,** 191–199.

27. Yerushalmy, J. The relationship of parents' smoking to outcome of pregnancy: Implications as to the problem of inferring causation from observed effects. *American Journal of Epidemiology,* 1971, **93,** 443–456.

28. Yerushalmy, J. Infants with low birth weight born before their mothers started to smoke cigarettes. *American Journal of Obstetrics and Gynecology,* 1972, **112,** 277–284.

29. Hardy, J. B. Rubella and its aftermath. *Children,* 1969, **16,** 91–96.

30. Leboyer, F. *Birth without violence.* New York: Knopf, 1974.

31. Scrimshaw, N. S. Early malnutrition and central nervous system function. *Merrill-Palmer Quarterly,* 1969, **15,** 375–388.

32. Birch, H. G. Functional effects of fetal malnutrition. *Hospital Practice,* March 1971, 134–148.

33. Lerner, M. I. *Heredity, evolution and society.* San Francisco: W. H. Freeman, 1968.

3 Physical and Mental Growth

PRINCIPLES OF PHYSICAL GROWTH

Direction of Growth

Differentiation and Integration

The Sequence of Development

PHYSICAL DEVELOPMENT DURING THE FIRST TWO YEARS OF LIFE

Infancy: The First Year

Infancy: The Second Year

MENTAL GROWTH

Quantitative Aspects of Mental Growth

Qualitative Aspects of Mental Growth

Perception

Language

Cognitive Processes

ESSAY

Parent Education and Infant Stimulation

BIOGRAPHY

Jean Piaget

SUMMARY

REFERENCES

Human development can be looked at as taking place in a series of stages that are related to age. During each stage there are certain characteristic and interrelated attainments in physical and mental growth as well as in personality and social development. Physical growth is the touchstone of development in general, and the principles that apply to physical growth often apply to mental, personality, and social development as well.

PRINCIPLES OF PHYSICAL GROWTH

Infancy is the period from birth to about 2 years of age. It is a time of extraordinarily swift growth and achievement in all areas of development. Because of the rapidity of infant growth, some of the general principles that govern human development at all stages of life are particularly clear during this period; these include (a) a characteristic growth rate, (b) a characteristic directionality, (c) a characteristic pattern of differentiation and integration, and (d) a characteristic sequence.

Growth Rate. For any given child, his or her physical development follows a certain growth rate that is relatively resistant to external environmental variations. Some children increase in height and weight at a regular, even pace, whereas others seem to grow in spurts. Even when unusual circumstances (such as illness or food deprivation) interfere with the normal pace of growth, there are self-regulatory processes that bring the infant back rather quickly to his or her original growth rate as soon as these conditions improve.

The hardiness of individual growth rates is particularly evident in the case of premature infants, those whose birth weight is less than 5½ pounds. Despite their low weight and small size, premature infants usually catch up with full-term babies in both height and weight within the first year of life (1, 2). However, youngsters whose birth weight is less than 4½ pounds may suffer permanent deficits not only in height and weight but also in intellectual ability (3–7). Thus, self-regulating processes will compensate for minor but not major deviations from the normal intrauterine growth.

In motor development as well, infants tend to mature at their own individual rate. Some children are consistently way ahead of the norm in learning to sit up, stand, and walk, whereas other children are always far behind the average. As in the case of physical growth, only the most severe environmental conditions can affect the rate of motor development. Mere restraint and lack of exercise, for example, do not affect it. The children of some American Indian tribes who spend most of the day strapped to a cradleboard nevertheless learn how to stand, walk, and crawl at about the same age as do children who are not restrained (8). Some years ago, one of the authors visited the Apache Indian reservation in the White Mountains of Arizona. He observed that many mothers carried their babies around on cradleboards during the day, but in the evening the children moved around freely on the floor in a manner that was appropriate to their age.

On the other hand, extra stimulation and special training also do not seem to have any lasting effects on individual growth rates. Infants trained in motor skills such as climbing may become more proficient in this activity than untrained children of the same age, but this advantage is short-lived since the untrained child soon catches up (9). Hilgard (10) conducted a typical study in this area by training 2-year-olds over the course of 12 weeks to climb ladders, button clothes, and use scissors. Another group who were matched with the trained children in age, sex, and IQ were able to attain scores that compared favorably with those of the trained group after having only 1 week of practice. Obviously, therefore, only extreme environmental circumstances can significantly accelerate or inhibit a child's inherent rate of maturation and the attainment of universal (crawling, walking, coordination) motor skills.

Direction of Growth

Growth also takes a certain direction that is characteristic of all mammals. In general it proceeds from the head downward and from the center of the body out to the periphery. Consistent with this principle, the brain at birth is closer to its eventual gross weight than any other organ of the body except the eyes. Furthermore, the brain develops more rapidly than any other part of the body. At birth the brain is about 25 percent of its adult weight; at 6 months it is nearly 50 percent; at 1 year, 60 percent; at 2½ years, about 75 percent; and at 10 years, 90 percent. These figures contrast sharply with those of weight and height. At birth an infant is only about 5 percent of his or her ideal adult weight and at age 10 he or she may be about 50 to 75 percent of his or her ideal weight; likewise, at birth he or she is about 33 percent of his or her adult height; at age 2, 50 percent, and at age 6, 60 percent (11).

The direction of growth from the trunk out to the periphery is also clearly apparent in young children. In general, they learn to coordinate the gross movements of their arms and legs, which are close to the trunk, before they learn the fine motor coordination of their fingers and toes, which are closer to the periphery. Thus, infants can lift and turn their heads before they are able to turn over entirely, and they can move their arms and legs before they are able to oppose their thumb and forefinger or push things with their toes. Similarly, they acquire strength in their arms and forearms before their fingers, which explains why young children *flail* with their arms when they are angry, whereas slightly older children *punch* with their fists.

Differentiation and Integration

Motor development generally proceeds according to two different but related mechanisms—differentiation and integration. **Differentiation** is the process by which gross, over-all patterns of behavior are broken down into fine and more functional actions. **Integration,** on the other hand, is the process of coordinating various segments of behavior patterns with one another.

An example of the differentiation of motor behavior can be seen in how an infant orients himself or herself to stimuli in the environment. At the appearance of new sights or sounds, very young infants will orient themselves by moving their whole bodies, whereas a few months later they will move only their heads (12, 13). The integration of motor movements is apparent in the typical development of reaching behavior. Young infants swat at objects they want to grasp because they have not yet learned to coordinate reaching and grasping actions. After a few months (usually when they are from 2½ to 7 or 8 months of age), however, they learn to integrate reaching with grasping so that they can reach for and grasp an object to bring it to their mouth (14—16).

Differentiation and integration can be observed at all levels of development and in the fields of social, cognitive, and personality development as well. Moreover, whereas differentiation and integration take place successively within a given area, they can take place simultaneously in two or more areas. An example of successive differentiation and integration is an infant's ability to differentiate the mother's voice from other sounds several months after birth. Later on, this differentiation is integrated with a differentiated visual impression of her face so that both are seen as belonging together. An example of simultaneous differentiation and integration in different areas is the attempt of 1-year-old children to coordinate their muscles for walking while also trying to differentiate their vocalizations enough to produce comprehensible sounds and words.

Figure 3.1 Sequential motor development. (*Source.* Adapted from Shirley, M. M. *The first two years: A study of twenty-five babies.* Postural and locomotor development. Vol. I. Minneapolis: University of Minneapolis Press, 1931. Institute of Child Welfare monographs.)

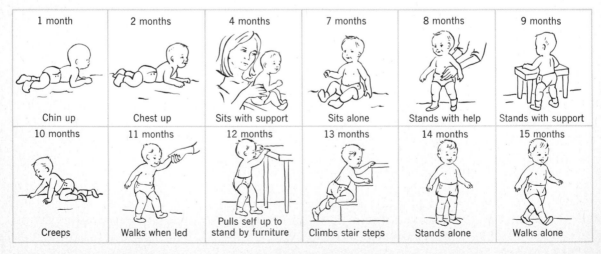

1 month	2 months	4 months	7 months	8 months	9 months
Chin up	Chest up	Sits with support	Sits alone	Stands with help	Stands with support

10 months	11 months	12 months	13 months	14 months	15 months
Creeps	Walks when led	Pulls self up to stand by furniture	Climbs stair steps	Stands alone	Walks alone

The Sequence of
Development

The various physical attainments of an infant during the first 2 years of life are not random, but rather they follow a sequence that is common to all human beings. The motor abilities that are required in learning how to walk follow the same sequence among the African bush children as among the children of Cambridge, Massachusetts. First children must learn how to sit without support, then crawl, then crawl while holding onto things, then pull themselves up with support, then walk with support, then stand alone, and finally walk alone (see Figure 3.1). Individual children, of course, will reach each phase at somewhat different ages, and parents should not worry too much about slight variations from the norm. Other examples of sequential development will be presented in our discussion of the evolution of concepts.

PHYSICAL
DEVELOPMENT
DURING THE FIRST
TWO YEARS OF
LIFE

Infancy: The First
Year

Although contemporary research demonstrates that a newborn infant has many competencies (17, 18), we should not forget that the neonate is still far from being a fully formed and functioning human organism. To be sure, the newborn infant has all of the necessary body organs, but the heart, lungs, and digestive tract still require further development before they can function under a wide range of circumstances. It will be many years before the infant's stomach can handle foods that are currently popular among school-age youngsters, hamburgers and pizza!

Similarly, although the infant's body structure is almost complete at birth, his or her bones are softer than those of older children and adults and they are shaped differently. Since the bones of the skull are not fully joined together, there is a soft spot on the top of the infant's head that is called the **fontanelle.** The bones will come together to form a completely hard skullcap somewhere between 9 months and a year. Another part of the bone structure, the teeth, is also incomplete at birth. In rare cases an infant may be born with erupted teeth, but the vast majority have only teeth buds that will not erupt until the middle or end of their first year (11).

The infant's nervous system also differs from that of older children and adults. While the infant's brain is similar in structure to that of the adult and has its full complement of neurons, these neurons have not acquired their insulating sheath of myelin. **Myelinization** enables specific pathways to be established between the muscles and the brain—which is required for all motor skills. Myelinization is fairly well established by 4 months of age, but it may continue well into early childhood.

Infant growth during the first year is rather rapid (11). At birth the average baby may weigh between 6 and 8 pounds and measure from 19 to 22 inches in length. By the end of 12 months the baby has usually tripled his or her birth weight and has grown one-third taller. Growth slows down gradually after that: by the end of the second year the child has reached about one-fourth of his or her ideal adult weight and about half of his or her eventual adult height.

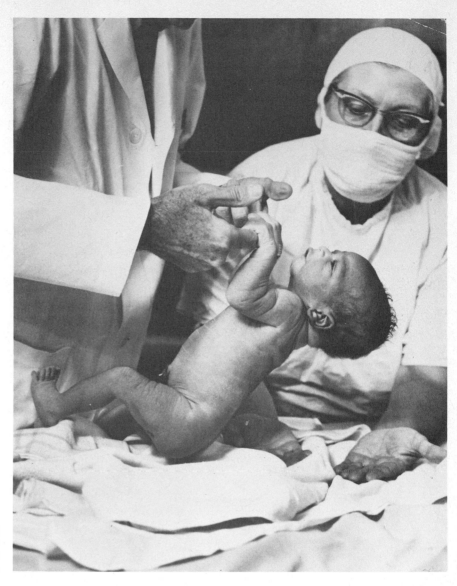

The grasp reflex is present from birth and makes up one of the infant's basic adaptive mechanisms.

At birth the infant has several well-established and easily discernible reflex patterns. One of these is the so-called **moro reflex.** This reaction can be observed if the infant is startled by a sudden loud noise or a sudden lack of support, particularly of the head, which the infant cannot hold alone. When the infant senses a loss of support, his arms reach out and clutch in a kind of "reining-in" movement that would appear to be an attempt to regain support. Another reflex pattern, the grasp reflex, occurs when the infant clutches his or her fist about an object; the infant, by grasping an adult's finger, can be lifted to a "sitting-up" position (11).

Infants attend to and enjoy brightly colored mobiles attached to the crib.

Muscular development during the first few months of life is also rather rapid. By the second month infants generally remain awake for longer periods and are more active. Their arms, legs, and fingers are not as spastic or "tight" as they had been at birth. At this age many infants start to lift their heads and chests a little, and many find their thumbs and begin to suck them. During the second month infants offer their first truly social smile (19). During the third and fourth months voluntary motor action becomes more efficient, probably because of the myelinization of the brain cells. Development during this period illustrates the "head to tail" direction of growth. While the 3-to-4-month-old can turn his or her head and reach for things, crawling and walking require further neuromuscular growth. With respect to the digestive system, improved neuromuscular control of the tongue and throat make it possible for the infant to begin to eat soft foods (11).

By 4 months of age, infants become interested in their fingers and toes and play with them. At this time, infants try to turn over and are usually able to accomplish this easily by the fifth month. Children can also sit up when held and keep their heads up long enough to look about and see what is going on. By five months infants begin making crawling movements when they are placed in a playpen or on the floor. Grasping, holding, and shaking are common movements, and infants begin to chew as they cut their first teeth at about 6 months of age (11).

During the second half of the first year, infants develop more independence of action and more responsiveness to their physical and social worlds. Motor control has reached the point where objects that are seen can be reached for, grasped, and either banged, shaken, or rattled. By the seventh month, newly strengthened back and abdominal muscles permit the infant to sit up without help and in many cases to crawl. By 8 months, the infant has developed enough fine motor control so that he or she can oppose thumb and fingers and pick up and hold small objects. At this time parents should be careful to keep small objects that can readily be popped into the mouth far away from the child's reach (20).

At 9 months the infant tries to increase his or her mobility and locomotion; he or she spends a lot of time practicing motor skills in the crib and playpen. Many parents are surprised to find that whereas they had left the baby sitting down in the crib when they went out of the room, he or she is standing up holding the side of the crib and smiling with considerable satisfaction when they return. Even though children at this age cannot walk, they can move amazingly fast by creeping and crawling; clearly, they should be carefully watched (20).

By 10 months babies can creep or crawl, sit up, and pull themselves erect. Motor independence is apparent in other areas as well. At this age most infants can drink from a cup and have enough teeth to be able to chew solid food; in fact many of them want to feed themselves. Although they usually mess up their food, they thoroughly enjoy themselves and perhaps get a little nourishment as well (20).

By the end of the first year infants have made substantial progress toward motor independence. They can move at will (and increasingly on two feet), grasp, hold, and let go, and they can chew, bite, and make a variety of sounds that approximate the language of their society. Although some of the special sensory and mental abilities of the infants will be described later, it must be remembered that progress in these other areas depends, at least in part, upon progress in motor development (21).

Infancy: The Second Year

After children learn to walk (toward the end of the first year), they move into a stage called "toddlerhood" that includes a whole new repertoire of motor activities. Within a few years they will begin to jump, run, and hop, as well as play with such equipment as balls and slides if they are avail-

Standing with support is
preparation for taking the
first step and usually
occurs towards the end of
the first year of life.

Climbing stairs is difficult for young children because of the size of the steps and because of their relative lack of coordination.

able. At this time hand, ear, and eye preferences also begin to emerge and to become established.

When children first attempt to walk, their feet are wide apart and their movement is irregular; indeed, the word "toddler" is an apt description. With increased practice, children bring their feet closer together and their steps become more even and rhythmical. They also begin to walk *straight* in the sense that they place the heel of the forward foot directly in front of the toes of the foot that is behind. Two-year-olds still need to monitor their feet visually as they walk in order to avoid obstacles, but this need disappears by the end of the third year (22).

Once children have confidence about walking, they begin to do variations and occasionally walk sideways and backward. One of the authors once watched a 2-year-old walking backward on a dock until, to his great surprise (and to that of the adults who were watching), he walked right off the end and fell into the water; needless to say, he was quickly rescued. Children of this age may also walk on tiptoe or try to become giddy by spinning about.

Toward the middle of the second year children may have a "hurried walk" that looks something like running. It is not true running, however, because toddlers do not have the leg power and balance to get off the ground with both feet at the same time; they usually cannot run until they are about 5 years of age. Children's efforts to jump parallel their efforts to run in that they have difficulty getting both feet to leave the ground simultaneously. Jumping often begins as children step off low objects such as stairs and boxes. In their first attempts young children sometimes step off with one foot but are reluctant to let go with the other; thus, they stand suspended, teetering on the brink. By 2 years of age children will take off from their jumping point with both feet (22). Other motor skills such as hopping, climbing, and catching and throwing balls require somewhat better visual motor coordination than 2-year-olds are capable of. To be sure, they may try to throw and catch, but they usually hold their arms out stiffly with their elbows pressed against their bodies. Coordinated throwing that includes the release of an object as part of the throwing motion cannot be achieved until children are somewhat older (22).

During the second year, but to some extent even during the first, children begin to show hand and eye preferences, which is an aspect of motor development. They tend to clutch objects with a particular hand and to favor one eye over the other in binocular vision. What brings about these preferences, which will become better established in later life, is not entirely clear, and many scientific and pseudoscientific theories have been offered to explain it. We do not yet understand the physiology of handedness or its relationship to other motor problems such as stuttering (22).

MENTAL GROWTH

The mental development of infants, like that of children and adults, can be seen from at least two points of view. One is that of quantitative mental testing, which asks, "How much mental ability does a particular infant have as compared with other infants his age?" The other is that of qualitative (or normative) developmental psychology, which asks, "What sorts of abilities and concepts do infants demonstrate, and how do these develop during the first 2 years or so of life?" We will discuss both the quantitative and the qualitative aspects.

Quantitative Aspects of Mental Growth

Tests of human intelligence usually include a number of subtests, each designed to measure different abilities. Within each subtest there are a number of items of increasing difficulty. The difficulty of any item is determined by the response of a large sample of subjects (the norm group)

The Gesell Developmental
Schedules are widely used
measures of infant
intelligence.

to the item. For example, suppose that an item on an infant intelligence test is "lifting head" and that 90 percent of a large sample of 3-month-old infants could do that. "Lifting head" would thus be an easy item for 3-month-olds. On the other hand, suppose that "letting go of objects" could be performed by only 10 percent of the 3-month-olds sampled; this would therefore be a difficult item for that age group. Most infant tests are constructed by choosing items that can be performed by 75 percent of the norm group at each successive month level, yielding a series of items of progressive difficulty (12, 13).

Most mental tests can be scored so as to yield a **mental age,** which is the age of the norm group that successfully completed the same number of items as the subject who was tested. An infant who correctly performs as many items as the 1-year-old norm group thus has a mental age of 1 year, regardless of chronological age. A child's mental age divided by the chronological age and multiplied by 100 yields the IQ (or **intelligence quotient**). This quotient is an index of the individual's relative brightness, which is independent of age. It is clear, therefore, that a child with a mental age that is greater than his or her chronological age is brighter than average and will have an IQ above 100, whereas a child whose mental age is less than his or her chronological age is not as bright as the average and will have an IQ below 100.

One of the continuing controversies in developmental psychology is whether or not infant intelligence tests are useful. There is abundant and consistent evidence that within the wide range of average intelligence, infant tests are not accurate measures of a child's intelligence nor can they predict how a child will do on other tests or at a later age (23, 24). If they are used in combination with other information, however, such as the socioeconomic level of the parents, infant intelligence tests have greater predictive value. And when they are used with clinical observation, these tests can accurately diagnose abnormalities such as brain injuries (25, 26).

Certain important facts about intelligence tests emerge when we consider why infant tests are such poor predictors of later performance. First of all, infant tests are quite different from those used to assess the mental ability of older children and adults. Infant tests measure such things as reaching, grasping, and following objects visually when the child is a few months old, and the ability to imitate, to fit blocks into holes of matching size and shape, and to recognize pictures when the child is about 1 year old. What is largely absent in infant intelligence tests, but plays a key role in such tests for older children and adults, is language. Older children and adults must follow verbal instructions given by the examiner as well as respond verbally themselves. Language skill is closely related to intellectual ability in general, and the fact that infant tests do not utilize language is probably one reason why they are not good predictors of a child's performance on later tests that do require language.

Another factor that contributes to the poor predictability of infant tests is the infants themselves. Testing presupposes cooperation on the part of the subject, but infants are usually wary of strangers and so they may or may not cooperate. Furthermore, their emotionality and distractibility make it difficult to determine whether their failure to perform a certain act is due to a lack of ability or a momentary distraction. Although there is a problem deciding whether performance accurately reflects competence in intelligence tests for any age group, it is particularly difficult in interpreting infant test responses.

A third factor that contributes to the poor predictability of infant tests also holds true for other intelligence tests as well: Intelligence is not a fixed quantity or ability since it is continually being influenced by environmental factors. Although there are probably limits beyond which the environment cannot modify an individual's endowment, these limits are not known. On the other hand, it is generally accepted that children who grow up in impoverished or sterile environments may not fully realize their intellectual potential (27). If, in the course of growing up, an infant's circumstances change and he or she moves from an enriched to an impoverished intellectual environment, or vice versa, his or her intelligence test performance will reflect this change—for better or for worse (28).

Qualitative Aspects
of Mental Growth

These aspects of mental growth include the development of **mental processes** and the accumulation of mental contents. Mental processes comprise such functions as perception, learning, problem-solving, reasoning, and language formation; **mental contents** are the results of these processes—knowledge, or what might be described as the contents of a child's mind. We will discuss the changes that take place in both mental processes and content during the first 2 years of life.

Perception

In general, perception pertains to the processes by which we read messages that are conveyed by our senses. The growth of perceptual ability includes both a gradually increasing sensitivity of a child's receptors (eyes, ears, and so forth) to the information provided by his or her environment and an increasing ability to register and interpret this information. Among the mental processes, perception probably makes the greatest progress during the first couple of years of life.

Vision. Of all of the senses, the vision of infants has been investigated the most extensively; we know more about the child's developing visual abilities than about any other sensory system. The eye itself is not fully formed at birth, and cellular changes continue to take place in the **fovea** (that part of the retina that deals with central vision) until the fourth month; this could affect the baby's visual acuity. In addition, because the distance between the lens and the retina is shorter than it will be when the child is somewhat older, the infant tends to be farsighted (29, 30). Other aspects of the visual system are also not complete (for example, the optic nerve has not been myelinized), and this too could affect the infant's basic visual capacities.

Visual **acuity,** which includes the ability to discriminate between lines of different widths, develops rapidly during the first year. Using a preference procedure (measuring the time an infant spends attending to different stimuli as a measure of discrimination ability), Robert Fantz and his colleagues found that infants could discriminate ½-inch stripes at a dis-

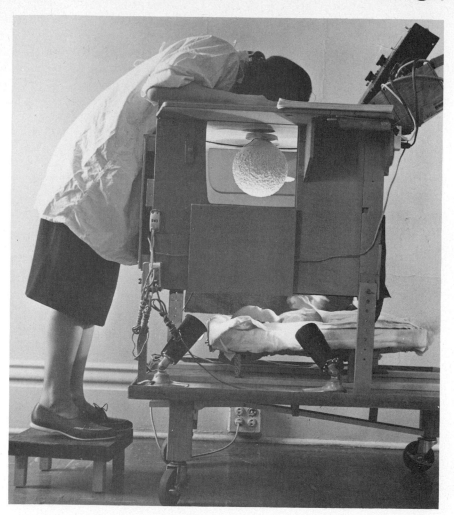

A looking chamber used to measure infants' attentiveness to different kinds of stimuli.

tance of 10 inches at 2 weeks of age (31), but could discriminate 1/64-inch stripes at 6 months (31). Similar progress is made in visual following or *pursuit* movements. While even a newborn infant is able to look toward a moving object with both eyes (32, 33), he or she cannot make smooth pursuit movements until 3 or 4 months of age (34).

Ethologists have observed that different species are programmed to respond selectively to different types of sensory stimulation. With respect to human infants, considerable work has been done to determine what kinds of visual stimuli they respond to and appear to prefer. Although it is difficult to know whether infants can actually see colors, the optical structures are there at birth (35) and it has been found that 4-month-old infants attend longer to the wavelengths for blue and red than they do to

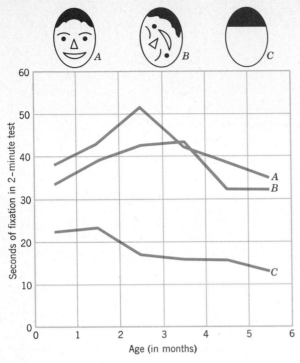

Figure 3.2 Fantz's test to determine the preference of young infants for a regular face (*A*), a distorted face (*B*), and a black-and-white oval (*C*). (*Source.* Fantz, R. L. The origin of form perception. *Scientific American:* 1961, **204,** 66–72.)

Figure 3.3 Visual preferences of newborn and older infants for black/white, colored, patterned, and unpatterned discs. (*Source.* Fantz, R. L. Pattern discrimination and selective attention as determinants of perceptual development from birth. In A. H. Kidd & J. I. Rivoire (Eds.), *Perceptual development in children.* New York: International Universities Press, 1966, 143–173.)

those for other colors (36). In addition, movement in the visual field and contour contrast (the large changes in reflected light where one figure begins and another ends) seem to be especially important in capturing the attention of young infants (37–39).

A number of studies have examined infants' attention to faces, hoping to discover when babies become attentive to them (69–72). It appears that infants begin to look at faces (especially the eye region) at about 6 or 7 weeks. By 4 months of age, infants seem to prefer faces that have regular features to those that are distorted or to non-face figures of comparable complexity (71). Thus, it would appear that a 4-month-old infant can recognize a face (70–73). It is still not clear, however, whether the child primarily pays attention to special features (such as the eyes and hairline) or to the total configuration.

There is some evidence that as infants become older, they prefer more complex stimuli. To assess infant preferences, two figures would be displayed in a uniform field above the infant's head. The infant's fixations on the figures could be observed through a peephole in the display board. By watching the reflection of the figure on the infant's retina, it was possible to know which figure the infant was looking at. And by measuring the time the infant spent looking at each figure, his or her preferences could be determined. Using a variety of patterns, including stripes, checkerboards, bull's-eyes, and solid colored figures, Fantz and his co-workers found that even very young infants preferred patterned to unpatterned stimuli. These researchers have also found that infants 2 months of age and under preferred stripes, whereas those beyond 2 months seemed to prefer the bull's-eye pattern (40–42). Other researchers have also demonstrated that by 13 weeks infants appear to prefer curves to straight lines and concentric to nonconcentric patterns (43, 44).

It should be noted that at present there is a certain amount of controversy over infants' perception of visual complexity. While it is generally agreed that very young infants prefer patterned to plain stimuli, the course of development after that is not clear. One of the problems is how to define "visual complexity" and "infant preference" (45–47).

Another facet of visual development is the perception of depth. In a classic study, Gibson and Walk (48) placed infants on a **visual cliff.** The cliff consists of a heavy glass plate, part of which rests on a table covered with checkerboard material and part of which extends across an open space to a supporting pair of legs. On the floor directly beneath the open space covered by the glass is more of the checkerboard material. Hence, at the edge of the table the child can look down at the checkerboard floor. Since the squares on the floor are farther away, they should provide the child with appropriate depth cues, if he or she can use them. It has been found that infants who are old enough to crawl (4 to 6 months) generally do not crawl over the "deep" side of the cliff. Therefore, it would appear that most children have depth perception by that age.

It is not known exactly when infants attain size and shape constancy (an automatic corrective process by the brain that enables us to "see" distant objects as being the same size as they are when they are closer and as retaining the same shape regardless of their orientation). One investigator, G. T. Bower (49, 50), claims that some aspects of size and shape constancy are already present during the first few months of life, but earlier researchers believed that these capacities did not emerge until about the end of the first year (for example, 51). One of the reasons for these discrepant views is that different investigators measure size and distance differently.

Audition. The auditory system of the newborn infant is functional but limited. Fluids from the amniotic sac remain for a time in the auditory canal, partially blocking the normal vibrations of the **ossicles** (the tiny bones of the middle ear that transmit vibrations from the eardrum to the cochlea, where the vibrations are transformed into nerve impulses). Movement of the ossicles is also temporarily impaired by connective

The "visual cliff" measures an infant's depth perception.

tissues; as these tissues degenerate, the ossicles become fully functional and responsive to a wide range of sounds (11).

Even with these constraints, the newborn can hear, particularly when the sounds are moderately loud. In a simple test for deafness, the obstetrician claps his or her hands loudly. If the infant responds with a startle pattern, this indicates that his or her auditory system is functioning. As the ossicles become free to move and the auditory nerves become myelinated, the young child's hearing improves so that soon he or she is responsive to the same range of sound stimuli (20 to 20,000 cycles per second)—with maximum acuity in the middle range (1000 to 3000 cps)—as adults.

According to Appleton, Clifton, and Goldberg (18), infants respond to sounds in several different ways. "They are soothed by them, are alert to them, or are distressed by them.'' Apparently stimuli that are not too intense and that are continuous can have a calming effect upon infants; this holds true for visual as well as auditory stimulation (52). Thus, a low-intensity light in an infant's room can be soothing, and so can rhythmic sounds. In one study it was found that tape-recorded heartbeats, a ticking metronome, and the singing of a lullaby were more soothing to an infant than silence, but these three were all about equal in their effects (53). The same principle applies in the case of those who place a small clock in the box of a newborn puppy; its repetitive sounds help to calm the young animal.

Human infants appear to be receptive to the sounds of the human voice. During their first 3 months, they can discriminate phonemes such as *ba* and *ga* (54) and *ba* and *pa* (55). They also seem to be receptive to the rhythm of adult speech. In one study, for example, newborn infants (12 hours to 14 days old) moved their bodies to the rhythm of adult speech, and they did this whether the parent was actually present or simply speaking by means of a tape recorder (56). In order to make sure that it was the voice pattern that produced this reaction, the researchers used both English and Chinese; they found syncopated motion in both cases! In contrast, these infants did not respond rhythmically to a tapping sound or to the utterance of disconnected vowels.

Finally, certain auditory stimuli appear to distress infants—sounds produced by pure tones above 4000 cps and by square waves of low frequency (these are staccato rather than continuous sounds) (57, 58). Sudden loud noises tend to produce startle reactions in infants (as they do in adults) as well as acceleration of the heart rate (59, 60). Apparently it is the suddenness that is disturbing, for if a sound is introduced gradually, these reactions do not occur (61).

Although a great deal of research has been done on the auditory abilities of young infants, much less has been done on older infants and young children. As Appleton, Clifton, and Goldberg point out, the reason for this may be that it is assumed that the development of auditory competence is little more than the attainment of enhanced discriminatory powers and lowered thresholds for sound. In fact, of course, auditory competence is an extremely complex cognitive process that requires translating the auditory messages into meaningful information (62).

Other Senses. We know much less about taste, smell, and touch than we do about vision and audition. These are relatively primitive senses in that they are fairly well developed at birth and show little maturation thereafter. Although these senses are simple, we agree with Gibson (63) that they constitute sensory *systems* to the extent that they interact with other sensory processes and with motoric actions. Both smell and taste, for example, are quickly associated with visual sensations and with the action of acceptance or rejection.

With respect to taste, the infant is born with developed taste buds on the tongue and complete nerve connections to the brain. At birth an infant cannot discriminate between sour, salt, and sweet, but after 2 or 3 months his or her gustatory preferences are fairly well developed, and he or she can tell if there has been a change in the milk mixture or in the amount of carbohydrates in the formula. At this age, babies sometimes show their dislike for certain tastes by spitting out these foods (64, 65).

Smell also develops quite early and even premature infants can detect certain differences in odor. Olfactory discrimination develops quite rapidly after birth. In one study it was found that newborn infants responded differentially (as measured by their gross motor activity) to five different-smelling alcohols (66). The more carbon molecules in the alcohol, the more vigorous and prolonged were the infant's actions. Other studies suggest that with increasing age there is little change in sensitivity to odor. Indeed, it appears that olfaction is not only one of the earliest senses to develop but one of the last to deteriorate with age (67, 68).

Language

Human language, like science and mathematics, is both a collective product and an individual achievement. As a collective product language consists of thousands of words and meanings that have been developed over time by a particular social group. No one individual could create an entire language or learn all that there is to be known about an existing one such as English or Russian. However, members of a given social group do learn the language of that group and how it can be used as an effective tool of social adaptation. We will discuss the individual's acquisition of language, rather than language as a social product.

Child psychologists continue to be interested in how children acquire language. Many of the baby biographers mentioned in Chapter 1 touched on this point with their subjects. In general, the study of language acquisition has focused on description (the *how*) and explanation (the *why*). These two aspects are closely related because the way in which an investigator describes language growth will depend in part on how he or she explains it. Indeed, the history of developmental studies of language can be described as a succession of concepts dictating the interaction between description and explanation.

In the first phase of the developmental study of language (from the time of the baby biographies until after World War II), it was assumed that children learned mainly by imitating adult speech. Therefore, the early descriptive studies of language (for example, 73) emphasized the age and sequence in which children learned the "parts of speech" and sentence construction. It was found, for example, that they learned nouns before pronouns, and verbs and adjectives before adverbs. They learned prepositions and conjunctions last of all. Likewise it was observed that they could speak simple sentences before complex ones, and so forth (73).

The late 1950s marked the second phase in the study of children's language, with the appearance of N. Chomsky's theory of "generative grammar" (74). He argued that sentences that are usually classified as different, such as:

Did the boy eat the apple?	(Interrogative)
The boy ate the apple.	(Declarative)
Boy, eat the apple.	(Imperative)
The boy ate the whole apple!	(Exclamatory)

were actually more alike than sentences that are usually classified as similar, such as:

The boy at the pie.	(Declarative)
The dog ran home.	(Declarative)
The girl was sick.	(Declarative)
The house was cold.	(Declarative)

Chomsky held that although the first group of sentences had different **surface structures** in that they reflected different sentence types, they had a common **deep structure** in that they all presented variations of the same basic information. In contrast, the second set of declarative sentences has a common surface structure but different deep structure—the grammar is the same, but the meanings differ.

What Chomsky accomplished, then, was to relate grammar (which has traditionally been a formal and empty discipline) to meaning and semantics. He held that the deep structures of language constituted a set of rules for organizing a fixed amount of information in different ways to convey different meanings. So, in addition to relating grammar to meaning, Chomsky suggested a new theory of language acquisition; accordingly, it was not only important to learn words but also to learn the deep structure rules for putting words together and for sorting out meanings.

The work of Chomsky (74) and of Harris (75) ushered in the second phase of child language studies. At this time there was an effort to describe the grammars that children develop as they mature, including the so-called "pivot grammars" (76, 77) where a child uses one word together with a variety of other words as in "Mommy up," "Mommy eat." But it has been found that such "pivot grammars" do not accurately describe the children's meaning and are surface rather than deep structure relationships (78–80). A child can use one word with a number of others to signify different meanings and grammatical relations. "Mommy up" reflects an actor-action relationship, whereas "Mommy purse" reflects a possessor-possession relationship.

In the 1970s more attention has been paid to Piaget's work (81) and to his view that, while language does include a set of generative rules, these are derived from the child's own actions and conceptualizations. Much of the research in this field in the 1970s has tried to relate language development to cognitive development. At present there is an emphasis on the total linguistic context of the child's utterances and not just on the form or content of his or her vocalizations (82).

Clearly, a great deal of information has been gathered on how children learn to speak. We will review the stages of vocalization, the development of receptive language, and contemporary research relating language growth to conceptual development.

Stages of Vocalization. From birth until about the end of the first month, the newborn infant engages in what has been called **undifferentiated crying** (83). This simply means that the adult listener cannot distinguish between cries of hunger, pain, fear, or general unhappiness. However, newborn infants appear to be sensitive to their own crying. In one study, tape recordings were played to newborns of their own crying as well as that of other newborns, and they tended to show a greater reaction and more reflexive crying to their own sounds than to those of other infants (83).

During the second month of life, the infant develops **differentiated crying**; that is, crying that is more distinguishable to the adult—signaling, for example, hunger or distress. Differentiated crying appears to be facilitated both in quality and quantity by adult vocalization and by social reinforcement in general (84, 85). Furthermore, a significant factor that leads to a decrease in crying during the first year appears to be the *promptness* with which a parent responds to the infant's crying. Such promptness not only reduces the amount and length of crying, but seems to enhance the infant's communication skills at 8 to 12 months of age (86). When possible, therefore, prompt attention to an infant's cries can have long-range beneficial effects.

The next stage is **babbling**, which may develop toward the end of the second month but then extends to the eighth or ninth month. At this time the infant begins to produce **phonemes,** the fundamental sound units of a language (87). Babbling appears to be related to physiological maturation and seems to be a universal phenomenon (88); it also makes linguistic shaping possible. By interacting with adults, the infant progressively eliminates the sounds that are not in the language of his or her parents (phonemic contraction) and progressively elaborates on the sounds that are in that language (phonemic expansion). Babbling thus enables the infant to begin to acquire the language of his or her particular society (89, 90).

During a later stage of babbling, around 6 to 8 months, the infant begins to make repetitive sounds such as *baba ba ba* or *mama mama,* which are sometimes called **lallation.** At this time the infant makes both vowel and consonant sounds. During the babbling stage, the infant does not produce sounds in order to communicate, but rather to play with his or her articulatory apparatus (91). During this period the infant's babbling is initiated by his or her own vocalization or by the speech of others who are nearby. In general, then, babbling sets the stage for the production of communicative language sounds.

Starting at about 10 months of age the infant moves into the last stage of the prelinguistic period, the stage of vocal imitation and comprehension of adult speech sounds (91). Although, as mentioned earlier, the young infant is able to distinguish his or her voice from that of other newborns, discrimination of specific speech sounds comes later, during the stage of babbling and lallation. But at about ten months the infant begins to distinguish and respond differentially to the words of adults. Indeed, some children at this age seem to be able to understand a few words such as "no," although these words may be accompanied by certain gestures and vocal intonations so that the child may be responding to the total situation rather than to the words themselves. One 10-month-old infant, for example, waved "bye-bye" when she heard her mother say "bye-bye" (91). By the end of the first year infants can discriminate among and reproduce the basic phonemes of the parental language.

Early Speech. At about the same time the child speaks his or her first meaningful word. It is not always easy to tell just when this occurs, however, because overeager parents may hear "words" that linguists would not consider meaningful. After the first word, vocabulary growth tends to be quite rapid. Although it is difficult to measure a child's total vocabulary, certain tests (that are designed to include words the child knows but may not use) indicate that a 2-year-old has a total vocabulary of about 250 words and that a 6-year-old has one ten times that large (93).

Growth in vocabulary size is relatively straightforward in comparison with estimates of the child's grammatical and communication competence. In fact, there is some controversy over how a young child's utterances should be described and interpreted. One position, advocated by Chomsky (74), holds that since linguistic structures are primary, linguistic ability precedes cognitive understanding. The other position, espoused by Piaget (81) and others (94–96), holds that linguistic structures are acquired (much like words) in an effort to code meanings that are nonlinguistic. In short, does language precede thought or does thought precede language?

Many contemporary psychologists, if not linguists, are now viewing language development as a progressively more complex attempt to code or to represent cognitive schemes (concepts) of the self and of the world. What these investigators claim, as opposed to Chomsky, is that grammar and syntax are not innate or preformed, but are rules constructed by the child in his or her effort to represent and communicate his or her experience. From this viewpoint, children learn syntax and grammar in the same way that they learn concepts: They abstract from adult usage the meaning of word order and inflection and try these out in their own speech (94–97).

The child's first words, like the first vocalizations, are undifferentiated; that is, the 1-year-old is not aware of saying a "word." Rather, the first words are global conglomerates of the meanings and constructions of the differentiated language used by older persons. The 1-year-old who says "Mommy" may mean "Look at Mommy" or "Pick up baby" or "I am hungry." It would be wrong to say that the child was implying a whole sentence since he or she does not understand what a sentence is. Rather, the infant's first words have been called **holophrastic**, and his or her varied usages of the same word are conveyed by different intonations, facial expressions, and so forth, which may be totally unconscious. Parents learn to interpret the infant's first words by considering the total context of the infant's behavior. Speech, at least initially, is only one aspect of the infant's total effort at communication (99, 100).

As the child moves into the second year of life, he or she begins to go beyond the undifferentiated holophrasic use of single words to the combination of two or more words. Two-word utterances reflect a new level of language differentiation in that it implies the child recognizes that word order as well as words and intonations convey meaning. But the young child's two-word utterances differ substantially from adult word combinations. Language usage at this time has been called *telegraphic speech* in the sense that the child usually leaves out articles, auxiliary verbs, and other connectives. A 21-month-old baby might say:

> Mommy book.
> Me show Mommy.
> This baby book.   (79)

Telegraphic speech can be understood by adults, but only if they look for other cues. Adults may attempt to check whether or not they have heard the child correctly by repeating, in more complete form, the substance of the child's words. Here is an actual record of how one mother responded to her child's telegraphic speech (79):

CHILD	MOTHER
Mommy eggnog.	Mommy had her eggnog.
Mommy sandwich.	Mommy will have a sandwich.
Sat wall.	He sat on the wall.

The fact that the young child is trying to use language to communicate ideas is reflected in another facet of early language, namely, repetition (101). For example, in attempting to formulate an idea more precisely, a child might say:

> Candy.
> Bobby candy.
> Mommy give candy.
> Mommy give Bobby candy.

Several kinds of events contribute to early language development. First there is the maturation and development of the articulation system that enables children to produce more precise sounds. Then there is the child's cognitive development by means of which he or she can conceptualize aspects of the self and the world. There is also the discovery of representation and the fact that words can stand for aspects of the child's experiences and concepts. Finally, there is the progressive conceptualization of language itself and the continuous effort to relate linguistic concepts to those derived from the world and the self. One of the authors has called this effort "connotative learning" (102). In short, the child begins to understand language at the same time that he or she is discovering the self and the world, and tries to relate language and thought while also elaborating each of them separately.

Before closing this section, something needs to be said about a neglected facet of language development, namely, receptive language, or language comprehension. Although language comprehension and language production are alike in some ways, they also differ. Obviously a listener has much less control over a communication than does a speaker (103). In general, receptive language precedes active speech, and the child understands language before he or she can speak it. Moreover, throughout life, our passive vocabulary (words that we understand but do not use) far exceeds our active vocabulary (words that we do use in everyday speech). Unfortunately, little research has been done on receptive language development; it would be desirable to have more information regarding receptive language to complement our rapidly growing understanding of language production.

Cognitive Processes
Although language is a cognitive process and could be included under this heading, we have maintained the tradition of treating it separately. Here we will discuss attentional processes, learning, problem-solving, and reasoning. These processes can be found among infants, serving as precursors to more advanced forms of cognition.

Orientation, Attention, and Habituation. In some ways, these behaviors are the cognitive or regulatory aspects of perception. In general, orientation pertains to movement in the direction of a suddenly occurring stimulus. A startle response to an unexpected sound is an undifferentiated orientation. When the stimulus is milder, the child usually turns in the direction of a sound or looks in the direction of a new sight. This is called an **orienting reflex** or **response** (OR). If an infant turns to look at his or her mother upon hearing her voice, this is an OR.

Attention is the selective focusing on one or another aspect of the stimulus field. The infant's world, no less than the adult's, is filled with all kinds of stimulation. In the nursery there are often pictures on the walls and a crib with toys in it or a mobile suspended over it; there are also the usual household noises—water running, doors opening and closing, telephones ringing, and, of course, human voices. Attentional processes allow the child to selectively focus upon one or another facet of the stimulus field so as to extract information from it.

In some ways, **habituation** is the complement of the OR. When a stimulus is new, an infant will respond to it with an OR. But if the stimulus is repeated, the OR will diminish. For example, if someone places a mobile above the infant's crib, the infant will pay close attention to it. But after several days the infant may look at it only occasionally—this is *habituation*. Among preschool children as well, a new toy may preoccupy them so much that they seem to have no time to eat or to do other things. But several days later the toy may lie neglected on the floor, a victim of habituation.

Orientation, attention, and habituation are important as concomitants of development and learning. For example, in the area of repeated visual stimuli, habituation becomes more rapid as infants grow older, particularly after 3 months of age (104–106). With respect to complex stimuli, some investigators have reported that infants orient first to one and then to another aspect of a complex configuration (107–109).

It has been claimed that orientation, attention, and habituation are not simple reflexes but are due to high-level brain activity. In that case these behaviors could be examined for signs of impairment of mental functioning (111); they have already been used to determine the effects of malnutrition in infants. Poorly nourished infants, in general, appear to be more difficult to arouse (they require more stimuli to produce orientation, attention, and habituation) than well-nourished infants (112).

Learning. In the most general sense learning is defined as occurring when there are behavior or thought modifications that can be traced to experience rather than to growth or maturation. Learning is not totally independent of growth and maturation, however, since growth and maturation make possible new modes of learning at later age levels. Learning tends to take place during relatively short periods of time, whereas growth and maturation tend to occur over somewhat longer periods. Clearly, the kinds of learning a child can undertake depend upon growth and maturation, but in any given case of learning, the result is almost totally a function of experience.

Perhaps the simplest form of learning is **classical conditioning.** Here there is an unconditioned response (UCR) such as an eyeblink; an **unconditioned stimulus** (UCS) such as a puff or air that "naturally" causes the eyeblink; the **conditioned stimulus** (CS) such as a tone of moderate intensity that does not elicit the eyeblink "naturally," and, finally, the **conditioned response** (CR) such as an eyeblink that can eventually be produced, through learning, by the CS.

In classical conditioning the CS (sound) is presented at about the same time as the UCS-UCR (puff of air–eyeblink) sequence. **Simultaneous conditioning** occurs when the CS and the UCS are presented at exactly the same time. **Delayed conditioning** occurs when the CS is presented before the UCS and also goes off before the UCS—that is, there is a period of time when the CS and the UCS are present by themselves.

It is not clear whether newborn infants can learn by means of classical conditioning (113); however, it is generally agreed that infants can be conditioned during their first month of life (114). In one study infants who were several days old were conditioned to give a sucking response to a tone (115). Some psychologists believe that there is an inevitable sequence in the sensory modes that are subject to classical conditioning. One Russian investigator, Kasatkin (116), holds that the first sense that could be conditioned is the vestibular system (which relates to body motion); this is then followed by stimuli that affect hearing, touch, smell, taste, and sight, respectively. Research in America, however, suggests that although there may be a sequence in the sensory modes in which infant behavior can be conditioned, the order may be determined as much by the UCR as by the particular mode (113). It should be noted that the existence of an order (whether of conditional stimuli or responses) indicates the relationship between development and learning. Development determines the structures (the order); learning determines the contents (the responses acquired).

Studies of infant conditioning indicate that it becomes easier as infants grow older. In one study, in which the CS was a noisemaking toy and the UCS was the mother's face and voice, it was found that older infants (5 months of age) showed more correct responses (head turning) in a shorter space of time than did younger infants (2 months of age) (117); this improvement with age is probably due to both accumulated experience and additional growth and maturation of the nervous system (113).

Another basic form of learning is **operant learning** (118). Much of the infant's behavior is spontaneous because one cannot know which UCS produced it. Some of the infant's behavior could be called *instrumental* in the sense that it serves some purpose. The child cries in order to get the parent's attention, looks at interesting events in the environment, and so forth. Once an operant response occurs, it is maintained or repeated only if it is *reinforced*. If the baby learns that its parent will come whenever it cries, it will cry whenever it wants attention; likewise, the baby will continue to look at novel events so long as these events provide new stimuli to explore. Operant learning is a very general form of learning employed by people of all ages.

When an investigator wants to control or regulate operant learning, he or she uses a procedure called *operant conditioning,* or more generally *behavior modification*. Here the experimenter chooses a behavior that the infant performs spontaneously and tries to modify (or shape) it by selective reinforcement. For example, an experimenter can get an infant to alter his or her rate of sucking by reinforcing the response on occasion with milk (119, 120) or a dextrose solution (121); other studies have shown that when adults smile and touch 4-month-old infants, there is more infant vocalization (122, 123). Children of 1 year have modified their behavior in order to turn on an interesting visual light display (124).

Operant conditioning can also be used to decrease the frequency of a behavior by not presenting the reinforcement that would normally follow the response. For example, in one study where an infant's smiling was not reinforced by the usual adult smiling and vocalization, the infant smiled less (125). This is called **extinction.** As the foregoing study indicates, operant learning is quite common in infancy and should be used appropriately by parents.

Problem-solving. **Problem-solving** is a form of learning in which the individual has to overcome some obstacle or barrier in order to reach a desired goal. Toward this end individuals typically use different *strategies.* Sometimes there is simple **trial and error.** This strategy may be used if we try to repair a piece of equipment that we really don't understand. Fooling around with the workings of a clock or radio in hopes that what is wrong will somehow become evident is a kind of trial and error strategy. Sometimes a problem is solved by **insight**—a kind of "aha" experience. If we can't find the screwdriver, we may suddenly decide that a coin could do the job. Finally, problem-solving can be systematic—it can comprise the progressive formation and testing of **hypotheses.**

As one might expect, problem-solving among infants is rudimentary, but it is possible to observe early forms of trial and error, insight, and hypothesis-testing. In a study by Papousek an apparatus was arranged so that the baby had to learn to turn his or her head to the right or to the left in order to obtain milk. A bell meant that milk was to come from the left, and a buzzer indicated that it would come from the right. When an infant learned to turn its head correctly to the bell and buzzer, the conditions were reversed.

The reversal produced a problem for the infants to solve. Papousek observed that they turned their heads in ways that suggested the following strategies:

> *1. The milk was expected to come from the side on which it had been presented in the preceding trial. 2. The milk was expected from the side on which it had been presented more frequently in the two preceding trials. 3. The milk was expected to come consecutively from the left and from the right, and vice versa. 4. The solution was to turn always to one side and to correct the response if the milk was not soon presented on that side.* [126]

Papousek noticed that not all of the infants used systematic strategies—some appeared to use random, even "chaotic," trial and error. Thus, individual differences in problem-solving were apparent at a very early age. From 3 months of age onward, some infants even showed a systematic approach to problem-solving in a simple learning situation (126).

With more complex tasks, however, systematic problem-solving does not appear until later. This reflects again the interaction between development and learning. In one study, infants from 12 to 24 months of age were given the task of securing a desired toy that was out of reach. Within their reach was a lever that, when rotated, would bring the toy within range of the child's hand. The youngest children either reached directly for the toy or used the lever in an ineffective way, whereas the oldest children could get the toy by manipulating the lever (127).

Reasoning. In a sense reasoning is also a form of learning since it allows us to extract new information from existing information by applying rules. For example, if we know that all candy is sweet and that this round ball is a piece of candy, we can deduce that it is sweet without actually tasting it. Such reasoning, which moves from the general to the specific, is called **deductive reasoning.** If, however, we taste a number of different pieces of candy and then conclude that all candy is sweet, we have used **inductive reasoning**, we have moved from the specific to the general.

Although infants are obviously limited in their reasoning, the development of these processes in the infant is of considerable interest because it reveals another competence and because it provides information about the development of reasoning in general.

Our present-day understanding of the development of reasoning in infants is largely due to the monumental work of the famed Swiss psychologist Jean Piaget (128–130). His studies of his own three children during their first 2 years of life have become classics in the literature of child development, and they have been a major factor in the large amount of infant research that has been undertaken since about 1960 (for example, 131–134). In Piaget's view, human intelligence, particularly reasoning, originates in an infant's early sensorimotor coordination. Piaget describes both how competent and how limited the infant is in dealing with the world.

Piaget, who calls the first 1½ to 2 years of life the **sensorimotor period,** believes that during this time there is a change from reflex action to "true" thinking. Piaget holds that a child can think if he can perform "mental experiments"; that is, sample actions on a small scale before actually performing them. Piaget has identified certain stages that mark the development of the infant's reasoning.

During the first stage, which lasts from birth to about 2 months, the child is primarily modifying certain reflex actions. As mentioned earlier, the newborn infant has a number of reflex patterns that can be elicited by appropriate stimuli. Modification would include the fact that the infant adjusts his or her mouth to the shape and size of the nipple. Piaget refers to such adjustments as **accommodation.** With age and practice the infant learns to distinguish among various things that are suckable, he or she may suck vigorously at a nipple that gives milk but reject an adult finger that does not. Such acceptance or rejection of environmental stimuli, according to the infant's own needs, Piaget refers to as **assimilation.** Accommodation and assimilation are the basic modes by which an individual interacts with and adapts to reality at various levels of development.

During the first stage of the sensorimotor period, the infant also learns to put its reflexes to new uses. Sucking, for example, can be used to identify and classify objects—those that can and cannot be sucked. The infant also distinguishes between objects that are to be sucked at different times or between nutrient and nonnutrient sucking. A satiated infant who rejects the nipple may nonetheless accept and suck on a finger or a pacifier.

From about 2 months to 4 months, the child begins to combine his modified reflex actions, which Piaget calls **schemes,** in various ways. The earliest combinations Piaget refers to as **circular reactions.** When a certain sequence of schemes happens by chance, the infant may like the result and thus try to reproduce it. For example, the infant may accidentally put his thumb into his mouth, suck it, and find it pleasurable. If the thumb falls out of his mouth, he will try to put it back in. Coordinating the sucking scheme with the thumb-movement scheme constitutes a higher order "thumb-sucking" scheme, which is a primary circular reaction: thumb in the mouth leads to sucking, which leads to putting the thumb into the mouth, which leads to sucking, and so forth.

Although the circular reaction represents an advance over the reflex, it has little cognitive significance. In a way it is a highly fortuitous coordination that happens to work and to bring pleasure. The child is not interested in the thumb except an object to be sucked. Piaget would say that the infant has made a kind of "functional" assimilation of the object to the self. Recognitive assimilation—that is, recognition of an object because of its own attributes—comes later.

From about the fourth month to the eighth—the third stage of the sensorimotor period—the child manifests what Piaget calls **secondary circular reactions.** This means that primary circular reactions, comprising only body schemes, are expanded to include outside objects and events. Piaget noted, for example, that while his baby son was kicking his legs, he happened to hit a toy that was suspended above the crib. Apparently his son got the same kind of pleasure from watching the toy move as he got from sucking his thumb, and so he kicked his feet again to make the toy move. Here the kicking scheme activated an object that activated the looking scheme; this led to further kicking, and so forth. In his observations Piaget was careful to make sure that his son's kicking was not simply a random excitement at seeing the toy, but a highly selective and directed response. At this stage, therefore, one can observe the beginnings of intentional actions.

Secondary circular reactions, by bringing objects into the child's action sequences, lead the child to accommodate himself or herself to the objects and their attributes and to be aware of the difference between self and objects. Yet, these reactions are still limited: They do not reflect "true" intentions, for if an infant discovers an interesting sight it is accidental, and the infant cannot yet invent or create interesting events.

During the last few months of the first year of life (Piaget's fourth stage) children begin to coordinate previously acquired schemes in order to attain a particular goal. That is to say, at this stage their intention begins to precede their action rather than follow it. At this age children typically begin to remove barriers or screens so that they can get desired objects. Piaget once hid his shiny watch under a pillow, and his son quickly moved the pillow in order to get the watch. The boy coordinated his looking scheme with his pushing (at the pillow) and grasping scheme in order to get to what he wanted.

The coordination of multiple schemes makes possible many new levels and types of actions. Perhaps the most important of these is imitation. During the last few months of the first year, the child begins to imitate actions performed by an adult. Indeed, when the infant removes a pillow that has been placed there by an adult, it is a kind of reverse imitation. In Piaget's view, imitation suggests a new level of mental activity and precedes true representation of all kinds, including language.

Early in the second year of life, the infant begins to show what Piaget calls **tertiary circular reactions,** marking the fifth stage of the sensorimotor period. At this time the infant appears to seek out and to create novelty rather than just repeating it after discovering it by accident. The infant actively explores objects to discover their features and properties. In this way the child begins to see himself or herself as a causal agent and to grasp certain concepts of cause and effect.

A tertiary circular reaction occurs when the child drops something outside the crib. This reaction includes the grasping and letting go schemes, the visual scheme of watching the object, and the auditory scheme of hearing it when it hits the floor. After the object has been retrieved (often by the parents), the child repeats the process but drops other objects (to see what they will do) or drops the same from a different height and with a different force to see what effects these variations will have.

Tertiary circular reactions enable children to learn that changes in their behavior can produce comparable changes in external events. They begin to understand that they can manipulate and control parts of their environment by their own actions. They are also learning (because they are toddlers and get into mischief) that their behavior can be controlled by others and that some of the novelties they produce are less than pleasing to their parents.

From the middle of the second year, children show evidence of what Piaget calls the *beginnings of thought,* marking the sixth and last stage of the sensorimotor period. At this time children perform what Piaget calls "mental experiments" in the sense that they try out certain actions "in their heads" before doing them in reality. If children want to solve a problem but cannot do so by trial and error, they may introduce a scheme that they learned in a different activity. Children at this stage do what Kohler's (136) apes apparently did when they secured bananas that were outside their cage by putting together bamboo poles and reaching outside to bring the bananas closer.

Piaget describes his daughter's attempts to remove an attractive chain from a partially open matchbox; she could see the chain, but she could not insert her fingers through the opening to get it. In trying to solve the problem, she first used a scheme that had worked in the past, namely, she tried to put her fingers into the box, but this didn't work. While she was studying the problem, Piaget noticed that she was also opening and closing her mouth, each time opening it a bit wider than she had before. After a few moments of this, she was able to open the box by pulling it wider and got the attractive chain. One can visualize the mouth movements as a sort of preparatory and exploratory action that could be applied to the box.

It is important to add that Piaget does not believe that the child's "mental experiments" utilize language. For one thing, the child's language at this age is not advanced enough for him or her to be able to understand or describe the problem verbally. Although the child can label objects and communicate wishes, his or her language is imbedded in a context of gestures and intonations; it is not yet independent of the social context. The beginning of thought is the mental experimenting that precedes specific action.

The mode of thinking that is available to the 2-year-old is, of course, very limited; it generally deals with the here and now and with the relationship between things. Since thought is also limited by the kinds of miniature actions the child can perform, it deals with the functions of things and not their attributes or qualities. By the age of 6 or 7, the child can conceptualize the properties and attributes of things as well as their functions.

At the outset of the sensorimotor period, the child is only capable of modifying his or her reflexes, but by the progressive differentiation and integration of schemes the child is finally able to explore objects deliberately and discover new means for attaining desired ends. Now the child is ready to move into the area of representation. It is clear that the emergence of cognitive abilities goes hand-in-hand with the child's construction of basic concepts about the world, of objects, of causality, and of space and of time.

Basic Concepts. Piaget's observations suggest that the young infant cannot distinguish between the world and itself. From the infant's point of view, there is no difference between a disappearance of the mother's face because she moved her head and a disappearance brought about by the infant moving its own head. During the first 2 months of life, a baby will stop looking for an object when it moves out of sight and look at something else instead. Peter Wolff (135) has noted that when an infant has been looking at an adult's face, it will cry when the face disappears, but it will not look for the face to reappear. In this case crying would seem to indicate that something pleasant has gone and will not return. During this first sensorimotor stage, the child has only a rudimentary notion of causality, space, and time. Causality is scarcely more than awareness of a sequential change in an existing state, and space is limited to awareness of the body and immediate environment.

During the stage of primary circular reactions, the child appears to have "passive expectations." After the end of the second month, he or she will gaze at the place where an object has disappeared as if waiting for it to reappear. The child does not actively search for the object, however, and there is no evidence that the child understands that the object exists apart from the ongoing action. If an infant is sucking at a pacifier and it falls to the floor, he or she may continue sucking as if waiting for it to reappear, but the infant does not actively look for it.

This passive expectancy expands the child's sense of causality somewhat in that he or she is beginning to separate the object from the action. Likewise the child is beginning to understand space better as he or she differentiates and locates different schemes with respect to the body. Time, too, is elaborated to the extent that the infant expects an event to happen again. We can only infer what the child's concepts of space and time are from his actions.

During the next 4 months, the stage of secondary circular reactions, the child begins to anticipate the trajectory of an object and to look for it at its expected landing place. Usually this occurs when the child has dropped or thrown the object himself or herself. At this time, too, the infant will look for partially hidden objects. When a rattle is partially covered with a bedspread, the infant will push away the bedspread or simply pull the rattle out. But if the rattle is completely covered, the child will not look for it.

At this stage the child can make a finer distinction between the object and the action and understand that there is a connection between his or her actions and what happens to the object. Spatial relations are also becoming more clearly defined. As the child reaches for a partially covered object, he or she begins to understand the concept of "over" and "under"; watching an object fall also contributes to the idea of "up" and "down." The infant also begins to understand time intervals as he or she throws an object and expects to hear or see the results immediately.

From the eighth to the twelfth month, the child will look for objects that have been completely hidden from view. When Piaget hid a piece of candy in his hand, his son Laurent tried to open the fist to get the candy. But when Piaget put his hand (holding the candy) under a hat and left the candy there, the child could not find it—he continued to look in Piaget's hand, unable to deal with the double displacement. Although the boy had begun to understand that objects could exist even though not seen, his experience had been limited to a single place; he could not understand how the candy could be out of sight in any other place.

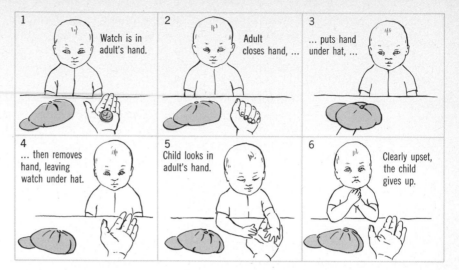

Figure 3.4 Illustration of a child who does not yet understand double displacement (*Source.* Adapted from Bower, T.G.R., *Development in infancy.* San Francisco: Freeman, 1974.)

Piaget tells a similar story about his infant daughter Jacqueline. Piaget's study overlooked a garden, and his daughter often looked up at him in his window from her carriage, which was in the garden on warm days. One day Piaget came through the garden on his way home. As Piaget bent over the carriage, Jacqueline looked up; first she looked at him and then at his study window. It was as if she assumed that his place was in the study window and not in the garden.

A child's concept of space, time, and causality all improve complementarily during this period. The child's directed action leads him or her to seek for desired objects and to understand relationships as he or she uses intermediaries to attain his or her ends. Space is further differentiated as the child begins to identify various spaces and places. Places become differentiated according to what can be done in them or what belongs in them. Time is further elaborated as the child differentiates between the intervals required for various actions and events.

Toward the middle of the second year the child begins to look for objects that have been both hidden and displaced, for example, the candy in the hand that is placed under the hat. The fact that a child can search for a double-displaced object signals the end of the sensorimotor period. The child now understands that objects have a permanence beyond his or her immediate experience and that objects are not associated with particular places. The concepts of self and world are now separate and independent.

The child also can now recognize causal sequences apart from those in which he himself is involved. Space, too, has become separated from action, and the child sees objects (including himself) as being in various places and yet seaparate from them. Concepts of time also show the same independence: Temporal sequences can occur apart from the child's own actions, and hence the child begins to achieve an objective, nonpersonal sense of time.

In summary, the child starts out viewing himself or herself at the center of the universe; everything else is measured from his or her own standpoint and in terms of his or her own actions. At the end of 2 years, the child sees himself or herself as merely a part of the universe, which has its independent objects, space, time, and causality. The child is now ready to enlarge his or her perspectives vis-à-vis other human beings.

Essay

PARENT EDUCATION AND INFANT STIMULATION

Since the 1960s psychologists have been participating to an increasing extent in programs of parent education and infant stimulation (for example, 137–143). Such programs have been established on the assumption that most modern parents have not had the opportunity to observe a wide variety of child-rearing practices, that effective parenting is critical during infancy for the healthy growth and development of the child, and that effective parenting can be taught.

Programs of parent education and infant stimulation try to promote better interaction between parents and children during the formative years. The need for such programs was emphasized for one of the authors on a cross-country flight when he observed a young couple who were traveling with their 3-month-old infant. The parents appeared to be intelligent, college-educated people who obviously cared for their baby. But while they were talking to each other, they didn't bother to talk to or smile at the baby. When the baby began to cry, the father picked it up and walked up and down the aisle holding the baby in front of him and by the waist so that the father was looking at the back of the baby's head while the baby was looking ahead down the aisle.

Such parents, well-intentioned though they were, could have benefited from some instruction on more effective ways to relate to their infant. It must be emphasized, however, that the goal of such programs is to *facilitate* rather than to accelerate growth—to allow children to develop as fully as possible without undue parental inhibitions or constraints.

While parent education and infant stimulation programs can be beneficial, one possible drawback is that if something goes wrong and the child does not adapt very well socially or academically, the parents may conclude that it is their fault. Certainly parents' attitudes and actions can help children live fuller, more rewarding lives, but the parents are not the only determinants of the child's future life. His or her abilities, temperament, and various external factors are also important. Accordingly, parent education and infant stimulation programs should try to help parents feel more confident about their child rearing without leading them to feel that they are totally responsible for their child's fate.

It should be said, too, that at all age levels there are many things parents can do to enrich the child's experience. During infancy, holding, rocking, playing with, and talking to baby are all important. Providing colorful mobiles above the crib and busy boxes (with buttons to push and so on) within the crib are also useful materials for infants to play with and to learn from. As the child gets older, investment in a set of sturdy blocks is worthwhile. Such blocks will be used again and again whereas other more complicated toys will be quickly discarded.

As children get older and approach school age there are other things parents can do to enrich the child's experience and to complement school learning. An important activity is reading to preschool children, so that they come to appreciate books. Taking walks and going on trips are useful, particularly if the parents take the time to point out new things, such as animals, and to label them. As children move into school, parents can help children with their spelling words, correct the grammar of their compositions and their math homework. Parents should not *do* the child's homework but should help the child to do the best job he or she is capable of doing.

Biography

JEAN PIAGET It is probably fair to say that the single most influential psychologist writing today is Swiss developmentalist Jean Piaget. His work is cited in every major textbook in psychology, education, sociology, and psychiatry — and in other disciplines such as chemistry and music. His research and theory have stimulated literally thousands of other investigations both experimental and theoretical. It is simply a fact that no contemporary social scientist can deem himself or herself fully educated without some exposure to Piaget's thinking.

Piaget was born in a small village outside of Lausanne. His father was a professor of history, in the University of Lausanne, who was particularly well known for his gracious literary style. Piaget's mother was an ardently religious woman who was often at odds with her husband's free thinking and lack of piety. Growing up in this rather conflictual environment, Piaget turned to intellectual pursuits, in part because of his natural genius, but perhaps also as an escape from a difficult and uncomfortable life situation.

As often happens in the case of true genius, Piaget showed his promise early in life. When he was ten he observed an albino sparrow and wrote a note about it which was published in a scientific journal. Thus was launched a career of publications that has had few equals in any science. Although Piaget had a natural bent for biological observation, he was not

inclined to experimental biology. The reason, according to Piaget, was that he was "mal adroit," or not well enough coordinated to perform the delicate manipulations required for experimental biology. Piaget's special talents appeared to lie in controlled observation of natural phenomena, not in experimental design and methodology.

After obtaining his doctorate, Piaget explored a number of traditional disciplines for one that would allow him to combine his philosophical interest in epistemology (the branch of philosophy concerned with the question of how we know reality) and his interest in biology and natural science. Piaget spent a brief period of time at the Burgholzli, the Psychiatric Clinic in Zurich where Carl Gustav Jung had once worked. In those years, Piaget was much impressed by Freudian theory, although he never had any desire to be a clinician and left the Burgholzli after less than a year.

From Zurich Piaget traveled to Paris, where he worked in the school that had once been used as an experimental laboratory by Alfred Binet. Piaget was given the chore of standardizing some of Sir Cyril Burt's reasoning tests on French children. Although the test administration was boring for the most part, one aspect of the work did capture Piaget's interest. Often when children responded to an item they came up with unusual or unexpected replies. Although these replies were "wrong" or "errors" for test purposes, they fascinated Piaget. In addition, when children came up with the wrong answer to questions like "Helen is darker than Rose and Rose is darker than Joyce, who is the fairest of the three," Piaget was curious about the processes by which the wrong response was arrived at. It seemed to Piaget that the contents of the children's errors and the means by which they arrived at wrong solutions were not fortuitous but systematic and indicative of underlying mental structures which generated them.

These observations suggested to Piaget that the study of children's thinking might provide some of the answers he sought on the philosophical plane, particularly those having to do with wholes and parts. He planned to pursue some investigations in this area and then move on to other problems. But the study of children's thinking became his life-long preoccupation. After Paris, Piaget moved to Geneva and undertook some investigations of children's thinking at the Jean Jacques Rousseau Institute, where he had taken an assistantship under Eduard Claparéde. On Claparéde's retirement, Piaget was appointed to his chair at the University of Geneva. He continued to hold this and other administrative positions until his own recent retirement.

As a person, Piaget is quite extraordinary. With his ring of white hair and scorched meerschaum, he looks somewhat like a latter-day Epstein. Up close his blue eyes have a merry twinkle, but they also convey an idea of his remarkable capacity for depth and penetration. One of the authors once attended a conference chaired by Piaget and attended by persons representing many disciplines — mathematics, philosophy, cybernetics,

Table 3.1 Piaget's Stages of Mental Development

Age Period	Emergent Abilities	Accomplishments Attributable to These New Abilities
0-2	Sensorimotor coordinations	Beginning concepts of space, time, causality, intentionality, object permanence
2-6	Pre-operations	Symbolic activities including language, conservation of properties such as shape and form, transductive (proximity) reasoning
6-11	Concrete operations	Conservation of quantity, syllogistic reasoning, hierarchical (boys + girls = children) reasoning, rule learning
11-15	Formal operations	Conceptualization of thought, understanding of historical time, geographical space, simile, metaphor, propositional logic, and experimental thinking

medicine, and physics. Piaget, who appeared to be dozing through most of the presentations, came to quickly when it was his turn to summarize the papers. His masterful integration of many complex concepts from various disciplines attests to his exceptional mental powers.

Piaget leads an extraordinarily disciplined life. Although he no longer teaches and has given up his administrative duties, he maintains a robust schedule of research and invited lectures. Each afternoon he takes a walk, usually up the small mountain behind his house, in order to sort out the ideas that he will write down upon his return. Piaget tries to write at least four publishable pages each day, even when he is traveling. This helps to explain his remarkable productivity.

Piaget's work has had a significant impact on contemporary child psychology and education and has influenced research in cognitive and moral development, infancy, perceptual development, memory, language, and referential communication. Outside of child psychology, Piaget's work has also been influential in such fields as linguistics and physics. His is one of the great minds of the twentieth century, and we in psychology are most fortunate that he chose to focus his talents upon the study of children.

Summary

Human growth can be viewed as taking place in successive stages that are related to age. Within each stage, development is governed by a characteristic growth rate, a characteristic directionality, a characteristic pattern of differentiation and integration, and a characteristic sequence.

During the first year the infant makes remarkable progress in physical development and coordination; from a few reflexes such as the startle and grasp reflexes, the infant learns to crawl, stand, and take a few steps (holding on tightly) by the end of the year. During the second year (sometimes called "toddlerhood"), young children are not only mobile, but they learn how to manipulate materials and get into all kinds of mischief; they should be watched carefully.

Mental growth during the first 2 years is also rapid and noteworthy. Infant intelligence is measured largely by means of sensorimotor skills; although such tests are valuable for discovering children with difficulties, they are not good predictors of later intellectual growth or ability. This is due in part to the fact that later intelligence tests measure verbal abilities while infant tests do not. Also, intelligence is not a fixed quantity, but it varies according to a variety of maturational and environmental factors.

Certain perceptual abilities such as visual, auditory, and gustatory discrimination are present at birth, but the more elaborate perceptual skills develop gradually during the first year. Unusually sudden, abrupt sights or sounds upset infants, whereas constant or repetitive sights or sounds appear to be soothing.

During the first 2 years children make rapid progress in both receptive (passive) and productive (active) language. The child moves gradually from undifferentiated to differentiated crying (that is, from crying that all sounds the same to crying that signals different things to adults). Around the middle of the first year the infant begins to babble, producing all of the speech sounds of his or her native language (as well as those of other languages). This is followed by *lallation,* or repetitive babbling, in which both vowel and consonant sounds appear. About the end of the first year the infant begins verbal imitation, which leads to the first word and the imitation of true speech.

During the second year the child rapidly increases his or her vocabulary and progresses from one- to two-word utterances. The first words are holophrastic in the sense that they are undifferentiated expressions with much additional meaning. Adults interpret a young child's verbalizations by means of contextual cues such as facial expression, body position, and so forth. Initially speech is simply one aspect of a larger effort to communicate. A child's verbal comprehension always exceeds his or her verbal productivity.

Very young infants demonstrate that they can learn by means of both classical conditioning and operant learning. They also show orienting behavior to new stimuli, attention to particular stimuli, and habituation to continued stimuli. Even those of 3 or 4 months demonstrate rudimentary problem-solving as well as reasoning behavior. By the age of 2, toddlers can utilize a number of cognitive processes.

Piaget's work has focused on the development of reasoning in infants and on their construction of the conceptual world. Reasoning develops gradually during a child's first few years, from the most elementary circular reactions to tertiary circular reactions that include intention and anticipation. At the same time, the child is also developing simple concepts of objects, space, time, and causality. By the age of 2 the child has a rather well-elaborated set of reasoning abilities together with certain limited but functional concepts about the basic parameters of his or her world.

References

1. Parmalee, A. A., & Haber, A. Who is the "risk infant"? In H. J. Osofsky (Ed.), *Clinical obstetrics and gynecology*. In press.
2. Hess, J., Mohr, G., & Barteleme, P. F. *The physical and mental growth of the prematurely born child*. Chicago: University of Chicago Press, 1939.
3. Douglas, J. W. B. "Premature" children at primary schools. *British Medical Journal,* 1969, **I,** 1008–1013.
4. Drillen, C. M. *The growth and development of the prematurely born infant*. Baltimore: Williams & Wilkins, 1964.
5. Wiener, G. Psychologic correlates of premature birth: A review. *Journal of Nervous and Mental Diseases,* 1962, **134,** 129–144.
6. Wiener, G., Rider, R. V., Oppel, W. C., Fischer, L. K., & Harper, P. A. Correlates of low birth weight: Psychological status at 6–7 years of age. *Pediatrics,* 1965, **35,** 434–444.
7. Wiener, G., Rider, R. V., Oppel, W. C., & Harper, P. A. Correlates of low birth weight: Psychological status at eight to ten years of age. *Pediatric Research,* 1968, **2,** 110–118.
8. Dennis, W., & Dennis, M. G. The effect of cradling practices on the age of walking in Hopi children. *Journal of Genetic Psychology,* 1940, **56,** 77–86.
9. McGraw, M. B. *Growth: A study of Johnny and Jimmy*. New York: Appleton-Century, 1935.
10. Hilgard, J. R. Learning and motivation in preschool children. *Journal of Genetic Psychology,* 1932, **41,** 36–56.
11. Lowrey, G. H. *Growth and development of children*. Chicago: Yearbook Publishers, 1973.
12. Cattell, P. *The measurement of intelligence of infants and young children*. New York: Psychological Corporation, 1940.
13. Bayley, N. *Bayley scales of infant development*. New York: Psychological Corporation, 1969.
14. Bruner, J. S. Eye, hand and mind. In D. Elkind & J. H. Flavell (Eds.), *Studies in cognitive development: Essays in honor of Jean Piaget*. New York: Oxford University Press, 1969.
15. White, B. L., Castle, P., & Held, R. Observations on the development of visually directed reaching. *Child Development,* 1964, **35,** 349–364.
16. White, B. L. The initial coordination of sensorimotor schemas in human infants: Piaget's ideas and the role of experience. In D. Elkind & J. H. Flavell (Eds.), *Studies in cognitive development: Essays in honor of Jean Piaget*. New York: Oxford University Press, 1969.
17. Stone, J. L., Murphy, L. B., & Smith, H. T. (Eds.), *The competent infant*. New York: Basic Books, 1973.
18. Appleton, T., Clifton, R., & Goldberg, S. The development of behavioral competence in infancy. In F. D. Horowitz (Ed.), *Child development research*. Vol. 4. Chicago: University of Chicago Press, 1975.
19. Wolff, P. H. The development of attention in young infants. *Annals of New York Academy of Science,* 1965, **118,** 783–866.
20. Gesell, A., et al. *The first five years of life*. New York: Harper, 1940.
21. Piaget, J. *The origins of intelligence in infants*. New York: Basic Books, 1954.
22. Cratty, B. J. *Perceptual and motor development in infants and children*. New York: Macmillan, 1970.
23. Lewis, M., & McGurk, H. Evaluation of infant intelligence. *Science,* 1972, **178,** 1174–1177.
24. Bayley, N. Development of mental abilities. In P. H. Mussen (Ed.), *Carmichael's manual of child psychology*. Vol. 1. New York: Wiley, 1970.

25. Knobloch, H., & Pasamanick, B. Prediction from the assessment of neuromotor and intellectual status in infancy. In J. Zubin & G. Jervis (Eds.), *Psychopathology of mental development*. New York: Grune & Stratton, 1967.

26. Elkind, D. Infant intelligence. *American Journal of Diseases of Children,* May 1974, **127,** 759.

27. Skeels, H. M. Adult status of children with contrasting early life experience. *Monographs of the Society for Research in Child Development,* 1966, **31,** (3).

28. Scarr-Salapatek, S. Race, social class and IQ. *Science,* 1971, **714,** 1285–1295.

29. Mann, I. *The development of the human eye.* New York: Grune & Stratton, 1964.

30. Spears, W. C., & Hohle, R. H. Sensory and perceptual processes in infants. In Y. Brackbill (Ed.), *Infancy and early childhood.* New York: Free Press, 1967.

31. Fantz, R. L., Ordy, J. M., & Udelf, M. S. Maturation of pattern vision in infants during the first six months. *Journal of Comparative and Physiological Psychology,* 1962, **55,** 907–917.

32. Dayton, G. O., Jones, M. H., Steele, B., & Rose, M. Developmental study of conditioned eye movements in the human infant, II. An electrocellographic study of the fixation reflex in the newborn. *Archives of Ophthalmology,* 1964, **71,** 871–875.

33. Wickelgren, L. The ocular response of human newborns to intermittent visual movment. *Journal of Experimental Child Psychology,* 1969, **8,** 469–482.

34. Gesell, A. L., Ilg, F. L., & Bullis, G. O. *Vision: Its development in infant and child.* New York: Paul Hoeber, 1949.

35. Barnet, A. B., Lodge, A., & Armington, J. C. Electrocetonogram in newborn human infants. *Science,* 1965, **148,** 651–654.

36. Bornstein, M. H. Qualities of color vision in infancy. *Journal of Experimental Child Psychology,* 1975, 401–419.

37. Haith, M. M. The response of a human newborn to a visual movement. *Journal of Experimental Child Psychology,* 1966, **3,** 235–243.

38. Kessen, W., Salapatek, P., & Haith, M. The visual response of the human newborn to linear contour. *Journal of Experimental Child Psychology,* 1972, **13,** 9–20.

39. Salapatek, P., & Kessen, W. Prolonged investigation of a plane geometric triangle by the human newborn. *Journal of Experimental Child Psychology,* 1973, **15,** 22–29.

40. Fantz, R. L. Pattern vision in newborn infants. *Science,* 1963, **140,** 296–297.

41. Fantz, R. L. Visual perception from birth as shown by pattern selectivity. *Annals of the New York Academy of Science,* 1965, **118,** 793–814.

42. Fantz, R. L., & Miranda. S. B. Newborn infant attention to form of contour. *Child Development,* 1975, **46,** 224–228.

43. Ruff, H. A., & Birch, H. G. Infant visual fixation: The effect of concentricity, and number of directions. *Journal of Experimental Child Psychology,* 1975, **17,** 460–473.

44. Hutt, C. Specific and diversive exploration. In H. W. Reese & L. P. Lipsett (Eds.), *Advances in child development and behavior.* Vol. V. New York: Academic Press, 1970.

45. Kessen, W., Haith, M., & Salapatek, P. H. Human infancy: A bibliography and guide. In P. H. Mussen (Ed.), *Carmichael's manual of child psychology* (3rd ed.). Vol. 2. New York: Wiley, 1970.

46. Harter, M. R., & Switt, C. D. Visually-evoked cortical responses and pattern vision in the infant: A longitudinal study. *Psychonomic Science,* 1970, **18,** 235–237.

47. Karmel, B. Z. Complexity, amounts of contour, and visually dependent behavior in hooded rats, domestic chicks, and human infants. *Journal of Comparative and Physiological Psychology,* 1969, **69,** 649–657.

48. Gibson, E. J., & Walk, R. D. The visual cliff. *Scientific American,* 1960, **202,** 64–71.

49. Bower, T. G. R. The visual world of infants. *Scientific American,* 1966, **215,** 80–92.

50. Bower, T. G. R. *Development in infancy.* San Francisco: W. H. Freeman, 1974.

51. Cruickshank, R. M. The development of visual size constancy in early infancy. *Journal of Genetic Psychology,* 1941, **56,** 77–86.

52. Brackbill, Y. Continuous stimulation reduces arousal level: Stability of the effect over time. *Child Development,* 1973, **44,** 43–46.

53. Brackbill, Y., Adams, G., Crowell, D. H., & Gray, M. L. Arousal level in neonates and preschool children under continuous auditory stimulation. *Journal of Experimental Child Psychology,* 1966, **4,** 178–188.

54. Moffitt, A. Consonant cue perception by twenty to twenty-four week old infants. *Child Development,* 1971, **42,** 717–731.

55. Eimas, P. D., Siqueland, E. R., Jusczyk, P., & Vigorito, J. Speech perception in infants. *Science,* 1971, **171,** 303–306.

56. Condon, W. S., & Sander, L. W. Synchrony demonstrated between movements of the neonate and adult speech. *Child Development,* 1974, **45,** 456–462.

57. Huller, M. W. The reactions of infants to changes in the intensity of pitch of pure tone. *Journal of Genetic Psychology,* 1932, **40,** 162–180.

58. Hutt, C., Von Bernuh, H., Lenard, H. G., Hutt, S. S., & Prechtl, H. F. Habituation in relation to state in the human neonate. *Nature,* 1968, **39,** 35–52.

59. Graham, F. K., Clifton, R. K., & Hatton, H. Habituation of heart rate response to repeated auditory stimulation during the first five days of life. *Child Development,* 1968, **39,** 35–52.

60. Graham, F. K., & Jackson, J. C. Arousal systems and infant heart rate responses. In H. W. Reese & L. P. Lipsett (Eds.), *Advances in Child Development and Behavior.* Vol. 5. New York: Academic Press, 1970.

61. Jackson, J. C., Kantowitz, S. R., & Graham, F. K. Can newborns show cardiac orienting? *Child Development,* 1971, **42,** 107–121.

62. Eisenberg, P. B. Pediatric audiology: Shadow or substance? *Journal of Auditory Research,* 1971, **11,** 148–153.

63. Gibson, J. *The senses considered as a perceptual system.* Boston: Houghton Mifflin, 1966.

64. McGraw, M. B. *The neuromuscular maturation of the human infant.* New York: Columbia University Press, 1943.

65. Pratt, K. C., Nelson, A. K., & Sun, K. H. *The behavior of the newborn infant.* Columbus: Ohio State University Studies, 1930, No. 10.

66. Rovee, C. K. Psychophysical scaling of olfactory response to the alcohols in human neonates. *Journal of Experimental Child Psychology,* 1969, **7,** 245–254.

67. Rovee, C. K. Olfactory cross-adaptation and facilitation in human neonates. *Journal of Experimental Child Psychology,* 1972, **13,** 368–381.

68. Rovee, C. K., Cohen, R. Y., & Shlapack, W. Life span stability in olfactory sensitivity. *Developmental Psychology,* 1975, **11,** 311–318.

69. Bergman, T., Haith, M., & Mann, L. Development of eye contact and facial scanning in infants. Paper presented at the meeting of the Society for Research in Child Development. Minneapolis, 1971.

70. Caron, A., Caron, R., Caldwell, R., & Weiss, S. Infant perception of the structural properties of the face. *Developmental Psychology,* 1973, **9,** 385–399.

71. Kagan, J., Henker, B., Hen-Tow, A., Levine, J., & Lewis, M. Infants' differential reactions to familiar and distorted faces. *Child Development,* 1966, **37,** 519–532.

72. Hoaf, R. A., & Bell, R. Q. A facial dimension in visual discrimination by human infants. *Child Development,* 1967, **38,** 895–899.

73. McCarthy, D. Language development. In L. Carmichael (Ed.), *Manual of Child Psychology.* New York: Wiley, 1954.

74. Chomsky, N. *Syntactic structures.* The Hague: Mouton, 1957.

75. Harris, Z. Concurrence and transformations in linguistic structure. *Language,* 1957, **33,** 283–340.

76. Braine, M. The ontogeny of English phrase structure: The first phase. *Language,* 1963, **39,** 1–13.

77. Braine, M. On learning the grammatical order of words. *Psychological Review,* 1963, **70,** 323–348.

78. Brown, R. *A first language.* Cambridge, Mass.: Harvard University Press, 1973.

79. Bloom, L. *Language development: Form and function in emerging grammars.* Cambridge, Mass.: M.I.T. Press, 1970.

80. Bowerman, M. *Learning to talk: A cross linguistic study of early syntactic development with special reference to Finnish.* New York: Cambridge University Press, 1973.

81. Piaget, J. *Six psychological studies.* New York: Random House, 1967.

82. Bloom, L. Language development review. In F. D. Horowitz (Ed.), *Review of child development research.* Vol. 4. Chicago: University of Chicago Press, 1975.

83. Simmer, M. L. Newborn's response to the cry of another infant. *Developmental Psychology,* 1971, **5,** 136–150.

84. Routh, D. K. Conditioning of vocal response differentiation in infants. *Developmental Psychology,* 1969, **7,** 245–254.

85. Shwartz, A., Rosenberg, D., & Brackbill, Y. An analysis of the components of social reinforcement of infant vocalizations. *Psychonomic Science*, 1970, **20**, 323–325.

86. Bell, S. M., & Ainsworth, M. D. S. Infant crying and maternal responsiveness. *Child Development*, 1972, **43**, 1171–1190.

87. McNeil, D. The development of language. In P. H. Mussen (Ed.), *Carmichael's manual of child psychology*. Vol. 1. New York: Wiley, 1970.

88. Lennenberg, E. H. *Biological foundations of language*. New York: Wiley, 1967.

89. Latif, I. The physiological basis of linguistic development and the ontogeny of meaning, 1. *Psychological Review*, 1934, **41**, 55–85.

90. Latif, I. The physiological basis of linguistic development and the ontogeny of meaning, 2. *Psychological Review*, 1934, **41**, 153–176.

91. Nakazema, S. Phonemicitization and symbolization in language development. In E. H. Lennenberg and E. Lennenberg (Eds.), *Foundations of language development: A multidisciplinary approach*. Vol. 1. New York: Academic Press, 1975.

92. Ingram, D. Transitivity in child language. *Language*, 1971, **47**, 888–910.

93. Smith, M. D. An investigation of the development of the sentence and the extent of vocabulary in young children. *University of Iowa Studies in Child Welfare*, 1926, **3**, No. 5.

94. Bloom, L. *One word at a time: The use of single-word utterances before syntax*. The Hague: Mouton, 1973.

95. Macnamara, J. Cognitive bases for language learning in infants. *Psychological Review*, 1972, **79**, 1–13.

96. Sinclair, H. J. The role of cognitive structures in language acquisition. In E. H. Lennenberg and E. Lennenberg (Eds.), *Foundations of language development*. Vol. 1. New York: Academic Press, 1975.

97. Slobin, D. I., & Welsh, C. A. Elicited imitation as a research tool in developmental psycholinguistics. In C. A. Ferguson & D. I. Slobin (Eds.), *Studies of child language development*. New York: Holt, 1973.

98. Brown, R. W., & Hanlan, C. Derivational complexity and order of acquisition in child speech. In J. R. Hayes (Ed.), *Cognition and the development of language*. New York: Wiley, 1970.

99. Leopold, W. F. *Speech development of a bilingual child: A linguistic record*. Evanston: Northwestern University Press, 1939–1949.

100. Halliday, M. A. K. Learning how to mean. In E. H. Lennenberg & E. Lennenberg (Eds.), *Foundations of language development*. Vol. 1. New York: Academic Press, 1975.

101. Braine, M. D. S. On two types of models of the internalization of grammar. In D. Slobin (Ed.), *The ontogenesis of grammar*. New York: Academic Press, 1971.

102. Elkind, D. *Child development and education: A Piagetian perspective*. New York: Oxford University Press, 1976.

103. Friedlander, B. Z. Receptive language development in infancy: Issues and problems. *Merrill-Palmer Quarterly*, 1970, **16**, 7–52.

104. Jeffrey, W. E., & Cohen, L. B. Habituation in the human infant. In H. W. Reese (Ed.), *Advances in Child Development and Behavior*. Vol. 6. New York: Academic Press, 1971.

105. Wetherford, M. J., & Cohen, L. Developmental changes in infant visual preferences. Paper presented at meeting of the Society for Research in Child Development, Minneapolis, 1971.

106. Pomerleau-Malcuit, A., & Clifton, R. K. Neonatal heart rate response to tactile, auditory, and vestibular stimulation in different states. *Child Development*, 1973, **44**, 485–496.

107. Jeffrey, W. E. The orienting reflex and attention in cognitive development. *Psychological Review*, 1968, **75**, 323–334.

108. Horowitz, A. B. Habituation and memory: Infant cardiac responses to familiar and discrepant auditory stimuli. *Child Development*, 1972, **43**, 43–53.

109. Miller, D. J. Visual habituation in the human infant. *Child Development*, 1972, **43**, 481–494.

110. Sokolov, Y. N. *Perception and the conditioned reflex*. New York: Macmillan, 1963.

111. Brackbill, Y. The role of the cortex in orienting: Orienting reflex in an encephalic human infant. *Developmental Psychology*, 1971, **5**, 195–201.

112. Lester, B. M. Cardiac habituation of the orienting response to an auditory signal in infants of varying nutritional status. *Developmental Psychology*, 1975, **11**, 432–442.

113. Fitzgerald, H. E., & Brackbill, Y. Classical conditioning in infancy: Development and constraints. *Psychological Bulletin*, 1976, **83**, 353–376.

114. Lintz, L. M., Fitzgerald, H. E., & Brackbill, Y. Conditioning the eyeblink response to sound in infants. *Psychonomic Science,* 1967, **7,** 405–406.
115. Lipsett, L., & Kaye, H. Conditioned sucking in the human newborn. *Psychonomic Science,* 1964, **1,** 29–30.
116. Kasatkin, N. I. First conditioned reflexes and the beginning of the learning process in the human infant. In G. Newton & A. H. Riesen (Eds.), *Advances in Psychobiology.* Vol. 1. New York: Wiley Interscience, 1972.
117. Koch, J. Conditioned orienting reactions to persons and things in 2–5-month-old infants. *Human Development,* 1968, **11,** 81–91.
118. Skinner, B. F. *The behavior of organisms.* New York: Appleton-Century-Crofts, 1938.
119. Kron, R. E., Stein, M., Goddard, K. E., & Phoenix, M. D. Effect of nutrient upon the sucking behavior of newborn infants. *Psychosomatic Medicine,* 1967, **29,** 24–32.
120. Sameroff, A. J. Can conditioned responses be established in the newborn infant? *Developmental Psychology,* 1971, **5,** 1–12.
121. Lipsett, L. P., Kaye, H., & Bosack, T. N. Enhancement of neonatal sucking through reinforcement. *Journal of Experimental Child Psychology,* 1966, **4,** 163–168.
122. Rheingold, H. L., Gewirtz, J. L., & Ross, H. W. Social conditioning of vocalizations in the infant. *Journal of Comparative and Physiological Psychology,* 1959, **52,** 68–73.
123. Weisberg, P. Social and nonsocial conditioning of infant vocalizations. *Child Development,* 1963, **34,** 377–385.
124. Lipsett, L. P., Pederson, L. J., & DeLucia, C. A. Conjugate reinforcement of operant responding in infants. *Psychonomic Science,* 1966, **4,** 67–68.
125. Brackbill, Y. Extinction of the smiling response in infants as a function of reinforcement. *Child Development,* 1958, **29,** 115–124.
126. Papousek, H. Experimental studies of appetitional behavior in human newborns and infants. In H. W. Stevenson, E. H. Hess., & H. L. Rheingold (Eds.), *Early behavior: Comparative and developmental approaches.* New York: Wiley, 1967.
127. Koslowski, B., & Bruner, J. S. Learning to use a lever. *Child Development,* 1972, **43,** 790–799.
128. Piaget, J. *Play, dreams and imitation.* New York: Norton, 1951.
129. Piaget, J. *The origins of intelligence in children.* New York: International Universities Press, 1952.
130. Piaget, J. *The construction of reality in the child.* New York: Basic Books, 1954.
131. White, B. L. The initial coordination of sensorimotor schemas in human infants: Piaget's ideas and the role of experience. In D. Elkind & J. H. Flavell (Eds.), *Studies of cognitive development: Essays in honor of Jean Piaget.* New York: Oxford University Press, 1969.
132. Schaffer, H. R. *The growth of sociability.* Baltimore: Penguin, 1971.
133. Bower, T. G. R. Stages in the development of the object concept. *Cognition,* 1972, **1** (No. 1).
134. Brunskill, A. Some studies of object permanence with children and monkeys. Unpublished honors thesis. Edinburgh University.
135. Wolff, P. H. The development of attention in young infants. *Annals of New York Academy of Science,* 1965, **118,** 783–866.
136. Kohler, W. *The mentality of apes.* New York: Harcourt Brace, 1925.
137. White, B. L., Watts, J. C., *et al. Experience and environment.* Vol. 1. Englewood Cliffs, N.J.: Prentice-Hall, 1973.
138. Gordon, I. J. *The infant experience.* Columbus, Ohio: Merrill, 1975.
139. Huntington, D., Provence, S., & Parker, R. *Daycare #2, Serving infants.* Washington, D.C.: Office of Child Development, U. S. Department of Health, Education and Welfare, 1972.
140. Heber, R., *et al. Rehabilitation of families at risk for mental retardation.* University of Wisconsin: Rehabilitation Research and Training Center in Mental Retardation. Progress Report to HEW.
141. Gordon, I. J., & Jester, R. Instructional strategies in infant stimulation. *Selected Documents in Psychology,* 1972, **2,** 122.
142. Gordon, I. J. Stimulation via parent education. *Children,* 1969, 57–59.
143. Gordon, I. J. *The Florida parent education early intervention projects: A longitudinal look.* Gainesville, Fla.: Institute for Development of Human Resources, University of Florida, 1973.

144. Shirley, M. M. The first two years. A study of twenty-five babies: I Postural and locomotor development. *Inst. Child Welfare Res. Monogr. Ser. No. 6.* Minneapolis: University of Minnesota Press, 1931.

145. Fantz, R. L. The origins of form perception. *Scientific American,* 1961, **204,** 66–72.

4 Personality and Social Development

SIGNALING AND ORIENTING BEHAVIORS

    Crying

    Gazing

    Smiling

    Babbling

    Imitation

    Factors That Affect Signaling and Orienting Behaviors

ATTACHMENTS TO PEOPLE

    Behaviors That Foster Attachment

    Stranger Anxiety

    Separation Anxiety

THEORIES OF THE ORIGINS OF INTERPERSONAL ATTACHMENTS

DETACHMENT AND INDIVIDUATION

    The Beginnings of Individuation

    Maternal Responses to Individuation

ATTITUDES TOWARD THE WORLD

    Infants' Influences on the Care They Receive

    Implications for Child Rearing

    Short-Term and Long-Term Effects of Infant-Care Practices

ESSAY

    On the Care and Spoiling of Infants

BIOGRAPHY

    John Bowlby

SUMMARY

REFERENCES

Personality is the sum of an individual's socially relevant thoughts, feelings, and actions. Personality and social development begin in infancy, when young children start to form habitual ways of relating to others and distinctive patterns of thinking and feeling about people, including themselves. These aspects of personality appear mainly in *expressive* behavior, and the growth of expressive behavior reflects in many ways the growth of personality.

Expressive behavior follows the principles of differentiation and integration that we introduced in Chapter 3. During the early months of life infants differentiate a number of expressive behaviors that *orient* them toward the world and *signal* their needs and interests; at about 6 months of age they begin to differentiate these behaviors into specific patterns of attachment to and detachment from the people around them; and by the age of 2 infants have begun to integrate these patterns into attitudes toward their world.

SIGNALING AND ORIENTING BEHAVIORS

Infants make social contact chiefly through five signaling and orienting behaviors: gazing (an orienting behavior) and crying, smiling, babbling, and imitation (signaling behaviors). Each type of behavior appears of its own accord, as a natural event. Over time, however, each is influenced by what a child experiences. Each becomes aimed toward people rather than objects and toward certain people rather than others.

Crying

Infants' cries are literally the first impact they make on their environment, and for the first several months of life crying is the main way in which they *signal* their needs. Crying differs in two important respects from the other four early social behaviors. Gazing, smiling, babbling, and imitation are mutual behaviors in which both infants and their parents engage; they are also pleasurable behaviors that parents enjoy and encourage. Crying, on the other hand, is usually neither mutual nor pleasurable as far as parents are concerned, nor is it behavior that they encourage.

Yet crying, more than any other activity in early life, brings parents to the infant's side and gets attention from them. This attention can mean anything from being fed and diapered to the social experience of being picked up, held, caressed, and talked to. All of these actions tend to stop an infant's crying: interestingly enough, it has been found that picking infants up is more likely to reduce their crying than feeding them (1).

Early in life babies cry mainly when they are hungry or in pain. There is some evidence that these two kinds of distress produce different kinds of crying; a gradually developing and rhythmical crying that is usually associated with hunger, and a sudden, irregular crying that generally means pain (2). As we noted in Chapter 3, however, the cries of young infants do not communicate much about how or what they are feeling. Although mothers may at times believe that they can tell from the sound of their infants' cries just what is disturbing them, these beliefs are based more on what they know of their child's state at the time (such as how long it has been since the last feeding) than on the nature of the cry they hear (3–5). Yet infants do have very distinctive cries, and many mothers are able to recognize their own baby's cries as early as 48 hours after birth (6).

During the first year of life infants gradually begin to cry for shorter periods of time and to use crying for communication. For example, Bell and Ainsworth report that infants up to 3 months of age spend more time crying when they are alone than when their mothers are holding them or are in view; between 9 and 12 months, however, infants cry more when they can see but not touch their mothers than when they are being held or when they are alone. Thus crying, which is at first brought about by distress and is only incidentally social, becomes by age 1 a mode of communication; it is now directed at specific people who are nearby and is intended to produce a social response. Bell and Ainsworth also found that 1-year-olds cry almost 50 percent less than they did at 3 months (1). As crying decreases, both infants and their parents have more time for the mutual and pleasurable behaviors of gazing, smiling, babbling, and imitation.

Gazing   Gazing is the first behavior in which infants *orient* themselves to their world and begin to take in information about it. One classic view held that infants perceive their world as a "booming, buzzing confusion"; yet research evidence since the early 1960s shows that children are born with highly developed visual capacities. As we noted in Chapter 3, infants only a few days old can focus on objects and follow them with their eyes. They can also tell the difference among objects by size, shape, and patterning, and even in the first week of life they prefer to look at patterned rather than plain objects and at novel rather than familiar stimuli (7–11).

These perceptual preferences help to orient infants toward the people in their world, since the most complex and changing stimuli they see are the moving and animated faces of their parents and others who take care of them. By the age of 4 weeks babies clearly prefer to look at faces more than at objects; by 4 or 5 months, when they have become capable of rather fine perceptual discriminations, they look at their mother's face in preference to the faces of other people (12–14).

When infants begin to gaze fixedly at the face—especially the eyes—of adults, a new and special kind of relationship arises. Eye-to-eye contact is an intense experience. Many mothers report that when they first really lock eyes with their offspring, around the end of the first month, they begin to regard their babies as people rather than objects. Before that,

Infants at 4-6 weeks begin to make direct eye contact with people, giving mothers their first sense of caring for a real person rather than an object. By 3 months, infants have also learned to look away as a means of avoiding or ending social contacts.

mothers tend to think of their infants in vague and impersonal terms. But with the beginning of face-to-face gazing, mothers experience markedly stronger feelings of affection toward their babies and take increasing delight in caring for them (14–16).

Besides promoting social relationships, gazing also gives infants their first chance to exert control in dealing with others. By 3 months of age infants have already become just about as adept as adults in focusing and averting their gaze. Whereas gazing elicits responses from others, looking away discourages social contacts. Having learned this, young infants close their eyes or look away not only to vary the amount and kind of perceptual stimulation they receive but also to terminate social contacts they find intrusive or overstimulating (17–20).

Smiling Smiling develops in three fairly distinct stages: *reflexive smiling, unselective social smiling,* and *selective social smiling.* From birth infants smile spontaneously in response to various internal states. During the first month smiling can also be elicited by high-pitched sounds, especially the sound of a female voice (14). These reflexive smiles are fleeting and unformed, however, and they convey little in the way of warmth or social awareness.

At around 4 to 6 weeks of age infants' smiling changes dramatically. They hold their smiles for longer periods of time, they smile more broadly, and they form smiling facial expressions that light up their eyes. Now, instead of smiling reflexively in response to sounds or internal states, they are more likely to smile in response to an animated, moving face accompanied by the sound of a human voice (21–23).

This warmly expressive social smiling appears at the same time that babies start to prefer looking at faces rather than at objects and to engage in mutual gazing with people. Yet, despite the feeling of many a mother that her baby now really "knows" her, social smiling in the early months is *unselective.* That is, babies will smile as readily at the faces of strangers as at the faces of members of their family. Not until infants are 5 or 6 months of age and learn to distinguish among faces does social smiling become *selective.* At that point babies begin to smile more at familiar than at strange faces. In fact, as we shall mention shortly, they become wary of strangers.

Babbling Babies cry, moan, and whimper in reaction to pain or pleasure during the early weeks of life. At 4 to 6 weeks of age they begin to coo and gurgle in response to the sound of voices and the sight of a moving face. Like social smiling, then, after the first month an infant's sounds begin to signal social interest and to bring attention and affection from others. Smiling soon becomes a response primarily to sights, but sounds continue to be cued by what infants hear as well. The human female voice is especially likely to elicit sounds from babies, and there is some evidence that 1-month-olds have already learned to recognize certain characteristics of their mothers' voice (2, 14, 24). Unlike smiling, moreover, which is visible only to others, infants can hear the sounds they are making; as a result, their vocalizing becomes self-perpetuating—that is, it leads to babbling even when they are left to themselves.

Babbling progresses through several stages that pave the way for later language development, as we indicated in Chapter 3. By the third or fourth month coos and gurgles begin to include the distinct sounds of vowels and consonants; by 6 months infants are beginning to repeat their own accidental sounds, and beginning at 9 or 10 months infants will repeat or even initiate sounds they have heard others make (25, 26). Aside from what it means for language development, this imitative aspect of infant babbling introduces a more general pattern of imitation by which babies signal their expanding social interest.

Imitation

Imitation is one of the most important ways in which children learn to become adults; we will discuss in several later chapters how copying their elders helps youngsters at all stages of development to acquire social skills. Although infants are not yet actively learning social skills, they do begin at about age 1 to display numerous imitative behaviors that enhance their social interactions. These start with imitative babbling and soon include imitation of others' movements. Now parents are dealing with a young person who not only looks and smiles at them but also "converses" with them by echoing the sounds they make. It does not matter that 1-year-olds do not understand what they are saying; when they make the sounds *ma* and *da* parents hear themselves being addressed and respond with expressions of pleasure and affection that enrich their infant's social experience.

Infants' tendency to imitate what they see as well as what they hear leads after the first year or so to many new and playful patterns of parent-child interaction. Parents find that if they raise their arms high above their heads and say "So-o-o big," babies will raise their arms and vocalize *o-o* or *bi-i*, and an enjoyable game will have begun. Thus, imitation is both a clear expression of social interest and an effective way of getting a social response (27).

Imitative behavior does not go through an unselective phase as smiling does. Rather, it is directed from the start at selected, familiar people toward whom the infant has developed some specific *attachment*. The mutually rewarding interactions that accompany imitative behavior usually strengthen these attachments.

Before turning to the differentiation of expressive behaviors into specific attachments, however, it may be helpful to summarize their beginnings (see Figure 4.1) and then examine briefly certain factors that affect the signaling and orienting behaviors that precede attachment.

Factors that Affect Signaling and Orienting Behaviors

Crying, gazing, smiling, babbling, and imitation are all natural events in the sense that they emerge spontaneously. Some theorists, influenced by the work of John Bowlby, a British psychiatrist, view the spontaneous emergence of these signaling and orienting behaviors as instinctive reactions that promote survival of the species. Bowlby argues that people, like other animals, need a repertoire of innate behaviors to keep themselves alive early in life until they have learned how to fend for themselves. Among babies this repertoire includes signaling and orienting behaviors,

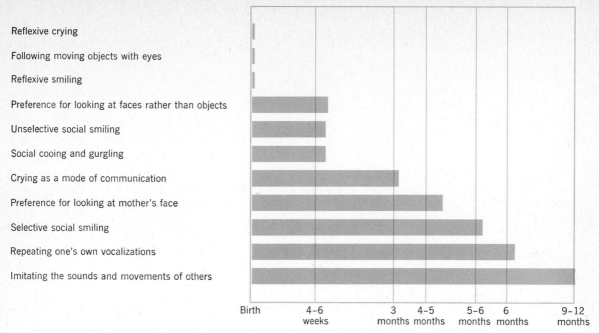

Figure 4.1 Approximate beginnings of expressive behavior.

which have survival value because they attract the attention of parents or other adults who feed, hold, and take care of them (28, 29).

Although it cannot be proved that the signaling and orienting behaviors of infants are specifically intended to bring about life-sustaining responses from others, it is clear that all normal infants develop these expressive behaviors in response to what they hear, see, and feel. And once they appear, these behaviors are strongly affected by the way in which others respond to them.

For example, experimental studies with babies ranging from 2 to 7 months of age have found that their vocalizations can be increased by smiling, saying something ("Yeah"), chucking them under the chin, or stroking their abdomens whenever they coo, gurgle, or babble; when the experimenters in these studies stopped responding and merely stared impassively, the infants gradually stopped making sounds and often looked away (30–34). Similarly, infants smile more when they are smiled at, talked to, or picked up, and they stop smiling when they no longer receive this kind of attention (35, 36).

Yarrow and his colleagues at the National Institute of Child Health and Human Development have supplemented these laboratory studies with home observations of 5- to 6-month-old infants and their mothers (37). They found that responsiveness influences infant behavior most when it is

Table 4.1 Significant Relationships between Maternal and Infant Behavior in
5- to 6-Month-Olds

Amount or Frequency of Maternal Behavior	Infant Variables			
	Social Respon-siveness	Goal Direct-edness	Reaching and Grasping	Secondary Circular Reactions
Tactile stimulation (touching)	No	Yes	No	Yes
Kinesthetic stimulation (moving)	Yes	Yes	No	Yes
Visual stimulation	Yes	No	No	No
Auditory stimulation	Yes	No	No	No
Contingent response to distress	No	Yes	Yes	Yes
Expression of positive affect	Yes	Yes	No	Yes
Smiling	Yes	No	No	Yes
Play	Yes	Yes	No	No
Level of social stimulation	Yes	Yes	No	Yes
Variety of social stimulation	Yes	Yes	Yes	Yes
Variety of play objects provided	No	Yes	Yes	Yes

Source: Based on data reported by Yarrow, L. J., Rubenstein, J. L., & Pedersen, F. A., *Infant and environment: Early cognitive and motivational development.* New York: Halsted, 1975.

contingent, that is, when it comes directly after the behavior. Thus, how much infants vocalize has little to do with how much their mothers talk to them; rather, it depends upon a mother saying or doing something in direct response to her infant's vocalizing—a **contingent response.**

Yarrow and his co-workers also found numerous relationships between the amount of stimulation mothers provide and their infant's social responsiveness, goal directedness, reaching and grasping, and secondary circular reactions (see Table 4.1). From these and other findings, there is good reason to believe that mothers who are physically and emotionally responsive to their infants encourage not only social initiative, but active exploration of their environment as well (37, 38).

The available evidence, then, demonstrates that infants need social stimulation in order to develop normal social responsiveness (38–40). When an infant is rarely caressed, smiled at, or talked to by adults, its expressive behaviors may not become differentiated into selective and mutually rewarding relationships with people. Fortunately, this does not happen to many infants, but when it does—as in some institutions or in the case of unusually cruel or neglectful parents—there may be serious and irreversible failures in social development. Such abnormal developments—known as *social isolation syndromes*—will be discussed in Chapter 6.

Ethical considerations do not permit infants to be deprived of social

Human and monkey infants need social stimulation to develop normal social behaviors. This infant monkey was reared in total isolation for the first 3 months of life and is unresponsive to the presence of other monkeys.

stimulation for research purposes. However, there is impressive evidence of the harmful effects of social isolation in animal studies, especially the research carried out by Harry Harlow and his co-workers at the University of Wisconsin Primate Center. Harlow's extensive work with monkeys has provided numerous insights into the early development of social relationships (41–44).

For example, infant monkeys who are reared alone in bare wire cages that allow them to see and hear other monkeys but not make physical contact with them fail to develop usual monkey social responses. If, after a year of such partial social isolation, these monkeys are placed with other monkeys, they spend most of their time huddling in a corner of the cage, rocking and clasping themselves, and they show no interest in play or other social encounters. These severe effects of early social isolation continue into the adulthood of such experimental monkeys and prevent them from assuming normal social roles (45–49). Conclusions about people must always be drawn cautiously from studies of animals. Nevertheless, the Harlow data would seem to bear grim testimony to the importance of social stimulation in sustaining normal expressive behavior.

ATTACHMENTS TO PEOPLE

As infants become selective in their signaling and orienting behaviors, they begin to develop special **attachments** to the familiar people in their world. These attachments include both love and dependence: infants display their attachment to people by seeking to be close to them, by striving to gain their attention and approval, and by becoming upset when they are separated from them. Some psychologists refer to the unselective gazing, smiling, and babbling of early infancy as attachment behaviors, since they attract attention and bring people close. However, it is not until expressive behavior becomes selective that infants truly become attached to specific people and sensitive to their presence or absence.

Attachment behavior has been studied in many parts of the world, including Israel, Scotland, Uganda, and the United States (50–56). From these studies we know that most infants develop selective attachments by 6 to 8 months of age. Infants focus their attachment on just one person at first, typically whoever has been most responsive to their social signals. Usually this person is the mother, although in some studies as many as one-third of the infants formed their first attachment to their father. First attachments are soon followed by other attachments, however, and infants usually become attached to both of their parents within a month of forming their first attachment to one of them.

Later on older brothers and sisters, grandparents, aunts and uncles, and even family friends may be selected as attachment figures if they regularly stimulate an infant and respond to his or her expressive behavior. Multiple attachments are common by the end of the first year, and by 18 months almost all babies have become psychologically attached to several different people.

On the other hand, the person toward whom infants form their first attachment tends to play a critical role in personality development from about 8 to 24 months of age. Up until 8 months, before infants have made selective social attachments, they develop normally so long as they receive adequate physical care and social stimulation from any number of people who may be caring for them. However, once they have formed a strong attachment to their mother, father, or other person, their psychological well-being depends in many ways upon close and continued contact with that person; the sheer amount of attention received from others is no longer enough to keep them happy. To understand these developments more fully, we need first to look at behaviors that foster the development of attachments and then describe two behavior patterns that often result from selective attachments—*stranger anxiety* and *separation anxiety*.

Behaviors That Foster Attachment

Attachment, like expressive behavior, is fostered when parents stimulate their infants and when they respond promptly and lovingly to their signals, especially crying. Conversely, the less stimulation parents provide and the less warmly responsive they are, the longer babies take to develop attachments and the weaker these attachments are (57). For example,

Ainsworth, Bell, and Stayton report that infants whose mothers pick them up affectionately and hold them long and tenderly during the first 3 months enjoy being picked up at 9 to 12 months and cuddle and embrace their mothers; by contrast, infants whose mothers have picked them up abruptly and held them briefly and carelessly dislike physical contact at 9 to 12 months and fuss and squirm in their mother's arms (53). Beckwith has observed in a similar study that 7-to-10-month-olds whose mothers ignore their signals show little interest in being held by them (58).

Hence, both the amount and the kind of care infants receive influence their attachments. However, it is important to emphasize that even limited social interaction does more to foster attachment than extended periods of routine feeding and physical care. On the communal farms in Israel (*kibbutzim*), for example, infants are cared for by a nursemaid (*metapelet*) and see their parents only briefly in the evening and on the Sabbath. Yet these infants become attached to their parents and not to the metapelet, apparently because the metapelet is busy with the physical care and supervision of a number of babies, whereas the parents can devote all of the time they have with their children to play and other social activities (59–61). Around the age of 2, kibbutz-reared children are about as attached to their parents as are home-reared American children (54). Studies of American infants who have been placed in daycare centers also show that, so long as they can be with their parents in the evenings and on weekends, they develop the same kinds of parental attachments as do home-reared babies (62).

As these observations demonstrate, intensive one-to-one care is not necessary in order for infants to become attached to people; attachments are formed not to those who spend the most time with an infant, but to those who are most stimulating and responsive. If parents are socially attentive and responsive while they are with their offspring, they need not worry about placing their child in a nursery or daycare center. The key fact here is that the *quality* rather than *quantity* of parental care is the crucial determinant of infant social behavior. In this regard, there is no evidence that infants will suffer any psychological harm if both their parents are employed, provided that the children have stable and adequate substitute care while their parents are away at work (63–67). Taking care of infants can also be shared among several different members of a family without interfering with the formation of attachments (50, 51, 55).

Stranger Anxiety   Once they have begun to form selective attachments, infants often show signs of anxiety in the presence of strangers. Between 5 and 8 months of age, most infants begin to become wary when strangers approach, and within a short time they are likely to frown, cry, or pull away when unfamiliar people make social overtures. **Stranger anxiety** usually reaches

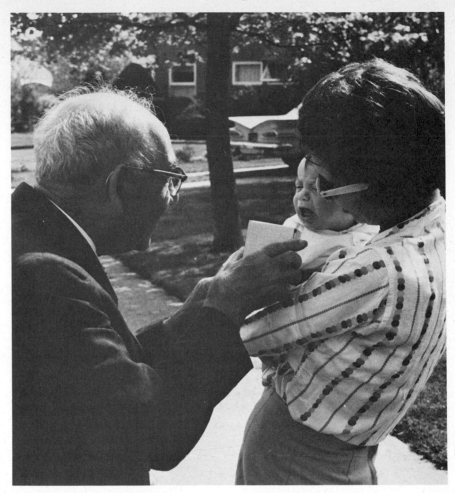

Many infants become wary of strangers between 5 and 8 months of age. A 4-month-old may enjoy being handed back and forth among several unfamiliar people who fondle him or her; but a 12-month-old is likely to become very upset upon being handed to a stranger, even if to a doting grandparent whom the infant has not had a chance to get to know.

a peak around the end of the first year and then gradually diminishes, as infants begin to learn that they do not have to fear people just because they are unfamiliar (56, 68–71).

Stranger anxiety can come as an unwelcome surprise to an infant's parents if they are not prepared for it. A mother who has enjoyed handing her 5-month-old daughter to friends and watching her smile and gurgle at them ("Isn't she adorable!") may be upset a few months later when the baby starts wailing and must be handed back ("What's the matter with her, anyway?"). Likewise, an occasional visitor who used to enjoy playing with a happy and receptive baby boy may later on be puzzled and disappointed by the fact that he no longer wants to be handled or even approached ("I thought he liked me. Am I doing something wrong, or has something happened to him?").

Not all infants experience stranger anxiety, and those who do get over it quickly—especially when they have a chance to become familiar with an adult who at first frightened them (56, 72). Nevertheless, it is helpful for parents to be aware that stranger anxiety may develop during the second half of the first year, since there are steps they can take to minimize their child's distress. For example, if strangers loom abruptly into an infant's line of vision, make loud noises that seem unfriendly, and snatch the infant up in their arms, the child is likely to be afraid. On the other hand, if an unfamiliar person approaches gradually, speaks softly, has a pleasant facial expression, and does not pick the baby up too quickly, the child may remain calm even if this happens at the height of its stranger-anxiety period (73–75). Infants are also less likely to display stranger anxiety and they may even be interested in the stranger if they are in familiar surroundings and their mother is nearby (68, 74). This is especially true if their mother is holding them when the unfamiliar person approaches; in one study infants showed more distress at the approach of a stranger when their mother was only 4 feet away than when she was holding them on her lap (68).

Parents can also minimize their child's distress by arranging for them to have positive social experiences during the first 6 months. The more social stimulation infants receive early in life by being touched, held, talked to, and played with, the less upset they are likely to become with strangers later on (76, 77). In an interesting study of this effect, Tizard and Tizard compared 30 2-year-old children who had been reared from the age of 4 months or earlier in a residential nursery with 30 children of the same age who had been brought up at home. As mentioned earlier in the case of the kibbutz and daycare children, these nursery children had become attached primarily to their parents, since they visited at least once a week. However, parental visits in this residential nursery were very limited compared with the regular evening and weekend get-togthers of the kibbutz and daycare children. Hence, these nursery children had very little chance to interact with their preferred attachment figures. At the age of 2, they were found to be significantly more fearful of unfamiliar people than the home-reared children, whose infantile stranger anxiety had all but disappeared (78).

Separation Anxiety Soon after they become wary of strangers, most infants also begin to develop anxiety about being separated from their parents or others to whom they are attached. **Separation anxiety** usually reaches its height between 13 and 18 months of age, at which time stranger anxiety has already begun to diminish (70).

Since infants are already creeping or even walking when separation anxiety appears, they can show their distress not only by crying but also by trying to stay close to someone who is moving away from them. Because there is a close relationship between attachment and separation anxiety, one can determine whether infants are attached to a particular person by observing what happens when that person leaves and returns. If infants cry and try to follow someone who is leaving and then later on approach that person warmly when he or she returns, it can be inferred that they have become attached to that particular individual (29, 39).

Such separation reactions have been studied by Bell and Ainsworth in a specially designed play situation in which mothers sit with their babies in a playroom, leave the room for a while, and then return. It was found that 1-year-olds left by their mothers for just a few minutes in this situation would cry, go to the door or look around the room as if following or searching for their mother, and lose all interest in the playroom and the toys there. When their mothers returned, they would stop crying, clamber up on her lap, clutch her tightly, and resist being put down (79, 80). These same responses to separation and reunion have been observed by many other researchers who have used this type of play situation with infants from 10 to 18 months of age (81–85).

Infant monkeys also show distress when they are separated from their mothers. Because in research with monkeys the separation can be extended longer than would be ethical with human infants, some interesting additional findings have emerged. When infant monkeys are placed together in a cage from which they can see and hear their mothers in another cage but cannot have any physical contact with them, they initially scream, run around, jump up and down, and look at them much of the time. After 3 weeks of separation, however, this "protest" gives way to "despair." The monkeys become inactive, stop playing with each other, and even stop looking at their mothers. If they are then reunited with their mothers, they go through a period of intense clinging before they begin to behave normally again (86–88).

When human babies must be separated from their parents for several days or longer, they tend to show the same kind of "protest" and "despair" as experimental monkeys. At first they cry and search for their absent parents, then they become irritable and lethargic, and later they may regress in some of their previously learned skills. Parents who return from a long vacation trip may find their 8-to-24-month-old children subdued and withdrawn as if they were depressed, or they may be creeping again even though they had learned to walk, or they may be soiling their clothes again even though they had learned bowel control (89–91).

Unlike young monkeys, however, human babies do not greet their returning parents so affectionately when there has been a separation of days or weeks rather than just minutes or hours. Instead, they are likely to appear detached. They may cry, turn or walk away when their parents approach them, and even seem not to recognize their parents—in short, to treat them as if they were strangers. After a few hours or days, depending upon the length of the separation, this detachment gives way to apparent ambivalence: children begin to approach their parents with warmth again and even cling to them, but they are also unusually demanding, defiant, and ornery. From the parents' point of view, it is as if their child were trying to get even with them, to punish them for having gone away, and this may very well be the case. Fortunately, this ambivalence disappears within a week or two after the parents' return, and the children become themselves again (65).

Children's reactions to brief separations dramatize how important primary attachment figures are to them. However, the distress infants experience when separated from their parents is minimized if they can remain in familiar surroundings, have familiar people and possessions around them, and be cared for by attentive substitute parents (92–95). For example, if a mother is going to the hospital to have a new baby, it is usually better to have a familiar person such as an aunt or grandmother serve as the mother substitute for a 1- or 2-year-old rather than a stranger. If possible, the substitute should move in rather than take the baby to her own home; if the child has to be moved, as many as possible of his or her accustomed toys and pieces of furniture (crib, highchair, playpen) should be taken along. If the baby has an older sibling, it is generally better for the children to stay together while their mother is away, rather than be cared for by separate relatives.

THEORIES OF THE ORIGINS OF INTERPERSONAL ATTACHMENTS

Although child specialists substantially agree as to *how* infants begin to show attachments to people, they have had different theories about *why* these attachments develop. Traditional psychoanalytic and social learning theories hold that social interests arise from biological needs. In the language of psychoanalysis, for example, infants begin to "cathect" or feel love toward their mother because they associate her with the pleasurable experience of being fed (96–98). In social learning terms, "primary drive reduction" provided by a mother, as in feeding her baby, causes the baby to develop secondary drives to be close to and dependent on her (99–101). Once love or dependency toward the mother is firmly established, these theories continue, the social interest it produces generalizes to other people as well.

Because of the influence of these theories, psychologists for many years made a distinction between primary (biological) and secondary (social) motives in human behavior. Since the 1960s, however, newer theories have held that social interest is a primary human characteristic in its own right. The most important of these theories has been formulated by John Bowlby, whose work we mentioned earlier. Bowlby argues that interpersonal attachments arise from infants' signaling and orienting behaviors and the personal attention these behaviors bring from others; it is the social responses of adults that shape an infant's expressive behaviors into patterns of interpersonal attachment. As we have seen, research findings tend to favor Bowlby's views over the more traditional need-reduction

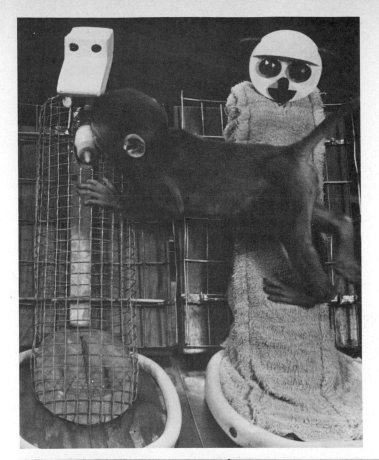

Infant monkeys reared with wire and terry cloth "mothers" prefer being close to the terry cloth "mother," even if they have been fed only from a bottle attached to the wire "mother." When frightened by a wooden "spider," they run and cling to the terry cloth "mother," apparently because of the sense of comfort and reassurance that comes from physical contact with "her."

128

theories of social development. Thus, when the kibbutz children become attached to their parents, who fondle and play with them for a little while each day, rather than to the metapelet who feeds them, they are showing that social stimulation rather than biological needs lead to the development of strong interpersonal ties.

Further evidence of this phenomenon has emerged from Harlow's animal work, particularly from observations that infant monkeys form very strong attachments even though they are not being fed. In these classic studies, infant monkeys were placed with two kinds of wire mesh "mothers," one consisting only of bare wire and the other covered with terrycloth. Both "mothers" had bottles set into the "chest" area from which the monkeys were fed. Between feedings all of the monkeys preferred to be with and to cling to the terrycloth "mother" even if they had been "fed" only by the bare wire "mother." Furthermore, when a large wooden "spider" was placed in the cage, the monkeys ran in apparent fright to the terrycloth "mother," again regardless of which one was "feeding" them (44, 102).

Because of this kind of evidence from human and monkey infants, many psychoanalytic and social learning theorists are shifting toward Bowlby's position. In psychoanalysis today, "object relations" theorists are viewing infants as being innately "object seeking," so that social motivations appear of their own accord rather than as a result of biological drives (103–105). Social learning theorists are paying less attention to "secondary drive" concepts of attachment and are concentrating on how emerging social interests are shaped by the environment (106–108).

DETACHMENT AND INDIVIDUATION

As infants become preschoolers, their early attachment figures become less important. Many new people enter the child's world, enriching it with new social interests. Young children thus outgrow the stranger and separation anxiety of infancy. From 10 to 18 months of age there is little change in reactions to brief separations, but 2-year-olds are less upset than 1-year-olds when their mother leaves them for a few minutes, 3-year-olds are much less upset, and 4-year-olds are hardly affected at all (54, 81). Along with the growing capacity to tolerate strangers and separation, young children begin to seek **detachment** and **individuation** from their parents; these developmental events pave the way for children to assert themselves as independent persons (109).

The Beginnings of Individuation

Through most of their first year infants stay pretty much where their mother puts them. Any "misbehavior," such as thrashing around when she is trying to diaper them, knocking a glass off the table, or making noise while she is on the telephone, is largely accidental and unrelated to feelings they have toward their mother. In the second year, however, two things happen: children become increasingly skillful in handling objects and in moving about on their own, and they also begin to understand that their behavior affects their parents. Parents and others who care for young children still wield enormous power. They are physically dominant, and they control most of the rewards and punishments in the child's life. But now infants realize that they can affect how their parents feel.

Their new motor skills and their dawning awareness of their impact on others lead infants to make their initial declarations of independence. Frustrated or provoked by their mother, they may "pay her back" by spilling their milk, refusing to hold still while she is dressing them, or keeping up a tantrum that drives her to distraction. Furthermore, as young children learn to speak, they begin to state their own needs and wants. Language is at first a means of pleasurable exchange between parents and children, but it also becomes a means of conflict when children learn to say "no." Once children learn this word, they use it often with good effect. They say "no" not so much because they do not want something or are unwilling to do something as because they want to assert themselves as persons in their own right.

It is by opposing their parents that children begin to stake out their independent identity. Negativism and rebelliousness are often disturbing to parents, but they are a necessary and inevitable part of growing up. If oppositional behavior does not occur by the end of the second year, there may exist what is known as a **symbiotic mother-child relationship.** Symbiotic children exist only as an extension of their mother; they make little or no progress toward establishing themselves as separate and distinct persons. Although symbiosis is normal in early infancy, its persistence at age 2 is often an early sign of abnormal development (110–112).

Maternal Responses
to Individuation

Clinical observations by psychoanalysts Margaret Mahler and Therese Benedek reveal that parents, especially mothers, respond differently to their child's individuation (113–115). Ideally, mothers should be pleased to have their children become increasingly independent. Although they may feel some nostalgia for the early close ties with their infant, they should welcome his or her new achievements and enjoy having a more self-reliant child. Mothers who can adapt to these changes tend to provide a fairly constant quality of care as their child matures.

Some mothers, however, enjoy caring for infants who are totally dependent on them, but lose interest when their children begin to mature as separate individuals. Babies gratify these women by serving as an extension of their own body and personality and by being completely under their control. When normal individuation interrupts this symbiosis and requires them to deal with children who have minds of their own, these women may look elsewhere for gratification. This may mean getting pregnant again and having a new infant to care for when their youngest child approaches the preschool years. In other cases it may mean turning the child over to a substitute caretaker and becoming heavily involved in one or another activity outside the home. In either case, the quality of maternal care provided by these mothers is likely to decline substantially when their offspring begin to assert their independence.

Another group of mothers have strong needs of their own to be dependent and cared for. These women do not enjoy taking care of a totally dependent infant, but they become more interested as their offspring mature. They are pleased when their child's individuation and increased ability to communicate relieve them of the burden of interpreting and responding to infant signals of distress. When their children reach preschool age, these mothers enjoy carrying on a conversation with them and having their companionship. Clearly, mothers of this kind tend to become more devoted to their children after they have become detached from them.

ATTITUDES TOWARD THE WORLD

By the age of 2 children are beginning to form general attitudes toward their world. The first of these attitudes to appear is what Erik Erikson has called a **sense of trust**—a general feeling that one's needs will be met and that the world is a safe and friendly place (116, 117). How much trust or mistrust children develop in the first 2 years of life depends upon how they are cared for; specifically, parents shape their children's attitudes toward the world by the way in which they respond to their needs.

For example, mothers who enjoy caring for their infants are likely to feed them in a relaxed and leisurely manner, probably cuddling and playing with them at the same time as well; on the other hand, mothers who resent or dislike their infants' demands may feed them in a hurried, mechanical, and disinterested fashion. These different maternal behaviors can affect whether children come to expect a warm and pleasant reception from others or a cold and grudging response. In this way infants develop either a sense of trust in their world—seeing it as a dependable source of comfort and support—or insecurity about what lies in store for them (38, 118).

Considerable research confirms the roles that parents play in promoting a child's sense of trust. These studies show that the more sensitive mothers are to their infant's needs and the more affectionate, responsive, and stimulating they are in caring for them, the more likely the infants are to develop secure rather than insecure attitudes toward the world (119–121). Children who are defined as ''secure'' in these studies make relatively few demands on their mother, feel comfortable in leaving her side to explore their surroundings, and tolerate brief separations without becoming too upset; ''insecure'' children, on the other hand, tend to cling to their mother and demand attention, are hesitant to explore their environment, and become markedly upset by separation. Secure children are confident that care and protection will be there when they need it; they know that they do not have to seek it out constantly or remain close to its source. Insecure children do not have this sense of trust.

The influence parents have on their children's personality development is determined in part by inborn differences among children that affect how their parents treat them. Children differ from birth in several aspects of their behavior, including their level of activity, eating and sleeping habits, and sensitivity to stimulation. Some babies are noisy, irritable, and difficult to satisfy, while others are placid and undemanding. Some display a lot of affection as well as rapid mental and physical growth, while others are emotionally reserved and slow to develop.

The effects of these inborn differences on parents are well known. Infants who are easy to manage, who mature rapidly, and who are cheerful about being cared for tend to make their parents feel good about taking care of them, which they demonstrate through expressions of love and affection. On the other hand, children who are by nature more or less active than their parents would like them to be, who are irritable to the point of crying constantly or becoming colicky, or who seldom smile, babble, or cling to their parents tend to fare less well. They frequently aggravate or frustrate their parents who, in turn, stop expressing warmth and concern (16, 121, 122). Thus, parents may become cold and rejecting in response to their infant's apparent coldness and rejection, and not because they are basically cold and rejecting people. In this and other ways, children can shape their parents' behavior almost as much as their parents influence them (123–128).

How active and emotional people are makes up part of their **temperament.** Although we will talk about temperament primarily in the chapters on individual variations, it is relevant to mention here some research on temperamental differences among infants that are likely to affect parental behavior. Having made repeated observations of infants with their mothers, Schaffer and Emerson classified certain infants as "cuddlers" and others as "noncuddlers." The "cuddlers" sought and enjoyed physical contact with their mothers, whereas the "noncuddlers" disliked and struggled against being held, even when they were frightened or seemed to need comforting. These differences between the two groups of infants bore no relationship to how their mothers were treating them; hence, they were apparently temperamental differences, which would more likely affect the mothers' behavior than be affected by it (129).

In an extensive series of studies with infants and older children, Thomas, Chess, and Birch described three temperamental styles that begin early in life: the *easy child,* the *difficult child,* and the *slow-to-warm-up child* (130–133). The largest group is the *easy* children; they eat and sleep regularly, adapt readily to change, approach new situations comfortably, and display moods that are generally positive in tone and mild to moderate in intensity. Parents tend to respond to these infants positively and often pride themselves on their child's smooth development, even though this has little to do with what kind of parents they are.

A smaller group, the *difficult* children, show just the opposite characteristics. They eat and sleep irregularly, which makes it difficult to feed them or keep them asleep; they adapt to change slowly, which means that they are likely to become distressed in new situations and around strange people; and they are often in a bad mood, crying and throwing tantrums even when they are only mildly frustrated. Because of such behaviors, the parents of difficult children feel negatively toward them, and they also feel guilty or worried that they may be responsible for the problem. In fact, however, parents are no more responsible for the temperament of a difficult child than for that of an easy child. Furthermore, difficult infants can adapt just as well as easy infants when they are a little bit older if their parents have enough patience to help them learn to overcome their initially limited tolerance for frustration.

Slow-to-warm-up children also find it difficult to adapt to new people and situations, but they express themselves quietly rather than loudly. They fuss mildly about new things or offer passive resistance, as by letting a new food dribble out of their mouth rather than spitting it out violently as a difficult child would do. These youngsters can also outgrow their potential personality difficulties if their parents are patient, do not push them to grow up faster than they are able to, and do not lose interest in caring for them.

Implications for Child Rearing

In view of the kinds of research we have just described, child development specialists have come to appreciate that during every stage of childhood certain aspects of youngsters' innate temperament and their rate of maturation interact with their parents' personality to determine the parents' child-rearing style (134–138). This process of parent-child interaction accounts for the fact that children who have been reared in the same family do not necessarily have the same kinds of experiences with their parents (139). Inborn differences among siblings tend to elicit different responses from their parents, which in turn have different effects on their personality development.

With respect to the broader issue of bringing up children, the role of temperament in personality development has two significant implications. First, there is no single or best way to bring up a child. Whether a child will benefit most from being held often or just occasionally, for example, will depend upon whether that child is more of a "cuddler" or a "noncuddler" by nature. Whether a child will thrive on being exposed to many new experiences or will fare better with a regular routine and a slowly changing environment will depend upon whether he or she is basically an "easy" or a "slow-to-warm-up" child.

Whatever child-rearing practice is being considered (such as feeding, providing stimulation, disciplining) and whatever child-rearing goal is intended (such as helping children feel secure, enabling them to be loving and affectionate, promoting their independence strivings), the most beneficial and effective way of caring for them will vary according to the child's basic temperament. Hence a good "fit" between an infant's temperament and the child-rearing style of its parents is the key to positive personality development, and any statement that there is one best way to care for all children must be taken with a grain of salt.

Second, in studying the effects of child-rearing practices, one must make allowances for differences in temperament. Too often research in this field has assumed that children are basically alike, so that a certain kind of parental behavior should affect each child the same way. The result in many cases has been apparently inconsistent findings: sometimes most of the children in a study show the expected effect and sometimes they do not. From what we now know about temperament, we can see the error in such research of not taking parent-child interaction into sufficient account. The question that should always be addressed in these studies is "What kinds of child-rearing practices *used with what kinds of children* produce what kinds of personality patterns?"

Short-Term and Long-Term Effects of Infant-Care Practices

Thus far, we have been discussing how parents affect their children's behavior while they are infants. These are short-term effects, as illustrated by the fact that infants whose mothers are affectionate and responsive show secure attitudes toward the world. It is well established that early life experiences have a significant influence on how infants feel and act. However, whether these early experiences have long-term effects—that is, whether there is a *continuity* of personality development from infancy to later childhood and beyond—is another matter. The available evidence would seem to advise caution in predicting later behavior from what infants are like or how they are cared for.

Taken together, studies of the long-term effects of infant-care practices have not provided consistent results (140). Many of these studies are flawed, however, because they are based on mothers' recollections of what their children were like as infants or how they cared for them. The results of such **retrospective research** are not very reliable, since human memory is both imperfect and convenient—people often remember what they want to remember, and not necessarily what actually happened. Only **observational research,** in which investigators see and record parent-child interactions while they are happening, provides reliable data for assessing the long-term effects of these interactions (38, 39, 140, 141).

Since there are very few long-term observational studies, much work remains to be done in identifying the later effects of infant experience. The few observational studies that have been made so far show little relationship between infant behavior and personality characteristics in adolescence and adulthood; generally speaking, it is not until the ages 6–10 that a moderately strong relationship between child and adult behavior begins to appear (142–145). These findings suggest that the attitudes that begin to form in infancy are far from fixed. Later experiences shape new kinds of attitudes, as we shall see, and they also modify or even reverse the old ones. Nevertheless, there is some continuity in personality development from infancy for the following reasons:

1. Even though children *can* change dramatically, they may not. If they grow up under very stable circumstances, with few changes from year to year in the kinds of people and situations they are exposed to, they may demonstrate a highly consistent personality style over time (143).

2. There appears to be more continuity at the extremes of a personality characteristic than in the middle range. Thus, a mildly insecure infant may become more secure if he or she has positive experiences later on in childhood, whereas a markedly insecure infant is less likely to change in response to later experience (142).

3. There appears to be continuity in a child's *temperament,* although not necessarily in his or her motivations. Temperament refers to the manner in which a child moves, talks, or thinks; motivation refers to what the child actually does, says, or thinks (146, 147). One example of consistent temperament would be a child's activity level, which remains fairly stable—a passive infant is likely to become a dependent adolescent and adult (143, 148).

4. Even though a child's attitudes at one age do not necessarily mean that he or she will have the same attitudes at a later age, they do set the stage for what is likely to happen next. Two-year-olds with a firm sense of trust in their world may or may not continue as optimistic people, depending upon the nature of their later experiences; however, they will respond differently from insecure children of the same age to the developmental tasks of the preschool years.

Essay

ON THE CARE AND SPOILING OF INFANTS

It is often said that a pampered child will become a spoiled child. According to this folklore, allowing infants to have their own way encourages them to become demanding and disobedient. John Watson, the founder of behavioristic psychology, suggested a scientific rationale for this belief, namely, that gratifying infants on demand has the effect of rewarding and reinforcing demanding behavior. Therefore, Watson cautioned mothers to feed their infants on a strictly determined time schedule and not in response to their hunger cries in order not to spoil them (149). Publications of the U.S. Children's Bureau have also said that picking up babies when they cry tends to encourage their crying behavior and make it more likely to recur, and hence that it contributes to spoiling (150).

Despite the popularity of these beliefs, all available evidence points in the other direction. Research studies indicate that parents who respond to their infants' cries are likely to provide conditions of warmth and nurturance that will stop the crying, enable their children to feel secure, and make them less likely to cry or demand unreasonable attention in the future. On the other hand, parents who ignore or delay responding to their infants' cries during the first few months of life tend to have babies who do a great deal of fussing and crying later on. Likewise, infants whose parents are more interested in controlling and disciplining them than in gratifying them tend to become unresponsive to parental commands by their second year. But babies whose cries are heard and responded to promptly and with loving care tend to become relatively undemanding, easily satisfied, and well-behaved infants (38, 39, 151, 152).

JOHN BOWLBY

Biography

John Bowlby is an English psychiatrist best known for his work on the attachment (emotional bonding) between parents and children. In Bowlby's view, disruptions of emotional attachment during childhood can be a cause of mental illness, and maintenance of affective bonds between parent and offspring is an important bulwark of mental health. Bowlby's work first came to international prominence when, in 1951, he published a report entitled "Child Care and the Growth of Love." The study was sponsored by NATO and in it Bowlby reported the results of his study of children separated and orphaned by World War II. In that book, which has become something of a classic, Bowlby introduced the concept of "maternal deprivation" and gave evidence of the effects of such deprivation on the growing child. It was the start of much contemporary work on attachment behavior.

Although Bowlby is best known for his work in attachment behavior, his interests and accomplishment are broad. He was one of the early advocates of family therapy and was the first to publish a paper on that subject in English. Likewise, Bowlby was one of the first behavioral scientists to recognize the value of the methods as well as of the approaches of ethnologists such as Tinbergen and Lorenz. Bowlby has always been appreciative of the contributions of social workers and psychologists and has organized and worked with interdisciplinary research and therapeutic settings.

In some respects, John Bowlby illustrates in his own life, the role of attachment, not only to people but also to places. He was born in the Hampstead district of northwest London in 1907 and has continued to live and work in that section of the city for most of his life. His father was a surgeon, and after a brief flirtation with a career in the Navy and a stint as a teacher in a small British infant school, Bowlby completed his studies of medicine at Cambridge. But he was interested in psychiatry rather than in physical illness and took his psychiatric training at the famed Maudsley Hospital in London.

Bowlby had developed an interest in Freud's psychoanalytic theories, but these were not highly regarded at the Maudsley. Nonetheless Bowlby felt his training there was valuable and grounded him in the conventional theories and diagnostic procedures of psychiatry. The critical attitude toward psychoanalysis may also have helped Bowlby to free himself from the doctrinaire attitudes of so many Freudians and to move in the new directions that his observations suggested.

After the war, Bowlby became Head of the Children's Department at the Tavistock Clinic in northwest London, a position he held until his recent retirement. Anna Freud, too, was at the Tavistock, and it soon came to be regarded as psychoanalytically oriented.

It was at the Tavistock Clinic that Bowlby undertook the observations and investigations that underlie his conception of attachment. For Bowlby attachment is both a more basic and a more powerful dynamic than the sexual drives posited by Freud. He believes strongly that a stable mothering relationship is beneficial even to children whose emotional difficulties may be partly organic in nature. And Bowlby insists that attachment is quite different from what is usually described as "dependency" or "dependency needs."

Whereas dependency is usually conceived narrowly, as the need of one person to be cared for any another, attachment is a much broader concept. Bowlby sees attachment as having a biological component (not unlike imprinting in animals) and as being more specific and of longer duration than dependency needs. In addition, attachment is a learned organization of behavior that occurs most extensively in early childhood and that involves parental behavior and emotional interaction and engagement. In a recent three-volume work, *Attachment, Separation,* and *Loss,* Bowlby elaborates his theory in the context of psychiatric, psychological, sociological, and ethnological research.

In his semiretirement, John Bowlby maintains his active enthusiastic interest in the concerns that have dominated his professional life from its outset. He is still vitally interested in the relations between parents and children, how they become attached to one another, and the vicissitudes of those attachments. The durability of this interest was conveyed in a remark Bowlby made to his wife after World War II. She had asked him what he was going to do and he had replied that he was going to study childhood separation and its effects. When she asked him what else he was going to study, he replied, "I'm sure that separation studies can occupy me for the rest of my life" (*APA Monitor*, May 1977, **8**, 6, 7).

Summary

Personality development begins in infancy with the appearance of expressive behavior. At first expressive behavior consists of *gazing,* which is an orienting behavior, and *crying, smiling, babbling,* and *imitation,* which are signaling behaviors. These orienting and signaling behaviors appear of their own accord in all infants. Over time, however, each of these behaviors becomes directed toward the important people in a child's life, and each is influenced by how these people respond.

Early expressive behaviors tend to be repeated when parents and others who are caring for children provide them with pleasant stimulation, such as by smiling at them, talking to them, or picking them up. There is a strong relationship between the amount of stimulation infants receive in response to their expressive behavior and the amount of expressive behavior they show. Without such stimulation, infants may be slow to develop this behavior and thus lag in making social contact with others.

At about 6 to 8 months of age, infants begin to form special attachments to their parents and other familiar persons in their world. These attachments are not necessarily to those who spend the most time with infants or who take care of their physical needs. Rather, the attachments are to those persons who are most responsive to an infant's needs for social attention and stimulation. Hence, it is the *quality* and not the quantity of parental care that is crucial for infant personality development.

After infants have formed selective attachments, they often become wary of strangers. Stranger anxiety usually reaches its height at around 1 year of age and then gradually diminishes, as infants learn that they do not have to fear people just because they are unfamiliar. Beginning at around 8 months of age, infants are also likely to become upset when they are separated from those to whom they have become attached. This separation anxiety, which reaches a peak between 13 and 18 months of age, is expressed through crying and apparent efforts to look for the absent person. If the separation is relatively long, as when parents are away on a vacation trip, infants may lose interest in having social contact with anyone. However, these reactions usually disappear soon after the parents return. Parents can minimize the distress of 1-to-2-year-old children by arranging for them to be among familiar people and/or surroundings while they are away.

As children near the age of 2, they begin to detach themselves from their parents and to assert themselves as independent persons. This detachment becomes clear as children start to say "no" and do what they please regardless of what their parents may want. Since *individuation* is a necessary part of growing up, parents must allow and encourage these assertions of independence.

Two-year-olds also begin to form general attitudes toward their world, starting with a *sense of trust*—a feeling that the world is a safe and friendly place. Trust is fostered by parents who are sensitive to their children's needs and who are affectionate, responsive, and stimulating in caring for them. Parents who do not provide this kind of care tend to have children who are insecure—children who are clinging and demanding, who hesitate to explore their surroundings, and who are unusually upset by even brief separations.

Besides being influenced *by* their parents, infants also affect how their parents behave toward them. Especially important in this regard are inborn differences in temperament, including level of activity, regularity or irregularity in eating and sleeping, and placidity or irritability. These aspects of infant temperament interact with the personality style of their parents to influence how the parents feel about and care for their offspring.

There is no doubt that infants' experiences shape what they are like as babies. However, there are few fixed relationships between behavior in infancy and behavior later on. Extreme tendencies are likely to persist, and certain aspects of temperament such as activity level may remain fairly stable over the years. Within the average range, however, there is little continuity between infant behavior and what children are likely to think, say, and do when they are somewhat older. Later experiences influence many new kinds of behavior, and most children leave infancy with considerable potential for change.

References

1. Bell, S. M., & Ainsworth, M. D. S. Infant crying and maternal responsiveness. *Child Development,* 1972, **43**, 1171–1190.
2. Wolff, P. H. The natural history of crying and other vocalizations in early infancy. In B. M. Foss (Ed.), *Determinants of infant behavior.* Vol. 4. London: Methuen, 1969.
3. Bernal, J. Crying during the first ten days of life, and maternal responses. *Developmental Medicine and Child Neurology,* 1972, **14**, 362–372.
4. Muller, E., Hollien, H., & Murray, T. Perceptual responses to infant cry tapes. *Journal of Child Language,* 1974, **1**, 89–95.
5. Stark, R. E., Rose, Susan N., & McLagen, M. Features of infant sounds: The first eight weeks of life. *Journal of Child Language,* 1975, **2**, 205–221.
6. Formby, D. Maternal recognition of infant's cry. *Developmental Medicine and Child Neurology,* 1967, **9**, 293–298.
7. Fantz, R. L. Pattern vision in newborn infants. *Science,* 1963, **140**, 296–297.
8. Fantz, R. L. Visual perception and experience in early infancy: A look at the hidden side of behavior development. In H. W. Stevenson, E. H. Hess, & H. Rheingold (Eds.), *Early behavior: Comparative and developmental approaches.* New York: Wiley, 1967.
9. Fantz, R. L., Fagan, J. F., & Miranda, S. B. Early visual selectivity as a function of pattern variables, previous exposure, age from birth and conception, and expected cognitive deficit. In L. Cohen & P. Salapatek (Eds.), *Infant perception.* New York: Academic Press, 1975.
10. Fantz, R. L., & Nevis, S. Pattern preferences and perceptual-cognitive development in early infancy. *Merrill-Palmer Quarterly,* 1967, **13**, 77–108.
11. Wolff, P. *The causes, controls, and organization of behavior in the neonate.* New York: International Universities Press, 1966.
12. Carpenter, G. C. Visual regard of moving and stationary faces in early infancy. *Merrill-Palmer Quarterly,* 1974, **20**, 181–194.
13. Haaf, R. A., & Bell, R. Q. A facial dimension in visual discrimination by human infants. *Child Development,* 1967, **38**, 893–899.
14. Wolff, P. H. Observations on the early development of smiling. In B. M. Foss (Ed.), *Determinants of infant behavior.* Vol. 2. London: Methuen, 1963.
15. Robson, K. S. The role of eye-to-eye contact in maternal-infant attachment. *Journal of Child Psychology and Psychiatry,* 1967, **8**, 13–25.
16. Robson, K. S., & Moss, H. A. Patterns and determinants of maternal attachment. *Journal of Pediatrics,* 1970, **77**, 976–985.

17. Carpenter, G. C., Tecce, J. J., Stechler, G., & Friedman, S. Differential visual responses to human and humanoid stimuli in early infancy. *Merrill-Palmer Quarterly,* 1970, **16,** 91–108.
18. Stern, D. N. A micro-analysis of mother-infant interactions. *Journal of the American Academy of Child Psychiatry,* 1971, **10,** 501–517.
19. Stern, D. N. Mother and infant at play: The dyadic interaction involving facial, vocal, and gaze behaviors. In M. Lewis, & L. A. Rosenblum (Eds.), *The effect of the infant on its caregiver.* New York: Wiley, 1974.
20. White, B. L., Castle, P., & Held, R. Observations on the development of visually-directed reaching. *Child Development,* 1964, **35,** 349–364.
21. Ambrose, J. A. The development of the smiling response in early infancy. In B. M. Foss (Ed.), *Determinants of infant behavior.* Vol. 1. New York: Wiley, 1961.
22. Gewirtz, J. L. The course of infant smiling in four child-rearing environments in Israel. In B. M. Foss (Ed.), *Determinants of infant behavior.* Vol. 3. London: Methuen, 1965.
23. Spitz, R. A., & Wolf, K. W. The smiling response: A contribution to the ontogenesis of social relations. *Genetic Psychology Monographs,* 1946, **34,** 57–125.
24. Mills, M., & Melhuish, E. Recognition of mother's voice in early infancy. *Nature,* 1974, **252,** 123–124.
25. McNeil, D. The development of language. In P. H. Mussen (Ed.), *Carmichael's Manual of Child Psychology.* Vol. I. New York: Wiley, 1970.
26. Vetter, H. J. *Language behavior and communication.* Itasca, Ill.: Peacock, 1969. Chap. 4. The ontogenesis of language.
27. Parton, D. Learning to imitate in infancy. *Child Development,* 1976, **47,** 14–31.
28. Bowlby, J. The nature of the child's tie to his mother. *International Journal of Psycho-Analysis,* 1958, **39,** 350–373.
29. Bowlby, J. *Attachment and loss.* Vol. I, *Attachment.* New York: Basic Books, 1969.
30. Haugan, G. M., & McIntire, R. W. Comparisons of vocal imitation, tactile stimulation, and food as reinforcers for infant vocalizations. *Developmental Psychology,* 1972, **6,** 201–209.
31. Rheingold, H. L., Gewirtz, J. L., & Ross, H. W. Social conditioning of vocalizations in the infant. *Journal of Comparative and Physiological Psychology,* 1959, **52,** 68–73.
32. Routh, D. K. Conditioning of vocal response differentiation in infants. *Developmental Psychology,* 1969, **1,** 219–226.
33. Todd, G. A., & Palmer, B. Social reinforcement of infant babbling. *Child Development,* 1968, **39,** 591–596.
34. Weisberg, P. Social and non-social conditioning of infant vocalizations. *Child Development,* 1963, **34,** 377–388.
35. Brackbill, Y. Extinction of the smiling responses in infants as a function of reinforcement schedule. *Child Development,* 1958, **29,** 115–124.
36. Brossard, L. M., & Decarie, T. G. Comparative reinforcing effect of eight stimulations on the smiling response of infants. *Journal of Child Psychology and Psychiatry,* 1969, **9,** 51–60.
37. Yarrow, L. J. Research in dimensions of early maternal care. *Merrill-Palmer Quarterly,* 1963, **9,** 101–114.
38. Yarrow, L. J., Rubenstein, J. L., & Pedersen, F. A. *Infant and environment: Early cognitive and motivational development.* New York: Halsted, 1975.
39. Ainsworth, M. D. S. The development of infant-mother attachment. In B. M. Caldwell & N. Ricciuti (Eds.), *Review of child development research.* Vol. 3. Chicago: University of Chicago Press, 1973.
40. Bloom, K. Social elicitation of infant vocal behavior. *Journal of Experimental Child Psychology,* 1975, **20,** 51–58.
41. Harlow, H. F. The nature of love. *American Psychologist,* 1958, **13,** 673–685.
42. Harlow, H. F. The development of affectional patterns in infant monkeys. In B. M. Foss (Ed.), *Determinants of infant behavior.* Vol. 1. London: Methuen, 1961.
43. Harlow, H. F., & Harlow, M. K. Effects of various mother-infant relationships on rhesus monkey behaviors. In B. M. Foss (Ed.), *Determinants of infant behavior.* Vol. 4. London: Methuen, 1969.
44. Harlow, H. F., & Zimmerman, R. R. Affectional responses in the infant monkey. *Science,* 1959, **130,** 421–432.

45. Cross, H. A., & Harlow, H. F. Prolonged and progressive effects of partial isolation on the behavior of Macaque monkeys. *Journal of Experimental Personality Research,* 1965, **1**, 39–49.

46. McKinney, W. T. Primate social isolation: Psychiatric implications. *Archives of General Psychiatry,* 1974, **31**, 422–426.

47. McKinney, W. T., Suomi, S., & Harlow, H. F. Methods and models in primate personality research. In J. C. Westman (Ed.), *Individual differences in children.* New York: Wiley, 1973.

48. Sackett, G. P. Some persistent effects of differential rearing conditions on pre-adult social behavior of monkeys. *Journal of Comparative and Physiological Psychology,* 1967, **64**, 363–365.

49. Seay, W., Alexander, B. K., & Harlow, H. F. Maternal behavior of socially deprived Rhesus monkeys. *Journal of Abnormal and Social Psychology,* 1964, **69**, 345–354.

50. Ainsworth, M. D. The development of infant-mother interaction among the Ganda. In B. M. Foss (Ed.), *Determinants of infant behavior.* Vol. 2. London: Methuen, 1963.

51. Ainsworth, M. D. S. *Infancy in Uganda: Infant care and the growth of attachment.* Baltimore: Johns Hopkins University Press, 1967.

52. Ainsworth, M. D. S. Patterns of attachment behavior shown by the infant in interaction with his mother. *Merrill-Palmer Quarterly,* 1964. **10**, 51–58.

53. Ainsworth, M. D. S., Bell, S. M., & Stayton, D. J. Individual differences in the development of some attachment behaviors. *Merrill-Palmer Quarterly,* 1972, **18**, 123–143.

54. Maccoby, E. E., & Feldman, S. S. Mother-attachment and stranger reactions in the third year of life. *Monographs of the Society for Research in Child Development,* 1972, **37**, 1–86.

55. Schaffer, H. R., & Emerson, P. E. The development of social attachments in infancy. *Monographs of the Society for Research in Child Development,* 1964, **29**, 1–77.

56. Yarrow, L. J. The development of focused relationships during infancy. In J. Hellmuth (Ed.), *Exceptional infant.* Vol. 1. Seattle: Special Child Publications, 1967.

57. Martin, B. Parent-child relations. In F. D. Horowitz (Ed.), *Review of child development research.* Vol. 4. Chicago: University of Chicago Press, 1975.

58. Beckwith, L. Relationships between infants' social behavior and their mothers' behavior. *Child Development,* 1972, **43**, 397–411.

59. Kohen-Raz, R. Mental and motor development of kibbutz, institutionalized, and home-reared infants in Israel. *Child Development,* 1968, **39**, 489–504.

60. Miller, L. Child rearing in the kibbutz. In J. G. Howells (Ed.), *Modern perspectives in international child psychiatry.* New York: Brunner/Mazel, 1971.

61. Pelled, N. On the formation of object-relations and identifications of the kibbutz child. *Israel Annals of Psychiatry,* 1964, **2**, 144–161.

62. Caldwell, B., Wright, C., Honig, R., & Tannenbaum, J. Infant day care and attachment. *American Journal of Orthopsychiatry,* 1970, **40**, 397–412.

63. Caldwell, B. M., & Smith, L. E. Day care for the very young—prime opportunity for primary prevention. *American Journal of Public Health,* 1970, **40**, 397–412.

64. Etaugh, C. Effects of maternal employment on children: A review of recent research. *Merrill-Palmer Quarterly,* 1974, **20**, 71–98.

65. Moore, T. W. Stress in normal childhood. *Human Relations,* 1969, **22**, 235–240.

66. Robinson, H. B., & Robinson, N. M. Longitudinal development of very young children in a comprehensive day-care program. *Child Development,* 1971, **42**, 1673–1684.

67. Wallston, B. The effects of maternal employment on children. *Journal of Child Psychology and Psychiatry,* 1973, **14**, 81–95.

68. Bronson, G. W. Infants' reactions to unfamiliar persons and novel objects. *Monographs of the Society for Research in Child Development,* 1972, **37**, 1–46.

69. Morgan, G. A., & Ricciuti, H. N. Infants' responses to strangers during the first year. In B. M. Foss (Ed.), *Determinants of infant behavior.* Vol. 4. London: Methuen, 1969.

70. Tennes, K. H., & Lampl, E. E. Stranger and separation anxiety. *Journal of Nervous and Mental Disease,* 1964, **139**, 247–254.

71. Waters, E., Matas, L., & Sroufe, A. I. Infants' reactions to an approaching stranger: Description, validation, and functional significance of wariness. *Child Development,* 1975, **46**, 348–356.

72. Ross, H. S. The effects of increasing familiarity on infants' reactions to adult strangers. *Journal of Experimental Child Psychology,* 1975, **20**, 226–239.

73. Bronson, G. W. The development of fear in man and other animals. *Child Development,* 1968, **39**, 409–431.

74. Decarie, T. G. *The infant's reaction to strangers.* New York: International Universities Press, 1974.

75. Rheingold, H. L., & Eckerman, C. O. Fear of the stranger: A critical examination. In H. W. Reese (Ed.), *Advances in child development and behavior.* Vol. 8. New York: Academic Press, 1973.

76. Moss, H. A., Robson, K. S., & Pederson, F. Determinants of maternal stimulation of infants and consequences of treatment for later reactions to strangers. *Developmental Psychology,* 1969, **1**, 239–246.

77. Rubenstein, J. Maternal attentiveness and subsequent exploratory behavior in the infant. *Child Development,* 1967, **38**, 1089–1100.

78. Tizard, J., & Tizard, B. The social development of two-year-old children in residential nurseries. In H. R. Schaffer (Ed.), *The origins of human social relations.* New York: Academic Press, 1971.

79. Ainsworth, M. D. S., & Bell, S. M. Attachment, exploration and separation: Illustrated by the behavior of one-year-olds in a strange situation. *Child Development,* 1970, **41**, 49–68.

80. Ainsworth, M. D. S., & Wittig, B. A. Attachment and exploratory behavior of one-year-olds in a strange situation. In B. M. Foss (Ed.), *Determinants of infant behavior.* Vol. 4. London: Methuen, 1969.

81. Coates, B., Anderson, E. P., & Hartup, W. W. Interrelations in the attachment behavior of human infants. *Developmental Psychology,* 1972, **6**, 218–230.

82. Cox, F. N., & Campbell, D. Young children in a new situation with and without their mothers. *Child Development,* 1968, **39**, 123–131.

83. Rheingold, H. L. The effect of a strange environment on the behavior of infants. In B. M. Foss (Ed.), *Determinants of infant behavior.* Vol. 4. London: Methuen, 1969.

84. Smith, L. Effects of brief separation from parents on young children. *Journal of Child Psychology and Psychiatry,* 1975, **16**, 245–254.

85. Willemsen, E., Flaherty, D., Heaton, C., & Ritchey, G. Attachment behavior of one-year-olds as a function of mother vs. father, sex of child, session, and toys. *Genetic Psychology Monographs,* 1974, **90**, 305–324.

86. Kaufman, I. C., & Rosenblum, L. A. The reaction to separation in infant monkeys: Anaclitic depression and conservation-withdrawal. *Psychosomatic Medicine,* 1967, **29**, 648–675.

87. Seay, B., Hansen, E., & Harlow, H. F. Mother-infant separation in monkeys. *Journal of Child Psychology and Psychiatry,* 1962, **3**, 123–132.

88. Seay, W., & Harlow, H. F. Maternal separation in the Rhesus monkey. *Journal of Nervous and Mental Disease,* 1965, **140**, 434–441.

89. Bowlby, J. Some pathological processes set in train by early mother-child separation. *Journal of Mental Science,* 1953, **99**, 265–272.

90. Heinecke, C. Some effects of separating two-year-olds from their parents: A comparative study. *Human Relations,* 1956, **9**, 105–176.

91. Heinecke, C., & Westheimer, I. *Brief separations.* New York: International Universities Press, 1966.

92. Bowlby, J. *Attachment and loss.* Vol. II, *Separation.* New York: Basic Books, 1973.

93. Robertson, J., & Robertson, J. Young children in brief separation: A fresh look. *Psychoanalytic Study of the Child,* 1971, **26**, 264–315.

94. Ross, G., Kagan, J., Zelazo, P., & Kotelchuck, M. Separation protest in infants in home and laboratory. *Developmental Psychology,* 1975, **11**, 256–257.

95. Yarrow, L. J., & Goodwin, M. S. The immediate impact of separation: Reactions of infants to a change in mother-figures. In L. J. Stone, H. T. Smith, & L. B. Murphy (Eds.), *The competent infant: A handbook of readings.* New York: Basic Books, 1974.

96. Edgcumbe, R., & Bugner, M. Some problems in the conceptualization of early object relationships. Part I: The concepts of need satisfaction and need-satisfying relationships. *Psychoanalytic Study of the Child,* 1972, **27**, 283–314.

97. Ferenczi, S. (1913) Stages in the development of the sense of reality. *Sex in psychoanalysis.* New York: Dover, 1956.

98. Freud, S. (1915) Instincts and their vicissitudes. Standard Edition, Vol. XIV. London: Hogarth, 1957.

99. Beller, E. K. Dependency and independence in young children. *Journal of Genetic Psychology,* 1955, **87**, 25–35.

100. Gewirtz, J. A learning analysis of the effects of normal stimulation, privation and deprivation on the acquisition of social motivation and attachment. In B. M. Foss (Ed.), *Determinants of infant behavior*. Vol. 1. London: Methuen, 1961.

101. Sears, R. R., Whiting, J. W. M., Nowlis, W., & Sears, P. S. Some child rearing antecedents of dependency and aggression in young children. *Genetic Psychology Monographs,* 1953, **47**, 135–234.

102. Harlow, H. F., & Harlow, M. H. Learning to love. *American Scientist,* 1966, **54**, 244–272.

103. Fairbairn, W. R. D. *An object relations theory of the personality*. New York: Basic Books, 1954.

104. Guntrip, H. J. S. *Psychoanalytic theory, therapy, and the self*. New York: Basic Books, 1971.

105. Winnicott, D. W. The theory of the parent-infant relationship. *International Journal of Psychoanalysis,* 1960, **41**, 585–595.

106. Bijou, S. W., & Baer, D. M. *Child development*. Vol. 2, *Universal stage of infancy*. New York: Appleton-Century-Crofts, 1965.

107. Gewirtz, J. L. Mechanisms of social learning: Some roles of stimulation and behavior in early human development. In D. A. Goslin (Ed.), *Handbook of socialization theory and research*. Chicago: Rand-McNally, 1969.

108. Sears, R. R. Attachment, dependency, and frustration. In J. L. Gewirtz (Ed.), *Attachment and dependency*. Washington, D.C.: Winston, 1972.

109. Rheingold, H. L., & Eckerman, C. O. The infant separates himself from his mother. *Science,* 1970, **168**, 78–83.

110. Mahler, M. S. *On human symbiosis and the vicissitudes of individuation*. Vol. 1, *Infantile psychosis*. New York: International Universities Press, 1968.

111. Mahler, M. S. Symbiosis and individuation. *Psychoanalytic Study of the Child,* 1974, **29**, 89–106.

112. Mahler, M. S., Pine, F., & Bergman, A. The mother's reaction to her toddler's drive for individuation. In E. J. Anthony & T. Benedek (eds.), *Parenthood: Its psychology and psychopathology*. Boston: Little, Brown, 1970.

113. Benedek, T. Motherhood and nurturing. In E. J. Anthony & T. Benedek (Eds.), *Parenthood: Its psychology and psychopathology*. Boston: Little, Brown, 1970.

114. Mahler, M. S. Thoughts about development and individuation. *Psychoanalytic Study of the Child,* 1963, **18**, 307–324.

115. Mahler, M. S., Pine, F., & Bergman, A. *The psychological birth of the human infant: Symbiosis and individuation*. New York: Basic Books, 1975.

116. Erikson, E. H. Growth and crises of the healthy personality. *Psychological Issues,* 1959, **1**, 50–100.

117. Erikson, E. H. *Childhood and society*. (2nd ed.) New York: Norton, 1963.

118. Yarrow, L. J., & Pedersen, F. A. Attachment: Its origins and course. In W. W. Hartup (Ed.), *The young child: Reviews of research*. Vol. 2. Washington, D.C.: National Association for the Education of Young Children, 1972.

119. Ainsworth, M. D. S. Attachment and dependency: A comparison. In J. L. Gewirtz (Ed.), *Attachment and dependency*. Washington, D.C.: Winston, 1972.

120. Ainsworth, M. D. S., Bell, S., & Stayton, D. Individual differences in strange-situation behavior of one-year-olds. In H. R. Schaffer (Ed.), *The origins of human social relations*. New York: Academic Press, 1971.

121. Clarke-Stewart, K. A. Interaction between mothers and their young children: Characteristics and consequences. *Monographs of the Society for Research in Child Development,* 1973, **38**, 1–108.

122. Moss, H. A. Sex, age, and state as determinants of mother-infant interaction. *Merrill-Palmer Quarterly,* 1967, **13**, 19–36.

123. Bell, R. Q. A reinterpretation of the direction of effects in studies of socialization. *Psychological Review,* 1968, **75**, 81–95.

124. Bell, R. Q. Stimulus control of parent or caretaker by offspring. *Developmental Psychology,* 1971, **4**, 61–72.

125. Bell, R. Q. Contribution of human infants to caregiving and social interaction. In M. Lewis & L. A. Rosenblum (Eds.), *The effect of the infant on its caregiver*. New York: Wiley, 1974.

126. Harper, L. V. The scope of offspring effects: From caregiver to culture. *Psychological Bulletin*, 1975, **82**, 784–801.

127. Thoman, E. B. Some consequences of early infant-mother-infant interaction. *Early Child Development and Care*, 1974, **3**, 249–261.

128. Yarrow, M. R., Waxler, C. Z., & Scott, P. M. Child effects on adult behavior. *Developmental Psychology*, 1971, **5**, 300–311.

129. Schaffer, H., & Emerson, P. Patterns of response to physical contact in early human development. *Journal of Child Psychology and Psychiatry*, 1964, **5**, 1–13.

130. Chess, S., & Thomas, A. Temperament in the normal infant. In J. C. Westman (Ed.), *Individual differences in children*. New York: Wiley, 1973.

131. Thomas, A., Birch, H. G., Chess, S., Hertzig, M. E., & Korn, S. *Behavioral individuality in early childhood*. New York: New York University Press, 1963.

132. Thomas, A., Chess, S., & Birch, H. G. *Temperament and behavior disorders in children*. New York: New York University Press, 1968.

133. Thomas, A., & Chess, S. *Temperament and development*. New York: Brunner/Mazel, 1977.

134. Buss, A. H., & Plomin, R. *A temperament theory of personality*. New York: Wiley, 1975.

135. Freedman, D. G. Personality development in infancy: A biological approach. In S. L. Washburn & P. C. Jay (Eds.), *Perspectives in human evolution*. New York: Holt, 1968.

136. Korner, A. F. Individual differences at birth: Implications for early experience and later development. *American Journal of Orthopsychiatry*, 1971, **41**, 608-619.

137. Korner, A. F. The effect of the infant's state, level of arousal, sex, and ontogenetic stage on the caregiver. In M. Lewis & L. A. Rosenblum (Eds.), *The effect of the infant on its caregiver*. New York: Wiley, 1974.

138. Osofsky, J. D., & O'Connell, E. J. Parent-child interaction: Daughters' effects upon mothers' and fathers' behaviors. *Developmental Psychology*, 1972, **7**, 157–168.

139. Kogan, K. L. Specificity and stability of mother-child interaction styles. *Child Psychiatry and Human Development*, 1972, **2**, 160–168.

140. Caldwell, B. M. The effects of infant care. In M. L. Hoffman & L. W. Hoffman (Eds.), *Review of child development research*. Vol. 1. New York: Russell Sage, 1964.

141. Escalona, S. K., & Corman, H. H. Early life experience and the development of competence. *International Review of Psychoanalysis*, 1974, **1**, 151–168.

142. Clarke, A. M., & Clarke, A. D. B. The formative years. In A. M. Clarke & A. D. B. Clarke (Eds.), *Early experience: Myth and evidence*. New York: Free Press, 1977.

143. Kagan, J. Resilience and continuity in psychological development. In A. M. Clarke & A. D. B. Clarke (Eds.), *Early experience: Myth and evidence*. New York: Free Press, 1977.

144. Kagan, J., & Moss, H. *From birth to maturity*. New York: Wiley, 1962.

145. Sameroff, A. J. Early influences on development: Fact or fancy? *Merrill-Palmer Quarterly*, 1975, **21**, 267–294.

146. Escalona, S. K., & Heider, G. M. *Prediction and outcome*. New York: Basic Books. 1959.

147. Kohlberg, L., LaCrosse, J., & Ricks, D. The predictability of adult mental health from childhood behavior. In B. B. Wolman (Ed.), *Handbook of child psychopathology*. New York: McGraw-Hill, 1972.

148. Halverson, C. F., & Waldrop, M. F. Relations between preschool activity and aspects of intellectual and social behavior at age 7½. *Developmental Psychology*, 1976, **12**, 107–112.

149. Watson, J. B. The psychological care of infant and child. London: Allen & Unwin, 1928.

150. U. S. Children's Bureau. *Infant care*. (Rev.) Washington, D.C.: Children's Bureau Publication No. 8, Care of Children Series No. 2, 1940.

151. Bell, S. M., & Ainsworth, M. D. S. Infant crying and maternal responsiveness. *Child Development*, 1972, **43**, 1171–1190.

152. Stayton, D. J., Hogan, R., & Ainsworth, M. D. S. Infant obedience and maternal behavior: The origins of socialization reconsidered. *Child Development*, 1971, **42**, 1057–1069.

5 | Infant Variations

GENETIC ENDOWMENT

THE GENETIC CONTRIBUTION TO IQ AND TEMPERAMENTAL TRAITS

NUTRITION
Malnutrition
Obesity

SEX DIFFERENCES

SOCIAL CLASS

FAMILY CONSTELLATION AND HOME ENVIRONMENT
Birth Order
Home Environment
Intervention Program
Reversibility of Early Deprivation

CULTURAL DIFFERENCES
Latin America and the Caribbean
Europe
Africa
Japan
India
Israel

ESSAY
Daycare

SUMMARY

REFERENCES

In Chapter 3 we described the physical and mental growth of "average" infants and suggested a "normal" range of variations. Here and in the succeeding "variations" chapters, we will examine some of the ways in which individuals vary and some of the factors that contribute to normal variations in children. In the next chapter and in succeeding ones on abnormal development, we will describe exceptional variations and some of the causative factors that produce them.

GENETIC ENDOWMENT

As a result of research in genetics since the 1950s, we now have a number of new concepts that enable us to be more precise in discussing the genetic components of physical and behavioral characteristics—an issue that arises in nearly every dimension of human variability.

Most of the new concepts deal with the events that intervene between the *genotype* (the genetic material received by the individual from his or her parents) and the *phenotype* (the physical or behavioral characteristic that can be attributed to this genetic material). Although genes provide a general blueprint or plan, it is not entirely understood how this plan regulates the individual's physical characteristics and behaviors. One of the new concepts pertaining to the path from genotype to phenotype is that of the **canalization** of traits that are developmental in nature. C. H. Waddington (1) holds that each phenotype takes a certain path toward realization (**creode**) but can be deflected; its susceptibility to deflection depends upon the degree of genotypic control, the force of deflection, and the timing of the deflection. In general, traits that are highly canalized are less susceptible to environmental modification than those that are moderately canalized. Ronald Wilson (2) has suggested that intelligence is highly canalized during infancy but is much less so at later ages.

Another new concept, called the **range of reaction,** relates to developmental and nondevelopmental characteristics such as skin color and allergies. What this means is that every genotype can be "expressed" in a variety of ways depending upon an individual's internal and external conditions. Skin color, for example, has a large reaction range. The actual skin color that is expressed as a phenotype will vary with the distance from the tropical sun. Pale skins in northern latitudes reflect the fact that the potential for skin pigmentation is not fully expressed in regions that do not have strong sunlight.

It is also important to recognize that the same phenotype can also be produced by different genotypes. An individual who grows up in a northern latitude may have the same skin color as one who grows up near the equator, but his or her skin color would have been much darker if he or she, too, had come from an equatorial country. In the same way, two individuals may have the same intelligence test score but for different reasons. One may do well on perceptual-spatial tasks such as puzzles while the other may do well on verbal tasks such as vocabulary. Both

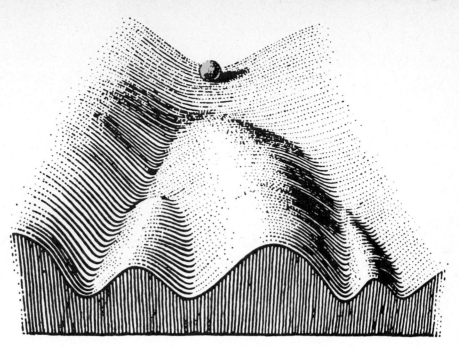

Figure 5.1 Waddington's genetic landscape showing possible routes of phenotypic expression for a given genotype. (*Source.* Waddington, C. H., *The strategy of the genes*. London: Allen and Unwin, 1957.)

have the same phenotype with respect to IQ test scores, but they probably have different genotypes in the area of intelligence.

Another example of the interaction between the genotype and the environment to produce a particular phenotype is provided by the biologist Medawar (3):

> *The tiny water shrimp* Sammavis chevruxi *is extruded from the brood pouch with red eyes, but usually ends up with black eyes— because of the black coloring matter melanin. Coloration of the eye is also affected by a number of other environmental factors: certainly the temperature and probably (though I don't know for sure) the dietary availability of such substances as tyrosine and phenylalanine or their precursors.*
>
> *Among these various factors, temperature is perhaps the most instructive, for it is possible to choose a genetic makeup such that coloration of the eye will appear to be wholly under environmental control: black at relatively high temperature of development and reddish or dusky at lower temperature. It is also possible to choose an ambient temperature at which red eyes or black eyes are inherited as straightforward alternatives according to Mendel's laws of heredity. Thus to make any pronouncement about determination of eye color it is necessary to specify both the genetic makeup and the conditions of upbringing: neither alone will do, for the effect of one is a function of the effect of the other. It would therefore make no sense to ask what percentage of the coloration of the eye was due to heredity and what percentage was due to environment [3, p. 14].*

What is true for the eye color of the water shrimp holds to an even greater extent for human intelligence. Mental ability is not a fixed trait; unlike eye color, the interaction between heredity and intelligence is a dynamic, ongoing one that continues throughout life. At an older age, for example, the abilities that an individual retains depend upon the extent of their use throughout life. Teachers, for example, retain their verbal skills to a greater extent than do laborers (4).

THE GENETIC CONTRIBUTION TO IQ AND TEMPERAMENTAL TRAITS

It used to be customary to cite studies of identical twins reared apart as evidence of the substantial contribution of heredity to intelligence. Inasmuch as identical twins share the same genetic endowment, correlations between their IQ scores should reveal the relative part played by heredity, especially in the case of twins reared in quite different environments. In general it was found that the mean differences in IQ scores were about 6.60 points for identical twins reared apart and about 5.0 points for identical twins reared together. But Kamin (5) has recently challenged the interpretation of these findings. He demonstrated that a substantial amount of the correlation between the test scores of identical twins reared together is simply due to the fact that both members of the pair are the same chronological age! Although it is obvious that heredity contributes to intelligence, it is not clear whether one can be sure exactly how much (6–8). It is our view that intelligence is such a complex trait that any single number, such as an IQ score, cannot completely represent the abilities in question. Moreover, since the IQ score represents many different abilities, each of which may have its own range of reaction, it is really impossible to determine heredity's role in intelligence with any great precision. At best one could give general reaction ranges that would probably apply to most of the traits represented by IQ scores. Some experimental investigations of altered environments have provided general estimates of the reaction range of human intelligence.

In one investigation, Heber (9, 10) took a group of 6-month-old children whose mothers had IQs of 70 or below and placed them in a very intensive enrichment program. The mothers were trained in both child rearing and vocational skills. After several years the children's IQ increased more than 30 points. Whether these changes are permanent will have to be determined by follow-up studies. Evidence that such gains could be long-lived was provided by Skeels (11). In that study institutionalized infants with low IQs were given over to be cared for by retarded but warm and nurturing women. Within a few years the children made IQ gains of 30 points or more, and these gains were maintained at least 30 years after their placement. Comparable children who remained in the institution continued to have low IQs.

One of the most dramatic demonstrations of the interaction between genotype and environment was provided by a study of cross-racial adop-

Table 5.1   IQ Scores for Adopted Children by Race

Children	IQ Scores			
	n	*M*	*SD*	Range
All adopted Black and interracial	130	106.3	13.9	68–144
White	25	111.5	16.1	62–143
Asian/Indian	21	99.9	13.3	66–129
Early-adopted Black and interracial	99	110.4*	11.2	86–136
White	9	116.8	13.4	99–138
Asian/Indian**				

*The average IQ for blacks of comparable genetic background but reared in low-income homes is about 90.
**Only 3 cases.
Source: Scarr-Salapatek, S., & Weinberg, R. A. IQ performance of black children adopted by white families. *American Psychologist,* 1976, **10,** 726–739.

tion (28) in which white middle-class parents in the Minneapolis–St. Paul area adopted black children. The effects of this adoption upon the children's IQ are shown in Table 5.1. As can be seen, the mean IQ scores for black adopted children is above the average (of 100) for nonadopted white children and about 10 points higher than that of the average black child. This demonstrates again the wide reaction range of human intelligence and how phenotypic test scores depend upon the environment for their realization. One can assume, of course, that had low-income white children been adopted by middle-class black parents, there would have been a comparable increase in IQ for the white adoptees.

A related question, but one for which there are very few data, is how much can the reaction range be pushed by an unusually rich environment. W. Fowler (12) believes that if young children can be provided with extensive intellectual stimulation, their IQs can be raised far beyond what would normally be expected in an ordinary environment. Englemann and Englemann have even written a book entitled *Give your child a superior IQ* (13). The evidence for the effects of such "super enrichment" is, however, not very substantial. It is probably easier to raise IQs that have been depressed by impoverished environments than it is to raise normally expressed IQs by super enrichment.

In addition to IQ the following physical attributes seem to be passed down from parents to children through several generations:

ability to roll the tongue
ability to taste the chemical phenylthiocabamide

astigmatism (a moderate visual deficit)
earlobes free along the lower edge
bass or soprano voice
hair on the middle section of the finger
tendency to fold the hand with the left thumb next to the body
nonred hair
"widow's peak" hairline
eyefold of the Mongolian race
high convex nose
dimpled cleft chin
freckles [14]

Since these traits are all dominant, they are likely to appear in successive generations.

The behavioral patterns of infants as well as physical characteristics, may have a hereditary component. Many investigators (for example, 15–17) have pointed out that infants differ a great deal from one another from the moment of birth. Consistent individual differences have been found in several areas such as infant responsiveness to loud and soft sounds, cold discs applied to the skin, and a pacifier inserted into the mouth. Some infants who are a few days old will respond vigorously, others moderately, and still others mildly or hardly at all (18).

Another type of temperamental difference that may have a hereditary component has been explored by Shaffer and Emerson (19, 20); as we mentioned briefly in Chapter 4, they defined certain infants as being "cuddlers" and others as being "noncuddlers." They categorized the infants after observing them at home and while being cuddled, stroked, kissed, and held on the knee. They also observed how the infants responded over time and with respect to inanimate objects. Shaffer and Emerson ruled out the mother's actions as a determinant of cuddling and noncuddling. They found that the noncuddlers were consistently faster than the cuddlers in learning motor skills, but that they were consistently less interested in self-stimulating activities. Some of these data are shown in Tables 5.2 and 5.3.

In summarizing their research, the investigators concluded:

The non-cuddler's avoidance of close physical contact is concerned with a phenomenon that is not peculiar to the relationship with the mother or indeed to social relationships in general. These children, it appears, were distinguished by a general behavioral characteristic affecting a wide range of functions and apparent in non-social as well as social situations. In the absence of any positive evidence that the mothers of the two contact groups could be clearly distinguished . . . and in view of our failure to find signs of a frustrated need (for cuddling) seeking other outlets, we are inclined to regard the congenital explanation as the more likely of the two hypotheses considered [19, p. 13].

Table 5.2 Age When Motor Skills and Developmental Quotients* Were Attained in the Two Contact Groups

	Sitting		Standing		Crawling		Walking		D.Q.	
	Mean (Wks)	S.D. (Wks)	Mean (Wks)	S.D. (Wks)	Mean (Wks)	S.D. (Wks)	Mean (Wks)	S.D. (Wks)	Mean	S.D.
Cuddlers	30.11	2.91	37.18	5.01	43.43	5.17	55.08	7.02	110.36	9.76
Noncuddlers	27.80	1.85	31.33	4.35	36.83	3.89	51.72	4.66	122.50	12.74
t	1.82		2.26		2.12		1.15		2.43	
p	<0.10		<0.05		<0.05		N.S.		<0.05	

*The developmental quotient is like an IQ but reflects the child's status on a variety of social and behavioral measures.
Source: Schaffer, H. R., & Emerson, P.E. Patterns of response to physical contact in early human development. *Journal of Child Psychology and Psychiatry,* 1964, **5,** 1–13.

Table 5.3 Use of Cuddly Toys and Incidence of Self-Stimulating Activities among Cuddlers and Noncuddlers

	Use of Cuddly Toys		Autoerotic Activities	
	Reported	Not reported	Reported	Not reported
Cuddlers	10	9	9	10
Noncuddlers	1	8	0	9
p	0.10		0.10	

Source: Schaffer, H. R., & Emerson, P. E. Patterns of response to physical contact in early human development. *Journal of Child Psychology and Psychiatry,* 1964, **5,** 1–13.

It has also been found that infants differ with respect to general temperament, which may have some genetic underpinnings. In a large-scale, longitudinal investigation, Thomas, Chess, and Birch (21) distinguished between infants who could effectively cope with the vicissitudes of their everyday experience and those who could not. They made observations in nine different areas: activity level, rhythmicity, adaptability, approach-withdrawal, intensity of reactions, quality of mood, distractibility, threshold level, and persistence-attention.

Children who were defined as having difficulty dealing with the ups and downs of everyday life were deviant in one or more of the areas listed above. For example, an infant who fell asleep and awoke at about the same time each night would be considered rhythmic, whereas a child who

Some infants are cuddlers and often initiate and enjoy body contact.

had an irregular sleep pattern would be viewed as arrhythmic—a sign of the child's lesser ability to cope. Likewise children with high activity levels, vis-à-vis their peers, got along less well than those with low activity levels. Intensity of reaction was also considered to be an index of coping behavior: A child who overreacts by "crying loud and long when the sun gets in his eyes" demonstrates less ability to cope than a child who has a milder reaction to such a situation.

One of the major findings of the Thomas, Chess, and Birch study was that children who had more difficulty dealing with the ups and downs of everyday life were more likely to become emotionally disturbed than were children who were able to cope. The authors state that it is not the child's temperament itself that causes the emotional disturbance, but rather the reactions of parents and teachers to the child's coping attempts. Parents who understand their child's difficulties and who treat him or her with patience, humor, and sympathy are much more helpful than those who become impatient or angry. If some of the child's emotional problems are due to the interaction between the child's temperament and the reactions of parents and other adults, then these problems would be one expression of the reaction range of temperamental genotypes.

Some of the differences among infants may, then, be due to the interaction of genotype and experience. As children mature, the persistence of these characteristics will not remain the same but will always reflect the expression of genetic potential within a given environment.

NUTRITION

Human growth and development is a complex biochemical process that requires a number of different nutriments. When these nutriments are missing or undersupplied, growth and development can be seriously hampered. Overfeeding may also have deleterious long-range effects. Some of the consequences of malnutrition will be discussed, as well as one of the possible consequences of overfeeding.

Malnutrition

In general, malnutrition means not only insufficient calories but also insufficient nutriments, particularly protein. Even children who have enough calories in their diet may be malnourished if they do not have enough fat and protein. The most general consequence of malnutrition is retarded physical, behavioral, and intellectual growth (22–24). Many biochemical processes are also interrupted; in the case of malnourished children, water distribution, fat absorption, and the metabolism of various substances resembles that which takes place in younger children. Malnourished children often show metabolic defects that closely resemble genetic defects (22).

Although controlled studies of human infants are obviously not possible, some animal studies are suggestive. Because the brain is somewhat close to its adult size at birth, it is one of the organs that is most affected by malnutrition of the mother during pregnancy and of the infant during the first months of life. Animals who do not consume enough calories and protein during the period when the brain is growing most rapidly have smaller brains than animals who receive an adequate diet (25, 26). The brains of adult rats that had been malnourished in infancy are smaller in size than those of comparable rats and show degenerative changes as well (27).

There is some evidence of similar effects of human infants. An early study by Cravioto and Robles (29) emphasized the harmful effects of malnutrition during the period of rapid brain growth—the last trimester of pregnancy and the first 6 months after birth. The children studied were those admitted to a children's hospital in Mexico with severe protein-calorie malnutrition. Their initial symptoms included severe dehydration and acute infections. After these conditions had been treated, the children were given tests that assessed four areas: motor behavior, adaptive behavior, language, and personality. The tests were repeated at 2-week intervals throughout the children's stay at the hospital.

The results showed that, in general, as the children recovered from malnutrition, their test performance improved. This was not true, however, in the case of children who were admitted to the hospital for malnutrition before the age of 6 months. Furthermore, they had to remain in the hospital longer than the older children—an average of 6½ months. These data suggest that severe malnutrition occurring early in life can have lasting effects.

Similar findings were reported from a study done in Jamaica (32). The subjects were 72 boys, all of whom had been treated in a hospital for severe malnutrition before they were 2 years of age. On the average the children stayed in the hospital for 8 weeks and were followed for 2 years afterward in their homes. As a comparison group, the investigators used the boys' siblings and classmates. At the time of the study, the subjects were about 6 years of age.

Both the previously malnourished and the comparison children were given a standardized intelligence test, the results of which are presented in Table 5.4. As can be seen, the malnourished children had lower scores than either the sibling or comparison (classmate) groups. Certain control procedures indicated that these differences could not be attributed to age variations between the groups or to sibling position. In contrast to the Cravioto and Robles study reported above, however, these investigators found no relationship between the child's age when admitted to the hospital and the severity of the malnutrition effects. Those who were hospitalized before 8 months of age were not significantly different from those who were hospitalized at a later age. Of course, it is possible that those who were hospitalized after 8 months of age had been malnourished beforehand. But these data suggest that one should be cautious in stating when malnutrition will be most harmful to human beings.

Another study of malnutrition compared undernourished children living

Children who are undernourished for long periods of time tend to be small in stature and to have poor health and low intelligence.

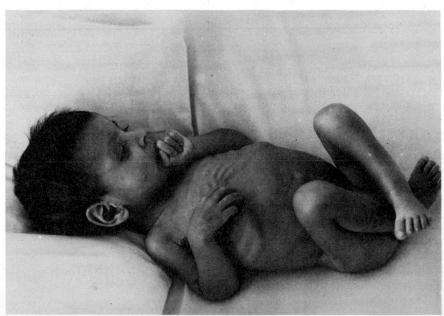

Table 5.4 Intellectual Levels of Malnourished Children, Siblings, and Comparison Children*

		Malnourished Children	Siblings	Comparison Children
	N	71	38	71
Mean Score	Full Scale IQ	57.72	61.84	65.90
	Verbal IQ	64.92	71.03	73.70
	Performance IQ	56.30	58.03	63.69
S.D.	Full Scale IQ	10.75	10.82	13.59
	Verbal IQ	11.80	12.87	14.55
	Performance IQ	11.85	10.47	13.30

Source: Hertzig, M. E., Birch, H. G., Richardson, S. A., & Tizard, J. Intellectual levels of school children severely malnourished during the first two years of life. Pediatrics, 1972, **49,** 814–824.
*Perhaps because of the cultural bias of the test even the comparison children scored at the retarded level.

in Cape Town, South Africa, with adequately nourished children of comparable background in the same area. The children in the chronically undernourished group came from homes that were described as "destitute" and many of these children were illegitimate. The adequately nourished children lived in a housing project and were all legitimate. The investigators measured both the undernourished children and the comparison group on intelligence, head circumference, height, and weight. The first testing was done when the children ranged from 10 months to 3 years of age and was continued until the children were 7 or 8 years of age.

Initially it was found that the undernourished children were shorter in height and lighter in weight than the well-nourished children. In addition, the mean head circumference and the mean IQ of the undernourished group were significantly less than that of the comparison group. In a follow-up study some 11 years later, essentially the same results were found. And when they were 18 years of age, the undernourished children still had smaller head circumferences and lower IQs, and they were still shorter and lighter than the better-nourished comparison group (30, 31).

The effects of poor nutrition are, of course, aggravated by such related factors as poor home environment, neglect, and illness. Since poor nutrition is often simply one aspect of a larger pattern of inadequate infant care, corrective efforts should be directed toward improved infant care. The earlier such efforts are undertaken the better, for, according to Graham and co-workers:

The younger the child at the onset of malnutrition, the more severe will be the growth deficit and the less likely will the child be able to make it up over the years. The duration of malnutrition has an

In some countries the diet is quite limited in variety and yet provides adequate nourishment for healthy growth.

equally important lasting effect on growth—much more than its severity at any given moment [33].

Poor nutrition can have other ill effects as well, for malnourished children are more vulnerable to all kinds of infection than are well-nourished children. Some infections can and do produce permanent defects in hearing, sight, and motor functions.

Obesity   Overfeeding an infant or young child is also detrimental to its health and well-being. Overfeeding in childhood can lead to lifelong obesity because the number of fat cells in the body is not fixed by heredity but will be increased by overfeeding during the early years of life. The number of fat cells will be permanent once physical growth comes to an end — in late adolescence. It is the number of fat cells and not their size that predisposes an individual to obesity; dieting can only reduce the size but never the *number* of fat cells (34, 35).

In America, overnutrition may be a greater problem than undernutrition; it is estimated that one out of five children in this country is overnourished. This figure is important because four out of five overweight children become overweight adults. And obese individuals are much more subject than those of average size to such problems as hardening of the arteries, high blood pressure, and diabetes mellitus (36). The psychological hazards of obesity, which are equally great, include feelings of self-rejection and overdependency upon others for acceptance.

Considering the physical and psychological drawbacks that are associated with obesity, parents should not overfeed their children. Food should not be used to pacify an infant, particularly if he or she has just recently been fed. Nor should infants be overfed in the mistaken belief that fat babies are healthy babies. A certain amount of baby fat is healthy, but an overfed infant is not. One way to help prevent obesity in adulthood is not to overfeed infants.

Only now are we beginning to appreciate the full importance of nutrition in human growth and development. It may well be that some of the differences in intellectual functioning that had been attributed to race or social-class differences may be mediated by the nutritional practices that separate these groups. And, of course, now we recognize the relationship between childhood and adult obesity.

SEX DIFFERENCES
Behavioral differences between boys and girls begin to appear in early infancy. With respect to sex differences in behavior, there is an extraordinarily complex interaction between genetic factors and environmental events. The child's sex, which *is* determined by heredity, can elicit sex-specific behaviors in the mother which can bring out latent behavioral phenotypes that are, in part, genetic. For example, the potential for aggression in girls may be almost as great as it is in boys, but this phenotype may not appear as often in girls because of the way they are treated in childhood (37).

One behavior that differentiates boys from girls during the first month of life is the amount of babbling that is elicited by human faces and voices. In the case of girls, babbling to faces and voices during their first year of life is a more consistent response and a better predictor of later cognitive skills than it is for boys. There is some evidence that babbling to faces and voices may be differentially conditioned. For example, middle-class and better-educated mothers seem to engage in more face-to-face vocalization and more imitative vocalization with their infant daughters than with their infant sons (37, 38). It is possible, though, that the range of reaction for vocalization differs for the two sexes and that environmental factors can elicit vocalization more easily in girls than in boys. It is clear that boy and girl babies differ with respect to the consistency of vocalization, but conflicting reasons are offered in explanation.

Varied interpretations have also been made of other behavioral differences between boys and girls in infancy. In one large-scale investigation (40) 400 infants were assessed immediately after birth and again at 8 months of age. At birth the infants were tested on such motor behaviors as strength of pull and on such adaptive behaviors as their reactions to a piece of cotton or cellophane placed lightly over their nose or mouth. At 8 months they were given a battery of tests that measured their physical development, social-emotional development, fine motor development, and over-all behavior.

The correlational results showed that there was a relationship between some of the neonatal measures and those made at 8 months for both boys and girls. The neonatal measures of girls were most closely related to their social-emotional development at 8 months, whereas the neonatal measures of boys were most closely related to their motor development at 8 months. The reasons for this are not clear. In a way the findings confirm the common observation that girls are, in most cases, more socially and emotionally mature than boys of the same age, but it is not known to what extent this difference is due to genetic makeup and to what extent it can be attributed to different parental attitudes and actions.

The play behavior of 13-month-old infants also reveals consistent sex differences. According to Goldberg and Lewis:

Observation of the children's behavior indicated that girls were more dependent, showed less exploratory behavior and their play behavior reflected a more quiet style. Boys were independent, showed more exploratory behavior, played with toys requiring gross motor activity, were more vigorous and tended to run and bang in their play [43].

To explain such differences Moss (44) has suggested that early in life boy and girl infants respond differently to their mother who, in turn, acts differently toward them. Thus, the infant "shapes" the mother's behavior just as much as the mother "shapes" the infant's. Indeed, something like this probably does take place, and infants may signal their parents to respond differentially in order to produce an environment that will enable them to realize certain behaviors. Far from being simply passive recipients of environmental stimuli, infants play an important role in structuring their environment and in regulating their parents' behavior.

Evidence exists that some of the social-emotional differences between boys and girls that are observed in infancy can predict later behavior. In one study (45) measures of shyness to 10 to 15 months were correlated with measures of shyness at 2 to 3½ years, 4 to 6 years, and 6½ to 8½ years (see Table 5.5). Shyness was measured by determining the amount

Table 5.5   Correlations between Ratings of Shyness at 10 to 15 Months of Age and Ratings of Shyness at Later Ages

Group	Age Period (in Years)		
	2-3½	4-6	6½-8½
Boys	.56 (N = 26)	.46 (N = 26)	.41 (N = 26)
Girls	.21 (N = 24)	.18 (N = 24)	.28 (N = 21)

Source: Bronson, S. W. Fear of visual novelty: Developmental patterns in males and females. *Developmental Psychology,* 1970, **2,** 33–40.

of wariness, reserve, or crying in the presence of strangers. At later ages rating scales of shyness were employed. As Table 5.5 indicates, shyness or fear behavior was a much more consistent trait for boys than it was for girls. As with the other sex differences described above, social-emotional differences are likely to reflect varying reactions to a number of environmental stimuli that are, at least in part, conditioned by the child himself or herself from the earliest days of life.

SOCIAL CLASS   In studying social-class differences, researchers typically look at the various parental practices and speculate about what behavioral differences might result. Since social-class differences are, however, also related to IQ variations, it is difficult to separate the effects of social class from those of heredity. It is also difficult to separate social-class differences from language and cultural factors. Social class always interacts with other factors in determining behavior.

As an example of this interaction, 45 black, low-income mothers were observed while they were interacting with their infants, and the mothers' behaviors were rated and scored (41). It was found that the sex of the infant influenced the mother's behavior: boy babies were rubbed, patted, touched, kissed, rocked, and talked to more than girl babies. These mothers also talked more to their sons than to their daughters. This appears to be a social-class difference since Thoman *et al.* (42) found that middle-class mothers who breast-fed their babies talked more to their daughters than to their sons. Although it is not clear just what the behavioral consequences of such maternal practices are, it seems likely that they will affect the behavior of the children at a later time.

Sometimes, despite differences in the home environment, no differences can be observed in the performance of infants. A study was made of year-old infants from disorganized slum families, low-income families, and middle-income families in which the infants were tested for object permanence (the understanding that an object continues to exist when it is no longer present to the senses) following Piaget's example. It was found that the infants from these diverse backgrounds all performed at about the same level (46). One explanation for this is that the effects of a child's home environment might be delayed; that is, the effects of early language stimulation (which would differ for the three groups) might not show up until the children really began to use language.

Evidence supporting this interpretation can be found in the research of Wachs, Uzgiris, and Hunt (47), who tested children from several different socioeconomic levels. They also found no significant differences among the infants on the cognitive measures, but they did find that on a test of vocal imitation, infants (15 and 22 months) from middle-class homes gave a larger number of words and more appropriate words than did infants from low-income homes. Some of the conclusions from this study are particularly interesting because they suggest what aspects of the home environment may significantly affect intellectual growth:

> *High intensity stimulation from which the infant cannot escape and involuntary exposure to an excessive variety of circumstances are negatively correlated with several aspects of psychological development. . . . Such findings are highly dissonant with the view that cultural disadvantage associated with poverty is analogous to the stimulus deprivation of isolated animals or to the unchanging homogeneity of input found in orphanage rearing. The present findings suggest that the hampering effects of slum rearing upon psychological development may lie in stimulus bombardment of the child rather than in stimulus deprivation [47, p. 317].*

In short, the effects of social class on infant behavior and mental ability may not be immediately apparent. This is true because some of these effects may not appear until the children are older and also because certain parental practices cut across social class and ethnic lines. From this point of view, it is the quality of parenting and not the family's economic level as such that is the crucial family variable.

FAMILY CONSTELLATION AND HOME ENVIRONMENT

One set of factors that contributes to individual variations is the child's position in the family and the parents' values and patterns of child rearing. Although these factors interact with others such as sex, social class, and ethnic background, certain studies have suggested how family constellation and home environment contribute to individual differences.

Birth Order

With respect to birth order, the effects of this factor are not clear during infancy. Nevertheless, it is probably true that parents are more experienced and less anxious in dealing with their later children than with their first-born. This could help to account for the birth-order differences that are observed at later ages. In general, parental expectations (and anxieties) about achievement tend to be greater for the first-born than for later-born children, and this helps to explain the high achievement orientation and competitiveness of first-borns.

Home Environment   In some ways the factor of home environment is unrelated to socioeconomic or ethnic considerations. For example, the quality of the environment may be better in some low-income homes than it is in some middle-income homes. And the quality of the environment in many black homes may be better than it is in many white homes. The quality of the home environment depends upon the kind of interactions that take place between children and parents, and good parental practices can be found among parents of all socioeconomic levels and in all ethnic groups.

To assess the quality of the home environment, one group of investigators (48–50) worked out a "home inventory scale"; it contains 45 items in six areas: (a) emotional and verbal responsiveness of the mother, (b) absence of restriction and punishment, (c) organization of the physical and temporal environment, (d) provision of appropriate play materials, (e) maternal interaction with the child, and (f) opportunities for variety in daily stimulation. Assessing a home environment was based on both observational and interview data.

In one study (48) infants were tested on an infant-development scale at 6 and 12 months of age and on the Stanford-Binet Intelligence Scale at 36 months of age. Each infant's home environment was assessed when he or she was 6, 12, and 24 months of age. In general the results showed that there was a high correlation (.54) between the child's home environment score at 6 months of age and his or her IQ at 3 years of age. That is, children who came from homes where there was more emotional and verbal responsiveness, appropriate play materials, and so forth, did better than children who came from homes with fewer of these things. In a follow-up study, the same investigators found that increases and decreases in IQ during the early years of life were also related to home environment:

Infants who come from homes rich in appropriate kinds of experiences have mental test scores that show a progressive increase during the first three years of life. By comparison, infants who come from homes poor in certain kinds of experiences have mental scores that progressively decrease. [48, p. 76]

In still another follow-up of the same children (50), the investigators looked at the correlations between home environment scores and mental ability scores when the children were 4½ years of age. Again they found that the child's home environment score during his or her first 2 years of life was positively correlated with the child's Stanford-Binet IQ score at

Table 5.6 Correlations between 54-Month-Old Children's Stanford-Binet Performance and Scores on the Home Inventory Scale Obtained at 6 and 24 Months

Home Inventory Scale	Correlations between Stanford-Binet at 54 Months and Home Inventory Scale	
	At 6 Months	At 24 Months
1. Emotional and verbal responsiveness of mother	.27	.50**
2. Absence of restriction and punishment	.10	.28*
3. Organization of physical and temporal environment	.31*	.33*
4. Provision of appropriate play materials	.44**	.56**
5. Maternal interaction with child	.28*	.55**
6. Opportunities for variety in daily stimulation	.30*	.39**
Total score	.44**	.57**
Correlation of all home inventory subscales with Binet scores	.50*	.63**

*$p < .05$.
**$p < .01$.

Source: Bradley, R. H., & Caldwell, B. M. The relation of infants' home environment to mental test performance at fifty-four months: A follow-up study. *Child Development,* 1976, **47,** 1172–1174.

age 4½. As Table 5.6 shows, the emotional and verbal responsiveness of the mother, appropriate play materials, and maternal interaction with the child seemed to be highly correlated with the child's mental ability at age 4½.

These results are consistent with other findings suggesting that "parental behavior does relate to IQ level during childhood" (51). In the past, perhaps we were too concerned with general differences between social classes and ethnic groups, thereby ignoring the large variations within each group. By focusing on how parents interact with their children regardless of social class or ethnic background, current research may be coming closer to the truly meaningful variables in child rearing—those that bring about individual variations.

Another study has suggested that a child's home environment remains rather stable over time (52). Hanson used another schedule of home environment that assessed both parent behaviors (direct teaching of language, emphasis on independence, and so forth) and the richness of the intellectual milieu (the existence of such teaching aids as alphabet cards, story books, and puzzles). Hanson correlated these environmental variables with measures of intelligence at 0 to 3, 4 to 6, and 7 to 10 years. As in the study mentioned earlier, the correlations between home environment and intelligence became apparent among the older rather than the younger children. In addition, because the home environment measures were made at each of the time intervals, it was possible to assess their consistency of the home variables over time. In general, Hanson found great consistency during the 7-to-10-year period, and the correlations with intelligence ranged from .462 to .953.

**Intervention
Programs**

The growing awareness of the importance of the early years of life for later intellectual development and psychological adjustment has led to some government-sponsored intervention programs. One of these, described as a "home visitor" approach for the mothers of young infants, was directed by Ira Gordon in Florida:

On a regularly scheduled basis a home visitor would demonstrate a technique of interacting with the baby or the use of a toy. She would leave some material with the mother with the expectation that, in the interval between home visits, the mother would carry on the activity with her baby. The focus was on a one-to-one relationship, and on strengthening and enhancing the mother's skill and the home as an effective learning center [53, p. 113].

This intervention program began when the infants were 3 months of age, and individual families remained in the program for 1, 2, or 3 years. It was assumed that mothers could become more effective with specialized training and that they would be willing and eager to learn. This, indeed, turned out to be the case. It also became apparent, as mentioned earlier, that even without training there were many effective parents in every social class and ethnic group.

To assess the impact of this home visitor program, a comprehensive survey, including observation and testing, was undertaken. With respect to mental ability, the results were impressive: The children who had been in the program for 2 consecutive years outperformed comparable children who had not been in the program on intelligence tests and other measures of cognitive ability. The mothers of these children were more likely than the control mothers to:

have a clear-cut system for handling praise and punishment; make a more conscious effort to improve children's language; have more reading materials such as books and children's books as well as newspapers and magazines in the home; make more effort to teach their children outside the home; provide more materials and . . . have library books in the home [53, p. 116].

Several other programs arrange for infants to spend some time at a center as well as provide special instruction for parents (54–56). In the Syracuse program (54, 55), for example, infants spend half a day every day at the center, where there is one adult for every four infants. The program focuses on intellectual stimulation as well as the child's emotional needs. When the children reach 15 months, they enter a full-day program. In comparing the children in this program with comparable children outside, it has been found that the former are more relaxed, more comfortable with their peers,and less conformist than the latter (55).

Perhaps the most extensive and intensive intervention project, which was described briefly earlier (9, 10, 65), is the family rehabilitation project. The children were born to women of low-income background and below-average intelligence (IQ 70). Some of these children were assigned to the stimulation program and a comparable group served as controls. The experimental program of full-day, year-round stimulation was begun when the infants were 6 months of age. At the outset there was a one-to-one ratio between infant and paraprofessional trainer, but this changed as the children became older. The children were exposed to an elaborate sensorimotor and receptive-speech program by the paraprofessionals. In addition, the mothers of the infants were trained in academic subjects as well as in practical nursing. The mothers' training was completed before the children were 3 years of age, but the children's program continued until they entered first grade.

The results of this study have been quite dramatic. The experimental children have scored significantly higher than the control children on measures of intellectual functioning (including IQ) and on measures of discrete learning tasks. The mother-child interactions have also changed: Children from the experimental groups have participated in more verbal and less physical information-gathering and have been more positive in their relationships with their mothers than the control children. Likewise, in helping their children solve problems, the experimental mothers have been more positive, less negative, and less physically controlling that the control mothers. Clearly, the family rehabilitation project has been beneficial in several areas.

It is really too early to assess the long-term effects of these various intervention programs. The results may be of enduring benefit if they change the mother's behavior and her mode of interacting with her child. In general, then, most long-term behavioral changes require lasting changes in the environment. This was essentially the conclusion that was reached by a government panel that evaluated the impact of infant intervention programs (57). It would be worthwhile to have longitudinal studies that follow the same children over long periods of time (66).

Reversibility of Early Deprivation

Even if children do not receive much mental and physical stimulation during their earliest years, they may not be permanently handicapped. It has been found that some children from rather deprived backgrounds can make remarkable gains if their environment is changed (58)—even at a later age.

An interesting case from Czechoslovakia concerns identical twin boys who were born in 1960 (59, 60). Their mother died soon after their birth and so they lived in a children's home for the first 11 months. Thereafter, the boys lived briefly with a maternal aunt and then went back to the children's home. When the boys were about 2 years of age, their father remarried and took custody of them. The new family included the twins' two older sisters (who had lived with their father after their mother's death) and the two children (a boy and a girl) of their stepmother. After their marriage the couple bought a small house in a village where they lived from about 1962 to 1967, when the plight of the twins was discovered. Apparently the stepmother was a deranged woman; the situation in which the boys lived for 5 years was described as follows:

The central figure in the family, and in the tragedy of the twins, was the stepmother. All the investigations, and especially the trial at the district and regional court, showed that she was a person of average intelligence but egocentric, remarkably lacking in feeling, possessing psychopathic character traits and a distorted system of values. The father was a person of low average intellect, passive and inarticulate; the stepmother dominated the family. Her own two children (the first of which was illegitimate and the second the product of a disturbed marriage which ended in divorce) were reared in early childhood by their maternal grandmother. The stepmother, therefore, had little experience with small children and showed no interest in them.

When the twins joined the family, she fed them but the other aspects of their care were left to their father. This disinterest developed into active hostility towards the twins and she induced a similar attitude towards them in other members of the family. The other children were forbidden to talk to the twins or to play with them. The father, who worked on the railways, was often away from home and took little interest in the boys. He probably realized that they were not receiving proper care but he was incapable of changing the situation. The twins therefore grew up lacking emotional relationships and stimulation, and were totally excluded from the family. Relationships between other members of the family were also unnaturally cool due to the mother's abnormal personality. The elder children were well dressed, their homework was supervised and so on, but these measures seem to have been motivated by the mother's ambitions. She accepted the two stepdaughters into the family though she preferred her own children, but with none of the children did she have a genuine maternal relationship.

The boys grew up in almost total isolation, separated from the outside world. They were never out of the house or into the main living rooms of the flat, which were tidy and well furnished. They lived in a small unheated closet, and were often locked up for long periods in the cellar. They slept on the floor on a polyurethane sheet and were cruelly chastised. They used to sit at a small table in an otherwise empty room, with a few building bricks which were their only toys. When one of their natural sisters was later examined for another reason she depicted this scene in a drawing entitled, 'At home!' [59, pp. 109–110].

The deplorable circumstances of the twins were discovered in 1967, when the father took one of the boys to a pediatrician to have him declared unfit for school. When the pediatrician had the home situation investigated, the criminal neglect was discovered. The boys were removed from the home and taken to a hospital where they were given a thorough examination. Because they suffered from rickets, they could barely walk; with shoes, it was impossible for them to walk at all since they had never worn shoes before. They communicated with one another largely by gesture, for they had learned very few words. They exhibited surprise and fear upon seeing mechanical toys and television and upon hearing the sounds of traffic; they could not understand the function or meaning of pictures.

Eventually the twins were adopted by a caring family. After being placed in a preschool, they made regular progress in language, cognitive, and social skills. In 1969 they entered a class for retarded children but soon surpassed their classmates in reading and writing. Finally, they were transferred into a regular school where, in 1972, they were about 3 years behind their appropriate grade level; by 1976 they were only 1½ years behind in schoolwork (60). Table 5.7 shows the IQ gains made by the twins in the years following their discovery and rehabilitation.

Other reports have also suggested that the effects of early deprivation are not necessarily irreversible. Jerome Kagan (61–63), for example, pointed out that the children in some Guatemalan villages are severely deprived of verbal stimulation, play materials, opportunities to explore, and even full daylight. On tests, they receive lower scores than American infants. After infancy, however, the children are incorporated into the culture and participate in all kinds of food-gathering and food-preparation activities. In adolescence, Kagan reports, the children do not differ from American young people on a variety of perceptual and memory tasks. Although this report presents certain difficulties (e.g. different groups of children were tested in infancy and adolescence), it suggests that limited early experiences can be corrected by a later environmental change.

Table 5.7   Gains in IQ Made by Twins Deprived of
Mental Stimulation after Adoption

Age (in Years)	Twin P. (IQ)	Twin J. (IQ)
9	80	72
10	91	89
11	95	93
12	95	104
13	98	100
14	100	101

Source: Koluchova, J. The further development of twins after severe and prolonged deprivation: A second report. In A. M. Clarke & A. D. B. Clarke (Eds.), Early experience: Myth and evidence. Glencoe, Ill.: The Free Press, 1977.

A similar conclusion can be drawn from the work of Wayne Dennis in foundling homes in Lebanon (64). Initially these homes kept orphans through their sixteenth year. However, as adoption began to be socially accepted in Lebanon, the age at which children could be adopted was gradually lowered. Accordingly, because there were children in the community who had been adopted at every age from infancy through adolescence, it was possible to evaluate the effects of adoption at different age levels. What Dennis found was that children who were adopted before the age of 2 tended to overcome their earlier retardation quickly; that is, they made more than a 1-year gain in intellectual functioning within a year. This was not true for the children who were adopted after the age of 2; these children simply progressed from where they were; that is, they made a 1-year gain in mental growth in a year.

What is the meaning of these findings? On the one hand, early intervention seems to work, for parents who are taught to be more stimulating have children who do better on IQ tests than children whose parents have not had such instruction. On the other hand, children who have had deprived and traumatic infancies can still overcome the effects of these experiences. Enriched environments, such as those provided by intervention programs, elicit one phenotype, whereas deprived environments elicit another. If the environment changes, then the phenotypic expression will change as well. These data are consistent with the view that intelligence is not a static entity that is fixed at birth, but a dynamic trait whose phenotypic expression is always a product of the environment at any given time interacting with the individual's genetic endowment.

CULTURAL DIFFERENCES

Culture is made up of the traditions, values, beliefs, practices, and language that characterize groups that have lived for a long time in a particular geographic region. Within various larger cultures there may be many subcultures. For example, in the United States we have a general culture in that English is the dominant language and we share a belief in certain democratic ideals. Nevertheless, there are many subcultures such as the American Indians, Catholics, Jews, Puerto Ricans, Mexican-Americans, and so forth. Each subculture may have its own religion, traditions, language, and values.

Cultures tend to differ from one another in their child-rearing practices. We will review some of the research on the sensorimotor development of infants in different cultures as these relate to varying child-rearing practices. This discussion can only touch upon some of the more significant effects that culture, as mediated by parents, can have on behavior, personality, and intelligence.

In most cross-cultural studies of infants, investigators have used one of several standardized infant scales such as the Gesell Developmental Scale (67) or the Bayley Scales of Infant Development (68). Many of these scales are similar in that they measure sensorimotor rather than language abilities. In some sense, therefore, these tests are more "culture fair" than tests that measure language and particular types of knowledge. Since motor development is universal, it would seem reasonable to ascribe differences there, at least in part, to various child-rearing practices.

Latin America and the Caribbean

An extensive study of Latin American infants was carried out by Brazelton, Robey, and Collier (72). The Zinacantico Indians of southern Mexico have successfully resisted assimilation into the larger culture, and they live now much as they have for centuries past. The Zinacanticos have small communities, engage in farming and hunting, and spend much time making hand-wrought objects. Their diet is apparently adequate with respect to total calories and with respect to the various nutrients.

Infants are reared in a way radically different from the way they are in the United States. Almost from birth the infant is carried about in a large shawl (called a *rebozo*) that is draped over the mother's breast or back and knotted behind her neck. The mother wears a woven shirt that is cut at the sides, permitting the infant to have easy and immediate access to the breast. So, although the Zinacantico infant has very little face-to-face social interaction and visual stimulation during its first year, it experiences almost constant touch and movement stimulation. This description of the mother-infant interactions was provided by the investigators:

> The infants were rarely placed on the floor or the bed, except when kept supine and swaddled beside the mother during the month of her postpartum confinement. . . . Breast feedings were notably frequent, as high as nine times in a 4-hour period. In four families, siblings were fed as many as ten times. The primary purpose of feeding appeared to be to quiet the child's restlessness. . . . The most striking feature of infant activity was the paucity of vocalizations. Indeed, during three observations, no vocalizations were heard. Cries were brief and were quickly terminated by the mother's quieting activities [72, p. 278].

Despite the lack of stimulation for developing motor and vocal skills, Zinacantico children followed the same developmental pattern as North American children but at a somewhat slower pace. Clearly, their development was not seriously retarded through lack of motor stimulation and social play. The investigators concluded that from birth Zinacantico infants are quieter, more rhythmic, and less abrupt in their movements and reactions than North American infants. They believe that this temperamental difference is brought about in part by the child-rearing practices that may, in turn, reflect the particular temperament of this culture. A culture may thus accentuate the temperamental predispositions of the social/genetic group that it encompasses.

Studies of infant development in several Latin American and Caribbean countries have reported a different phenomenon — that newborn babies

The *rebozo* enables the Indian woman to move freely while keeping her baby safe and in close physical contact with her.

from small villages in Jamaica (69), Guatemala (70), and Mexico (71) are motorically 2 weeks ahead of infants in the United States. One explanation is that the infants in the Latin American and Caribbean samples were, on the average, smaller and lighter. Some forms of motor behavior may be easier for small, light babies than for heavy ones.

The early motor precocity of infants from small villages in Jamaica, Guatemala, and Mexico was not found in certain large cities of South

America. In one large-scale study in São Paulo, Brazil (73), infants who had poor homes and illiterate parents were compared with those whose homes were more well-to-do and whose parents had some education. It was found that the infants from the poorer homes were retarded with respect to crawling, standing, and walking when compared with the infants from the more well-to-do homes. The infants from the poorer families also had a lower birth weight; their retardation could have been due, at least in part, to poor nutrition.

Europe

Other researchers have investigated the psychomotor development of infants in Europe (74, 75). In England, for example, infants appear to mature motorically at about the same rate as in the United States. However, on items that test for fine motor coordination (for example, uncovering a square box), British infants score a month or two ahead of American infants (74). The researchers suggest that this may be due to the fact that British infants are generally given more freedom to explore their surroundings than are American infants. Belgian infants appear to be somewhat heavier at birth and to walk somewhat earlier than French, Swiss, or British infants (75). The differences among these infants were not great and did not seem to reflect any significant cultural or nutritional variations.

Africa

Many studies have been made of motor development of infants in various African countries (71–82). It has consistently been found that African infants are motorically more advanced than American infants. American infants, however, have usually caught up by the end of the first year or the beginning of the second. The findings on black African infants have been reported from Uganda (76, 77), Senegal (78, 79), Cameroon (80), Nigeria (81), and South Africa (82, 83).

In her extensive study of Ugandan infants, Mary Ainsworth (77) suggested certain reasons for their motor precocity. In general, she found that the attainment of certain motor behaviors, such as sitting alone, was important to Ugandan mothers. The naming ceremony, for example, was postponed until the child could sit alone. (This illustrates very nicely the interaction between cultural traditions and child-rearing practices.) Walking alone is also important, because it is taken as a sign that the infant is ready to be weaned. Not surprisingly, therefore, Ugandan mothers encouraged their babies to learn to sit and walk alone. For example, they would sometimes seat their baby on the ground with its legs stretched out to either side and with its trunk bent forward supported by its hands against the ground. Although wobbly, the infants managed to "sit" in this position; thus, they were being trained in motor skills.

The fact that American infants typically catch up in motor skills with African infants by the end of the first year may also be due to child-rearing practices. When American infants begin to walk and talk, they have more interactions with their parents, but it seems that just the opposite happens in Africa. Marcelle Geber (76), who has done extensive work in Africa, suggests that the decline in their motor prococity is due to the rapid weaning and decline of mother-child interactions that accompanies it. Often this occurs because of the arrival of another baby. And Ainsworth claims that the African mother's focus on infants of less than a year leads her to pay far less attention to her older children.

Japan In one study of urban, middle-class Japanese infants (84), it was found that they were somewhat behind comparable American infants in their motor behavior—American infants tended to be more vocal and active than Japanese babies. Observations of the way in which Japanese mothers interacted with their infants suggested a possible reason for this. Japanese mothers seemed to assist, soothe, and guard their babies, whereas American mothers tended to talk to and play with their infants. These different parental patterns could have long-range effects upon how the children learn to interact with others.

India In contrast to Japan, which is heavily industrialized and westernized, India is primarily rural and abysmally poor. A longitudinal study of Indian children from different social classes as well as from both rural and urban areas showed that they were *all* generally superior to American children in their psychomotor development (85, 86). However, this superiority was short-lived, seldom beyond the first year of life, and the infants from rural and poor backgrounds lost their advantage much more quickly than did those from urban, middle-class homes.

The temporary superiority of Indian infants may be due to a number of factors. One is undoubtedly the low birth weight of Indian babies, which is one of the lowest in the world. As pointed out earlier, low birth weight may facilitate certain sensorimotor coordinations. Another factor may be the permissiveness of Indian mothers, who take their babies with them wherever they go, breast-feed them on demand, and allow them to crawl around freely both in the house and in the yard. The scarcity of electrical appliances and other dangerous objects in Indian homes makes them safer places for infants to explore than is true in America.

Israel Many studies have examined the psychomotor development of Israeli children. One study compared infants who were reared in three different settings — institutions, homes, and kibbutzim (where infants are cared for by trained personnel in something like a daycare center). There were 405 infants in this study: 166 were from urban, middle-class homes; 151 from kibbutzim; and 88 from institutions. The children were from 1 to

27 months of age, and all were tested with the Bayley Scales of Mental Development (87).

The results of this study showed that the kibbutz- and home-reared infants were at about the same level with each other and with American infants in their psychomotor development. The fact that there is a temporary drop in the kibbutz infants' scores toward the end of their first year is, in all likelihood, due to changes in the children's life at that time—they are transferred from "infant" to "toddler" houses, where they are cared for by different personnel. In contrast, the psychomotor scores of infants reared in institutions were significantly lower than those for children raised at home and in kibbutzim. The institutionalized infants from 1 to 27 months were all less coordinated and motorically adept than were the comparison children. The reason for this is undoubtedly due to the limited care and attention they received in relation to the other children.

In summary, although infants from certain African and Asian countries sometimes show an initial superiority in psychomotor development over American infants from western Europe (88), their superiority is generally lost by their second year. In part, their initial superiority reflects their generally lower birth weights and may reflect permissive child-rearing practices. Their early psychomotor superiority, however, may be "purchased" at the price of later retardation in mental and psychomotor development for the very conditions (poor nutrition, low technology, permissive parental practices) that lead to acceleration in infancy may also result in slower development later on.

Essay

DAYCARE

Currently there are more than six million children under the age of 6 whose mothers work full or part time. About half of these children are cared for by relatives in their own homes. An additional 35 percent are cared for in homes other than their own, an arrangement usually called *family daycare*. Only about 10 per cent of the children are cared for in rooms or buildings specifically set aside and provisioned for children— what is usually meant by a *daycare center*. The remaining children are cared for in a variety of ways. Some accompany their mothers to work, while others are left to their own devices. It is generally recognized that the care received by more than half of these children is substandard.

The widespread need for quality daycare is now recognized at all levels of government as well as by businesses and by religious organizations of all denominations. The task of providing quality daycare for all those children who need it, however, presents a wealth of problems that reflect the bureaucratic complexity and socioeconomic and ethnic diversity of our society. There are no easy and simple answers to the question of what constitutes "quality" daycare, how it should be provided, or for whom it should be provided. Nor is there any clear consensus regarding who is to bear the major share of the costs if a mother works and her young children are cared for by others. How far we have come in a decade is shown by a yearly survey of college women which indicates that from the middle sixties until the present time there has been a regular increase in the number of women who said that they would go to work and leave their young children in the care of others.

The question of what constitutes "quality" daycare illustrates the complexity of the daycare issues. Programs for young children can be described on a continuum from "developmental" to "custodial" care. Total developmental care would include the provision of well-balanced meals, opportunities and equipment for physical exercise and recreation, arrangements for medical or nursing attention, directed learning experiences, and constructive social interactions with other children (such as "show and tell"). As the number of these components decreases, the program moves from total developmental to barely custodial. A program that provided only hot meals and some exercise would thus be called "custodial."

Where on this continuum does quality daycare lie and how much developmental daycare do children need to realize their full physical and intellectual potential? The question is important because total developmental care, which requires the services of professionals, is clearly more expensive than custodial care, which does not. It would be relatively simple to answer this and other questions about daycare if there were some hard and fast evidence on the questions at issue, but unfortunately there is not. Daycare and family-care programs differ so much—one from another, in the populations they serve, in the adequacy of their facilities, in the quality of staffing—that it is virtually impossible to generalize from the effects of one daycare program to the effects of another. Results of studies are more suggestive than definitive, and the conclusions reached are determined as much by the investigators' theoretical biases as they are by the data. It is not surprising, then, that child development specialists are in disagreement as to how much of a developmental program is essential for healthy physical and mental growth and can serve as a standard for "quality" daycare.

Beyond that, there is no consensus on how the daycare needs are to be met. Opinions range from suggesting the provision of no additional monies for child care to advocacy of comprehensive programs that would provide not only daycare for children of working mothers but also for the special needs of handicapped children as well as health services for pregnant women and young children. Given current fiscal realities, some sort of compromise seems essential. What is needed is legislation that would provide daycare of reasonable quality to those children who are most in need of it—children currently in substandard family-care settings.

Like the question of daycare quality, the question of how child care should be provided cannot be answered simply. There are both advantages and disadvantages to many of the daycare arrangements currently used by parents. Nonprofit daycare centers are an example. Such centers are usually supported by a combination of federal and local funds and are often located in rented quarters such as church buildings. Because the centers are subsidized, they can provide developmental care at low cost and usually charge parents on a sliding scale according to income level. For all-day, five-days-a-week care, some parents may pay as much as $40 per week per child whereas another parent may pay as little as $5 per child.

Proprietary daycare centers are more variable in quality than the non-profit centers. In the late 1960s a number of companies planned to set up franchised child-care centers. Most of these efforts cam to naught. Although there were many reasons for these failures, the basic reason, which most companies eventually discovered, is that it is impossible to provide quality daycare at fee levels parents can afford and still make a profit. They also discovered that providing a human service is different from selling a product. One company we know about billed parents as they did their other customers and sent dunning letters if tuition was not paid on time. Parents got angry at this impersonal and hostile treatment from a company they thought was on their side. Many parents quit the program as a result.

The form of daycare that accommodates more children than any other is family daycare. Although there are licensing laws for daycare homes in most states, only about 10 percent of existing homes are actually licensed. There are many different reasons for this and they speak to some of the pros and cons of family daycare facilities. One of the reasons that family daycare centers do not apply for licensing is that the buildings would not meet state building codes without extensive and costly renovation. In addition, most state licensing laws limit the number of children a home can accommodate, ranging from two or three to eleven or twelve. Many daycare proprieters take in many more children than the state laws permit. Finally if the home was licensed the fees would have to be reported as income and a careful accounting of expenditures and income would have to be kept. All of these reasons militate against the daycare proprieter applying for licensing if his or her prime motivation is monetary.

There are advantages and disadvantages to all of the daycare delivery systems, including nonprofit and proprietary daycare centers and family-care settings. It is probably a virtue to have a variety of alternatives to accommodate the diversity of daycare needs and finances. Other facilities include daycare programs in high schools and at factories. What does seem necessary and most urgent, nevertheless, is the establishment of mechanisms for the enforcement of minimum standards for all daycare facilities. It is our belief that this can be most readily and effectively done if daycare is made part of the public education system. This would permit the use of existing school buildings, which are safe and build upon the states existing licensing system. While there are dangers to this approach, particularly the bureacratization of daycare practice, it seems to us to be the most sensible and practical solution at this time.

Summary

Genetic endowment contributes in many ways to individual and group variations in intelligence. A person's genetic endowment for a particular trait has a range of reaction so that the same genotype can be expressed as different phenotypes, depending upon the environmental circumstances. Human intelligence is a complex trait with a wide reaction range. Children from homes with little mental stimulation can make remarkable gains in IQ if they are exposed to enriched environments. Children who come from homes with substantial mental stimulation, however, are not likely to gain very much by additional enrichment.

Temperamental differences in infants are apparent soon after birth: Some infants respond vigorously to stimulation while others do not; some infants are "cuddlers" while others are distinctly "noncuddlers." Infants can also be grouped according to their ability to cope with the normal ups and downs of everyday life. Those who have difficulty dealing with such matters can be helped by patient, caring parents who understand but do not blame their children for their coping problems.

Nutrition, particularly early in life, has long-range as well as immediate effects upon health, physical stature, and intelligence. Poorly nourished children, even those who consume enough calories but not enough protein, are generally smaller, less intelligent, and less energetic than those who are well nourished. There is some evidence that the effects of poor nutrition of the mother during pregnancy and of the baby during its first 6 months of life may be less reversible than the effects of poor nutrition suffered later. Poor nutrition can also contribute to the higher incidence of serious disease. Overnutrition is likewise unhealthy, and evidence exists that overfeeding an infant can predispose him or her to be obese in later life.

Boy-girl differences during the first 2 years of life can be observed in several different areas, but it is not clear to what extent these differences are attributable to social conditioning and how much to genetic factors. Girls appear to babble more consistently than boys, but this may be due in part to the fact that mothers vocalize more with their infant daughters than with their infant sons. Girls also appear to be more socially and emotionally mature than boys by the end of the first year. Boys, on the other hand, seem to show more independent exploratory play than do girls, and boys also seem to be consistently more shy than girls.

Social class can affect children to the extent that it relates to various parental practices such as the amount of verbal interaction. It is possible, however, that the quality of the home environment is more important than social class. Several studies suggest that homes in which parents provide play materials, allow their children to explore freely, and interact verbally with their children are more conducive to the children's intellectual development than homes in which parents do not do these things. Intervention programs that are designed to encourage the mother to provide her infant with an enriched environment appear to be successful, at least in the short run, in producing significant gains in the child's mental functioning. Evidence also exists showing that early deprivation may be reversible and that children can sometimes make up later what they seem to have lost in infancy.

Cross-cultural studies of infant behavior have focused upon differences in sensorimotor performance. A general conclusion from studies of infants in certain Asian and African countries is that during their first year they tend to be smaller and motorically more advanced than children from North America and western Europe. But the latter children tend to catch up with and surpass the Asian and African children by the end of the first year. The very conditions (poor nutrition, low technology, permissive parental practices) that bring about an acceleration of psychomotor development in infancy may lead to a slower development later on.

References

1. Waddington, C. H. *The strategy of the genes*. London: Allen & Unwin, 1957.
2. Wilson, R. S. Twins: Early mental development. *Science*, 1972. **175**, 914–917.
3. Medawar, P. B. Unnatural Science. *New York Review of Books*, February 3, 1977, pp. 13–18.
4. Horn, J. L. Human abilities: A review of research and theory in the early 1970's. In M. R. Rosenzweig & L. W. Porter (Eds.), *Annual Review of Psychology*, 1976, 437–486.
5. Kamin, L. J. Heredity, intelligence, politics and psychology. In N. J. Block & G. Dworkin (Eds.), *The I.Q. controversy*. New York: Pantheon, 1976.
6. Lewontien, R. C. Race and intelligence. In N. J. Block & G. Dworkin (Eds.), *The I.Q. controversy*. New York: Pantheon, 1976.
7. Jensen, A. R. Race and the genetics of intelligence: A reply to Lewontien. In N. J. Block & G. Dworkin (Eds.), *The I.Q. controversy*. New York: Pantheon, 1976.
8. Scarr-Salapatek, S. Unknowns in the I.Q. equation. *Science*, 1971, **174**, 1223–1228.
9. Heber, R. Rehabilitation of families at risk for mental retardation. Madison: Regional Rehabilitation Center, University of Wisconsin, 1969.
10. Stuckland, S. P. Can slum children learn? *American Education*, 1971, **7**, 3.
11. Skeels, H. M. Adult status of children with contrasting early life experiences: A follow-up study. *Child Development Monographs 31*, No. 3 (Scrial no. 105), 1966.
12. Fowler, W. A developmental learning approach to infant care in a group setting. *Merrill-Palmer Quarterly*, 1972, **18**, 145–177.
13. Engelmann, Z., & Engelmann, T. *Give your child a superior mind*. New York: Simon & Schuster, 1966.
14. Swanson, H. D. *Human reproduction: Biology and social change*. New York: Oxford University Press, 1974.
15. Brown, J. L. States in newborn infants. *Merrill-Palmer Quarterly*, 1964, **10**, 313–327.
16. Brown, J. Precursors of intelligence and creativity: A longitudinal study of one child's development. *Merrill-Palmer Quarterly*, 1970, **16**, 117–137.

17. Kron, R. E., Ipsen, J., & Goddard, K. E. Consistent individual differences in the nutritive sucking behavior of the human newborn. *Psychosomatic Medicine,* 1968, **30,** 151–161.

18. Birns, B. Individual differences in human neonates, responses to stimulation. *Child Development,* 1965, **36,** 249–256.

19. Schaffer, H. R., & Emerson, P. E. Patterns of response to physical contact in early human development. *Journal of Child Psychology and Psychiatry,* 1964, **5,** 1–13.

20. ———————— ———————— The development of social attachments in infancy. *Monographs, Society for Research in Child Development,* 1964, **29** (Serial no. 94).

21. Thomas, A., Chess, S., & Birch, H. G. *Temperament and behavior disorders.* New York: New York University Press, 1968.

22. Eichenwold, H. F., & Fry, P. G. Nutrition and learning. *Science,* 1969, **163,** 644–648.

23. Jackson, R. L. Effect of malnutrition on growth in the preschool child. Washington, D.C.: National Academy of Science–National Research Council Publication No. 1282, 1966.

24. Rao, K. S., Swaminathan, N. C., & Pathwardan, V. N. Protein malnutrition in South India. *Bulletin,* WHO, 1959, 603–639.

25. Dickerson, J. W. T., Dobbing, J., & McCance, R. A. The effect of undernutrition on the postnatal development of the brain and cord in pigs. *Proceedings of the Royal Society,* 1967, **166,** 396–407.

26. Widdowson, E. M., Dickerson, J. W. T., & McCance, R. A. Severe undernutrition in growing and adult animals. IV. The impact of severe undernutrition on the chemical composition of the soft tissues of the pig. *British Journal of Nutrition,* 1960, **14,** 457–470.

27. Widdowson, E. M., & McCance, R. A. The effect of finite periods of undernutrition at different ages on the composition and subsequent development of the rat. *Proceedings of the Royal Society* 1963, **158,** 329–342.

28. Scarr-Salapatek, S., & Weinberg, R. A. I.Q. performance of black children adopted by white families. *American Psychologist,* 1976, **10,** 726–739.

29. Cravioto, J., & Robles, B. Evolution of adaptive and motor behavior during rehabilitation from kwashiorkor. *American Journal of Orthopsychiatry,* 1965, **35,** 449.

30. Stock, M. B., & Smythe, P. M. Does undernutrition during infancy inhibit brain growth and subsequent intellectual development? *Archives of Diseases of Children,* 1963, **38,** 546.

31. ——————— ———————. Undernutrition during infancy and subsequent brain growth and intellectual development. In N. S. Scrimshaw & J. E. Gordon (Eds.), *Malnutrition, learning and behavior.* Cambridge, Mass.: M.I.T. Press, 1968.

32. Hertzig, M. E., Birch, H. G., Richardson, S. A., & Tizard, J. Intellectual levels of school children severely malnourished during the first two years of life. *Pediatrics,* 1972, **49,** 814–824.

33. Graham, G. G., Cordano, A., Baertl, J. M., & Morales, E. Programs for combating malnutrition in the pre-school child in Peru. In *Pre-School Child Malnutrition.* National Academy of Sciences Research Council Publication No. 1282. Washington, D.C.: National Research Council, 1966.

34. Albrink, M. J. Overnutrition and the fat cell. In P. K. Bandy (Ed.), *Diseases of Metabolism* (6th ed.) Vol. 2, Philadelphia: Saunders, 1972.

35. Williams III, G. Growing up fat. *Science Digest,* December 1974, 60–65.

36. Kannel, W. B., Pearson, G., & McNamara, P. M. Obesity as a force of morbidity and mortality. In F. P. Heald (Ed.), *Adolescent nutrition and growth.* New York: Appleton-Century Crofts, 1969.

37. Murphy, L. Development in the first year of life: Ego and drive development in relation to mother infant tie. In L. J. Stone, H. T. Smith, & L. Murphy (Eds.), *The competent infant.* New York: Basic Books, 1973.

38. Kagan, J. Continuity in cognitive development during the first year. *Merrill-Palmer Quarterly,* 1969, **13,** 101–119.

39. Osofsky, J. D. Neonatal characteristics and mother-infant interaction in two observational situations. *Child Development,* 1976, **47,** 1138–1147.

40. Rosenblith, J. F. Relations between neonatal behaviors and those at eight months. *Developmental Psychology,* 1974, **10,** 779–792.

41. Brown, J. V., *et al.* Interactions of black inner-city mothers with their newborn infants. *Child Development,* 1975, **46,** 677–686.

42. Thoman, E. B., Leiderman, P. H., & Olson, J. P. Neonate-mother interaction during breast feeding. *Developmental Psychology,* 1972, **6,** 110–118.

43. Goldberg, S., & Lewis, M. Play behavior in the year-old infant: Early sex differences. *Child Development,* 1969, **40,** 21–32.

44. Moss, H. A. Sex, age and state as determinants of mother-infant interactions. *Merrill-Palmer Quarterly,* 1967, **13,** 19–36.

45. Bronson, G. W. Fear of visual novelty: Developmental patterns in males and females. *Developmental Psychology,* 1970, **2,** 33–40.

46. Golden, M., & Birns, B. Poverty and infant experience. *Merrill-Palmer Quarterly,* 1968, **14,** 139–149.

47. Wachs, T. D., Uzgiris, I. C., & Hunt, J. McV. Cognitive development in infants of different age levels and from different environmental backgrounds: An exploratory investigation. *Merrill-Palmer Quarterly,* 1971, **17,** 283–317.

48. Elardo, R., Bradley, R. H., & Caldwell, B. M. The relation of infants' home environment to mental test performance from 6 to 36 months: A longitudinal analysis. *Child Development,* 1975, **46,** 71–76.

49. Bradley, R. H., & Caldwell, B. M. Early home environment and changes in mental test performance in children from 6 to 36 months. *Developmental Psychology,* 1976, **12,** 93–97.

50. Bradley, R. H., & Caldwell, B. M. The relation of infants' home environment to mental test performance at fifty-four months: A follow-up study. *Child Development,* 1976, **47,** 1172–1174.

51. McCall, R. B., Appelbaum, M. I., & Hogarty, P. S. Developmental changes in mental performance. *Monographs of the Society for Research in Child Development,* 1973, **38,** 3.

52. Hanson, R. A. Consistency and stability of home environmental measures related to IQ. *Child Development,* 1975, **46,** 470–480.

53. Gordon, I. J. *The infant experience.* Columbus, Ohio: Merrill, 1975.

54. Lully, J. Quality care for infants. *Sharing,* Summer 1973, pp. 31–39.

55. Caldwell, B., & Richmond, J. "The Children's Center in Syracuse, New York." In C. Chandler, R. Lourie, and A. Peters (Eds.), *Early child care: The new perspectives.* New York: Aldine, 1968.

56. Huntington, D. Programs for infant mothering to develop sense of self and competence in infancy. Paper presented at the Laurence K. Frank Symposium, Society for Research in Child Development, Minneapolis, Minnesota, April 3, 1971.

57. Stedman, D., *et al.* How can effective early intervention programs be delivered to potentially retarded children? Report to Secretary, HEW, October 1972.

58. Clarke, A. M., & Clarke, A. D. B. (Eds.). *Early experience: Myth and evidence.* Glencoe, Ill.: Free Press, 1977.

59. Koluchova, J. Severe deprivation in twins: A case study. *Journal of Child Psychology and Psychiatry,* 1972, **13,** 107–114.

60. _____ . The further development of twins after severe and prolonged deprivation: A second report. In A. M. Clarke & A. D. B. Clarke (Eds.), *Early experience: Myth and evidence.* Glencoe, Ill.: Free Press, 1977.

61. Kagan, J., Klein, R. E., Haith, M. M., & Morrison, F. J. Memory and meaning in two cultures. *Child Development,* 1973, **44,** 221–223.

62. Kagan, J., & Klein, R. E. Cross cultural perspectives on early development. *American Psychologist,* 1973, **28,** 947–961.

63. Kagan, J. Resilience and continuity in psychological development. In A. M. Clarke & A. D. B. Clarke (Eds.), *Early experience: Myth and evidence.* Glencoe, Ill.: Free Press, 1977.

64. Dennis, W. *Children of the creche.* New York: Appleton-Century-Crofts, 1973.

65. Fallender, C. A., & Heber, R. Mother child interaction and participation in a longitudinal intervention program. *Developmental Psychology,* 1975, **11,** 830–836.

66. Kuhn, D. Inducing development experimentally: Comments on a research paradigm. *Developmental Psychology,* 1974, **10,** 590–600.

67. Gesell, A., & Amatruda, C. S. *Developmental diagnosis* (2nd ed.). New York: Hoeber, 1947.

68. Bayley, N. *Bayley scales of infant development: Manual.* New York: Psychological Corporation, 1969.

69. Granthan-McGregor, S. M., & Bark, E. A. Gross motor development in Jamaican infants. *Developmental Medicine and Child Neurology,* 1971, **13,** 79–87.

70. Cravioto, J. Motor and adaptive development of premature infants from a preindustrial setting during the first year of life. *Biologia Neonatorum,* 1967, **11,** 151–158.

71. Cravioto, J., Birch, H., Delicardie, E., Rosales, L., & Vega, L. The ecology of growth and development in a Mexican preindustrial community. Report I: Method and findings from birth to one month of age. *Monographs of the Society for Research in Child Development*, 1969, **34,** 128.

72. Brazelton, T. B., Robey, J. S., & Collier, G. Infant development in the Zinacanteco Indians of Southern Mexico. *Pediatrics*, 1969, **44,** 274–290.

73. Schmidt, B. J., Maciel, W., Boskowitz, E. P., Rosenberg, S., & Cury, C. P. Une enquete de pediatrie sociale dans une ville brasilienne. *Courrier*, 1971, **21,** 127–133.

74. Francis-Williams, J., & Yule, W. The Bayley infant scales of mental and motor development: An exploratory study with an English sample. *Developmental Medicine and Child Neurology*, 1967, **9,** 391–401.

75. Hindley, C. B. Growing up in five countries: A comparison of data on weaning, elimination training, age of walking and IQ in relation to social class from five European longitudinal studies. *Developmental Medicine and Child Neurology*, 1968, **10,** 715–724.

76. Geber, M., & Dean, R. F. A. Le developpement psychomoteur et somatique des jeunes enfants africains en Auganda. *Courrier*, 1964, **14,** 425–437.

77. Ainsworth, M. D. S. *Infancy in Uganda: Infant care and the growth of love*. Baltimore: Johns Hopkins Press, 1967.

78. Falade, S. Le developpement psycho-moteur du jeune africain originaire du Senegal. *Concours Medical*, 1960, **82,** 1005–1013.

79. Bardet, C., Masse, G., Moreigne, F., & Senecol, M. J. Application du test de Brunet-lezine à un groupe d'enfants Oulofs de 6 mois à 24 mois. *Bulletin Societe Medicine d'Afrique Noire*, 1960, **5,** 334–356.

80. Voulloux, P. Etude de la psycho-motricité des enfants africains au Cameroun. Test de Gesell et reflexes archaiques. *Journal de la Soci*été d'Africanistes, 1959, **29,** 11–18.

81. Poole, E. The effect of westernizaton of the psychomotor development of African (Yoruba) infants during the first year of life. *Journal of Tropical Pediatrics*, 1969, **15,** 172–176.

82. Liddicoat, R. Development of Bantu children. *Developmental Medicine and Child Neurology*, 1969, **11,** 821–822.

83. Meredith, H. V. Body size of contemporary groups of one year old infants studied in different parts of the world. *Child Development*, 1970, **41,** 551–600.

84. Candell, W., & Weenstein, H. Maternal care and infant behavior in Japan and America. *Psychiatry*, 1959, **32,** 12–43.

85. Phatak, P. Mental and motor growth of Indian babies: 1–30 months. (Longitudinal growth of Indian children). Department of Child Development, Faculty of Home Sciences, M.S. University of Baroda, India, 1970.

86. Phatak, P. Motor growth patterns of Indian babies and some related factors. *Indian Pediatrics*, 1970, **7,** 619–624.

87. Kohen-Raz, R. Mental and motor development of kibbutz, institutionalized and home reared infants in Israel. *Child Development*, 1968, **39,** 489–504.

88. Werner, E. E. Infants around the world: Cross-cultural studies of psychomotor development from birth to two years. *Journal of Cross Cultural Psychology*, 1972, **3,** 111–134.

6 | Abnormal Development

IDENTIFYING AND CLASSIFYING ABNORMAL BEHAVIOR

MENTAL RETARDATION
Categories of Mental Retardation
Causes of Mental Retardation

INFANTILE AUTISM
Characteristics of Infantile Autism
Origins of Infantile Autism
Outcome and Treatment

SOCIAL ISOLATION SYNDROMES
The Nature of Social Isolation Syndromes
Recovery from Social Isolation Syndromes

ESSAY
Special or Regular Classes for the Mildly Retarded?

SUMMARY

REFERENCES

Aside from being important in its own right, the study of abnormal behavior is helpful in understanding the nature and limits of normal development in children. After discussing how abnormal behavior is identified and classified, we will consider three kinds of disturbance that begin early in life: mental retardation, infantile autism, and social isolation syndromes. In this chapter, as well as in the other chapters on abnormal development, we hope to show how psychopathology relates to normal development and what studies of handicapped and disturbed children can reveal about the causes of behavior.

IDENTIFYING AND CLASSIFYING ABNORMAL BEHAVIOR

In order to identify abnormal behavior, one must decide whether to define normality as *average, ideal,* or *adjustment* (1). Normality as *average* is a statistical definition; it means that the most common behaviors among a group of people are considered normal for that group, and any significant deviation is regarded as abnormal. Although this approach makes normality easy to define and measure for research purposes, it is not very useful for dealing with actual people and situations. For, if normal is defined as average, then gifted as well as retarded persons, creative as well as unproductive people, and those who are extremely happy as well as those who are extremely sad must be viewed as abnormal. Furthermore, those who remain calm and clear-headed in an emergency must be considered abnormal, because they are not displaying the panic of others around them. Contrary to this approach, we should keep in mind that being *different* does not necessarily mean being *abnormal*.

Defining normality as *ideal* means that it is a state of perfection that people strive for but rarely achieve. The popular expression "nobody is perfect" fits this definition well; it implies that all of us have certain limitations or "hangups" that prevent us from becoming the completely contented, mature, and successful people we would like to be. Although this approach can help people recognize ways of improving themselves and enjoying life more, it sheds no light on the study and treatment of psychological disturbances. For, if virtually everyone is considered abnormal, how can we determine which kinds of "abnormality" can be left alone and which kinds require professional assistance from trained clinicians?

Most clinicians define normality as *adjustment*. Being adjusted means being able to function effectively in coping with life experiences; more specifically it consists of being able to enjoy rewarding interpersonal relationships and to work productively toward self-fulfilling goals. In this approach abnormal behavior is a state of mind or way of acting that impairs a person's ability to function effectively in these ways.

The adjustment approach to normality helps clinicians identify which people need their help, and it also helps psychopathologists decide which conditions to study. In the chapters on abnormal development, we discuss the most common and/or widely researched conditions that prevent children from relating well to others, performing to capacity in school, and acting in self-fulfilling ways.

It is generally agreed that psychopathology comprises four broad categories of disturbance: neurosis, personality disorder, psychosis, and problems associated with mental retardation or organic brain dysfunction (2–4). Of these, the first two do not arise early in life. Young children do not have the mental and emotional complexity to develop neurotic symptoms, and their personalities are not developed enough to become systematically disordered. Further maturation is required before they can display the subtle shades of neurosis and personality disorder that appear in older children and adults. Mental retardation, on the other hand, is largely due to events that occur early in life, as are the other two conditions discussed in this chapter—infantile autism and social isolation syndromes—both of which are comparable in severity to adult psychosis.

MENTAL RETARDATION

As defined by the American Association on Mental Deficiency, **mental retardation** refers to "significantly subaverage general intellectual functioning existing concurrently with deficits in adaptive behavior" (5). Although mental retardation is produced by events that take place before or soon after birth, it is seldom identified before children enter school. School makes many demands for learning and social adaptation, and as these demands increase over the years children with below-average intelligence fall noticeably behind their peers. Before the age of 4 only one child in 1000 is diagnosed as retarded; however, mental retardation is detected increasingly during middle childhood, so that by the age of 10 to 14, 30 out of 1000 are identified as retarded. This 3-percent incidence of below-average intelligence is the general estimate for the population at large (6–8).

Categories of Mental Retardation

Mentally retarded persons are commonly classified as being mildly, moderately, severely, or profoundly retarded (5). Those who are *mildly* retarded have an IQ between 55 and 69 on the Wechsler scales, which are the most widely used measures of intelligence in children and adults. They constitute 89 percent of all mentally retarded people and are often called **educable retardates.** They may lag behind somewhat in their early development, but they are seldom identified as retarded until they enter elementary school (see Table 6.1). At this time their limitations become apparent, and they need special educational approaches in order to learn basic academic skills. With suitable instruction these children can usually reach between a third- and sixth-grade level of education by the time they

Table 6.1 Developmental Characteristics of the Mentally Retarded

Degree of mental retardation	Wechsler IQ range	Age 0-5: Maturation and Development	Age 6-20: Training and Education	Age 21 and over: Social and Vocational Adequacy
Mild (89% of retardates)	55-69	Can develop social and communication skills; minimal retardation in sensorimotor areas; often not distinguished from normal until older	Can learn academic skills up to approximately 6th grade level by late teens; can be guided toward social conformity	Can usually learn adequate social and vocational skills for minimum self-support but may need guidance and assistance when under unusual social or economic stress
Moderate (6% of retardates)	40-54	Can talk or learn to communicate; poor social awareness; fair motor development; benefits from training in self-help; can be managed with moderate supervision	Can profit from training in social and occupation skills; unlikely to progress beyond 2nd grade level in academic subjects; may learn to travel alone to familiar places	May be able to support self in unskilled or semiskilled work under sheltered conditions; needs supervision and guidance when under mild social or economic stress
Severe (3½% of retardates)	25-39	Poor motor development; minimal speech; generally unable to benefit from training in self-help; little or no communication skills	Can talk or learn to communicate; can be trained in simple health habits; benefits from systematic habit training	May contribute in part to self-support under complete supervision; can develop some self-protection skills in a controlled environment
Profound (1½% of retardates)	Below 25	Gross retardation; minimal capacity for functioning in sensorimotor areas; needs nursing care	There is some motor development; may respond to minimal or limited training in self-help	There is some motor and speech development; may learn a little self-care; needs nursing care

Source: Based on R. Heber (Ed.), A manual on terminology and classification in mental retardation. *American Journal of Mental Deficiency Monograph Supplement,* 1959, **64**, No. 2.

leave school. As adults they are usually able to do unskilled or semiskilled work and meet the routine demands of social living; they often impress others as being "slow" but not necessarily abnormal (9).

Moderately retarded persons have an IQ between 40 and 54 and are called **trainable retardates.** These individuals, who constitute 6 percent of all retarded people, lag behind noticeably in developing communication and motor skill during the preschool years. In school they usually cannot master functionally useful academic skills. Hence the most that can be done for trainable retardates is to help them develop some capacity for self-care and social adjustment within a restricted environment. They may eventually be able to support themselves by means of some semiskilled or unskilled work in a sheltered workshop or other protected environment.

Many moderately retarded youngsters must be placed in institutions, however. As they grow up, it becomes clear that they cannot exercise the judgment and independence that are expected of young people their age. If and when these children will be institutionalized depends upon a number of factors. The lower their measured IQ (especially if it is below 50), the more physical disabilities and health problems they have, and the more supervision they require, the more likely they are to be placed in an institution. The more uncomfortable their parents are about having them at home and the greater the availability of institutions that their parents can accept and afford, the sooner they are likely to be placed (10–12).

On the other hand, parents who can tolerate and provide for a moderately retarded child at home and who dislike the idea of a residential placement may delay institutionalization indefinitely. Sometimes such a decision is best for all concerned. These parents may really enjoy having their youngster at home and they can avoid the feelings of guilt and loss that often come from sending a child off to an institution. Moreover, moderately retarded children who are kept at home may live more happily with their family than they would in an institution, and they may be spared the feelings of having been rejected.

Yet at other times the decision to keep a moderately retarded child at home is made ill-advisedly and benefits no one. Parents who feel guilty for having given birth to a retarded child may feel duty-bound to provide for the child's total care, even if doing so disrupts their lives, fills them with resentment that causes them to be poor parents, and deprives their other children of a normal home life. Retarded youngsters who are kept at home under these circumstances may be more unhappy than if they were in an institution; they may also have less opportunity at home than in an institution to learn skills that would help them function as partially self-sufficient adults later on.

Unfortunately, the decision to send a child to an institution for the mentally retarded is commonly believed to be a lifetime commitment. Although this may have been the case in the past, it is far from being so now. Many of these institutions are overcrowded and without adequate resources, but they have also adopted new policies since the early 1960s.

Now it is agreed that moderately retarded youngsters should not be institutionalized for custodial care; rather, they should be placed in an institution to help them develop and mature, and they should remain there only as long as required to achieve this purpose. Good institutional programs also try to keep children in close contact with their families and with nonresidential child-care agencies in the community (13). Being institutionalized during the school years, therefore, may improve rather than diminish the prospects for moderately retarded youngsters to learn how to support themselves as adults in sheltered but noninstitutional settings.

Severely retarded individuals have an IQ between 25 and 39 and represent 3½ percent of all mentally retarded; they are also called **untrainable** or **custodial retardates.** These people are largely incapable of taking care of themselves and require institutionalization, usually early in life. Under careful supervision they may eventually learn such basic self-care skills as feeding and dressing themselves, but they never outgrow their need for an institutional environment.

In Chapter 4 we noted that infants need close contact with familiar and stimulating adults in order to develop normal social responsiveness. For this reason, severely retarded children may adjust better in an institution if they have spent their infancy at home. It is especially important for untrainable retardates to remain with their family until they have learned to distinguish between people and have formed attachments to them. Although institutionalizing young children just at that point may be quite painful for parents and siblings, it seems to be best for the welfare of a severely retarded child.

The IQ of *profoundly* retarded person is below 25 and may not even be measurable. These people, who constitute the remaining 1½ percent of all retardates, need total nursing care throughout life. Because of their limited motor abilities, they may not ever be able to feed themselves, control their bowels, or walk. As in the case of severely retarded children, they may benefit from staying at home during their early life before entering an institution although their gross and obvious handicaps often make it very difficult for parents to care for them adequately.

Causes of Mental Retardation

Mental retardation has many different causes. About 25 to 35 percent of retarded individuals have biological defects that account for their mental limitations, whereas the remaining 65 to 75 percent have what is known as **familial retardation.** In familial retardation there are no obvious biological abnormalities, but there is a family history of one or both parents being retarded (17, 18). It is not yet known whether familial retardation is due primarily to genetic factors or to the experience of being reared by retarded parents. First we will look at some known biological causes of

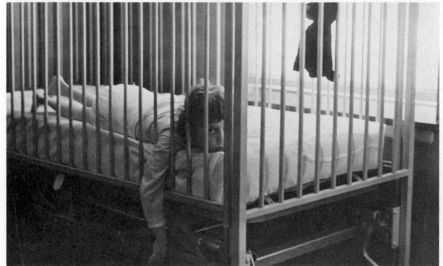

The future prospects of retarded children vary considerably with the degree of their handicap. The mildly retarded children above are in a special class for educable retardates. The profoundly retarded girl below is 12 years old and requires total nursing care.

retardation and then summarize some different opinions about genetic and experiential factors in familial retardation.

Known Biological Causes of Retardation. The most common inborn biological disorder that results in mental retardation is Down's syndrome, or *mongolism*, which we mentioned briefly in Chapter 2. Most children with mongolism have IQs below 60, and mongolism is responsible for 10 to 30 percent of all cases of moderate or severe retardation. Like most biological defects that arise during pregnancy or birth, mongolism is more common among children of older mothers. It occurs in only 1 out of 1500

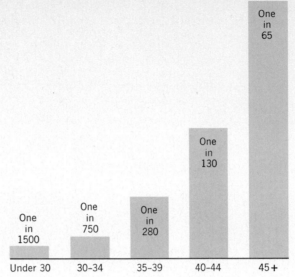

One in 65

One in 130

One in 280

One in 750

One in 1500

| Under 30 | 30–34 | 35–39 | 40–44 | 45+ |

Figure 6.1 Mother's age at baby's birth

children born to women under 30, but in 1 out of 65 children born to women over 45 (see Figure 6.1) (19–22).

Mongolism is an irreversible condition that becomes apparent at or soon after birth from several distinctive characteristics: small, egg-shaped eye sockets that give the impression of slanting; a wide, flat nose; a large, fissured tongue; and short, broad, square-shaped hands and feet (see page 191). Sometimes these children are described as placid, cheerful youngsters who are easy to manage at home; at other times they are described as being unable to adapt to family life and needing early and long-term institutionalization. Neither description is always true, however, since these children are found to differ widely as to what they are like as people and in their capacity for social adaptation (23, 24).

Aside from such specific conditions as mongolism, mental retardation can also be due to physical factors that interfere with normal biological development early in life. Before birth a mother's health has much to do with her child's mental growth, especially during the first 3 months of pregnancy when the central nervous system is being formed. Most significant in this regard are *rubella* (German measles), poor nutrition, exposure to radiation, and heavy drug use, each of which increases the risk that the child will be retarded (25–30).

Certain birth complications also increase this risk. Infants who are born prematurely (which is defined as weighing less than 5½ pounds at birth) have a higher-than-average chance of being mentally retarded, and the lower the birth weight, the greater the likelihood of retardation (31, 32).

Other potential sources of retardation at birth are *anoxia* (an inadequate supply of oxygen to the brain), which can occur when there are difficulties

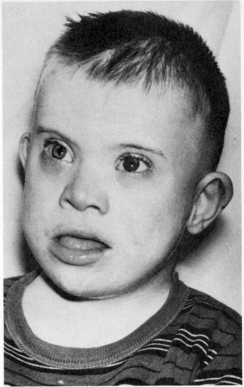

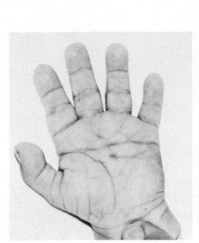

Down's syndrome (mongolism) is a biological disorder that involves mental retardation. This mongoloid child shows many of the physical features of the disorder, including unusually shaped eye sockets, an overly large tongue that results in a preference for leaving the mouth open. These children's hands are usually square-shaped and both shorter and broader than would be expected.

getting a newborn to start breathing; and birth injuries caused either by instruments used in the delivery or by problems arising from the infant's passage through the birth canal (33–35). A well-known condition that is due to birth injury is **cerebral palsy,** in which damage to the brain produces motor difficulties and frequently a mental handicap as well. Children with cerebral palsy suffer from various kinds of muscle paralysis, weakness, poor coordination, and involuntary movement, and 45 to 60 percent of them are mentally retarded (36, 37).

Events that occur after birth are less likely to cause mental retardation than problems of pregnancy and the birth process itself; in 9 out of 10 cases in which damage to the brain results in mental retardation, the damage has been done by the time the child is born (38). Nevertheless, certain infectious diseases accompanied by prolonged high fever—especially encephalitis and meningitis—may cause permanent damage to the brain if they occur early in life; the same is true of head injuries and nutritional deficiencies that stunt the growth of the central nervous system (39–43). Lead poisoning has also come to attention as a cause of mental retardation, since it poses a particular threat to children who are inadequately supervised or who live in dilapidated buildings. Swallowing even a small amount of lead in paint that is flaking from the walls or that comes off nursery toys can cause severe mental retardation (44).

Familial Retardation. As mentioned earlier, familial retardates have no obvious biological defects. They have an IQ between 50 and 69 and a family history of retardation, but the specific cause of their condition is not known. Most authorities regard familial retardation as a handicap that is passed through the genes from retarded parents to their children (17, 45). This opinion is based on fairly substantial evidence that 50 to 75 percent of the variability among people in IQ test scores can be accounted for by their genetic inheritance (46, 47). This means that the closer the blood relationship between two people, the greater the similarity in their measured intelligence. For example, identical twins are much more similar in intelligence than fraternal twins, even if they have been reared in different homes. Likewise, the IQs of adopted children are more like those of their biological parents than those of their adoptive parents (48, 49).

Nevertheless, some writers argue that intelligence is determined largely by a child's experiences, rather than by his or her inheritance, and that retardation in the absence of any obvious biological disorder is due to psychosocial factors (50–52). Since it is known that infants who are deprived of adequate psychosocial stimulation may not develop normal intelligence, some researchers maintain that being reared by one or more retarded parents can lead to below-average intelligence. They hold that familial retardation is due to the limited intellectual stimulation provided by retarded parents as well as the deprived sociocultural environment in which they live.

This view is supported in part by the fact that familial retardation occurs more often among lower-class than among middle-class families, especially when the family is living in a disadvantaged neighborhood. On the other hand, being in a lower socioeconomic class can be regarded as an *effect* rather than a *cause* of retardation in families. From this point of view—known as the **cultural drift hypothesis**—families whose retardation is inherited tend to drift toward a lower socioeconomic class because of their limited social and vocational capacities. Hence, their poverty can be seen as due to their limited genetic endowment, rather than as a reason for their own retardation or that of their children (53, 54).

Very few researchers regard below-average intelligence as due to either biological or psychosocial factors alone, however; most believe that it is the *interaction* between genetic and environmental influences that determines whether and how much a particular child will be retarded (55, 56). For example, the motivational and emotional aspects of retardates' lives

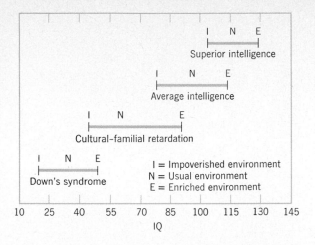

Figure 6.2 The functioning of children at different levels of intelligence is likely to depend on whether they are growing up in an enriched or an impoverished environment. This chart indicates the possible range of variability among Down's syndrome children, familial retardates, and children of average and superior intelligence. (*Source.* Baroff, G. S. *Mental retardation: Nature, cause, and management:* New York: Halsted, 1974.)

are extremely important in determining their level of functioning (57). Moreover, the intellectual functioning of both below-average and normally intelligent persons is affected by whether they have been reared in a stimulating or impoverished environment. Figure 6.2 suggests how children at several intellectual levels might vary in their IQ test scores depending upon how much their environment has encouraged or inhibited the use of their intellectual capacity. Consistent with this figure, we noted in Chapter 5 that there is preliminary evidence to indicate that early enrichment programs may help children whose family history would lead to the expectation of familial retardation to achieve intelligence test scores in the normal range (58).

INFANTILE AUTISM

Infantile autism is a very serious disorder of mental and social development that begins at or soon after birth. Autism occurs in no more than 1 or 2 children per 10,000, which makes it a very rare condition (59, 60). It merits our attention, though, because a great deal has been written about it and because it illustrates further the difficulties of separating biological and psychosocial causes of abnormal development. After describing the characteristics of autism, we will discuss its origins, outcome, and treatment.

Characteristics of Infantile Autism

Infantile autism was first described by Leo Kanner, a distinguished physician who is often referred to as the "father" of child psychiatry in the United States (61, 62). Kanner identified the two chief characteristics of the condition: interpersonal isolation and an abnormal concern with the preservation of sameness. *Interpersonal isolation* refers to the fact that autistic children are strikingly unresponsive to other people. As infants they lag far behind in beginning to show such signs of social interest as following people with their gaze, making direct eye contact, and smiling; some may never develop these responses. In addition, autistic children often do not make the kinds of anticipatory movements normally seen in

As infants, many autistic children hold themselves stiff and dislike being picked up even by their own mothers. Such resistance to being cuddled is often recalled by parents as the first indication of their child's abnormal development.

babies who are about to picked up, and, when they are picked up, they tend to keep their bodies stiff rather than cuddle up against the person who is holding them. More than anything else, autistic children are content to be left alone; they rarely notice whether other people are around or not (63–67).

Preservation of sameness describes the limited tolerance autistic children have for changes in their environment. Sometimes these children seem to have no interest in what is going on around them. They may sit motionless for hours, staring off into space. At other times they may become intensely absorbed in odd, repetitive behaviors, such as turning a vacuum cleaner switch on and off, passing a toy back and forth from one hand to the other, or touching each side of their crib or playpen over and over in succession. In either case, whether they are doing nothing or performing some ritual, autistic children cannot bear to be interrupted. They show no response when people speak to them or otherwise try to get their attention. If someone should forcibly interrupt them, say, by picking them up or taking an object away from them, they are likely to throw a violent temper tantrum. These children may also become frantic if their physical surroundings are changed—for example, as by moving their playpen or taking a piece of furniture out of their bedroom (68–70).

Most autistic children are first identified between the ages of 2 and 4, which is when their interpersonal isolation and need for sameness become most obvious (71). The condition also becomes more evident at this time because of language abnormalities. About half of these youngsters cannot talk by the age of 5. Those who can typically have certain speech peculiarities: **echolalia**, which consists of automatically repeating words that have been spoken to them; **pronomial reversal**, such as using the word "you" for "I"; the literal and concrete use of words, as in "down" to mean "floor" and "tap-it" to mean a hammer; and **part-whole confusion** in the use of words. "Do you want some ketchup?" may be the statement made by an autistic boy to indicate that he wants his dinner (72–74).

Since almost all autistic children have language abnormalities, many specialists believe that cognitive and perceptual handicaps lie at the core of the disorder. From this point of view the unresponsive and self-preoccupied behavior of autistic children may be due to mental defects that interfere with these children's ability to understand sounds and produce language (75–77). It is also important to note that normal children may show aloofness and emotional isolation, repetitive and self-preoccupied behavior, and speech peculiarities from time to time; however, in normal children these characteristics come and go quickly, whereas in autistic youngsters they persist all day, every day, year after year.

Origins of Infantile Autism

The origins of infantile autism have been hotly debated by *psychogenetic* and *biogenetic* theorists. The psychogenetic position holds that autism is caused by personality defects in mothers that prevent them from being warm and loving toward their infants (78, 79). The biogenetic position regards autism as caused by inborn cognitive and perceptual defects (80–83). Much of what is known about autism can be interpreted either way, as can be seen in the following examples:

First, the mothers of autistic children are frequently described as being emotionally cold and detached from their disturbed youngsters. From the psychogenetic point of view this observation confirms the role of inadequate mothering in producing autism. However, biogenetic theorists point to the fact that a mother who is indifferent to her child may well have become that way because of her child's unresponsiveness to her.

Second, fewer than 5 percent of the siblings of autistic children have serious psychological disturbances; in other words, most mothers of autistic children have other children who are neither autistic nor disturbed in other ways (60, 84). Biogeneticists interpret these findings as proof that inadequate mothering is not responsible for the disorder; otherwise, these other children would also be disturbed. However, psychogenetic theorists account for these findings by pointing to another feature of family life we mentioned in Chapter 4: namely, that all children in a family do not necessarily receive the same treatment from their parents, so that it is quite possible for one child to be loved and another ignored under the same roof.

Much research remains to be done to identify the origins of infantile autism. Recent findings seem to be pointing more and more to biological factors, however. Most importantly, there appear to be many mothers of autistic children who are *not* cold and detached, and who communicate with their children the same way other mothers do (71, 83-86). Without the support of evidence that all or at least most mothers of autistic children are unable to show warmth toward their infants, the psychogenetic explanation has few legs to stand on.

Outcome and Treatment

The outcome of infantile autism depends upon the severity of the individual child's disorder. Mildly autistic children may overcome their social isolation when they reach middle childhood, and they may also outgrow some of their speech peculiarities and odd behaviors. Yet, even with marked improvement, these youngsters as adolescents are likely to be cold, reserved, and socially immature, and to have difficulty making friends and becoming self-supporting later on (90–92).

Furthermore, even these modest improvements occur in only a small percentage of autistic children. Only about 25 percent of all autistic children make any substantial educational or social progress, and of these just a few can really be said to be functioning well academically and socially. The majority of autistic children show a steady decline over the years, falling further and further behind their peers in school and in personality development. Approximately half of all autistic children are institutionalized by their late teens, and this fate is almost inevitable for those whose IQ falls below 60 or who have not learned to talk understandably by the time they enter school (93–95).

On the other hand, clinicians have been working very hard during the 1970s to find ways of reducing at least the most serious symptoms of this disorder. Preliminary evidence indicates some success in these efforts, especially in helping youngsters who appear to be showing signs of outgrowing their autism. Long-term residential psychotherapy is being used to encourage emotional warmth and social responsiveness in these children; educational and reinforcement techniques are being used to teach them language and academic skill; and parents are being counseled to work with professional therapists in promoting their child's improvement (78, 96–100).

SOCIAL ISOLATION SYNDROMES

Social isolation syndromes consist of arrested development that occurs when infants do not receive enough stimulation from their environment. If steps are not taken to reverse these syndromes, children can be permanently retarded in their physical and mental growth as well as suffer from abnormal personality and social development.

The Nature of Social Isolation Syndromes

Social isolation syndromes among infants were first described in detail by René Spitz, an eminent psychoanalyst. In the mid-1940s Spitz reported that he had observed infants in a South American orphanage who were wasting away despite the fact that they were receiving adequate physical care. These infants lagged behind in their physical growth and failed to develop an interest either in people or in playing with toys. Later on they were slow in learning to talk and gave evidence of progressive mental retardation. Spitz attributed the mental and physical condition of these infants to the fact that they were separated from their families and were being reared in an emotionally sterile environment (101, 102).

In 1951 John Bowlby, whose important work on infant attachments we discussed in Chapter 4, was asked by the World Health Organization to prepare a report on the mental health of homeless children. Bowlby concluded in this report that the abnormal development observed by Spitz and others among institutionalized infants was due to "maternal deprivation"—that is, by the fact that these infants had no close physical and emotional contact with their mothers during the period in their lives when it was essential (103).

In support of Bowlby's conclusion, it has often been found that institutionalized infants show the same kinds of social defects that are associated with a failure to develop attachments to people; besides social unresponsiveness, these include a failure to distinguish between strange and familiar people and an indifference to being separated from familiar people (104–107). Thus, the term **maternal deprivation** was used for many years to describe what we are calling social isolation syndromes, and it is still fairly common. However, it is now recognized that persons other than infants' mothers can become the first or most important persons to whom they become attached and that a first attachment is soon followed by meaningful attachments to others. Hence, it is misleading to attribute any developmental problems of institutionalized babies solely to their being separated from their mothers.

Some authorities have even argued that social isolation syndromes have nothing at all to do with attachments to people, but rather are caused by the extent to which institutionalized babies are deprived of normal sensory stimulation (108, 109). Spitz's description of the orphanage in which he made his first observations bears grim testimony to this possibility:

The infants lay in cots with bed sheet hung over the railings so that the child was effectively screened from the world. . . . Probably owing to the lack of stimulation, the babies lay supine in their cots for many months and a hollow is worn into their mattresses [101, p. 63].

Two kinds of data support this "sensory deprivation" view of social isolation syndromes. First, when special steps are taken to provide sensory stimulation for institutionalized babies, they show less developmental arrest than infants who do not receive this attention (110). Second, infants who are born blind—and thus deprived by nature of much sensory input—are less likely to exhibit developmental arrest if their parents make an effort to keep them stimulated and physically active (111).

However, social isolation syndromes cannot be attributed to sensory deprivation alone, any more than to maternal deprivation alone. Although sensory deprivation can prevent a child from developing his or her normal mental capacities, there is little evidence that it leads to the child's lack of interest in other people that occurs in social isolation syndromes (112). Moreover, sensory stimulation by itself does not prevent the appearance of social isolation syndromes, and the stimulation of institutionalized babies does more to improve their intellectual and social functioning when it is done in a personalized, mothering way than when it is done in an impersonal, automatic way (107, 110, 113).

Social isolation syndromes have been studied mainly in institutions, but developmental arrest can occur wherever infants are deprived of social and sensory stimulation (112, 114–116); even among babies who are reared at home and given adequate physical care, emotional deprivation can bring about a failure in growth and a physical wasting away (117–120). It is the quality of care infants receive, not where they receive it, that determines if they will grow normally. In well-staffed institutions where children receive individual attention and have an abundance of toys, games, and planned activities, they are just as likely as children reared at home to show average physical and mental development, although they are less likely to form close attachments to adults (121, 122). Furthermore, the older children are before they enter an institution and the shorter their stay, the less likely they are to suffer from the experience (106, 107, 123, 124).

Recovery from Social Isolation Syndromes

A dramatic aspect of social isolation syndromes is the speed with which children can recover from them if their environment is enriched. As soon as institutionalized babies with this disorder are placed in adequate foster homes, they begin to catch up in their physical development, their mental capacities improve, and they develop an interest in their surroundings— sometimes to the point of becoming overactive and overly affectionate to others (112, 125–129).

One of the earliest demonstrations of recovery from social isolation syndromes was reported in 1939 by Skeels and Dye (130), whose work we mentioned briefly in Chapter 5. Their subjects were infants in an overcrowded and understaffed orphanage; the babies were kept in sheet-covered cribs, which limited their perceptual stimulation and contact with each other, and they had few toys and little attention from adults. Because of the overcrowding, 13 children who were considered mentally retarded (their average IQ was 64.3) were transferred to an institution for mental defectives when they were around 19 months of age. Here in this new environment these children were cared for individually by mentally retarded young women, who "adopted" the children and gave them a great deal of emotional and sensory stimulation.

When Skeels and Dye reassessed these "mentally retarded" children 18 months after they had been transferred to the more stimulating environment, they found that the children's average IQ had increased *more than 27 points*—to 91.8. During this same period of time, a comparison group of similarly aged children who remained at the orphanage experienced a *drop of 26 points* in their average IQ, from 86.7 to 60.5. In other words, transferring socially isolated children who appeared to be mentally defective into a more stimulating environment enabled them to attain an average IQ in less than 2 years, while the continuing social isolation of a comparison group during this same period of time reduced their intellectual level from dull-normal to mildly retarded. At the end of 4 years, the transferred youngsters' IQ had climbed to 101.4, and most of them had been adopted and left the institution. When Skeels followed up on this group almost 30 years later, he found that they were no different from the general population in their level of education, occupation, and income, or in the intellectual level of their own children (131).

Skeels's study demonstrates that social isolation syndromes can be prevented in institutions and that, when they do occur, personalized attention can bring about a recovery. The methods used in this early research have often been criticized; however, as we indicated in our discussion in Chapter 5 of the reversibility of early deprivation, such findings have largely been confirmed by others (132). It should be pointed out, though, that children who recover from social isolation syndromes may continue to show lingering effects of the disorder. Their language development may be slow, their thinking may be somewhat rigid and concrete, and their deprivation experience may leave them more than usually sensitive to future threats of separation. Even in adolescence they may still do poorly on intelligence tests, and their limited social skills may be a handicap in establishing close friendships (133).

Because children with social isolation syndromes resemble autistic children in their indifference to other people, some psychologists have suggested that there might be a close relationship between these conditions. However, three major distinctions make any such relationship unlikely. First, emotionally deprived children often show retarded growth and physical wasting away, whereas autistic children typically eat well and exhibit normal physical growth (74). Second, socially isolated children lose interest in everything, objects as well as people, whereas autistic children are often very busy carrying out their usual routines and are very attached to certain toys and objects (134). Third, and most important, autistic children do not exhibit the dramatic recovery that is often seen in socially isolated children when they are placed in a more favorable environment.

Essay

SPECIAL OR REGULAR CLASSES FOR THE MILDLY RETARDED?

In the 1920s public schools in the United States began to pay attention to the needs of intellectually limited children. During the next 40 years special classes for educable mental retardates were established in the schools as rapidly as money could be found for this purpose. By the late 1960s, however, many special educators began thinking that it would be preferable to put mildly retarded youngsters into regular classes rather than having them in separate classes. This idea, which is called **mainstreaming**, holds that segregating school children from their peers, unless it is absolutely necessary, can do more harm than good (135–138).

Arguments between special-class and "mainstream" educators continue to this day. For example, mainstreamers point out that special classes appear to hinder rather than to improve learning; that is, children with a low IQ are generally found to do better academically in *regular* classes than in special classes (139–141). Some special educators have tried to explain away these disappointing results, on one or more of the following grounds: (a) children who have been selected for special-class placement are usually those who are troublesome or low-achieving to begin with, and not those who could benefit the most from the special class; (b) special-class teachers are often inadequate or poorly trained, rather than teachers qualified to make a special-class program succeed; (c) special-class teachers generally do not expect very much of their students and therefore do not help them work up to their potential (142, 143). However, when steps are taken to rule out these possible sources of poor results, special-class students are still found to lag behind academically when compared with mildly retarded children left in their regular classes (144, 145).

Why have special classes, then? The answer is that mildly retarded children appear to adjust better and to feel better about themselves in these classes, where they are competing and interacting only with youngsters of the same ability, than in regular classes, where they are constantly overshadowed and outstripped by their brighter peers (146–149). Furthermore, although educators are concerned about the stigma that may be attached to these children by being called "retarded" and placed in a special class, there is no evidence that these things have any long-lasting harmful effect; school-age children tend to judge each other more according to how they perform than according to how they are labeled (150–152). With respect to their personality development, then, it may be better to put mildly retarded children into a special class, even if this hinders their academic achievement. Indeed, it could be argued that social adjustment and not intellectual accomplishment should be the major educational goal for the mildly retarded.

There are no easy answers to the question of how schools can best meet the needs of their mildly retarded pupils. As this essay implies, decisions must be made not only on the basis of research findings (for example, which methods work best for what purposes?) but also in terms of educational philosophy (for example, is the primary purpose of the public school to teach children academic skills or to foster their positive personality and social development?). Schools should also make placement decisions on an individual basis, in light of each child's particular academic and social needs, whatever his or her precise IQ. At present some schools are trying to combine both alternatives by keeping mildly retarded children in their regular class, but arranging for them to spend part of each day with a special-education teacher who helps them with particular academic problems.

Summary

Abnormal behavior is a state of mind or way of acting that impairs a person's ability to function effectively, especially with respect to being able to enjoy rewarding interpersonal relationships and work productively toward self-fulfilling goals. It is widely agreed that psychopathology comprises four broad categories of disturbance: neurosis, personality disorder, psychosis, and problems associated with mental retardation or organic brain dysfunction. Of these, mental retardation and behavior disorders that are comparable to adult psychosis are the two conditions that are most likely to arise during infancy.

Mental retardation consists of significantly subaverage intellectual functioning that begins very early in life. It affects approximately 3 percent of the population, although almost 90 percent of those affected are only mildly retarded. Mental retardation is caused by several different biological and psychosocial factors. Only 25 to 35 percent of all retarded individuals have definite biological abnormalities that account for their conditions, however. The remaining 65 to 75 percent have familial retardation, which means that they have a family history of retardation but that the precise origin of their handicap is not known. Opinions differ as to whether familial retardation is passed on genetically from parent to children, or whether it is due simply to the experience of being reared by retarded parents. Available evidence tends to point to a genetic explanation. However, most researchers agree that it is the interaction between genetic and environmental influences that determines whether and how much a particular child will be retarded.

A rare but extremely serious psychotic disorder that begins at or soon after birth is known as infantile autism. Children with this disorder fail to develop normal attachments to people. While remaining indifferent and unresponsive to others, however, they are extremely sensitive to and unable to tolerate changes in their environment. The fact that most autistic children have speech peculiarities suggests that the disorder is due to cognitive and perceptual defects that interfere with the children's ability to understand sounds and produce language. Yet some specialists believe that autism results solely from personality defects in mothers that prevent them from being warm and loving toward their infants. Although more research needs to be done, recent findings seem to be pointing to biological factors as the cause of infantile autism. Some children outgrow this disorder, while others can be helped by various kinds of treatment to overcome its more serious effects. In general, however, the prognosis for infantile autism is poor. Only about 25 percent of all autistic children make any substantial educational or social progress; the majority show no improvement, and about half of them are institutionalized by their late teens.

Another serious abnormality that occurs in infancy is social isolation syndromes, which consist of retarded physical and mental growth and a total lack of interest in people, objects, or play. Some researchers have argued that these syndromes, which are found most often in institutionalized babies, result from being deprived of loving parental care. Other researchers have said that this condition is caused simply by the sensory deprivation that infants experience in sterile environments, whether in an institution or at home with neglectful parents. It now appears that there is some truth in both views—social isolation syndromes do not arise when infants receive abundant sensory stimulation from warm and devoted parents or other caretakers. Moreover, such attention can produce rapid recovery from social isolation syndromes, especially in institutionalized infants who are placed in good foster homes.

References

1. Offer. D., & Sabshin, M. *Normality: Theoretical and clinical concepts of mental health.* (Rev. ed.) New York: Basic Books, 1974.
2. American Psychiatric Association. *Diagnostic and statistical manual of mental disorders.* (2nd ed.). Washington, D.C.: American Psychiatric Association, 1968.
3. Group for the Advancement of Psychiatry. *Psychopathological disorders in childhood: Theoretical considerations and proposed classification.* New York: Aronson, 1974.
4. Kessler, J. W. Nosology in child psychopathology. In H. E. Rie (Ed.), *Perspectives in chlld psychopathology.* Chicago: Aldine-Atherton, 1971.
5. Grossman, H. J. (Ed.) *Manual on terminology and classification in mental retardation.* (Rev. ed.) Washington, D.C.: American Association on Mental Deficiency, 1973.
6. Gruenberg, E. M. Epideminology. In H. A. Stevens & R. Heber (Eds.), *Mental retardation: A review of research.* Chicago: University of Chicago Press, 1964.
7. Scheerenberger, R. C. Mental retardation: Definition, classification, and prevalence. *Mental Retardation Abstracts,* 1964, **1**, 432–441.
8. Office of Mental Retardation Coordination. *Mental retardation sourcebook.* Washington, D.C.: U. S. Department of Health, Education, and Welfare, 1972.
9. Baller, W. R., Charles, D. C., & Miller, E. L. Mid life attainments of the mentally retarded. *Genetic Psychology Monographs,* 1967, **75**, 235–329.
10. Eyman, R. K., O'Conner, G. O., Tarjan, G., & Justice, R. S. Factors determining residential placement of mentally retarded children. *American Journal of Mental Deficiency,* 1972, **76**, 692–698.
11. Graliker, B. V., Koch, R., & Henderson, R. A. A study of factors influencing placement of retarded children in a state residential institution. *American Journal of Mental Deficiency,* 1965, **69**, 553–559.
12. Hobbs, M. T. A comparison of institutionalized and non-institutionalized mentally retarded. *American Journal of Mental Deficiency,* 1964, **69**, 206–210.
13. Baumeister, A. A., & Butterfield, E. C. (Eds.) *Residential facilities for the mentally retarded.* Chicago: Aldine, 1970.
14. Tarjan, G., Wright, S. W., Eyman, R. K. & Keeran, C. V. Natural history of mental retardation: Some aspects of epidemiology. *American Journal of Mental Deficiency,* 1973, **77**, 369–379.

15. Thurman, S. K., & Thiele, R. L. A viable role for retardation institutions: The road to self-destruction. *Mental Retardation,* 1973, **11**, 21–23.

16. Wolfensberger, W. Will there always be an institution? II. The impact of new service models—residential alternatives to institutions. *Mental Retardation,* 1971, **9**, 31–37.

17. Jensen, A. R. A theory of primary and secondary familial mental retardation. In N. R. Ellis (Ed.), *International review of research in mental retardation.* Vol. 4. New York: Academic Press, 1970.

18. Zigler, E. Familial mental retardation: A continuing dilemma. *Science,* 1967, **155**, 292–298.

19. Abramowicz, H. K., & Richardson, S. A. Epidemiology of severe mental retardation in children: Community studies. *American Journal of Mental Deficiency,* 1975, **80**, 18–39.

20. Benda, C. E. *Down's syndrome: Mongolism and its management.* New York: Grune & Stratton, 1969.

21. Koch, R., & de la Cruz, F. F. (Eds.) *Down's syndrome.* New York: Brunner/Mazel, 1975.

22. Smith, S. W., & Wilson, A. A. *The child with Down's syndrome (mongolism).* Philadelphia: Saunders, 1973.

23. Belmont, J. M. Medical-behavioral research in retardation. In N. R. Ellis (Ed.), *International review of research in mental retardation.* Vol. 5. New York: Academic Press, 1971.

24. Menolascino, F. J. Changing developmental perspectives in Down's syndrome. *Child Psychiatry & Human Development,* 1974, **4**, 205–215.

25. Apgar, V. Drugs in pregnancy. *Journal of the American Medical Association,* 1964, **190**, 840–841.

26. Birch, H. G., & Gussow, J. D. *Disadvantaged children: Health, nutrition and school failure.* New York: Harcourt, 1970.

27. Chess, S., Korn, S. J., & Fernandez, P. B. *Psychiatric disorders of children with rubella.* New York: Brunner/Mazel, 1971.

28. Sever, J. L., Nelson, K. B., & Gilkeson, M. R. Rubella epidemic, 1964: Effect on 6000 pregnancies. *American Journal of Diseases of Children,* 1965, **110**, 395–407.

29. Tizard, J. Early malnutrition, growth and mental development in man. *British Medical Bulletin,* 1974, **30**, 169–174.

30. Wood, J. W., Johnson, K. G., & Omori, Y. In utero exposure to the Hiroshima atomic bomb. An evaluation of head size and mental retardation twenty years later. *Pediatrics,* 1967, **39**, 385–892.

31. Drillien, C. M. The incidence of mental and physical handicaps in school age children of very low birth weight. II. *Pediatrics,* 1967, **39**, 238–247.

32. Wiener, G., Rider, R. V., Oppel, W. C., Fischer, L. K., & Harper, P. A. Correlates of low birth weight: Psychological status at six to seven years of age. *Pediatrics,* 1965, **35**, 434–444.

33. Gottfried, A. W. Intellectual consequences of perinatal anoxia. *Psychological Bulletin,* 1973, **80**, 231–242.

34. Graham, F. K., Ernhart, C. B., Thurston, D., & Craft, M. Development three years after perinatal anoxia and other potentially damaging newborn experiences. *Psychological Monographs,* 1962, **76** (Whole No. 522).

35. Morgan, H. S., & Kane, S. H. An analysis of 16,327 breech births. *Journal of the American Medical Association,* 1964, **187**, 262–264.

36. Hohman, L. B., & Freedheim, D. K. Further studies on intelligence levels in cerebral palsy children. *American Journal of Physical Medicine,* 1958, **37**, 90–97.

37. Stephen, E. Cerebral palsy and mental defect. In A. M. Clarke & A. D. Clarke (Eds.), *Mental deficiency: The changing outlook.* New York: Free Press, 1958.

38. Yannet, H. Classification and etiological factors in mental retardation. *Journal of Pediatrics,* 1957, **50**, 226–230.

39. Fabian, A. A. Prognosis in head injuries in children. *Journal of Nervous and Mental Disease,* 1956, **123**, 428–431.

40. Gibbs, F. A. Mental retardation following common forms of encephalitis: Electroencephalographic aspects. In H. V. Eichenwald (Ed.), *The prevention of mental retardation through the control of infectious disease.* Washington, D.C.: USPHS Publication No. 1692, 1966.

41. Hertzig, M. E., Birch, H. G., Richardson, S. A., & Tizard, J. Intellectual level of school children severely malnourished during the first two years of life. *Pediatrics,* 1972, **49**, 814–824.

42. Lawson, D., Metcalfe, M., & Pampiglione, G. Meningitis in childhood. *British Medical Journal,* 1965, **1**, 557–562.
43. Winick, M. *Malnutrition and brain development*. New York: Oxford University Press, 1976.
44. Moncrieff, A. A., Koumides, O. P., & Clayton, B. E. Lead poisioning in children. *Archives of Diseases of Children,* 1964, **39**, 1–13.
45. Burt, C. The inheritance of mental ability. *American Psychologist,* 1958, **13**, 1–15.
46. Loehlin, J. C., Lindzey, G., & Spuhler, J. N. *Race differences in intelligence*. San Francisco: W. H. Freeman, 1975.
47. Scarr-Salapatek, S. Genetics and the development of intelligence. In F. D. Horowitz (Ed.), *Review of child development research*. Vol. 4. Chicago: University of Chicago Press, 1975.
48. Erlenmeyer-Kimling, L., & Jarvik, L. F. Genetics and intelligence: A review. *Science,* 1963, **142**, 1477–1479.
49. Munsinger, H. The adopted child's I.Q.: A critical review. *Psychological Bulletin,* 1975, **82**, 623–659.
50. Girardeau, F. L. Cultural-familial retardation. In N. R. Ellis (Ed.), *International review of research in mental retardation*. Vol. 5. New York: Academic Press, 1971.
51. Kamin, L. J. *The science and politics of I.Q.* New York: Erlbaum, 1974.
52. Zajonc, R. B., & Markus, G. B. Birth order and intellectual development. *Psychological Bulletin,* 1975, **82**, 74–88.
53. Burt, C. Intelligence and social mobility. *British Journal of Psychology,* 1961, **14**, 3–24.
54. Herrnstein, R. J. *IQ in the meritocracy*. Boston: Little, Brown, 1973.
55. Baroff, G. S. *Mental retardation: Nature, cause, and management*. New York: Halsted, 1974.
56. Robinson, N. M., & Robinson, H. B. *The mentally retarded child*. (2nd ed.) New York: McGraw-Hill, 1976.
57. Zigler, E. Motivational aspects of mental retardation. In R. Koch & J. C. Dobson (Eds.), *The mentally retarded child and his family*. New York: Brunner/Mazel, 1971.
58. Heber, R. F., Garber, H., & Falender, C. The Milwaukee Project: An experiment in the prevention of cultural-familial retardation. September 1973 (mimeographed). See also *APA Monitor,* September/October, 1976, 4–5.
59. Lotter, V. Epidemiology of autistic conditions in young children. I. Prevalence. *Social Psychiatry,* 1966, **1**, 124–137.
60. Treffert, D. A. Epidemiology of infantile autism. *Archives of General Psychiatry,* 1970, **22**, 431–438.
61. Kanner, L. Autistic disturbances of affective contact. *Nervous Child,* 1943, **2**, 217–250.
62. Eisenberg, L., & Kanner, L. Early infantile autism, 1943–1955. *American Journal of Orthopsychiatry,* 1956, **26**, 556–566.
63. Freitag, G. An experimental study of the social responsiveness of children with autistic behaviors. *Journal of Experimental Child Psychology,* 1970, **9**, 436–453.
64. Hutt, C., & Ounsted, C. Gaze aversion and its significance in childhood autism. In S. J. Hutt & C. Hutt (Eds.), *Behavior studies in psychiatry*. New York: Pergamon, 1970.
65. Richer, J. M., & Coss, R. G. Gaze aversion in autistic and normal children. *Acta Psychiatrica Scandinavica,* 1976, **53**, 193–210.
66. Block, M. B., Freeman, B. J., & Montgomery, J. Systematic observation of play behavior in autistic children. *Journal of Autism and Childhood Schizophrenia,* 1975, **5**, 363–371.
67. Rimland, B. Infantile autism: Status and research. In A. Davids (Ed.), *Child personality and psychopathology: Current topics*. Vol. 1. New York: Wiley, 1974.
68. Prior, M., & Macmillan, M. B. Maintenance of sameness in children with Kanner's syndrome. *Journal of Autism and Childhood Schizophrenia,* 1973, **3**, 154–167.
69. Ritvo, E. R., Ornitz, E. M., & LaFranchi, S. Frequency of repetitive behaviors in early infantile autism and its variants. *Archives of General Psychiatry,* 1968, **19**, 341–347.
70. DeMyer, M. K., Mann, N. A., Tilton, J. R., & Loew, L. H. Toy-play behavior and use of body by autistic and normal children as reported by mothers. *Psychological Reports,* 1967, **21**, 973–981.
71. Ornitz, E. M., & Ritvo, E. R. Medical assessment. In E. R. Ritvo (Ed.), *Autism: Diagnosis, current research and management*. New York: Halsted, 1976.
72. Baker, L., Cantwell, D. P., Rutter, M., & Bartak, L. Language and autism. In E. R. Ritvo (Ed.), *Autism: Diagnosis, current research and management*. New York: Halsted, 1976.

73. Simon, N. Echolalic speech in autistic children: Consideration of possible underlying loci of brain damage. *Archives of General Psychiatry,* 1975, **32**, 1439–1446.

74. Wing, J. K. Diagnosis, epidemiology, aetiology. In J. K. Wing (Ed.), *Early childhood autism.* (2nd ed.) London: Pergamon, 1976.

75. Bartak, L., Rutter, M., & Cox, A. A comparative study of infantile autism and specific receptive language disorder. I. The children. *British Journal of Psychiatry,* 1975, **126**, 127–145.

76. Rutter, M. The description and classification of infantile autism. In D. W. Churchill, G. D. Alpern, & M. K. DeMyer (Eds), *Infantile autism.* Springfield, Ill.: Thomas, 1971.

77. Rutter, M. The development of infantile autism. *Psychological Medicine,* 1974, **4**, 147–163.

78. Bettelheim, B. *The empty fortress: Infantile autism and the birth of the self.* New York: Free Press, 1967.

79. Ekstein, R. *Children of time and space, of action and impulse.* New York: Appleton-Century-Crofts, 1966.

80. Lockyer, L., & Rutter, M. A five- to fifteen-year follow-up of infantile psychosis: IV. Patterns of cognitive ability. *British Journal of Social and Clinical Psychology,* 1970, **9**, 152–163.

81. Rimland, B. *Infantile autism.* New York: Appleton-Century-Crofts, 1964.

82. Rutter, M., & Bartak, L. Causes of infantile autism: Some considerations from recent research. *Journal of Autism and Childhood Schizophrenia,* 1971, **1**, 20–32.

83. Ornitz, E. M., & Ritvo, E. R. The syndrome of autism: A critical review. *American Journal of Psychiatry,* 1976, **133**, 609–621.

84. Lotter, V. Epidemiology of autistic conditions in young children. II. Some characteristics of the parents and children. *Social Psychiatry,* 1967, **1**, 163–173.

85. DeMyer, M. K., Pontius, W., Norton, J. A., Barton, S., Allen, J., & Steele, R. Parental practices and innate activity in normal, autistic, and brain-damaged infants. *Journal of Autism and Childhood Schizophrenia,* 1972, **2**, 49–66.

86. DeMyer, M. K. Research in infantile autism: A strategy and its results. *Biological Psychiatry,* 1975, **10**, 433–452.

87. Hingten, J. N., & Bryson, C. Q. Recent developments in the study of early childhood psychoses: Infantile autism, childhood schizophrenia and related disorders. *Schizophrenia Bulletin,* 1972, No. 5, 8–53.

88. Kolvin, I. Studies in the childhood psychoses. *British Journal of Psychiatry,* 1971, **118**, 381–419.

89. Wolff, W. M., & Morris, L. A. Intellectual and personality characteristics of parents of autistic children. *Journal of Abnormal Psychology,* 1971, **77**, 155–161.

90. Eisenberg, L. The autistic child in adolescence. *American Journal of Psychiatry,* 1956, **112**, 607–612.

91. Kanner, L. Follow-up study of eleven autistic children originally reported in 1943. *Journal of Autism and Childhood Schizophrenia,* 1971, **1**, 119–145.

92. Rutter, M. Autistic children: Infancy to adulthood. *Seminars in Psychiatry,* 1970, **2**, 435–450.

93. DeMyer, M. K., Barton, S., DeMyer, W. E., Norton, J. A., Allen, J., & Steele, R. Prognosis in autism: A follow-up study. *Journal of Autism and Childhood Schizophrenia,* 1973, **3**, 199–246.

94. Lotter, V. Factors related to outcome in autistic children. *Journal of Autism and Childhood Schizophrenia,* 1974, **4**, 263–277.

95. Kanner, L., Rodriguez, A., & Ashenden, B. How far can autistic children go in matters of social adaptation? *Journal of Autism and Childhood Schizophrenia,* 1972, **2**, 9–33.

96. Freeman, B. J., & Ritvo, E. R. Parents as paraprofessionals. In E. R. Ritvo (Ed.), *Autism: Diagnosis, current research and management.* New York: Halsted, 1976.

97. Lovaas, O. I., Schreibman, L., & Koegel, R. L. A behavior modification approach to the treatment of autistic children. In E. Schopler & R. J. Reichler (Eds.), *Psychopathology and child development: Research and treatment.* New York: Plenum, 1976.

98. Schopler, E., & Reichler, R. J. Parents as cotherapists in the treatment of psychotic children. *Journal of Autism and Childhood Schizophrenia,* 1971, **1**, 87–102.

99. Stevens-Long, J., & Lovaas, O. I. Research and treatment with autistic children in a program of behavior therapy. In A. Davids (Ed.), *Child personality and psychopathology: Current topics.* New York: Wiley, 1974.

100. Wenar, C., & Ruttenberg, B. A. Therapies for autistic children. In J. H. Masserman (Ed.), *Handbook of psychiatric therapies*. New York: Aronson, 1973.
101. Spitz, R. A. Hospitalism: An inquiry into the genesis of psychiatric conditions in early childhood. *Psychoanalytic Study of the Child,* 1945, **1**, 53–74.
102. Spitz, R. A., & Wolf, K. M. Anaclitic depression. *Psychoanalytic Study of the Child,* 1946, **2**, 313–342.
103. Bowlby, J. *Maternal care and mental health*. Geneva: World Health Organization, 1952.
104. Bakwin, H. Emotional deprivation in infants. *Journal of Pediatrics,* 1949, **35**, 512–521.
105. Fischer, L. Hospitalism in six month old infants. *American Journal of Orthopsychiatry,* 1952, **22**, 522–533.
106. Freud, A., & Burlingham, D. T. *Infants without families*. New York: International Universities Press, 1944.
107. Rheingold, H. L. The modification of social responsiveness in institutional babies. *Monographs of the Society for Research in Child Development,* 1956, **21**, No. 63.
108. Casler, L. Maternal deprivation: A critical review of the literature. *Monographs of the Society for Research in Child Development,* 1961, **26**, No. 2.
109. Freedman, D. A. The influence of congenital and perinatal sensory deprivations on later development. *Psychosomatic Medicine,* 1958, **9**, 272–277.
110. Casler, L. The effects of extra tactile stimulation on a group of institutionalized infants. *Genetic Psychology Monographs,* 1965, **71**, 137–175.
111. Fraiberg, S. Intervention in infancy: A program for blind infants. *Journal of the American Academy of Child Psychiatry,* 1971, **10**, 381–405.
112. Rutter, M. *The qualities of mothering: Maternal deprivation reassessed*. New York: Aronson, 1974.
113. Saltz, R. Effects of part time "mothering" on IQ and SQ of young institutionalized children. *Child Development,* 1973, **9**, 166–170.
114. Caldwell, B. M. The effects of psychosocial deprivation on human development in infancy. *Merrill-Palmer Quarterly,* 1970, **16**, 260–277.
115. Provence, S., & Lipton, R. C. *Infants in institutions*. New York: International Universities Press, 1962.
116. Yarrow, L. J. Maternal deprivation. *Psychological Bulletin,* 1961, **58**, 459–490.
117. Bullard, D. M., Glaser, H. H., Heagarty, M. C., & Pivchik, E. C. Failure to thrive in the "neglected" child. *American Journal of Orthopsychiatry,* 1967, **37**, 680–690.
118. Clancy, H., & McBride, G. The isolation syndrome in childhood. *Developmental Medicine and Child Neurology,* 1975, **17**, 198–219.
119. Pollitt, E., Eichler, A. W., & Chan, C. Psychosocial development and behavior of mothers of failure-to-thrive children. *American Journal of Orthopsychiatry,* 1975, **45**, 525–537.
120. Patton, R. G., & Gardner, L. I. *Growth failure in maternal deprivation*. Springfield, Ill.: Thomas, 1962.
121. Powell, G. F., Brasel, J. A., & Blizzard, R. M. Emotional deprivation and growth retardation. *New England Journal of Medicine,* 1967, **276**, 1271–1283.
122. Tizard, R., & Rees, F. A comparison of the effects of adoption, restoration to the natural mother, and continued institutionalization on the cognitive development of four-year-old children. *Child Development,* 1974, **45**, 93–99.
123. Tizard, B., & Rees, J. The effect of early institutional rearing on the behavior problems and affectional relationships of four-year-old children. *Journal of Child Psychology and Psychiatry,* 1975, **16**, 61–73.
124. Dennis, W., & Najarian, P. Infant development under environmental handicap. *Psychological Monographs,* 1957, **71**, No. 436.
125. DuPan, R. M., & Roth, S. The psychologic development of a group of children brought up in a hospital type residential nursery. *Journal of Pediatrics,* 1955, **47**, 124–129.
126. Ainsworth, M. D. The effects of maternal deprivation: A review of findings and controversy in the context of research strategy. In *Deprivation of maternal care: A reassessment of its effects*. Geneva: World Health Organization 1962.
127. Clarke, A. D. B., & Clarke, A. M. Formerly isolated children. In A. M. Clarke & A. D. B. Clarke (Eds.), *Early experience: Myth and evidence*. New York: Free Press, 1977.
128. Koluchova, J. Severe deprivation in twins: A case study. *Journal of Child Psychology and Psychiatry,* 1972, **13**, 107–113.

129. Koluchova, J. The further development of twins after severe and prolonged deprivation: A second part. *Journal of Child Psychology and Psychiatry,* 1976, **17,** 181–188.
130. Skeels, H. M., & Dye, H. A study of the effects of differential stimulation on mentally retarded children. *Proceedings of the American Association on Mental Deficiency,* 1939, **44,** 114–136.
131. Skeels, H. M. Adult status of children with contrasting early life experiences. *Monographs of the Society for Research in Child Development,* 1966, **31,** No. 3.
132. Clarke, A. D. B., & Clarke, A. M. Studies in natural settings. In A. M. Clarke & A. D. B. Clarke (Eds.), *Early experience: Myth and evidence.* New York: Free Press, 1977.
133. Goldfarb, W. Emotional and intellectual consequences of psychologic deprivation in infancy: A re-evaluation. In P. H. Hoch & J. Zubin (eds.), *Psychopathology of childhood.* New York: Grune & Stratton, 1955.
134. Provence, S., & Ritvo, S. Effects of deprivation on institutionalized infants: Disturbances in the development of relationship to inanimate objects. *Psychoanalytic Study of the Child,* 1961, **16,** 189–205.
135. Brenton, M. Mainstreaming the handicapped. *Today's Education,* March/April 1974, 20–25.
136. Dunn, L. M. Special education for the mildly retarded—is much of it justifiable? *Exceptional Children,* 1968, **35,** 5–24.
137. MacMillan, D. L., Jones, R. L., & Meyers, C. E. Mainstreaming the mildly retarded: Some questions, cautions, and guidelines. *Mental Retardation,* 1976, **14,** 3–10.
138. Goodman, J. F. The developmental class: Best of both worlds for the mentally retarded. *Psychology in the Schools,* 1976, **13,** 257–265.
139. Fitzgibbon, W. C. Public school programs for the mentally retarded. In A. A. Baumeister (Ed.), *Mental retardation: Appraisal, education, and rehabilitation.* Chicago: Aldine, 1967.
140. Guskin, S. L., & Spicker, H. H. Educational research in mental retardation. In N. R. Ellis (Ed.), *International review of research in mental retardation.* Vol. 3. New York: Academic Press, 1968.
141. Stanton, J. E., & Cassady, V. M. Effectiveness of special classes for educable mentally retarded. *Mental Retardation,* 1964, **2,** 8–13.
142. Quay, L. C. Academic skills. In N. R. Ellis (Ed.), *Handbook of mental deficiency.* New York: McGraw-Hill, 1963.
143. Sparks, H. L., & Blackman, L. S. What is special about education revisited: The mentally retarded. *Exceptional Children,* 1965, **31,** 242–247.
144. Carroll, A. W. The effects of segregated and partially integrated school programs on self-concept and academic achievement of educable mental retardates. *Exceptional Children,* 1967, **34,** 93–99.
145. Goldstein, H. The efficacy of special classes and regular classes in the education of educable mentally retarded children. In J. Zubin & G. A. Jervis (Eds.), *Psychopathology of mental development.* New York: Grune & Stratton, 1967.
146. Gottlieb, J., Gampel, D. H., & Budoff, M. Classroom behavior of retarded children before and after integration into regular classes. *Journal of Special Education,* 1975, **9,** 307–315.
147. Bruininks, R. H., Rynders, J. E., & Gross, J. C. Social acceptance of mildly retarded pupils in resource rooms and regular classes. *American Journal of Mental Deficiency,* 1974, **78,** 377–383.
148. Goodman, H., Gottlieb, J., & Harrison, R. H. Social acceptance of EMRs integrated into a nongraded elementary school. *American Journal of Mental Deficiency,* 1972, **76,** 412–417.
149. Schurr, K. T., Joiner, L. M., & Towne, R. C. Self-concept research on the mentally retarded: A review of empirical studies. *Mental Retardation,* 1970, **8,** 39–43.
150. Gottlieb, J. Attitudes toward retarded children: Effects of labeling and academic performance. *American Journal of Mental Deficiency,* 1974, **79,** 268–273.
151. MacMillan, D. L., Jones, R. L., & Aloia, G. F. The mentally retarded label: A theoretical analysis and review of research. *American Journal of Mental Deficiency,* 1974, **79,** 241–261.
152. Cook, J. W., & Wollersheim, J. P. The effects of labeling of special education students on the perceptions of contact versus noncontact peers. *Journal of Special Education,* 1976, **10,** 187–198.

PART 3

Preschool Years

7 | Physical and Mental Growth

PHYSICAL GROWTH

MENTAL GROWTH
  Assessment of Intelligence
  Perceptual Development
  Memory
  Discrimination Learning
  Conservation Behavior
  Language Development
  Theories of Attainment
  Referential Communication

THE CONCEPTUAL WORLD OF THE YOUNG CHILD

ESSAY
  Early Childhood Education

BIOGRAPHY
  Maria Montessori

SUMMARY

REFERENCES

The years from 2 to 5—the preschool years—are much less dramatic than the first 2 years of life with respect to motor development. Nothing in a preschooler's physical growth could match the drama of an infant who is sitting, standing, or walking for the first time. This is not to say that motor development stops during the preschool years, but just that it is more gradual, more varied, and more closely related to specific patterns of experience and practice than it was in infancy. In contrast, there are greater changes in mental growth during the preschool period than in infancy, and there is considerable elaboration of learning, perception, reasoning, memory, and language.

PHYSICAL GROWTH

Growth in height and weight is less rapid during the preschool years than in infancy, but both height and weight continue to increase at a faster pace than in middle childhood. At about age 2 children are roughly half their final adult height, so that a toddler who is 36 inches tall has a good chance of becoming a 6-foot adult. By 5 the average child is 43 to 44 inches in height. This means that during the first 2 years of life infants (who start at 20 to 21 inches in length) grow about 7 to 8 inches a year, whereas from age 2 to 5 they average only 3 to 4 inches per year. Weight gain also slows down and may even stop for a while in the case of heavy toddlers, who may become taller and thinner without gaining much weight during part of the preschool period (1).

Effective toilet training occurs only after children have attained sufficient muscular control of bowel and bladder, usually toward the end of the second year.

One of the major motor accomplishments of the preschool years is toilet training. Typically bowel training precedes bladder training, mainly because it is easier for children to control their bowel movements than it is for them to hold their urine. Although some children reverse this sequence, the majority establish bowel control before they completely stop wetting, especially at night. Most children tend to be bowel and bladder trained by the age of 3, but there are wide differences that are related to the maturity of the muscles controlling the sphincter and anus, to the child's sex, and to parental attitudes. Children cannot be toilet trained until they are physically able to control their bowel and sphincter muscles. Girls generally achieve toilet training earlier than boys, while boys are more likely to continue to wet the bed for a longer time than girls. However, both boys and girls may occasionally have "accidents" throughout the preschool years.

Many girls and some boys train themselves simply by beginning to tell their parents when they need to go to the bathroom. For other youngsters the age of toilet training depends upon how soon the parents begin training and how vigorously they pursue it, say, by taking their child to the toilet at regular intervals or whenever he or she appears to need to go. Children who continue to wet the bed or to soil their clothes into middle childhood may suffer from late development of the muscular system, from emotional problems, or from some combination of the two (2). Parents of such children should discuss this problem with their pediatrician or other health professional with whom the family has regular contact.

The preschool child's development is evident in other areas as well. By the age of 2 most children are feeding themselves, and by the age of 3 they are using forks and spoons with some effectiveness. Using a knife to cut meat or to spread butter requires more advanced coordination, however, and so this is usually not mastered until a few years later. By the age of 3, many children are able to undress themselves somewhat, and by the age of 4 many are able to dress themselves in part, including the use of buttons and zippers. The ability to put on snow pants, boots, and shoes (including tying shoelaces) is usually not accomplished until about the age of 5 or 6 (3). Since children have to be taught to hold forks, spoons, and knives in the socially.accepted manner, this instruction usually should not be given until they have appropriate motor ability, typically about the age of 6 or 7. Parents simply have to be patient with their young children's awkward use of spoons, knives, and forks.

Among the large motor accomplishments during the preschool period are balancing, climbing, and throwing a ball. With respect to balancing, most 3-year-olds can walk a reasonably straight path on the floor but ordinarily they cannot follow a circular path until about a year later (4, 5). Again, while standing on the ground, most children cannot stand on one foot with their arms folded across their chest for a few seconds until they are about 5 years of age. Girls appear to be better at this and can stand in the position longer than boys (6).

Performance on a "balance board"—a beam suspended a little above the floor—also shows a regular progression with age. Two-year-old children are only able to make an attempt to stand on the beam. Slightly older children try to walk on the beam, but with one foot off and one foot on. Three-year-old children can alternate feet and move partway along a 7½-meter length. By the age of 4½, children can walk the balance beam quickly and without hestitation (4–7).

In the area of climbing, there is also a regular developmental progression, involving emotional as well as motor factors. One of the emotional elements in both balancing and climbing is the fear of falling. Climbing is usually first observed in infants who try to crawl up any available and accessible stairs. Once children begin to walk, they will climb the stairs upright but without alternating feet. By the age of about 4½, however, they generally begin to alternate steps. Children will usually not try to go downstairs alone (8). Children's ability at throwing progresses in a similar manner during the early childhood years, as illustrated in Figures 7.1 and 7.2.

Hopping is a fairly advanced form of motor coordination that can be observed in early childhood.

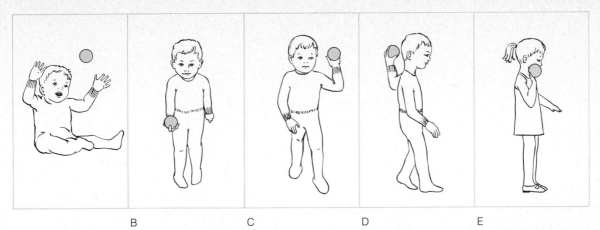

B   C   D   E

Figure 7.1 Stages in the development of throwing. The sequence is: accidental letting-go in an 18-month child (A), variable performance of a 2- to 4-year-old (B), throwing while stepping with the same-side foot (C), making the correct mechanical effort while stepping with the foot opposite the throwing arm (D). Into late childhood, a girl is less likely to involve her entire body in the action (E), than is a boy. (*Source.* Adapted from Cratty, B. J., *Perceptual and motor development in infants and children.* New York: Macmillan, 1970.)

Play activities also reflect preschool children's maturing motor abilities. On the playground, they can climb up and go down small slides, they can sit on swings and allow themselves to be pushed, and they can use a variety of other outdoor equipment such as jungle gyms, sleds, and roller skates. Tricycle riding is popular among preschoolers, and most 3-year-olds can learn to coordinate pedaling and steering in a matter of minutes. Riding a two-wheeler is more difficult, and it is usually not even possible until about the age of 5 or 6. Again, children may be afraid to ride

Figure 7.2 Stages in the ability to walk a balance beam. The sequence is: walking lines for short distances and standing on wide balance beams (A and B), walking curved lines (C), assuming more difficult postures (D), and walking narrower balance beams (E,F). (*Source.* Adapted from Cratty, B. J., *Perceptual and motor development in infants and children.* New York: Macmillan, 1970.)

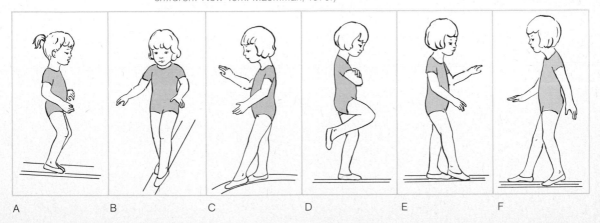

A   B   C   D   E   F

Riding a tricycle is one of the many new motor skills that become possible in early childhood.

a two-wheeler because of the possibility of falling. This fear may be as much of a hindrance for some children as the matter of balance and coordination.

In the area of small motor play, preschool children can hold brushes and paint lines and circles; they can cut paper and paste collages; and they can color with crayons. Once they have learned how to hold pencils and crayons, children begin to draw spontaneously, and this drawing shows a regular age-related progression (9). They begin with scribbles and soon progress to the **named scribble stage**, which has been described as follows:

> *A four year old put three blobs of paint on a paper but said "come see my big fierce jungle bird!" Children paint and use their painting as symbols for something they have thought about. Sometimes it will be a painting of a "big red bus" and on another occasion it will be "my mother"* [10].

After this comes the **controlled scribble stage**, in which children make the scribbles go in a desired direction such as diagonally or in a circle. Between about 4 and 7 years of age many children make **preschematic**

The first stage of drawing is that of the "scribble" characterized by predominantly circular lines.

drawings, in which they try to represent something they see. Usually children begin with the head and then try to add the eyes, nose, and mouth, but not necessarily in their usual location! In the **schematic stage**, which may appear by the age of 5, youngsters try to represent the entire human figure, usually themselves or their mother or father (9). To encourage the development of these motor skills, parents should provide crayons and paints for their children to experiment with, as well as an appropriate place and suitable clothes that can get "messed up." But parents should

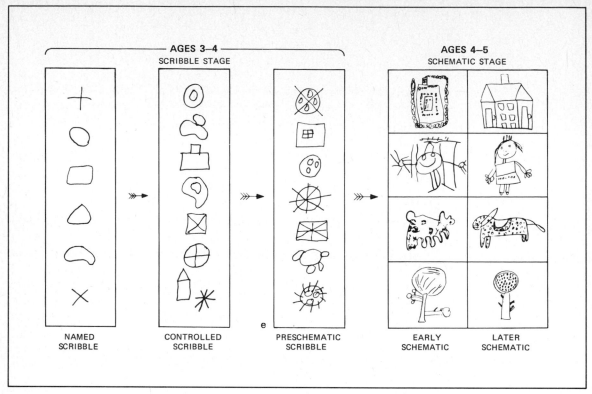

A chart depicting shape, design, and stages in the development of children's drawings.

avoid telling children what to draw and demanding that children tell them what they have painted. It should be mentioned that the preschool child's play activities, like all motor skills acquired during this period, are used increasingly for social and pragmatic purposes. In contrast to infants, who engage in much repetitive skill play simply to develop motor coordination, preschoolers tend to direct their motor play at furthering some general goal. Although preschool children sometimes run, sing, and dance out of sheer exuberance, more often they run as part of a game of tag, they build blocks to make a garage, and they dress dolls as part of playing house. Because of this functional, socially oriented dimension in young children's play, the famed Italian educator Maria Montessori said that "play is the young child's work" (11). But play can sometimes simply be play for fun and for personal expression; it is not always directed at social adaptation.

Although child psychologists agree about the descriptive details of motor development as it appears in self-help activities, locomotion, and play, they disagree about how these patterns of action are acquired. Some investigators (12–15) argue that children develop skilled patterns of movement by means of information-processing activities. That is to say, the child might try out one movement, for example the balance beam, and correct it according to the feedback he or she receives from his or her foot. According to this view, skilled actions become more economical and less variable as the individual develops proficiency.

Other investigators, however, insist that the acquisition of skilled patterns of action is due as much to the task itself as to the information processing in the child. According to this view, the child builds up a standard reaction to particular stimuli which he or she then varies to accommodate to new situations. On the balance board, for example, the child would try out the same walking steps he or she normally uses on the ground but increase his or her control and balance to fit the new stimulus situation. This **construction standard** theory suggests that the child constructs standard schemas for various types of motor skills and that new motor skills are acquired by modifying older ones (16–18).

Still a third approach suggests that the acquisition of skilled actions is comparable to cognitive development in general and especially to language. In one study (19) the investigators began by describing three directions that mark the growth of children's language: that it becomes hierarchically more complex (children recognize that Fords, Buicks, and Dodges are all cars); involves more interruptions (that is, includes subordinate clauses within the sentence); and reflects more role changes (the same word serves more than one function in a sentence) with increasing age. The investigators devised play activities that would test for hierarchical organization, interruptions, and variable role-playing and presented them to children of different ages. They found that, on the tasks they created, play developed in the same directions that are observed in the evolution of language and thought.

It should be noted that these three approaches do not necessarily contradict one another and may even be complementary in certain ways. As yet, the theories are not sufficiently developed, nor are there enough data to favor one or the other. What all these theories share in common, though, is the view that skilled action is a complex accomplishment that develops gradually and that may follow along the same general lines as the acquisition of logically organized thought and language.

MENTAL DEVELOPMENT

The growth of mental abilities during the preschool period is as remarkable as the growth of physical and motor abilities during infancy. At this time children develop the pattern of skills that we call "general intelligence," which can be assessed by standardized tests comparable to those used with older children and adults. In addition, particular skills such as perception, memory, learning, problem-solving, and language all become established during this period. Because of these changes in intellectual power, the child's conceptual world is considerably broadened and deepened as compared with what it was in infancy. The remainder of this chapter will review some of these extraordinary changes in intellectual prowess.

Assessment of Intelligence

Intelligence tests were originally devised for preschool and school-age children and reflected the pattern of abilities such children demonstrated in adapting to new situations. Some of the subtests of the Stanford–Binet test (the current version of the first intelligence test) indicate the range of abilities young children (aged 2 to 5) are expected to have. These subtests include perceptual motor coordination such as a three-hole form board in which children are asked to insert a wooden square, a triangle, and a circle into their appropriate places on a cutout board. In another task children are asked to build a tower of blocks. Verbal tests require youngsters to identify objects (dog, ball, bed, and so forth) by name and another test asks children to identify pictures of common objects. A further test instructs children, after waiting a short time, to find an object that has been hidden under one of the three objects; hence it requires memory (20). Some of the test items are depicted in the accompanying photograph.

In establishing this test, which was originally intended to distinguish between normal and retarded children, Binet assumed that a person could be considered average if he or she could do the things persons of his or her

A child being tested on the Stanford-Binet Intelligence Test.

age normally do (21). Thus, the test was designed on a psychological rather than a physical scale. Test items were assigned to particular age levels according to the number of children in a normative sample who correctly answered each item. For example, 15 percent of the 2-year-old children tested by Binet could solve the three-hole form-board problem. Very few 1-year-olds but nearly all 3-year-olds could solve the problem; thus, the test was placed at the 2-year level.

In general, there are six tests at each age level, and passing any one of the tests earns the child 2 months of credit. In actual testing, the examiner usually starts at a level at which he or she believes the child will correctly answer all of the items. This is called the **basal age**. A 4-year-old child, for example, might be given all the tests at the 3-year level. If the child correctly answered all of the 3-year items, he or she would automatically receive credit for all the preceding years (or items) as well. The testing is continued until the child fails all of the items at a particular age level; this is called the child's **ceiling**. The child's score is the basal score plus the number of months earned above it. The total attained score in years and months is the child's **mental age**.

Although Binet thought that mental age was a useful concept in indicating a subject's absolute level of mental growth, other investigators wanted a measure that would show a child's brightness in relation to other children. The German psychologist William Stern then introduced the concept of **intelligence quotient**, which was defined as follows:

$$\text{Intelligence quotient} = \frac{\text{Mental age (M.A.)}}{\text{Chronological age (C.A.)}} \times 100$$

To illustrate, if a child with a C.A. of 4 years and 2 months attains a mental age of 5 years, his or her intelligence quotient would be, in months:

$$IQ = \frac{60}{50} \times 100 = 120$$

Conversely, a child with a C.A. of 7 years and 6 months but a mental age of 5 years and 3 months would have the following intelligence quotient, in months:

$$IQ = \frac{63}{90} \times 100 = 70$$

In general, the average IQ (of the population at large) is 100 and scores above and below that average become less frequent the further they are from the average.

A somewhat different approach to intelligence assessment was taken by David Wechsler (22), who did away with the concept of mental age and used a point scale of intelligence. That is to say, instead of scoring a subject's performance in months and years, as on the Binet test, his or her performance is scored in points that are then converted directly to IQs. The Wechsler scales (for adults, children, and more recently preschool children) yield three IQs—a verbal IQ, a performance IQ, and a total IQ.

Some examples from Wechsler's recently introduced preschool test (23) may help to clarify what abilities are required for the verbal and performance scales. One of the verbal scales deals with general information and includes questions such as "How many ears do you have?" and "What lives in water?" Another verbal test—of vocabulary—asks children to define a list of words. The test begins with "shoe" and "knife," and then goes on to more difficult words such as "microscope" and "gamble." One of the performance tests asks children to tell what is missing in pictures of familiar objects (the teeth on a comb, and so forth). Another requires the child to build a design with blocks like one that is shown on a card.

Although the Binet and Wechsler scales use somewhat different items, test procedures, and scoring methods, they correlate about .75 with one another (23). This suggests that both scales are measuring some over-all capacity, or general intelligence, as well as specific abilities required by the different test items. Other tests of intelligence that are more limited in the range of abilities they assess, such as the Peabody Picture Vocabulary Test (24), do not correlate as highly with the Binet and Wechsler scales as the latter two do with each other. Therefore, if one needs a comprehensive assessment of a young child's intellectual abilities, the Binet or Wechsler scales are preferable.

Why is intelligence testing of preschool and school-age children much more reliable and valid than of infants? The main reason is that young children have the verbal abilities that make it possible for them to respond to verbal directions and to give verbal responses to test items. These children are also socially more adept than infants and less self-centered in their concerns. Nonetheless, testing young children takes considerable skill because they must feel comfortable with an adult in order to perform well.

The relationship between feeling comfortable and a child's test performance was demonstrated in a study of Head Start children. The investigators felt that the fact that disadvantaged children performed poorly on intelligence tests was due more to "debilitating motivational factors" than to low intellectual ability. Such factors include a wariness of strange adults, little motivation to be correct for the sake of correctness, and a willingness to settle for low levels of achievement. Any improvement in the test performance of children enrolled in programs such as Head Start might reflect changes in these motivational factors as much as changes in mental ability per se.

To examine this possibility, culturally disadvantaged children from two nursery schools were compared with a control group of children who did not attend nursery school. All of the children were given *two* intelligence tests at the beginning of the nursery school year and two again at the end of the school year. One of these was administered in the standard way—that is, according to the prescribed rules—in which the examiners remained neutral but friendly toward the children throughout the test. The second intelligence test was administered according to "optimizing procedures," in which the examiner established a pleasant social interaction between herself and the child, allowing the child to experience considerable success with the easy items, minimizing the child's wariness of herself (the tester), and trying to motivate him or her to achieve.

The study provided a number of interesting results, which are shown graphically in Figure 7.3. First of all, during the testing at the beginning of the school year, the disadvantaged children performed much better under the optimizing conditions than under standard conditions. This difference, the largest noted in the study, suggests that standard procedures often undercut the culturally deprived child's intellectual potential to perform. When these children are truly motivated, they can do better on the test. Furthermore, the children who attended nursery school showed significant gains in IQ from the beginning to the end of the year (7 months), while the other children did not. But this gain appeared only on the tests that were given under standard conditions, not on the tests that were given under optimizing conditions.

By the end of the school year, the nursery-school children's average IQ, as measured by standard testing, had increased significantly over what it had been at the outset. This was not true for the control children, however. Apparently, when disadvantaged children enter nursery school, they do not have the motivation to do well in cognitive tasks—nor perhaps the attention and emotional readiness as well—so that they do not demonstrate their maximum abilities when tested under standard conditions. But the "debilitating motivational factors" appear to diminish after several months at nursery school, which results in much better performance

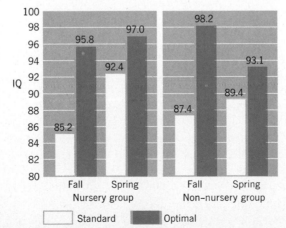

Figure 7.3
Intelligence-test performance of children under standard and optimal conditions. The IQs of nursery and non-nursery school children for standard and optimal fall and spring testing. (*Source*. Zigler, E. & Butterfield, E. C. Motivational aspects of deprived nursery school children. *Child Development*, 1968, **39**, 1–14.)

under standard testing procedures. From this we might conclude that nursery-school attendance modifies the attitudes and motivations of disadvantaged children rather than their cognitive abilities. Nevertheless, there is little doubt that "the demonstrated improvement in their standard IQ indicates that these children were generally more competent by the end of the nursery-school year" (25).

We have discussed this study at length because it illustrates so well the hazards of interpreting intelligence test data without a full understanding of the circumstances under which the testing was done. One of us vividly recalls testing a 6-year-old girl who was suspected of having minimal brain injury. She was angry and negativistic throughout the entire procedure and clearly was not doing her best. The test would have been rescheduled but the results were needed immediately. Later it was learned that the child's father had told her he was taking her horseback riding—her favorite activity—but then brought her to the clinic instead. Not surprisingly, her anger and frustration were vented on the test and the examiner. The test results obtained under such circumstances had to be interpreted with caution. Test scores, then, are not physical measurements, and they can reflect motivation and attitudes as much as intellectual ability. We shall return to the problems of intelligence testing in our discussion of individual variations.

Before concluding this section on intelligence testing, we should mention that some psychologists have challenged the meaning and the worth of intelligence tests (26, 27). They argue that intelligence tests do not measure native "brightness" but simply a limited set of competencies that tend to be valued by the middle class. These competencies include attentional and verbal skills, attitudes toward achievement, test-taking strategies, and so forth. Because these skills are acquired and are not part of a child's native endowment, the middle class child has an unfair advantage over the lower-class child on intelligence tests. This may explain why middle-class children regularly score higher then lower-class children.

Perceptual Development

Perception encompasses the processes by which we read the information that comes to us via our senses. The general outlines of perceptual development during the preschool years are reasonably well established. Perception develops somewhat as follows: The perception of a young child tends to be caught and held by the dominant features of a stimulus configuration. With increasing age and maturing perceptual abilities, the child's perception gains greater freedom from its earlier dependence upon particular dominant features, so that the child can survey and organize the configuration as a whole (28–30). This change can be seen in the way children perform on a number of different perceptual tasks.

One of these tasks is illustrated in Figure 7.4. These "part-whole" drawings were shown to 195 children from 4 to 9 years of age who were

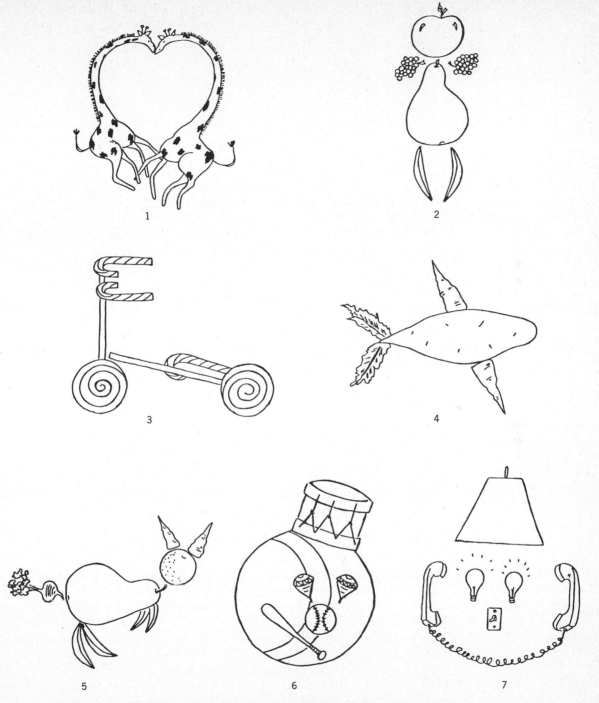

Figure 7.4 Picture integration test. (*Source.* Elkind, D., Koglar, R., & Go, E. Studies in perceptual development II: Part-whole perception. *Child Development,* 1964, **35,** 81–90.

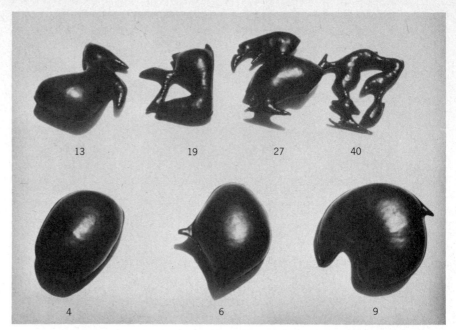

Figure 7.5
Three-dimensional objects
varying in complexity.
(*Source*. Switzky, H. N.,
Haywood, C., & Isett, R.
Exploration, curiosity, and
play in young children.
*Developmental
Psychology*, 1974, **10,**
321–329.)

asked to describe what they saw. It was found that the youngest children
either focused upon the parts (for example, the apple, grapes, and pear in
Drawing 2) and ignored the whole, or focused upon the whole (the man)
but ignored the parts. By the age of 8 or 9, however, most children
described Drawing 2 as ''a man made out of fruit'' and Drawing 3 as ''a
bike made out of candy.'' The ability of the older children to see the parts
and the whole simultaneously also supports the view that perceptual organization becomes more rapid as well as more integrated with increasing
age (31, 32).

The development of perception is also evident in the fact that the child
prefers more complex stimulus arrays as he or she becomes better able to
cope with them. It is generally accepted that complexity and novelty are
two stimulus characteristics that elicit exploratory behavior on the part of
children (32–35). Accordingly, one might expect that as children grow
older and become increasingly able to deal with more complicated stimuli,
they would become more curious about them and prefer them to less
complex stimuli. This is actually what happens. When figures (such as
those depicted in Figure 7.5) are generated by increasing the number of
turns, older children will explore and prefer the more complex, many-
sided figures, whereas younger children will not (36–38).

Another facet of perceptual development that attests to the older child's
increased competence has been called *cross-modal transfer*. This transfer
is the comparison between what has been experienced in one sense modality and what has been experienced in another. For example, a child

might be shown an object with a certain shape and then asked to find it among others by touch (usually the child has to put his hand into a box so that he or she cannot see what he or she is touching). Or a child might be asked to handle a form and then to identify it when presented visually. Although there is some dispute about whether tactile discriminations are as easy as visual ones (39, 40), the answer may depend upon the forms that are used. In one study, for example, a change in line curvature was distinguished at an earlier age by eye than it was by hand. But just the reverse was true for a change in figure orientation (41). In any case, the cross-modal transfer improves steadily with age, or at least during childhood (42).

Some of the developmental processes that occur in cross-modal matching are revealed when children are asked to match an auditory (temporal) series with a spatial (visual) series. For example, when 4- and 5-year-old children are asked to reproduce—using dots on a sheet of paper—a pattern of auditory taps they have heard, young children cannot distinguish the temporal from the spatial series. If they hear the following series: •• •• they write: •• ; then, after the pause, they add another couple of dots and end up with: ••••. First- and second-grade children can represent the tapped pattern correctly, but they sometimes try to copy the physical features of the sound and write as follows: OoOo. By the age of 7 or 8 most children understand how to represent a temporal series spatially and do not try to copy the physical features of the sound (43–45). Older children can take a pattern in one modality and translate it into a different type of pattern in another modality.

The work on cross-modal transfer indicates that perception does not develop in isolation but rather interacts with other mental processes, motivations, and so forth. An interesting example of such interaction is shown in Figure 7.6. Children between 4 and 8 years of age were asked to draw pictures of Santa Claus periodically before Christmas and for 2 weeks afterward. As can be seen, the pictures of Santa grow larger as Christmas draws near and become smaller as the holiday fades in memory (46). The effects of motivation on perception are not always this clear-cut; indeed, they become extraordinarily complex in response to stimuli such as the Rorschach inkblot test (47). We simply wanted to emphasize that a child's perception may be affected by motivational and personality factors as well as perceptual ability and the characteristics of the stimuli.

Perceptual development is also related to growth in language ability. For 4-year-old children, actively saying the names of figures helps them to recall these figures better than if they merely hear someone else say the names for them. At the same time, however, hearing someone else say the names of pictures facilitated recall to a greater extent than not hearing the names at all. For 6-year-old children similar results were obtained except that saying and hearing the names of pictures were equally effective in facilitating recall. It seems reasonable to suppose that for 4-year-old chil-

Figure 7.6 Changes in three children's drawings of Santa Claus before and after Christmas. (*Source.* Solley, C. M. & Murphy, G. *Development of the perceptual world.* New York: Basic Books, 1960.)

dren saying a word mobilizes their attention to a greater extent than merely hearing the word spoken by someone else.

Language may be helpful to young children in making perceptual discriminations because of the difficulty they have focusing their attention selectively (50). Older children are more likely than younger children to use selective attention and ignore secondary perceptual features that are irrelevant to a given task. But language, as suggested above (49), seems to help young children pay attention to relevant stimuli and avoid distraction. It should be noted, however, that the parental admonition "Look at what you are doing!" needs to be specific in order to be effective. Parents would do better to say "Watch the top of your glass when you are pouring juice."

 Memory How well do young children remember what they have heard or seen? That is not an easy question to answer. It depends in part upon the type of material that is to be recalled (verbal or pictorial). But it also depends upon whether one is referring to relatively **short-term memory** (for example, recalling a telephone number you have just looked up long enough to dial it) or **long-term memory** (recalling your own phone number or address). What children remember also depends upon their level of development and the cognitive abilities and systems at their disposal.

If a child is supposed to remember an object, is it better to present the object itself, the object's name, or the name and the object? In other words, do young children store experiences visually, verbally, or by some combination of the two? In general, preschool children's ability to remember pictures of objects tends to be quite extraordinary and to far surpass their memory for object names (51–54). In one study (53), 4-year-old children recognized 93 percent of the 16 figures that had been presented to them visually but recalled only 71 percent of the items that had been presented verbally. But it is also true that children spontaneously try to label objects that have not been named by the experimenter. Thus, while children's memory for pictures is better than it is for names, this memory may be helped by the fact that they make up names spontaneously (55).

So far we have considered children's ability to recognize lists of unrelated pictures and words. But what about more complicated prose material? Will young children recall more ideas from a prose passage in which the ideas are related to one another than from one in which they are not? The results for young children are clear: Preschool children recall meaningful, connected discourse much better than they do nonconnected discourse (56–60). In this regard, then, their performance is like that of older children and adults; the only difference is that young children cannot recall as much material.

How do young children remember anything—a list of words, a prose passage, or a series of pictures? In general, they do not have too many strategies available for memorizing material. Older children and adults often relate individual elements to a more general category (since dog, cat, and cow are all animals, they can more easily be recalled by thinking of the larger category). But preschool children do not have such general categorical skills and subject groupings. They might put a dog and a cat, but not a cow, together because they both "bite." It is not until about the age of 6 or 7 that children can effectively group or "cluster" materials to be memorized according to objective categories (61–67).

However, young children do have a few techniques for memorizing material, although these are more limited and more primitive than the categorizing and clustering strategies. For example, when 3-year-old children were told to "remember" where a toy dog was hidden, they looked at the place where the dog was hidden more often than if they had not been told. With 2-year-old children, however, the instruction to "remember" made no particular difference (68). For children from about 3 to 5 years of age, therefore, asking them to "remember" helps to direct their attention to the relevant stimuli, even though they cannot yet use categorical strategies.

Thus far we have largely been discussing short-term memory, in which only a few moments elapsed between presentation of the material and its recall or recognition. What about a young child's recall of events over a longer period of time? Some truly surprising results have been reported by Jean Piaget and Barbel Inhelder (69). They have argued that memory is not a copy of an experience that has simply been stored and then retrieved. Rather, they have argued that memory is, in fact, an active process and that the original experience can undergo many different transformations before it is recalled. Therefore, what a child recalls may not resemble very closely the original experience.

The idea that memory is an active process is not a new idea. Early investigators such as Sir Frederick Bartlett (70) and Sigmund Freud (71) demonstrated that material stored in the memory undergoes spontaneous transformations. Bartlett showed that when subjects recalled stories they elaborated or **sharpened** certain parts (namely, gory details such as blood oozing out of a victim's mouth), but standardized or **leveled** other points (a "mountain" became a "hill," 5½ days became a "week," and so forth). Freud, in turn, noted that many of the memories his patients recalled were fabrications (or "screens") that they had unconsciously constructed to hide or obscure painful events.

What Piaget and Inhelder added to this description of the transformations of memory was a developmental dimension. In a series of studies they demonstrated that children's memories for quantitative displays changed spontaneously with the development of their mental abilities for dealing with quantitative relationships. In one study, for example, 4-, 5-, and 6-year-old children were shown a set of eight sticks that formed a size-graded series; they were arranged from the smallest to the largest. The children were first asked to copy the series and then to draw the pattern from memory, immediately after seeing it, a week later, and then 6 months later.

The 4-year-olds had trouble copying the series and remembering it. Frequently they drew pairs of sticks, one bigger than the other. The 5- and 6-year-olds were more accurate and usually made correct copies. The dramatic finding was that the 4-year-old children, when asked to draw the series 6 months later, showed a significant improvement over their initial drawings. And this was true despite the fact that they had not been asked to draw the series in the interim. Piaget and Inhelder concluded that these children's memory of the series had been transformed in accordance with their newly developed capacity to arrange different-sized sticks in a series. These findings and interpretations have generally been supported by other investigators (72–76).

Piaget and Inhelder thus provided new evidence for viewing memory as an active rather than a passive process. Furthermore, while Bartlett (70) and Freud (71) had argued that memory activity was basically a distorting process, Piaget and Inhelder demonstrated that this was not necessarily the case. For growing children, memories of past experiences may improve with age as the child reconstructs those memories with more mature mental operations and concepts.

With respect to adult memory for early childhood experiences, most adults cannot remember this period in their lives very well. We may have one or two striking memories of the period and some vague intuitions, but it is largely a blank. The reason for this is probably related to intellectual maturity. Memories are stored in a spatial and temporal framework. The famous question "Where were you on the night of . . .?" asks for time and place and thus provides a reference for searching one's memory. But young children have only vague concepts of space and time, and so they cannot store these memories in a systematic framework. This lack of a comprehensive system of space-time coordinates probably accounts in large measure for adults' "amnesia" regarding their preschool years.

Discrimination Learning One of the basic adaptive tasks of young children is to learn to identify and distinguish among various objects and properties of objects in their everyday world. Children need to learn to identify red Winesap and green pippins as apples, and they must learn to distinguish apples from oranges, squares from circles, and so forth. As the foregoing examples suggest, discrimination is one way in which children learn **concepts** when these are defined as "common responses to diverse stimuli." Some aspects of discrimination learning were mentioned in the discussion of perception, but here we will focus upon the learning aspects of discrimination.

One of the most substantiated findings pertaining to the learning of young children is that a qualitative change occurs between the ages of 4 and 6 (76). This change in discrimination learning has been demonstrated by the reversal shift problem (see Figure 7.7) (77). In this task the subjects are first trained to make a discrimination along one dimension (for example, color) and to ignore variations in another (for example, form.) Once the discrimination has been learned (by rewarding the "correct" responses

Figure 7.7 Figures used in reversal-shift training. This discrimination-shift model involves a comparison between a reversal (RS) and an extradimensional shift (EDS). For each pair of figures, plus indicates reinforcement, minus indicates nonreinforcement. As a control measure each figure cue (black, white, circle, and triangle) is correct for one-fourth of the subjects during both preshift and postshift problems. (*Source.* Kendler, H. H. & Kendler, T. S. Discrimination and development. In W. K. Estes (Ed.), *Handbook of learning and development*, New York: Halsted, 1975.)

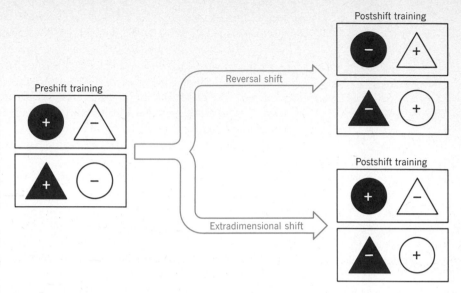

and not rewarding the "incorrect" responses), the subjects are exposed to one of the two post-training discriminations. In a **reversal shift** (RS) the correct and the incorrect responses of the initial training are reversed (in the example, black would be incorrect, white correct). In an **extradimensional shift** (EDS) the previously irrelevant dimension (form) becomes relevant, with one of its values being rewarded as correct.

The reversal shift problem has been presented to animals as well as to children and adults (78–88). Young children and animals have more difficulty with a reversal shift than with an extradimensional shift. But older children and adults find reversal shifts to be easier than extradimensional shifts. According to the Kendlers (78), the reason for this is that for young children discrimination learning means learning something about a particular stimulus whereas for older children and adults discrimination learning means learning a concept or a "mediating" response. In short, young children learn that black is "right" and white is "wrong," whereas older subjects learn that color is "right" and form is "wrong." In the reversal shift condition young children must overcome their tendency to respond to "black," but older children and adults do not have to change their response to "color" as the appropriate dimension. In contrast, on the extradimensional shift young children do not have to alter their negative response to "white" since another dimension is involved. But older children and adults need to recognize that the previously positive dimension is now negative and vice versa.

It is important to point out that the "mediation" that marks the performance of older children and adults does not have to be verbal. Indeed, for Jean Piaget (89) the mediating processes would be internalized actions (or "mental operations"); these will be discussed in detail later in the chapter, pp. 00, and also in Chapter 00. In addition, a subject's failure to use mediation may be due to a lack of ability (**mediation deficiency**) or to a lack of utilization (**production deficiency**). That is to say, in a particular situation (for example, a crossword puzzle) a subject may not get a word either because he or she does not know it (mediation deficiency) or because he or she does not think of it in connection with the definition (production deficiency). In other words, subjects may not always use the mediational processes at their disposal (89, 90).

In another well-researched discrimination task, which is called **transposition,** children are trained to respond to the larger of two stimuli, such as the larger of two circles. Then, in the second (or test) phase of the experiment, the smaller circle of the original pair is replaced by a third circle that is larger than either of the original two. In this situation will the child choose the original circle (the stimulus choice) or the larger circle (the relational choice)? More precisely, in learning a discrimination, does the child learn to respond to a particular stimulus or to the relationship between the stimuli?

The answer to this question depends, in part, upon the distance (dimension) between the stimuli that are originally used to train the child and the distance used in testing him or her subsequently. Young children make relational choices when the newly introduced stimulus (for example, the circle) is not much larger than the original one. But when it is substantially larger, they choose the original stimulus and no longer respond on a relational basis (91, 92). It would seem that with large distances transposition requires symbolic mediation analogous to that which is required for reversal shifts.

It should be said, however, that even 3-year-olds can make relational choices with large dimensional differences if they have been trained to respond to stimulus relations (93–95). On the other hand, training young children to make verbal responses to the relations does not help them transpose across large dimensional differences (95–97). Apparently verbal mediation calls for more than the capacity to say or repeat words; it requires representational abilities that most preschool children do not have. Usually transposition on a relative basis depends upon a number of stimulus and training conditions as well as mediation (98).

Conservation Behavior

A very different approach to human learning has been taken by Jean Piaget (88), who has attempted to trace the development of children's thinking from infancy through adolescence. Some of Piaget's work on the emergence of infants' concepts about the world was discussed in Chapter 3. Piaget believes that a child learns about the world by progressively subordinating perception to reason. This is, of course, what characterizes the march of science generally. The roundness of the earth, for example, is not self-evident, but has to be deduced from such cues as the earth's shadow on the moon and the disappearance of a ship over the horizon. It took humankind thousands of years to overcome our perceptual impressions that the earth was flat and that the sun revolved around the earth.

In order to determine how much of the child's world is ruled by perception and how much by reason, Piaget devised certain conservation tasks in which the child is confronted with a stituation where perceptual and logical judgments contradict one another. For example, he or she might be shown two wide beakers of orangeade filled equally high, and a third tall, narrow, empty beaker. The child is then asked whether "there is the same amount to drink" in the two wide beakers. Once the child is satisfied that the quantities are the same, the experimenter pours the orangeade from one of the wide beakers into the tall, narrow one and asks the child whether there is the same amount to drink in the wide beaker as in the tall, narrow one.

It is important to note that there appears to be more orangeade in the tall beaker than in the wide one, but this is an illusion. To overcome the illusion, the child has to use logic and realize that since the two quantities had been the same before and nothing was added or taken away, they must still be the same. If the child responds to the illusion and says that one of the beakers contains less orangeade. Piaget claims that the child lacks conservation of the quantity in question. If, on the other hand, the child judges the quantities to be equal, he or she has demonstrated conservation; that is, shown that his or her reason has triumphed over his or her perception.

Piaget and his colleagues have devised conservation tasks for many different concepts including number, space, time, quantity, movement, speed, and geometry (99–104). In general, most children below the age of 6 or 7 do not demonstrate conservation in any of the areas that have been studied by Piaget. According to Piaget, preschool children lack the mental capacity—the reasoning abilities—to overcome the illusions presented by perception. Many of these studies have now been replicated all over the world with strikingly comparable results (105–108).

On the other hand, some investigators have argued that young children have more ability than Piaget would acknowledge. Two problems have attracted particular attention: transitive inferences and the young child's conception of number. We shall see that, as in the research on reversal-shift and transposition learning, young children's success or failure on these tasks may depend upon many different variables.

Transitive Inferences. Suppose that you show a child two sticks of different lengths, A and B, such that $A > B$, and you ask him or her to judge which is longer. Then suppose that you show him or her another pair of sticks, one from the previous pair and a new one, such that $B > C$, and you ask him or her again which is longer. Finally, suppose you ask the child, without allowing him or her to compare the sticks directly, whether A is longer than C. Knowing that $A > B$ and that $B > C$, if the child concludes that A > C, he or she is said to have made a transitive inference.

Piaget (102–104) has argued that young children below the age of 5 or 6 do not make transitive inferences. Other investigators, some of whom come from traditions quite different from Piaget's, have also found that young children have great difficulty in making inferences from premises (109–111). But in the past ten years, still other investigators have claimed that children as young as 3 or 4 years of age can make transitive inferences and that they are cognitively more competent than Piaget and his co-workers contend (112–115).

The evidence for transitive inferences in preschool youngsters comes from studies in which they are trained on the various pairs before the inference is made. One of the procedures used for training was as follows (114): Children were taught that A > B, B > C, C > D, and D > E by using five sticks of varying lengths and different colors. A was 7 inches long, B 6 inches, C 5 inches, D 4 inches, and E 3 inches. The colors were blue, red, green, yellow, and white. A block of wood was also used that had holes drilled to different depths; the depths were such that when any two sticks were placed in the board, they only extended above it by 1 inch. The children were asked to choose which of the two sticks was longer (when any two were in the board), and then they were shown the actual lengths by removing the sticks from the board. Thus, the children learned to identify the different lengths by color, and they learned these comparisons easily. On the test trial the children were asked to compare B and D while they were in the board. More than 75 percent of the 4-year-old children did so correctly. The results have also been replicated by others (115).

Can young children be trained to make transitive inferences? It is possible that during the training the children "overlearned" the sizes of the sticks, each of which was associated with a particular color. The children may have built up mental images of the sticks during the training and then reviewed the mental images in their heads when asked to compare B and D. If so, they would not be making the correct comparisons by means of transitive reasoning but by means of mental imagery (116). Thus, it is still not clear whether preschool children can be trained to make transitive inferences. Without training, however, most young children do not appear to use such inferences spontaneously.

Number Conservation. In one of Piaget's (119) experiments to determine a child's conception of number, a conservation problem was employed. A child was presented with a row of six plastic chips and was asked to take the "same number" from a nearby pile of chips, and to "make a row just like this." Piaget found a regular age-related progression of responses. Children of 4 years (who had no independent conception of "sixness") copied the spacing of the elements but ignored their length, and so they made a row that was longer and which had more chips than the model. Or they sometimes copied the length but ignored the spacing, therefore putting in too many chips again. Children of 5 and 6, however, were able to copy the model with respect to both length and spacing.

In any event, Piaget did not believe that copying the model was a good test of the child's conception of number. Once the two rows were similar, Piaget arranged the chips in one row so that it was longer (but less dense) than the other. Under these conditions both the 4-year-old children and the 5-year-old children (who had correctly copied the row) said that the longer row had "more" chips even though both rows still had six. Even more striking was the fact that some of the children who counted the chips correctly in the original and longer rows still said that the longer row had more chips than the short one!

Piaget argued that the child only attains a true sense of number when he or she can overcome the perceptual illusions of numbers with the aid of reason. For Piaget, reasoning in children develops because of the progressive internalization of actions. Once internalized, actions operate as a system (such as the operations of arithmetic). One characteristic of arithmetic operations is that they are reversible; the sum of $6 + 6 = 12$ can be reversed by subtracting $12 - 6 = 6$. Multiplication and division are also reversible. The reversibility of intellectual operations allows the child to return to the starting point in the conservation experiment and recognize that the transformation of spreading the chips is also reversible and hence that the number of chips remains constant. There are other ways that reversible operations can lead the child to conservation. He or she might discover that what the row gained in length, it lost in density, or that nothing was added or taken away. The attainment of mental operations makes the reversibility of thought, and hence conservation, possible.

Piaget's (119) demonstration of the development of number conservation has now been replicated with comparable results (for example, 118, 119). But, as in the case of transitive inferences, some investigators have not been willing to accept the idea that a preschool child believes that the number of chips increases when the row is lengthened. Many studies have attempted to show that by varying the procedures used by Piaget, or by training children, number conservation can be found in children below the age of 5 (119–121).

One of the challenges to Piaget's interpretation of the development of number was the reported finding of number conservation in 2-year-old children (122). The procedure employed, however, differed from that used by Piaget. No transformation was presented to the children; the number of elements employed was smaller and sometimes differed. When the experiment was repeated with proper controls, other investigators could not replicate these findings on conservation in young children. Furthermore, still other investigators have demonstrated that very young children do not even understand the terms "same" and "more" in the same way that 4- and 5-year-old children do (123–126). Clearly, there are many methodological problems in demonstrating conservation in young children.

Some of the controversy as to whether or not young children have a concept of number stems from the failure to recognize that there are levels of conceptualization. The 3- or 4-year-old child has a concept of number but it differs from the concept held by older children and adults (the same is true for many other concepts as well). Children of 3 and 4 years of age have a **global** concept of number in the sense that they judge number or quantity in terms of perceptual aggregates rather than units. This kind of number concept is also found in animals that can make numerical judgments on the basis of the *size* of the aggregates rather than their number. On the standard number conservation task, however, children cannot judge by size of aggregate because the two aggregates are numerically the same. Therefore, they resort to centering upon length or density and thus they make errors. Either they center upon length, and make the rows too dense, or they center upon density and make the rows too long.

At the next stage (usually ages 4½ to 5½) children demonstrate an **intuitive** concept of number in the sense that they begin to grasp that some sort of unit is involved. Hence, with a little trial and error they are able to construct a one-to-one correspondence and match one set of 6 counters with another. But this notion of unit is only intuitive because it is destroyed when the one-to-one relation is perceptually altered by lengthening one of the rows. When this happens, a child with an intuitive concept of number slips back to judging number by perceptual attributes such as length or density.

At the third stage (usually observed in youngsters from 5½ to 6½) children demonstrate a **true** sense of number. They can both construct a one-to-one correspondence rapidly and without error, and can recognize that this correspondence will hold even when the perceptual correspondence is no longer intact. At this stage children have a *unit* conception of number since their estimation of number will depend upon an accounting of individual elements. Studies (for example, 128, 129) demonstrating that very young children have or can learn a concept of number must specify whether this concept is global, intuitive, or true in the sense of including a notion of unit. Otherwise these investigators may be attributing true, abstract concepts of number to 3- and 4-year-old children, although no recent study has supported such an extreme ascription of intellectual power to children of this age (130).

A similar pattern can be found in the development of young children's ability to construct class concepts (131). When they are given a set of colored plastic geometric forms (circles, arcs, triangles, and rectangles) and are asked to group together the ones that are the same, they typically construct **graphic** collections, that is, they construct such things as houses out of the forms rather than grouping them according to their properties. At a second stage, comparable to the intuitive stage in the development of number, children begin to group the objects together according to form, but they are not consistent and may assemble five rectangles and a triangle. During the last stage children can systematically group objects according to their form and color (131).

Thus, 3- and 4-year-olds do have some concepts of quantity and class, but these are global or general and undifferentiated. Only with increasing age, active manipulation of many kinds of material, and social stimulation will children progressively construct concepts of quantity and class comparable to those held by older children and adults.

Language
Development

The growth of language during the preschool years is quite dramatic. From the first one-word utterances that occur during the second year of life, the child progresses to rather elaborate and complex verbal constructions by the age of 4 or 5. Those parents who could not wait for their children to begin speaking often wish that they would keep still. As we noted in our discussion of language in Chapter 3, those who study language do not completely agree about how this transformation in verbal skill and language production comes about. However, they do agree that naturalistic studies of how children actually acquire and use language are the proper method for examining language development. Therefore, most of the research in the field uses longitudinal studies of the language development of just a few children. We will review certain aspects of language growth during the preschool years and some of the theories that attempt to explain this growth.

Language Acquistion. One dimension of language development that has received considerable attention is the length of the verbal utterance. As children grow older their verbal utterances become longer, thereby providing a rough gauge of their verbal competence. Two-word phrases, such as ''Bobby up'' or Mommy drink,'' are a marked improvement over single words in communicative efficiency. Children who use two words can choose any combination of subject, verb, or object in their two-word utterances, but the subject-verb unit appears to be more common than any other combination (132, 133).

As children progress to three- and four-word utterances, more variation is possible in linguistic construction, and children begin to develop consistent individual differences in their mode of language acquisition. For example, some children use only themselves as the agent: ''I throw ball'' or ''I want candy.'' Other children, however, recognize that others can also be the agents of action: ''Daddy, new book'' or ''Mommy change sheets.'' Therefore, while language growth is marked by longer utterances, broader vocabulary, and more varied constructions, there are distinct differences in how children acquire language.

Besides the length of the utterance, language growth is also marked by a steady increase in active as well as passive vocabularies. Although it is difficult to estimate vocabulary size, most 3- and 4-year-old children probably have passive vocabularies of several thousand words. Their active vocabularies—the words children actually use—tend to be considerably smaller than that. The acquisition of vocabulary is not uniform with respect to all types of words, however, since some words are acquired earlier or more easily than others. A number of studies on language growth have dealt with the acquisition of particular words.

Of special interest are words that are opposite in meaning, but of unusual difficulty from the child's standpoint—for example, the words "more" and "less." It has been found that while young children understand the term "more," they often assume that "less" means the same thing. When asked to manipulate a cutout display so that a tree would have "more" or "less" apples, young children *added* apples in both cases (135). This finding has been replicated in some studies (136, 137), but not in others (138). Actually, some children demonstrate this confusion in all studies while others do not.

Children's use of time concepts has also been investigated. As noted earlier, young children do not possess an elaborate system of spatial and temporal concepts. Their rudimentary grasp of temporal sequences is reflected in their language as well. They begin to understand the words "before" and "after" during the preschool years, although they usually grasp "before" somewhat earlier than "after." Again, as in the case of "more" and "less," some children cannot distinguish between these words and assume that they are synonymous (139, 140). It is interesting to note that children appear to understand "yesterday" better than they do "tomorrow" (141).

Children of 3 and 4 apparently do not have much difficulty with definite and indefinite articles. When tested with stories such as the one that follows, they generally used the correct definite and indefinite articles.

> *Once there was someone who wanted to have an animal. He went out to a pond. He saw bunches of animals, lots of frogs and lots of turtles (or two animals, a frog and a turtle). He went up with his box, and he put (one of) them into his box. What did he put into his box?*

With this story young children generally said "the frogs" or "the turtles" when the story was about "lots" of frogs and turtles and "a frog" or "a turtle" when the story was about individual animals (142).

Theories of Attainment
Various theories have been offered to explain the development of children's linguistic abilities. Each of them may contribute something to our understanding of language development, but none of them is comprehensive enough to cover all aspects of language growth.

One theory holds that language development reflects the *maturation* of language structures that are more or less innate and therefore are shared by all members of the human species (143, 144). According to this view, children are destined to talk and while the particular language will depend upon each child's culture, the underlying structure will be comparable in all cultures. In learning his or her own language the child would make use of a **language acquistion device** that includes not only the features that are common to all languages, but also a set of hypotheses or strategies that would enable him or her to learn those aspects that are unique to his or her own native language (143). In short, these researchers believe that children are born with certain linguistic competencies. Some cross-cultural data support this position by showing comparable patterns of language growth in children who are learning languages as different as English and Russian (145).

At the other extreme are those researchers who claim that language is acquired almost entirely by learning (146–148). From this viewpoint much of what a child learns about language comes from modeling what he or she hears from the reinforcement (or lack of it) from others. From this perspective verbal behavior is no different from other behavior and is learned in the same way. Some of the researchers who uphold this position have softened their stand somewhat but still insist that learning is important in language development. Evidence supporting this theory comes from studies such as those in which the frequency with which children ask questions is increased by the readiness of adults to answer them (149).

A third theory that has become prominent in the last decade emphasizes the activity of the child in learning language. Those who advocate this position look at the ways in which children actually learn words and grammar (133–135). One hypothesis that is currently held among this group of researchers is that language development, in its manner of construction, is similar to cognitive development. That is, the child learns words and grammatical constructions in order to express what he or she has learned from active exploration of the environment. For example, consider some of the cognitive attainments of the infant just before he or she develops language. As described in Chapter 3, the infant now knows that objects exist, that they disappear, and that they can reappear. These discoveries are among the first aspects of the child's experience to be coded linguistically. For example, children learn the names of things (the existence of objects), descriptions of change like ''all gone'' (their disappearance), and demands for replenishment—''more cookie'' (their reappearance)—which corresponds with his or her early cognitive attainments (134).

Data exist, therefore, to support all three theories of language development, and perhaps all three contain elements of truth. Some aspects of language may be more or less innate and others more or less entirely learned. Still other aspects of language may be constructed on the model presented by the child's own cognitive development. Language is such a multifaceted accomplishment that perhaps there can be no one, all-encompassing explanation of its attainment—at least at our present, limited state of knowledge.

**Referential
Communication
Skills**

Language is first and foremost a communication tool, and one important aspect of language development is the child's growing ability to use it to convey ideas. To communicate effectively, however, the child must, to some extent, take into account the listener's perspective. That is, in using speech to communicate, the child must also acquire skills which enable him or her to take the listener's point of view. These skills are called "referential communication skills."

One of the first investigators to pay attention to referential communication skills was Jean Piaget (150). In an early work he noted that young children often speak *at* rather than *to* one another; speech often appears to be simply that which accompanies action and not an effort at communication. Two 3-year-olds playing together might say:

TOM: My Mommy bought me these new shoes.
SUE: This dumb thing, why doesn't it work?

Young children often engage in parallel play, with each child totally involved with his or her activity. At such times children often talk at, rather than to one another.

Piaget called such language **egocentric speech** and observed that it comprised a substantial part of a young child's communication with peers but was not so predominant when he or she was talking to adults (150).

Piaget argued that the young child was egocentric in the sense that he or she could not take the position of another person when it differed from his or her own. Although Piaget arrived at his conclusion from naturalistic observations, other investigators have confirmed it by means of experimental referential communication tasks (for example, 151–153).

In one such task, preschool children were initially shown some unique geometric forms and asked to give them names. Young children did this easily, giving them such names as "kitty," "apple," and so forth. Furthermore, if the experimenter used one of these names to refer to a form, the child was able to select it from a group. That is, young children give idiosyncratic names to geometric forms, but the names are not idiosyncratic to the child who can use them to correctly identify the objects.

Children who were trained to give names to objects were individually paired with another child who sat facing him or her across a table. A small partition was placed in the middle of the table so that neither child could see the tabletop on the other side. Both children had a set of the same geometric forms in front of them. The child who had previously assigned names to the forms now had the task of telling the other child which form he or she had chosen. Children of 3 and 4 did not describe the form to the other child but merely used the idiosyncratic name; they could not appreciate the fact that the name meant nothing to the other child (142, 143). Children of 6 or 7, however, could describe the forms so that the other child would know which ones had been chosen (153).

Although 3- to 5-year-olds have difficulty communicating with others when the latter have a different viewpoint, they still have rudimentary referential communication skills. For example, 4-year-old children will simplify their language when they are speaking to 2-year-olds. But they will not do this when they speak to peers or adults (154). In some instances, then, young children can appreciate the differences between themselves and others in communicative ability even if not in their perspectives on the world.

While we do not completely understand how linguistic and communicative competencies are achieved, we can appreciate their scope and complexity, as well as the young child's notable accomplishment in attaining these symbolic skills.

THE CONCEPTUAL WORLD OF THE YOUNG CHILD

In reviewing the details of the intellectual accomplishments of the child of 3 to 5 years, it is easy to lose perspective and to view his or her world as an assortment of unrelated bits and pieces. In fact, it is not like that at all, and the young child's thought has its own system and organization. While it differs from that of adults, it is not totally unfamiliar to us because on occasion we all revert back to more subjective modes of thought; it is these modes that characterize the thinking of young children.

The broad outlines of young children's thinking were first presented systematically by Jean Piaget (155–157). But the same findings have also been replicated by others. It should be noted that because young children look at the world somewhat differently from adults, their behavior is sometimes misunderstood. For example, a young child's failure to share his or her toys reflects his or her belief that the toys are a part of himself or herself and that sharing is, in fact, giving away part of himself or herself. Understanding a young child's conceptual world, therefore, can help us evaluate his or her behavior more objectively.

One characteristic of young children's thinking is what Piaget calls **phenomenalistic causality**. In this mode of thinking the child assumes that there is a causal relationship between two things that happen simultaneously. For example, a child might be frightened by a strange noise and hold onto a warm blanket for comfort. Because the blanket is associated with a feeling of relief, the child believes that the blanket brought protection. The next time the child feels frightened he or she will again look for the blanket. Teddy bears and blankets tend to be dear to young children partly because of phenomenalistic causality.

Phenomenalistic causality is but one product of a kind of reasoning that characterizes young children and some adults as well; it is called **transductive reasoning** and can be described as follows:

A and B occur together
A is present
B must be present

Much "stubbornness" in the young child can be traced to transductive reasoning. A child who refuses to try a new food because he or she didn't like the last new food he or she tried is engaging in transductive reasoning: "New food and an unpleasant experience occurred together in the past. This is a new food, therefore it will produce an unpleasant experience."

In adults, transductive reasoning often leads to superstition. A salesman who happens to cross his fingers before successfully making a sale may feel that this will always work. And a student who happens to take a bath before an exam on which he or she does well may feel that he or she should bathe before every exam.

Another characteristic of young children's thinking is **animism**, the belief that the inanimate world is alive. This comes about because the child tends to model the physical world upon his or her own experience. Since he sometimes feels pain, hot, cold, and so forth, he or she assumes that stones, trees, and dolls also experience the same feelings. One aspect of animistic thinking is the belief that feelings are physical in the same sense that colors are physical. One of the authors had the following conversation with a young child:

A: Tom, why are you holding your cheek?

TOM: Because I have toothache.

A: Oh, does it hurt much?

TOM: Yes, can't you feel it?

Not surprisingly, in light of our earlier discussion of children's concepts of "more" and "less" and "before" and "after," young children believe that life and death are synonyms. For 3- and 4-year-olds, death is not the absence of life because life is a permanent property of things such as their hardness or color. Thus, they believe that death is like a physical disappearance, which is only temporary. Again it may help to clarify this mode of thinking with another conversation between one of us and a young child.

RICK: Why do they bury dead people in the ground?

A: I dunno, where do you think they should be buried?

RICK: In the garbage can.

A: Why in the garbage can?

RICK: Well, when they get out it will be easier and they won't be as dirty.

By middle childhood children begin to learn that death is the termination of life in the physiological sense. When this concept of death is attained, it is often a frightening experience.

A last characteristic of young children's thinking is **purposivism**. Since they believe that everything in the world was made by and for man, they believe that everything has a purpose. Children's famous "why" questions should be understood from that point of view. When a child asks why the sun shines or the grass is green, he or she really wants to know the purposes. Therefore, appropriate answers are "To keep us warm" and "To hide the green caterpillars so the birds won't eat them." Such answers are not entirely wrong, and they make sense to the child. On the other hand, by reciting lengthy facts about heat and light to explain why the sun shines would not help the child understand the real question he or she was asking.

The purpose of this brief description has been simply to underline the fact that the young child does have a full, conceptual world that is every bit as rich as, although different from, that of the adult. The young child's mind, then, is not an empty tablet to be filled in by experience. At each stage the child constructs his or her own conceptual world. Part of growing up is learning about the conceptual world of adults, and also the gradual giving up of the conceptual world of early childhood.

Essay

The age range from about 2 to 5, the preschool period, is one of very rapid intellectual growth. By the end of the period, in addition to mastering language, young children also have conceptualized the fundamental properties of the world (form, size, color, and so on) and have acquired rudimentary notions of time, space, and causality. Although there is general agreement among psychologists and educators regarding the intellectual achievements of young children, there is much less agreement about the sort of educational program most appropriate to this age level (158).

The range of opinions among professionals on this issue is very broad indeed. At one end of the spectrum are those who see the preschool years as the crucial ones for educational intervention (e.g., 159, 160). They argue that young children learn easily and are very motivated to learn. They claim further that if this period is not capitalized upon, a golden opportunity for raising children's IQ and eventual level of academic attainment will be lost. At the other end of the spectrum are those who see the preschool years as extraordinarily delicate ones for the formation of the concepts of self and personality. These investigators argue for the importance of interaction between child and mother (or careperson) and argue that educational intervention (particularly during the third year) could be damaging to the child if it interferes with the interpersonal relationship (e.g., 161–163).

Between these two extremes of formal education on the one hand and personality development on the other are a range of intermediate positions. The traditional nursery school, which stems from the educational work of Froebel, Pestalozzi, and Montessori, reflects a moderate approach. Children come to school for several mornings or afternoons a week and participate in a balanced program of play and educational activities. Such schools seek to further the child's intellectual as well as personality growth.

What type of program is best suited for young children? The answer is difficult not only because the findings in this field are not clear-cut, but also because children vary so much in background and personality. Programs that may be appropriate for one child may not be appropriate for another. In short, programs for young children are neither "good" nor "bad" in themselves, but rather appropriate or inappropriate for particular children. A very bright child, for example, might profit from a program that offered many educational opportunities. A shy child, by contrast, might benefit the most from a program that emphasized social interaction and personal growth.

Accordingly, it seems best to recognize that the preschool years are important for both intellectual and personality growth. Educational programs can facilitate this growth, but they will not accelerate it. Which program is best for a particular child can only be determined with respect to that child's special needs and abilities.

Biography

MARIA
MONTESSORI

Maria Montessori was born in Chiaravalle, near Ancona, Italy, in 1870. As in the case of many geniuses, there was evidence of her promise early in life. As a young adolescent she was interested in mathematics and thought about becoming an engineer. She even attended classes at a technical school for boys (in those days an unheard-of thing for a young woman to do). Later she became interested in biology and decided to study medicine. Against the advice of everyone, including her parents, she persisted. As the only woman at medical school, she experienced many discriminations and indignities. For example, since she was the only woman in her class, she was forced to do her dissections alone at night since it was not considered proper for males to be present at such a time. But she persisted and won the respect of faculty and students alike. When Montessori gave her first student lecture before the faculty, she did it with such poise and skill that she won an ovation.

At the age of 26, Montessori graduated from medical school with academic honors, to become the first woman medical doctor and surgeon in Italy. One of her first medical positions was in an insane asylum, where she found mental retardates confined with the mentally ill. She worked to get the retardates into a separate facility, of which she became the director. For 2 years she worked with these people, using the methods developed by Itard and Seguin. Montessori was extraordinarily successful, and many of her mentally retarded patients learned to read and to write and to become useful members of society.

Montessori was impressed by the progress made by the retardates but also by the fact that the level of literacy they had achieved was the same as or better than that of many poor children in Italy. What achievements could these children of average or above-average mental ability attain if they received the same schooling? Montessori was given the opportunity to find out when she was asked to design a facility for children in a housing settlement for working-class parents. In 1906 she established the first of her *casa di bambini* (children's houses) in the San Lorenzo district of Rome. There, utilizing the techniques she had developed with retardates, she devised a program of early-childhood education that was so successful that it is now used all over the world.

Basic to the Montessori method is the concept of a "prepared environment." Perhaps Montessori's greatest contribution was the wide array of self-teaching materials that constituted the prepared environment of the Montessori classroom. Montessori also introduced child-sized chairs and tables, as well as methods for teaching very young children to wash themselves, to button their clothes, tie their shoelaces, and so forth. The Montessori materials were child-centered in that they were adapted to the developmental level and capacities of the children. In that sense, Montessori's work is quite modern and in keeping with the contemporary emphasis on adapting curriculum materials to children's level of comprehension.

Summary

Physical growth slows down during the preschool years but children make remarkable gains in coordination; by the age of 5 they can climb, throw objects, and balance themselves with proficiency. Because of their new verbal abilities, children are now able to take standard intelligence tests such as the Stanford-Binet and Wechsler scales, which can predict later intelligence and academic achievement. In perception children make progress in the systematic exploration and organization of stimulus configurations. They are also able to transfer discriminations made in one sensory domain to another; this is called *cross-modal transfer*.

The young child's ability to remember also improves. He or she can remember pictorial material more easily than verbal material. Although preschool youngsters do not organize things to be remembered categorically, they do regulate their attention in trying to learn something. Young children's memory for certain configurations may simply improve with age and without any practice. They also make gains in discimination learning, particularly reversal-shift and transposition learning. Although young children find reversal shifts easier than extradimensional shifts, the opposite is true for older children. Likewise, young children can transpose size relationships across small dimensional differences but not across large ones.

With respect to conservation learning, it is not clear what young children are able to do and what concepts they have. Piaget and his followers claim that preschool youngsters cannot make *transitive inferences* and that they lack *conservation of number*. Other investigators suggest that these children can be trained to make transitive inferences and to conserve number. Some of the controversy arises from differences in definition and terminology. Although it is true that young children can be trained to make transitive inferences and number-conservation judgments, they do not seem to make such judgments spontaneously.

Language development is very rapid during the preschool years. Two-word utterances can demonstrate grammatical complexity; although they can be comprised of any combination of subject, verb, or object, subject-verb combinations are the most common. Three-word utterances are considerably more complex and also begin to reflect individual differences in mode of language acquisition. Certain words are learned more readily than others. "More" is learned before "less," and "before" is learned earlier than "after." Theories of language acquisition range from those that emphasize innate structures to those that stress learning. A middle position focuses on the child's own activities in the construction of language. Another aspect of language development is *referential communication skills*—one's ability to take the point of view of the listener. Young children have these skills only at a very rudimentary level.

The conceptual world of preschool youngsters is, in many ways, different from that of adults. Young children see the world according to phenomenalistic causality: they believe that there is a causal relationship between things that occur together. They also tend to view inanimate objects as alive. Finally, they assume that everything in the world is made *by* and for man—that everything has a purpose. Although adults have given up these modes of thought, they still revert to them occasionally during periods of emotional stress.

References

1. Stoudt, H. W., Damon, A., & McFarland, R. A. Heights and weights of young Americans. *Human Biology,* 1960, **32**, 331–341.
2. Baller, W. R. *Bed Wetting* New York: Pergamon, 1975.
3. Gesell, A., *et al. The first five years of life: A guide to the sudy of the preschool child.* New York: Harper, 1940.
4. Bayley, N. A. The development of motor abilities during the first three years. *Monographs of the Society for Research in Child Development,* 1935, **1**, 1–26.
5. Wellman, B. L. Motor achievements of preschool children. *Childhood Education,* 1937, **13**, 311–16.
6. Cratty, B. J., & Martin, M. M. *Perceptual motor efficiency in children.* Philadelphia: Lea & Febiger, 1969.
7. Keogh, J. F. *Motor performance of elementary school children.* Monograph, University of California, Los Angeles, Department of Physical Education, March 1965.
8. Cratty, B. J. *Perceptual and motor development in infants and children.* New York: Macmillan, 1970.
9. Lowenfeld, V., & Lambert, B. *Creative and mental growth.* New York: Macmillan, 1970.
10. Marsh, L. *Alongside the child.* New York: Harper, 1970.
11. Montessori, M. *Spontaneous activity in education.* New York: Schodan, 1965 (first English publication 1917).
12. Bruner, J. Organization of early skilled action. *Child Development,* 1973, **44**, 1–11.
13. Flershman, A. E. *The structure and measurement of physical fitness.* Englewood Cliffs, N.J.: Prentice-Hall, 1964.
14. Gardner, E. B. The neuromuscular base of human movement: Feedback mechanism. *Journal of Health, Physical Education and Recreation.* 1965, **36**, 61–62.
15. Hogan, J. C., & Hogan, R. Organization of early skilled action: Some comments. *Child Development,* 1975, **46**, 233–236.
16. Eckert, H. M. A developmental theory. In H. M. Eckert (Ed.), *Motor development symposium.* Berkeley: University of California, 1971.
17. Eckert, H. M., & Eichorn, D. H. Construct standards in skilled action. *Child Development,* 1974, **45**, 439–445.
18. Keogh, B. K. Pattern copying under three conditions of an expanded spatial field. *Developmental Psychology,* 1971, **4**, 25–31.
19. Goodson, B. D., & Greenfield, P. M. The search for structural principles in children's manipulative play: A parallel with linguistic development. *Child Development,* 1975, **46**, 734–746.
20. Terman, L. M., & Merrill, M. A. *Stanford-Binet intelligence scale.* Cambridge, Mass.: The Riverside Press, 1960.
21. Binet, A., & Simon, T. Le development de intelligence des enfants. *L'Annee psychologique,* 1908, **14**, 1–94.
22. Wechsler, D. *The measurement and appraisal of adult intelligence.* (4th ed.) Baltimore: Williams & Wilkins, 1958.
23. Wechsler, D. *Wechsler preschool and primary scale of intelligence.* New York: The Psychological Corporation, 1967.
24. Dunn, L. M. *Expanded manual for the Peabody picture vocabulary test.* Circle Pines, Minn.: American Guidance Service, 1965.

25. Zigler, E., & Butterfield, E. C. Motivational aspects of changes in IQ test performance of culturally deprived nursery school children. *Child Development*, 1968, **39**, 1–14.
26. DeVries, R. Relationships among Piagetian IQ and achievement assessments. *Child Development*, 1974, **45**, 746–756.
27. McClelland, D. C. Testing for competence rather than for "intelligence." *American Psychologist*, 1973, **28**, 1–14.
28. Elkind, D. Perceptual development in children. *American Scientist*, 1975, **63**, 533–541.
29. Maccoby, E. E. The development of stimulus selection. In Vol. 3. J. P. Hill (Ed.), *Minnesota Symposia on Child Psychology*. Minneapolis: University of Minnesota Press, 1969.
30. Piaget, J. *The mechanisms of perception*. London: Routledge & Kegan Paul, 1969.
31. Elkind, D., Koegler, R. R., & Go, E. Studies in perceptual development II: Part-whole perception. *Child Development*, 1964, **35**, 81–90.
32. Whiteside, J., Elkind, D., & Golbeck, S. Duration and part-whole perception in children. *Child Development*, 1976, **47**, 498–501.
33. Berlyne, D. Curiosity and exploration. *Science*, 1966, **153**, 25–33.
34. Haywood, H. C. Relationships among anxiety-seeking of novel stimuli and level of assimilated percepts. *Journal of Personality*, 1961, **29**, 105–114.
35. Hull, C. How children explore. *Science Journal*, 1970, **6**, 68–71.
36. Isett, R. Object Exploration: Effects of age exposure to complexity levels. Unpublished doctoral dissertation. George Peabody College, 1973.
37. Munsinger, H., & Kessen, W. Uncertainty structure and preference. *Psychological Monographs*, 1964, **78** (Whole No. 586).
38. Switzky, H. N., Haywood, H. C. & Isett, R. Exploration, curiosity and play in young children: Effects of stimulus complexity. *Developmental Psychology*, 1974, **10**, 321–329.
39. Rose, S. A., Blank, M. S., & Bridger, W. H. Intermodal and intramodal retention of visual and tactile information in young children. *Developmental Psychology*, 1972, **6**, 482–486.
40. Bryant, P. E., & Raz, I. Visual and tactual perception of shape in young children. *Developmental Psychology*, 1975, **4**, 525–526.
41. Gibson, L. J., Gibson, J., Pick, A. D., & Osser, H. A developmental study of the discrimination of letter-like forms. *Journal of Comparative and Physiological Psychology*, 1962, **55**, 897–906.
42. Birch, H. G., & Lefford, A. Visual differentiation, intersensory integration and voluntary motor control. *Monographs of the Society for Research in Child Development*, 1967, **32** (Serial No. 110).
43. Birch, H. G., & Belmont, L. Auditory visual integration, intelligence and reading ability in school children. *Perceptual and Motor Skills*, 1965, **20**, 295–305.
44. Goodnow, J. Auditory-visual matching: modality problem or translation problem *Child Development*, 1971, **42**, 1187–1202.
45. Stambak, M. Trois epreuves de rhythme. In R. Zazzo (Ed.), *Psychologie de l'enfant et methode genetique*, Neuchatel: Dalacaux & Niestle, 1962.
46. Solley, C. M., & Haigh, G. A note to Santa Claus. *TPR*, The Menninger Foundation, 1951, **18**, No. 3, 4–5.
47. Eriksen, B. A., & Eriksen, C. W. *Perception and personality*. Morristown, N.J.: General Learning, 1972.
48. Kendler, H. H., Kendler, T. S., & Marken, R. S., Developmental analysis of reversal and half reversal shifts. *Developmental Psychology*, 1969, **1**, 318–326.
49. Yussen, S. R., & Santwik, J. W. Comparison of the retention of preschool and second grade performers under three verbalization conditions. *Child Development*, 1974, **45**, 821–824.
50. Hagen, J. W., & Hale, S. A. The development of attention in children. In A. Pick (Ed.), *Minnesota Symposia on Child Psychology*. Minneapolis: University of Minnesota Press, 1973.
51. Brown, A. L., & Campione, J. C. Recognition memory for perceptually similar pictures in preschool children. *Journal of Experimental Psychology*, 1972, **95**, 55–62.
52. Corsini, D. A., Jacobus, K. A., & Leonard, S. D. Recognition memory of preschool children for pictures and words. *Psychonomic Science*, 1969, **16**, 192–193.
53. Jones, H. R. The issue of visual and verbal memory processes by three year old children. *Journal of Experimental Child Psychology*, 1973, **15**, 340–351.

54. Perlmutter, M., & Myers, N. A. Recognition memory development in two to four-year olds. *Developmental Psychology,* 1974, **10**, 447–450.
55. Perlmutter, M., & Myers, N. A. Young children's coding and storage of visual and verbal material. *Child Development,* 1975, **46**, 215–219.
56. Brown, A. L. Progressive elaboration and memory for order in children. *Journal of Experimental Child Psychology,* 1975,
57. Brown, A. L. The development of memory: Knowing knowing about knowing how to know. In H. W. Reese (Ed.), *Advances in child development and behavior.* Vol. 10. New York: Academic Press, 1975.
58. Brown, A. L. Recognition, reconstruction and recall of narrative sequences by preoperational children. *Child Development,* 1975, **46**, 156–166.
59. Christie, D. J., & Shumacher, G. Developmental trends in the abstraction and recall of relevant versus irrelevant thematic information from connected verbal materials. *Child Development,* 1975, **46**, 598–602.
60. Korman, T. A. Differences in verbal semantic memory of younger and older preschoolers VII, 1945, cited by Yendovitskayz, T. V., Development of Memory. In A. V. Zaporozhets & D. B. Elkonin (Eds.), *The psychology of preschool children.* Translated by J. Shybert and S. Simon, Cambridge, Mass.: M.I.T. Press, 1971.
61. Appel, L. F., Cooper, R. G., McCarrell, N., Sims-Knight, J., Yussen, S. R., & Flavell, J. H. The developing of the distinction between perceiving and memorizing. *Child Development,* 1972, **43**, 1365–1381.
62. Flavell, J. H., Frederichs, A. G., & Hoyt, J. D. Developmental changes in memorization processes. *Cognitive Psychology,* 1970, **1**, 324–340.
63. Kreutzer, M. A., Leonard, C., & Flavell, J. H. An interview study of children's knowledge about memory. *Monographs of the Society for Research in Child Development,* 1970, **40**, (1, Serial No. 159).
64. Neimark, E., Slotnick, N. S., & Ulrich, T. The development of memorization strategies. *Developmental Psychology,* 1971, **5**, 427–432.
65. Ryan, S. M., Hegron, A. G., & Flavell, J. H. Nonverbal mnemonic mediation in preschool children. *Child Development,* 1970, **41**, 539–550.
66. Tomlinson-Keasey, C., Crawford, D. G., & Miser, A. L. *Developmental Psychology,* 1975, **11**, 409–410.
67. Yussen, S. R. The distinction between perceiving and memorizing in the presence of category cues. *Child Development,* 1975, **46**, 763–768.
68. Wellman, A. M., Ritter, K., & Flavell, J. H. Deliberate memory behavior in the delayed reactions of very young children. *Developmental Psychology,* 1975, **11**, 780–787.
69. Piaget, J., & Inhelder, B. *Memory and intelligence.* London: Routledge & Kegan Paul, 1973 (First French edition, 1968).
70. Bartlett, F. *Remembering.* Cambridge: Cambridge University Press, 1932.
71. Freud, S. Screen memories. In *Collected papers,* Vol. 5. London: Hogarth, 1953.
72. Altmeyer, R., Fulton, D., & Berney, K. Long term memory improvement: Confirmation of a finding by Piaget. *Child Development,* 1969, **40**, 845–857.
73. Dablem, N. Reconstructive memory in children revisited. *Psychonomic Science,* 1969, **40**, 845–857.
74. Furth, H., Ross, B., & Youness, J. Operative understanding in children's immediate and long term reproductions of drawings. *Child Development,* 1974, **45**, 63–70.
75. Liben, L. Operative understanding of horizontality and its relation to long term memory. *Child Development,* 1974, **45**, 416–424.
76. Liben, L. Evidence for developmental difference in spontaneous seriation and its implications for past research in long-term memory improvement. *Child Development,* 1975, **11**, 121–125.
77. White, S. H. Evidence for a hierarchical arrangement of learning processes. In L. P. Lipsett, and C. C. Spiker (Eds.), *Advances in child behavior and development.* Vol. 2. New York: Academic Press, 1965.
78. Kendler, H. H., & Kendler, T. S. Discrimination and development. In W. K. Estes (Ed.), *Handbook of learning and cognitive processes.* New York: Halstead, 1975.
79. Brookshire, K. H., Warren, J. M., & Ball, G. G. Reversal and transfer learning following overtraining in rat and chicken. *Journal of Comparative and Physiological Psychology,* 1961, **54**, 98–102.

80. Campione, J. C. Optimal intradimensional and extradimensional shifts in children as a function of age. *Journal of Experimental Psychology,* 1970, **84,** 296–300.

81. Campione, J. C., Hyman, L., & Zeaman, D. Dimensional shifts and reversals in retardate discrimination learning. *Journal of Experimental Child Psychology,* 1965, **2,** 255–263.

82. Dickerson, D. J. Performance of preschool children on three discrimination shifts. *Psychonomic Science,* 1966, **4,** 417–418.

83. Johnson, P. J., & White, R. M., Jr. Concept of dimensionality and reversal shift performance in children. *Journal of Experimental Child Psychology,* 1967, **5,** 223–227.

84. Kendler, H. H., Glasman, L. D., & Ward, J. W. Verbal labeling and cue training in reversal shift behavior. *Journal of Experimental Child Psychology,* 1972, **13,** 195–209.

85. Kendler, H. H., & Kendler, T. S. Reversal shift behavior: some basic issues. *Psychological Bulletin,* 1969, **72,** 229–232.

86. Kendler, H. H., Kendler, T. S., & Ward, J. W. An ontogenetic analysis of optional intradimensional and extradimensional shifts. *Journal of Experimental Psychology,* 1972, **95,** 102–109.

87. Kendler, T. S. Verbalization and optional reversal shifts among kindergarten children. *Journal of Verbal Learning and Verbal Behavior,* 1964, **3,** 428–436.

88. Kendler, T. S. The effect of training and stimulus variables on the reversal-shift ontogeny. *Journal of Experimental Child Psychology,* 1974, **17,** 87–106.

89. Piaget, J. *The psychology of intelligence.* London: Routledge & Kegan Paul, 1950.

90. Flavell, J. H., Beach, D. R., & Chinsky, J. M. Spontaneous verbal rehearsal in a memory task as a function of age. *Child Development,* 1966, **37,** 283–299.

91. Reese, H. W. Verbal mediation as a function of age level. *Psychological Bulletin,* 1962, **59,** 502–509.

92. Alberts, E., & Ehrenfreund, D. Transposition in children as a function of age. *Journal of Experimental Psychology,* 1951, **51,** 30–38.

93. Kuenne, M. R. Experimental investigation of the relation of language to transposition behavior in young children. *Journal of Experimental Psychology,* 1946, **36,** 471–490.

94. Johnson, R. C., & Zara, R. C. Relational learning in young children. *Journal of Comparative Physiological Psychology,* 1960, **53,** 594–597.

95. Hunter, I. M. L. An experimental investigation of the absolute and relative theories of transposition behavior in children. *British Journal of Psychology,* 1952, **43,** 113–128.

96. Sherman, M., & Stunk, J. Transposition as a function of single versus double discrimination training. *Journal of Comparative and Physiological Psychology,* 1964, **58,** 449–450.

97. Marsh, J. G., & Jones, R. L. Verbal mediation of transposition as a function of age level. *Journal of Experimental Child Psychology,* 1966, **4,** 90, 98.

98. McKee, J. P., & Riley, D. A. Auditory transposition in six year old children. *Child Development,* 1962, **33,** 469–476.

99. Zeiler, M. D. Solution of the two stimulus transposition problem by four and five year old children. *Journal of Experimental Psychology,* 1966, **71,** 576–579.

100. Stevenson, H. L. Learning in children. In P. H. Mussen (Ed.), *Carmichael's manual of child psychology.* Vol. 1. New York: Wiley, 1970.

101. Piaget, J., & Szeminska, A., *The child's conception of number.* New York: Humanities Press, 1952.

102. Piaget, J., & Inhelder, B. *The child's conception of space.* London: Routledge & Kegan Paul, 1956.

103. Piaget, J. *The child's conception of time.* New York: Basic Books, 1970.

104. Piaget, J., & Inhelder, B. *Le developpement des quantities chez l'enfant.* Neuchâtel: Delachaux et Niestle, 1941.

105. Piaget, J. *The child's conception of movement and speed.* New York: Basic Books, 1969.

106. Piaget, J., Inhelder, B., & Szeminska, A. *The child's conception of geometry.* New York: Basic Books, 1960.

107. Bovet, M. Cognitive processes among illiterate children and adults. In J. W. Berry (Ed.), *Culture and cognition: Readings in cross cultural psychology.* London: Methuen, 1969.

108. Goodnow, J. Problems in research on culture and thought. In D. Elkind and J. H. Flavell (Eds.), *Studies in cognitive development.* New York: Oxford University Press, 1969.

109. Peluffo, N. Les notions de conservation et de causalité chez enfants provenant de differents milieux physiques et socioculturels. *Archives de Psychologie* (Geneve, 1962), **38**, 75–90.
110. Vernon, P. E. *Intelligence and cultural environment.* London: Methuen, 1969.
111. Achenbach, T. M., & Weisz, J. R. A longitudinal study of developmental synchrony between conceptual identity, seriation and transitivity of color, number and length. *Child Development,* 1975, **46**, 840–848.
112. Kendler, H. H., & Kendler, T. S. Inferential behavior in young children. In L. P. Lipsett and C. C. Spiker (Eds.), *Advances in child development and behavior.* Vol. III. 1967.
113. Smedslund, J. The development of concrete transitivity of length in children. *Child Development,* 1963, **34**, 389–405.
114. Brainerd, C. J. Training and transfer of transitivity, conservation and class inclusion of length. *Child Development,* 1974, **45**, 324–334.
115. Bryant, P., & Trabasso, T. Transient inferences and memory in young children. *Nature,* 1971, **232**, 456–458.
116. Bryant, P. *Perception and understanding in young children.* New York: Basic Books, 1974.
117. Harris, P., & Bassett, E. Transitive inferences in four year old children. *Developmental Psychology,* 1975, **11**, 6, 875–876.
118. deBorgson-Bardies, B., & O'Rogan, K. What children know in spite of what they do. *Nature,* 1973, **246**, 531–534.
119. Piaget, J., & Szeminska, A. *The child's conception of number.* New York: Norton, 1959.
120. Elkind, D. The development of quantitative thinking. *Journal of Genetic Psychology,* 1961, **98,** 37–46.
121. Wohlwill, J., & Lowe, R. C. Experimental analysis of the development of the conservation of number. *Child Development,* 1962, **33**, 153–167.
122. Mehler, J., & Bever, T. G. Cognitive capacity of very young children. *Science,* 1967, **158,** 141–142.
123. Beilin, H. Cognitive capacities of young children: A replication. *Science,* 1968, **162,** 920–921.
124. Calhoun, L. G. Number conservation in very young children: The effect of age and mode of responding. *Child Development,* 1971, **42**, 561–572.
125. Piaget, J. Quantification, conservation and nativism. *Science,* 1968, **162**, 976–979.
126. Rothenberg, B. B., & Courtney, R. G. Conservation of number in very young children: A replication and comparison with Mehler and Bever's study. *Journal of Psychology,* 1968, **70**, 205–212.
127. Lorenz, K. *King Solomon's ring.* New York: Crowell, 1952.
128. Brainerd, C., & Allen, T. Experimental inductions of the conservation of "first-order" quantitative invariants. *Psychological Bulletin,* 1971, **75**, 128–144.
129. Gelman, R. Conservation acquisition: A problem of learning to attend to relevant attributes. *Journal of Experimental Child Psychology,* 1967, **7**, 167–187.
130. Kuhn, D. Inducing development experimentally: Comments on a research paradigm. *Developmental Psychology,* 1974, **10**, 590–600.
131. Piaget, J., & Inhelder, B. *The early growth of logic in the child.* New York: Humanities Press, 1964.
132. Bloom, L. *Language development: Form and function in emerging grammars.* Cambridge, Mass.: M.I.T. Press, 1970.
133. Brown, R. *A first language.* Cambridge, Mass.: Harvard University Press, 1973.
134. Bloom, L., Lightbown, P., & Hood, L. Structure and variation in child language. *Monographs of the Society for Research in Child Development,* 1975, **40** (No. 160).
135. Donaldson, M., & Wales, R. On the acquisition of some relational terms. In J. Hayes (Ed.), *Cognition and the development of language.* New York: Wiley, 1970.
136. Palermo, D. S. More about less: A study of language comprehension. *Journal of Verbal Learning and Verbal Behavior,* 1973, **12**, 211–221.
137. Palermo, D. S. Still more about the comprehension of less. *Developmental Psychology,* 1974, **10**, 827–829.
138. Weiner, S. L. On the development of more and less. *Journal of Experimental Child Psychology.* 1974, **17,** 271–287.

139. Bever, T. The comprehension and memory of sentences with temporal relations. In G. B. Flores d'Arcais & W. J. M. Levelt (Eds.), *Advances in psycholinguistics*. New York: American Elservier, 1970.

140. Clark, E. On the acquisition of the meaning of before and after. *Journal of Verbal Learning and Verbal Behavior*, 1971, 266–275.

141. Harner, L. *Children's understanding of linguistic reference to past and future*. Unpublished doctoral dissertation. Columbia University, 1973.

142. Maratsos, M. P. *Preschool children's use of definite and indefinite articles*. Cambridge, England: Cambridge University Press, 1976.

143. Chomsky, N. *Aspects of a theory of syntax*. Cambridge, Mass.: M.I.T. Press, 1965.

144. McNeil, D. *The acquisition of language: the study of developmental psycholinguistics*. New York: Harper, 1970.

145. Slobin, D. I. *The acquisition of Russian as a native language*. Cambridge, Mass.: M.I.T. Press, 1966.

146. Braine, M. On learning the grammatical order of words. *Psychological Review*, 1963, **70**, 323–348.

147. Skinner, B. F. *Verbal behavior*. New York: Appleton-Century-Crofts, 1957.

148. Staats, A. Linguistic-mentalistic theory versus an explanatory S-R learning theory of language development. In D. I. Slobin (Ed.), *The ontogenesis of grammar*. New York: Academic Press, 1971.

149. Endsley, R. C., & Clarey, S. Answering young children's questions as a determinant of their subsequent question-asking behavior. *Developmental Psychology*, 1975, **11**, 363.

150. Piaget, J. *The language and thought of the child*. New York: Harcourt, 1926.

151. Flavell, J. H., Botkin, P. T., Fry, C. L., Wright, J. C., & Jarvis, P. E. *The development of role-taking skills in children*. New York: Wiley, 1968.

152. Glucksberg, S., Krause, R. M., & Weisberg, R. Referential communication in nursery school children. *Journal of Experimental Child Psychology*, 1966, **3**, 333–342.

153. Sussevein, B. J., & Smith, R. F. Perceptual discriminability and communication performance in preschool children. *Child Development*, 1975, **46**, 954–957.

154. Shantz, M., & Gelman, R. The development of communication skills: Modifications in the speech of young children as a function of listener. *Monographs of the Society for Research in Child Development*, 1973, **38**, (Serial No. 152).

155. Piaget, J. *The child's conception of the world*. New York: Harcourt, 1929.

156. Piaget, J. *Judgment and reasoning in the child*. New York: Harcourt, 1928.

157. Piaget, J. *The child's conception of physical causality*. New York: Harcourt, 1930.

158. Hess, R. D., & Bear, R. R. (Eds.) *Early education*. Chicago: Aldine, 1968.

159. Engelmann, S. The effectiveness of direct instruction in IQ performance and achievement in reading and arithmetic. In J. Hellmuth (Ed.), *Disadvantaged Child*. Vol. 3 New York: Bruner/Mazel, 1970.

160. Fowler, W. Cognitive learning in infancy and early childhood. *Psychological Bulletin*, 1962, **59**, 116–152.

161. Moore, R. S., & Moore, D. N. *Better late than early*. New York: Readers Digest Press, 1975.

162. Rohwer, W. D. Prime time for education: Early childhood or adolescence? *Harvard Educational Review*, 1971, **41**, 316–341.

163. White, B. L., et al. *Experiences and environment: Major influences on the development of the young child*. Englewood Cliffs, N.J.: Prentice Hall, 1973.

8 Personality and Social Development

SELF-AWARENESS AND SELF-ATTITUDES

Awareness of the Body

Feelings of Mastery

EXPANDING FAMILY AND SOCIAL RELATIONSHIPS

Role of the Father

Relationships with Siblings

Contacts with Peers

SOCIALIZATION

Discipline

Identification

ESSAY

The Impact of Television on Aggressive and Altruistic Behavior in Children

BIOGRAPHY

Erik Erikson

SUMMARY

REFERENCES

Between the ages of 2 and 5 the expressive behaviors acquired in infancy begin to crystallize into individual patterns, and children develop many distinctive attitudes, preferences, and ways of acting. First of all, pre-school children become increasingly aware of themselves as individuals and begin to form certain positive and negative attitudes toward themselves. Secondly, they come into contact with increasing numbers and types of people, with whom they experience many new kinds of social interactions. Finally, early childhood is a crucial period for various disciplinary and role-modeling activities by which parents socialize their youngsters and transmit their culture to them.

SELF-AWARENESS
AND
SELF-ATTITUDES

As one very important consequence of their physical and cognitive maturation, young children become increasingly aware of themselves and form new self-attitudes. In particular, they show a growing awareness of their body and the emergence of feelings of mastery.

Awareness of the
Body

During the first 2 years of life, infants gradually realize that they are distinct persons with a body that belongs to them. They learn that various limbs and organs are *theirs,* because they can control the movements of these limbs and organs, such as by raising their arm or closing their eyes, and also because they are affected by whatever happens to these limbs and organs, such as by feeling pain when their hand touches a hot stove. Preschoolers, having achieved this basic recognition of possessing a body, now become acutely aware of changes that occur in it and how it differs from others' bodies.

For example, children between the ages of 2 and 5 frequently express pride or concern about their size ("Look how big I'm getting"; "Will I be big as Mommy?"); they eagerly anticipate opportunities to be weighed or measured, whether at home or in the doctor's office; and they are fascinated with the course and outcome of bruises, scabs, mosquito bites, and other temporary conditions that affect the appearance of their bodies ("How come my fingers get wrinkled when I'm having a bath?").

Preschoolers also recognize physical differences between the sexes and begin to sense their identity as male or female. At 2½ most children are not positive about their sex, but by age 3, two-thirds of them know whether they are boys or girls. Games consisting of undressing or sexual exploration are common by age 4, and most 4- to 5-year-olds ask their parents questions about sexual matters. Boys may want to know why they can't have babies, and girls may ask if they will have penises when they grow up (1–4). In "Mister Rogers' Neighborhood," a popular television program for preschoolers, such concerns are deftly met with the following lines from a song:

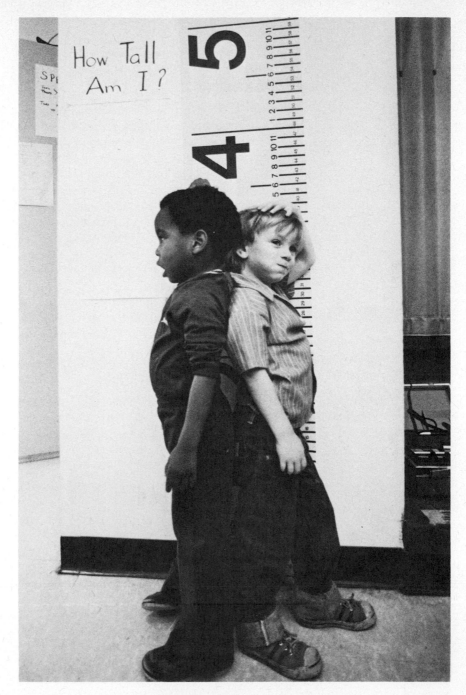

Children from 2 to 5 tend to be very interested in how their bodies are growing, especially with regard to how tall they are getting to be.

> Boys are fancy on the outside,
> Girls are fancy on the inside;
> Everybody's fancy, everybody's fine,
> Your body's fancy and so is mine.

Young children are also likely to voice special concerns about damage to their body or the loss of body parts. Youngsters who are not otherwise fearful or physically cautious may become very upset at losing a fingernail or chipping a tooth, and they often exaggerate the possible consequences of injury or rough treatment. A boy who is being spanked by his father may cry, "Stop it, you're killing me." Girls seem less inclined than boys to be concerned about loss of or injury to specific body parts. Psychoanalytic theorists feel that this apparent sex difference is due to boys' belief that girls have had their penises removed and that they, too, might suffer a similar fate. Psychoanalysts call this fear **castration anxiety** (5, 6).

How parents react to the increasing body awareness of their offspring is likely to affect the children's attitudes toward themselves. Parents who express pleasure at their children's growth help them feel proud and self-confident. Positive self-attitudes are also fostered when parents can respond to questions about sex without embarrassment and with information tailored to a child's level of understanding. On the other hand, parents who ignore or make light of children's normal interest in physical growth can make them feel foolish and unimportant, and parents who discourage sexual curiosity—or worse yet, punish their children for it—can foster negative self-attitudes, self-consciousness, and uneasiness with respect to sex.

Feelings of Mastery

Children's feelings of mastery begin to be shaped during infancy by the pleasure they get from becoming able to control their environment. For example, infants have been observed to coo, smile, and even laugh upon mastering such tasks as learning to operate a mobile (7, 8). Because the mastery of new skills provides pleasure, it tends to encourage further attempts at mastery, and in this sense it is a self-perpetuating activity.

In addition, there are several ways in which parents can foster their infants' attempts at mastery. Research studies show that even very young children are influenced to make more attempts at mastery if their parents encourage, help, and praise them in acting independently, as in feeding themselves (9–11).

Children do not become capable of feeling any lasting sense of accomplishment until the preschool years, however, when their cognitive maturation allows them to recognize the difference between past and present levels of skill. The ability to apply standards of excellence to their own behavior—that is, to realize that they are doing something well or better than before—results in children viewing some of their experiences as *achievements*. Achievement experiences in turn now begin to generate feelings of mastery that can have a lasting influence on an individual's sense of personal competence (12–14).

This aspect of personality development accelerates rapidly between the ages of 2 and 5. Children's increasing cognitive and motor skills during these years enable them to do much more for themselves than they could before, which enlarges their opportunities to experience mastery. Furthermore, their language skills enable children to gain a better idea than before of the impact they are capable of having on their environment. Parents too play an important role in helping preschoolers develop strong feelings of mastery. The nature of this parental influence has been identified in research on achievement motivation, instrumental competence, and self-esteem.

Achievement motivation refers to the inclination to strive for success and the capacity to experience pleasure in being successful. Research on the origins of the motivation to achieve, which was stimulated by the contributions of David McClelland (15) and John Atkinson (16), has yielded two definite findings. First, high achievement motivation is fostered during the preschool years by strong parental encouragement of achievement accompanied by moderate demands for independence and a warm, supportive parent-child relationship. In other words, the more preschoolers are urged and helped to do as much as they can on their own, without being expected to do more than they are capable of, the more likely they are to become self-confident individuals who respond eagerly to the challenge of new experiences. Second, the development of achievement motivation is directly related to the amount of specific training in achievement activities that parents provide their children during the preschool years (17–21).

Instrumental competence has been defined in a series of studies by Diana Baumrind as behavior that is socially responsible and independent (22–24). In studying preschool children and their parents, Baumrind found that the children who were most reliant, self-controlled, explorative, and contented had parents who were socially responsible, self-assertive, and self-confident and who exercised *authoritative* control; that is, they set and enforced specific limits on their children's behavior but were also warm and nonrejecting—they were willing to explain and reconsider their rules for behavior, and they encouraged their children to take on challenges.

Children who were relatively discontent, withdrawn, and distrustful, Baumrind found, had parents who were detached and *authoritarian*. These parents were highly controlling, restrictive, and protective. They left little room for discussion or variation, and they denied their children opportunities to take risks, to try new things, and to make decisions. A third group of children, who were the least self-reliant, explorative, and

Table 8.1   Relations between Patterns of Parental Authority and Preschoolers'
Levels of Instrumental Competence

Parental Pattern of Authority	Level of Children's Instrumental Competence
Authoritative: firm but warm and nonrejecting; willing to explain and reconsider rules	Most competent; self-reliant, self-controlled, explorative, and content
Authoritarian: detached, highly controlling, restrictive, and overprotective; unwilling to discuss or reconsider rules	Less competent; relatively discontent, withdrawn, and distrustful
Permissive: noncontrolling and nondemanding; no firm rules established	Least competent; relatively dependent, aimless, and irresponsible

Source: Based on Baumrind, D. Current patterns of parental authority. Developmental Psychology Monographs, 1971, 4, Part 2, 1–103.

self-controlled, had warm but *permissive* parents. By adopting a noncontrolling and nondemanding stance, these parents failed to set any definite standards against which their children could judge the adequacy of their behavior, and they also failed to encourage their children to accept any challenges (see Table 8.1). These and other findings on instrumental competence parallel what has been learned about the origins of achievement motivation: namely, parents who consistently urge their children to accomplish as much as they can, while supporting their efforts with praise and encouragement, produce high levels of instrumental competence (25).

Self-esteem is the value people place on themselves and the extent to which they anticipate success in what they do. The most thorough study of factors leading to self-esteem has been reported by Coopersmith, whose results are consistent with those on achievement motivation and instrumental competence. Parents whose children are high in self-esteem tend to be warmly accepting people who establish clearly defined limits for their children's behavior but allow them some latitude within these limits. As did Baumrind, Coopersmith found a significant modeling effect: namely, that the parents of children with high self-esteem tend to be active, poised, and relatively self-assured themselves (26).

It may seem surprising that so far in our discussion of feelings of mastery we have not made a distinction between boys and girls. There are some widely cited research findings that seem to identify sex differences in achievement-related behavior, with boys being motivated to achieve primarily by mastery strivings and girls being motivated mainly by the need for social approval (27–29). This apparent difference has been attributed to certain sex-role stereotypes in our society: namely, that boys

Mastery of new skills and the pleasure of achievement become important parts of children's lives during the preschool years.

should be aggressive, independent, and competitive, whereas girls should be passive, dependent, and cooperative. Because of these stereotypes, it is said, little girls are overprotected and are not encouraged to master difficult tasks, so that they often grow up to be less self-confident, less industrious, and less successful in task-oriented activities than boys of equal ability (29–31).

In opposition to such beliefs, Maccoby and Jacklin have concluded from a comprehensive review of the available data that boys and girls do *not* differ in their striving for achievement, and that boys in our society are *not* receiving more encouragement toward mastery than girls (32). Unfortunately, not all of the research on which Maccoby and Jacklin base their conclusions has been well done. In some cases investigators have relied on measures that were too crude to detect sex differences even if they were present. In other cases only preschool children have been studied, which fails to make allowance for the fact that actual sex differences may not become clear-cut until middle childhood or adolescence (33). Hence the most that can be said currently about sex differences in feelings of mastery is (a) that prominent authorities can be quoted to support the position either that they do or do not exist, and (b) that additional, more carefully designed studies are necessary before firm conclusions can be drawn one way or the other.

The formulations of Erik Erikson may be useful to mention again at this point. In Chapter 4 we noted Erikson's view that what infants experience in their relationship with their parents influences whether they develop basic feelings of trust or mistrust in their world and in their future. With respect to early childhood, Erikson suggests that the aspects of parent-child interaction we have been discussing here determine whether **autonomy** or **shame and doubt** will emerge as persistent personality traits. If parents can recognize and encourage preschool children's pride in their accomplishments and their wish to do as much for themselves as possible, the children develop a sense of autonomy, a feeling that they can control themselves and their environment. But if parents prevent their children from doing certain reasonable things on their own or if they demand more of their children than they are capable of, the youngsters are likely to experience shame about their capacities and doubt about their ability to influence their own destiny (34).

EXPANDING
FAMILY AND
SOCIAL
RELATIONSHIPS

In the United States there used to be rather sharp distinctions between maternal and paternal roles in child rearing. Mothers remained at home to care for the children, while fathers worked outside the home to support the family. A mother was not expected to be a wage-earner unless the family was financially hard-pressed or the father was disabled or unemployed; a father was not supposed to change diapers, feed the baby at night, or take care of the routine needs of the children unless his wife was

ill or away. Such mutually exclusive role definitions are disappearing
now. Increasing numbers of women work outside the home to find self-
fulfillment in utilizing their talents, as well as to earn money, and in most
families child care is viewed as a responsibility to be shared by both
parents (35).

Nevertheless, in the typical family children form their first attachments
to their mother, and she generally remains the most important person in
their life during the preschool years. Many women postpone looking for
full-time jobs until their children have reached school age, or they may
interrupt their careers, at least in part, while their children are young.
Hence, as infants, children usually spend much more time with their
mother than with anyone else, and her behavior is the most important
environmental influence on their personality and social development.
During the preschool years, however, mothers begin increasingly to share
this influence with the child's father, siblings, and peers.

Role of the Father

As we noted in Chapter 4, fathers may take on many responsibilities for
infant care, especially if their children are bottle-fed, and infants often
form early attachments to their fathers as well as to their mothers (36–40).
But it is during the preschool years that most men really emerge as active
participants in their children's lives. Whereas infants may be napping
when their father leaves for work in the morning and asleep for the night
when he returns, preschool children are awake much of the time when
their father is home. Because of their maturation, preschoolers have more
opportunities to interact with their father, such as sitting with the family at
mealtimes, playing various kinds of games, and engaging in conversation.
Preschoolers are also likely to be interested in trips and other opportunities their fathers may provide, such as piggyback rides, trips to the zoo or
a circus, or the repairing of a broken toy.

The interest of preschool children in their fathers has been demonstrated in a simple but meaningful study by Lynn and Cross (41). They
asked a large number of 2-to-4-year-old children which of their parents

Figure 8.1 Preschool
children's preference for
playing with their mothers
or fathers. (*Source.* Based
on data reported by Lynn,
D. B. & Cross, A. DeP.
Parent preferences of
preschool children.
*Journal of Marriage and
the Family,* 1974, **36,**
555–559.)

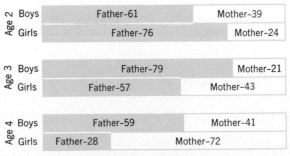

Figures in percentages

(sitting in the next room) they wanted to have play with them in several different kinds of games. The boys at all three ages (2, 3, and 4) gave a clear preference for playing with their fathers. Among the girls, the fathers were also strongly preferred by the 2-year-olds. However, at age 3 the girls showed a diminishing preference for playing with their fathers, and at age 4 they clearly preferred their mothers. It seems likely that this trend among the girls reflects the tendency of children to begin identifying with their same-sexed parent as they approach middle childhood, which is a topic we will consider later in the chapter.

Preschool children's increased interaction with their fathers is generally believed to help them recognize that they have two distinct parents to take care of them, rather than just one. Whereas formerly they sought only their mother's attention, now they seek attention from both parents; they also begin to direct some kinds of concerns mainly toward their mother and others mainly toward their father. For example, a boy may ask his father for candy because he has learned that his father is likely to give him some but that his mother will probably say ''no'' because she is concerned about his teeth. Similarly, a girl who has accidentally broken a dish may confess to her mother because she knows she will be sympathetic, rather than to her father, whom she expects to scold her for being careless.

Preschool children's ability to perceive differences in their parents' attitudes and personality style sometimes leads them to try to play off one parent against the other. Children at this age may become skillful at belittling the judgment of one parent in light of what the other may have said (''*Mommy* lets me do it''); at rejecting one parent's authority in favor of what the other may have decreed (''I don't have to do what you say, 'cause *Daddy* says I can do what I want''); and at expressing favoritism in an outright effort to manipulate the behavior of one parent or the other (''You're too mean; I want *Mommy* to do it for me''; ''Mommy, why don't you go to work so *Daddy* can stay home and take care of us?'').

It is usually better for children if their parents can resist being played off against each other. Although there is no one best way to rear all children, parents should try to agree on and stick to the ways they intend to use. A united parental front helps children develop internalized standards of conduct, for reasons we will explain in our discussion of discipline; in addition, parental firmness prevents children from thinking they can always get their own way simply by demanding it.

Extensive research by Henry Biller and others indicates that fathers play a particularly important role in child development during the preschool years. Compared to children who are reared only by their mothers, preschoolers who also have attentive fathers tend to have a more positive self-concept, to feel better about being a boy or girl, to get along better with other children and adults, and to function more effectively in achievement-related situations (42–46).

Children whose fathers are absent or neglectful are especially susceptible to uncertainty or conflicts about their sex role. For example, some
preschool boys without fathers are reported to act in a "feminine" way
(being dependent and nonassertive) and then, in middle childhood, to
become "hypermasculine" (being overaggressive, bullying smaller children, and avoiding activities that could be considered "girlish" or
"sissy"), as if to cover up or compensate for an underlying sense of
inadequate masculinity (47–50).

Attentive fathers also contribute to their daughters' feeling comfortable
in their sex role. By showing pleasure at having a daughter and by treating
their daughters as they feel girls should be treated, fathers help them
develop a positive feminine self-concept. Preschool girls who are deprived of a close relationship with their fathers often fail to develop a clear
sense of what it means to be a female. Although this failure may pass
unnoticed during childhood, these girls are often found as adolescents to
have difficulties relating to boys because they feel uncertain and insecure
in a feminine role (51–53).

Needless to say, the adequacy of paternal care children receive cannot
be measured simply by the amount of time their fathers spend at home.
Detached or disinterested fathers are unlikely to provide adequate care,
even if they are constantly around the house. On the other hand, fathers
whose work prevents them from spending much time with their families
may be excellent parents because they share a close, positive relationship
with their children when they are with them.

As we have already stressed in Chapter 4, it is the quality and not the
quantity of care children receive that holds the key to their positive personality and social development. Unfortunately, many studies of father
absence have not taken this fact into account. Although research findings
generally support what we have said about the possible consequences of
inadequate fathering, many inconsistent data appear in numerous studies
in which it was mistakenly assumed that the amount of good paternal care
children receive is directly related to how much time their fathers spend at
home (38, 43, 54).

Moreover, the extent to which children suffer ill effects from their
fathers' being away varies with the circumstances. For one thing, father
absence appears to have less of an impact on a child's development if it
begins in middle childhood or adolescence, rather than the preschool
years. Second, the evidence suggests that preschoolers can adjust more
easily to their fathers' being away for unavoidable reasons, such as death,
hospitalization, or extended business trips, than because of desertion,
separation, or divorce. Third, if parents have (or had) a good marital
relationship, so that the mother speaks well of the father when he is away,
and if the mother-child relationship is warm and supportive, so that she
encourages and reinforces her child's appropriate sex-role behavior, there
may be relatively few negative results from the father's absence. And

finally, preschool children may be able to avoid entirely the problems of not having a father if there are other males available to assume the father's role with them, such as a stepfather, uncle, or much older brother (42, 45, 49, 54, 55).

Relationships with Siblings

During the preschool years important relationships with siblings usually begin. Most firstborn children experience the arrival of baby brothers and sisters, and later-born children become involved in new kinds of interactions with their older siblings. These sibling relationships normally include some feelings of jealousy and rivalry, which are dramatized in many works of literature. In the Bible Cain slays his brother Abel, Jacob plots to steal Esau's birthright, and Jacob's favorite son Joseph is sold into slavery by his resentful brothers; in Greek mythology the sons of Oedipus kill each other off in their competition to become King of Thebes; and in a fairy tale the sisters of Cinderella, jealous of her beauty, force her into the role of a servant. Although sibling relationships rarely lead to such extreme results in the real world, they often challenge a preschool child's sense of well-being and require sensitive parental handling.

Arrival of a New Baby. A new brother or sister is almost always a disturbing event in the life of a preschool child, especially for firstborns who had been enjoying an exclusive claim on their parents' attention. Numerous observations indicate that the new arrival is likely to be viewed as an intruder and troublemaker (56). Preschoolers tend to communicate their unhappiness about a new brother or sister indirectly, as by making "innocent" remarks that suggest eliminating the new arrival from the family ("When are we going to give the baby back to the hospital?"). In other instances they may regress in some of their learned skills, such as by asking for the bottle again after having given it up or by losing bowel control after toilet training has been well established. These regressions usually reflect a temporary longing to be considered a baby again and to receive the total care their new sibling is getting.

However, family studies also identify many ways in which parents can help preschoolers avoid or overcome negative reactions to a new baby. It is especially helpful if parents include their preschool children in making preparations for the baby's arrival and permit them to help in caring for it, such as by holding the bottle during a feeding. Many preschoolers also need to be reassured that their toys or other favorite possessions will not be taken away and given to the baby. These and similar actions bolster the preschoolers' sense of being important and having a rightful place in the family, which makes it easier for them to adjust to sharing attention with the newcomer (56).

Interactions with Older Siblings. The relationship of preschool children to older brothers and sisters commonly alternates between compan-

Preschoolers often envy and try to compete with their older brothers and sisters, but they also enjoy opportunities to learn from them.

ionship and rivalry. Younger children learn to respect the older ones, to enjoy being with them, and to turn to them for help and protection. But they also resent their privileges (''Why do I have to go to bed when she doesn't?''), and they compete with them for attention and approval (''Look what *I* can do''). Thus, preschoolers may be very pleased when their older siblings agree to play with them or teach them something, but they may also welcome opportunities to inform their parents of an older child's misbehavior. Preschoolers' fondness for tattling, which often annoys parents as much as it does an older child being tattled on (''Why are you such a little snitch?''), can be understood as an attempt to increase their share of their parents' affection by pointing out the unworthiness of an older sibling.

Parents can usually help siblings get along well together by establishing age-appropriate responsibilities and privileges for each of their children. Preschoolers can then recognize that what they are allowed or expected to do now and in the future depends only on how old and how capable they are, and not on their having to compete with their brothers and sisters. If parents do not treat their children as individuals, but instead try to prevent rivalry by treating them all alike, they often make matters worse rather than better. Older children who are restricted to privileges appropriate to a younger sibling are likely to feel babied and to lose confidence in their abilities; younger children who are given the same responsibilities as older ones may become frustrated, because they cannot meet their parents' unrealistic expectations, or they may develop an exaggerated sense of what they are capable of.

Contacts with Peers During the preschool years children establish their first important contacts with their peers. Now that they are physically agile, eager to explore the world outside their home, and less in need of constant supervision, they enter into the bustling world of childhood play. Infants who play in groups largely tend to ignore each other, except for occasionally exchanging toys in an impersonal manner. Often they pay more attention to adults who are present than to their playthings. By the age of 2, however, children in play groups are spending more time with their playmates and playthings than with adults, and they are also beginning to play together rather than side by side—including arguing over possession of a toy instead of just crying about not having it.

Eckerman and her colleagues used an experimental play situation to map this development of social play during the second year of life (57). Children at three different ages (10 to 12 months, 16 to 18 months, and 22 to 24 months) were placed with their mothers in a playroom, together with another child of the same age and the other child's mother. The experimenters then observed for 20 minutes how much the children played alone, how much with each other, how much with their own mother, and

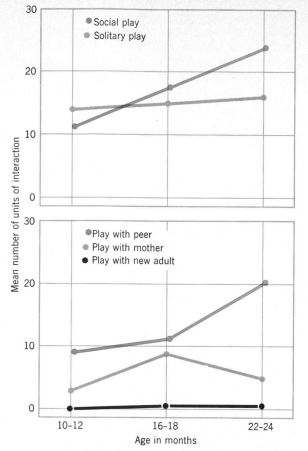

Figure 8.2 The growth of social play in the second year of life; by age 2 most children have become much more interested in playing with their peers than in playing alone or with their mothers. (*Source.* Eckerman, C. O. *et al.* The growth of social play with peers during the second year of life. *Developmental Psychology,* 1975, **11,** 42–49.)

how much with the other child's mother. As summarized in Figure 8.2, the results demonstrated the appearance of social play by age 2 and the growing interest of children in playing with each other rather than their mothers.

Other research indicates that, once social play begins, children spend increasing amounts of time with each other and start to play in groups of three or more as well as in pairs. By the time preschoolers reach the age of 4 or 5, moreover, they are turning increasingly to their peers rather than to adults for attention and praise. Whereas earlier they depended solely on their parents for rewards, they now begin to reward each other with signs of acceptance, approval, and affection (58–60).

This widening interaction with their age-mates enables preschool children to become increasingly aware that they differ from each other. They see that some children are bigger than themselves and that some are smaller; some are obviously stronger or braver or wilder, and others are not; some have brown skin, some yellow, some white, and so forth.

Preschoolers also gradually discover that children come from a variety of family situations that may differ from their own. Some have siblings, some do not; some have young parents, some have old parents, some have one parent missing; other children have different mealtimes, different toys, and different parental rules and regulations for their behavior. This growing social participation with peers is thus a tremendously broadening experience, and most preschool children begin to besiege their parents with seemingly endless questions about how and why life is different in other families ("How come I don't have any brothers or sisters?"; "Why can't I have a big dollhouse like Mary has?"; "Why doesn't Johnny have any daddy—will our daddy go away too?").

Preschool children additionally begin to recognize differences among themselves in their native talents and personality traits. They learn that some children are more advanced than others in their language and motor skills; some are quicker than others to grasp and remember new ideas; some are more aggressive, selfish, considerate, or timid than others, and so forth. They see the emergence of those who are the leaders and those who are followers, of those who are shy and those who are self-confident, of the bullies and the cowards, of the crybabies and the daredevils, and of a host of other distinctive behavior patterns, each reflecting basic attitudes young people are forming toward themselves and their world.

As one result of preschoolers showing distinctive personality characteristics, some of them become more popular with their peers than others. Research studies identify clearly the characteristics associated with popularity: nursery-school boys and girls who are most liked by their peers are those who are perceived as being friendly and cooperative, who frequently provide the kinds of attention and approval young children crave from each other, and who adapt well to the group situation. On the other hand, children tend to be disliked if they are socially withdrawn or hostile; if they ignore or make fun of others' efforts to win praise; or if they are cantankerous, unruly, and disruptive in the group (60–62). In middle childhood and adolescence the very same characteristics lead to being liked—friendliness, sociability, helpfulness, cooperativeness, adaptability, and conformity to group norms (60).

Play is especially important for social and personality development during the preschool years. Through the use of toys and games youngsters learn about each other as people and about how to handle interpersonal relationships. Children who do not have opportunities to play with agemates miss out on a vital social learning experience; as a result they may be slower than other children to become confident and sure of themselves in relating to people outside their family. As a case in point, Halverson and Waldrop found a significant relationship between the amount of social participation shown by boys and girls at age 2½ and the extent of their peer interaction at age 7½ (63).

In addition to this general carryover of social participation from the preschool years to middle childhood, preschoolers can also benefit from experiencing peer-group interactions away from home and from their parents' supervision. Whether in a nursery school or some similar situation, being away from home for brief periods to meet and play with new companions is good preparation for the school years to come. Children who have rarely been away from their parents' side may find the transition to kindergarten and the first grade a source of considerable anxiety. We will consider some specific effects of fears about going to school or socializing with peers in Chapter 14.

SOCIALIZATION

Socialization is the process through which children acquire the social judgment and self-control necessary for them to become responsible adult members of their society. Children are not born with a concept of right and wrong or with an understanding of what behavior is permissible and what is frowned upon. The cognitive maturation that takes place during the preschool years and middle childhood gradually increases children's capacity to make social judgments and to control their behavior in light of these judgments. However, the *content* of socialization—that is, the specific notions children form of proper and improper behavior—is determined not by maturation but by what children experience. Most of all, social judgment and self-control are shaped by how parents discipline their children and by the examples they set in their own behavior. In this way parents transmit to their children the sociocultural attitudes, traditions, and values to which they subscribe. These include standards of morality common to their society as well as subcultural values related to the parents' race, religion, ethnic origin, social class, and political leanings.

Children respond to their parents' influence by forming two complementary sets of internalized standards. First, as they incorporate prohibitions and taboos imposed by their parents (''You're not supposed to take things that belong to other people''), they begin to develop **conscience**, an inner voice that continues to say ''no'' even in their parents' absence. Second, as they incorporate the positive goals and values endorsed by their parents (''You were a good boy to pick up your toys''), they begin to develop an **ego-ideal**, which is an inner sense of aspiration and of what they ought to do. The emergence of conscience subjects children to feelings of guilt for behaving in ways they should not; their developing ego-ideal causes feelings of shame when they fall short of doing what they think they should (64).

Socialization proceeds most effectively when parents (a) discipline their children in ways that will help them form an adequate but not overly strict conscience, and (b) serve as models of social judgment and self-control with whom their children can identify. Discipline and identification can thus be considered the two key factors in socialization.

Discipline   It has been widely demonstrated that discipline, whether in the form of
rewards or punishments, helps children modify their behavior and learn
self-control. In one common way of studying discipline in the laboratory,
children are given the opportunity to reach for either an attractive or an
unattractive toy. When they reach for the unattractive toy they are given
praise ("Good!") and a piece of candy; when they reach for the attractive
toy they receive no reward. Later, when they are left alone with the toys,
children who have gone through this experimental procedure tend to deny
themselves the attractive toy and reach for the unattractive one
(65, p. 130).

Similar results are found if children in this kind of situation are punished
with a reprimand whenever they reach for the attractive toy ("No, that's
not for you"). That is, children left alone with attractive toys tend to resist
touching them if they have previously been scolded for doing so (66).
Interestingly, the effects of both reward and punishment in these studies
are greater if they occur while the children are reaching for the toys rather
than after they have already begun playing with them. This would seem to
imply that discipline will be more effective during the early phase of some
behavior than after the behavior has already been going on for a while.

Once we leave the laboratory, however, it is difficult to make generalizations about the effects of discipline on children's behavior. In addition to the timing of discipline and whether it takes the form of rewards or
punishments, many other factors influence the impact it has, including
who administers it, how appropriate it is to the particular situation, and
how sensitive an individual child is to being praised or rebuked. For this
reason, most reviews of the research on discipline advise a cautious interpretation of the findings (19, 67, 68). On the other hand, it has been
fairly clearly demonstrated that children benefit most from discipline that
is (a) administered consistently, (b) instructive rather than merely punitive, and (c) directed at their behavior and not at themselves as persons.

Consistent Discipline. From experimental studies of learning we know
that behavior that is rewarded sometimes but not always (**partial reinforcement**) becomes more firmly entrenched and resistant to change than
behavior that is always rewarded. Likewise, it has been found that consistent punishment of such behavior as aggression will reduce it more
effectively than punishing it sometimes and ignoring it the rest of the time,
apparently because allowing certain behavior from time to time acts as an
implicit partial reinforcement.

Deur and Parke demonstrated this partial reinforcement effect in a
study in which children punched a large Bobo doll under three different
training conditions (69). One group received a continuous reward of mar-
bles for punching the doll; a second group received the reward half of the
time and no reward the other half of the time; and a third group was
rewarded half of the time but punished the other half of the time with a
loud buzzing sound, which they were told indicated they were playing the

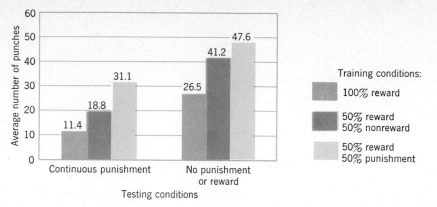

Figure 8.3 Persistence of aggressive behavior (punching a Bobo doll) under conditions of continuous punishment or ignoring (neither punishment nor reward) following training sessions involving inconsistent rewards and punishments. (*Source*. Based on data reported by Deur, L. & Parke, R. D. The effects of inconsistent punishment on aggression in children. *Developmental Psychology*, 1970, **2**, 403–411.)

game "badly." In a subsequent testing session, it was observed how long the children in each of these groups would continue to punch the doll when they received either no reward or continuous punishment.

The results shown in Figure 8.3 indicate that, regardless of whether aggressive behavior was being ignored or consistently punished, the children who had previously received 50 percent rewards and 50 percent punishment for punching the doll continued to punch it longer than the other two groups. In fact, children with the previous experience of mixed punishment and reward subsequently punched the doll longer in the face of continuous punishment (an average of 31.1 times) than children with a previous 100 percent reward whose punches were subsequently being ignored (an average of 26.5 times).

What this suggests is that parents can help their children learn good judgment and self-control by agreeing on standards of conduct and regularly enforcing these standards. If, on the other hand, parents disagree about how their children should behave or punish certain acts sometimes but not always, children may persist in such unsocialized behavior as aggressive, inconsiderate, impulsive, and irresponsible actions toward others.

The ways in which inconsistent discipline leads to inadequate socialization are not fully understood. One reasonable hypothesis is that children who are faced with inconsistent discipline tend to conclude that their parents are unreliable people who do not say what they mean or mean what they say, and that whatever rewards and punishments they receive are due not to their behavior but to unpredictable circumstances over which they have no control. Children with this view of the world have difficulty establishing what Rotter has called an **internal locus of control**; instead, they behave primarily according to how they see external events (70–73).

People who have an **external locus of control** usually fail to develop an adequate conscience. They see their destiny as being in the hands of fate or of those who wield power, and their morality generally consists of doing whatever they believe they can get away with. Their main reason for deciding not to act in an illegal or immoral fashion is usually fear of being caught and punished. By contrast, people with internalized standards of morality believe they have some control over their destiny, and their decisions about how to act stem from their own sense of right and wrong rather than from fear of external consequences.

Studies with children indicate that those who are developing an internalized sense of morality are more likely to feel guilty when their behavior is harmful to others than children whose actions are governed primarily by external controls. They are also more likely to accept blame when they are at fault, to confess misdeeds that have gone undetected, and to resist encouragement by others to commit immoral or inconsiderate acts (74). Hence, children who are being helped by consistent parental discipline to develop an internal locus of control are being helped to mature into responsible adults.

Instructive Discipline. Discipline is instructive when it is administered in a reasonably calm manner, when it is based on a specific misdeed, and when it is appropriate for the act. By contrast, angry scoldings and spankings that are not related to the deed or are too severe for the offense are simply punitive.

When parents are excessively or indiscriminately punitive, children are found to respond in one of two ways, depending on their personality. Preschoolers who are passive or timid and perhaps physically frail are often cowed by severe punishment into becoming overly compliant and fearful of asserting themselves. On the other hand, young children who are energetic, self-confident, and physically robust are likely to respond to parental browbeating by becoming hostile, aggressive, and short-tempered—in other words, they are likely to model themselves after the way their parents are treating them (75–77).

Modeling is one aspect of identification, and it accounts for the fact that parents whose discipline is based on a "do what I say" approach may be surprised at the results they get. Children do what their parents *do* as well as what they *say,* and parents who rely on punitive discipline are likely to experience precisely the opposite outcome of the one they were seeking.

The differences between instructive and punitive discipline have been elaborated by Martin Hoffman (74, 78). He describes two kinds of punitive discipline: *power assertion,* which includes actual or threatened physical punishment or deprivation of material objects or privileges; and *love withdrawal,* in which parents express anger or disapproval by ignoring their children, refusing to speak or listen to them, or threatening to leave them or give them away. Instructive discipline, on the other hand, involves *induction* techniques, whereby parents explain to their children why they want them to change their behavior. In one variation of this technique—*other-oriented induction*—parents call attention to ways in which the child's behavior is harmful to others ("It makes me sad when you break things"; "Teasing your brother makes him feel bad inside"; "When you dig a hole in the neighbor's yard, they have to fill it in and put all new grass in, and it's very hard work for them").

Studies of power assertion, love withdrawal, and induction techniques reveal that the method chosen has a significant effect on whether a child develops an internalized code of conduct (strong morality) or an external locus of control (weak morality). The use of power assertion is associated with weak moral development in children, whereas induction techniques, especially when they are other-oriented, correlate with advanced moral development. It would appear that giving children explanations helps them form an internal set of rules and expectations that aids them in controlling their behavior. Finally, love withdrawal has not been found to bear any consistent relationship to indices of moral development (75, 79–83; see Table 8.2). As we shall see next, however, positive expressions of affection do regularly help to foster internalized codes of conduct.

Behavior-directed Discipline. Discipline can be directed either at a child's behavior ("That's a bad *thing* to do") or at the child as a person ("Why are *you* so bad?"). Generally speaking, discipline directed at their behavior helps children preserve their self-respect, whereas discipline aimed at their person tends to make them feel unloved and incompetent. As Haim Ginott stressed in *Between Parent and Child*, parents should distinguish between their children as persons (whom they always love) and their children's actions (which they may or may not like) (84). This allows children to tolerate discipline better and learn more from it than if they interpret criticism to mean they are unloved and unlovable.

It is not difficult to see how discipline administered with a warm and

Table 8.2   Relations between Techniques of Discipline and Moral Development in Children

Technique	Description of Technique	Kind of Morality Likely to Develop
Power assertion	Punitive discipline; physical punishment or material deprivation	Weak morality; external locus of control
Love withdrawal	Punitive discipline; verbal rebuke or deprivation of attention and affection	No consistent relationship demonstrated
Induction	Instructive discipline; explanation of reasons for desired behavior change	Strong morality; internal locus of control

Source: Based on Hoffman, M. L. Moral development. In P. H. Mussen (Ed.). *Carmichael's manual of child psychology.* Vol. 2 (3rd ed.). New York: Wiley, 1970.

loving attitude helps children internalize standards of conduct. Accepting parents are more reliable sources of reward than rejecting parents and hence more effective teachers of social judgment and self-control. Likewise, disapproval from loving parents has more impact on behavior than disapproval from cold and distant parents, since a child has more to lose from their being displeased with how he or she is acting. Presumably for these reasons, the research in this area confirms that parents who administer discipline in a warm, nurturant, and loving manner generally encourage their children to develop an internal locus of control, whereas discipline without warmth and support generally encourages externalized morality (19, 73, 75, 85).

Identification

Identification is a process in which people respond to the feelings, attitudes, and actions of others by adopting them as their own. Identification, which was first described by Freud and other psychoanalytic writers (86), is largely an unconscious process; that is, people who are identifying with someone else are not necessarily aware of taking on that person's characteristics. Hence identification differs from the conscious imitation of one person by another, although both processes contribute to personality development.

As we noted briefly in Chapter 4, children begin early in life to imitate their parents' speech, gestures, and preferences. At the dinner table, for example, young children may brush away crumbs when they see their mother brushing away crumbs, or they may say "I don't like peas either" if they hear their father remark that he doesn't like peas. Such early imitative behaviors are fostered by subtle or not-so-subtle encouragement from parents, who are usually pleased to have their children follow their own example and reinforce it ("Isn't that cute?"; "He sure takes after me").

During the preschool years these acts of imitation gradually develop into an identification process, as children progress from merely doing what their parents do to actually being like their parents (87–89). In particular, they begin to act as their parents would, or as they think they would, even when the parents are not present. A boy, for example, may sit in his father's favorite chair and say, "I'm the daddy now," or he may scold a sibling for behaving in a way he thinks his mother would disapprove. Children at this age also begin to say things that indicate an eagerness to identify with their parents, such as "I want to be a mommy, too, when I grow up," or "When will I be able to shave like you do and drive the car?"

Not all specialists in child development make a distinction between identification and imitation. Such prominent social learning theorists as Bandura and Walters argue that all of a person's tendencies to model the actions and attitudes of others are determined by the same principles of

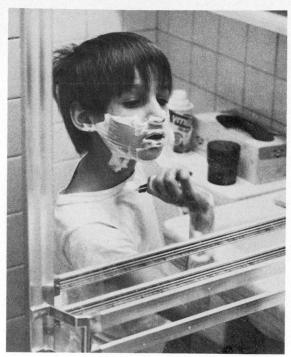

Young children imitate their parents, as shown by the boy on the left; gradually they begin to identify with them, as shown by the boy on the right, who is acting as his father would even though his father is not present.

learning, and hence that the concept of imitation fully explains this aspect of personality development (90). However, we feel there are some good reasons for the more common practice of using the word *imitation* to mean the mimicking of specific acts of others (which begins in infancy) and *identification* to mean assuming the general role of another person (which begins during the preschool years).

First, imitation does not require certain cognitive capacities that are necessary for identification to occur. People can mimic the specific acts of others simply by rote, but they cannot take on other people's roles unless they can empathize with them—that is, put themselves in those people's shoes and appreciate how they think and feel. Research studies indicate that children first begin to develop this role-taking capacity at about the age of 3 or 4 (91, 92). This information provides a basis for distinguishing earlier imitative behavior from identification, which does not become possible until role-taking capacity appears.

Second, identification and imitation differ with respect to the range of people who serve as models. As we will explain shortly, identification occurs primarily in the context of a close, ongoing relationship between two people, whereas imitation can take place as a result of brief, relatively unimportant, and even impersonal observations of others. Hence, pre-schoolers identify almost exclusively with their parents, but they readily imitate many other people, including peers, nursery school teachers, and characters in cartoons, in the movies, and on television.

Much of the research on children's identification with their parents has been concerned with factors that contribute to the strength of role-modeling. This work indicates that modeling is especially likely to be fostered by *warmth* and *power* (93, 94). Children appear to identify more strongly with parents whom they feel love and accept them (nurturant models) than with parents who make them feel disliked or unwanted (rejecting models). As for parental power, parents who exhibit competent problem-solving in their daily behavior foster stronger identification than parents who seem unable to cope with problems or to exert much control over their circumstances.

Three other factors have been found to influence children's identification with their parents. First, identification occurs more readily when there are perceived similarities between children and their parents; this is simply a matter of one person being able to assume the role of another more easily if there are certain apparent likenesses between them at the outset. Sometimes children perceive similarities to their parents on their own ("I eat with my left hand just like you do, Mommy"). At other times they are made aware of a resemblance by what other people say; for example, a doting grandparent may remark to a preschool girl, "You look just like your mother did when she was your age." On occasion young children may even consciously imitate some of their parents' actions in order to become more like them, thereby promoting their own identifications.

Second, it is easier for children to identify with parental models when they can perceive clearly what these models are. In order to try to be like someone else, one needs to know how that other person thinks and feels. This means that children cannot easily identify with parents who are not available to them because of death, divorce, separation, or frequent absences from the home. Children also have difficulty identifying with parents who do not give them much opportunity to learn what they are like as people; that is, parents who keep their thoughts, opinions, hobbies, experiences, and even the nature of their work to themselves.

Third, identification (like imitation) is reinforced by parents who show pleasure and approval whenever their children act or say they want to be like them. When a boy who is sitting in his father's chair says, "I'm the daddy now," and his mother responds, "I'm sure you'll make a good daddy when you grow up," the process of taking on his father's role is strengthened. On the other hand, parents who ignore or discourage such efforts at identification ("You know you're not supposed to sit in that chair with dirty shoes on"; "With all the trouble you give me, I don't think you'll ever grow up"; "What in the world would you want to be like him for?") tend to weaken the identification process (95–97).

We have illustrated some of the effects of child-rearing practices on identification because strong identification promotes effective socialization. The more children identify with their parents, the more likely they are to internalize their parents' codes of conduct. In a sense, identification is the *implicit* agent of socialization, whereas discipline is its *explicit* agent. With discipline parents spell out specific standards of behavior for their children; with identification, however, they establish a model with their own behavior. The more nurturant and powerful this model is, the more likely children are to adopt various aspects of their parents' conscience and ego-ideal as their own.

Three aspects of personality development during the preschool years—aggression, altruism, and sexual identification—provide clear examples of how identification and imitation act together to influence the kind of person a child becomes.

Aggression. All people act aggressively at times, and aggressive behavior may be an inevitable aspect of the human condition. Numerous theories attempt to explain the origins of human aggression—that it is an inherent trait, that it develops in response to frustrations experienced in childhood, or that it is learned from parental reinforcement or other social rewards (76, 77). Yet, despite extensive research, we still know very little about how and why children act aggressively. What we do know is that aggression in children varies with age and that aggressive behavior is stimulated by observing aggressive models; that is, by imitation and identification.

Before describing age differences in children's aggression, we must distinguish between two kinds of aggressive behavior: **hostile aggression,** which is aimed at other people and is accompanied by angry feelings toward them, and **instrumental aggression,** which is aimed at attaining or retrieving some object, territory, or privilege but which is largely impersonal, even though others may suffer as a result of it (98, 99). Two interesting sets of observations that were reported 40 years apart point to consistent age variations in these two kinds of aggression. In 1934 Dawes examined 200 quarrels among nursery-school children aged 18 to 65 months, and in 1974 Hartup studied the interactions within several groups of preschool (4 to 6 years of age) and elementary-school (6 to 7 years of age) children during a 10-week period (100, 101).

The Dawes and Hartup studies both show the following: (a) although aggressive interactions among preschoolers are primarily instrumental (for example, quarrels over the possession of a toy), from about the age of 2 to about the age of 5 children gradually display less instrumental aggression; (b) with the decline of instrumental aggression, there is an increase in hostile aggression (for example, fighting with or shouting at others); and (c) both of these trends continue into middle childhood, with 6- to 7-year-olds displaying less total aggression than preschoolers but being more likely to show hostile aggression when they are behaving aggressively.

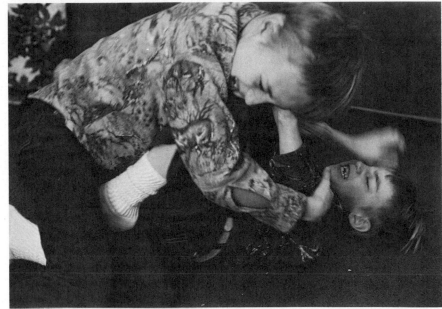

As preschool children become more aware of each other as people, their aggressive behavior toward each other changes from being primarily *instrumental* to being primarily *hostile*. The boys at the top are showing instrumental aggression; they are fighting over possession of the toy but not paying much direct attention to each other. The older boys below are showing hostile aggression which involves direct expression of anger toward another person.

These changes in aggressive behavior can be accounted for by the socialization process. In the first place, as children internalize social sanctions against behaving aggressively, they learn to restrain such urges. Second, as they become capable of role-taking behavior, they become more likely to attribute frustrations to the actions or intent of other people ("It's your fault") rather than to such impersonal circumstances as not

Children readily imitate the aggressive behavior of adults. The children shown above are treating the inflated doll in the same aggressive way as they observed in an adult model.

having a toy. Hence, 5-year-olds can generally be expected to behave aggressively less often than they did at age 2, but more often to direct their aggression toward others.

As for observational learning, aggressive behavior increases when children identify with parents who act aggressively and also as a result of their imitating aggressive acts they see in others. The readiness of children to copy aggressive behavior has been demonstrated in a series of studies by Bandura and his colleagues. In one of these studies half of a group of nursery-school boys and girls observed an adult behaving aggressively toward a Bobo doll (hitting it, knocking it down), while the other half observed an adult who ignored the doll. When the children were later left alone with the doll, those who had observed the aggressive model treated the doll more aggressively than those who had observed a nonaggressive model (102).

Bandura obtained similar results by showing nursery-school children some filmstrips in which people were behaving either aggressively or nonaggressively toward each other. Children who viewed an aggressive film behaved more aggressively in a subsequent play situation than those who had watched a nonaggressive film (103). Many other studies confirm that watching aggressive films increases the amount of aggression children show in play, and furthermore that this effect can last for several months after seeing the film (104–106). These findings have obvious implications for the possible impact of televised violence on aggressive behavior in children, which we discuss in the essay for this chapter (see page 284).

Altruism. **Altruism** refers to behavior that is kind, considerate, generous, and helpful to others. Like aggression, altruism is a trait that shows some consistency over time and some generality; that is, some people are regularly more altruistic than others, and people who are altruistic in one way tend to be altruistic in others. The generality of altruism begins to appear during the preschool years. For example, Baumrind found a close relationship in preschool children among their degree of sympathy, supportiveness, and helpfulness toward others, and Yarrow and Waxler observed consistent patterns of sharing, helping, and comforting behaviors among 3- to 7-year-olds at play (24, 107).

The early appearance of such patterns of altruistic behavior has suggested to some writers that children have an underlying disposition to be kind and considerate. From this point of view, altruism begins as soon as children become capable of appreciating the feelings of others and recognizing their needs for help (108). Others believe that altruism is learned as a standard of moral conduct; that is, without necessarily being disposed toward kindness, children learn helpfulness from being taught that it is the right thing to do (109, 110). However, just as we do not yet know for sure how and why people come to act aggressively, we have no firm understanding of the origins of altruism.

It is also difficult to determine how altruism changes with age. Around age 2, when children are beginning to show aggressive behavior toward each other, they also begin to share toys and candy and to offer sympathy (111). For example, a 20-month-old boy described by Hoffman insisted on giving his favorite Teddy bear to a friend who was crying because his parents were away from home (108). Numerous studies report that such sharing and generosity increases with age, from the preschool years up to age 10 to 12 (112–114). However, the laboratory situations used in many of these studies may not provide a good measure of real-life behavior.

In a typical laboratory study of generosity, children are allowed to win tokens for playing a game, with the understanding that the more tokens they win, the better the prize they will be able to exchange them for. Then, before the exchange is made, the children are given an opportunity to donate some of their tokens "to help needy children." School-age children will generally donate more tokens in this situation than preschoolers, and 11-year-olds more than 7-year-olds. On the other hand, when children are observed in the naturalistic setting of playground activities, 3-to-5-year-olds show just as much helpfulness toward each other as 8-to-10-year-olds (115).

One possible explanation that has been suggested for this difference is that children are becoming more competitive as well as more altruistic from age 2 to 12 (113). Thus 10-year-olds may be more sensitive to others' needs for help than 5-year-olds, but they may also refrain from being helpful because of concerns about achievement and independence. This real-life interaction between wanting to help others but also wanting to surpass them can make it much more difficult to describe age changes in altruism than laboratory studies suggest; we always need to be cautious in taking behavior in an artificial laboratory situation as indicative of behavior that is likely to occur in natural situations.

Despite current uncertainty about why altruism begins and how it changes with age, we know definitely that it can be encouraged and shaped by observing altruistic models. In laboratory situations children who witness acts of giving and helpfulness show increased generosity and helpfulness themselves. This modeling effect is found whether the model is another child or an adult and whether the modeling is done live or with a film presentation (116, 117). In addition, naturalistic observations indicate that nursery-school children imitate altruistic acts of their peers, and that altruistic behavior in children is directly related to having at least one parent who models kind and helpful behavior (118, 119).

It is finally interesting to note that the modeling of altruistic behavior has much more effect on children than the preaching of it. When children are told "It's good to give" by adults who are not themselves displaying generosity, they are not nearly as likely to become more generous as when they observe generous acts (120–122). The implication of such findings is similar to the point we made earlier with respect to identification: children do what their parents do, not necessarily what they say.

Sexual Identification. Sexual identification is the process by which people form a concept of themselves as male or female. We mentioned earlier that preschool boys and girls recognize differences in their anatomy and in their eventual destinies as adult men and women. Identification expands this sexual awareness by virtue of the fact that children tend to identify primarily with their same-sexed parent and with his or her sex-related role.

Although many theories have been advanced to account for the primary identification of a boy with his father and a girl with her mother, research findings point to *similarity* and *reinforcement*—the basic sources of all observational learning—as the simplest explanation. First, biological differences make children more similar to their same-sexed parent and hence able to identify with them more easily. Second, most parents encourage and reward what they consider to be sex-appropriate behavior, while discouraging its opposite (45, 123, 124).

The kinds of distinctions children make between masculinity and femininity vary from one family to the next. Moreover, exclusive sex-role definitions appear to be disappearing in our society, as we have already noted. Even so, some traditional viewpoints and stereotypes about sex-appropriate behavior are proving to be remarkably persistent. Preschoolers, for example, still tend to believe that fathers work while mothers take care of the house and children, and even children whose mothers work outside the home are likely to express this view (125). Judith Bardwick, who has written extensively about the psychology of women, calls special attention to the fact that, at a time when parental roles are becoming less mutually exclusive, when 40 percent of all women are in the labor force, and when women are permitted or encouraged to undertake many presumably masculine pursuits ranging from engineering to race-car driving, children still hold traditional notions about sex roles (30).

It also appears that, despite numerous outward signs of changing sex roles, socialization practices in many societies are still producing distinctive behavior patterns in preschool boys and girls. Boys are expected and observed to be relatively active, aggressive, and domineering, whereas girls are found to be relatively passive and dependent and more interested in giving and seeking help in their relationships with others than in controlling them (126, 127).

As children become more acutely aware of the personality characteristics of their parents and older siblings, their identifications direct them toward increasingly specific roles and attitudes associated with their sex. We will trace this further progress toward sex-role identity in our discussion of middle childhood.

Essay

THE IMPACT OF
TELEVISION ON
AGGRESSIVE AND
ALTRUISTIC
BEHAVIOR IN
CHILDREN

In the United States 99 percent of all households in which there are children have one or more television sets, which are turned on an average of 6 hours per day. Children begin watching television at 1½ to 2 years of age and gradually increase their viewing time to an average of 3 or 4 hours daily during the elementary-school years. Television watching drops off during adolescence, but it is estimated that by age 16 most children in the United States have spent more time watching television than going to school (128–130).

Preschoolers are particularly susceptible to the influence of television. They are old enough to have the capacity and inclination to model themselves after others, but too young to exercise good judgment about whom to imitate. It has been demonstrated, for example, that young children tend to regard television characters either as real people or as like real people; not until late childhood or even adolescence do they recognize discrepancies between real life and life as portrayed on the television screen (130). Hence, indiscriminate modeling after what is seen on television, for better or worse, is especially likely to occur among young children—a prospect that has raised considerable public concern about such matters as the possible influence of televised violence on aggressive behavior.

One view—the **catharsis hypothesis**—holds that viewing aggression can serve as a fantasy outlet for aggressive urges in children, thus decreasing the amount of aggression displayed in their daily lives. Feshbach and Singer seemed to find support for this viewpoint in a well-known study in which they arranged for one group of 8- to 18-year-old boys to watch a schedule of aggressive programs (for example, "Superman," "The FBI") and another group to watch mainly nonaggressive programs (for example, "Bewitched," "The Flintstones"). During a period of 6 weeks the boys who saw primarily nonaggressive programs were observed to become more aggressive, both verbally and physically, while those who watched aggressive programs showed no changes in their behavior (131).

Although widely cited as demonstrating the harmlessness or even the value of having children watch aggressive television, the Feshbach and Singer study had many flaws. First of all, it is possible that the group who were limited to nonaggressive programs became angry simply because they were not being allowed to watch some of their favorite programs. Second, the response of 8- to 18-year-olds may not reflect accurately the impact of television on younger children.

Indeed, in research with preschool youngsters the potential for televised violence to increase aggressive behavior has been regularly demonstrated. In one such study Leifer and Roberts compared groups of preschoolers who watched a film of 12-year-olds who were either displaying aggression toward toys and toward one another or who were playing constructively with toys and with each other. In a subsequent play session those children who had watched the aggressive film were more likely to behave aggressively, as in hitting an inflated clown, and they were more likely to say they would use aggression to resolve a conflict with another child (132).

In a second study, Steuer, Applefield, and Smith watched pairs of preschoolers playing together for several sessions both before and after one member of the pair had seen a violent television cartoon while the other child had viewed a nonviolent cartoon. As compared with their earlier actions, those children who had seen the violent cartoon were more likely to hit, kick, choke, or push their playmate, whereas those who had watched the nonviolent cartoon did not become more aggressive (133).

In a third study Friedrich and Stein observed nursery-school children over a 9-week period during which some of them were regularly shown aggressive television cartoons (for example, "Superman," "Batman"). Those who saw the cartoons, but not the rest of the children, became markedly less obedient, less willing to exert self-control, and less able to tolerate minor frustrations (134).

These and numerous other studies have cast serious doubt on the validity of the catharsis hypothesis. In a detailed assessment of whether children who watch televised violence will be less hostile, Berkowitz concludes that "the weight of evidence presses overwhelmingly for a 'no' answer'' (135). With regard to the possibility that televised violence may increase aggressive behavior, Liebert, Neale, and Davidson provide the following summary of available research:

> *There is, then, a remarkable degree of convergence among all of the types of evidence that have been sought to relate violence viewing and aggressive behavior in the young: laboratory studies, correlational field studies, and naturalistic experiments all show that exposure to television can, and often does, make viewers significantly more aggressive...* [136, p. 87].

It is sometimes suggested that such effects depend on a child's disposition; that is, children who are influenced toward aggression by watching television were aggressive to begin with. There appears to be some basis for this belief. Children who are high in aggression generally show more of an increase in aggressive behavior following televised modeling of aggression than low-aggressive children. By no means, however, does this finding explain away the potential influence of television. The impact of televised violence in increasing the aggressive behavior of young children is observed in low-aggressive as well as high-aggressive children, even though it is greater in the latter group; moreover, the high-aggressive children who are most influenced include a large percentage of perfectly normal children and do not constitute any deviant minority (137).

There is also reason to be concerned about the long-term effects of viewing aggression on television, even among 8- and 9-year-olds. In contrast to the Feshbach and Singer study, many researchers have found increased aggression or acceptance of aggression following exposure to violent television programs among school-age boys (138–140). In a longitudinal study of several hundred children, Eron and his colleagues found that third-graders who preferred violent television programs were more aggressive in school, as rated by their peers, than those who preferred less violent programs; 10 years later third-grade preference for violent television was still predictive of aggressive behavior. In fact, there was a higher correlation between viewing violence at the age of 9 and aggressive behavior at age 19 (.31) than between watching violent programs at age 19 and aggressive behavior at that same age (-.05; see Figure 8.4) (141, 142).

Because this impact of television appears due to children's imitative behavior, it follows that programs can be designed to encourage altruism as well as aggression. Indeed, ample evidence exists that children imitate models of charity and self-control that they see on television as well as aggressive models. For example, it has been found that kindergarten children who watched just a few segments of ''Misterogers' Neighborhood'' afterward obeyed rules more readily, tolerated delays better, worked more persistently at various tasks, and demonstrated more helping, sharing, and sympathetic behavior (143–146). In one study Sprafkin, Liebert, and Poulos measured the helping behavior of first-graders in an experimental situation after they had watched one of three television programs:

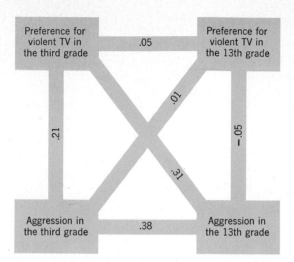

Figure 8.4 The correlations between a preference for violent television and peer-rated aggression for 211 boys over a 10-year lag. (*Source.* Eron, L. D. *et al.* Does television violence cause aggression? *American Psychologist,* 1972, **27,** 253–263.)

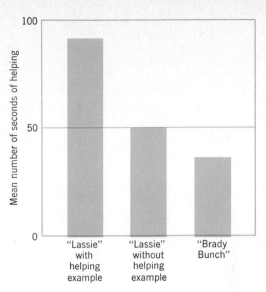

Figure 8.5 Mean number of seconds of helping by children who had viewed the prosocial "Lassie," neutral "Lassie," and "Brady Bunch" programs. (*Source.* Liebert, R. M. & Poulos, R. W. Television and personality development: The socializing effects of an entertainment medium. In A. Davids (Ed.), *Child personality and psychopathology: Current topics.* Vol. 2. New York: Wiley, 1975.)

an episode of "Lassie" that included a dramatic example of a boy helping a dog; a "Lassie" episode without any such example; and an episode of "The Brady Bunch," a family situation comedy. As indicated in Figure 8.5, the first of these programs had an especially strong effect in promoting altruistic behavior (147).

The implication of these findings on aggressive and altruistic behavior seems clear. Television can exert a powerful influence on children through its modeling effects, especially during the preschool years. It thus behooves the television industry to exercise care in the kinds of programs it prepares for children, and parents to exercise responsibility in supervising what kinds of programs their children watch.

Biography

ERIK H. ERIKSON

Erik Erikson would be the first to acknowledge that his preoccupation with the problem of ego identity originates with his own personal history. He was born in Germany of Danish parents, but his father abandoned his mother before he was born. When Erikson was several years old, his mother married her Jewish pediatrician, who adopted Erikson—thus he bears the middle name Homburger. As a youth of Aryan appearance, but with one Jewish parent, he was rejected by both Gentile and Jewish peers. After completing

Table 8.3 Erikson's Stages of Psychosocial Development

Age Period	Focal Crisis	Determinants
0-2 years	Trust vs. mistrust	If parents meet the preponderance of the infant's needs, the child develops a stronger sense of trust than of mistrust.
2-4 years	Autonomy vs. shame or doubt	If parents reward the child's successful actions and do not shame his or her failures (say in bowel or bladder control), the child's sense of autonomy will outweight the sense of shame and doubt.
4-6 years	Initiative vs. guilt	If parents accept the child's curiosity and do not put down the need to know and to question, the child's sense of initiative will outweight the sense of guilt.
7-12 years	Industry vs. inferiority	If the child encounters more success than failure at home and at school, he or she will have a greater sense of industry than of inferiority.
13-18 years	Identity vs. role diffusion	If the young person can reconcile diverse roles, abilities, and values and see their continuity with past and future, the sense of personal identity will not give way to a sense of role diffusion.
19-35 years	Intimacy vs. isolation	With a sufficiently strong sense of personal identity, one can give much of oneself to another person without feeling a loss of identity. The person who cannot do this experiences a sense of loneliness.
35-55 years	Generativity vs. stagnation	The individual who has had children or produced some meaningful work invests much in those children and/or work as continuities of personal identity that will persist when the personal identity no longer does. The person who cannot so invest himself or herself experiences a sense of stagnation, of standing still rather than of growing.
55-	Integrity vs. despair	The individual who has attained a sense of personal identity, intimacy, and generativity can look back upon life as having been well spent and can accept death without regrets. But the individual who reaches old age without having involved himself or herself in other people or works experiences a sense of despair at a life ill spent.

high school, he spent several years traveling about as an itinerant artist finding his own "moratorium" (a period of time in which the young person is finding himself or herself rather than pursuing a career).

An old school friend, Peter Blos, invited him to come to Vienna, where he first worked as a tutor with a family who knew the Freuds. During this period (the late 1920s), Erikson was trained as a Montessori teacher and taught in an experimental school. But he was also part of the psychoanalytic circle and was accepted for training as a lay analyst. He specialized in the psychoanalysis of children and worked closely with Anna Freud, who was also treating young people. While in Vienna, Erikson courted and wed a Canadian-born dance student, Joan Moivat Serson, who became both an artist and a writer who in addition to her own work, edits all of her husband's writings.

As the threat of Hitler was felt in Austria, Erikson moved to Boston where, as New England's only child analyst, he was very welcome. He received an appointment at Harvard, where he met and befriended some of the leading thinkers of his day, particularly the anthropologists Margaret Mead, Ruth Benedict, and Scudder McKeel. As a result of the anthropologists' influence, Erikson made a number of field trips to the Sioux Reservation at Pine Ridge, South Dakota, and later visited the salmon-fishing Yurok Indians of northern California. Erikson has a unique sense of empathy with people of different cultures, and this has enabled him to appreciate some of the emotional conflicts of these Indians as they, themselves, have experienced them.

What became apparent to Erikson was that the problems suffered by American Indians had less to do with repressed sexual impulses than with the way in which they were thinking about themselves, their families, and their tribes. It was their inability to reconcile the traditions of their tribes with the ignoble position in which they found themselves among white people that drove many of them to drink and not a few to suicide. Here was clear evidence that cognitive conflict was just as potent a determination of emotional distress as the unconscious conflicts of the drives that Freud had emphasized.

In 1942 Erikson moved to the University of California at Berkeley, where he both taught and carried on clinical work. While he was treating servicemen in a veterans' hospital, he was able to confirm the observations that he first made among the Indians. Many of these men were troubled because they could not reconcile their role as soldiers (killers) with their previous role as civilians (law-abiding citizens). Here again Erikson noted that conflicts within the ego could produce emotional distress that was just as severe as that produced by sexual drives. Although Erikson remained loyal to Freudian theory, he felt compelled to expand this theory to include disorders produced by "identity conflicts." He made his first comprehensive statement of his position in *Childhood and*

Society (1950), which was the culmination of more than a decade of clinical observation and research. This book is widely viewed as a classic and is now standard reading in many college courses. In that book Erikson describes his conception of the eight stages of man (see Table 8.3) which soon made him world famous.

Erikson left Berkeley in 1950, when he refused to sign the loyalty oath that was required of all University of California professors at that time (due to the influence of McCarthyism). Erikson joined a group of psychiatrists and psychologists who were taking over a small residential treatment center in the Berkshires—The Austen Riggs Center, Inc.—which they hoped would become a therapeutic community for disturbed adolescents. At Austen Riggs, Erikson did more work on substantiating and elaborating his original theories of ego development. In 1960 Erikson accepted a chair in developmental psychology at Harvard University, where he taught courses but retained his affiliation with The Austen Riggs Center.

In 1970 Erikson won both a Pulitzer Prize and a National Book Award for *Gandhi's Truth,* a book in which he characterizes the man who eliminated the British from India without bloodshed and without dividing India into warring camps. *Gandhi's Truth* is no mere idealization of Gandhi, for Erikson discusses the Mahatma's weaknesses at considerable length. It is to that unique ability in people to be able to transcend human weaknesses and to be able to identify with all mankind that Erikson speaks in *Gandhi's Truth*. Indeed, it is Erikson's own genius for intuiting the feelings of people from different cultures and of people at different stages of life that has given his work such universal appeal.

Summary

Between the ages of 2 and 5 children become increasingly aware of themselves as people, they experience many new kinds of interpersonal relationships, and they begin to recognize and adopt socially approved patterns of behavior. In the process, they form many distinctive attitudes, preferences, and ways of acting.

With respect to self-awareness, preschoolers pay close attention to their physical growth and appearance. They learn their sexual identities as male or female, and they form positive or negative attitudes toward themselves in response to what others say about how they look and how their bodies are growing. These self-attitudes are also shaped by how other people respond to the many new cognitive and motor skills preschoolers are developing. Young children who are encouraged to master skills and act independently tend to become self-confident persons who enjoy challenge and anticipate success; on the other hand, children who are overprotected or belittled may come to doubt themselves and expect failure in what they try to do.

As for new kinds of interpersonal relationships, preschoolers distinguish between their mother and father much more clearly than they did as infants and develop different ways of interacting with each parent. Fathers appear to play a particularly important role in helping preschool children form a positive self-concept and function well in achievement-related situations. Although adverse effects are not inevitable in a father-less home, preschoolers without fathers frequently have difficulty in arriving at a sex-appropriate self-concept and in getting along socially with other children and adults.

Most young children have to learn to share their parents' affection either with a new baby, who seems to get more attention, or with older siblings, who seem to have more privileges, or both. Parents can usually help preschoolers sustain their self-esteem and sense of competence in the face of these sibling rivalries by safeguarding their rights and reassuring them of their personal worth. Young children must also learn to share and compete with their peers, whom they meet in neighborhood play groups, nursery schools, and daycare centers. In these situations preschoolers make comparisons between themselves and their playmates that influence how they feel about themselves, for better or worse, and they also begin to adopt characteristic interpersonal styles, such as being shy or outgoing, timid or brash, a leader or a follower. Opportunities to meet and play with many different children and to be away from home for brief periods of time help prepare children for entering kindergarten and first grade.

Finally, early childhood is a crucial period for *socialization,* the process by which children acquire the social judgment and self-control necessary for becoming responsible adults in their society. Children are socialized primarily through *discipline* and *identification.* Discipline is most effective when parents administer it consistently, when they attempt to teach rather than merely punish their children with it, and when they direct it toward their children's behavior rather than their worth as persons. Such discipline ordinarily helps young people develop an internal sense of right and wrong and behave according to its dictates. Inconsistent, punitive, and person-directed discipline, on the other hand, is likely to lead to external morality, in which acceptable behavior is considered to be whatever one can get away with.

Identification consists of adopting the feelings, attitudes, and actions of others as one's own. The more nurturant and powerful parents are as models, and the greater the similarities between parents and their children, the more strongly the children will identify with them. Strong identifications help the socialization process, because the more children attempt to be like their parents, the more they tend to internalize parental codes of conduct. Besides their parents, children also model themselves after other adults, siblings, playmates, and television characters. The models to which children are exposed affect many important aspects of their emerging personality style, including how aggressive and/or altruistic they are in their relationships with others and how they progress toward an adequate sex-role identity.

References

1. Fraiberg, S. *The magic years: Understanding and handling the problems of early childhood.* New York: Scribner, 1959.
2. Gesell, A., Halverson, H. M., Thompson, H., Ilg, F. L., Castner, B. M., Ames, L. B., & Amatruda, C. S. *The first five years of life.* New York: Harper, 1940.
3. Kreitler, H., & Kreitler, S. Children's concepts of sexuality and birth. *Child Development,* 1966, **37,** 363–378.
4. Rutter, M. Normal psychosexual development. *Journal of Child Psychology and Psychiatry,* 1971, **11,** 259–283.
5. Balint, A. *The early years of life: A psychoanalytic study.* New York: Basic Books, 1954.
6. Conn, J. H., & Kanner, L. Children's awareness of sex differences. *Journal of Child Psychiatry,* 1947, **1,** 3–57.
7. Sroufe, L. A., & Wunsch, J. A. The development of laughter in the first year of life. *Child Development,* 1972, **43,** 1326–1344.
8. Watson, J. S. Smiling, cooing, and "The Game." *Merrill-Palmer Quarterly,* 1972, **18,** 323–340.
9. Appleton, T., Clifton, R., & Goldberg, S. The development of behavioral competence in infancy. In F. D. Horowitz (Ed.), *Review of child development research.* Vol. 4. Chicago: University of Chicago Press, 1975.
10. Bronson, W. C. Mother-toddler interactions: A perspective on studying the development of competence. *Merrill-Palmer Quarterly,* 1974, **20,** 275–301.
11. White, B. L. Critical influences in the origins of competence. *Merrill-Palmer Quarterly,* 1975, **21,** 243–266.
12. Veroff, J. Social comparison and the development of achievement motivation. In C. P. Smith (Ed.), *Achievement-related motives in children.* New York: Russell Sage, 1969.
13. White, R. W. Motivation reconsidered: The concept of competence. *Psychological Review,* 1959, **66,** 297–333.
14. White, R. W. Competence and the psychosexual stages of development. In M. Jones (Ed.), *Nebraska symposium on motivation.* Lincoln: University of Nebraska Press, 1960.
15. McClelland, D. C., Atkinson, J. W., Clark, R. A., & Lowell, E. L. *The achievement motive.* New York: Appleton-Century-Crofts, 1953.
16. Atkinson, J. W. (Ed.). *Motives in fantasy, action, and society.* Princeton, N. J.: Van Nostrand, 1958.
17. Crandall, V. Achievement behavior in young children. *Young Children,* 1964, **20,** 77–99.
18. Crandall, V., Preston, A., & Rabson, A. Maternal reactions and the development of independence and achievement behavior in young children. *Child Development,* 1960, **31,** 243–251.
19. Martin, B. Parent-child relations. In F. D. Horowitz (Ed.), *Review of child development research.* Vol. 4. Chicago: University of Chicago Press, 1975.
20. Rosen, R., & D'Andrade, R. The psychosocial origins of achievement motivation. *Sociometry,* 1959, **22,** 185–218.
21. Smith, C. P. The origin and expression of achievement-related motives in children. In C. P. Smith (Ed.), *Achievement-related motives in children.* New York: Russell Sage, 1969.
22. Baumrind, D. Child care practices anteceding three patterns of preschool behavior. *Genetic Psychology Monographs,* 1967, **75,** 43–88.
23. Baumrind, D. Socialization and instrumental competence in young children. *Young Children,* 1970, **26,** 104–119.
24. Baumrind, D. Current patterns of parental authority. *Developmental Psychology Monographs,* 1971, **4,** Part 2, 1–103.
25. Baumrind, D. The contributions of the family to the development of competence in children. *Schizophrenia Bulletin,* 1975, No. 14, 12–37.
26. Coopersmith, S. *The antecedents of self-esteem.* San Francisco: W. H. Freeman, 1967.
27. Garai, J. E., & Scheinfeld, A. Sex differences in mental and behavioral traits. *Genetic Psychology Monographs,* 1968, **77,** 169–299.
28. Tyler, F. B., Rafferty, J. Y., & Tyler, B. B. Relationships among motivations of parents and their children. *Journal of Genetic Psychology,* 1962, **101,** 69–81.
29. Hoffman, L. W. Early childhood experiences and women's achievement motives. *Journal of Social Issues,* 1972, **28,** 129–155.

30. Bardwick, J. M. *The psychology of women: A study of biosocial conflict*. New York: Harper, 1971.

31. Berens, A. E. Sex-role stereotypes and the development of achievement motivation. *Ontario Psychologist*, 1973, **5**, 30–35.

32. Maccoby, E. E., & Jacklin, C. N. *The psychology of sex differences*. Stanford, Calif.: Stanford University Press, 1974.

33. Block, J. H. Issues, problems, and pitfalls in assessing sex differences. *Merrill-Palmer Quarterly*, 1976, **22**, 283–308.

34. Erikson, E. H. *Childhood and society*. (2nd ed.) New York: Norton, 1963.

35. Mason, K. O., Czajka, J. L., & Arber, S. Change in U. S. women's sex-role attitudes, 1964–1974. *American Sociological Review*, 1976, **41**, 573–596.

36. Burlingham, D. The preoedipal infant-father relationship. *Psychoanalytic Study of the Child*, 1973, **28**, 23–47.

37. Kotelchuk, M. The infant's relationship to the father: Experimental evidence. In M. E. Lamb (Ed.), *The role of the father in child development*. New York: Wiley, 1976.

38. Lamb, M. E. The role of the father: An overview. In M. E. Lamb (Ed.), *The role of the father in child development*. New York: Wiley, 1976.

39. Pedersen, F. A., & Rabson, K. S. Father participation in infancy, *American Journal of Orthopsychiatry*, 1969, **39**, 466–472.

40. Schaffer, H. R., & Emerson, P. E. The development of social attachments in infancy. *Monographs of the Society for Research in Child Development*, 1964, **29**, No. 3, 1–77.

41. Lynn, D. B., & Cross, A. DeP. Parent preference of preschool children. *Journal of Marriage and the Family*, 1974, **36**, 555–559.

42. Biller, H. B. *Father, child, and sex role: Paternal determinants of personality development*. Lexington, Mass.: Heath, 1971.

43. Biller, H. B. Paternal deprivation, cognitive functioning, and the feminized classroom. In A. Davids (Ed.), *Child personality and psychopathology: Current topics*. Vol. 1. New York: Wiley, 1974.

44. Biller, H. B. The father and personality development: Paternal deprivation and sex-role development. In M. E. Lamb (Ed.), *The role of the father in child development*. New York: Wiley, 1976.

45. Lynn, D. B. *The father: His role in child development*. Monterey, Calif.: Brooks/Cole, 1974.

46. Radin, N. The role of the father in cognitive, academic, and intellectual development. In M. E. Lamb (Ed.), *The role of the father in child development*. New York: Wiley, 1976.

47. Biller, H. B. *Paternal deprivation*. Lexington, Mass.: Heath, 1974.

48. Crumley, F. E., & Blumenthal, R. S. Children's reactions to temporary loss of the father. *American Journal of Psychiatry*, 1973, **130**, 778–782.

49. Hetherington, E. M., & Deur, J. L. The effects of father absence on child development. In W. W. Hartup (Ed.), *The young child: Review of research*. Vol. 2. Washington, D.C.: National Association for the Education of Young Children, 1972.

50. Santrock, J. W. Relation of type and onset of father-absence to cognitive development. *Child Development*, 1972, **43**, 455–569.

51. Biller, H. B. Fathering and female sexual development. *Medical Aspects of Sexuality*, 1971, **5**, 126–138.

52. Biller, H. B., & Weiss, S. D. The father-daughter relationship and personality development of the female. *Journal of Genetic Psychology*, 1970, **116**, 79–93.

53. Hetherington, E. M. Effects of father absence on personality development in adolescent daughters. *Developmental Psychology*, 1972, **7**, 313–326.

54. Herzog, E., & Sudia, C. E. Children in fatherless families. In B. M. Caldwell & H. N. Ricciuti (Eds.), *Review of child development research*. Vol. 3. Chicago: University of Chicago Press, 1973.

55. Oshman, H. P., & Manosevitz, M. Father absence: Effects of stepfathers upon psychosocial development in males. *Developmental Psychology*, 1976, **12**, 479–480.

56. Legg, C., Sherick, I., & Wadland, W. Reaction of preschool children to the birth of a sibling. *Child Psychiatry and Human Development*, 1974, **5**, 3–39.

57. Eckerman, C. O., Whatley, J. L., & Kutz, S. L. Growth of social play with peers during the second year of life. *Developmental Psychology*, 1975, **11**, 42–49.

58. Bronson, W. C. Developments in behavior with age-mates during the second year of life. In M. Lewis & L. A. Rosenblum (Eds.), *Friendship and peer relations*. New York: Wiley, 1975.

59. Charlesworth, R., & Hartup, W. W. Positive social reinforcement in the nursery school peer group. *Child Development,* 1967, **38,** 993–1002.

60. Hartup, W. W. Peer interaction and social organization. In P. H. Mussen (Ed.), *Carmichael's manual of child psychology.* Vol. 2 (3rd ed.). New York: Wiley, 1970.

61. Hartup, W. W., Glazer, J. A., & Charlesworth, R. Peer reinforcement and sociometric status. *Child Development,* 1967, **38,** 1017–1024.

62. Moore, S. G. Correlates of peer acceptance in nursery school children. In W. W. Hartup & N. L. Smothergill (Eds.), *The young child: Reviews of research.* Vol. 1. Washington, D.C.: National Association for the Education of Young Children, 1967.

63. Halverson, C. F., & Waldrop, M. F. Relations between preschool activity and aspects of intellectual and social behavior at age 7½. *Developmental Psychology,* 1976, **12,** 107–112.

64. Piers, G., & Singer, M. *Shame and guilt: A psychoanalytic and cultural study.* Springfield, Ill.: Thomas, 1953.

65. Aronfreed, J. *Conduct and conscience. The socialization of internalized control over behavior.* New York: Academic Press, 1968.

66. Parke, R. D. Effectiveness of punishment as an interaction of intensity, timing, agent, nurturance, and cognitive structuring. *Child Development,* 1969, **40,** 211–235.

67. Higgins, J. Inconsistent socialization. *Psychological Reports,* 1968, **23,** 303–336.

68. Parke, R. D. Some effects of punishment on children's behavior. In W. W. Hartup (Ed.), *The young child: Reviews of research.* Vol. 2. Washington, D.C.: National Association for the Education of Young Children, 1972.

69. Deur, J. L., & Parke, R. D. The effects of inconsistent punishment on aggression in children. *Developmental Psychology,* 1970, **2,** 403–411.

70. Rotter, J. B. Generalized expectancies for internal versus external control of reinforcement. *Psychological Monographs,* 1966, **80** (Whole No. 609).

71. Rotter, J. B. Some problems and misconceptions related to the construct of internal versus external control of reinforcement. *Journal of Consulting and Clinical Psychology,* 1975, **43,** 56–67.

72. Lefcourt, H. M. *Locus of control: Current trends in theory and research.* New York: Erlbaum, 1976.

73. MacDonald, A. P. Internal-external locus of control: Parental antecedents. *Journal of Consulting and Clinical Psychology,* 1971, **37,** 141–147.

74. Hoffman, M. L. Moral internalization, parental power, and the nature of parent-child interaction. *Developmental Psychology,* 1975, **11,** 228–239.

75. Hoffman, M. L. Moral development. In P. H. Mussen (Ed.), *Carmichael's manual of child psychology.* Vol. 2 (3rd ed.). New York: Wiley, 1970.

76. Feshbach, S. Aggression. In P. H. Mussen (Ed.), *Carmichael's manual of child psychology.* Vol. 2 (3rd ed.). New York: Wiley, 1970.

77. Feshbach, N., & Feshbach, S. Children's aggression. In W. W. Hartup (Ed.), *The young child: Reviews of research.* Vol. 2. Washington, D.C.: National Association for the Education of Young Children, 1972.

78. Hoffman, M. L. Childrearing practices and moral development: Generalizations from empirical research. *Child Development,* 1963, **34,** 295–318.

79. Allinsmith, W. Moral standards: II. The learning of moral standards. In D. R. Miller & G. E. Swanson (Eds.), *Inner conflict and defense.* New York: Holt, 1960.

80. Forehand, R., Roberts, M. W., Doleys, D. N., Hobbs, S. A., & Resick, P. A. An examination of disciplinary procedures with children. *Journal of Experimental Child Psychology,* 1976, **2,** 109–120.

81. Hoffman, M. L., & Saltzstein, H. D. Parent discipline and the child's moral development. *Journal of Personality and Social Psychology,* 1967, **5,** 45–57.

82. Lytton, H., & Zwirner, W. Compliance and its controlling stimuli observed in a natural setting. *Developmental Psychology,* 1975, **11,** 769–779.

83. Sears, R. R., Maccoby, E. E., & Levin, H. *Patterns of child rearing.* Evanston, Ill.: Row, Peterson, 1957.

84. Ginott, H. *Between parent and child.* New York: Macmillan, 1965.

85. Parke, R. D., & Walters, R. H. Some factors determining the efficacy of punishment for inducing response inhibition. *Monographs of the Society for Research in Child Development,* 1967, **32,** No. 109.

86. Bronfenbrenner, U. Freudian theories of identification and their derivatives. *Child Development,* 1960, **31,** 15–40.

87. Gewirtz, J. L., & Stingle, K. G. Learning of generalized imitation as the basis for identification. *Psychological Review,* 1968, **75,** 374–397.

88. Hartup, W. W., & Coates, B. Imitation: Arguments for a developmental approach. In R. D. Parke (Ed.), *Recent trends in social learning theory.* New York: Academic Press, 1972.

89. Schafer, R. *Aspects of internalization.* New York: International Universities Press, 1968.

90. Bandura, A., & Walters, R. H. *Social learning and personality development.* New York: Holt, 1964.

91. Flavell, J. *The development of role-taking and communication skills in children.* New York: Wiley, 1968.

92. Selman, R. L. Taking another's perspective: Role-taking development in early childhood. *Child Development,* 1971, **42,** 1721–1734.

93. Hetherington, E. M., & Frankie, G. Effects of parental dominance, warmth, and conflict on imitation in children. *Journal of Personality and Social Psychology,* 1967, **6,** 119–125.

94. Masters, J. C., Anderson, E. P., & Fitzpatrick, L. J. Effects of relative nurturance and social power on observational learning and imitation. *Journal of Research in Personality,* 1975, **9,** 200–210.

95. Bandura, A. Social learning theory of identificatory processes. In D. Goslin (Ed.), *Handbook of socialization theory and research.* Chicago: Rand-McNally, 1969.

96. Kagan, J. The period of identification: 3 to 6 years. In I. L. Janis, G. F. Mahl, J. Kagan, & R. R. Holt, *Personality: Dynamics, development, and assessment.* New York: Harcourt, 1969.

97. Sears, R. R., Rau, L., & Alpert, R. *Identification and child rearing.* Stanford, Calif.: Stanford University Press, 1965.

98. Feshbach, S. The function of aggression and the regulation of aggressive drive. *Psychological Review,* 1964, **71,** 257–272.

99. Rule, B. G. The hostile and instrumental function of human aggression. In W. W. Hartup & J. de Wit (Eds.), *Determinants and origins of aggressive behaviors.* The Hague: Mouton, 1974.

100. Dawes, H. C. An analysis of two hundred quarrels of preschool children. *Child Development,* 1934, **5,** 139–157.

101. Hartup, W. W. Aggression in childhood: Developmental perspectives. *American Psychologist,* 1974, **29,** 336–341.

102. Bandura, A., Ross, D., & Ross, S. Transmission of aggression through imitation of aggressive models. *Journal of Abnormal and Social Psychology,* 1961, **63,** 575–582.

103. Bandura, A., Ross, D., & Ross, S. A. Imitation of film-mediated aggressive models. *Journal of Abnormal and Social Psychology,* 1963, **66,** 3–11.

104. Bandura, A. The role of the modeling process in personality development. In W. W. Hartup & N. L. Smothergill (Eds.), *The young child: Reviews of research.* Vol. 1. Washington, D.C.: National Association for the Education of Young Children, 1967.

105. Hicks, D. J. Imitation and retention of film-mediated aggressive peer and adult models. *Journal of Personality and Social Psychology,* 1965, **2,** 97–100.

106. Kniveton, B. H. The very young and television violence. *Journal of Psychosomatic Research,* 1974, **18,** 233–237.

107. Yarrow, M. R., & Waxler, C. Z. Dimensions and correlates of prosocial behavior in young children. *Child Development,* 1976, **47,** 118–125.

108. Hoffman, M. L. Developmental synthesis of affect and cognitions and its implications for altruistic motivation. *Developmental Psychology,* 1975, **11,** 607–622.

109. Bryan, J. H., & London, P. Altruistic behavior by children. *Psychological Bulletin,* 1970, **73,** 200–211.

110. Krebs, D. L. Altruism: An examination of the concept and a review of the literature. *Psychological Bulletin,* 1970, **73,** 258–302.

111. Rheingold, H. L., Hay, D. F., & West, M. J. Sharing in the second year of life. *Child Development.* In press.

112. Bryan, J. H. Children's cooperation and helping behaviors. In E. M. Hetherington (Ed.), *Review of child development research.* Vol. 5. Chicago: University of Chicago Press, 1975.

113. Rushton, J. P. Socialization and the altruistic behavior of children. *Psychological Bulletin,* 1976, **83,** 898–913.

114. Rushton, J. P., & Wiener, J. Altruism and cognitive development in children. *British Journal of Social and Clinical Psychology,* 1975, **14,** 341–349.

115. Severy, L. J., & Davis, K. E. Helping behavior among normal and retarded children. *Child Development,* 1971, **42,** 1017–1031.

116. Bryan, J. H. Why children help: A review. *Journal of Social Issues,* 1972, **28,** 87–104.

117. Yarrow, M. R., Scott, P. M., & Waxler, C. Z. Learning concern for others. *Developmental Psychology,* 1973, **8,** 240–260.

118. Hartup, W. W., & Coates, B. Imitation of peers as a function of reinforcement from the peer group and the rewardingness of the model. *Child Development,* 1967, **38,** 1003–1016.

119. Hoffman, M. L. Altruistic behavior and the parent-child relationship. *Journal of Personality and Social Psychology,* 1975, **31,** 937–943.

120. Bryan, J. H., & Walbek, N. H. The impact of words and deeds concerning altruism upon children. *Child Development,* 1970, **41,** 747–757.

121. Midlarsky, E., & Bryan, J. H. Affect expression and children's imitative altruism. *Journal of Experimental Research in Personality,* 1972, **6,** 195–203.

122. Rushton, J. P., & Owen, D. Immediate and delayed effects of TV modeling and preaching on children's generosity. *British Journal of Social and Clinical Psychology,* 1975, **14,** 309–310.

123. Kagan, J. Sex typing during the preschool and early school years. In I. L. Janis, G. F. Mahl, J. Kagan, & R. R. Holt, *Personality: Dynamics, development, and assessment.* New York: Harcourt, 1969.

124. Mischel, W. Sex-typing and socialization. In P. H. Mussen (Ed.), *Carmichael's manual of child psychology.* Vol. II. New York: Wiley, 1970.

125. Dubin, R., & Dubin, E. R. Children's social perceptions: A review of research. *Child Development,* 1965, **36,** 809–838.

126. Buss, A. H., & Plomin, R. *A temperament theory of personality development.* New York: Wiley, 1975.

127. Whiting, B., & Edwards, C. P. A cross-cultural analysis of sex differences in the behavior of children age three through 11. *Journal of Social Psychology,* 1973, **91,** 171–188.

128. Liebert, R. M., & Poulos, R. W. Television and personality development: The socializing effects of an entertainment medium. In A. Davids (Ed.), *Child personality and psychopathology: Current topics.* Vol. 2. New York: Wiley, 1975.

129. Lyle, J., & Hoffman, H. R. Children's use of television and other media. In E. A. Rubinstein, G. A. Comstock, & J. P. Murray (Eds.), *Television and social behavior.* Vol. IV, *Television in day-to-day life: Patterns of Use.* Washington, D.C.: U.S. Government Printing Office, 1972.

130. Murray, J. P. Television and violence: Implications of the Surgeon General's research program. *American Psychologist,* 1973, **28,** 472–478.

131. Feshbach, S., & Singer, R. *Television and aggression.* San Francisco: Jossey-Bass, 1971.

132. Leifer, A., & Roberts, D. Children's responses to television violence. In J. P. Murray, E. A. Rubinstein, & G. A. Comstock (Eds.), *Television and social behavior.* Vol. II, *Television and social learning.* Washington, D.C.: U.S. Government Printing Office, 1972.

133. Steuer, F. B., Applefield, J. M., & Smith, R. Televised aggression and the interpersonal aggression of preschool children. *Journal of Experimental Child Psychology,* 1971, **11.** 442–447.

134. Friedrich, L. K., & Stein, A. H. Aggressive and prosocial television programs and the natural behavior of preschool children. *Monographs of the Society for Research in Child Development,* 1973, **38,** No. 4, 1–64.

135. Berkowitz, L. Control of aggression. In B. M. Caldwell & H. N. Ricciuti (Eds.), *Review of child development research.* Vol. 3. Chicago: University of Chicago Press, 1973.

136. Liebert, R. M., Neale, J. M., & Davidson, E. S. *The early window: Effects of television on children and youth.* New York: Pergamon, 1973.

137. Stein, A. H., & Friedrich, L. K. Impact of television on children and youth. In E. M. Hetherington (Ed.), *Review of child development research.* Vol. 5. Chicago: University of Chicago Press, 1975.

138. Cisin, I. H., Coffin, T. E., Janis, I. L., Klapper, J. T., Mendelsohn, H., & Omwake, E. *Television and growing up: The impact of televised violence.* Washington, D. C.: U.S. Government Printing Office, 1972.

139. Liebert, R. M., Sobol, M. P., & Davidson, E. S. Catharsis of aggression among institutionalized boys: Fact or artifact? In G. A. Comstock, E. A. Rubinstein, & J. P. Murray (Eds.), *Television and social behavior*. Vol. V, *Television's effects: Further explorations*. Washington, D.C.: U. S. Government Printing Office, 1972.

140. Thomas, M. H., & Drabman, R. S. Toleration of real life aggression as a function of exposure to televised violence and age of subject. *Merrill-Palmer Quarterly*, 1975, **21**, 227–232.

141. Eron, L. D., Lefkowitz, M. M., Huesmann, L. R., & Walder, L. O. Does television violence cause aggression? *American Psychologist*, 1972, **27**, 253–263.

142. Eron, L. D., Huesmann, L. R., Lefkowitz, M. M., & Walder, L. O. How learning conditions in early childhood—including mass media—relate to aggression in late adolescence. *American Journal of Orthopsychiatry*, 1974, **44**, 412–423.

143. Coates, B., Pusser, H. E., & Goodman, I. The influence of "Sesame Street" and "Mister Rogers' Neighborhood" on children's social behavior in the preschool. *Child Development*, 1976, **47**, 138–144.

144. Friedrich, L. K., & Stein, A. H. Prosocial television and young children: The effects of verbal labeling and role playing on learning and behavior. *Child Development*, 1975, **46**, 27–38.

145. Liefer, A. D., Gordon, N. J., & Graves, S. B. Children's television: More than mere entertainment. *Harvard Educational Review*, 1974, **44**, 213–245.

146. Stein, G. M., & Bryan, J. H. The effect of a television model upon rule adoption behavior of children. *Child Development*, 1972, **43**, 268–273.

147. Sprafkin, J. N., Liebert, R. M., & Poulos, R. W. Effects of a prosocial televised example on children's helping. *Journal of Experimental Child Psychology*, 1975, **20**, 119–126.

9 Preschool Variations

INTELLIGENCE: THE CONTRIBUTIONS OF HEREDITY AND ENVIRONMENT

Group Differences in IQ

Patterns of Ability within Racial/Ethnic Groups

SEX DIFFERENCES

Mental Abilities

Personality Characteristics

FAMILY CONSTELLATION

Birth Order
Father Absence

SOCIAL AND CULTURAL DIFFERENCES

Social Class Differences in Language

Social and Cultural Variations in Reinforcement Styles

Child-Rearing Practices in Three Countries

INTERVENTIONS AT THE PRESCHOOL LEVEL

ESSAY

Life and Death: The Feelings and Concepts of Children

SUMMARY

REFERENCES

During the preschool years, individual and group variations become apparent in many areas and a number of these differences are due to closely related and interacting factors. For example, many differences may be accounted for according to ethnic group or social class. For purposes of discussion we will examine some of these factors separately, but their considerable interactions need to be kept in mind.

INTELLIGENCE: THE CONTRIBUTIONS OF HEREDITY AND ENVIRONMENT

In discussing infant intelligence (Chapter 4), we described the limitations of infant intelligence tests. Such tests cannot really be used to predict individual or group differences at a later age. By the time children are 3 or 4, however, intelligence tests do become better predictors of later intellectual performance (1–3) since these tests are reliable and consistent measures of individual and group differences in mental ability. Because of the relative stability of IQ performance during this period, intelligence tests can be used to assess the contribution of environmental factors to intelligence test performance.

Before we describe some of the experimental procedures for ascertaining the contribution of various factors to the IQ, we must introduce the concept of **heritability.** As in genetics, heritability presupposes that there is a measurable trait that is normally distributed in a given population. The height of 10-year-old boys in Chicago in 1973–1974 would be such a trait. The heritability of a trait is the degree of variation in the trait that can be attributed to genetic factors.

Studies of the heritability of a trait are usually designed to control for genetic endowment and to measure the amount of variability in the trait that remains. For example, suppose that the range of heights among 10-year-old boys was about 24 inches, but that the average difference between any two boys selected at random was 2 inches. Now, suppose that we compared the heights of identical and fraternal 10-year-old twin boys. If the average difference for both types of twins was also 2 inches, we would say that height had zero heritability and was determined completely by the environment. If, however, the difference between the identical twins was negligible and only about half an inch for the fraternal twins, we might regard height as having a heritability of .90 or better; that is, as being almost completely due to heredity.

The heritability of intelligence is studied in much the same way. Investigators select pairs of identical twins, fraternal twins, and siblings and administer intelligence, achievement, or other tests to them. One refinement of this procedure is to test identical twins who have been reared apart so that a more exact assessment of the role of the environment can be made. Other variations of the technique are to study children of biracial marriages, or twins from different socioeconomic groups. In all cases, however, the genetics are the independent variable, which is controlled by selection, and the measured trait is the dependent variable whose heritability is to be assessed.

Table 9.1 Median Values of Intelligence-Test-Score Correlations Obtained in 56
Studies Conducted between 1911 and 1962

Number of Samples	Biological Relationship	Condition of Rearing	Median Correlation
15	Monozygotic twins	Same family	.88
4	Monozygotic twins	Separate families	.75
21	Dizygotic twins	Same family	.53
39	Siblings	Same family	.49
3	Siblings	Separate families	.46
7	Unrelated	Same family	.17

Source: Jarvik, L. F., & Erlenmeyer-Kimling, L. Survey of familial correlations in measured intellectual functions. In. J. Zubin & G. A. Jervis (Eds.). *Psychopathology of mental development.* New York: Grune & Stratton, 1967.

Many studies have now been carried out to assess the IQ of identical twins (reared together and apart), of fraternal twins, of siblings, of parents and children, and of unrelated persons. Although variations can obviously be found from one study to another, the results are quite consistent. A summary of 56 such studies is given in Table 9.1 (4). The table confirms the point we made in Chapter 5, that there is a direct relationship between genetic similarity and the similarity of performance on IQ tests. It is also true that there is a direct relationship between the similarity of rearing and similarity of IQ scores. But the environmental factor seems to be less significant than the genetic one as indicated by the high correlation between IQs of identical twins reared apart, in presumably dissimilar environments. That is to say, the similarity in IQ of persons living together may vary from .17 to .88, whereas the similarity in IQ between parents and children varies only between .46 and .88.

In order to get a more exact estimate of the heritability of IQ, some investigators (5) have taken the data from Table 9.1 and divided them into the components and suggest that the total heritability of IQ is .75. Not all investigators agree on these figures, however; at least one (6) asserts that IQ heritability is higher, while others maintain that it is considerably lower (7–9). As we have indicated in Chapter 5, because of the many unknowns (population differences, errors of measurement, and so forth) and the dynamic interaction between IQ and experience, it is probably not possible or even necessary to obtain an exact numerical estimate of IQ heritability. Much more important is the unavoidable conclusion that a significant portion of IQ variability within specified groups must be attributed to genetics (10–12).

It is important, however, to stress that while IQ scores may provide a reasonable measure for estimating heritability, within groups, they are not reasonable measures for assessing genetic differences between groups. We shall discuss this issue in much more detail in a later section. At this point, it just needs to be said that when the IQ is used to compare groups from different backgrounds, it is best thought of as a measure of environmental factors more or less conducive to test performance. This is how the IQ is interpreted in the assessment of environmental interventions (see Chapter 3), and this is how we believe it should be thought of in the assessment of social class and racial/ethnic group differences.

Group Differences in IQ

Studies of the heritability of IQ (as discussed above) have mostly been within comparable groups. Comparisons between groups that are not comparable are much more difficult because there is no way to control for genetic endowment. Consequently, any differences between groups can be attributed to different genetic endowments *or* to different environments *or* to some combination of the two. It is important, therefore, to keep in mind the concept of within and between group differences. Within-group differences can be used to assess heritability; between-group differences cannot.

Socioeconomic Status (SES). A general finding is that IQ is positively related to socioeconomic status. Socioeconomic status is generally measured by a combination of the levels of educational attainment and income of the parents. The IQs of children from different SES groups have been obtained for both blacks and whites. For preschool children the correlations in one study were .24 for blacks and .33 for whites (10). Similar correlations between SES and achievement scores have also been obtained for Orientals (13). For American Indians, however, among whom SES differences are minimal, the correlations between ability and SES were not significant (13).

Many investigators (14–17) have compared the mean IQs of whites and blacks from both higher and lower social classes; a summary of those studies is presented in Table 9.2 (5). While it is clear that group differences exist, the reasons why are not so obvious. It is probably true that a certain amount of intelligence is required for economic success in our society and this may account for the SES and IQ correlations. But children at high SES level may acquire certain skills, such as relating to strange adults, that have nothing to do with intelligence but which nonetheless are reflected in intelligence test performance.

Racial/Ethnic Differences in IQ. In the late 1960s an emotion-laden hypothesis was offered to explain black/white differences in intelligence. As can be seen in Table 9.2, black children generally score below the mean (which is 100) of white children on such tests. In 1969 Arthur Jensen (19–22) suggested that the difference might be due more to genetics than to the environment, and marshaled a great deal of statistical evidence as a possible factor to support his hypothesis. Jensen's hypothesis that black/white differences in intelligence are largely genetic in origin has created a great deal of controversy (23–29).

As we have already suggested, however, the IQ cannot be used to assess the contribution of genetics to differences between groups. In our

Table 9.2   Comparison of Average Wechsler-Bellvue (W-B) IQs for Higher and Lower Socioeconomic Groups (H-L) That Are Defined the Same Way for Black and White (B-W) Samples in Various Studies

Study	Average IQ				W-B IQ Difference, within Class		H-L IQ Difference, within Race	
	LB	LW	HB	HW	L	H	B	W
Six earlier studies	82	94	92	112	12	20	10	18
Wilson (1967)	94	101	95	109	7	14	1	8
Tulkin (1968)	91	94	108	113	3	5	17	19
Sitkei & Meyers (1969)	77	93	96	106	16	10	19	13
Nichols (1970)	92	97	102	107	5	5	10	10
Scarr-Salapatek (1971a)	82	88	87	101	6	14	5	13
Nichols & Anderson (1973)	101	102	103	111	1	8	2	9
Nichols & Anderson (1973)	91	94	96	104	3	8	5	10

Source: Loehlin, J. C., Lindsey, G., & Spuhler, J. N. *Race differences in intelligence.* San Francisco: W. H. Freeman, 1975.

view, this is the fundamental flaw in Jensen's argument. The clearest rationale for our position has been given by the population geneticist Richard C. Lewontin, who writes:

If two populations have high heritabilities for a character and there is an average difference between them, is the difference mostly geneti-cal? One possibility is that the populations differ genetically because of a previous history of differential selection of a type that causes genetic variation to be stabilized. Another possibility is that the popu-lations may differ genetically because of historical accidents of genetic sampling (genetic drift) without differentiated selection. A third possibility is that the populations are genetically alike but live in environments that differ from each other in some critical limiting factor. All of these situations occur in nature and again, no a-priori likelihood can be assigned to them. . . .

An underlying assumption of Jensen's argument is that the ob-served direction of difference between black and white populations reveals an underlying average genetic difference in the same direc-tion. But this is an unjustified assumption. Even if there were non-trivial genetic differences between Blacks and Whites for genes in-

fluencing IQ, it does not follow that elimination of environmental differences would result in simply narrowing the gap in performance. It could easily result in simply narrowing the gap in the other direction, with Blacks outperforming Whites on the average. Which group would have the better average performance in a uniform environment depends upon the particular form of relationship between environment and the phenotype characteristics of the genes in question. [There is absolutely no evidence of any kind on this issue] [27, p. 109].

From a psychological standpoint, we find Jensen's argument faulty for comparable reasons. He assumes that the IQ is a measure which is equally valid for between-group as well as within-group differences that are partly genetic in origin. But as we have insisted earlier, tests measure different characteristics between groups than they do within groups. Piaget's conservation tests, for example, give a reasonable assessment of cognitive development for children of comparable backgrounds. But when children from different backgrounds are tested—say, from Bush Africa and Cambridge, Mass.—any differences between the groups would reflect development *and* background. As in the examples suggested by Lewontin, there is really no way to determine how much, if any, of the difference between the groups is due to environment and how much, if any, of the difference is due to genetics.

For within-group comparisons, where background can be assumed to be constant, the IQ is a reasonable measure for the determination of the contributions of heredity and environment. That is why we reviewed the data on twins and parents and their offspring. But the IQ cannot be used to assess the contribution of heredity and environment for between-group differences. The "IQ Controversy," the question of racial differences in intelligence rests, therefore, on a false assumption. Perhaps, if it were recognized that the IQ cannot legitimately be used to assess the contribution of genetics to between-group differences, the controversy would diminish.

Patterns of Ability within Racial/ Ethnic Groups

Intelligence tests assess a broad range of skills and abilities. Such tests can yield a profile, or pattern, depicting an individual's (or group's) performance on various measures. On the Wechsler Intelligence Scale for children (WISC), for example, children can be compared on verbal and performance IQ's, as well as on such subtests as vocabulary and general information.

One way to analyze the pattern of abilities in different groups is to use **factor analysis**—a statistical procedure. If a group has been tested on vocabulary, reasoning, problem-solving, memory, perception, and so forth, the data can be analyzed to see whether the various test scores can be described more economically by means of several underlying or ''common'' factors. For example, reasoning and problem-solving might have a high correlation, thus constituting a ''cognitive'' factor. Similarly, measures of discrimination and spatial orientation might have a high correlation, thereby constituting a ''perceptual'' factor. These factors have been used like scores to describe an individual or group's pattern of abilities.

This factor-analytic procedure has been employed to see whether the pattern of mental abilities is consistent in comparing various racial/ethnic groups. In general the pattern has been found to be consistent. For example, one study of 5-to-9-year-old black and white children found that the performance of both groups yielded the same factors (30). Another study of persons of Japanese and European ancestry showed that their performance too, gave rise to comparable factors (31). Other studies (10, 11, 32) suggest that there is little, if any, difference in the factorial *pattern* of abilities among various racial/ethnic groups. But what about relative differences in the ability *level* of the different groups? That is to say, since every racial/ethnic group has a verbal, a reasoning, a spatial visualization factor, and so forth, do the groups do equally well on these factors?

A study attempting to answer this question was conducted in 1965 (33). The subjects were first-grade children of Chinese American, Jewish, black, and Puerto Rican ancestry. There were equal numbers of boys and girls, and the children were equally divided between middle- and lower-class backgrounds for each racial/ethnic group. First of all, the children were given aptitude tests that had been modified somewhat so that they would be relevant to the children's past experience. The tests were administered in such a way as to maximize the children's rapport with the examiners giving the tests and minimizing any group differences in the matter of simply taking tests.

The four tested abilities and the results are presented in Table 9.3. One can see that there are substantial differences between the groups in ability level. It is also important to note that there was a definite relationship between SES and the scores but not with the over-all ordering of abilities. That is, the relative standing of the groups on the four tests of ability remained the same across differences in SES. This study was replicated in another city (34), and the results were comparable. Although these findings have been challenged (35), we feel that the investigator's reply (36) adequately answers the criticism and indicates that the data are reasonably correct.

Another, similar, study (37) compared 4-year-old disadvantaged children living in New York who were of Chinese, Italian, black, and Puerto Rican backgrounds. In four tests the youngsters were required to construct mosaics, identify and show that they understood parts, copy geometric figures, and demonstrate verbal fluency. The results showed that the Chinese children performed best in constructing mosaics and identifying body parts, and the Puerto Rican children did exceptionally well on the

Table 9.3 Scores of First-Grade Children of Different Backgrounds on Four Tests of Ability

Social Class	Verbal				
	Chinese	Jewish	Black	Puerto Rican	Mean
Middle	76.8	96.7	85.7	69.6	82.2
Lower	65.3	84.0	62.9	54.3	66.6
Mean	71.1	90.4	74.3	61.9	74.4

Social Class	Reasoning				
	Chinese	Jewish	Black	Puerto Rican	Mean
Middle	27.7	28.8	26.0	21.8	26.1
Lower	24.2	21.6	14.8	16.0	19.1
Mean	25.9	25.2	20.4	18.9	22.6

Social Class	Number				
	Chinese	Jewish	Black	Puerto Rican	Mean
Middle	30.0	33.4	24.7	22.6	27.7
Lower	26.2	23.5	12.1	15.7	19.4
Mean	28.1	28.5	18.4	19.1	23.5

Social Class	Space				
	Chinese	Jewish	Black	Puerto Rican	Mean
Middle	44.9	44.6	41.8	37.4	42.4
Lower	40.4	35.1	27.1	32.8	33.8
Mean	42.7	39.8	34.4	35.1	38.0

Source: Lesser, G. S., Fifer, G., & Clark, D. H. Mental abilities of children from different social class and cultural groups. *Monographs of the Society for Research in Child Development,* 1965, **30,** No. 4.

test of verbal fluency. Since these children were somewhat younger than those who participated in the studies mentioned above (33, 34), this might account for some of the discrepancies in the findings.

Many investigations have sought to compare black and white youngsters regarding their patterns of ability (30, 38–40). In much of this research the WISC has been used, and black and white children have been compared on verbal and performance IQs and on particular subtests. The results obtained with the WISC have been quite consistent. Black children attain higher scores on the verbal subtests than they do on the performance subtests. This appears to be true for older children and adults as well (5). Whites, upon whom the test is standardized, perform equally well on the verbal and performance subscales.

On the Stanford-Binet tests, 4-year-old black and white children performed differently. Black children scored higher on the tests requiring concentration and memory, whereas white children did better on the tests requiring judgment and reasoning (11). In another study of 4-year-old black and white children, a somewhat different pattern was found. The six factors assessed were verbal comprehension, ideational fluency, perceptual speed, figural reasoning (reasoning about pictures), memory span, and picture memory. The only test on which the white children did better than the black children was verbal comprehension (15).

The evidence reviewed above suggests that while the set of mental abilities (which make up IQ test performance), is about the same for various racial/ethnic groups in the United States, the groups do differ with respect to their level of attainment on particular abilities within this set. In our opinion, as we urged before, there is no way to determine whether the between-group differences are due to genetic, nutritional, or social/cultural factors, or to a complex interaction of these factors. Differences between groups in special abilities are no easier to interpret than between group differences in IQ.

SEX DIFFERENCES

During the preschool years boy/girl differences become much more varied and prominent than they had been in infancy. The extent to which these differences are determined by genetic or hormonal factors and by social or cultural conditioning probably varies from trait to trait. The body configuration of girls vis-à-vis boys (smaller average stature, less muscle, more fat, and so forth) is biologically determined. Differences in mental abilities may be due in part to biology and in part to cultural and social factors. With respect to personality traits, these may be almost entirely due to the social millieu.

Mental Abilities

It is frequently generalized that girls do better on verbal tasks while boys do better on spatial tasks (41, 42). While this generalization may be warranted, the differences are not as consistent or significant as they were once thought to be. What can be said is that when there are differences between boys and girls on verbal tests, for example, girls tend to do better (43–45). Maccoby and Jacklin, who have compiled and integrated a large amount of recent data on sex differences (46), suggest that there are distinct phases of language development. Girls are often superior until about the age of 3, at which time boys catch up. At about the age of 11, girls again begin to outperform boys on tests of verbal ability.

The assumption that there are consistent and substantial differences between boys and girls in spatial abilities also does not seem to be well founded (46). One of the problems is trying to define what spatial ability is and how it should be measured. Some of the tasks that are usually assumed to measure this ability include building designs with blocks from a pictured model, reasoning about spatial relationships, and reproducing geometric figures. In general, when there are differences between boys and girls on spatial tasks, boys tend to do better. Maccoby and Jacklin (46) argue that the male advantage in spatial visualization, to the extent that there is one, appears in adolescence and is maintained throughout adulthood.

In reviewing the research on sex differences in quantitative ability, analytic thinking, and reasoning, Maccoby and Jacklin found no sex differences up until adolescence. Even at that time most studies show few sex differences, with the notable exception of Piagetian tasks. We shall discuss those differences in Chapter 17. At this point it is only necessary to say that at the preschool level there do not appear to be any significant differences between boys and girls on general or specific measures of mental ability.

Personality
Characteristics

Certain aspects of behavior that are usually considered to be part of a child's personality show sex differences, but these are significantly related to children's sociocultural experience. We will review research on sex differences in field independence, play, and aggression.

As described in Chapter 1, **field independence** is the tendency to orient to one's immediate environment in terms of inner cues, while **field dependence** is the tendancy to use external cues for such orientation. A child who looked to other children or to adults for cues about how to act in a particular social situation would be field-dependent, whereas a child who usually assessed a situation independently before acting would be field-independent. Field independence/dependence is a fairly consistent trait that can be observed in many different types of behavior (47).

A much replicated finding among older children and adults is that women are more field-dependent than men (48–50). Some investigators have interpreted this as an example of cultural stereotyping and of the pressures upon women in our society to conform (47). This interpretation was made because it has been found that among the Eskimos (where men

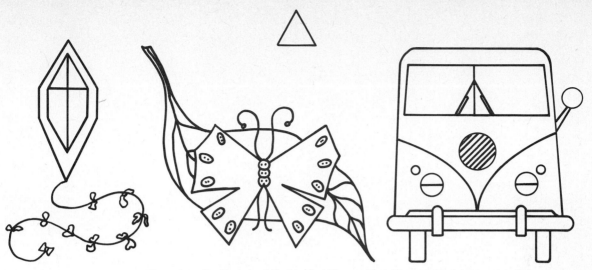

Items from the Preschool Embedded Figures Test. The child is instructed to find the triangle in each of the figures.

and women are treated as equals), there are no sex differences in tests of field independence. On the other hand, among the Temne of East Africa (where the women are dependent) the men were significantly more field-independent than the women (51).

Although field independence/dependence was first measured in older children and adults, a new test was introduced to assess this trait in children (52) (the Preschool Embedded Figures Tests or PEFT). The test requires the child to find a simple form that is embedded in a more complex form. Presumably the field-independent child is less bothered or misled by contextual clues than the field-dependent child. In using the PEFT with preschool children, it was found (although not consistently) that among 4- and 5-year-old children, girls are generally more field-independent than boys (53).

As we suggested above, field dependence appears to be associated with the passive orientation that is traditionally associated with women's role in many societies. The fact that preschool girls show more independence than boys—although this relation is reversed in later childhood and adulthood—also suggests that this trait is more a matter of social conditioning than of genetic makeup.

In the area of play, boy/girl differences were first noted by (among others) the distinguished psychoanalyst Erik Erikson (54). As we mentioned in Chapter 1, he reported that girls seemed to be especially interested in open, inner spaces. They built structures representing the interiors of homes—without walls—using elaborate entrances such as ornamental gateways. In contrast, boys built towers, turrets, and roadways. Girls seemed to be anxious about having their inner spaces invaded, and

In the nursery school boys and girls often gravitate to sex-role-stereotyped activities.

boys seemed to be anxious about the possible collapse of their erected structures.

The sexual symbolism in these play activities, as described by Erikson, is clear enough. What is not clear is the origin of these play preferences. Some investigators (55, 57) contend that sex differences in play are socially conditioned by the toys and rewards children are given. Typically girls receive dolls and other housekeeping materials and are rewarded for playing with them. Boys usually receive construction materials, trucks, cars, and so forth, and they are rewarded for playing in "masculine" ways. In a replication of Erikson's work (58), however, Cramer and Hogan present a persuasive argument against the learning theory of sex differences in play behavior; they contend (with Erikson) that children's play, at least in part, reflects fundamental themes associated with boy/girl differences in body configuration.

In our view there is probably some truth in both positions. It would be strange, indeed, if children's play were not affected by the toys and rewards they are given. On the other hand, the significant differences between the bodies of boys and girls evoke considerable curiosity and concern. It would be surprising if children did not act out some of their concerns about their bodies in play since, more than most other activities, play allows for the free expression of inner concerns.

Closely related to these differences in play are sex differences in social orientation and aggressiveness. These differences appear early: by the age of 1, boys show more aggressiveness and exploratory behavior than do girls (59, 60). These tendencies become more prominent during the pre-school years. Observational studies of young children suggest that "boys are interested in things and girls in people" (61, p. 159). Such studies also suggest that boys spend twice as much time in aggressive interaction as girls, and that boys tend to be the initiators and targets of attacks. When confronted, girls tend to give in or to quarrel rather than to fight, whereas boys tend to fight back (62).

These differences in boy/girl social interactions are related to subtle differentiations in ability that may entail more than simple social learning. Girls tend to use eye contact and physical proximity as indicators of social acceptance earlier than boys (63). And in confrontation situations, boys and girls act quite differently. Girls appear to be more afraid because they touch themselves more, smile ambivalently, and show apprehensive movements of the mouth. Boys appear to be less afraid because they turn their heads and bodies away; in a confrontation situation these actions are more likely to encourage a physical contest than girls' reactions (64). Boy/girl differences in play and in social interactions appear to be quite complex. These differences are partly due to social conditioning and stereotyping, and partly due to differences in body conformation and possibly to spontaneous differences in bodily orientation to social situations.

A child's awareness of his or her sexual role and of sexual stereotypes develops quite early, as we noted in Chapter 8; by the end of the third year most boys and girls know what sex they are and understand the major aspects of stereotyped sex-role behaviors. Even 3-year-old children can correctly identify pictures of clothing, toys, tools, and appliances as to whether they belong to men or women (65).

FAMILY CONSTELLATION

By the time children are of preschool age, patterns of parent-child and sibling interactions have become well established, and these often have important effects. Here we will discuss birth order and father absence.

Birth Order

Considerable evidence has been accumulated showing that first-born children differ in significant ways from later-born children. In general the first-born (and to a lesser extent only children) tend to score higher on measures of academic achievement and intelligence than do the later-born (66–68). In this regard, we might mention that nearly all (21 out of 23 who went to the moon) of America's astronauts have been first-born children (69). The reason for this phenomenon is not known, but many explanations have been offered (70–72).

In one study of the birth-order differences in achievement, three samples of students who had participated in the National Merit Scholarship Qualification Test were chosen. One sample was randomly selected from

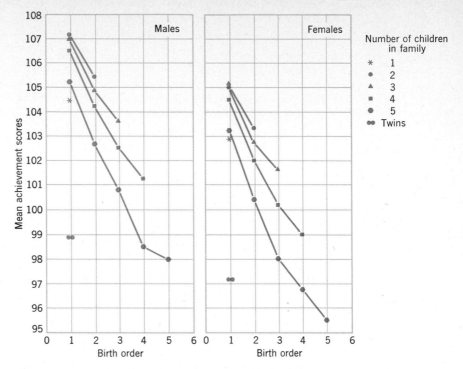

Figure 9.1 Mean National Merit Scholarship scores for young people of different birth order. (*Source.* Breland, H. M. Birth order, family configuration, and verbal achievement. *Psychological Bulletin,* 1974, **45,** 1011–1019.)

among all the students who took the examination; this was the "normative" sample. The second sample was a randomly selected group of high-scoring students. The third sample consisted of all the students who took the National Merit Scholarship Qualification Test in 1965.

The National Merit Scholarship examination has five subjects: English usage, mathematics usage, social studies reading, natural science reading, and word usage. It was found that in all three samples the first-borns from small families had the highest scores while the last-borns from large families had the lowest scores (73). Although not shown in Figure 9.1, first-borns showed less superiority to later-borns on tests requiring math skills.

In a cross-cultural study of birth-order effects, data were obtained from 39 unrelated societies in different parts of the world on the treatment and prerogatives afforded first-born children. The authors concluded:

In a world-wide sample of 39 societies, the birth of a first child of either sex is more likely than the birth of other children to increase parent status, stabilize parent marriage, and provide a parental tek-nonym.* First-borns are likely to receive more elaborate birth cere-monies and, in childhood, first-born daughters are likely to receive more respect from siblings than other daughters, and first-born sons, in comparison to other sons, are likely to have more authority over

*A person to take the parents' place should the parent die.

*siblings, more control of property, more power or influence over
others; to be respected more by siblings, and to head a kin group
[74, p.53].*

Among the many explanations offered for the different effects of birth
order, Schachter (75) proposed a "social comparison" theory. He held
that first-born children seek to measure themselves in terms of parental
achievements. Because the discrepancies are so great, at least initially,
first-borns become highly achievement-oriented in order to catch up with
their parents.

Other investigators have suggested that parents may treat first-born
children differently than they do later-born children (76, 77). Several
studies indicate that parents exert more pressure upon, are more inconsistent with, and expect more from their first-borns (78–80). And first-born
children appear to be more dependent or help-seeking than later-born
children (75, 78, 80, 81). The actions of first-borns may help to shape
parent behavior, just as parent behavior influences child behavior (76).

Other data also point to the interactions between first-borns and others
to explain their behavior. Studies that take into account the sex relationships among siblings show that the affiliation tendencies of first-borns
depend upon their sibling roles. First-born boys who have younger
brothers show the expected adult orientation, including dependence and
achievement striving, but their younger brothers do not. First-born girls
with younger brothers also show the expected pattern, but girls with older
brothers do not. However, first-born girls with younger sisters and first-
born boys with younger sisters do not show the achievement orientation
and dependence that characterize other first-born children (82–84).

Probably any generalizations about first-born children should be qualified by such considerations as the sex of other siblings in the family, the
age differences between siblings, and so forth (85). While many first-borns
show the paradoxical combination of high achievement orientation and
high affiliation, many others do not.

Father Absence

This area has been extensively researched because it has been assumed
that the father's presence in the home is essential for a child's (particularly a boy's) normal development. As we indicated in Chapter 8, it has
been found that the effects of father absence depend upon the age of the
children at the time the father leaves, whether his absence is permanent or
temporary, whether it is due to divorce or death, the financial stability of
the family, the solidarity and happiness of the marriage, and whether
there is an extended family and community support (86).

As an illustration of such variations, it is interesting to examine some
discrepant findings from two comparable studies of sailors' families—one
in Norway (87) and the other in Italy (88). In both studies the children
were given doll play tests (for assessing masculine or feminine behavior)

and the mothers were interviewed. Compared to a control group, the Norwegian sons of absent-sailor fathers showed insecure masculine identification, compensatory overmasculinity, and difficulties with peer adjustment. The mothers were described as overprotective of their sons and as having few interests outside the home (87).

A replication of the study with the families of Italian (Genoese) sailors did not corroborate these findings. The sons of sailors did not differ in masculinity from the control males with whom they were compared. In fact it appeared that the women whose husbands were home were more protective of their sons than the women whose husbands were away. In both cases the authors attribute the behavior of the boys to the effect their father's absence had on their mother, and the social context of father absence, rather than to the fact of father absence per se.

That is to say, in Genoa the society confers considerable independence upon women who are responsible for family finances and management. Moreover, there is a large extended family and considerable social interaction and support are provided by relatives and friends (87, 89). In contrast, the Norwegian mothers had less responsibility and independence and were less likely than the Italian mothers to be employed outside the home. Also, the Norwegian mothers did not have extended family and friends. It seems reasonable to conclude, therefore, that the effects of father absence upon the child are largely mediated through the attitudes, behavior, and personality of the mother (90).

SOCIAL AND CULTURAL DIFFERENCES

Young children are subjected to many different social and cultural influences that can significantly affect their thought and behavior. In this section we will discuss the following influences: language, reinforcement patterns, and general child-rearing practices. Because social and cultural factors are so general, strong experimental data are not always available. This is especially the case with respect to child-rearing practices in the Soviet Union, China and Israel. While the information from these countries is largely comprised of anecdotal observations by visitors, we believe it is important to include information from these societies in order to get a better perspective on our own parenting practices.

Social Class Differences in Language

Among American social scientists there is dispute about the meaning of social class differences in language. On the one hand, there are those who, following the English *socio*linguist Basil Bernstein (91), argue that lower-class children have different verbal skills. Bernstein holds that lower-class children communicate by means of a *restricted code* in which much information is conveyed nonverbally. In contrast, middle- and upper-class children communicate by means of an *elaborated code,* in which almost all information is communicated verbally. In Bernstein's view, differences in language provide different orientations to other areas of life, including education, work, and interpersonal relationships. Language shapes social interactions.

Following Bernstein's work in England, investigators have also found social class differences in language usage and patterns of interaction among middle-class and lower-class families in America (92–94). In one such investigation (95) middle- and lower-class mothers were asked a number of questions as, for example, ''Let's just imagine that (name of her child) is old enough to go to school for the first time. How do you think you would prepare him?'' The following are two typical replies:

First of all I would take him to see his new school, we would talk about the building, and after seeing the school, I would tell him that he would meet new children who would be his friends, he would work and play with them. I would explain to him that the teacher would be his friend, would help him and guide him in school and that he should do as she tells him to. That she will be his mother while he is away from home.

Well I would tell him he is going to school and he have to sit down and mind the teacher and be a good boy, and I show him how when they give him milk, you know, how he's supposed to take his straw and do, and not put nothing on the floor when he get through. [95, p. 96].

It is clear that the second mother spoke in terms of imperatives—unqualified commands—while the first mother spoke in terms of instructions—information about the rules to be obeyed; she also explained the rules and why they should be followed. In this study the mothers were also asked to instruct their children on certain tasks such as sorting objects by color. Middle-class mothers tended to give their children full explanations, whereas lower-class mothers tended to say simply ''put this here'' or ''this here'' without explaining very much.

The authors concluded:

The cognitive environment of the culturally disadvantaged child is one in which behavior is controlled by imperatives rather than by attention to the individual characteristics of a specific situation, and one in which behavior is neither mediated by verbal cues which offer opportunities for using language as a tool for labelling, ordering, and manipulating stimuli in the environment, nor mediated by teaching that relates events to one another and the present to the future. The meaning of deprivation would thus seem to be a deprivation of meaning in the early cognitive relationships between mother and child [95, p. 103].

This view of the significance of social class differences in language has been sharply disputed by psycholinguists (96–98). They hold that the language of lower-class blacks (and of lower-class whites as well) is not restricted but simply different. Black English, they contend, is every bit as rich and variegated as standard English. It is not seen or heard in testing situations such as those described above because lower-class subjects feel inhibited under such circumstances. On the street, however, or in comfortable surroundings and with friends, black children display a large language repertoire. The syntax and vocabulary differ from that spoken by middle-class children but their language is just as complex in structure and extensive in vocabulary.

There is some research evidence supporting this rejection of the "cultural deprivation" hypothesis about lower-class children. As noted in Chapter 7, several studies were made of preschool children, in which disadvantaged youngsters were tested under "optimum" conditions; that is, where they were familiar with the examiner and with the setting. It was found that their intelligence test performance improved over what it had been under standard testing conditions (99). One could conclude that when disadvantaged children feel comfortable, they are more likely to speak up and reveal their "elaborated code." It seems to us that what these conflicting studies demonstrate—more than anything else—is that the entire situation must be taken into consideration in assessing social class differences in language and cognition.

Social and Cultural Variations in Reinforcement Styles

One of the difficulties in cross-cultural research is to find a measurable behavioral dimension that is common to various social and cultural groups. One such dimension is the rewards and punishments parents use to teach their children.

Much of the data on this topic was collected by Norma D. Feshbach (100) and her collaborators. Typically a mother would be asked to teach her child to put together a puzzle. Reinforcement would be measured by counting the number of positive or negative statements the mother would make to her child during the instruction period. Neutral statements were not counted. Positive comments would include the following: "Yes, that's right," "good," while negative comments consisted of phrases like "not like that," "that's wrong, can't you see?" Thus, different investigators could classify the verbal statements as positive or negative with nearly perfect agreement.

At first, Feshbach and her colleagues used these procedures with American middle- and lower-class white and black mothers (103). It was found that the white middle-class mothers used more positive reinforcement than the black middle-class mothers; both the white and black lower-class mothers used about the same amount of positive reinforcement. The black lower-class mothers used significantly more negative reinforcement than the mothers in any of the other three groups; whose use of negative reinforcement was about the same.

An innovative feature of these studies was that the investigators asked the preschool children of these mothers to teach a younger child how to put together a simple puzzle (103). As in the case of the mothers, each child's positive and negative statements were counted in order to determine their use of rewards and punishments. In general, the results paralleled those of their mothers. Middle-class children used proportionately more positive than negative reinforcement, while the opposite was true for lower-class black children. Middle-class black children and lower-class white children used about the same number of rewards and punishments.

The same procedures were then followed with Israeli and English children and their mothers (100, 102). The results obtained for the mean number of positive and negative reinforcements used by 4-year-olds in teaching younger children are shown in Table 9.4, and the results for the American, Israeli, and English mothers in Table 9.5. In general, the results suggest that in these three societies, middle-class parents tend to use more positive than negative reinforcement, whereas the opposite is true for lower-class parents, and that children mirror the performance of their parents in providing reinforcement.

These data can be variously interpreted. Feshbach (100) argues that lower-class parents, simply because of their financial situation, experience greater privation, illness, and general stress than do middle-class parents:

The lower class parent who is trying to maintain at least a marginal level of social and economic adjustment is confronted with more daily pressures and demands (including more pregnancies and children) than is the middle class parent. Under these circumstances we might expect lower class parents to be less tolerant and more critical of their child's errors and other deviant behavior. In brief, the economic circumstances under which lower and middle class families live render it likely that the lower class family will make greater use of negative reinforcement than the middle class family [100, p. 107].

Table 9.4   Mean Frequencies of Reinforcement Administered by American, Israeli, and English 4-Year-Old Teachers

Culture	Middle-Class White	Middle-Class Black	Lower-Class White	Lower-Class Black
Positive Reinforcement				
American (study 1)	2.3	.2	.8	.7
American (study 2)	2.4	.08	1.9	.08
Israeli	1.8		.6	
English	1.8		.7	
Negative Reinforcement				
American (study 1)	1.6	1.3	1.7	2.1
American (study 2)	2.3	.4	2.6	1.6
Israeli	1.2		1.0	
English	2.4		2.5	

Source: Feshbach, N. D. Cross cultural studies of teaching styles in four year olds and their mothers. In A. D. Pick (Ed.) *Minnesota Symposia on Child Psychology.* Volume 7, Minneapolis: The University of Minneapolis Press, 1973.

Table 9.5   Mean Frequencies of Reinforcement Administered by American, Israeli, and English Mothers

Culture	Middle-Class White	Middle-Class Black	Lower-Class White	Lower-Class Black
Positive Reinforcement				
American	6.4	4.6	4.7	4.7
Israeli	6.7		4.3	
English	4.4		3.0	
Negative Reinforcement				
American	1.4	1.8	2.2	5.4
Israeli	2.9		3.8	
English	1.5		2.0	

Source: Feshbach, N. D. Teaching styles in four-year-olds and their mothers. In J. F. Rosenblith & W. Allensmith, *The causes of behavior.* (3rd ed.) Boston: Allyn & Bacon, 1972.

Child-Rearing Practices in Three Countries

Child-rearing customs in any society reflect, among other things, how that society values parenthood and children. In the case of both the Soviet Union and China, a new political ideology has been introduced that was not necessarily consistent with the cultural traditions of both societies. Although the evidence is scant, it appears that communal early childhood education, which is advocated by Communist ideology, is much more congenial to the Chinese historical tradition than to the Russian tradition. In Israel the communal ideology which underlay kibbutz education in the past is now being modified in keeping with longstanding traditions of Jewish child rearing.

Child-Rearing Practices in Russia. In the Soviet Union the schools for young children (from infancy through 6 years of age) provide total care, including meals, naps, outdoor exercise, and various types of supervised work and play. Children are left there by their parents on their way to work in the morning and then picked up on their way home in the evening. In principle, these schools are charged with indoctrinating children with the dominant values and morals of the society. The teaching and instructional materials have been explicitly designed to accomplish this (104, 105).

Actually, however, only about 10 percent of all Russian infants and 20 percent of children below 7 years of age are enrolled in these early childhood programs. The reason is partly because of tradition. In a questionnaire study, 66 percent of the mothers who sent their children to these nurseries said that they did so because there was no babushka (grandmother) or neighbor to care for them at home or in the neighborhood. Only 33.7 percent said they enrolled their children in the nursery to provide them with a more advantageous learning experience (105).

Despite much public propaganda and exhortation for husbands to

In many ways programs for young children in Russia are quite like those provided for young children in America.

"share the family burdens," child rearing is still regarded by men to be the responsibility of women. And Russian mothers whose children are in day nurseries express the same kinds of concern as American mothers whose children are in daycare centers:

> *The management undoubtedly knows that I have two children. But no one has ever totaled up the number of days I stay home from work when they are sick. . . . I worry about the children and about my work. Doctors write in the certificate "acute inflammation of the bronchial tubes." The doctors are in a hurry. I am also in a hurry; we take the children back to kindergarten before they are completely well. . . .*
>
> *There are twenty-eight children in the group, and the teacher does not have the strength to pay attention to everyone. Who invented the norms? Probably people who do not have children themselves.*
>
> —Natalya Baranskaya, "A week like
> any other," Moy Mir [105]

Although the programs are supposed to be identical in all day nurseries throughout the Soviet Union, this does not appear to be the case. As in America, the programs tend to vary according to the staff, children, and

Chinese children at school. Education in China is highly politicized and regimented.

facilities available. For example, one kindergarten teacher admitted that her pupils were learning English because the parents (who were professionals) wanted them to. The teacher said that at another school where she had worked, English was not taught because the parents did not demand it.

At the practical level of everyday child care, Soviet preschool programs probably do not differ very much from such programs in America. Indeed, variations in the program within each country are probably greater than the general differences between the two countries (105).

Child-Rearing Practices in China. In Communist countries, the family is sometimes regarded as an impediment to the purposes of the state. The individual's loyalty is supposed to be first and foremost to the larger community rather than to the family. One of the purposes of the communal rearing of infants has been to wean them from their close attachment to their parents. In the Soviet Union, as we have just mentioned, this aim has not been successfully realized. Collective child rearing, like collective farming, seems to conflict with the more abiding family and property traditions of the society (106).

Communal child rearing seems to be more successful in China. This is

Chinese children at play
that may also have
political overtones.

surprising because both the Chinese tradition and religion held that the
individual's primary loyalty was to his or her family. Ancestor worship
was but one example of the veneration accorded the Chinese family. Mao
Tse-tung attempted to change that and to reorganize child rearing and
education so that the primary loyalty of an individual would be to his or
her country (107). The "cultural revolution" of the 1960s was remarkable
because, for the first time, Chinese youth were berating and informing
upon their parents and teachers.

This change in loyalties was brought about by an extraordinary indoctrination campaign. Even at the nursery-school level, children's games are interpreted in political terms. When, for example, young children climb over chairs, climb through hoops, and cross a play bridge, they are told that this symbolizes Chairman Mao's Long March. One observer noted that when a teacher was trying to help the losing team in a game of tug-of-war, she said, in effect, "If you don't do better, you are going to be imperialists" (107).

Educators and psychologists who have visited China in the last few years have mixed opinions about the regimentation in the schools. Some fear that it will produce a generation of persons who will be totally subservient to government authority and have no personal will or initiative. Others note that the children seem to be happy and healthy and that they are well integrated within the society. Perhaps the regimentation is not too detrimental. According to one expert on China:

> *The thing for Westerners to remember is that although Mao has wrought many drastic changes in the Chinese way of life, he has not tampered with the Chinese sense of groupness. The Chinese have always felt a part of something larger than themselves and today that something is the state [107].*

Among the Chinese, there has long been a tradition of cohesiveness and self-regulation; this is also found among those of Chinese background living in the United States. For example, there is proportionately less delinquency among Chinese adolescents than among other groups here (108). It has been speculated that the reason for this is that Chinese parents teach their children not to express physical aggression; the parents try to facilitate this by removing their frustrations and by encouraging them to express aggression verbally (109, 110). The low rate of delinquency may also be due to the fact that the Chinese adolescent is readily accepted by his family and community.

Child-Rearing in Israeli Kibbutzim. The communal rearing of children on Israeli collective farms (kibbutzim) differs from the communal rearing in China and the Soviet Union. The first Jews to emigrate to Israel came from urban ghettos in Eastern Europe. In Israel they hoped to return to the soil and to get away from the mercantile pursuits that had been their lot for centuries. They hoped to establish work-cultural communities in which the property and labor would be shared in common. In some ways the traditional family, as an economic unit, was not congenial to this communal ideal and so its significance was played down.

Child rearing was also regarded as a communal responsibility. Children lived in "children's houses," where they were cared for by a trained teacher called a *metapalet*. The children would eat, sleep, play, and go to school at the children's houses. The parents would spend 2 hours in the afternoon with their children and then put them to bed at night. Some-

Lunch at a children's house on an Israeli kibbutz. The *metapalet* serves as surrogate mother and teacher.

times the children would spend a weekend with their parents. As the children grew older, they would move from one children's house to another; they would also participate more in the everyday work of the kibbutz, perhaps spending a few hours in school, a few hours picking fruit, and so forth. The entire kibbutz was regarded as both a vast playground and an educational environment for children, who were encouraged to explore and study it by congenial and sympathetic adults.

In 1969, Bruno Bettelheim, a well-known psychoanalyst, spent 7 weeks studying the kibbutz, after which he wrote an influential book entitled *Children of the Dream* (111). He concluded that young people who had grown up in a kibbutz were group-oriented, lacked independence, and were inhibited and conformist. Other observers have challenged his conclusions (112, 113). In fact, some studies show that kibbutz-reared children have as much individuality and variability as other children, but far less psychopathology (114–116).

The past decade or so, there have been a number of changes in the kibbutz. For one thing, native-born "kibbutzniks" do not need to react against urban ghettos as their parents did. Farm life has been their only experience. In addition, with increased mechanization, those living on the kibbutz are moving further and further away from the soil. When one is riding a tractor he or she is literally several feet from the earth. In at least some kibbutzim today, children are staying in their parents' homes at night—a practice unheard of a decade ago. Family life is becoming more prominent. On the kibbutz, as in the Soviet Union and China, longstanding cultural values and traditions have eventually asserted themselves despite political philosophies and social proscriptions. It would appear that no human group can ever be entirely made over by a new social form that has been imposed upon it.

INTERVENTIONS AT THE PRESCHOOL LEVEL

In 1964 the United States government initiated an ambitious program of remedial education for disadvantaged children. The program, known as Head Start, was based on the premise that poor children lacked certain experiences that are required for successful academic work. In part this view was derived from research with animals that showed the lasting effects of early stimulus deprivation. It was also derived from investigations that indicated language impoverishment among poor children (91–95).

In establishing Head Start programs, several different theories on the relationship between cognitive development and experience emerged and

Head Start programs have provided good preschool education for many children whose parents could otherwise not afford it.

The Montessori schools provide a very structured educational program for young children, requiring that materials be used in specific ways and according to fixed sequences.

were implemented. These theories ranged from the traditional "enrichment" (117, 118) of early childhood to the "didactic" approach most recently associated with the behavior modification tradition (119, 120). Because of the haste with which most Head Start programs were set up and because of their pragmatic aims, experimental evaluation of these programs was seldom possible.

One notable exception was an investigation made by Miller and Dyer (121); theirs was one of the most systematic and carefully controlled studies of early childhood education that has ever appeared in the literature. We will discuss what their study showed about the lasting effects of different methods of educating young, disadvantaged children.

Four different models of early childhood education were investigated. One of these, the Bereiter Engelmann (BE) program, is remedial and seeks to help children acquire basic academic skills such as reading and arithmetic and to increase their IQs (119, 120). The program has a clearly defined curriculum, and instruction is usually carried out by means of small groups using "patterned drill." The teacher would model a certain behavior, for example, the pronunciation of a word, and then the children would respond in unison. In general, the classroom atmosphere is businesslike and task-oriented.

The second program that was investigated was devised at the George Peabody College in Nashville, Tennessee (122), and is called DARCEE

(Demonstration and Research Center for Early Education). This program is also remedial but, besides trying to improve children's academic skills, it also focuses upon their feelings and attitudes toward school. Thus, extensive work is done with the parents as well. The curriculum is based upon an information-processing model, utilizes (a) input, (b) association activities, and (c) output. Children are helped to attend to stimuli (input), relate these to other material (association), and then communicate their experiences (output). This program also emphasizes small groups, but the groups use games rather than responding in unison.

The third method investigated was the Montessori (MONT) approach (pp. 246–248). As compared with the two programs already mentioned, Montessori's method has more general and more long-term goals (123). It attempts to develop (a) the senses, (b) concepts, (c) competence in daily activities, and (d) character. Montessori always stressed the importance of using teaching materials that were appropriate to the child's given level of physical and mental development. The environment is "prepared" in the sense that it contains teaching materials for the children to select from and to manipulate in very specific ways. The atmosphere in the Montessori classroom is quiet, as each child is busy working at one or another self-selected learning task.

The fourth program that was studied has been called the traditional (TRAD) "enrichment" approach. Here there is humanistic emphasis and the over-all aim is the total development of the child. This program is not a preparation for something else, and the child's immediate life experiences are held to be just as important as the later ones. There is no specific curriculum, but an attempt is made to provide experiences and activities that are unfamiliar and interesting to children. Disadvantaged children are regarded in the same fashion as other children with respect to their basic needs, interests, and abilities; they simply need the chance to discover the world and themselves. The classroom atmosphere is generally busy with small groups of children participating in such activities as baking bread, reading, or doing dramatic play. Occasionally the groups come together for storytelling or show and tell (talking about important events such as new babies, trips, new cars, and so forth) (124).

In setting up their study, the investigators selected 12 teachers who had been working in Head Start programs and who had some previous academic training and sent them to be trained in the four programs as described above. Although these teachers were not of the same age or intelligence (those in the MONT program were younger and brighter), they had basically similar attitudes toward children, and were about equal in such personality variables as anxiety, emotional poise, and extroversion.

The children who participated in the programs were selected from the low-income population of a large borderline Southern community (Louisville, Kentucky) and randomly assigned to one of the four programs or to a control group that did not attend any Head Start Program. There were no significant differences among the groups on such variables as parental age, income, education, and so forth. All children participated in the program for a full year prior to kindergarten; that is, during their fourth year.

The study planned to compare the groups at various times over a 4-year period as well as to evaluate the programs themselves. Program evaluation was done to make sure that there was a relationship between the stated purpose and the actual teaching of each program; a high degree of congruence was found.

To assess the children's accomplishments in the various programs, a wide variety of instruments was employed. Some of the results are shown in Table 9.6. It can be seen from this table that while the programs seem to have had some effects upon the children, these effects had all but disappeared by the end of the second grade. There were no significant differences between the four groups and the control children; by the end of the second grade, the control children were doing just as well as those who had participated in Head Start for a full year.

What is the meaning of these results? Is preschool education of no value? Certainly these findings are consistent with other research which has also found no evidence of any long-term effects on early education (125). Possibly the investigators failed to measure meaningful aspects of behavior. Perhaps the children had made gains in self-confidence, poise, and strategies of problem-solving that were not measured by the tests. Or perhaps other methods of educating young children, not explored in this investigation, would have had lasting and beneficial results. Finally, as we have discussed elsewhere, to be effective such programs must be continued into the school years or the quality of parent-child interaction must be permanently changed.

As we interpret these results, we think that Americans have expected too much of education. As the works of Jencks (7) and others (e.g. 18)

Table 9.6   Mean Stanford-Binet IQs for Five Groups of Children from Prekindergarten through Second Grade.

	BE	DAR	MONT	TRAD	CONT
	Stanford-Binet				
Pre-k—fall	92.93	96.12	92.11	89.98	89.07[a]
Pre-k—spring	98.35	96.61	97.04	96.44	90.87
Kindergarten	93.65	94.39	94.54	94.33	95.00
Grade 1	89.78	93.65	94.75	93.12	92.97
Grade 2	86.85	91.00	92.96	89.81	92.80

[a]CL-1 only.

Source: Miller, L. B. & Dyer, J. L. Four preschool programs: Their dimensions and effects. *Monographs for the Society for Research on Child Development*, 1975, **40**, 162.

suggest, it is the socioeconomic status of the child (and not just education) that seems to correlate substantially with academic and vocational success. The real lesson to be learned from this study (and similar ones) is that socioeconomic inequities cannot be removed or significantly altered simply through well-supported educational programs for disadvantaged children.

Essay

Life and death are topics of great interest to children because they pose certain problems and riddles. ''Why can't the bird fly any more?'' and ''Why do they have to kill the turkey?'' are the type of questions that parents and teachers are inevitably asked by young children. Death is a particularly difficult topic to discuss, in part because of our own emotional attitudes toward the subject. It is helpful, therefore, to understand how children at different ages think and feel about death in order to deal with the subject at their level.

Evolution of Children's Conceptions of Life and Death

A number of investigators have explored the evolution of children's conceptions of life and death and have arrived at comparable conclusions. Most investigators agree that conceptions develop in stages that are roughly related to age. Until about the age of 5, children do not understand the meaning of death and do not regard it as discontinuous with, or in opposition to, life. At the second stage, usually from ages 6 to 9, children begin to consider death as discontinuous with life but as reversible and not applicable to everyone. Then, beginning at about the age of 11 or 12, children begin to view death as irreversible in medical/biological terms (126–130).

In order to do full justice to the evolution of children's conceptions of life and death, however, we need to put them into the context of the general systems of thought that characterize intelligence at different age levels. For this purpose, the general stages of intellectual development described by Piaget (131) are appropriate. Piaget's stages pertain in part to how children conceptualize space, time, and causality—all of which are central to the child's understanding of death. For example, unless the child understands the meaning of the future, the anticipation of death cannot appear frightening.

The Preoperational Child. Children at this stage of development (usually from ages 3 to 6) tend to see the world in *anthropomorphic* terms (132); that is, they believe that many physical objects are alive and have feelings, intentions, and purposes. They also believe that plants and animals, as well as houses and automobiles, were made by and for man. They perceive every event such as falling rain and moving clouds as having purpose; there is no such thing as accident or chance. Past and future are scarcely understood at this age; the here-and-now looms very large in children's thinking.

Thus it is really not surprising that young children do not understand death as the termination of life. The responses of young children to questions on the meaning of death reflect their thinking. Children may say that to be dead means that you "didn't have any supper" or that you "go to sleep" (126). At best preschool children understand death as a kind of changed state, such as being hungry or asleep, but still continuous with life.

The Concrete Operational Child. At around the age of 6 or 7, most children acquire what Piaget (131) calls concrete operations; that is, an internalized set of actions that allows them to do in their heads what they had previously had to do with their hands. In trying to solve a pencil maze, for example, the concrete operational child will examine the various paths before putting his pencil on the paper. By contrast, the preschool child will try to solve the puzzle by trial and error, first following one path with his pencil and then another. Concrete operations also make it possible to understand space, time, and quantity as measurable dimensions. Concrete operations give rise to a *pragmatic* orientation toward the world, which is reflected in many different aspects of elementary-school children's behavior, including their conceptions of life and death.

One of their conceptions is that while death is the end of one life, it is also the beginning of another. Here are some examples of what children have said:

A child has just viewed a coffin and says, "Of course the person who went away [in the coffin] will become a baby." What makes you think so? "Of course he will, won't he?" I don't know. "When John [the child's baby brother] was born someone must have died" (126).

What happens when you die? "You don't feel anything." Anything else? "There are many people who go there." And when they go there what happens? "Sometimes they become an animal." How does that happen? "There is a force, a force which changes you into an animal after you have been in a cemetery" (130).

Another conception of the concrete operational child is that while death happens to some people, it does not happen to everyone. The child is not always clear about which people are to die and which people are to live:

Are there people who never die? "Sometimes." Who are the people who never die? "The parents." Why don't they die? "Because they take care of the children . . . and the policemen too." Why the policemen too? "Because they take us to prison and put handcuffs on." And they never die? "No." Would you like to be a policeman? "No, I would like to be a teacher." Would some of your friends like to be a policeman? "I don't know." If some of your friends became policemen, would they not die? "There are some people who die and some people who don't" (130).

Toward the end of the concrete operational period, however, the child discovers death in a very personal sense. It suddenly occurs to the child that he or she will die, and this comes as a startling and terrifying revelation. The child's realization that his parents will also die adds to his or her consternation. So traumatic is the discovery of death that many adults still remember the occasion quite vividly.

The Formal Operational Period. Beginning at about the age of 11 or 12, children acquire what Piaget (131) calls formal operations. These operations make possible new modes of thought and the acquisition of more abstract ideas of space, time, and causality. Adolescents can begin to understand concepts of historical time, celestial space, and probabilistic causality. They can also grasp metaphor and simile and participate in intellectual discussions about ideals, values, and attitudes. At this stage, young people arrive at a scientific view of the world that reflects itself in their views of life and death.

At about the age of 11 or 12, children begin to understand life and death in biological/medical terms. In one study (126) adolescents defined death as "A body that has no life in it" or "When you have no pulse, no temperature, and can't breathe." Adolescents appear to accept death as a fact of nature without undue emotional distress. They know that they themselves and their loved ones will die. But their understanding of time is such that they also recognize that these events are, in all probability, far in the future and thus need not be worried about now. In addition, formal operations allow adolescents to shift perspectives and look at death from different viewpoints, including the religious and the dramatic. This ability to shift perspectives, together with the young person's newfound sense of time units, makes the consciousness of his or her own mortality easier to bear than when it was first discovered at the end of the concrete operational period.

Talking with Children about Death

It is useful and necessary to discuss death with a child when the child has actually suffered the loss of a loved one, witnessed a death, or in some other way experienced the death of another person. Children may also become curious about death for other reasons. The crucial difference between these two sets of circumstances is the emotional state of the particular adults and children.

When a death occurs in the family, the children's world is thrown into a turmoil. Those whom they love begin to behave in strange and difficult ways. Familiar sources of emotional support are shaken, the children begin to fear that their previously comfortable world is about to fall apart. They need to be reassured that although the adults in their world are unhappy and upset now, this will pass. They need to hear that the adults in their world will continue to love them and that there will be few, if any, major changes in their way of life. In short, at a time of bereavement, what children need most to hear is that their immediate world—especially the love and protection of their parent or parents—will continue. A first rule, therefore, in talking with children about death is to give them ample reassurance about the continuity of life.

A second general rule is to avoid figurative language. Often, what seems to the adult to be supportive has just the opposite effect and thus causes the child additional fear and anxiety. Since children do not understand figurative language, they often take it quite literally. A child who is told that "Grandma has gone to sleep and won't wake up" may develop a dread of going to sleep for fear that he or she won't wake up either. Likewise, a child who is told that "Jesus took Daddy because he was so good" may decide never to be good for fear of being taken by Jesus. A child who is told that "Grandpa died because he was sick" may associate all sickness with death and become terrified at catching cold, and child who is told that his mother has "gone on a long trip" may believe that he or she has simply been abandoned.

In talking with bereaved children about death, it is important to be honest, simple, and direct. It is appropriate to use the words "death" and "dead" because the child understands these terms best, and they are least likely to be misunderstood. More emphasis should be given to reassuring the child about the continuation of his/her world than to explaining the nature of death. Similar guidelines apply when talking with nonbereaved children about death. In such instances, however, it is instructive to ask the child to try to answer his or her own questions. As indicated earlier, young children have quite elaborate ideas about death that they are quite willing to expound. Listening to nonbereaved children talk about death, we should show the same concern for their needs as when we offer reassurance to bereaved children. In both cases, what children learn about death is far less important than what they learn about life from those who love and care for them.

Summary

During the preschool years individual variations become more pronounced than they were during infancy. Preschool children are able to take intelligence tests, and their performance becomes predictive of later intellectual ability. Although intelligence has a genetic component (heritability), there is disagreement about how much genetics contributes to IQ variations between individuals and groups. Individuals and groups differ not only in overall ability but also in the patterns of subabilities measured by intelligence tests. Again it is not clear what sort of heredity-environment interaction contributes to these patterns.

During early childhood there are only insignificant differences between boys and girls on measures of mental ability. Personality differences are more marked. There appear to be some boy-girl differences in cognitive style, play behavior, body language, and aggressiveness. These differences are probably due to the interaction of body configuration and social conditioning.

Two aspects of family configuration have particular significance for individual variations at the preschool level: birth order and father absence. First-born children often show a pattern of high achievement and high need for affiliation. But whether a first-born will show this pattern will depend on such factors as the sex and spacing of siblings. Father absence need not be traumatic for children, and its effects will depend on such things as the mother's personality and the support provided by family and community in child rearing.

During early childhood social-class and cultural differences can be observed in language, reinforcement styles, and in child-rearing practices. There is disagreement as to whether lower-class people have a more restricted code than upper-class people. Lower-class parents do seem to use proportionately more negative than positive reinforcement in child rearing. Child rearing practices in Russia, China, and Israel are supposedly dictated by political ideology. However, cultural traditions of long standing will often determine how the ideology gets translated into practice.

References

1. Bayley, N. Consistency and variability in the growth of intelligence from birth to eighteen years. *Journal of Genetic Psychology,* 1949, **75,** 165–196.
2. Bradway, K. P. I.Q. constancy in the revised Stanford Binet from the preschool to the junior high school level. *Journal of Genetic Psychology,* 1944, **65,** 197–217.
3. Skodak, M., & Skeels, H. M. A final follow-up study of 100 adoptive children. *Journal of Genetic Psychology,* 1949, **75,** 85–125.
4. Jarvik, L. F., & Erlenmeyer-Kimling, L. Survey of familial correlations in measured intellectual functions. In J. Zubin & G. A. Jervis (Eds.), *Psychopathology of mental development.* New York: Grune and Stratton, 1967.
5. Loehlin, J. C., Lindzey, G., & Spuhler, J. N. *Race difference in intelligence.* San Francisco: W. H. Freeman, 1975.
6. Jensen, A. R. *Genetics and education.* New York: Harper, 1972.
7. Jencks, C., *et al. Inequality: A reassessment of the effect of family and schooling in America.* New York: Basic Books, 1972.
8. Kamin, T. Heredity, intelligence, politics and psychology. In N. J. Block & G. Dworkin (Eds.), *The IQ controversy.* New York: Pantheon, 1976.
9. Tayzer, D. Heritability analyses of IQ scores: Science or numerology. *Science,* 1974, **183,** 1259–1266.
10. Nichols, P. L. The effects of heredity and environment on intelligence test performance in 4 and 7 year old white and Negro sibling pairs. (Doctoral Dissertation, University of Michigan.) Ann Arbor, Michigan: *University Microfilms,* 1970, **No. 71-18,** 874.
11. Scarr-Salapatek, S. Race, social class and IQ. *Science,* 1971, **174,** 1223–1228.
12. Osborne, R. T., & Gregor, A. J. Racial differences in heritability estimates for tests of spatial ability. *Perceptual and Motor Skills,* 1968, **27,** 735–739.
13. Coleman, J. S., *et al.* Equality of educational opportunity. Washington, D.C.: U.S. Office of Education, 1966.
14. Nichols, P. L., & Anderson, V. E. Intellectual performance, race and socioeconomic status. *Social Biology,* 1973, **20,** 367–374.
15. Sitkei, E. G., & Meyers, C. E. Comparative structure of intellect in middle and lower

class four year olds of two ethnic groups. *Developmental Psychology,* 1969, **1,** 592–604.

16. Tulkin, S. R. Race, class, family and school achievement. *Journal of Personality and Social Psychology,* 1968, **9,** 31–37.

17. Wilson, A. B. Educational consequences of segregation in a California community. In report of U.S. Commission on Civil Rights. *Racial Isolation in Public Schools.* Vol. 2, Appendices, Washington, D.C.: U.S. Government Printing Office, 1967.

18. McClelland, D. C. Testing for competence rather than for intelligence. *American Psychologist,* 1973, **28,** 1–14.

19. Jensen, A. R. How much can we boost IQ and scholastic achievement? *Harvard Educational Review,* 1969, **39,** 1–123.

20. Jensen, A. R. *Genetics and education.* New York: Harper, 1972.

21. Jensen, A. R. *Educability and group differences.* New York: Harper, 1973.

22. Jensen, A. R. The differences are real. *Psychology Today,* 1973, **7,** 80–86.

23. Layzer, D. Science or Superstition? A physical scientist looks at the I.Q. controversy. *Cognition,* 1973, **1,** No. 2.

24. Thoday, J. M. Educatility and group differences. *Nature,* 1973, 245.

25. Lewontin, R. Race and intelligence. In N. J. Block & G. Dworkin (Eds.), *The I.Q. controversy.* New York: Pantheon, 1976.

26. Bereiter, C. Genetics and educability: Educational implications of the Jensen debate. In N. J. Block & G. Dworkin (Eds.). *The I.Q. controversy.* New York: Pantheon, 1976.

27. Lewontin, R. Further remarks on race and the genetics of intelligence. In N. J. Block & G. Dworkin (Eds.), *The I.Q. controversy.* New York: Pantheon, 1976.

28. Jensen, A. R. A reply to Lewontin. In N. J. Block & G. Dworkin (Eds.), *The I.Q. controversy.* New York: Pantheon, 1976.

29. Bane, M. J., & Jencks, C. Five myths about your I.Q. In N. J. Block & G. Dworkin (Eds.), *The I.Q. controversy.* New York: Pantheon, 1976.

30. Semler, I. J., & Iscoe, I. Comparative and developmental study of learning abilities of Negro and white children under four conditions. *Journal of Educational Psychology,* 1963, **54,** 38–44.

31. DeFries, J. C., *et al.* Near identity of cognitive structure in two ethnic groups. *Science,* 1974, **183,** 338–339.

32. Humphreys, L. S., & Taber, T. Ability factors as a function of advantaged and disadvantaged groups. *Journal of Educational Measurement.* 1973, **10,** 107–115.

33. Lesser, G. S., Fifer, G., & Clark, D. H. Mental abilities of children from different social class and cultural groups. *Monographs of the Society for Research in Child Development,* 1965, **30,** No. 4.

34. Stodolsky, S. S., & Lesser, G. Learning patterns in the disadvantaged. *Harvard Educational Review,* 1967, **37,** 546–593.

35. Feldman, D. Problems in the analyses of patterns of abilities. *Child Development,* 1973, **44,** 12–18.

36. Lesser, G. S. Problems in the analyses of patterns of abilities: A reply. *Child Development,* 1973, **44,** 19–20.

37. Leifer, A. Ethnic patterns in cognitive tasks. *Proceedings* of the 80th Annual Convention of the American Psychological Association, 1972, **7,** 73–74.

38. Caldwell, B. M., & Smith, T. A. Intellectual structure of Southern Negro children. *Psychological Reports,* 1968, **23,** 63–71.

39. Nichols, P. L., & Anderson, V. E. Intellectual performance, race and socioeconomic status. *Social Biology,* 1973, **20,** 367–374.

40. Osborne, R. T. Stability of factor structure of the WISC for normal Negro children from preschool to first grade. *Psychological Reports,* 1966, **18,** 655–664.

41. McCarthy, D. Language development in children. In L. Carmichael (Ed.), *Manual of Child Psychology.* (2nd ed.) New York: Wiley, 1954.

42. Maccoby, E. E. Sex differences in intellectual functioning. In E. E. Maccoby (ed.), *The development of sex differences.* Stanford, Calif.: Stanford University Press, 1966.

43. Matheny, A. P., Jr. Heredity and environmental components of competency of children's articulation. Paper presented at the biennial meeting of the Society for Research in Child Development. Philadelphia, 1973.

44. Sharan (Singer), S., & Weller, T. Classification patterns of underprivileged children in Israel. *Child Development,* 1971, **42,** 581–594.

45. Shipman, V. C. *Disadvantaged children and their first school experience.* Educational Testing Service Head Start Longitudinal Study, 1971.

46. Maccoby, E. E., & Jacklin, C. *The psychology of sex differences*. Stanford, Calif.: Stanford University Press, 1974.

47. Witkin, H. A., *et al. Psychological differentiation*. New York: Wiley, 1962.

48. Bieri, J., Bradburn, W., & Salinsky, M. Sex differences in perceptual behavior. *Journal of Personality*, 1958, **26**, 1–12.

49. Morf, M. E., Kavanaugh, R. D., & McConville, M. Intratest and sex differences on a portable Rod-and-Frame test. *Perceptual and Motor Skills*, 1971, **32**, 727–733.

50. Vaught, S. M. The relationship of role identification and ego strength to sex differences the Rod-and-Frame Test. *Journal of Personality*, 1965, **33**, 271–283.

51. Berry, J. W. Temne and Eskimo perceptual skills. *International Journal of Psychology*, 1966, **1**, 207–229.

52. Coates, S. *The preschool Embedded-Figures test (PEFT)*. Palo Alto, Calif.: Consulting Psychologists Press, 1972.

53. Coates, S. Sex differences in field independence among preschool children. In R. C. Friedman, R. M. Richart, & R. L. VandeWiele (Eds.), *Sex differences in behavior*. New York: Wiley, 1974.

54. Erikson, E. H. Sex differences in the play configurations of preadolescents. *Journal of Orthopsychiatry*, 1951, **21**, 667–692.

55. Brown, D. G. Masculinity-femininity development in children. *Journal of Consulting Psychology*, 1957, **21**, 197–202.

56. Lynn, D. B. Sex differences in masculine and feminine identification. *Psychological Review*, 1959, **66**, 126–135.

57. Mischel, W. A social-learning view of sex differences in behavior. In E. Maccoby (Ed.), *The Development of Sex Differences*. Stanford, Calif.: Stanford University Press, 1966.

58. Cramer, P., & Hogan, K. A. Sex differences in verbal and play fantasy. *Developmental Psychology*, 1975, **2**, 145–154.

59. Goldberg, S., & Lewis, M. Play behavior in the one year old infant: Early sex differences. *Child Development*, 1969, **40**, 21–31.

60. Hutt, C. Specific and diverse exploration. In H. Reese and L. Lipsitt (Eds.), *Advances in child development and behavior*. Vol. 5. New York: Academic Press, 1970.

61. Hutt, C. Sex differences in human development. *Human Development*, 1972, **15**, 153–170.

62. Brindley, C., Clover, P., Hutt, C., Robinson, I., & Wethle, E. Sex differences in the activities and social interactions of nursery school children. In R. P. Michael and J. H. Crook (Eds.), *Comparative ecology and behavior of primates*. New York: Academic Press, 1972.

63. Post, B., & Hetherington, E. M. Sex differences in the use of proximity and eye contact in judgements of affiliation in preschool children. *Developmental Psychology*, 1974, **10**, 881–889.

64. Stern, D. N., & Bender, E. P. An ethological study of children approaching a strange adult: Sex differences. In R. C. Friedman, R. M. Richart, & R. L. VandeWiele (Eds.), *Sex differences in behavior*. New York: Wiley, 1974.

65. Thompson, S. K. Gender labels and early sex role development. *Child Development*, 1975, **46**, 339–347.

66. Belmont, T., & Marolla, F. A. Birth order, family size and intelligence. *Science*, 1973, **182**, 1096-1101.

67. Eysenck, H. J., & Cookson, D. Personality in primary school children: Three family background. *British Journal of Educational Psychology*, 1969, **40**, 117–131.

68. Record, R. G., McKeown, T., & Edwards, J. H. The relation of measured intelligence to birth order and maternal age. *Annals of Human Genetics*, 1969, **33**, 61–69.

69. *The New York Times*, December 24, 1968.

70. Schooler, C. Birth order effects: not here, not now! *Psychological Bulletin*, 1972, **78**, 161–175.

71. Breland, H. M. Birth order effects: a reply to Schooler. *Psychological Bulletin*, 1973, **80**, 210–212.

72. Schooler, C. Birth order effects: a reply to Breland. *Psychological Bulletin*, 1973, **80**, 213–214.

73. Breland, H. M. Birth order, family configuration and verbal achievement. *Child Development*, 1974, **45**, 1011–1019.

74. Rosenblatt, P. C., & Skoogberg, E.L. Birth order in cross cultural perspective. *Developmental Psychology*, 1974, **10**, 48-54.

75. Schachter, S. *The psychology of affiliation.* Stanford, Calif.: Stanford University Press, 1959.

76. Osofsky, J. D., & Oldfield, S. Children's effects on parental behavior: Mothers' and fathers' responses to dependent and independent child behaviors. *Proceedings of the 79th Annual Convention, American Psychological Association,* 1971, **6**, 143–144.

77. Sutton-Smith, B., & Rosenberg, B. G. *The sibling.* New York: Holt, 1970.

78. Cushna, B. Age and birth order differences in very early childhood. Paper presented at the annual meeting of the American Psychological Association, New York, 1966.

79. Lasko, J. K. Parent behavior towards first and second children. *Genetic psychology monographs,* 1954, **49**, 97–137.

80. Hilton, I. Differences in the behavior of mothers towards first and later born children. *Journal of Personality and Social Psychology,* 1967, **7**, 282–290.

81. Gewirtz, J. L. Succorance in young children. State University of Iowa, Iowa City. Unpublished Ph.D. thesis, 1948.

82. Koch, H. L. The relation of certain family constellation characteristics and the attitudes of children towards adults. *Child Development,* 1954, **25**, 209–223.

83. Bragge, B. W. E., & Allen, V. L. Ordinal position and conformity. Paper presented at the annual meeting of the American Psychological Association, New York, September 1966.

84. Sampson, E. E. The study of ordinal position: antecedents and outcomes. In B. Maher (Ed.), *Progress in experimental personality research.* Vol. II. New York: Academic Press, 1965.

85. Koch, H. L. Some emotional attitudes of the young child in relation to characteristics of his sibling. *Child Development,* 1956, **27**, 393–426.

86. Herzog, E., & Sudia, C. E. Children in fatherless families. In B. M. Caldwell & H. N. Riccuiti (Eds.), *Review of child development research.* Vol. 3. Chicago: University of Chicago Press, 1973.

87. Tiller, P. O. Father absence and the personality development of children in sailor families. A preliminary research report II. In N. Anderson (Ed.), *Studies of the family.* Gottingen: Vandenhoeck and Ruprecht, 1957.

88. Cincona, L., Cesa-Bianchi, M., & Bouquet, F. Identification with the father in the absence of a paternal model. *Archivo di Psicologia, Neurologia e psichiatria,* 1963, **24**, 339–361.

89. Gimseth, E. The impact of father absence in sailor families upon personality structure and social adjustment of adult sailor sons. In N. Anderson (Ed.), *Studies of the family.* Part I. Gottingen: Vandenhoeck and Ruprecht, 1957.

90. Tiller, P. O. Father absence and personality development in children of sailor families. *Nordesk Psyckologis Monograph Series No. 9.* Oslo: Bokhyrnet, 1958.

91. Bernstein, B. Elaborated and restricted codes: Their social origins and some consequences. *American Anthropologist,* 1964, **66**, 55–69.

92. Cherry-Persach, E. Children's comprehension of teacher and peer speech. *Child Development,* 1965, **30**, 467–480.

93. Krauss, R. M., & Rotter, G. S. Communication abilities of children as a function of status and age. *Merrill-Palmer Quarterly,* 1968, **14**, 161–173.

94. Whiteman, M., Brown, B. R., & Deutsch, H. Some effects of social class and race on children's language and intellectual abilities. In M. Deutsch *et al.* (Eds.), *The disadvantaged child.* New York: Basic Books, 1967.

95. Hess, R. D., & Shipman, V. C. Maternal influences upon early learning; The cognitive environments of urban preschool children. In R. D. Hess and R. M. Bear (Eds.), *Early education.* Chicago: Aldine Press, 1968.

96. Baratz, J. C. Language in the economically disadvantaged child: A perspective. *Journal of the American Speech and Hearing Association, ASHA,* 1968, **10**, 143–145.

97. Labov, W. Academic ignorance and black intelligence. *Atlantic Monthly,* June 1972, **229**, 59–67.

98. Stewart, W. A. Urban Negro speech: Sociolinguistic factors affecting English teaching. In R. W. Shuey (Ed.), *Social dialects and language learning.* Champaign, Ill.: National Council of Teachers of English, 1964.

99. Zigler, E., Abelson, W. D., & Seitz, V. Motivational factors in the performance of economically disadvantaged children on the Peabody Picture Vocabulary Test. *Child Development,* 1973, **44**, 294–303.

100. Feshbach, N. D. Cross-cultural studies of teaching styles in four year olds and their

mothers. In A. D. Pick (Ed.), *Minnesota symposia on child psychology*. Vol. 7. Minneapolis: The University of Minnesota Press, 1973.

101. Feshbach, N. D. Teaching styles in four year olds and their mothers. In J. F. Rosenblith & W. Allensmith (Eds.), *The causes of behavior: Readings in child development and educational psychology*. (3rd ed.) Boston: Allyn & Bacon, 1972.

102. Feshbach, N. D. Teaching styles of Israeli four year olds and their mothers: A cross-cultural comparison. Paper presented at the meeting of the American Educational Research Association, New Orleans, February 1973.

103. Feshbach, N. D., & Devor, G. Teaching styles in four year olds. *Child Development*, 1969, **40**, 183–190.

104. Bronfenbrenner, U. *Two Worlds of Childhood: U.S. and U.S.S.R.* New York: Russell Sage, 1970.

105. Jacoby, S. Who raises Russia's children? *Saturday Review*, August 1971.

106. *Time* magazine, February 27, 1976.

107. Coming of Age in Communist China, *Newsweek*, February 21, 1972.

108. Sollenberger, R. T. Chinese American child rearing practices and juvenile delinquency. *Journal of Social Psychology*, 1968, **74**, 12–23.

109. Hsu, F. L. K., Watrous, B., & Lord, E. Culture pattern and adolescent behavior. *International Journal of Social Psychiatry*, 1960–1961, **7**, 33–53.

110. Niem, Tien-Ing Chyou, & Collard, R. R. Parental discipline of aggressive behaviors in four year old Chinese and American children. In H. C. Lindgren (Ed.), *Children's behavior*. Palo Alto, Calif.: Mayfield, 1975.

111. Bettelheim, B. *Children of the dream*. New York: Macmillan, 1969.

112. Bronfenbrenner, U. The dream of the kibbutz. *Saturday Review*, 1969.

113. Marcus, J., Thomas, A., & Chess, S. Behavioral individuality in kibbutz children. *Israel Annals of Psychiatry and Related Disciplines*, 1969, **7**, 43–54.

114. Kaffman, M. Survey of opinions and attitudes of kibbutz members towards mental illness. *Israel Annals of Psychiatry and Related Disciplines*, 1967, **5**, 17–31.

115. Kaffman, M. A comparison of psychopathology: Israel children from kibbutz and from urban surroundings. *American Journal of Orthopsychiatry*, 1965, **35**, 509–520.

116. Kaffman, M. Characteristics of the emotional pathology of the kibbutz child. *American Journal of Orthopsychiatry*, 1972, **4**, 692–709.

117. Branche, C. F., & Overly, N. V. Illustrative descriptions of two early childhood programs. *Educational Leadership*, 1971, **28**, 821–826.

118. Cowles, M. Four views of learning and development. *Educational Leadership*, 1971, **28**, 790–795.

119. Bereiter, C., & Englemann, S. *Teaching disadvantaged children in the preschool*. Englewood Cliffs, N. J.: Prentice-Hall, 1966.

120. Englemann, S. The effectiveness of direct instruction on IQ performance and achievement in reading and arithmetic. In J. Hellmuth (Ed.), *Disadvantaged child*. Vol. 3. New York: Brunner/Mazel 1970.

121. Miller, L. B., & Dyer, J. L. Four preschool programs: Their dimensions and effects. *Monographs of the Society for Research on Child Development*, 1975, **40**, (Serial No. 162).

122. Gray, S. W., & Klauss, R. A. An experimental preschool program for culturally deprived children. *Child Development*, 1965, **36**, 887–898.

123. Montessori, M. *The Montessori method*. New York: Schocken, 1964.

124. Hymes, J. L., Jr. *Teaching the child under six*. Columbus, Ohio: Merrill, 1968.

125. Westinghouse Learning Corporation, Ohio University. *The impact of Head Start, an evaluation of the effects of Head Start on children's cognitive and affective development*. Vol. 1, text and appendices A.–E. Washington, D.C.: Clearing House for Federal Scientific and Technical Information, Department of Commerce, National Bureau of Standards, 1969.

126. Anthony, S. *The child's discovery of death*. New York: Harcourt, 1940.

127. Gesell, A., Ilg, F. L., & Ames, L. B. *Youth: The years from ten to sixteen*. New York: Harper, 1956.

128. Melear, J. D. Children's conceptions of death. *Journal of Genetic Psychology*, 1973, **123**, 359–360.

129. Nagy, M. The child's theories concerning death. *Journal of Genetic Psychology*, 1948, **73**, 3–27.

130. Wallon, H. *Les origines de la pensée chez l' enfant*. Paris: Presses Universitaires de France, 1946.
131. Piaget, J. *The psychology of intelligence*. London: Routledge & Kegan Paul, 1950.
132. Piaget, J. *The child's conception of the world*. London: Routledge & Kegan Paul, 1929.

10 | Abnormal Development

MINIMAL BRAIN DYSFUNCTION (MBD)

Manifestations of MBD

Maladaptive Consequences of MBD

Causes of MBD

Treatment of MBD

CHILDHOOD SCHIZOPHRENIA

Symptoms of Childhood Schizophrenia

The Origin of Schizophrenia

Prognosis and Treatment

PHOBIAS AND RITUALS

Fears and Phobias

The Disposition to Early Childhood Phobias

The Focus of Phobic Reactions

Routines and Rituals

Treatment

ESSAY

Stimulant Drugs for Hyperactive Children:
A Blessing or a Curse?

SUMMARY

REFERENCES

The major psychological disturbances of early childhood, like those of infancy, can be grouped into just a few broad categories. In this chapter we will discuss three such categories of disturbance that are likely to make their first appearance during the preschool years: minimal brain dysfunction, childhood schizophrenia, and phobias and rituals.

MINIMAL BRAIN DYSFUNCTION

Minimal brain dysfunction (MBD) is a disorder of behavioral and cognitive functioning that is presumed to involve some impairment of the central nervous system. Although child specialists generally agree that this condition exists, opinions differ as to what it should be called. Most prefer MBD, the term we are using (1-3). However, because the condition is often characterized by a heightened level of activity and can occur without detectable brain damage, it is also commonly referred to as **hyperactive child syndrome** (4, 5).

Despite considerable variation in the criteria used to identify MBD, surveys consistently reveal its presence in 5 to 10 percent of all children examined (6–8). This makes MBD by far the most common behavioral disorder among young people; it means further that probably no fewer than 3 million children in the United States, and perhaps as many as 6 million, suffer from impairments associated with MBD. From 30 to 50 percent of children referred to child guidance clinics are found to have some form of this disorder (3, 5).

For reasons that are not clear, MBD is at least three or four times more common among boys than among girls (8). One possibility that researchers are considering is that this sex difference in susceptibility to MBD is due to some inborn sex-linked determinant of the condition.

MBD is usually present from birth or soon afterward. Like mental retardation, however, it is often not identified until middle childhood, when the academic and social demands of being in school make an MBD child's limitations more obvious than before. Nevertheless, it is during the preschool years that the primary manifestations of the disorder first become apparent, and growing recognition of this fact is resulting in increasing research attention to MBD preschoolers. Books addressed to parents (for example, *Raising a Hyperactive Child, Why Your Child Is Hyperactive)* are also making the general public more sensitive than in the past to indications of MBD among 2- to 5-year-olds (4, 9–11).

Manifestations of MBD

MBD consists of several distinctive behavioral and perceptual-cognitive impairments that lead in turn to various academic, social, and emotional difficulties.

Behavioral Impairments. More than anything else, MBD children have problems controlling and coordinating their motor activity. In addition to being hyperactive, most MBD children are awkward and clumsy in their gross motor movements and slow in learning to sit up, stand, walk, skip, and run. These children also tend to be conspicuously distractible, impulsive, and excitable. They have a limited span of attention and limited ability to concentrate; they have a low tolerance for frustration and little self-control; and they overreact to stimulation and show rapid, unpredictable changes in mood (2, 5, 12–15).

MBD children tend to be constantly on the go, dashing from one place to the next, crashing into people and things with reckless abandon, and making a general nuisance of themselves. They almost always appear tense and keyed-up. Even when they sleep, which is less often than other children their age, they are restless and unable to relax.

Because of their ceaseless squirming and fidgeting, MBD children often require herculean efforts on the part of their parents to wash, dress, and otherwise care for them. They sometimes burst into tears or throw violent temper tantrums over little or nothing, and they may alternate tears and tantrums with silly giggling or uproarious laughter, all in rapid succession. No person, toy, game, television program, or other diversion can keep them occupied for very long, and the task of keeping them entertained, much less under control, tries the patience of even the most accepting and easygoing adults. With their quick temper and poor self-control, MBD children are likely to kick, punch, push, bite, or pummel their parents, siblings, playmates, and baby sitters at the slightest provocation, or even with none at all.

Perceptual-Cognitive Impairments. MBD children are often impaired in their spatial perception, eye-hand coordination, memory, speech, and hearing. They have difficulty learning right from left and frequently confuse the two. They are inept at putting blocks or puzzles together and slow to master the intricacies of buttoning buttons, drawing circles, and catching a ball that is thrown to them. They are less able than other youngsters to remember past events and recent happenings. Because of mild hearing losses or difficulty in discriminating sounds, they may be slow to develop language and may have minor speech defects (8, 16–18).

Impaired fine motor coordination, visual-motor difficulties, and poorly articulated speech are among the ''soft signs'' used by neurologists to identify brain dysfunction in the absence of ''hard'' evidence of damage to the central nervous system (such as a paralysis or loss of feeling in some area of the body). These soft signs can be detected by such simple tests as asking children to stand still, to stand or hop on one foot, or to touch their thumbs to each of their fingers in rapid succession. Neurological examinations of MBD children are likely to reveal pronounced developmental lags involving imbalance, incoordination, confused handedness, and reflexes that are asymmetrical (uneven on the two sides of the body) or hyperactive (stronger or quicker than normal). From 50 to 60 percent of all MBD children show such neurological soft signs, which rarely occur in children who do not display the behavioral impairments associated with MBD (8, 19, 20).

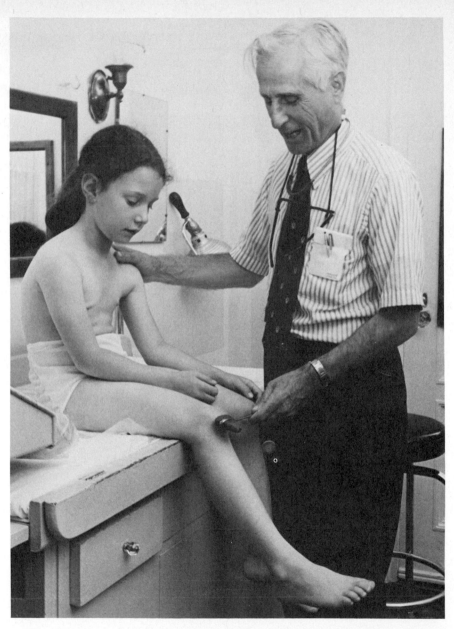

Most physical examinations include testing of reflexes with a rubber hammer.

Maladaptive Consequences of MBD

MBD children frequently do poorly in school. Their restlessness and distractability make it difficult for them to pay attention in the classroom, and, because of their problems with visual and motor functioning, they often fall behind other children in learning to read and write. It is estimated that one-half to two-thirds of all MBD children suffer from some form of learning disability, and MBD is the most frequent cause of learning problems among children who have adequate intelligence and educational opportunities (2, 8, 21, 22; see Chapter 14).

MBD children usually become painfully aware of their shortcomings and find it hard to maintain their self-esteem. Their parents and teachers are impatient with their slow learning and restlessness; their playmates mock their awkwardness and poor coordination; and they themselves worry about their uncontrollable outbursts of temper and aggression. The criticism and rejection MBD youngsters encounter typically result in their feeling depressed and inadequate (23, 24).

Two other maladaptive consequences of MBD may occur. First, these youngsters may become so frustrated at their inability to do what others expect of them that they give up trying to control their behavior. When this happens, they tend to become even more unpredictable and disorderly than would otherwise be the case. Second, in an effort to gain some feelings of worth and importance, they may engage in a variety of silly, wild, reckless, provocative, and inconsiderate acts that are intended to draw attention to themselves.

MBD children typically get into social and interpersonal difficulties. Their quick tempers and aggressive ways win them few friends. Their disruptiveness in groups and lack of self-control make them unpopular with their peers, teachers, and other adults. As they become more and more isolated from other people, and as their academic and emotional frustrations mount, MBD children become increasingly likely to engage in such antisocial acts as fighting, stealing, lying, and cheating (25).

Thus the prominent characteristics of MBD vary with age, as is summarized in Table 10-1. This characteristic course of MBD is not inevitable, however, especially with regard to how severe the symptoms are.

Table 10.1   Changing Characteristics of Minimal Brain Dysfunction (MBD)

Developmental Stage	Most Prominent Characteristics
Infancy	MBD is rarely identified; it is manifest in irritability, overalertness, colic, and difficulty in being soothed.
Preschool years	MBD begins to be diagnosed by pediatricians and family doctors; it is manifest primarily in hyperactivity, temper tantrums, poor self-control, and inability to tolerate frustration.
Middle childhood	MBD is most frequently identified at this time, primarily due to difficulties in school; the child is unable to pay attention and gets along poorly with other children, and specific learning problems often develop by the third grade.
Adolescence	MBD may be overlooked at this time if it has not already been identified; learning problems persist, but they are overshadowed by antisocial behavior, chronic low self-esteem, and episodes of depression.

Follow-up studies indicate that only one-fourth to one-third of MBD children continue to suffer the same severity of disturbance. About one-half show moderate improvements in response to treatment or to their own maturation, and the remaining children improve at least slightly (26, 27).

Yet MBD is a chronic disorder, and symptomatic improvement does not constitute a cure. MBD children who have improved still tend as adolescents to be more restless, distractible, impulsive, and excitable than their peers. They also tend to have more difficulty with their schoolwork and to behave more aggressively. Antisocial behavior is observed in 25 to 60 percent of MBD adolescents in various studies, and a large percentage of these youngsters report having negative feelings about themselves (28–31).

Causes of MBD

MBD is a condition of multiple etiology—meaning that, like mental retardation, it has many possible causes. These include most of the same prenatal and postnatal events that can result in mental retardation: (a) poor nutrition, infections, irradiation, and drug abuse affecting the mother during her pregnancy; (b) such birth complications as prematurity, injury by surgical instruments during delivery, and anoxia (an insufficient oxygen supply to the brain when the infant does not begin breathing promptly); and (c) head injuries, prolonged high fever, malnutrition, or lead poisoning during the first few years of life (32–36).

Of particular interest with respect to preventing MBD are studies suggesting that heavy drinking or smoking by mothers while they are pregnant may increase the risk of their children being hyperactive, and that certain chemicals added to food for artificial coloring or flavor may be responsible for some cases of hyperactivity and learning disabilities (37–39). Feingold (39) found that almost one-third of a group of hyperactive children showed dramatic improvement when they were placed on diets free of these food additives; improvement among the 3- to 5-year-olds he studied occurred in just a few days on the new diet.

Other research has found that many MBD children have parents who are behaviorally disturbed and appear to have been MBD children themselves. Significantly, this finding is limited to the biological parents of MBD children. Parents with adopted MBD children are no more likely than the parents of normal children to have current psychological problems or a history that suggests MBD (40–44).

This evidence for a genetic component in MBD is supported by studies of siblings and half-siblings who have been reared apart by different sets of parents or foster parents. Siblings reared apart show a 50 percent concordance for MBD—that is, if one sibling has the disorder, there is a 50 percent likelihood that a full sibling will have it as well; half-siblings reared apart show only a 14 percent concordance (45, 46).

It is also possible that some of the long-term consequences of social isolation (see Chapter 6), especially impaired concentration and self-control, are manifestations of MBD. Hence, psychosocial deprivation too may be a potential cause of MBD in those rare cases where the deprivation is sufficiently severe and prolonged to produce lingering mental and emotional handicaps. Taken together, then, available evidence suggests that there is no single cause of MBD, but rather that different causative agents are responsible for its occurring in different children (47).

Treatment of MBD Fortunately, many of the academic, emotional, and behavioral problems of MBD can be minimized through treatment programs involving some combination of drugs, psychotherapy, parent counseling, and educational planning.

Drugs. For reasons that are not fully understood, stimulant drugs have proved helpful in reducing the hyperactivity and distractibility of MBD children. In particular, dextroamphetamine (Dexedrine) and methylphenidate (Ritalin) have a calming effect on these youngsers; those who respond favorably show improved eye-hand coordination, a longer attention span, less restless and disruptive behavior, and improved relationships with their parents and peers (5, 48–51). No single drug or combination of drugs always gives these results, however, nor is there any known way of predicting in advance whether a specific child will benefit from drugs, or from which drug, or from what amount of the drug.

It is also impossible to predict how long the medication will have to be continued. In some cases lasting benefit can be achieved with only a few months' treatment, whereas other MBD children may have to continue their medication until or even during adolescence. Despite these uncertainties, clinical reports indicate that drugs are the most commonly used and most effective single treatment for MBD: 35 to 50 percent of these children show prompt and dramatic improvement when they are placed on appropriate stimulant medication, another 30 to 40 percent show moderate improvement, and only the remaining 15 to 20 percent show no benefit (5, 52–55).

Because stimulants usually reduce the hyperactivity of MBD children, this drug effect has often been called "paradoxical." Yet there is now reason to believe that the observed overactivity of MBD results from an underactive or underaroused level of nervous-system functioning. Just as children who are overtired often grow restless or irritable, it may be that less than optimal activity of the nervous system leads to the distractibility, emotionality, and impulsivity of MBD. Hence, stimulant drugs calm MBD children not because they sedate them, which would be a paradoxical effect, but because they increase the children's level of nervous-system arousal, which allows them to concentrate better, keep their emotions fairly calm, and exercise greater control over their behavior (1, 56–59).

Its widespread use notwithstanding, many concerns have been raised about drug treatment of MBD children. Do stimulant medications have dangerous side effects in young children? Do they lead to later dependence on or abuse of drugs? Do they represent a means of achieving social control at the expense of depriving people of their individuality? We will return to such concerns in the essay with this chapter. It should be noted here, however, that even among therapists who favor using drugs with MBD children, most use them only in conjunction with other treatment methods, and many do not consider using them at all until other methods have proved inadequate.

Psychotherapy. Traditional psychotherapy has little effect on the basic manifestations of MBD, and it is rarely used to treat the disorder in its early stages. After MBD children enter school, however, psychotherapy may become important in helping them overcome negative self-attitudes and avoid the feelings of failure and alienation that often lead these children into antisocial behavior during adolescence (60–63).

Therapists can also increase the self-control of MBD children by systematically rewarding it. The systematic use of reward and punishments to alter disturbed behavior is known as **behavior therapy.** Behavior therapists do not concentrate as much as traditional psychotherapists on the origins of disturbed behavior. Instead, they try to modify behavior through education and training, and a number of behavioral techniques have been utilized successfully in working with MBD children (64–69).

Parent Counseling. The adjustment difficulties of MBD children can also be eased if their parents are appropriately counseled about the condition and about what they can realistically expect of their youngsters. Parents often blame themselves when one of their children has a defect from early in life, and parents may feel especially overwhelmed if the defect manifests itself in unpredictable, unmanageable behavior. Both self-blame and feelings of helplessness interfere with constructive parental care, and both can be relieved through parent counseling. Parents can learn to supplement and eventually even take over certain functions of the professional therapist, particularly in caring for their child in ways that will encourage positive growth rather than an intensified behavioral disorder (70–72).

Among the helpful responses parents can learn from effective counseling are to reward their youngsters for what they are able to accomplish and not to make excessive demands on them; to accept their children's handicap without subjecting them to countless evaluations in the hope of finding an expert who will refute the MBD diagnosis; and to allow them to do as many things as possible that other children do, rather than overprotect them or accentuate their sense of being different. Such constructive parental management preserves the self-esteem of MBD children and also helps them benefit more from whatever other treatment they are receiving (73, 74).

Educational Planning. Special kinds of training such as speech therapy, remedial reading, and exercises in perceptual-motor coordination can help MBD children function more effectively and feel more adequate. The effectiveness of such training usually depends upon how closely it relates to actual tasks that children are expected to master. For example, perceptual-motor training using contrived exercises is not nearly as helpful as training in such specific skills as reading, writing, dancing, and catching and throwing balls (75, 76).

Similarly, efforts to improve the concentration of MBD schoolchildren by having them work in windowless rooms or semi-isolated cubicles (where they will have few distractions) may do more harm than good. Such a contrived situation deprives children of the opportunity to learn to handle the potentially distracting stimulation of the real world. Moreover, it has been found that both normal and distractible children function better in learning situations that include ordinary background sights and sounds (77–79).

CHILDHOOD SCHIZOPHRENIA

Schizophrenia is primarily a disorder of adolescence and adulthood, and it is found in no more than 4 to 5 per 10,000 preschool and elementary-school children (80). Whereas MBD accounts for 30 to 50 percent of all psychiatric referrals among children, schizophrenia is diagnosed in only about 10 percent of 2- to 12-year-old children seen in psychiatric clinics and hospitals (81, 82). Nevertheless, as a precursor of adult schizophrenia, **childhood schizophrenia** offers an important developmental glimpse into one of our major mental health problems.

Numerous studies indicate that schizophrenia occurs in 1 percent of the population, and the National Institute of Mental Health estimates that 2 percent of all persons born in the United States will suffer from this disorder sometime during their life. One-half of the beds in mental hospitals and almost one-quarter of all the hospital beds in the United States are occupied by schizophrenic patients. The cost of schizophrenia—including lack of productivity by schizophrenic patients and the expense of treating and rehabilitating these patients—is estimated at $11.6 to $19.5 billion annually (83–86).

Because preschool schizophrenic youngsters exhibit many of the same behavioral peculiarities as the autistic children we discussed in Chapter 6, some psychologists and psychiatrists make no distinction between the two conditions. In the view of such prominent clinicians as Lauretta Bender and Bruno Bettelheim, for example, autism is just one of several forms of childhood schizophrenia and exists on a continuum with adult schizophrenia (87, 88). However, there seem to be several useful ways of distinguishing between childhood schizophrenia and infantile autism.

First, the onset of schizophrenic symptoms after age 2 involves with-

Table 10.2 Ratio of Boys to Girls Receiving Treatment for
Psychological Disorders in the United States

	Age		
	5-9	10-14	15-19
Psychotic disorders (excluding organic psychoses)	2.13	1.18	1.03
All psychological disorders	2.56	1.22	.91

Source: Based on data reported by Gove, W. R., & Herb, T. S., Stress and mental illness among the young: A comparison of the sexes. *Social Forces,* 1974, **53,** 256–265.

drawal from people and disturbed mental functioning following a period of normal psychological development. In infantile autism, on the other hand, disturbance is present almost from birth, with virtually no period of normally developing mental or social capacities (89, 90). Second, among children born to schizophrenic mothers, 25 to 40 percent exhibit serious psychological disturbances beginning in later childhood or adolescence, whereas very few suffer disturbances from birth on, as in autism (91).

Third, autistic children hardly ever grow up to become schizophrenic adolescents or adults. Those who do not recover either continue to exhibit the symptoms of infantile autism or develop the primary symptoms of mental retardation, epilepsy, or aphasia (an organically caused impairment of the ability to understand or express verbal concepts) (92, 93). By contrast, long-term follow-up studies indicate that approximately 90 percent of schizophrenic children subsequently show evidence of adult schizophrenia (81, 94–96).

Interestingly, however, there is a clear sex difference in the incidence of schizophrenia among children and adults. Schizophrenia occurs with equal frequency among adult men and women, but it is diagnosed more than twice as often among boys as among girls (97, 98). As indicated in Table 10.2, this sex difference is part of a general trend for boys to be more susceptible than girls to psychological disorders of all kinds, and for girls gradually to become more susceptible as they approach maturity, when sex differences are no longer apparent.

One possible explanation for this sex difference is that boys experience more psychological stress than girls, partly because greater social expectations are placed on them and partly because they do not mature as fast biologically. With maturity, boys catch up biologically and girls encounter increasing social pressures; therefore, they become equal in their susceptibility to psychological disturbances (99). Further research is needed to determine whether this hypothesis is accurate or whether some other explanation must be sought.

Table 10.3   Personality Impairments in Schizophrenia

Type of Capacity	Related Impairments
Cognitive	1. Disconnected thinking 2. Illogical reasoning 3. Peculiar patterns of concept and language formation 4. Inaccurate or distorted perceptions of the environment and of one's own body
Interpersonal	5. Poor social skills 6. Withdrawal from people
Integrative	7. Blunted or inappropriate emotional reactions 8. Inability to suppress anxiety-provoking thoughts 9. Inadequate control over aggressive, antisocial, and self-destructive impulses

Symptoms of Childhood Schizophrenia

Schizophrenia consists of a serious breakdown in the cognitive, interpersonal, and integrative capacities of the personality, leading to the kinds of impairments listed in Table 10.3 (100–102). Although these impairments characterize schizophrenia at all ages, the manifest symptoms of the disorder tend to vary with the developmental stage of the disturbed person.

Preschool-age schizophrenics exhibit many of the same behavioral peculiarities that are observed in autistic children, as we have mentioned: ritualistic, repetitive actions and an intolerance for change in the environment; strange, incomprehensible speech patterns or even a total loss of previously established language skills; excessive, diminished, or unpredictable responses to sensory stimulation; a poor grasp of their bodily integrity and of their identity as a distinct person; overactivity or bodily rigidity and strange posturing; aloofness from people and a tendency to treat people as if they were inanimate objects; and periods of unaccountably severe anxiety and violent temper tantrums (103–105).

Child specialists disagree about whether preschool children are likely to exhibit such grossly abnormal behavior unless, like autistic children, they have been disturbed from birth. Rutter, for example, maintains that serious psychological disturbances are likely to appear either before the age of 3 (autism) or after the age of 7 (schizophrenia), and that psychoses seldom ever begin between the ages of 3 and 6 (106). However, in a large group of schizophrenic children studied by Bender, 55 percent became disturbed between the ages of 2 and 6, and numerous other clinical and research studies have confirmed that children can and do become disturbed at this age following an apparently normal infancy (104, 107–109).

During the elementary-school years schizophrenic children commonly develop delusions and hallucinations that heighten their detachment from reality and disrupt even further their interpersonal relationships. For example, beginning at about the age of 5, these children may become unrealistically fearful that other children are "out to get them," and they may tell bizarre stories about what these supposedly dangerous enemies are doing to them and about imaginary friends or powers they can rely on for protection. Between 5 and 8 they may have the delusion of being an animal, and they may have difficulty differentiating dreams from reality. At around 8 years of age, they may develop delusions about their own bodies, such as believing that they are a machine or that they do not have certain vital organs, and they may also begin to see and hear things that do not actually exist.

Initially these delusional and hallucinatory experiences come and go quickly, and they change from one moment to the next. As schizophrenic children approach adolescence, however, their distortions of reality become more organized and persistent. Unless there is some effective treatment, the condition is likely to become stable by the age of 12 or 13 and merge into the schizophrenia of adolescence and adulthood (104, 110).

The Origin of Schizophrenia

The cause of schizophrenia is not yet fully understood. Some clinicians and researchers believe that it is due to inherited or acquired biochemical abnormalities or neurophysiological defects. Others are convinced that schizophrenia is the result of faulty social learning that occurs in disorganized families. Schizophrenia has been studied more extensively than any other psychological disorder, and proponents of both points of view report research findings in support of their position.

Biogenetic theorists call attention to a well-established fact that schizophrenia runs in families. The more closely two people are related, the more likely they are to be concordant for schizophrenia; that is, if one has the disorder the other will also. To be specific, schizophrenia occurs in 1 percent of the general population; it is found in 9 to 16 percent of those who have one schizophrenic parent; and it occurs in 40 to 68 percent of those who have two schizophrenic parents. Similarly, schizophrenia is found in 5 to 16 percent of those who have schizophrenic siblings or dizygotic (nonidentical) twins, but in 20 to 75 percent of those who have schizophrenic monozygotic (identical) twins (111; see Table 10.4).

To support further the biogenetic view, many schizophrenic children exhibit neurological abnormalities or have a history of prenatal or birth complications that could have caused brain damage. Such direct or indirect evidence of neurological dysfunction has been found in up to 70 percent of schizophrenic children in some studies. Taken together, these neurological data and the incidence of schizophrenia in families have led many investigators to conclude that biological defects, whether inherited or acquired, are most often the cause of schizophrenia (81, 82, 112–117).

Yet psychosocial theorists use many of these same data to support their

Table 10.4 Incidence of Schizophrenia in Families as Found in Various Studies

Relationship to Schizophrenic Person	Incidence of Schizophrenia (in Percentages)
Child of one schizophrenic parent	9–16
Child of two schizophrenic parents	40–68
Sibling of schizophrenic	8–14
Dizygotic (nonidentical) twin of schizophrenic	5–16
Monozygotic (identical) twin of schizophrenic	20–75
General population	0.85

Source: Based on data summarized by Zerbin-Rudin, E. Genetic research and the theory of schizophrenia. *International Journal of Mental Health,* 1972, **1,** 42–62.

viewpoint. The fact that schizophrenic individuals often have schizophrenic parents can be interpreted as confirming that schizophrenic parents are more likely than normal parents to rear their children in a disorganized fashion; likewise, the high concordance of schizophrenia among siblings and twins can be seen as reflecting the fact that the closer the relationship is between two people, the more likely they are to have the same social-learning environment, for better or for worse.

Psychosocial theorists also emphasize that, depending upon which study from Table 10.4 is looked at, up to 60 percent of the children who have both parents schizophrenic and up to 80 percent of the identical twins of schizophrenics do *not* become schizophrenic. With regard to neurological dysfunction, a substantial percentage of schizophrenic children are either free from any evidence of biological defect or, along with having some neurological dysfunction, they show even more striking evidence of having been reared in a disordered psychosocial environment.

In offering evidence for their position, psychosocial theorists have identified a high frequency of disturbed communication in the families of people who become schizophrenic. For example, parents may continually say one thing when they mean another, which makes it difficult for their children to develop a firm sense of reality and feel certain about what they should think or do. Thus a mother may say to her son "Stand on your own two feet" while her actions encourage him to remain dependent on her. Such maternal behavior puts the child in a double bind about how to act, and these kinds of disturbed communications could be responsible for children learning schizophrenic ways of adapting to their world (118–124).

However, the findings of psychosocial theorists can also be interpreted in other ways. For example, disturbed family interactions can be viewed as a result of having a schizophrenic child in the family rather than as a cause of the schizophrenic disturbance. Furthermore, most studies reporting poor communication in the families of schizophrenic persons also include many families in which there are no apparent psychosocial problems, and several investigators have found no differences in attitude or patterns of communication in families with and without schizophrenic children (95, 113, 125–127).

Two relatively new research methods are currently being used to sort out these issues in what causes schizophrenia. One of these, the **cross-fostering method,** consists of comparing children born to and reared by schizophrenic parents with children born to schizophrenic parents but, as a result of adoption or foster-home placement, reared by psychologically normal parents. This method distinguishes fairly clearly between hereditary and environmental influences: if heredity is more significant, then children born to schizophrenic parents should have a higher-than-usual incidence of schizophrenia regardless of whether they are reared by their biological parents or by psychologically normal adoptive parents; if the environment is more important, children born to schizophrenic parents but reared by normal parents should be no more likely than the general population to develop schizophrenia (128–131).

The second method, called **risk research,** utilizes longitudinal studies of children who are considered at risk for developing schizophrenia. A wide range of biogenetic and psychosocial factors are evaluated in children who are considered more likely than the average person to become psychologically disturbed (usually because other members of their family are disturbed). As time passes and some of these children develop schizophrenia while others do not, it is possible to examine factors that may have made some of these children vulnerable. Since the data collected in risk research precede the onset of the disorder, circumstances that appear to lead to schizophrenia can be separated from those that appear to arise as a result of it (132–136).

Findings from these new approaches are making it increasingly clear that neither biogenetic nor psychosocial explanations can account for all cases of schizophrenia. Work by Heston indicates that children born to schizophrenic parents but placed for adoption early in life and reared by normal parents are significantly more likely to develop schizophrenia and other personality disorders by age 35 than adopted children born to normal biological parents (137–139; see Figure 10.1). In fact, the incidence of schizophrenia among Heston's foster-home-reared children of schizophrenic mothers (11 percent) is as high as the incidence found when children are reared by as well as born to schizophrenic mothers (9 to 16 percent; see Table 10.4). These findings are extremely difficult to explain in psychosocial terms.

Furthermore, the same kinds of family background and crisis situation that appear to cause schizophrenia in some persons produce different disorders in others, which may mean that there are constitutional factors that contribute to particular kinds of personality breakdown. Yet, since

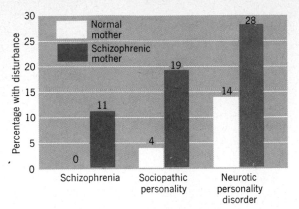

Figure 10.1 Disturbances in adult offspring separated at birth from their schizophrenic or normal mothers. (*Source.* Based on data reported by Heston, L. L. Psychiatric disorders in foster home reared children of schizophrenic mothers. *British Journal of Psychiatry*, 1966, **112**, 819–825.)

the majority of children with a family history of schizophrenia (including those who have a schizophrenic identical twin) do not become schizophrenic, there can be little doubt that other factors play a role in the development of schizophrenia.

It currently seems likely that schizophrenia is due to a combination of biogenetic predisposing and psychosocial developmental and precipitating factors. This interaction view, called the **diasthesis-stress model** of schizophrenia, is becoming the most widely held view of schizophrenic causality, and it is endorsed by many researchers who favor a primarily biogenetic or psychosocial approach (119, 140–142). The stronger the biogenetic predisposition (diasthesis) to the disturbance, the more likely it is to arise in response to minimal psychosocial stress. Conversely, those with little or no predisposition to schizophrenia are usually able to cope adequately with severe family disorganization and crisis situations; in the case of a breakdown, they develop other forms of psychopathology.

Prognosis and Treatment

As we have already noted, schizophrenic children usually grow up to become schizophrenic adults. Nevertheless, their prognosis for making a social adjustment outside an institution is somewhat better than in infantile autism. About one-third are able to make a moderately good social adjustment during adolescence, and another one-third can adjust at least marginally to life at home or in the community. The remaining one-third of schizophrenic youngsters, like 50 percent of autistic children, face the prospect of progressive psychological decline and more or less permanent residential care (81, 143).

Generally speaking, the older children are when they become schizophrenic and the sooner professional help is obtained, the better their chances are for recovery. It is also favorable if they are free from any neurological dysfunction and if they have reasonably well-adjusted parents. On the other hand, children who develop schizophrenia soon after the age of 2 and do not receive treatment, who also have neurological abnormalities, and whose parents are seriously disturbed themselves are the least likely to escape continuing psychological distress, chronic academic and social incompetence, and eventual institutionalization (81, 82).

As of the 1970s, the most promising type of treatment for schizophrenic children is a **therapeutic milieu.** In this type of therapy children are placed in a residential or a daycare facility where they can be immersed in a varied and intensive program of activities. Every member of the staff, every feature of the environment, and every aspect of the daily routine is utilized to help the children overcome their personality handicaps. The aim of such a total therapeutic environment (milieu) is what Goldfarb calls "corrective socialization," which means providing schizophrenic children with social experiences that will improve their self-awareness, self-control, accurate perception of reality, and ability to get along with other people (144, 145).

In addition to being a living experience, milieu programs typically include individual psychotherapy and behavior modification sessions. Individual psychotherapy by itself is seldom effective with schizophrenic children, especially in severe cases. However, used in conjunction with full or partial residential care, it plays an important role in facilitating the progress these youngsters are able to make (145–148).

Behavior modification techniques can be very useful in helping schizophrenic children improve their social skills and overcome some of their specific symptoms. For example, well-conceived exercises can train these children to communicate more clearly, use better judgment, keep their emotions under control, and feel less anxious (149, 150).

Drug therapy, which is common in the treatment of MBD, is not used very much with schizophrenic children. In some instances a tranquilizer may be given to reduce anxiety, so that the child can participate more fully in the programs of a treatment milieu. By and large, however, drugs are not regarded as having much beneficial effect on the personality impairments from which these children suffer (82, 105).

PHOBIAS AND RITUALS

Specific neurotic disturbances first begin to appear during the preschool years. **Neurotic behavior** consists of repetitively immature, inappropriate, or maladaptive ways of responding to people and situations. Although most neuroses do not form until middle childhood or later, two neurotic patterns that can occur among preschool children are phobias and rituals, which are exaggerated expressions of normal fears and routines.

Fears and Phobias

Preschoolers normally become fearful of a wide range of objects and events that threaten them with physical injury, such as dogs, robbers, imaginary creatures, storms, and being alone in the dark. Some of these fears are rational, learned reactions to potential danger (moving cars, snarling dogs). Other common but less rational fears of early childhood are acquired by observing and identifying with parents who are themselves frightened by storms, the dark, or visits to the doctor. Like so many other shared experiences of young children, such normal fears are captured by a nursery rhyme:

> *Little Miss Muffet sat on a tuffet,*
> *Eating her curds and whey;*
> *Along came a spider and sat down beside her*
> *And frightened Miss Muffet away.*

Various surveys indicate that preschoolers typically have an average of about three different fears. Although fearfulness tends to decrease with maturity, almost half of all elementary-school children are also likely to display some distinct fear at one time or another. In most cases these fears come and go quickly, cause relatively little anxiety, and do not interfere very much with children's lives. However, about 5 percent of children are likely to develop an excessive, incapacitating fear of some object or event, which constitutes a phobia (151–153).

Phobias, then, are unrealistic, disruptive fears of relatively harmless situations. Phobic dread serves no obvious protective purpose, as does the fear of a speeding car. It is typically far out of proportion to any actual danger, and it cannot be erased by explanations or reassurances that there is nothing to fear (154). A boy with a phobia of dogs may panic at the sight of a small puppy and run to his mother's side, trembling and weeping, and efforts to "cure" him by forcing him to confront the dog only intensify his terror.

Phobic reactions can become so intense that they completely dominate a child's life. A boy with a dog phobia may hesitate to go outside to play, for fear there might be a dog in the neighborhood; he may refuse to go shopping or visiting with his mother, on the off chance that they might encounter a dog along the way; he may lose interest in his picture books or his favorite television programs because they sometimes feature dogs. Phobias can also generalize, so that an irrational fear of dogs turns into an irrational fear of cats, squirrels, hamsters, and perhaps eventually all four-legged animals.

Phobias vary in degree. In mild cases they may cause a child only moderate distress and become apparent only in specific situations. For example, a boy may feel threatened only by large dogs, or he may be able to remain calm near dogs so long as his mother or father is holding his hand. In such mild cases it is often difficult to distinguish a normal childhood fear from a phobic neurotic reaction, and careful assessment is necessary to decide whether the child needs professional help (155, 156).

The Disposition to Early Childhood Phobias

As we discussed in Chapter 8, 2- to 5-year-olds recognize that they are distinct individuals with special physical features that distinguish them as boys or girls, and they are fascinated with and proud of how their bodies are growing. Consequently, they are disposed to worrying about physical harm that might come to them, and phobias at this age are simply the exaggeration of such worries into an actual anticipation of bodily damage or destruction. Such worries are particularly well illustrated by a common fear among young children of objects that make things disappear, such as toilets, drains, and vacuum cleaners. Preschoolers have matured enough cognitively to realize that they are small, weak, and helpless in relation to amost everything else in their environment, but they have not yet matured enough to comprehend which objects realistically threaten their safety or existence.

This still-limited comprehension of the real world increases the susceptibility of young children to fears of physical harm. The more frightened they are and the less they feel they can protect themselves, the more likely they are to develop phobic reaction patterns. Research studies have confirmed a strong direct relationship between specific fears in preschool boys and girls and their physical timidity or anxiety prior to the onset of excessive fearfulness (156, 157). Because being physically timid or anxiety-prone can be influenced by a person's basic temperament, it is conceivable that biogenetic factors also play a role in disposing children to phobic neurosis. However, it is primarily children's life experiences, and not their constitution, that lead them to exaggerate normal worries into a phobic reaction pattern.

The Focus of Phobic Reactions

The specific focus of children's phobic reactions depends upon a number of real or imagined mishaps. For example, being bitten by a dog may lead to a persistent, unreasoning, and overgeneralized fear of dogs that bears no relationship to the actual likelihood of being bitten again. The learning of a phobia from a frightening experience was reported in 1920 by John Watson, the founder of behavioristic psychology, in a classic experiment. Working with Albert, an 11-month-old boy, Watson made a loud banging noise (of which Albert was afraid) every time the boy reached out toward a white rat (of which he was initially not afraid). Over a 7-day period Albert gradually came to show fear in the presence of the white rat, without any noise being made, and this fear subsequently generalized to include all furry objects. Watson's experiment proved that excessive or unreasonable fears can be learned from unpleasant experiences not only directly (as in becoming afraid of dogs after having been bitten by one) but also indirectly, by association with some fear-provoking event (158).

Phobias can develop without the occurrence of obvious frightening experiences, however. We have already mentioned that children can develop excessive fears simply by identifying with parents who are extremely fearful themselves. In other cases children may become terrorized by the dire warnings of older children or adults that "garbage trucks gobble up little boys" or that "spiders like to scratch and bite little girls."

Such teasing of a phobia-prone preschooler may generate fears of garbage trucks or spiders that generalize to all moving vehicles or all insects and cause the child to remain within the safety of his or her home.

In the case of other phobic children, the dreaded object may have no particular significance other than as a convenient representation for something else that is feared. The process of transferring a fear from its real source to a previously neutral object is called **displacement,** and it was first described by Sigmund Freud in one of the most famous case histories in the psychoanalytic literature.

Writing in 1909, Freud described his lengthy conversations with the father of "Little Hans," a 5-year-old boy who was afraid of horses. Freud's analysis of the information he obtained suggested (a) that Little Hans's real fear was that his father was angry at him and intended to harm him, and (b) that Hans had displaced this fear onto horses. By so doing, he had been able to minimize his anxiety, since it was easier for him to avoid horses than his father; he had also been able to maintain a reasonably comfortable relationship with his father, since he was not consciously aware of fearing him (159). The role of this displacement process in the formation of phobias is particularly clear in school phobias, which will be discussed in Chapter 14.

Routines and Rituals

Like phobias, the neurotic **rituals** of early childhood are exaggerated expressions of normal concerns about suffering harm. Most children from 2 to 5 go through a phase of insisting on certain kinds of routine and order in their daily lives. A particular doll or stuffed animal must be taken to bed every night, and no other toy will do; the shirt has to be put on before the pants because "that's the way it's supposed to be done"; a trip to the grocery store or Grandma's house must be along the same route each time without variation.

Such attention to regularity among young children emerges as an effort to control their environment and their own behavior. The more regular and predictable they can make their lives, the more secure they feel and the less they need to worry about some unexpected disaster taking place. Regularity also protects young children from letting their own impulses get out of hand; that is, by sticking to various routines they can more easily keep from doing things they fear they might be sorry about or punished for later on (155, 160).

The more children are concerned about being either the agent or the victim of physical violence, the more likely it is that their routines will become maladaptive rituals. Neurotically ritualistic children engage in numerous repetitive, nonproductive behaviors that occupy their waking hours and closely resemble the rituals of schizophrenic children, but do not involve a schizophrenic breakdown of interpersonal and reality contacts.

Treatment Phobias and rituals are the earliest disturbances to appear that are both relatively mild and largely due to psychosocial factors. As a result, they differ in two important respects from the more serious and/or largely biogenetically determined abnormalities we have discussed previously. First, childhood phobias and rituals have a high recovery rate, especially when children receive appropriate treatment. Second, the earlier phobias and rituals appear, the more likely they are to be short-lived and to respond quickly to therapy.

Among adults who develop phobias, approximately 20 to 30 percent recover completely, and an additional 30 percent or so show some improvement. In contrast, 90 percent or more of phobic children are likely to get over their excessive fears. The phobias of early childhood are especially likely to pass quickly, since children's physical growth (getting bigger and stronger) and their mental development (for example, coming to understand that they cannot be flushed down the toilet) help them master fears of physical harm that are common among preschoolers.

The phobias of later childhood, which pertain to more complex social and school concerns, are not so readily overcome but are still more easily mastered than phobias that begin in adolescence and adulthood. These later-beginning phobias are not simply an exaggeration of fears that are common to others of the same age, which helps explain why they are a more serious neurotic disturbance than childhood phobias and more likely to persist over time (161–164).

The relatively short duration and high recovery rate of childhood phobias does not mean that professional attention is unnecessary. A disturbance that lasts 6 months in the life of an adult may not be a particularly stressful experience, but 6 months for a 3-year-old represents one-sixth of a lifetime. Hence, a short-lived disturbance may have many more long-term negative effects on a young child than on an adult. This fact, together with ample evidence that treatment of various kinds can shorten the duration of a childhood phobia, makes it important that children with excessive fears receive some kind of treatment, even if only briefly (153, 165).

Several kinds of psychological treatment have proved effective in eliminating the phobic and ritualistic behavior of neurotic preschool children. These include psychoanalytic psychotherapy, in which children are helped to verbalize and to understand the nature of their basic fears; play therapy, in which children are encouraged to act out and gain control over their impulses; and behavior therapy, in which children are helped to relax and to enjoy pleasurable experiences while they are gradually exposed to the situation they fear, or in which they are systematically rewarded for nonphobic, nonritualistic behavior (166–170). When such treatment programs are instituted promptly, before these neuroses become well established and before they seriously undermine a child's self-concept and relationships with others, considerable impovement or complete cure is almost always possible.

Play therapy is an effective way of helping young children express concerns that are difficult for them to talk about directly.

Essay:

STIMULANT DRUGS
FOR HYPERACTIVE
CHILDREN:
A BLESSING OR
A CURSE?

In the summer of 1970 the Washington *Post* captured national attention with an article stating that 5 to 10 percent of the elementary-school children in Omaha, Nebraska, were being given stimulant drugs to improve their classroom behavior and learning potential. The article was grossly misleading, since the 5-to-10 percent figure was only an estimate of the number of Omaha schoolchildren with learning disabilities, not the number of children receiving stimulant drugs. Nevertheless, the public concern aroused by this article led to a congressional inquiry into the role of schools in encouraging drug treatment, and the Office of Child Development of the Department of Health, Education and Welfare subsequently convened a distinguished panel of scientists and educators to look into the facts of the matter (171, 172).

Despite the findings of this and other inquiries, it is difficult to know just how many schoolchildren are receiving stimulant medication. Most of the published information appears in newspaper and magazine articles that refer to "estimates" by "prominent authorities." Actual research findings by trained behavioral scientists are scant. One exception is a survey conducted in 1971 and repeated in 1973 by Krager and Safer, in which medical records were collected for 1894 elementary-school children in Baltimore County, Maryland. In 1971 1.07 percent of these children were receiving medication for hyperactivity, and in 1973 the figure had increased to 1.73 (173).

This actual figure of just under 2 percent of schoolchildren receiving stimulant drugs is not necessarily a cause for alarm. It has consistently been found that 5 to 10 percent of school children in the United States suffer disorders manifest in hyperactivity and learning problems, and the Office of Child Development concluded from its investigation that 60 to 70 percent of hyperactive children show improved attention and self-control when they take stimulant drugs. Hence the numbers of schoolchildren receiving these drugs does not appear to be out of proportion to the number who need and could benefit from them; however, a key question not answered by these figures is whether the *right* children are getting drugs.

The point here is that there are many different ways of treating children who have behavior and learning problems. Using stimulant drugs is effective primarily with children whose problems appear to be due to minimal brain dysfunction (MBD). Disorderly or unmanageable children with neurotic or psychotic disturbances, on the other hand, become worse when they are given stimulants. Among MBD children, furthermore, stimulants affect mainly their hyperactivity and distractibility and not the various perceptual impairments they may also have. This means that MBD children whose learning difficulties are largely caused by perceptual handicaps (and not hyperactivity or distractibility) are unlikely to benefit from medication (2, 3, 52, 55, 56).

Thus stimulant drugs are not appropriate for all children with learning and behavior problems, and they should be prescribed only when careful evaluation has indicated that the child probably has MBD with prominent hyperactivity. Regrettably, such evaluations are not always made before deciding to use drugs. In one school, for example, the teachers were asked which of their students had "behavior disorders" or "difficulty concentrating"; using these unverified impressions, the school subsequently called the parents of 20 percent of the entire student body and advised them to consider stimulant medication for their child (51). With such an amateur approach, there will undoubtedly be unnecessary and even harmful use of drugs. Even more distressing are documented cases in which parents have been threatened with having their child expelled from school unless they accepted a recommendation for drug treatment (55, 174).

But what about using stimulant medication for hyperactive children, after a careful evaluation of the child's problems and without violating the family's right to privacy—is it a blessing or a curse? Many people fear that these drugs will make zombies out of children, preserving peace at home and in the classroom at the expense of the children's spirit and self-determination, and that the drugs will lead young people into future drug abuse. Neither of these fears seems justified. Appropriate stimulant medication does not sedate or dehumanize hyperactive children. Rather, it increases the functioning of their nervous system in ways that give them more control over their behavior, and it reduces symptoms that are interfering with their efforts to make friends, learn in school, and develop a feeling of being a worthwhile person. As for long-term effects, there is no evidence that stimulant medication in childhood leads to drug abuse or addiction later on (8, 171, 175, 176).

Yet it cannot be said that stimulants are an unmixed blessing, even when properly administered. First, there are both short-term and long-term negative side-effects of these drugs. Many children experience insomnia, loss of appetite, sadness, nausea, headaches, and vomiting during the first week they are placed on stimulants. Although these reactions usually disappear within a few weeks, they need to be considered in making decisions to use drugs rather than rely on behavioral treatment methods that have no such undesirable side-effects (177).

The major long-term side-effect of stimulants that has been reported is a suppression of growth while children are taking the drugs. Children grow on the average at only 60 to 75 percent of their annual expected rate during the period they are on such medication. Fortunately, they show a rebound when the drugs are discontinued, so that their growth suppression is only temporary. However, it is not yet known if the rebound is sufficient to make up for all of the growth that is suppressed during long-term medication, nor has very much research yet been done to rule out other possible long-term side-effects (178–180).

Second, children are sensitive about having a condition that sets them apart from their peers and requires daily medication, whether it is insulin for diabetes, dilantin for epilepsy, or stimulants for MBD. While stimulants may enable MBD children to exercise greater self-control and thus feel better about themselves, they can also undermine the children's self-esteem by causing them to feel different.

Third, the dramatic reduction of hyperactivity in these children after they begin taking stimulants may prematurely convince their parents and teachers that the problem is solved. Seeing that their child is calmer and more self-controlled, parents may not recognize his or her continuing needs for understanding and help in coping with various social and emotional difficulties the condition may have caused. With a more attentive and less disruptive pupil, teachers may lose sight of the fact that medication neither corrects perceptual handicaps nor wipes out the learning deficits of children who may have fallen a year or more behind their classmates in reading, writing, and other basic academic skills (181–183).

What is needed, then, is both a careful evaluation of which children should receive stimulant medication and continuing attention to the social, emotional, and educational problems of these children even after the medication has taken effect. Neither the potential misuse of these drugs nor the limits of their therapeutic effect should constitute a reason for avoiding them or legislating against them. Further research on their long-term side-effects is necessary (as is true of many current medical treatments), and opportunities to treat these children effectively without using drugs should always be identified and acted on. Yet it also needs to be recognized that, as part of a multifaceted treatment program that includes sensitive counseling of MBD children and their parents and adequate remedial education, stimulant drugs may offer hope for a better life to many hyperactive children.

Summary

The major psychological disturbances that emerge during the preschool years are minimal brain dysfunction, childhood schizophrenia, and phobias and rituals. Minimal brain dysfunction (MBD) is a disorder of behavioral and cognitive functioning that is presumed to involve some impairment of the central nervous system. It occurs in 5 to 10 percent of children and is the most frequent behavior disorder for which young people are brought for professional help.

The major behavioral characteristics of MBD are hyperactivity, distractibility, impulsivity, and excitability. In addition, MBD children are often impaired in their spatial perception, eye-hand coordination, memory, speech, and hearing. As a result, MBD children are likely to learn poorly in school, feel depressed and inadequate, and exhibit aggressive and inconsiderate behavior. The characteristics of MBD change with age: during the preschool years, hyperactivity is the primary symptom; during middle childhood, difficulties in learning and social relationships are the major characteristics; and during adolescence, antisocial behavior is most prominent.

MBD has many possible causes, including genetic inheritance and many of the same prenatal and postnatal events that contribute to mental retardation. Although MBD is a chronic and potentially seriously handicapping condition, many of its academic, emotional, and behavioral consequences can be minimized or avoided entirely with prompt and appropriate treatment. Stimulant drugs are the most common and the most effective single treatment for the disorder. However, serious questions have been raised about the possible negative effects of prescribing stimulants for young children, and it is essential for their use to be coordinated with psychotherapy, parent counseling, and educational planning to provide maximum help to the individual MBD child.

Childhood schizophrenia is a rare but severely disabling disorder that resembles infantile autism in some of its outward manifestations but, unlike autism, begins after a period of apparently normal personality development. Although it occurs in no more than 4 or 5 children in 10,000, it is in many ways a precursor of adult schizophrenia, which afflicts 1 percent of the population and accounts for one-half of the beds in mental hospitals. In schizophrenia there is a breakdown in personality functioning that leads to disconnected thinking, illogical reasoning, inaccurate perception of reality, poor social relationships, inappropriate emotional reactions, and loss of control over thoughts and actions.

Strong arguments have been made for the role of both biogenetic and psychosocial factors in causing schizophrenia. The most widely accepted view of its origin is a *diasthesis-stress* model, according to which schizophrenia results from the combination of an inherited predisposition toward the disorder (diasthesis) with highly stressful life experiences. Despite the severity of the condition, about one-third of children with schizophrenia achieve a moderately good social adjustment during adolescence, and another one-third may be able to make a marginal social adjustment outside an institution. The older the child is when the disturbance begins and the sooner professional help is received, the better will be the chances for improvement or recovery.

Phobias and rituals are exaggerated expressions of the normal fears and routines of young children. Preschoolers typically develop a number of specific fears, pertaining mainly to objects or events that threaten them with physical harm. When these fears become unrealistic and incapacitating, and cannot be erased by explanations or reassurances, a phobic reaction exists.

The neurotic rituals of early childhood also develop from normal concerns about suffering harm. Most preschoolers enjoy routines that give a certain amount of regularity to their lives. However, when they become preoccupied with numerous repetitive and nonproductive rituals, they are displaying abnormal development.

Phobias and rituals are neurotic disturbances that arise chiefly from life experiences rather than from biogenetic causes. Hence, they are likely to be short-lived and to disappear as children develop a more mature understanding of what is realistically threatening to them. More than 90 percent of phobic children recover completely, and several forms of psychological treatment can help to hasten their recovery.

References

1. Connors, C. K. Minimal brain dysfunction and psychopathology in children. In A. Davids (Ed.), *Child personality and psychopathology: Current topics*. Vol. 2. New York: Wiley, 1975.
2. Wender, P. H. *Minimal brain dysfunction in children*. New York: Wiley, 1971.
3. Wender, P. H. The minimal brain dysfunction syndrome. *Annual Review of Medicine*, 1975, **26**, 45–62.
4. Ross, D. M., & Ross, S. A. *Hyperactivity: Research, theory, action*. New York: Wiley, 1976.

5. Safer, D. J., & Allen, R. P. *Hyperactive children: Diagnosis and management*. Baltimore: University Park Press, 1976.
6. Huessy, H. F. Study of the prevalence and therapy of the choreatiform syndrome or hyperkinesis in rural Vermont. *Acta Paedopsychiatrica*, 1967, **34**, 130–135.
7. Miller, R. G., Palkes, H. S., & Stewart, M. A. Hyperactive children in suburban elementary schools. *Child Psychiatry and Human Development*, 1973, **4**, 121–127.
8. Wender, P. H., & Eisenberg, L. Minimal brain dysfunction in children. In S. Arieti (Ed.), *American handbook of psychiatry*. Vol. II. (2nd ed.) New York: Basic Books, 1974.
9. Cantwell, D. P. Clinical picture, epidemiology and classifications of the hyperactive child syndrome. In D. P. Cantwell (Ed.), *The hyperactive child*. New York: Spectrum, 1975.
10. Feingold, B. F. *Why your child is hyperactive*. New York: Random House, 1975.
11. Stewart, M. A., & Olds, S. W. *Raising a hyperactive child*. New York: Harper, 1973.
12. Clements, S. D. *Minimal brain dysfunction in children*. Washington, D.C.: National Institute of Neurological Diseases and Blindness, Monograph No. 3, 1966.
13. Douglas V. I. Stop, look and listen: The problem of sustained attention and impulse control in hyperactive and normal children. *Canadian Journal of Behavioral Science*, 1972, **4**, 259–282.
14. Drash, P. W. Treatment of hyperactivity. *Pediatric Psychology*, 1975, **3**, 17–20.
15. O'Malley, J., & Eisenberg, L. The hyperkinetic syndrome. *Seminars in Psychiatry*, 1973, **5**, 95–103.
16. Aron, A. M. Minimal cerebral dysfunction in childhood. *Journal of Communication Disorders*, 1972, **5**, 142–153.
17. Chalfant, J. G., & Scheffelin, M. A. *Central processing dysfunctions in children: A review of research*. Washington, D.C.: National Institute of Neurological Diseases and Stroke, Monographs No. 9, 1969.
18. Conners, C. K. Psychological assessment of children with minimal brain dysfunction. *Annals of the New York Academy of Sciences*, 1973, **205**, 283–302.
19. Paine, R. S., Werry, J. S., & Quay, H. C. A study of minimal cerebral dysfunction. *Developmental Medicine and Child Neurology*, 1968, **10**, 505–520.
20. Werry, J. S., Minde, K., Guzman, A., Weiss, G., Dogan, K., & Hoy, E. Studies on the hyperactive child. VII: Neurological status compared with neurotic and normal children. *American Journal of Orthopsychiatry*, 1972, **42**, 441–451.
21. Dykman, R., Peters, J., & Ackerman, P. Experimental approaches to the study of minimal brain dysfunction. *Annals of the New York Academy of Sciences*, 1973, **205**, 93–108.
22. Hammar, S. L. School underachievement in the adolescent: A review of 73 cases. *Pediatrics*, 1967, **40**, 373–381.
23. Stevens-Long, J. The effect of behavioral context on some aspects of adult disciplinary practice and affect. *Child Development*, 1973, **44**, 476–484.
24. Weiss, G., Minde, K., Werry, J., Douglas, V., & Nemeth, E. Studies on the hyperactive child. VIII. Five-year follow-up. *Archives of General Psychiatry*, 1971, **24**, 409–414.
25. Cantwell, D. P. Natural history and prognosis in the hyperactive child syndrome. In D. P. Cantwell (Ed.), *The hyperactive child*. New York: Spectrum, 1975.
26. Mendelson, W., Johnson, J., & Stewart, M. Hyperactive children as teen-agers: A follow-up study. *Journal of Nervous and Mental Disease*, 1971, **153**, 273–279.
27. Minde, K., Lewin, D., Weiss, G., Lavigueur, H., Douglas, V., & Sykes, E. The hyperactive child in elementary school: A five-year, controlled follow-up. *Exceptional Child*, 1971, **38**, 215–221.
28. Campbell, S. B. Hyperactivity: Course and treatment. In A. Davids (Ed.), *Child personality and psychopathology*. Vol. 3. New York: Wiley, 1976.
29. Menkes, M., Rowe, J., & Menkes, J. A twenty-five year follow-up study on the hyperkinetic child with minimal brain dysfunction. *Pediatrics*, 1967, **39**, 392–399.
30. Minde, K., Weiss, G., & Mendelson, M. A five-year follow-up study of 91 hyperactive school children. *Journal of the American Academy of Child Psychiatry*, 1972, **11**, 595–610.
31. Stewart, M. A., Mendelson, W. B., & Johnson, N. E. Hyperactive children as adolescents: How they describe themselves. *Child Psychiatry and Human Development*, 1973, **4**, 3–11.
32. Denhoff, E. The natural life history of children with minimal brain dysfunction. *Annals of the New York Academy of Sciences*, 1973, **205**, 188–205.

33. National Institute of Child Health and Human Development. *Maturation, learning, and behavior.* Washington, D.C.: Department of Health, Education, and Welfare Publication No. (NIH) 76-1036, 1976.

34. Needleman, H. L. Lead poisoning in children: Neurological implications of widespread subclinical intoxication. *Seminars in Psychiatry,* 1973, **5,** 47–53.

35. Rubin, R., Rosenblatt, C., & Balow, B. Psychological and educational sequelae of prematurity. *Pediatrics,* 1973, **52,** 352–363.

36. Towbin, A. Organic causes of minimal brain dysfunction. *Journal of the American Medical Association,* 1971, **271,** 1207–1214.

37. Denson, R., Nanson, J. L., & McWatters, M. A. Hyperkinesis and maternal smoking. *Canadian Psychiatric Association Journal,* 1975, **20,** 183–187.

38. Jones, K. L., Smith, D. W., Streissguth, A. P., & Myrianthopolous, N. C. Outcome in offspring of chronic alcoholic women. *Lancet,* 1974, **1,** 1076–1078.

39. Feingold, B. F. Hyperkinesis and learning disabilities linked to artifical food flavors and colors. *American Journal of Nursing,* 1975, **75,** 797–803.

40. Cantwell, D. P. Psychiatric illness in the families of hyperactive children. *Archives of General Psychiatry,* 1972, **27,** 414–417.

41. Cantwell, D. P. Familial-genetic research with hyperactive children. In D. P. Cantwell (Ed.), *The hyperactive child.* New York: Spectrum, 1975.

42. Morrison, J. R., & Stewart, M. A. A family study of the hyperactive child syndrome. *Biological Psychiatry,* 1971, **3,** 189–195.

43. Morrison, J. R., & Stewart, M. A. The psychiatric status of the legal families of adopted hyperactive children. *Archives of General Psychiatry,* 1973, **28,** 888–891.

44. Willerman, L., & Plomin, R. Activity level in children and their parents. *Child Development,* 1973, **44,** 854–858.

45. Omenn, G. Genetic issues in the syndrome of minimal brain dysfunction. *Seminars in Psychiatry,* 1973, **5,** 5–19.

46. Safer, D. A familial factor in minimal brain dysfunction. *Behavior Genetics,* 1973, **3,** 175–187.

47. Dubey, D. R. Organic factors in hyperkinesis: A critical review. *American Journal of Orthopsychiatry,* 1976, **46,** 353–366.

48. Conners, C. K., Eisenberg, L., & Barcai, A. Effect of dextroamphetamine on children: Studies on subjects with learning disabilities and school behavior problems. *Archives of General Psychiatry,* 1967, **17,** 478–485.

49. Conners, C. K. Controlled trial of methylphenidate in preschool children with minimal brain dysfunction. *International Journal of Mental Health,* 1975, **4,** 61–74.

50. Hoffman, S. P., Engelhardt, D. M., Margolis, R. A., Polizos, P., Waizer, J., & Rosenfeld, R. Response to methylphenidate in low socioeconomic hyperactive children. *Archives of General Psychiatry,* 1974, **30,** 354–359.

51. Steinberg, G. G., Troshinsky, C., & Steinberg, H. R. Dextroamphetamine responsive behavior disorder in school children. *American Journal of Psychiatry,* 1971, **128,** 174–179.

52. Conners, C. K. Pharmacotherapy of psychopathology in children. In H. C. Quay & J. S. Werry (Eds.), *Psychopathological disorders of childhood.* New York: Wiley, 1972.

53. Fish, B. The "one child, one drug" myth of stimulants in hyperkinesis. *Archives of General Psychiatry,* 1971, **25,** 193–203.

54. Millichap, J. G. Drugs in management in minimal brain dysfunction. *Annals of the New York Academy of Sciences,* 1973, **205,** 321–334.

55. Sroufe, L. A. Drug treatment of children with behavior problems. In E. M. Hetherington, S. Scarr-Salapatek, & G. M. Siegel (Eds.), *Review of child development research.* Vol. 4. Chicago: University of Chicago Press, 1975.

56. Fish, B. Stimulant drug treatment of hyperactive children. In D. P. Cantwell (Ed.), *The hyperactive child.* New York: Spectrum, 1975.

57. Satterfield, J. H., Cantwell, D. P., & Satterfield, B. T. Pathophysiology of the hyperactive child syndrome. *Archives of General Psychiatry,* 1974, **31,** 839–844.

58. Satterfield, J. H. Neurophysiologic studies with hyperactive children. In D. P. Cantwell (Ed.), *The hyperactive child.* New York: Spectrum, 1975.

59. Zahn, T. P., Abate, F., Little, B. C., & Wender, P. H. Minimal brain dysfunction, stimulant drugs, and autonomic nervous system activity. *Archives of General Psychiatry,* 1975, **32,** 381–387.

60. Gardner, R. A. Psychotherapy of the psychogenic problems secondary to minimal brain dysfunction. *International Journal of Child Psychotherapy*, 1973, **2**, 224–256.

61. Gardner, R. A. Psychotherapy in minimal brain dysfunction. In J. H. Masserman (Ed.), *Current psychiatric therapies*. Vol. 15, New York: Grune & Stratton, 1975.

62. Gardner, R. A. Techniques for involving the child with MBD in meaningful psychotherapy. *Journal of Learning Disabilities*, 1975, **8**, 272–282.

63. Satterfield, J. H. Central and autonomic nervous system function in the hyperactive child syndrome: Treatment and research implications. In A. Davids (Ed.), *Child personality and psychopathology*. Vol. 3. New York: Wiley, 1976.

64. Allyon, T., Layman, D., & Kandel, H. J. A behavioral-educational alternative to drug control of hyperactive children. *Journal of Applied Behavioral Analysis*, 1975, **8**, 137–146.

65. Douglas, V. I. Are drugs enough: To treat or train the hyperactive child. *International Journal of Mental Health*, 1975, **4**, 199–212.

66. Meichenbaum, D. H., & Goodman, J. Training impulsive children to talk to themselves: A means of developing self-control. *Journal of Abnormal Psychology*, 1971, **2**, 115–126.

67. O'Leary, K. D., & Drabman, R. Token reinforcement programs in the classroom: A review. *Psychological Bulletin*, 1971, **75**, 379–398.

68. Patterson, G. R., Jones, R., Whittier, J., & Wright, M. A. A behavior modification technique for the hyperactive child. *Behavior Research and Therapy*, 1965, **3**, 217–226.

69. Palkes, H., Stewart, M., & Kahana, B. Porteus maze performance of hyperactive boys after training in self-directed verbal commands. *Child Development*, 1968, **39**, 817–826.

70. Berkowitz, B. T., & Graziano, A. M. Training parents as behavior therapists: A review. *Behavior Research and Therapy*, 1972, **10**, 297–317.

71. Feighner, A. Videotape training for parents as therapeutic agents with hyperactive children. In D. P. Cantwell (Ed.), *The hyperactive child*. New York: Spectrum, 1975.

72. Gross, M. B., & Wilson, W. C. *Minimal brain dysfunction: A clinical study of incidence, diagnosis and treatment in over 1,000 children*. New York: Brunner/Mazel, 1974.

73. Laufer, M. W., & Shetty, T. Organic brain syndromes. In A. M. Freedman, H. K. Kaplan, & B. J. Sadock (Eds.), *Comprehensive textbook of psychiatry*. (2nd ed.). Baltimore: Williams & Wilkins, 1975.

74. Loney, J., Comly, H. H., & Simon, B. Parental management, self-concept, and drug response in minimal brain dysfunction. *Journal of Learning Disabilities*, 1975, **8**, 187–190.

75. Mann, L. Perceptual training: Misdirections and redirections. *American Journal of Orthopsychiatry*, 1970, **40**, 30–38.

76. Mann, L. Perceptual training revisited: The training of nothing at all. *Rehabilitation Literature*, 1971, **32**, 322–327.

77. Forness, S. Educational approaches with hyperactive children. In D. P. Cantwell (Ed.), *The hyperactive child*. New York: Spectrum, 1975.

78. Turnure, J. E. Children's reaction to distractors in a learning situation. *Developmental Psychology*, 1970, **2**, 115–122.

79. Turnure, J. E. Control of orienting behavior in children under five years of age. *Developmental Psychology*, 1971, **4**, 16–24.

80. Mosher, L. R., & Gunderson, J. G. Special report: Schizophrenia, 1972. *Schizophrenia Bulletin*, 1973, No. 7, 12–52.

81. Bender, L. The life course of children with schizophrenia. *American Journal of Psychiatry*, 1973, **130**, 783–786.

82. Werry, J. S. Childhood psychosis. In H. C. Quay & J. S. Werry (Eds.), *Psychopathological disorders of childhood*. New York: Wiley, 1972.

83. Babigian, H. M. Schizophrenia: Epidemiology. In A. M. Freedman, H. I. Kaplan, & B. J. Sadock (Eds.), *Comprehensive textbook of psychiatry*. (2nd ed.) Baltimore: Williams & Wilkins, 1975.

84. Gunderson, J. G., & Mosher, L. R. The cost of schizophrenia. *American Journal of Psychiatry*, 1975, **132**, 901–906.

85. National Institute of Mental Health. *Schizophrenia: Is there an answer?* Washington, D.C.: Department of Health, Education and Welfare Publication No. (HSM) 73-9086, 1972.

86. Yolles, S. F., & Kramer, M. Vital statistics. In L. Bellak & L. Loeb (Eds.), *The schizophrenic syndrome*. New York: Grune & Stratton, 1969.

87. Bender, L. The nature of childhood psychosis. In J. G. Howells (Ed.), *Modern perspectives in international child psychiatry*. New York: Brunner/Mazel, 1971.

88. Bettelheim, B. *The empty fortress: Infantile autism and the birth of the self*. New York: Free Press, 1967.

89. Eisenberg, L. The classification of childhood psychosis reconsidered. *Journal of Autism and Childhood Schizophrenia*, 1972, **2**, 338–342.

90. Rutter, M. Concepts of autism: A review of research. *Journal of Child Psychology and Psychiatry*, 1968, **9**, 1–25.

91. Reider, R. O. The offspring of schizophrenic parents: A review. *Journal of Nervous and Mental Disease*, 1973, **157**, 179–190.

92. Rutter, M. Autistic children: Infancy to adulthood. *Seminars in Psychiatry*, 1970, **2**, 435–450.

93. Rutter, M. Relationships between child and adult psychiatric disorders. *Acta Psychiatrica Scandinavica*, 1972, **48**, 3–21.

94. Bennett, S., & Klein, H. R. Childhood schizophrenia: 30 years later. *American Journal of Psychiatry*, 1966, **122**, 1121–1124.

95. Bender, L., & Grugett, A. A study of certain epidemiological factors in a group of children with childhood schizophrenia. *American Journal of Orthopsychiatry*, 1956, **26**, 131–145.

96. Colbert, E. G., & Koegler, R. R. The childhood schizophrenic in adolescence. *Psychiatric Quarterly*, 1961, **35**, 693–701.

97. Goldfarb, W. Childhood psychosis. In P. H. Mussen (Ed.), *Carmichael's manual of child psychology*. Vol. 2. (3rd ed.) New York: Wiley, 1970.

98. Keith, S. J., Gunderson, J. G., Reifman, A., Buchsbaum, S., & Mosher, R. A. Special report: Schizophrenia, 1976. *Schizophrenia Bulletin*, 1976, **2**, 509–565.

99. Gove, W. R., & Herb, T. S. Stress and mental illness among the young: A comparison of the sexes. *Social Forces*, 1974, **53**, 256–265.

100. Arieti, S. *Interpretation of schizophrenia*. (2nd ed.) New York: Basic Books, 1974.

101. Bellak, L., Hurvich, M., & Gediman, H. K. *Ego functions in schizophrenics, neurotics, and normals*. New York: Wiley, 1973.

102. Weiner, I. B. *Psychodiagnosis in schizophrenia*. New York: Wiley, 1966.

103. Aug, R. G., & Ables, B. S. A clinician's guide to childhood psychosis. *Pediatrics*, 1971, **47**, 327–337.

104. Despert, J. L. *Schizophrenia in children*. New York: Brunner/Mazel, 1968.

105. Miller, R. T. Childhood schizophrenia: A review of selected literature. *International Journal of Mental Health*, 1974, **3**, 3–46.

106. Rutter, M. Childhood schizophrenia reconsidered. *Journal of Autism and Childhood Schizophrenia*, 1972, **2**, 315–337.

107. Arajarvi, T., & Alanen, Y. O. Psychoses in childhood. I. A clinical, family and follow-up study. *Acta Psychiatrica Scandinavica*, Supplement, 1964, **40**, 1–32.

108. Bender, L. The life course of schizophrenic children. *Biological Psychiatry*, 1970, **2**, 165–172.

109. Bomberg, D., Szurek, S., & Etemad, J. A statistical study of a group of psychotic children. In S. Szurek & I. Berlin (Eds.), *Clinical studies in childhood psychosis*. New York: Brunner/Mazel, 1973.

110. Jordan, K., & Prugh, D. G. Schizophreniform psychosis of childhood. *American Journal of Psychiatry*, 1971, **128**, 323–339.

111. Zerbin-Rudin, E. Genetic research and the theory of schizophrenia. *International Journal of Mental Health*, 1972, **1**, 42–62.

112. Gittelman, M., & Birch, H. G. Childhood schizophrenia: Intellect, neurologic status, perinatal risk, prognosis, and family pathology. *Archives of General Psychiatry*, 1967, **17**, 16–25.

113. Goldfarb, W. Distinguishing and classifying the schizophrenic child. In S. Arieti (Ed.), *American handbook of psychiatry*. Vol. 2. New York: Basic Books, 1974.

114. Mednick, S. A. Breakdown in individuals at high risk for schizophrenia: Possible predispositional perinatal factors. *Mental Hygiene*, 1970, **54**, 50–63.

115. Rosenthal, D. Genetics of schizophrenia. In S. Arieti (Ed.), *American handbook of psychiatry*. Vol. 3. New York:

116. Rutt, C. N., & Offord, D. R. Prenatal and perinatal complications in childhood schizophrenics and their families. *Journal of Nervous and Mental Disease,* 1971, **152,** 324–331.

117. White, L. Organic factors and psychophysiology in childhood schizophrenia. *Psychological Bulletin,* 1974, **81,** 238–255.

118. Arieti, S. An overview of schizophrenia from a predominantly psychological approach. *American Journal of Psychiatry,* 1974, **131,** 241–249.

119. Goldstein, M. J., & Rodnick, E. H. The family's contribution to the etiology of schizophrenia: Current status. *Schizophrenia Bulletin,* 1975, No. 14, 48–63.

120. Heilbrun, A. B. *Aversive maternal control: A theory of schizophrenic development.* New York: Wiley,1973.

121. Laing, R. D., & Esterson, A. *Sanity, madness, and the family.* (2nd ed.) New York: Basic Books, 1970.

122. Lidz, T. *The origin and treatment of schizophrenic disorders.* New York: Basic Books, 1973.

123. Schuham, A. I. The double-bind hypothesis a decade later. *Psychological Bulletin,* 1968, **68,** 409–416.

124. Wynne, L. C., Singer, M. T., Bartko, J. J., & Toohey, M. L. Schizophrenics and their families: Recent research on parental communication. In J. M. Tanner (Ed.), *Psychiatric research: The widening perspective.* New York: International Universities Press, 1975.

125. Hirsch, S. R., & Leff, J. P. *Abnormalities in parents of schizophrenics.* London: Oxford University Press, 1975.

126. Liem, J. H. Effects of verbal communications of parents and children: A comparison of normal and schizophrenic families. *Journal of Consulting and Clinical Psychology,* 1974, **42,** 438–450.

127. Waxler, N. E., & Mishler, E. G. Parental interaction with schizophrenic children and well siblings. *Archives of General Psychiatry,* 1971, **25,** 223–231.

128. Cunningham, L., Cadoret, R. J., Loftus, R., & Edward, J. E. Studies of adoptees from psychiatrically disturbed biological parents. *British Journal of Psychiatry,* 1975, **126,** 534–549.

129. Rosenthal, D. A program of research on heredity in schizophrenia. *Behavioral Science,* 1971, **16,** 191–201.

130. Wender, P. H. Adopted children and their families in the evaluation of nature-nurture interactions in the schizophrenic disorders. *Annual Review of Medicine,* 1972, **33,** 255–372.

131. Wender, P. H., Rosenthal, D., Kety, S., Schulsinger, F., & Welner, J. Cross-forstering: A research strategy for clarifying the role of genetic and experimental factors in the etiology of schizophrenia. *Archives of General Psychiatry,* 1974, **30,** 121–128.

132. Anthony, E. J. A clinical and experimental study of high-risk children and their schizophrenic parents. In A. R. Kaplan (Ed.), *Genetic factors in schizophrenia.* Springfield, Ill.: Charles C. Thomas, 1972.

133. Garmezy, N. The experimental study of children vulnerable to psychopathology. In A. Davids (ed.), *Child personality and psychopathology: Current topics.* Vol. 2. New York: Wiley, 1975.

134. Mednick, S. A., & Schulsinger, F. Factors related to breakdown in children at high risk for schizophrenia. In M. Roff & D. F. Ricks (Eds.), *Life history research in psychopathology.* Vol. I. Minneapolis: University of Minnesota Press, 1970.

135. Mednick, S. A., Schulsinger, H., & Schulsinger, F. Schizophrenia in children of schizophrenic mothers. In A. Davids (Ed.), *Child personality and psychopathology: Current topics.* Vol. 2. New York: Wiley, 1975.

136. Ragins, N., Schachter, J., Elmer, E., Preisman, R., Bowes, A. E., & Harway, V. Infants and children at risk for schizophrenia: Environmental and developmental observations. *Journal of the American Academy of Child Psychiatry,* 1975, **14,** 150–177.

137. Heston, L. L. Psychiatric disorders in foster home reared children of schizophrenic mothers. *British Journal of Psychiatry,* 1966, **112,** 819–825.

138. Heston, L. L. The genetics of schizophrenic and schizoid disease. *Science,* 1970, **167,** 249–256.

139. Rosenthal, D., Wender, P. H., Kety, S. S., Welner, J., & Schulsinger, F. The adopted-away offspring of schizophrenics. *American Journal of Psychiatry,* 1971, **128,** 307–311.

140. Gottesman, I. I., & Shields, J. A critical review of recent adoption, twin, and family studies of schizophrenia: Behavioral genetics perspectives. *Schizophrenia Bulletin,* 1976, **2,** 360–401.

141. Rolf, J. E., & Harig, P. T. Etiological research in schizophrenia and the rationale for primary intervention. *American Journal of Orthopsychiatry,* 1974, **44,** 538–554.

142. Rosenthal, D. *Genetic theory and abnormal behavior.* New York: McGraw-Hill, 1970.

143. Eisenberg, L. The course of childhood schizophrenia. *Archives of Neurology and Psychiatry,* 1957, **78,** 69–83.

144. Goldfarb, W. *Growth and change of schizophrenic children. A longitudinal study.* New York: Winston, 1974.

145. Goldfarb, W. Therapeutic management of schizophrenic children. In J. G. Howells (Ed.), *Modern perspectives in international child psychiatry.* New York: Brunner/Mazel, 1971.

146. Des Lauriers, A. M. *The experience of reality in childhood schizophrenia.* New York: International Universities Press, 1962.

147. Ekstein, R. Functional psychoses in children: Clinical features and treatment. In A. M. Freedman, H. I. Kaplan, & B. J. Sadock (Ed.), *Comprehensive textbook of psychiatry.* (2nd ed.) Baltimore: Williams & Wilkins, 1975.

148. Szurek, S. A., & Berlin, I. (Eds.) *Clinical studies in childhood psychoses.* New York: Brunner/Mazel, 1973.

149. DeMyer, M., & Ferster, C. Teaching new social behavior in schizophrenic children. *Journal of the American Academy of Child Psychiatry,* 1962, **1,** 443–461.

150. Leff, R. I. Behavior modification and the psychosis of childhood. *Psychological Bulletin,* 1968, **69,** 396–409.

151. Lapousse, R., & Monk, M. A. Fears and worries in a representative sample of children. *American Journal of Orthopsychiatry,* 1959, **29,** 223–248.

152. Miller, L. C., Barrett, C. L., Hampe, E., & Noble, H. Factor structure and childhood fears. *Journal of Consulting and Clinical Psychology,* 1972, **39,** 264–268.

153. Miller, L. C., Barrett, C. L., & Hampe, E. Phobias of childhood in a prescientific era. In A. Davids (ed.), *Child personality and psychopathology.* Vol. 1. New York: Wiley, 1974.

154. Marks, I. M. *Fears and phobias.* New York: American Press, 1969.

155. Anthony, E. J. Neuroses of children. In A. M. Freedman & H. I. Kaplan (Eds.), *The child.* Vol. 2, *The major psychological disorders and their treatment.* New York: Atheneum, 1972.

156. Poznanski, E. O. Children with excessive fears. *American Journal of Orthopsychiatry,* 1973, **43,** 428–438.

157. Berecz, J. M. Phobias of childhood: Etiology and treatment. *Psychological Bulletin,* 1968, **70,** 695–720.

158. Watson, J. B., & Rayner, R. Conditioned emotional reactions. *Journal of Experimental Psychology,* 1920, **3,** 1–14.

159. Freud, S. Analysis of a phobia in a five-year-old boy (1909). Standard Edition, Vol. X. London: Hogarth, 1955.

160. Kessler, J. W. Neurosis in childhood. In B. B. Wolman (Ed.), *Manual of child psychopathology.* New York: McGraw-Hill, 1972.

161. Agras, W. S., Chapin, H. N., & Oliveau, D. C. The natural history of phobia. *Archives of General Psychiatry,* 1972, **26,** 315–317.

162. Glick, B. S. Conditioning therapy with phobic patients: Success and failure. *American Journal of Psychotherapy,* 1970, **24,** 92–101.

163. Hampe, E., Noble, H., Miller, L. C., & Barrett, C. L. Phobic children one and two years post-treatment. *Journal of Abnormal Psychology,* 1973, **82,** 446–453.

164. Marks, I. M. Phobic disorders four years after treatment: A prospective follow-up. *British Journal of Psychiatry,* 1971, **118,** 683–688.

165. Bandura, A., Grusec, J. E., & Menlove, F. L. Vicarious extinction of avoidance behavior. *Journal of Personality and Social Psychology,* 1967, **5,** 16–23.

166. Bentler, P. M. An infant's phobia treated with reciprocal inhibition therapy. *Journal of Child Psychology and Psychiatry,* 1962, **3,** 185–189.

167. Kolansky, H. Treatment of a three-year-old girl's severe infantile neurosis: Stammering and insect phobia. *Psychoanalytic Study of the Child,* 1960, **15,** 261–286.

168. Rachman, S., & Costello, C. G. The etiology and treatment of children's phobias: A review. *American Journal of Psychiatry,* 1961, **118,** 97–106.

169. Sperling, M. Animal phobias in a two-year-old child. *Psychoanalytic Study of the Child,* 1952, **7,** 115–126.

170. Woltmann, A. G. Play and related techniques. In D. Brower & L. E. Abt (Eds.), *Progress in clinical psychology.* New York: Grune & Stratton, 1952.

171. Freedman, D. X. *Report of the conference on the use of stimulant drugs in the treatment of behaviorally disturbed children.* Sponsored by the Office of Child Development and the Department of Health, Education, and Welfare, Washington, D.C., January 11–12, 1971. Reprinted in the *National Elementary Principal,* 1971, **50,** 53–59.

172. Gallagher, C. C. *Federal involvement in the use of behavior modification drugs on grammar school children.* Hearing before a subcommittee of the Committee of Government Operations, House of Representatives, September, 29, 1970.

173. Krager, J. M., & Safer, D. J. Type and prevalence of medication in treating hyperactive children. *New England Journal of Medicine,* 1974, **291,** 1118–1120.

174. Grinspoon, L., & Singer, S. B. Amphetamines in the treatment of hyperkinetic children. *Harvard Educational Review,* 1973, **43,** 515–555.

175. Beck, L., Langford, W. S., MacKay, M., & Sum, G. Childhood chemotherapy and later drug abuse and growth curve: A follow-up study of 30 adolescents. *American Journal of Psychiatry,* 1975, **132,** 436–438.

176. Safer, D. J., & Allen, R. P. Stimulant drug treatment of hyperactive adolescents. *Diseases of the Nervous System,* 1975, **36,** 454–457.

177. Conners, C. K. Recent drug studies with hyperkinetic children. *Journal of Learning Disabilities,* 1971, **4,** 476–483.

178. Safer, D., & Allen, R. Factors influencing the suppressant effects of two stimulant drugs on the growth of hyperactive children. *Pediatrics,* 1973, **51,** 660–667.

179. Safer, D., Allen, R., & Barr, E. Growth rebound after termination of stimulant drugs. *Journal of Pediatrics,* 1975, **86,** 113–116.

180. Weiss, G., Kruger, E., Danielson, U., & Elman, M. Effect of long-term treatment of hyperactive children with methylphenidate. *Candian Medical Association Journal,* 1975, **112,** 159–165.

181. Rie, H. E., Rie, E. D., Stewart, S., & Ambuel, J. P. Effects of Ritalin on underachieving children: A replication. *American Journal of Orthopsychiatry,* 1976, **46,** 313–322.

182. Weithorn, C. J., & Ross, R. Stimulant drugs for hyperactivity: Some disturbing questions. *American Journal of Orthopsychiatry,* 1976, **46,** 168–173.

183. Schaefer, J. W., Palkes, H. S., & Stewart, M. A. Group counseling for parents of hyperactive children. *Child Psychiatry and Human Development,* 1974, **5,** 89–94.

PART 4

Middle Childhood

11 Physical and Mental Growth

PHYSICAL GROWTH
  Motor Skills
  Body Image

MENTAL DEVELOPMENT
  Academic Testing
  Perceptual Development
  Language Development
  Memory
  Conservation Behavior
  Moral Development

THE CONCEPTUAL WORLD OF CHILDHOOD

ESSAY
  Learning to Read

BIOGRAPHY
  Alfred Binet

SUMMARY

REFERENCES

Middle childhood is the period from about the age of 5 or 6 to about the age of 11 or 12. This is a time of leisurely growth between the more rapid growth of the preschool period and the onset of adolescence.

PHYSICAL GROWTH

By the age of 6, most children have lost their soft contours and their top-heavy stature that makes preschoolers so appealing to adults. In middle childhood the arms and legs grow faster than the trunk so that early in this period many youngsters have a "spindly" appearance. While girls tend to mature somewhat earlier than boys, boys still are somewhat taller and heavier than girls until about the age of 10.

The average North American 6-year-old is about 46 inches tall and weighs about 48 pounds. Each year during middle childhood the average youngster grows about 2 or 3 inches and gains between 3 and 6 pounds (1). There are wide individual differences, of course. Some 6-year-olds can be mistaken for 10-year-olds and vice versa. In general, by the time a child reaches this period in life, his or her relative size is fairly stable and predictable. A child who is small or large in relation to his or her peers will probably have the same position in adulthood (2).

Changes in body proportion at this time are accompanied by changes in facial configuration. As children lose their "baby fat," their faces tend to become slimmer and narrower, and this adds to the "gawky" appearance of this age group. Children also lose their baby teeth, the first one coming out at about the age of 6. With the appearance of permanent teeth and several molars, the shape of the child's face is changed. The transition

At the elementary school level children have the motor coordination and the intellectual ability required to engage in team sports and games.

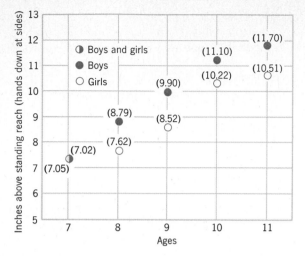

Figure 11.1 Vertical jump performance by age and sex. (*Source:* Johnson, R. D. Measurements of achievement in fundamental skills of elementary school children. *Research Quarterly*, 1962, **33,** 94–103.)

from temporary to permanent teeth is usually completed by about 11 or 12 years of age.

With respect to growth, sometimes not enough attention is paid to a child's eyes. At 6 years of age the eyes have not yet reached their final size and shape. Many children between 6 and 8 years of age are slightly farsighted, but this condition usually corrects itself spontaneously between the ages of 8 and 10 (3), when their eyes reach adult eye size and shape. One practical implication of this finding is that their early reading materials should be printed in large type.

Motor Skills During the preschool years children learn the smooth coordination of small and large muscles. During middle childhood this coordination is further refined and used in many activities ranging from reading and writing to playing team games.

Jumping. A good index of growth in motor coordination and strength is jumping. One measure of this activity is called vertical jumping; the child must stand flat-footed with his or her hands raised above the head and jump straight up. The results for boys and girls at several age levels are shown in Figure 11.1. As can be seen, after the age of 7, boys generally exceed girls in the height of their vertical jumps (4). In the standing broad jump boys also tend to surpass girls after 7 years of age.

On another task—jumping and hopping into grids (somewhat like hopscotch)—it is not until children reach the age of 6 that they can jump and hop with enough precision to move from one square to another. On this particular test girls are superior to boys. Children show rapid improvement in this skill from age 6 to 9, after which they appear to reach a plateau (4–6). With respect to hopping, Cratty makes the following summary:

The data from these investigations of simple and complex locomotor attributes suggest that, to the extent to which the task seems to require relatively straightforward, or upward manifestations of leg strength and power, the boys between the age of 6 and 12 years excel the girls. The girls, on the other hand, seem better than the boys in jumping and hopping tasks that require precision and accuracy. In part these differences in the simple tasks probably reflect superiority in the leg power and strength of the boys, whereas the girls excel in the more complex tasks because their visual motor coordinations, necessary to execute these activities, are more mature at earlier ages and because they more frequently engage in this type of task (hopscotch) in the American culture [7, pp. 198–199].

Skill in Ball Play. Elementary-school children play ball in many different ways. Participation in such activities is important to the child's socialization and self-concept.

By the age of 6 most children can throw a small ball forcefully and with some accuracy. With increasing age, however, children can throw a ball increasing distances. Not surprisingly, in view of their greater strength, boys surpass girls in the length of their throw at all ages from 6 to 12 (5). By the age of 10, children can throw twice as far as they did at age 6 and by the age of 12, they can throw three times as far (5). Accuracy of throwing also improves with age, and boys typically throw more accurately than girls (4).

As a general rule, catching is more difficult than throwing, and a child's skill depends in part on the size of the ball and speed with which it is thrown. In one study, which investigated children's ability to estimate when to catch a ball that had been thrown to them, regular age changes were found. Between the ages of 6 and 8 children were not too accurate in estimating a ball's trajectory. It was not until about the age of 10 that they could correctly anticipate the return path. On this task no boy-girl differences were found (8).

Not much data exist on changes in a child's ability to kick and bat balls. There is a little evidence, however, that boys usually surpass girls in kicking balls at horizontal targets (9). Boys also do better in batting a ball. As in the case of girls and hopscotch, however, the superiority of boys in kicking and batting balls may be due, in some degree, to the fact they often play games requiring these skills.

Reaction Time. Motor skills obviously require a sequence of actions and thus they have a temporal dimension; this is called the **reaction time** (RT), and it is generally made up of several components. One of these is the **movement time**, the time that passes between the beginning and the end of the action. Another is the **decision time**—the time that passes between the signal or stimulus to action and the first movement. Investigators have explored the age changes in children's decision and movement times.

In one study children from 4 to 16 years of age were given two RT tasks. On one task 10 high and 10 low tones were presented at intervals ranging from 10 to 25 seconds. The subjects were asked to press a button as quickly as possible to turn off the tone (movement RT). On the second task they were also asked to press a button as quickly as possible, but only when the high tones were presented (decision RT). Each child was given two scores—one for the speed of responses and the other for the variation in response from trial to trial.

It was found that there was a regular decrease in the child's reaction time with age. For the youngest children the movement RT was .75 seconds, and for the oldest .25 seconds. The greatest decreases in movement reaction time occurred among the 4- to 9-year olds. On the decision RT task, the results were similar—1.3 seconds for the youngest children and .35 seconds for the oldest. Again, the greatest gains were made among the 4- to 9-year-olds (10). The variability scores also changed regularly with age, with the younger children showing much more variation in their performance than the older ones. The greatest diminution in variability took place among the 4- to 9-year-olds.

Another study to test decision time required the subject to make a

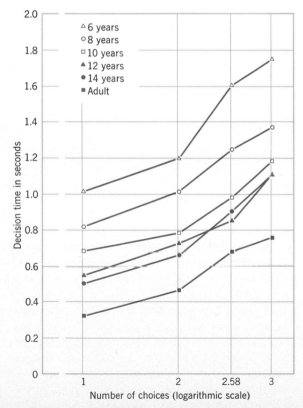

Figure 11.2 Decision time as a function of the number of alternatives per card for various age groups. (*Source.* Connolly, K. Response speed, temporal sequencing and information processing in children. In K. Connolly [Ed.], *Mechanisms of motor skill development.* New York: Academic Press, 1970.)

number of discriminations or decisions in sorting cards. The materials consisted of four decks of 24 cards each. One deck had three colors with eight cards per color. A second deck had four colors and six cards per color. A third deck had six different colors with four cards per color. The last deck contained eight different colors with three cards per color. Each subject was asked to sort the cards into piles according to color (two, four, six, or eight cards to a pile). The movement time was measured by having the subjects sort a deck of blank cards into piles of two, four, six, and eight cards. The decision time was the difference in time required to sort the colored and blank cards into the various piles.

The subjects in the study were males and females of the following ages: 6, 8, 10, 12, 14, and 24 years. The results, which appear in Figure 11.2, indicate that the decision time depended upon the age of the subject and the number of choices required. The oldest subjects virtually always took the shortest time regardless of the number of choices. Also, among every age group the decision time increased as the number of choices increased. Of the consecutive age groups shown in Figure 11.2, it would appear that the greatest shift in decision time occurs between the ages of 6 and 8 (11).

There is also a decrease in response variability during middle childhood. This development may be related to the gradual acquisition of motor skills, such as catching and hitting balls, playing hockey, croquet, and other games that call for decision-making as well as eye-hand coordination. It is possible that some children's poor performance in motor skills may be due to inhibited decision-making rather than immature eye-hand coordination.

Body Image

As children progressively acquire a more realistic conception of their environment, they also develop a more adequate conception of themselves. One aspect of this self-concept is the child's **body image.** Body image includes an awareness of the body and its parts but it also involves an evaluation of the adequacy of one's physical appearance and motor skills in comparison with one's peers. Although body image begins to be formed in infancy and early childhood, it becomes more conscious during middle childhood when the youngster can compare himself or herself with peers rather than with parents.

Body Perception. Table 11.1 presents a general idea of the development of the body concept (4). Such an assessment is made using a variety of techniques, including human figure drawing. If, for example, children are given an incomplete figure and asked to draw in the missing parts, their ability to do so will improve as they become older (14). Another method of assessment is to ask children to identify their own and other people's right and left sides (15–17). Although not mentioned in the table, the child's growing ability to inhibit motor actions of all kinds is another kind of evidence for growth in body perception (18).

Self-Concept. A long time ago George Herbert Mead (19), the famed

Table 11.1 Body Perception by Children

Age (in Years)	Perceptions
0–2	At the end of this period, the child can sometimes identify gross body parts verbally; can touch "tummy," back, arm, or leg when asked to do so; seems aware of toes before legs.
2–3	Becomes aware of front, back, side, head, and feet, and can locate objects relative to these body parts; begins to be aware of thumb, hand, feet, etc.; learns parts of the face.
4	Becomes aware that there is a right side and a left side of the body, but does not know which is which; has more detailed awareness of body parts; can name little finger and first fingers.
5	Is confused about which is the left and which is the right side of the body; can locate self in relation to objects, and objects in relation to self; trunk appears in figure drawings.
6	Begins to distinguish left and right body parts and to locate body in relation to the left and right of things and objects in relation to the left and right of the body; becomes aware of little finger and ring finger and can name them.
7–8	Concept of left/right well established; begins to distinguish correctly the left and right of other people and name correctly their left and right movements; facial expressions appear in figure drawings; limbs are filled in and details are added in figure drawings.
9–10	Adopts other people's spatial perspective with ease; can describe the arrangement of objects from another's point of view.

Source: Adapted from Cratty, B. J., & Martin, M. M. *Perceptual-motor efficiency in children.* Philadelphia: Lea & Febiger, 1969.

philosopher-sociologist, suggested that the individual's self-concept was derived from the "reflected appraisals" of others. But the child cannot grasp these reflected appraisals until his or her cognitive abilities are sufficiently developed. By the elementary-school years, the child becomes susceptible to the appraisals of peers and tends to evaluate himself or herself accordingly.

To study children's self-conceptions, investigators often use an adjective or phrase checklist, which includes both positive and negative words. The child either reads the list or it is read out loud by someone else. After each adjective or phrase, the child must say whether it is true for herself or himself. In general, the results of such studies do suggest that a child's self-concept depends to a large extent upon the appraisals of others (20–21). Children who are doing poorly in school and who may be looked down upon by parents and peers have a lower self-regard than children who are performing at the academic norm (22).

Actually, a child probably has many self-concepts, depending upon his

A child's self-concept is acquired, in part, from the reactions of other people to his or her behavior and appearance.

or her talents and interests. In addition to the body image, there is the self-concept as a pupil, as an athlete, as a friend, as someone with a special skill, and so forth. For example, a child may have a positive self-conception as a musician but a negative one as a chess player. Thus, a child who is unsuccessful in one area may be able to bolster his or her self-concept in another. However, the child who feels incompetent in all areas may become emotionally troubled. These matters are discussed more fully in the next chapter (Chapter 12).

MENTAL DEVELOPMENT

Around the age of 6 or 7, children develop certain new mental abilities that Piaget (23) calls **concrete operations.** Thanks to these operations, elementary-school children can form concepts of classes, relations, and numbers, thereby greatly expanding their conceptual world. Also, children who can perform concrete operations can learn and follow rules that have been formulated by others. Thus, middle childhood is a prime period for instructing children in certain skills and knowledge they will need in order to function effectively in their society.

We will discuss what children are able to accomplish once they have developed concrete operations. Since mental growth is often measured quantitatively, we will begin with testing; children usually cannot take group-administered tests of aptitude and achievement until they can perform concrete operations. Then we will look at the changes that take place in children's perception, language, memory, concepts of conservation, and moral development. A final section will briefly sketch the conceptual world of middle childhood, providing some examples of the language and lore that marks the highly original and persistent ''culture'' of this age period.

Academic Testing

As children learn to read and write, they are able to take group-administered tests; such tests are widely used for assessing **achievement** and **aptitude.** In theory, achievement tests measure past learning in a given area of instruction. Aptitude tests, by contrast, are supposed to be able to predict future learning (24, 25). An intelligence test is one kind of aptitude test.

During middle childhood children acquire the skills and ability to take group-administered tests.

The distinction between achievement and aptitude tests can be illustrated by means of the test items themselves. Items on an aptitude test are selected with the assumption that all children from a given background should have had an equal opportunity to have learned certain things. For example, one question might show a picture of a face with an eyebrow missing and ask, "What is missing in this picture?" It is assumed that most children have observed a large number of faces so that their success with the question should be a matter of general ability rather than specific instruction. Such questions are uncommon, however, and most items on an aptitude test require specific as well as general experience.

Achievement tests are designed to test what the child has learned from past instruction. Tests of reading, arithmetic, science, and so forth, sample bits of information a child should have learned in school, such as "2 × 2 = ?" or "What is the capital of Delaware?" For older children it becomes increasingly difficult to make a distinction between aptitude and achievement test items because it becomes less clear what has been acquired in school and what was acquired outside it.

Both achievement tests and aptitude tests are widely used in elementary schools to assess pupil progress. Most achievement tests are **norm-referenced;** that is, a given child's score is compared with that of a specified group. This same principle is used in college when examinations are graded on a "curve"; in this case, the class is the reference group. If there are many very bright students in that class, the average student will get a poorer grade than if the class had many poor students. Some achievement tests are norm referenced for a given state or for the whole nation. Thus, a child's or a school's performance can be evaluated in relation to the city, state, or nation.

Although achievement tests are useful for measuring pupil progress, they have many limitations that critics have been quick to note. Piaget (26), among others (27–29), believes that tests can have a negative effect upon education because they tend to dictate the contents of courses and the techniques used in the classroom. B. F. Skinner (30) argues that in order to make tests objective, responses are required that tap only the most superficial aspects of the child's knowledge. "Very often the responses which are most readily accepted as signs of knowledge are precisely those which are least likely to form part of a successful repertoire" (p. 245). In a recent, comprehensive review of achievement testing, Levine (31) says that while educators say that the aim of education is to acquire positive attitudes to learning and to develop skill in interpretation, achievement tests do not measure these attainments.

One way in which the shortcomings of achievement tests have been dealt with is through the introduction of **criterion-referenced** tests. At the college level, for example, some courses are now taught so that the student can move at his or her own pace with the aid of readily accessible videotapes. The student takes an exam when ready for it and retakes the exam, if necessary, until the course content is mastered. Criterion-referenced tests are thus intended to reveal what students can do or what they know, rather than to compare students with a norm. Such tests provide information that is immediately interpretable from the standpoint of an absolute standard of performance (32, 33).

Criterion-referenced tests are beginning to be used in elementary schools as well. A teacher who requires each child to complete ten book reports of a certain length is setting a criterion. Some educators are suggesting that records should be kept of each child's work and that teacher observations and work samples should be used to gauge pupil progress rather than tests (34). Although this type of evaluation is just beginning to appear in elementary schools, we believe it is a healthy development. Documentation of a child's work over a given period of time seems to us to be a much better index of his or her academic achievement than a test performance that measures only a superficial aspect of academic learning. On the other hand, if the criteria become too rigid and do not allow for individual differences, they can be as unsatisfactory as achievement tests.

Perceptual Development

Perceptual development, which is closely related to sensorimotor development, seems to follow a similar course in that major changes in perceptual processing seem to take place from about 4 to 9 years of age, with few, if any, significant changes occuring after that.

Search Strategies. One aspect of perception that does improve with age is the child's ability to search a stimulus array for particular items; the search becomes more rapid and more accurate with increasing age (35–39). There is also evidence that there are significant qualitative differences in the way in which younger and older children proceed with their search. These age differences are especially clear when the subjects compare perceptual stimuli or when they deal with relatively complex or ambiguous stimuli.

In one study, children of different ages were asked to compare drawings of the facades of houses that were alike or different in one or more respects (curtains in the windows, presence of a door, and so forth). Young children were much less successful than older children in making comparisons. Eye movement records suggested that the younger children compared just one feature. If the instances of that feature (for example, the windows) were alike, the children said the facades were the same without examining the other features (39). In a related study (40) it was found that teaching children what to look for in a comparison task was more helpful to the older ones than to the younger ones.

In a relatively free exploration task (Figure 11.3), age differences in search strategies are quite clear. When children are shown a card on which familiar figures are pasted in an ordered and a disordered array,

Figure 11.3 Picture exploration cards. (*Source.* Elkind, D., & Weiss, J. Studies in perceptual development III: Perceptual exploration. *Child Development,* 1967, **38,** 1153–1161.)

Ordered array

Disordered array

their ability to name the figures varies with their age and the pattern. Young children (4–5 years) do not name some figures and name others twice on the disordered array card. By contrast, older children (6–8 years) read the figures from left to right and from top to bottom and make no errors. On the ordered array (where the cards are pasted so that they form a triangle) young children make no errors because the path of exploration is clearly indicated by the figure itself (41, 42).

It was also found that in children's search strategies, younger children are more susceptible to distracting stimuli. In a couple of studies children were asked to compare the shapes and colors of wooden animal figures and to say whether they were the same or different when distracting features were added to those figures. The distracting features hindered the older children temporarily, but they constituted an absolute hindrance to younger children. Older children could more easily adjust their search strategies to look for new features than could younger children (43, 44). In short, during the early elementary-school years, children's search strategies become more rapid, efficient, and systematic with increasing age—at least until adolescence.

Logical Organization. As children mature, they are better able to organize perceptual information in logical ways. Older children can thus process more information and more complex information than is possible for younger children. Several studies by Eleanor Gibson and her colleagues demonstrate the emergence of cognitive processing in perception. In one study (45) groups of younger and older children had to learn to push buttons in relation to particular words. Some of the words rhymed and recognizing the rhyming rule could make learning easier. Significantly, more of the older children (age 11–12) than the younger children (7–8) made use of the rhyming rule to facilitate learning. In another study (46) fourth-grade children were able to use category knowledge to solve anagrams. Both of these studies suggest that with advancing age, children increasingly use cognitive processes to organize perception.

Evidence for the role of organizational cognition also comes from studies inspired by Piaget's (47) developmental theory of perception (which was described in Chapter 7). In Piaget's view (47) the ability to see the whole-part combinations shown in Figure 7.4 (48, 49) comes about because children can logically grasp the fact that one and the same form (for example, the apple shape in the "fruit man") can be *both* an apple *and* a head at the same time. This realization is comparable to understanding that someone can be both American and Protestant—that one person can belong to many different classes (48). The logical nature of this perceptual construction was demonstrated in another investigation. Children were grouped according to whether or not they could see whole-part combinations and then tested for skill in **logical multiplication**.

$$\left(\begin{array}{ccc} \text{The class of} \\ \text{Americans} \end{array} \times \begin{array}{c} \text{The class of} \\ \text{Protestants} \end{array} = \begin{array}{c} \text{The class of} \\ \text{American Protestants} \end{array} \right)$$

Those who could see whole-part combinations were significantly superior to the others in performing logical multiplication (50).

Decentering. Perceptual development can also be described according to the child's increasing freedom from the demands of a stimulus configuration; Piaget (47) calls this **decentering**. Young children tend to focus upon the dominant characteristics of visual configurations. These dominant aspects have been described by Gestalt psychologists (51, 52) as "closure, good form, continuity," and so forth. If dots are placed close together (contiguity), they appear to form a figure. An incomplete figure (for example, a circle with a segment missing) leads one to mentally fill in the missing part (closure). While these Gestalt principles operate at all levels of development, children can increasingly oppose these principles and construct alternative arrangements as they grow older.

Some of the studies already described provide evidence for decentering. For example, a child who says "a man made of fruit" to drawing number 2 in Figure 7.4 has decentered from viewing the head as only an apple, the body as only a pear, and so forth. In a somewhat different type of study, children were required to form concepts of a character, an activity, or a setting (background). When all three were present in the stimulus configuration (for example, a boy playing ball in the backyard), young children could abstract the boy, but they could not abstract the setting or the activity and respond to these facets of the configuration. Older children could conceptualize the activities and the settings as easily as the characters. In Gestalt terms, they could decenter from the figure (the character) to the ground (the activity or setting) (53).

In general, then, as children mature, their perception becomes increasingly more efficient, rapid, and subject to logical processes. In addition, they are gradually able to overcome the dominant aspects of the visual configuration and can select and organize information according to their own intentions and purposes.

Language Development

As we pointed out in Chapter 8, language growth during the preschool years is extraordinarily rapid. Indeed, superficially, the 5-year-old child seems to have mastered the basic syntactic structures of the language and to have a substantial vocabulary. Although it might appear that a child's language development is largely complete by the time he or she enters middle childhood, it is, in fact, far from ended and there is considerable growth in both vocabulary and syntactic understanding of language between the ages of 5 and 10 (54–56).

Growth in Language Utilization. One might suspect that the attainment of concrete operations would be accompanied by a new understanding of many terms and by the learning and using of new terms. This turns out to be the case. As children mature intellectually, their understanding of the words "more," "less," and "same" change dramatically. Young children understand terms such as "more," "less," or "same" as describing differences in things they can see, while older children realize that they pertain to nonperceptual differences as well.

A 4-year-old might say that ten pennies were more than four because he could see the difference visually, whereas a 6-year-old would give the same answer because he had mentally counted the coins. Both the 4-year-old and the 6-year-old made a successful discrimination and used the right terms, but their understandings of these terms differed. The child's ability to use language correctly does not necessarily indicate the depth of understanding. In this regard, the 5-year-old son of one of the authors once asked, "Dad, what is your true identity?" Being somewhat startled, the father asked in return, "I'm not sure. What do you mean by my 'true identity'?" The boy replied promptly, "Well, Clark Kent is Superman's true identity." The child had understood "true identity" in one sense, but certainly not in the same way as an adult who wonders "Who am I?"

A series of studies demonstrating the transformations in language understanding that are associated with transformations of cognitive ability was carried out by Sinclair-deZwart, a colleague of Piaget's (57, 58). In one study children were first asked to describe simple quantitative situations. They were then shown two pencils—a short thick one and a long thin one—and were asked to tell how they differed. To test their comprehension, children were asked to "Find a pencil that is shorter but thicker than this one." The children were also given measures of concrete operations and then were placed into two groups according to whether or not they could demonstrate operations; those who were in a transitional stage were placed into a third group.

It was found that there were no differences among the three groups on the comprehension tasks, but there were significant differences on the description tasks. Of the preoperational children, about 90 percent used such absolute expressions as "This one is thin and this one fat." However, all of the children who had achieved operations used comparative words: "This pencil is longer but thinner; this one is short but thick."

Sinclair-deZwart (57, 58) carried out an additional study to test the role of language in cognitive understanding. She tried to teach the children who had not attained operations the verbal expressions used by those youngsters who had. The teaching was not easy, and young children had the most trouble learning comparatives such as long *and* thin, short *and* fat. Of the children who learned the terms, however, only 10 percent showed progress in attaining concrete operations. In general, then, concrete operations seemed to be closely linked to the spontaneous use of comparatives rather than absolutes in verbal description.

Growth in Syntactic Knowledge. A relationship between cognitive development and comprehension can be demonstrated with respect to the syntactic aspects of language such as the passive voice. Passives are not used frequently in the spoken language; furthermore, they are both cognitively and grammatically more complex than the active voice because the noun-subject relations are irregular and must be translated into a standard form in order to be understood. The passive sentence "The man was bitten by the dog" has to be interpreted as "The dog bit the man." The noun-subject relations in passive sentences are particularly troublesome in a sentence that is reversible, that is, plausible if the sentence were reversed. ("The man was bitten by the dog" cannot really be reversed). While active sentences can also be reversible or nonreversible, reversibility is much more of a problem in passive than in active sentences (56).

In one study (59) four groups of children of 6, 8, 10, and 12 years of age and a group of college students were read reversible and nonreversible active and passive sentences. After each sentence was read to a subject, he or she was shown a picture of an action sequence described in the sentence. The subjects were asked to respond as quickly as possible after viewing each picture by pushing a "Right" or a "Wrong" button to show if it accurately depicted the sentence. It was found that the reaction time (RT) to the pictures for all sentences decreased with age. The 10- and 12-year-old groups performed at about the same level, but they were significantly faster than the younger children. The college students gave the fastest RT's of all. For all groups, the reversible sentences were more difficult than the nonreversible ones (the RT's were longer), and the passive reversible sentences were the most difficult of all (59). Very similar results were obtained by other investigators who used somewhat different procedures (60).

Developmental changes in children's syntactic understanding were also revealed in a series of studies by Carol Chomsky (61). Chomsky chose exceptions to usual linguistic constructions to determine the age at which children understood the exceptions as well as the general rules. She used verbs such as "to see" in which the reference of "see" is variable. In the sentence "John is easy to see," John is the referent, whereas in the sentence "John is eager to see," he is not. Likewise, the verbs "promise," "ask," and "tell" violate the general rules of syntax. Chomsky also examined children's understanding of pronouns.

In general, Chomsky found that for syntactical irregularities, children tended to improve each year between the ages of 5 and 10. There were wide individual differences, however; some children understood syntactical irregularities at age 5 while others did not understand them until age 10. This variability was not found in the matter of pronominal reference. With only a few exceptions, children below the age of 5 did not understand pronominal reference whereas nearly all of the children above the age of 5 did. Growth in the understanding of syntactical irregularities thus continues during the elementary-school years, while pronominal reference appears to be mastered by the age of 6.

According to Chomsky (61), growth in language during the elementary-school years seems to move in two directions. One is an increasing knowledge or semantic understanding of words. The other is an understanding of the syntactic rules governing the use of words. While preschool children are acquiring the basic rules of syntax, elementary-school children are slowly mastering the exceptions.

Referential Communication Skills. In Chapter 7 we pointed out that even young children can adapt their language to the developmental level of the listener. Such referential communication skills continue to improve as children mature socially as well as linguistically. Indeed, many experts in this field now argue that linguistic or psycholinguistic skills of the type discussed by Noam Chomsky are not the same as those that are needed to communicate (63–65). Apparently knowledge of a language and knowledge of how to use that language to communicate may require different abilities.

To illustrate the skills needed for referential communication, we will describe a two-person situation (briefly mentioned in Chapter 7) in which there is a *speaker* and a *listener* who can hear but not see one another; usually they are seated at opposite sides of a table, hidden from one another by a screen across the center. Both the speaker and the listener have identical sets of objects or pictures in front of them; one object or picture is selected to be the *referent* stimulus while the others are then known as the *nonreferent* stimuli. In general, the speaker must identify the referent stimulus to the listener by describing it so well that the listener can select it from the nonreferent stimuli. There is no single word that will identify the referent.

In this situation it would appear that a number of consecutive steps is required. First the speaker must decide which properties distinguish the referent from the nonreferents (for example, a green circle as opposed to circles of other colors and green objects of other shapes). Then the speaker must put this information into words that can be understood by the listener. Obviously the listener's attributes must be taken into account; for example, color would not be a meaningful word to a blind or a color-blind person. Clearly, these referential communication skills require more than just linguistic ability (64).

All of the studies of the growth in referential communication skills show that children make substantial progress during the elementary-school years (66–69). The relative success of younger children in communicating depends to some extent on the nature of the task. They perform satisfactorily as speakers if they share some information in common with the listener (70). They can also perform fairly well if they receive feedback as to how successful they are with the listener (71). It would appear that younger speakers require more contextual clues about the listener's understanding in order to be successful communicators than is true for older children and adults.

Several different theories have tried to explain an individual's skill in referential communication. One is essentially a learning theory and holds that a speaker's skill depends upon his or her verbal repertoire and the number of verbal associations at his or her disposal (72). The larger his or her repertoire, the greater his or her chance of making a connection with the verbal associations of the listener. One example of this would be charades. It could be predicted that the individual who has a large language repertoire would be more successful at this game than one who did not. A somewhat different theory was presented by Piaget (73) and more recently by Flavell and his co-workers (66). They argue that for referential communication a child must have the cognitive capacity to take the other person's perspective—a skill that is usually associated with concrete operations.

These two theories are not necessarily contradictory. Indeed, it would be surprising if referential communication did not depend upon a large verbal repertoire and the ability to see the world from another's point of view. Communicating effectively with another person is an extraordinarily difficult and complex task that is only now beginning to be studied.

Memory

During middle childhood one can differentiate at least three major phases of the memory process: the *encoding* (or initial learning) phase, the *storage* (or memory organization) phase, and the *retrieval* (or performance) phase. There are significant developmental changes in all three phases of the memory process during the elementary-school years.

Encoding and Taking in of Information. One important part of the encoding process is the subject's motivation to learn the given material. Generally, material that is intentionally learned is better remembered than material that is learned only incidentally. If you concentrate on learning other people's names at a party (by repeating them to yourself, using them in your own sentences, and so forth), you are much more likely to remember the names than if you just hear them but make no effort to remember them. Research tends to support this commonsense observation as well as the assumption that older children would be more effective than younger ones in using intentional encoding strategies (74–76).

In one study (74) groups of children aged 4, 7, and 11 participated in an intentional and incidental encoding task. Each child was tested under two conditions. In one condition the children were shown between 9 and 15 pictures of single objects and were told to *look* at the pictures carefully because this would be helpful in a later task. In the second condition, the same procedure was followed except that the children were told to *remember* the objects in the pictures. Later the children were asked to recall as many of the objects in the pictures as they could.

The results of the study showed a clear developmental progression. For both the *look* and the *remember* conditions, there was a regular increase with age in the number of objects recalled. The performance of the

4-year-old children was about the same for both the *look* and the *remember* conditions. For the 7- and 11-year-olds, however, they performed better under the *remember* condition than under the *look* condition. This experiment has been replicated (75) with 6-year-olds, and it has been found that they also recall more under *remember* than under *look* conditions. Possibly children's encoding strategies change around the age of 5 or 6 when they are also acquiring concrete operations.

Does the encoding process itself change with age? Do older children use different methods or strategies for encoding than younger children do? To some extent, of course, the answer will depend upon the material to be learned—recalling digits may require a different strategy than recalling names. A number of studies (for example, 77–79) suggest that as children grow older they not only have more memory strategies available but can select the most appropriate strategy or strategies for the material.

In one investigation (78) the material to be learned was the content and location of a number of pictures. Children of different ages were asked to memorize the pictures and their locations. The pictures were hidden below a screen and each was connected with a button that, when pushed, would raise the picture to a particular location on the screen. Observers noted that the children used a sequence of three strategies on this task. The first was to "name" the objects. Then the children began to "anticipate" the location before the picture appeared. Later on, the children began to "rehearse," which was a combination of naming and anticipating. In general, children between 6 and 9 years of age used all three strategies. Thus, elementary-school schildren are increasingly able to memorize material and utilize effective encoding strategies.

Storage and Memory Organization. Studies to determine how subjects store information for retrieval have to be indirect. They often focus on the organization of the material to be remembered in relation to the subjects' facility in remembering. It is generally assumed that a subject's ability to remember varies with his or her capacity to reproduce the organization. For example, suppose subjects are asked to recall a number of objects that can be grouped together under more general categories. Those subjects who use such higher-order categories—who "cluster" their responses—would be expected to remember more objects than those who do not.

Clustering—that is, putting information into higher-order categories—requires cognitive ability as well as memory strategies. In general, children improve in their ability to do this as they grow older. Accordingly, one might expect a regular improvement in children's memory for categorizable materials with age, and this is precisely what many investigators have found (77, 80–82).

In one memory study (77) children in grades 1, 3, 4, 5, and 6 as well as college students served as subjects. The stimuli consisted of 24 pictures that could be grouped under four general categories—animals, vehicles, furniture, and articles of clothing. The pictures were presented all at once, and the subjects were instructed to study the pictures for 3 minutes, after which they would be required to recall as many as possible. The subjects were also told that they could rearrange the pictures if they wanted to.

The subjects were scored not only for the number of pictures recalled, but also for their categorical rearrangement of the pictures during the study period. It was found that there was a regular increase with age in the subjects' tendency to arrange the pictures according to category. There was a corresponding increase in the number of pictures recalled. The mean recall score for the first-grade children was 11, for the third-grade children 16, and for the fourth-, fifth,- and sixth-graders it was about 19. The mean recall score for the college students was 23. The clustering scores suggested that, with age, children increasingly store information according to higher-level organizations whenever this is possible.

Retrieval. One way to view Piaget and Inhelder's theory of memory (83), discussed in Chapter 7, is in terms of storage and retrieval. Basically Piaget and Inhelder hold that what is stored in memory can be transformed during the retrieval process. They believe that stored material is a mental construction and that what the child recalls is the way the construction appears as a consequence of the mental operations available to him or her at a given point in his or her development. In other words, contrasted with the work discussed earlier, Piaget and Inhelder contend that the material can be organized *after,* rather than *before,* the information is stored. In Chapter 7 we reviewed some of the research supporting this theory, and there have been other studies with elementary-school children that also tend to support it (84, 85). Some theorists (86) are now arguing that what a subject knows influences memory.

A rather different approach to retrieval has been taken by Tulving (87), who holds that retrieval is related to the "cognitive environment" that exists during learning. He believes that the cognitive environment provides a set of cues that can assist retrieval. For example, one trick in trying to remember a person's name is to go through the alphabet thinking of names that begin with each letter. Sometimes the name itself or its first letter can be remembered in this way. Saying names that begin with each letter may reinstate cues that can facilitate recall. Likewise, in many mystery stories, the attempt to "reconstruct the crime" helps to jog witnesses' memories.

This conception of retrieval was tested in a rather ingenious way (88). The subjects for the study were children in grades 1, 3, and 6. The stimuli to be remembered consisted of 24 pictures of common objects; there were eight categories with three objects in each category. The novel aspect of this study was that the categories were not broader concepts but rather the *places* where the objects were normally found. A fruit stand, for example, was the category (cue) for such objects as grapes, pears, and bananas.

During the initial phase of this experiment the subjects were shown pictures of both the objects and the places where they might be found (for example, a camel, monkey, and bear as well as a zoo). At this time the experimenter indicated the relationship between the objects and the categories. During the second or recall phase of the experiment, three different conditions were introduced. Under the *free recall* condition, the children were simply asked to remember as many objects as they could. Under the *cue recall* condition, the subjects were given the categories by the experimenter as general aids to recall. Under the *directive cue* condition, the children were given the eight categories *and* were asked which objects went with each one.

As expected, the differences were age-related. For both the free recall and the cue recall conditions, the older children remembered more objects than did the younger ones. The first- and third-grade children performed about the same on free recall, but the sixth-graders did substantially better with cue recall than with free recall. The most interesting result was that with the directive cue condition, all age groups performed at essentially the same high level, remembering more than 75 percent of the objects. These and similar results from other studies (89–91) suggest that a young child's difficulties with retrieval may be related to problems in reconstructing the original "cognitive environment." When this is done by the experimenter, young children perform at about the same level as older children.

The fact that during middle childhood there is a gradual improvement in the encoding, storage, and retrieval of material that is to be recalled is probably due to the joint growth in the use of organizing strategies and in cognitive ability. When the organizing strategy is provided from outside, even young children can demonstrate good recall.

Conservation
Behavior

Conservation—one's ability to judge that a certain quantity remains the same despite a change in its appearance—becomes significant during middle childhood. Piaget (23) contends that conservation (as described above) does not appear until the child attains concrete operations. Children can, however, be taught to conserve before they attain concrete operations, but this tends to be a limited achievement that lacks the generalizability to be observed when concrete operations are attained spontaneously.

Types of Conservation. During the elementary-school years, children discover conservation in many different areas (23). They discover, for example, that amount, length, area, mass, weight, and volume remain the same despite changes in appearance. They also discover that time progresses uniformly no matter how it is measured. Some of these attainments will be described below.

At about 7 years of age, most children acquire the conservation of

A child presented with a
conservation task dealing
with the conservation of
continuous quantity
(liquid).

length; it is usually assessed as follows: The child is shown two uncut
pencils (or sticks) of the same length and is asked if they are equally long.
Once the child agrees to their equality—usually by placing the pencils
alongside one another so that the ends align—the experimenter moves one

of the pencils so that it is ahead of the other. The child is then asked whether the two pencils are equally long or whether one is longer than the other. (The experimenter typically uses language that is familiar to the child.)

The findings of this experiment are quite predictable, although the ages may vary depending upon the child's intelligence or background. At about 4 years of age, children say that one of the two pencils is longer than the other because it is "ahead" or because "it goes farther." Five-year-old children usually say that one of the pencils is longer while it is ahead of the other one but that if it were pushed back the two pencils would be equal again. Finally, around the age of 6 or 7, children typically say that the two pencils are the same length because "You just moved them; you didn't add anything or take anything away." By this age they understand that length does not change simply because an object's position has changed (92).

A particularly interesting sequence of understanding conservation occurs with mass, weight, and volume. Although the assessment procedure is the same for each concept, there is an age-related sequence of attainment. Children understand the conservation of amount at about 6 or 7 years of age, weight at about 8 or 9, and volume at about 11 or 12. Understanding the conservation of volume, however, is not uniformly achieved by all children (as is amount and weight) (93–96). Piaget (97) refers this separation as a **horizontal décalage**, meaning that the identical abilities are required to understand each concept but that the concepts themselves vary in difficulty. In the case of weight and volume, children have to overcome more subjective perspectives (such as measuring weight by how heavy things feel) than they do with amount.

Mass, weight, and volume conservation is usually tested by presenting the child with two balls of clay and asking if they contain the same amount (weight or volume). The child is allowed to add or subtract clay to "make them the same." (With weight conservation children are permitted to use scales, although many youngsters do not know how to read them.) Once the child agrees that the two balls contain the same amount (weight or volume) of clay, the experimenter rolls one of the balls into a "sausage" that is longer and thinner than the remaining ball and then asks the child if the two clay objects are still the same amount (weight or volume). A child who responds that the clay ball has the same amount (weight or volume) as the clay sausage is said to have conservation for that concept.

As mentioned earlier, there is a "horizontal decalage," with children understanding the conservation of amount first, then weight, and then volume. What is particularly interesting is that the explanation children offer for the conservation of amount ("nothing was added or taken away") holds equally well for weight and volume. And yet children fail to recognize this because they are involved in the conceptual problem and not with the materials of the experiment.

With respect to the conservation of area (92), Piaget and his colleagues often used a board to represent a farm, animals, and farm buildings. Children were asked whether the cows had "more to eat" when they were close together on the "field" than when they were spread apart. Before the age of 7 or 8 most children assumed that there was less to eat when the animals were spread over the field than when they were close together. Other investigators have demonstrated the same phenomena with other arrangements. Young children apparently perceive a crowded room as physically smaller than an empty one of the same size.

Because time, as a uniform progression regardless of how it is measured, is an abstract concept, children begin measuring it in more concrete ways. For example, one young lad told his father, "you don't need any more birthdays; you are already all grown up." Clearly, young children view growing older as synonymous with getting bigger. Once you have attained your full height, you don't need any more birthdays! In Piaget's experiments (98) children believed that low, wide trees were younger than tall, willowy ones because the tall ones were higher. Children usually do not understand that time is independent of physical size and motion until middle childhood.

During the elementary-school years, then, children progressively *quantify* their experience. They begin to understand that mass, weight, volume, space, time, number, length, and so on involve units that are not altered by a variety of changes in appearance.

Training in Conservation. Piaget's demonstration of conservation behavior has led to a number of related studies. Many of these have attempted to determine whether children who do not understand conservation can be trained to do so. Researchers have wanted to learn (a) whether children can be taught conservation at an earlier age than they would normally learn it, and (b) what processes enable children to learn conservation.

When Piaget's work first became popular in this country (during the early 1960s), a number of training studies were undertaken, but they were generally not successful (for example, 99–101). In the late 1960s and early 1970s, however, a "second wave" of such studies appeared showing that 4- to 5-year-old children who could not conserve before training were able to do so afterward (102–105). Although there is some controversy as to how to evaluate children's attainment of conservation, it is generally accepted today that this can be taught to some 4- to 5-year-old children.

The real value of the training studies was to reveal some of the processes by which conservation is learned. Many of the studies have focused on one or another process that was believed to be crucial for understanding conservation. In some cases Piaget (106) believed these processes were essential for conservation; in other cases the processes studied were not believed by Piaget to be essential.

One process that Piaget (106) believed was essential to the child's understanding of conservation is **reversibility**—that a ball of clay can be rolled into a "sausage" and then rolled back into a ball. Presumably by training children to pay attention to the reversible nature of conservation, they should learn that quantity does not vary in spite of apparent change. In one study (107) a number of objects were attached to an elastic band that could be stretched but that quickly returned to its original length, restoring the objects to their original spacing on the band. In this and other studies (108–110) children seem to have been successfully trained in reversibility and in conservation.

Another process that Piaget (106) felt was essential is **compensation**—that the loss of certain amount in one dimension (due to a transformation) is gained in another. A clay ball that is rolled into a "sausage" gains in length but loses in diameter, but the differences compensate for one another so that the quantity does not really change in amount. A number of studies have now been done in which children have been trained to attend to the compensatory aspects of transformation (for example, 111–113). Although the results are not uniform, they do indicate that compensation training can help children understand conservation. Its effectiveness may, however, depend in part on the nature of the conservation task; for example, it may be more useful for continuous quantities (such as clay and water) than for discontinuous ones (such as chips, beads, and peas).

In his early work Piaget (114) suggested that cognitive development may require *social interaction*. As children interact with one another, there is a self-corrective process. For example, a child who talks about Santa Claus as a man who lives at the North Pole would soon be corrected by other children. And a child who breaks a rule in a game is quickly informed of this by his or her friends. Since the 1960s several investigations have been conducted in which social interaction between two or three children was used to teach conservation. In some of these studies, children were asked to reach a joint decision as to whether or not a quantity was conserved when it was transformed. By including children who both do and do not understand conservation in such a group, the effect of social interaction can be assessed.

Again, although studies do vary in their results, it appears that social interaction can be helpful in teaching conservation (115–117). In one study (118) third-grade children who both did and did not understand conservation had a discussion to decide about the conservation of area. In 11 out of 14 pairs of children, those who could conserve prevailed over those who could not. Those who did not understand conservation but followed the lead of those who did were able to maintain their achievement for at least a month.

In Piaget's (23) view, the basic process required to understand all conservation is **equilibration**. This is a very general process, suggesting that growth occurs as a result of conflict or contradiction in judgments. Indeed, it is because reversibility, compensation, and social interaction all bring about some form of conflict or logical contradiction that they are helpful. In an extensive series of studies, some of Piaget's colleagues (105) have demonstrated that confronting children with contradictions and conflicts can enhance their ability to grasp conservation. They insist, however, that the effects of such training always depend upon the child's development. Older, more mature children profit more from such training than do younger, less mature children.

One of the processes that Piaget does not believe is essential for conservation, but that other investigators do, is language. Piaget emphatically holds that language does not determine conservation but that conservation or cognitive development determines language, at least at the concrete-operational level of development. Nevertheless, a number of studies have attempted to see whether children can be taught conservation using verbal rules about the effects of transformation. It appears that such training, particularly if it is coupled with feedback about the child's performance, can teach conservation (119–121).

Another approach that Piaget disagreed with is perceptual discrimination training. Some investigators have believed that the reason young children fail to understand conservation might be due to the fact that they do not pay attention to the proper cues. These investigators felt that if children could be taught to pay attention to the correct perceptual cues, they could be taught conservation. A number of such studies have now been carried out and many have successfully taught conservation to young (4- to 5-year-old) children (113, 122–124).

There are, then, many ways in which children can be taught conservation. While some of these approaches might seem to contradict Piaget's interpretation, this is not necessarily the case. What is called "language" or "perceptual training" may also include conflict and contradiction, hence there is equilibration. On the other hand, "reversibility," "compensation," and "conflict training" also require language and perception. These considerations have encouraged Piaget to broaden his conception of the origins of conservation to include static processes such as perceptual comparison (125).

Our discussion of conservation provides a nice example of the process of scientific work. A phenomenon is discovered and an initial theory is offered to account for it. More refined and extensive work confirms the theory in some respects, but disconfirms it in others. This, in turn, leads to modifications of the theory and to new directions in research. Perhaps this example will illustrate how complex certain human behavior is and how far we are from fully understanding how human beings learn even such an apparently simple concept as conservation.

The long-term value of brief training in conservation, however, does not seem to be very great (126). This is, after all, what might be expected. The ability to understand conservation reflects one's over-all cognitive development and individual differences in ability and rate of growth. One training experience is not likely to alter a child's over-all course of development. Parents or teachers who believe that they can accelerate children's growth by training them in a few particular conservation skills are probably wasting their time.

Moral Development

In one of his early books, *The Moral Judgment of the Child,* Piaget (114) described an age-related change in children's understanding of moral dilemmas. Piaget presented children with two stories, both of which described a child doing something that was potentially punishable. In one story, however, the child had accidentally committed a misdeed, whereas in the other, the child had deliberately done something wrong. After listening to the two stories, the children were asked to decide which child was more guilty. Their decision was made more difficult because more damage was done as a result of the accidental misdeed than by the deliberate transgression. Here are two of the stories presented by Piaget:

[A] *A little boy who is called John is in his room. He is called to dinner. He goes into the dining room. But behind the door there was a chair with a tray with fifteen cups on it. John couldn't have known that there was all this behind the door. He goes in, the door knocks against the tray, bang go the fifteen cups and they all get broken!*

[B] *Once there was a little boy whose name was Henry. One day when his mother was out he tried to get some jam out of the cupboard. He climbed up on a chair and stretched out his arm. But the jam was too high up and he couldn't reach it and have any. But while he was trying to get it he knocked over a cup. The cup fell down and broke.* [114]

After reading these stories to the children, Piaget asked them to repeat the stories to make sure that they had really understood them. Then Piaget asked: Are the two children equally naughty (to blame)? Which one is the naughtiest (most to blame)?

In general, the younger children (ages 6 and 7) said that the child who caused the most damage was the naughtiest (most blameworthy) and should be punished the most severely. However, most 8- or 9-year-old children judged the ''naughtiness'' of the action by the child's intention. They said that the child who was doing ''something he wasn't supposed to'' was the one who should be punished the most. Piaget concluded that young children have a more *objective* concept of moral behavior in the sense that they judge guilt according to the amount of damage done. By contrast, older children have a more *subjective* sense of moral behavior because they judge guilt according to the intention of the actor.

Piaget also explored the concept of **imminent justice**. Young children tend to believe that a person who gets hurt while engaging in a forbidden action (say, a child who gets burned while playing with matches—a forbidden activity) is actually being punished for his or her transgression.

Older children, however, realize that a person can engage in forbidden activity and get away with it—not be punished. These and other aspects of children's moral judgments have now been replicated by many other investigators with approximately the same results. In a review (127) of the studies done in Western countries (England, America, Western Europe), only one out of the 21 studies surveyed failed to report the sequence of moral development noted by Piaget.

Piaget's discussion of moral development has now been considerably amplified and differentiated by Lawrence Kohlberg (128). In Kohlberg's view, moral development takes place during six stages comprising three levels of moral orientation:

Premoral Level: Conduct is determined by external factors

Stage 1 Obedience and punishment orientation, deference to superior power and prestige

Stage 2 Naïve, hedonistic, and instrumental orientation; acts are defined as right that satisfy the self and sometimes others

Conventional Morality: Morality is defined as performing good acts and maintaining the conventional social order

Stage 3 Morality is held to be maintaining good relations; oriented toward selecting approval and toward pleasing and helping others

Stage 4 Oriented toward authority, law, duty, and maintaining the status quo (whether social or religious), which is assumed to be a primary value

Morality of Self-Accepted Principles: Morality is defined as conforming to shared or common standards, rights, or duties

Stage 5 Morality of contract, individual rights, and democratically accepted law

Stage 6 Morality of individual principles of conscience; oriented toward existing rules and standards as well as conscience as a directing agent

In testing for these stages, Kohlberg has used stories somewhat like those used by Piaget. But because the stages are more differentiated, there have been difficulties in knowing how to score the children's responses and thereby assign them to the appropriate stages; thus, there have been problems in validating Kohlberg's stages (129, 130). One of Kohlberg's students has been preparing an objective scale of moral development that can be more easily scored and validated (131, 132). Initial work with this new scale indicates that it overcomes some of the problems that were found with Kohlberg's original scoring scheme and that it will permit a more objective assessment of moral development than had been possible before. In general Kohlberg finds that children at the concrete operational level seldom go beyond his Stage 4. We shall discuss Kohlberg's stages as they pertain to adolescents in Chapter 15.

One dimension of moral judgment that was not explored by either

Piaget or Kohlberg was the matter of personal injury. In both the Piaget and Kohlberg stories, children are asked to judge the culpability of children who have inflicted large and small amounts of property damage either intentionally or unintentionally. But in law and in moral philosophy, personal injury is an important dimension of moral judgment. A recent study explored this aspect of moral judgment in children. Kindergarten, second-grade, and fourth-grade children responded to six story pairs corresponding to all possible combinations of intentionality (unintentional/intentional) and type of damage (personal injury/property damage). The types of personal injury were roughly equated to the types of property damage (for example, a bloody nose versus a flat tire).

The results (142) showed that when intentionality was held constant, children at all of the age levels studied said that personal injury was more serious than property damage. Young children (6 years of age) said that "it hurts more"; somewhat older children (8 years old) said that "it costs more" and the oldest children (10 years old) intimated that "persons are more valuable than things." When intentionality and type of damage varied at the same time, personal injury loomed larger in the child's judgments than did property damage. That is to say, when personal injury was involved, even 6-year-old children were able to respond to intentionality. Personal injury, therefore, is an important dimension of moral judgment that is just beginning to be explored.

THE CONCEPTUAL WORLD OF CHILDREN

When children attain concrete operations they are intellectually capable of learning the culture of childhood. This culture consists of an extensive language and lore pertaining to children's interests. There are rhymes to ward off unwanted events—"Rain, rain, go away, come again another day"—and taboos about performing certain actions—"Step on a crack and break you back."

There are jingles that ridicule adults and have a regional or national slant:

> Jingle bells, jingle bells
> Ford smells and Nixon ran away
> Oh what fun it is to ride
> In a Carter Chevrolet.

And ther are endless riddles that attest to children's new found sophistication.

Q: Where does a 900-pound gorilla sit?
A: Anywhere he pleases.

This language and lore of childhood seems to be common to most Western countries. Although the content of the riddles and chants may differ from country to country, they nonetheless always deal with chil-

dren's universal fantasies, fears, unhappiness, anger, and so forth. Furthermore, in any given country or community, this language and lore is
passed down verbally from generation to generation. Children today sing
rhymes and ask riddles that can be traced back hundreds of years. Finally,
although the culture of childhood probably serves many purposes, the
main one is to assimilate the child into the peer group. By learning the
appropriate rhymes and riddles, the elementary-school child becomes a
member in good standing of his or her peer group.

The culture of childhood is thus conservative in the sense that it per-
petuates the pattern presented by the next older age group without radical
change (in contrast to adolescents, who wish to radically alter the world of
adults). But children at this stage are far from being stolid and unimagina-
tive; quite the contrary. But the imagination and fantasy of school-age
children is not concerned with societal change—which is still beyond the
range of their mental capacities. What children are concerned with is
mystery and adventure which they find in books, television, movies, and
in their own play. Children love to explore abandoned houses, attics,
basements, and other places where adults are not usually about and where
hidden "treasures" of all sorts may be found. The sense of exploration
and mystery is prominent in the minds of school-age children.

A final component of the conceptual world of children is a perennial
optimism. Because children are not yet aware of the many constraints on
success in any endeavor, children believe that they can become what they
want to be—although they may not be sure what that is. And children are
not very critical of parents or school or society and are generally happy
with their world. This is largely because they live in the here and now,
because social pressures upon them are slight, and because they are really
unable to fully conceptualize and understand the many problems and
dangers (pollution, nuclear war, and so on) that trouble adolescents and
adults. Children still believe that the future will be what they wish it to be;
therein lies the basis of the eternal optimism of the childhood period.

Essay

LEARNING
TO READ

One of the most important skills children must learn during the early
elementary-school years is how to read. Reading is important not only for
every course in school—arithmetic, science, language arts, and social
studies—but for nearly every aspect of life as well. Despite its importance, however, there is still no generally accepted theory of reading or of
reading instruction (134). Consequently, in the United States reading is
taught in many different ways, ranging from an informal "language experience" (135) approach to a highly structured format (136).

With this multiplicity of approaches to reading instruction, parents and educators sometimes wonder at what age *formal* instruction should begin. Formal reading instruction typically includes phonics (such as sound blending) and spelling. On the other hand, informal instruction consists of such language-enrichment activities as listening to stories, dictating stories to be recorded by others, printing letters, and so forth. In general, formal instruction means learning a set of rules, whereas informal instruction means becoming familiar with printed letters and words.

Some investigators believe that formal instruction could be started as early as kindergarten (136). But others, including the authors of this book, hold that such instruction should wait until children have attained concrete operations—usually about the age of 6½. This discrepancy in viewpoint stems from different conceptions of the reading process. Those who support early reading instruction argue that reading is essentially a discrimination process, which is well within the capability of young children. Those who urge postponement until children are about 6½ believe that even the simplest reading requires complex reasoning processes that are beyond the capability of most preconcrete operational children.

Unfortunately, the data on this issue are not clear-cut. Durkin (137) found that children of average ability who learned to read early retained their superiority over children of comparable ability in the later grades of school. But two later studies have shown that early readers of average ability were children who had attained concrete operations whereas non-readers of comparable ability were those who had not (138, 139). Cross-cultural data also support the viewpoint on later reading instruction. In the Soviet Union and the Scandinavian countries, formal reading is not taught until children enter school at 7 years of age. Only a small number of children in these countries encounter reading difficulties. In France, however, where formal reading instruction begins at age 5, some 25 percent of the children repeat first grade because they have not learned to read (140).

A study done in the 1930s is still of value in demonstrating some of the possible fringe benefits associated with delaying formal instruction in reading. The study included two groups of fifth-grade children. One group had received formal reading instruction beginning at the start of the first grade. The second group had received informal instruction in the first grade (their teacher read to them, they dictated their own stories, and so forth). At the end of the year, those who had had formal instruction were superior in reading to those who had not. By third grade, however, those who had received informal instruction during the first grade had caught up with those having formal instruction (141).

Of particular interest in this study was a follow-up that was conducted when these children were in junior high school. The investigators selected naïve observers (persons who did not know the children or anything about the earlier study) and asked them to rate the children on various dimensions. It turned out that the children who did not begin formal reading instruction until second grade were clearly distinguishable from those who started it in the first grade—even by naïve observers. The former group was described as "curious," "enthusiastic," "joyous" learners whereas the latter group was not (141).

In short, there is no clear-cut evidence that early reading instruction is beneficial; on the contrary, some evidence shows that it may do some children considerable harm. While we believe that children who want to read before they are 6 or 7 should be helped and encouraged, we do not believe that formal instruction in reading is beneficial to most children until they have attained concrete operations.

Biography

ALFRED BINET

In the history of science, instruments have vied with theories in producing significant breakthroughs in various disciplines. The construction of the telescope in astronomy and the microscope in biology were instrumental innovations of revolutionary importance. It might not be farfetched to say that the intelligence scale, introduced by Alfred Binet and Theodore Simon, has become psychology's microscope. Like the microscope, the intelligence test is both a clinical tool of great diagnostic value and a research instrument of considerable precision and depth. And like the microscope, the intelligence scale has led to the development of other instruments—in this case, for example, achievement tests and personality scales. As a discipline, psychology is still identified in the popular mind with one or another form of testing.

Despite the value of their contributions, the inventors of instruments are less well known than their inventions. How many people can recall who invented the microscope or the telescope? In contrast, theorists tend to be much better known than their theories. Many people who have little understanding of the ideas of Freud, Darwin, and Einstein at least know their names. In view of this discrepancy in public awareness of theorists and inventors, it is not surprising that far more people know about intelligence tests than have ever heard of their originator, Alfred Binet.

Alfred Binet was born in Nice, France, in 1857; his father was a physician and his mother was an artist. Binet's parents separated when he was quite young, and Binet's father apparently played little or no role in his upbringing and education. After a somewhat erratic formal education in which he attempted both law and medicine, Binet began his own informal education as a reader in the National Library. It was there that he became interested in psychological issues. Since he had an independent means of support, he could afford to follow his own interests.

Binet began his scientific work in the laboratory of neurologist Jean Charcot. There he associated himself with Charcot's theories and methods on hypnosis. When Charcot was devastatingly attacked by methodologically sophisticated researchers, Binet had to reconsider his own methods as well as his theoretical orientation. After leaving Charcot's laboratory and before finding another professional affiliation, Binet published several papers on children's thinking, using data he had collected by observing his own two daughters. Hence, it may have been the necessity of finding his own subjects that turned Binet in the direction of the field where he was to realize his true talents—child psychology.

In one of his most important books, *L'Étude experimentale de l'intelligence,* Binet described 20 little "experiments" he had carried out with his two daughters. The experiments were ingenious and antedate many contemporary measurement devices. Binet's careful tests and observations revealed consistent individual differences between the two girls. One was a romantic dreamer and the other was a practical, reality-oriented achiever. Their orientations were evident in their descriptions of common objects, in their production of words, and in many other ways. Contemporary studies of "cognitive style" seem meager when compared with the wealth of data Binet obtained.

Although Binet was primarily interested in the nature of human intelligence, he also became caught up in the widespread search among psychologists for a brief and easily administered test of mental ability. Such a test was in great demand for educational reasons, primarily for the diagnosis of mental retardation. Prior to Binet, however, no one had succeeded in developing a useful intelligence scale. It required many years and many unsuccessful attempts before Binet and his co-workers were finally able to publish their first scale of 20 items in 1905.

The scale incorporated many of Binet's ideas about intelligence, a word that in French has much broader connotations than it does in English. Binet was convinced that intelligence revealed itself primarily in complex mental processes such as judgment, reasoning, and comprehension and not in simple sensory or motor skills. Hence, Binet's scale contained items that attempted to evaluate these higher-order abilities. In addition, Binet believed that one needed to measure intelligence in psychological rather than physical units. The difficulty of an item would be determined according to the number of children at a particular age who succeeded in answering it. Each item could then be assigned to the age at which a majority (75 percent) of the children passed it.

Revisions of the scale were published in 1908 and in 1911, the year of Binet's untimely death. Although these scales won Binet worldwide recognition and acclaim, his work was not appreciated in France; Binet never received an academic appointment at a French university. Indeed, intelligence tests and testing are only now beginning to be accepted and used in France. As in the case of many other prophets, Binet was not accorded the recognition he deserved in his own country.

Binet recognized and foresaw the possible dangers as well as the benefits of the tests he developed, but his cautions were not heeded. A methodology, once released, has a history of its own quite apart from the hopes and wishes of the originator. Binet also did significant work in the area of personality; hopefully his research in this field will become better known in the years ahead.

Summary

Growth is less rapid during middle childhood than during the preschool years, but significant achievements do occur. Since basic motor coordinations are well established, youngsters can put them to work in running, jumping, balancing, and throwing balls. Their reaction times are shorter for motor-skill tasks and games. Finally, a child's motor abilities, like his or her physical appearance, play an important part in his or her self-concept.

As children acquire concrete operations they are able to participate in formal instruction and take achievement tests. Norm-referenced tests have serious drawbacks that are not found in criterion-referenced tests. Perceptual development improves and children are better able to search visual displays systematically, to center their attention and avoid distracting stimuli, and to logically organize their perceptual constructions. Language development continues, though less rapidly, during the elementary-school years as children enlarge their vocabularies, learn exceptions to grammatical rules, and improve their referential communication skills.

With respect to memory, children are able to elaborate new and more logical strategies for encoding, storing, and retrieving material. Middle childhood is also a time par excellence for learning conservation concepts such as those of mass, weight, volume, length, and area. Studies aimed at training children in conservation, which is usually learned spontaneously, suggest that a number of methods can be used to teach them conservation before an age when they would be likely to acquire it on the own. It is not clear whether such early training has any lasting value.

Piaget's work on moral development has aroused substantial interest. His finding that young children judge moral situations according to the damage done while older children judge it according to a person's intention has been replicated many times with comparable results. Kohlberg's extension of Piaget's stages of moral development is of great interest, but it has presented empirical problems. Some of these are being worked out and a more objective test of his stages is now available. New work in this area suggests that personal injury is an important dimension of moral judgment.

Finally, the conceptual world of middle childhood is rich in language and lore that dates back hundreds of years. This is a hidden side of childhood that adults seldom see or hear very much of. Yet it is all-important to children because acquiring it is their foremost means of socialization and a passkey to their acceptance into the society of children.

References

1. Watson, E. H., & Lowry, G. G. *Growth and development in children*. Chicago: Yearbook Medical Publishers, Inc., 1967.
2. Tanner, J. M. Physical growth. In P. Mussen (Ed.), *Carmichael's manual of child psychology*. (3rd ed.), New York: Wiley, 1970.
3. Jenkins, D. D., Shacter, H. S., & Bower, W. B. *These are your children*. Glenview, Ill.: Scott, Foresman, 1966.
4. Cratty, B. J., & Martin, M. M. *Perceptual-motor efficiency in children*. Philadelphia: Lea & Febiger, 1969.
5. Keogh, J. J. Motor performance of elementary school children. Monograph, University of California, Los Angeles, Physical Education Department, October 1968.
6. Keogh, J. J. Physical performance test data for English boys ages 6–9. *Physical Education*, 1966, **5,** 65–69.
7. Cratty, B. J. *Perceptual and motor development in infants and children*. New York: Macmillan, 1970.
8. Williams, H. G. The perception of moving objects by children. Unpublished study. Perceptual Motor Learning Laboratory, University of California, Los Angeles, 1967.
9. Carpenter, A. Tests of motor educability for the first three grades. *Child Development*, 1940, **1,** 293–299.
10. Surwillo, W. W. Human reaction time and period of the EEG in relation to development. *Psychophysiology*, 1971, **8,** 468–482.
11. Connolly, K. Response speed, temporal sequencing, and information processing in children. In K. Connolly (Ed.), *Mechanisms of motor skill development*. New York: Academic Press, 1970.
12. Gardner, H. Children's duplication of rhythmic patterns. *Journal of Research in Music Education*, 1971, **19,** 355–360.
13. Rothoteim, A. L. Effect of age, feedback and practice on ability to respond within a fixed time interval. *Journal of Motor Behavior*, 1972, **78,** 459–486.
14. Ilg, F. L., & Ames, L. B. *School readiness*. New York: Harper, 1966.
15. Hecaen, H., & Ajuriaguerra, J. *Left-handedness, manual superiority and cerebral dominance*. New York: Grune & Stratton, 1964.
16. Piaget, J. *Judgement and reasoning in the child*. London: Routledge & Kegan Paul, 1951.
17. Elkind, D. The child's conception of right and left. *Journal of Genetic Psychology*, 1961, **99,** 269–276.
18. Constantini, A. F., & Hoving, K. L. The relationship of cognitive and motor response inhibition to age and IQ. *Journal of Genetic Psychology*, 1973, **123,** 303–319.
19. Mead, G. H. *Mind, self and society*. Chicago: University of Chicago Press, 1934.
20. Coopersmith, S. *The antecedents of self-esteem*. San Francisco: W. H. Freeman, 1967.
21. Kokenes, B. Grade level differences in factors of self esteem. *Developmental Psychology*, 1974, **10,** 954–958.
22. Black, F. W. Self concept as related to achievement and age in learning disabled children. *Child Development*, 1974, **45,** 1137–1140.
23. Piaget, J. *Six psychological studies*. New York: Random House, 1968.
24. Green, D. R. (Ed.). *The aptitude-achievement distinction*. Monterey, Calif.: McGraw-Hill, 1974.
25. Gage, N. L., & Berliner, D. C. *Educational psychology*. Chicago: Rand-McNally, 1975.
26. Piaget, J. *Science of education and the psychology of the child*. New York: Orion Press, 1970.
27. Glaser, R. Instructional technology and the measurement of learning outcomes: some questions. *American Psychologist*, 1963, **18,** 519–521.
28. Carver, R. C. Two dimensions of tests. *American Psychologist*, 1974, **29,** 512–518.
29. Tyler, R. W., & Wolf, R. M. (Eds.) *Crucial issues in testing*. Berkeley, Calif.: McCutchan, 1974.
30. Skinner, B. F. *The technology of teaching*. New York: Appleton-Century-Crofts, 1968.
31. Levine, M. The academic achievement test: Its historical context and social functions. *American Psychologist*, 1976, **31,** 228–238.
32. Popham, W. J., & Husek, T. R. Implications of criterion referenced measurement. *Journal of Educational Measurement*, 1969, **6,** 1–9.

33. Glaser, R., & Nitko, A. J. Measurement in learning and instruction. In R. L. Thorndike (Ed.), *Educational Measurement*. (2nd ed.). Washington, D.C.: American Council of Education,

34. Chittenden, E. A., & Busses, A. M. Open education: research and assessment strategies. In E. B. Nyquest & S. R. Howes (Eds.), *Open education: a sourcebook for parents and teachers*. New York: Bantam, 1972.

35. Liss. P. H., & Haten, M. M. The speed of visual processing in children and adults: Effects of backward and forward masking. *Perception and Psychophysics*, 1970, **8**, 396–398.

36. Miller, L. K. Developmental differences in the field of view during tachistascopic presentation. *Child Development*, 1971, **42**, 1543–1551.

37. Miller, L. K. Visual masking and developmental differences in information processing. *Child Development*, 1972, **43**, 704–709.

38. Miller, L. K. Developmental differences in the field of view during covert and overt search. *Child Development*, 1973, **44**, 247–252.

39. Vurpillot, E. The development of scanning strategies and their relations to visual differentiation. *Journal of Experimental Child Psychology*, 1968, **6**, 632–650.

40. Pick, A. D., Christy, M. D., & Frankel, G. W. A developmental study of visual selective attention. *Journal of Experimental Child Psychology*, 1972, **14**, 65, 175.

41. Elkind, D., & Weiss, J. Studies in perceptual development III: Perceptual exploration. *Child Development*, 1967, **38**, 1153–1161.

42. Kugelmass, S., & Leiblich, A. Perceptual exploration in Israeli children. *Child Development*, 1970, **41**, 1125–1132.

43. Pick, A. D., & Frankel, G. W. A study of strategies of visual attention in children. *Developmental Psychology*, 1973, **9**, 348–357.

44. Pick, A. D., & Frankel, G. W. A developmental study of strategies of visual selectivity. *Child Development*, 1974, **45**, 1162–1165.

45. Gibson, E. J., Poag, K., & Rader, N. The effect of redundant rhyme and spelling patterns on a verbal discrimination task. In appendix to final report, *The relationship between perceptual development and the acquisition of reading skill*. Ithaca: Cornell University and United States Office of Education, 1972.

46. Gibson, E. J., Tenney, Y. J., & Zaslow, M. Is discovery of structure reinforcing? The effect of categorizable context on scanning for verbal targets. In final report, *The relationship between perceptual development and reading skill*. Ithaca: Cornell University and the United States Office of Education, 1971.

47. Piaget, J. *The mechanisms of perception*. New York: Basic Books, 1969.

48. Elkind, D., Koegler, R., & Go, E. Studies in perceptual development II: whole-part perception. *Child Development*, 1964, **35**, 81–90.

49. Whiteside, J., Elkind, D., & Golbeck, S. Duration and part whole perception in children. *Child Development*, 1976, **47**, 498–501.

50. Elkind, D., Anagoslopoulou, I., & Malone, S. Determinants of part-whole perception. *Child Development*, 1970, **41**, 391-397.

51. Koffka, K. *Principles of Gestalt psychology*. New York: Harcourt, 1935.

52. Kohler, W. *Dynamics in psychology*. New York: Liverwright, 1940.

53. Elkind, D., Van Doorninck, W., & Schwarz, C. Perceptual activity and concept attainment. *Child Development*, 1967, **38**, 1153–1161.

54. Toban, W. *The language of elementary school children*. Champaign, Ill.: National Council of Teachers of English, Research Report No. 1, 1963.

55. Menyuk, P. Alteration of rules in children's grammar. *Journal of Verbal Learning and Verbal Behavior*, 1964, **3**, 480–488.

56. Palermo, D., & Molfese, D. Language acquisition from age five onward. *Psychological Bulletin*, 1972, **78**, 409–428.

57. Sinclair-deZwart, H. *Acquisition du langage et developpement de la pensee*. Paris: Dunod, 1967.

58. Sinclair-deZwart, H. Developmental psycholinguistics. In D. Elkind & J. H. Flavell (Eds.), *Studies in cognitive development*. New York: Oxford University Press, 1969.

59. Slobin, D. I. Grammatical transformations and sentence comprehension in childhood and adulthood. *Journal of Verbal Learning and Verbal Behavior*, 1966, **5**, 219–227.

60. Turner, E. A., & Rommetvert, R. The acquisition of sentence voice and reversibility. *Child Development*, 1967, **38**, 649–660.

61. Chomsky, C. *The acquisition of syntax of children from 5 to 10*. Cambridge, Mass.: M.I.T. Press, 1969.

62. Nelson, C. W. Comprehension of spoken language by normal children as a function of speaking rate, sentence difficulty, and listener age and sex. *Child Development*, 1976, **47**, 299–303.

63. Cazden, C. B. The situation: A neglected source of social class differences in language use. *Journal of Social Issues*, 1970, **26**, 35–60.

64. Glucksberg, S., Krauss, R., & Higgins, E. T. The development of referential communication skills. In F. D. Horowitz (Ed.), *Review of child development research*. Vol. 4. Chicago: University of Chicago Press, 1975.

65. Olson, D. R. Language and thought: Aspects of a cognitive theory of semantics. *Psychological Review*, 1970, **77**, 257–273.

66. Flavell, J. H., Botkin, P. T., Fry, C. L., Wright, J. C., & Jarvis, P. E. *The development of role taking and communication skills in children*. New York: Wiley, 1968.

67. Krauss, R. M., & Glucksberg, S. The development of communication: Competence as a function of age. *Child Development*, 1969, **40**, 255–256.

68. Krauss, R. M., & Glucksberg, S. Socialization of communication skills: the development of competence as a communicator. In R. Hoppe, E. Simmel, & G. Z. Milton (Eds.), *Early experience and the process of socialization*. New York: Academic Press, 1970.

69. Krauss, R. M., & Rotter, G. C. Communication abilities of children as a function of status and age. *Merrill-Palmer Quarterly*, 1968, **14**, 161–173.

70. Higgins, E. T. A social and developmental comparison of oral and written communication skills. Unpublished doctoral dissertation. Columbia University, 1973.

71. Fishbein, H. D., & Osborne, M. The effects of feedback variations in referential communication of children. *Merrill-Palmer Quarterly*, 1971, **17**, 243–250.

72. Rosenberg, S., & Cohen, B. D. Referential processes of speakers and listeners. *Psychological Review*, 1966, **73**, 208–231.

73. Piaget, J. *The language and thought of the child*. New York: Harcourt, 1926.

74. Appel, L., Cooper, R., Knight, J., McCarrell, N., Yussen, S., & Flavell, J. The development of the distinction between perceiving and memorizing. *Child Development*, 1972, **43**, 1365–1381.

75. Yussen, S. R., Gagne, E., Garguilo, R., & Kunen, S. The distinction between perceiving and memorizing in elementary school children. *Child Development*, 1974, **45**, 547-551.

76. Zinchenko, V. P., Chzhi-Tsin, V., & Tarakanov, V. V. The formation and development of perceptual activity. *Soviet Psychology and Psychiatry*, 1962, **2**, 3–12.

77. Neimark, E. D., Slotnick, N. S., & Ulrich, T. Development of memorization strategies. *Developmental Psychology*, 1971, **5**, 427–432.

78. Flavell, J. H., Frederichs, A. G., & Hoyt, J. D. Developmental changes in memorization processes. *Cognitive Psychology*, 1970, **1**, 324–340.

79. Worden, P. Effects of sorting on subsequent recall on unrelated items: A developmental study. *Child Development*, 1975, **46**, 687–695.

80. Conrad, R. The chronology of the development of covert speech in children. *Developmental Psychology*, 1971, **5**, 398–405.

81. Flavell, J. H. Developmental studies of mediated memory. In H. W. Reese & L. P. Lyssett (Eds.), *Advances in child development and behavior*. New York: Academic Press, 1970.

82. McCarver, R. B. A developmental study of the effect of organizational cues on short term memory. *Child Development*, 1972, **43**, 1317–1328.

83. Piaget, J., & Inhelder, B. *Memory and intelligence*. London: Routledge & Kegan Paul, 1973.

84. Paris, S. G., & Carter, A. Semantic and constructive aspects of sentence memory in children. *Developmental Psychology*, 1973, **9**, 189–197.

85. Prawatt, R. S., & Cancelli, A. Constructive memory in conserving and nonconserving first graders. *Developmental Psychology*, 1976, **12**, 47–50.

86. Jenkins, J. Remember that old theory of memory? Well, forget it! *American Psychologist*, 1974, **29**, 785–795.

87. Tulving, E. Cue dependent forgetting. *American Scientist*, 1974, **62**, 74–82.

88. Kobasigawa, A. Utilization of retrieval cues by children in recall. *Child Development*, 1974, **45**, 127–134.

89. Halperin, M. S. Developmental changes in the recall and recognition of categorized word lists. *Child Development*, 1974, **45**, 144–151.

90. Worden, P. E. The development of the category recall function under three retrieval conditions. *Child Development*, 1974, **45**, 1054–1059.
91. Arlen, M., & Brody, B. Effects of spatial presentation and blocking on organization and verbal recall at three age levels. *Developmental Psychology*, 1976, **12**, 113–118.
92. Piaget, J., Inhelder, B., & Szeminska, A. *The child's conception of geometry*. London: Routledge & Kegan Paul, 1960.
93. Elkind, D. Children's discovery of the conservation of mass, weight and volume. *Journal of Genetic Psychology*, 1961, **98**, 219–227.
94. Elkind, D. Quantity conceptions in junior and senior high school students. *Child Development*, 1961, **32**, 551–560.
95. Graves, A. J. Attainment of mass, weight and volume in minimally educated adults. *Developmental Psychology*, 1972, **7**, 223.
96. Hobbs, E. D. Adolescents' concepts of physical quantity. *Developmental Psychology*, 1973, **9**, 431.
97. Piaget, J., & Inhelder, B. *Le development des quantities chez l'enfant*. Paris: Delachaux et Niestle, 1941.
98. Piaget, J. *The child's conception of time*. New York: Basic Books, 1970.
99. Beilin, H. Learning and operational convergence in logical thought development. *Journal of Experimental Child Psychology*, 1965, **2**, 317–339.
100. Smedslund, J. Patterns of experience and the acquisition of conservation of length. *Scandinavian Journal of Psychology*, 1963, **4**, 257–264.
101. Wohlwill, J. F., & Lowe, R. C. Experimental analysis of the development of conservation of number. *Child Development*, 1962, **33**, 153–167.
102. Brainerd, C. J., & Chillen, T. W. Experimental inductions of the conservation of "first order" quantitative invariants. *Psychological Bulletin*, 1971, **75**, 128–144.
103. Gelman, R. Conservation acquisition: A problem of learning to attend to relevant attributes. *Journal of Experimental Child Psychology*, 1969, **7**, 167–187.
104. Bucher, B., & Schneider, R. E. Acquisition and generalization of conservation by preschoolers, using operant training. *Journal of Experimental Child Psychology*, 1973, **16**, 187–204.
105. Inhelder, B., Sinclair, H., & Bovet, M. *Apprentissage et structures de la commaissance*. Paris: Presses Universitaires de France, 1974.
106. Piaget, J. *The psychology of intelligence*. New York: Harcourt, 1950.
107. Schnall, M., Alter, E., Swanlund, T., & Schwentzer, T. A sensory-motor context affecting performance in a conservation task: A closer analogue of reversibility than empirical return. *Child Development*, 1972, **43**, 1012–1023.
108. Roll, S. Reversibility training and stimulus desirability as factors in conservation of number. *Child Development*, 1970, **41**, 501–507.
109. Carey, R. L., & Steffe, L. P. An investigation in the learning of equivalence and order relations by four and five year old children. Athens: University of Georgia, Research and Development Center in Educational Stimulation, research paper no. 17, 1968.
110. Whiteman, M., & Pesach, E. Perceptual and sensorimotor supports for conservation tasks. *Developmental Psychology*, 1970, **2**, 247–256.
111. Curcio, F., Katlef, E., Levine, D., & Robbins, O. Compensation and susceptibility to conservation training. *Developmental Psychology*, 1972, **7**, 259–265.
112. Gelman, R., & Weinberg, D. H. The relationship between liquid conservation and compensation. *Child Development*, 1972, **43**, 371–383.
113. Sheppard, T. L. Compensatory and combinational systems in the acquisition and generalization of conservation. *Child Development*, 1974, **65**, 717-730.
114. Piaget, J. *The moral judgement of the child*. Glencoe, Ill.: Free Press, 1948.
115. Murray, J. P. Acquisition of conservation through social interaction. *Developmental Psychology*, 1972, **6**, 1–6.
116. Murray, J. P. Social learning and cognitive development: modeling effects on children's understanding of conservation. *British Journal of Psychology*, 1974, **65**, 151–160.
117. Silverman, I. W., & Geringer, E. Dyadic interaction and conservation induction: A test of Piaget's equilibrium model. *Child Development*, 1973, **44**, 815–820.
118. Silverman, I. W., & Stone, J. M. Modifying cognitive functioning through participation in a problem solving group. *Journal of Educational Psychology*, 1972, **63**, 603–608.
119. Beilin, H. *Studies in the cognitive bases of language development*. New York: Basic Books, 1975.

120. Siegler, R. S., & Liebert, R. M. Effects of presenting relevant rules and complete feedback on the conservation of liquid quantity task. *Developmental Psychology,* 1972, **7,** 133–138.

121. Zimmerman, B. J., & Rosenthal, T. L. Conserving and retaining equalities and inequalities through observation and correction. *Developmental Psychology,* 1974, **10,** 260–268.

122. Boersma, F., & Wilton, K. M. Eye movements and conservation acceleration. *Journal of Experimental Child Psychology,* 1974, **17,** 49–60.

123. Christie, J. F., & Smothergill, D. W. Discrimination and conservation of length. *Psychonomic Science,* 1970, **21,** 336–337.

124. Miller, P. H. Attention to stimulus dimensions in the conservation of liquid quantity. *Child Development,* 1973, **44,** 129–136.

125. Piaget, J. Address to the Jean Piaget Society. Philadelphia, June 1975.

126. Bearison, D. J. Is school achievement enhanced by teaching children operational concepts? In G. Lubin, J. Magary, & M. Paulsen (Eds.), *Piagetian theory and the helping professions.* Los Angeles: University of Southern California, 1975.

127. Hoffman, M. L. Moral development. In P. H. Mussen (Ed.), *Carmichael's manual of child psychology.* New York: Wiley, 1970.

128. Kohlberg, L. From is to ought. In T. Mischel (Ed.), *Cognitive development and epistemology.* New York: Academic Press, 1971.

129. Kurtines, W., & Grief, E. B. The development of moral thought: Review and evaluation of Kohlberg's approach. *Psychological Bulletin,* 1974, **81,** 453–470.

130. Turiel, E. An experimental test of the sequentiality of developmental stages in the child's moral judgement. *Journal of Personality and Social Psychology,* 1966, **3,** 611–618.

131. Rest, J. R. The hierarchical nature of stages of moral judgement. *Journal of Personality,* 1973, **41,** 86–109.

132. Rest, J. R., Cooper, D., Coder, R., Masanz, J., & Anderson, D. Judging the important issue in moral dilemmas — an objective measure of development. *Developmental Psychology,* 1974, **10,** 491–501.

133. Opie, I., & Opie, P. *The lore and language of school children.* London: Oxford University Press, 1959.

134. Miller, S. A. (Ed.) *Linguistic communication: perspectives for research.* Newark, Del.: Univ. of Delaware Press, 1974.

135. Moss, J. The bedtime story and language development. *American Journal of Diseases of Children,* 1976, **130,** 180–184.

136. Bereiter, C., & Englemann, S. *Teaching disadvantaged children in the preschool.* Englewood Cliffs, N.J.: Prentice-Hall, 1966.

137. Durkin, D. *Children who read early.* New York: Teachers College Press, 1966.

138. Briggs, C., & Elkind, D. Cognitive development in early readers. *Developmental Psychology,* 1973, **9,** 279–280.

139. Briggs, C., & Elkind, D. Characteristics of early readers. *Perceptual and Motor Skills,* 1977, **44,** 1231–1237.

140. Downing, J. (Ed.) *Comparative reading: Cross natural studies of behavior and processes in reading and writing.* New York: Macmillan, 1973.

141. Washburne, C. W., & Marland, S. P. *Winnetka: the history and significance of an educational experiment.* Englewood Cliffs, N.J.: Prentice-Hall, 1963.

142. Elkind, D., & Dabek, R. Personal injury and property damage in the moral judgements of children. *Child Development,* 1977, **48,** 518–522.

12 Personality and Social Development

ENTRY INTO SCHOOL

Attitudes toward School

The Sense of Industry or Inferiority

INCREASING IMPORTANCE OF THE PEER GROUP

Self-Perceptions and Popularity

Individualism, Conformity, and Other Ways of
Dealing with People

Feelings of Belonging or Alienation

Changes in the Structure of Peer-Group Relationships

SEX-ROLE IDENTITY

Psychosexual "Latency"

FAMILY RELATIONS

Parental Adjustment to a School-Age Child

Reassessment of Parents by School-Age Children

ESSAY

The Feminized Classroom

BIOGRAPHY

Sigmund Freud

SUMMARY

REFERENCES

Children enter middle childhood as semisocialized little boys and girls who play at being mommy or daddy; they leave it as preadolescent youths ready to grapple realistically with adult roles and responsibilities. During the intervening elementary school years the developmental pace is slow and steady, the strains relatively few, and the pleasures many. No longer in need of close parental supervision, school-age children are off on their own much of the time, playing, exploring their world, learning about people and things, and touching home base only to rest, refuel, and occasionally seek comfort or reassurance. Unburdened by major responsibilities, they are free to live for the joys of the moment. Although frustrations and disappointments may cloud this idyllic picture from time to time, elementary-school children are generally content with their lot and satisfied that theirs is a good age to be. The early school years are often referred to as the golden years of childhood, and most adults recall this period of their life fondly and with vivid memories of friends known and things done.

With respect to personality and social development, two major and permanent changes occur at this time that have an important effect on what kind of individuals children will become. First, they enter school, where they will spend half of their waking hours for the next ten years or more. With few exceptions, youngsters continue in school until they are ready to earn a living, and once children start school they are never again as intimately and exclusively lodged in the bosom of their family as they had been before.

Second, as children start school and become less dependent on their families, the focus of their interpersonal relationships gradually shifts from their parents to their peers and the larger community. School-age children begin to spend more time with their peers than with their family, and peer attitudes become an increasingly important influence in how they feel about themselves. In addition, teachers, playground directors, clergymen, policemen, and other adults who are visible in the community, on television, or in the movies begin to share the role-modeling and socialization functions that previously belonged to the parents.

In this chapter we will discuss the impact of classroom, peer-group, and community experiences on personality development during middle childhood, following which we will extend our earlier coverage of sex-role identity and family relations.

ENTRY INTO
SCHOOL

Entry into school confronts children with a host of new challenges and opportunities. Above all, they must give up much of their earlier dependence on their parents and their home environment. Each weekday requires them to spend several hours in a new environment presided over by unfamiliar adults and populated for the most part by unfamiliar children. In this setting they do not have the unconditional acceptance of their parents or any established position of authority or respect they may have earned with their neighborhood playmates. In school children start with a clean slate and are judged and responded to on the basis of their merits as students and classmates. How they are judged and responded to significantly influences their attitudes toward school and whether they develop a sense of industry or a sense of inferiority.

Attitudes toward School Most children look forward eagerly to beginning school because it gives them a feeling of importance and maturity and a chance to learn and do many new things (1, 2). Now they will be "grown up," able to walk to school or ride on the school bus with the "big kids," and they will be sharing in the exciting activities they have heard older siblings or neighborhood children talk about. Despite their typical complaints about school ("Do I *have* to go today?") and their joy when summer vacation arrives ("No more papers, no more books, no more teachers' dirty looks"), most elementary-school children look forward to the start of each new year, priding themselves on being promoted to each higher grade and finding satisfaction in their mastery of increasingly difficult subject matter.

There are some important exceptions to this generally positive view of school. Sometimes overly dependent children are fearful of going to school because they dread being separated from their parents. Such excessive fears constitute a special pattern of abnormal development in middle childhood (school phobia) that we will discuss in Chapter 14. In other instances children living in disadvantaged neighborhoods, especially the ghetto areas of large cities, may have good reason to regard the school as a hostile environment that has little to offer them. We will consider in this chapter and in Chapter 14 some of the special problems of these disadvantaged schoolchildren. At the same time, however, we need to recognize that their problems are not typical of American youth. Data from the White House Conference on Children indicate that only 8.2 percent of elementary school children live in poverty areas of large cities (3).

It is understandable that the majority of children are enthusiastic about school, for it plays a major role in their intellectual and social development. Here they learn the basic skills of reading, writing, and arithmetic; they come to understand more about their culture and their environment; they develop social relationships with large numbers of adults and agemates; and they are challenged to exercise their initiative and mastery. It is the school, then, that provides children their central forum for learning, for feeling a sense of accomplishment, for meeting new people, and for having fun. Whether children's enthusiasm for school continues, however, is influenced by the kind of school they attend and by their parents' attitudes toward education.

Influence of the School. Among the many aspects of a school that

Differences among elementary schools in class size and available facilities influence how much opportunity children have for getting individual attention and for participating in activities that make the school day interesting and enjoyable.

affect children's attitudes are its size and its educational policies. The size of the school is important because it determines how much opportunity there is for children to participate. The more students there are in a classroom, for example, the less chance each of them has to ask questions, work on projects, assist the teacher, or receive individual attention. Likewise, the larger the student body, the fewer opportunities there may be for children to become involved in such activities as sports, band, chorus, and school plays.

In some research on school size Barker and Gump confirmed that students in smaller schools are much more likely than large-school students to be encouraged to take part in activities and to become involved in leadership and functionary positions. Small-school students were also found to report more positive feelings of developing competence, being valued by others, and participating in important group efforts (4, 5). These and similar findings suggest that the less opportunity children have to participate in school activities, the less important school becomes to them as a focus for new learning and social experiences and the more likely their initial enthusiasm for it will be to fade (6, 7).

The influence of school size is a bit more complex than this, however. For one thing, children vary in how they respond to school size. Talented and outgoing boys and girls will usually find a place for themselves regardless of the size of their school, and it is primarily retiring children with modest or limited talents who tend to be shut out of enriching and rewarding activities in a large school. In relatively small schools, on the other hand, marginal students are found to report just as much sense of involvement in school activities as their more able classmates (8).

For another thing, opportunities for participation in the classroom and in extracurricular activities are meaningful only in relation to what a school can offer. Schools that are too small to have art, music, and physical education programs or a decent library disadvantage their students. Similarly, schools with inadequate teaching aids or recreational facilities may not sustain children's enthusiasm whatever the size of the student body.

Even more crucial in influencing how children feel about school are the educational policies followed in the classroom. Curriculum planning and teaching methods that make learning a lively, exciting, and meaningful adventure kindle curiosity and interest, whereas teaching that is dull, routine, and unrelated to what is going on in the world eventually dampens a child's enthusiasm for school.

Such negative effects are described in Charles Silberman's *Crisis in the Classroom*. Silberman believes that far too many elementary schools are oriented toward "education for docility." These schools emphasize order, discipline, and conformity in the classroom, rather than the fostering of self-expression, self-reliance, sensitivity, intellectual curiosity, and a sense of values. As a result, Silberman concludes, large numbers of children become bored and restless in school and fail to develop their full intellectual and personal potential (9).

A major example of poor educational policy is the use of bland, uninteresting reading materials that have little to do with the actual life children are familiar with. Numerous surveys of the traditional "Dick and Jane" books that were used to teach reading to generations of American children have found that they present an obviously unreal world, one in which everybody is good and lives happily ever after; where no one is poor, hungry, deprived; and where there are no such things as violence, dishonesty, racial tension, unemployment, or even politics (10–13).

Fortunately, these evaluations of children's readers have had a constructive influence on the schools. Children are more likely now than in the past to be given reading that is true to life and that deals with social issues children know to exist, either from their own experience or from television and the movies. The difference these changes can make in children's reading has been demonstrated in two interesting studies. In one study Wiberg and Trost compared the reading that was assigned to a group of first-graders in their classroom with the books they themselves chose in the library. It was found that the children's assigned reading emphasized such Dick-and-Jane themes as play and perfect happiness, whereas the books they chose in the library consisted of either folktales depicting good and evil in people or stories of real-life events having sad as well as happy outcomes (14).

In the other study Asher and Markell tested fifth-graders for their reading ability on two passages, one that was of low interest to them and the other that was of high interest. These students had significantly higher reading scores on the passage that interested them. Furthermore, whereas the girls in the study read substantially better than the boys (which is a common finding among elementary-school pupils), the difference between them was more pronounced on the reading material of low interest. On the passage of high interest (which, for the boys, was about airplanes and astronauts), the boys read almost as well as the girls (see Figure 12.1). The implication is clear that the reading skills of poor readers in particular could be improved by assigning more interesting reading material (15).

Generally speaking, the matter of "education for docility" is part of the larger issue of traditional versus modern approaches to education. The

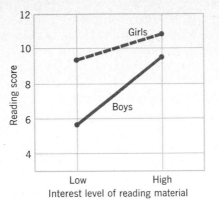

Figure 12.1 Reading level of boys and girls with low- and high-interest material. (*Source*. Based on data reported by Asher, S. & Markell, R. A. Sex differences in comprehension of high and low interest reading material. *Journal of Educational Psychology*, 1974, **66**, 680–687.)

traditional approach emphasizes established knowledge and judges students by their academic performance. In traditional schools teachers are *learning-oriented;* that is, they function as authority figures whose job is to convey facts and maintain order in the classroom. It is assumed that children are motivated to learn because they are competing with each other to do well and because they want their teacher's approval for doing good work.

By contrast, the modern educational approach is *student-oriented*. The emphasis is on helping children develop themselves socially and psychologically as well as intellectually. Modern schools accordingly make use of exploration, experimentation, and discussion of subject matter to arouse students' imagination and curiosity. Teachers in these schools study with their students rather than talk down to them, and it is assumed that a child will be motivated to learn if the teacher is successful in making learning an exciting and useful experience.

Although many people have been tempted to view traditional education as all bad and modern education as all good, no such conclusion is really justified. Rather, both approaches have their strengths and their weaknesses. Patricia Minuchin and her colleagues at the Bank Street College of Education in New York have reported an extensive study of fourth-graders in two traditional and two modern schools. It was found that children in the modern schools generally were able to describe themselves more clearly, were more self-accepting, were more content with being children, and were more flexible in their view of sex-role differences. On the other hand, the children in traditional schools tended to be somewhat impersonal rather than distinctly individualistic, future-oriented rather than enjoying their status as children, and socially conventional rather than open with respect to sex roles (16).

One might conclude from these findings that modern schools tend to shape children as open-minded individualists while traditional schools encourage them to be stilted conformists; yet one could also conclude that modern schools foster immaturity and uncertainty whereas traditional schools provide children with a sense of stability and direction that helps them ultimately find a meaningful place in society. In addition, the Minuchin study came up with some surprising data that made it very difficult to draw black-and-white distinctions between learning-oriented and student-oriented approaches to education. Specifically, it was found that there were no consistent differences in cognitive skills between children in the traditional and the modern schools. Despite the modern schools' emphasis on imagination and experimentation, for example, the children from these schools did not perform any better than those from traditional schools on problem-solving tasks that required flexible, exploratory thinking. The children from the modern schools did perform somewhat better than the other children on group problem-solving tasks; however, the traditionally educated children outperformed those from the modern schools on individual achievement tests.

Obviously, good and bad things can be said about both approaches to education; furthermore, it is not clear if there is a good or bad educational environment for *all* children. Because school-age children have individual personalities, an environment that encourages maximum intellectual and psychological growth in some children may interfere with such growth in others. As a case in point, Minuchin reports that several bright children in one of the modern schools surveyed by her group were floundering, unable to study effectively or perform at the level of their abilities. These children seemed to be suffering from the lack of structure in their classroom experience; because of their personality style, they would probably have done better in a more routinized classroom with a more authoritarian teacher. Generally speaking, then, the attitudes children form toward school and the extent to which they realize their academic potential will depend not only upon the characteristics of the school they attend, but also upon how well these characteristics fit their individual needs and interests.

Influence of the Parents. Children readily identify with their parents' feelings about school and education. Parents who value the educational process and respect the efforts of their child's teachers encourage positive attitudes, whereas parents who belittle teachers or brag about how much they have accomplished without much schooling often encourage negative attitudes. Similarly, parents who *say* that education is important but who show no interest in reading, learning, or intellectual discussions may discourage their children from having any interest in school. As we noted in Chapter 8, children tend to do what their parents *do* rather than what they *say*.

Using data from extensive longitudinal studies of child development conducted by the Fels Institute, Virginia Crandall has demonstrated some clear relationships between how parents feel about learning in school and how they react to the educational experiences of their elementary-school children. The greater the value parents place on their own intellectual attainments, the more they value the intellectual attainments of their children and the more they participate in intellectual activities with them. Interestingly, however, parents are more likely to communicate the importance of learning to their daughters than to their sons during elementary school, but they set higher standards for their sons' than for their daughters' achievements. In other words, academically oriented parents tend to expect better school performance from their daughters, but they are more willing to accept a lower performance from them than from their sons (17–19).

Crandall attributes these sex differences to commonly held sex-role stereotypes. According to these stereotypes, boys should not get too wrapped up in their studies at the expense of more "masculine" activities lest they become "bookworms" or "sissies"; however, it is all right for girls to enjoy school, for schoolwork is a natural and appropriate activity for them from an early age. Yet traditional sex-role stereotypes also hold that doing well in school is more important for boys than for girls in the long run, since it is primarily the boys who will have to qualify for jobs and earn a living. From these stereotypes comes the apparently inconsistent result that parents provide more support for their daughters' viewing school as important while at the same time expressing more concern with the actual school performance of their sons.

The parents' social class is also likely to be a factor affecting children's attitudes toward school. Middle- and upper-class parents tend to be well educated themselves and to regard school as a way of preparing for life, socially and psychologically as well as vocationally. Hence they typically speak in positive terms about what school has to offer; they follow closely what their children are doing in school; they appreciate and discuss with them the significance of what they are learning; and they reward them for their academic accomplishments. There is evidence to suggest that lower-class parents, on the other hand, tend to have minimal education, to regard school as an alien and hostile institution, and to view their children's attendance as little more than a legal requirement or perhaps as a route toward getting a better-paying job. They are less likely than white-collar parents to discuss school activities with their children, to understand and help them with their studies, or to praise their achievements in the classroom (20, 21).

As a consequence, children from lower-class families may have a less positive feeling toward school and be less influenced by it than middle- or upper-class children. Yet we must be careful to avoid any glib or overgeneralized social-class contrasts. In the first place, the school may in fact be a hostile environment for children in some lower-class or disadvantaged neighborhoods, independently of their parents' attitudes. There is reason to think that labeling children as "culturally disadvantaged" has the effect in some classrooms of leading teachers to expect less of them and consequently to give them less attention, encouragement, and support than middle-class children (22). In one interesting study of this phenomenon, Richer found that lower-class children were likely to receive special attention in student-oriented classrooms, but in learning-oriented classrooms they tended to have significantly less than their share of interactions with the teacher (23).

Second, parents within any social class may differ widely and convey totally different attitudes to their children. For example, Greenberg and Davidson found many differences between the parents of lower-class black fifth-graders who were doing well in school and the parents of a similar group of children who were doing poorly. The parents of the achieving children were more interested in their child's education, more knowledgeable about the school system, more likely to regard high school as preparation for college, and more likely to have books and adequate study space in the home (24).

Third, lower-class parents who do not encourage or support school activities may still foster positive attitudes toward verbal communication, which have been found to correlate significantly with achievement among inner-city elementary-school children (25). In addition, the influence of older siblings, aunts and uncles, and adults in the neighborhood who value education may help children form positive feelings about school regardless of the attitudes of their parents. Teachers who fail to consider such possibilities may wrongly assume that their lower-class pupils will not like or do well in school. As we have just noted, any expectation that lower-class children will be indifferent or troublesome in class can become a self-fulfilling prophecy working to the disadvantage of those with intellectual potential.

The Sense of Industry or Inferiority

During the preschool years children strive to master the basic motor and social skills they need to get along in the world. As they become more socialized, independent, and cognitively mature during the elementary-school years, this striving for mastery is replaced by a more complex orientation consisting of a motivation to achieve specific future goals, an interest in competition, and feelings of competence about their acquired skills and their ability to cope with new situations.

Erikson accordingly speaks of the elementary-school years as the time when children form either a **sense of industry** or a **sense of inferiority** (26). To the extent that children's achievement motivation, competitiveness, and feelings of competence are reinforced by some degree of success, they will develop a sense of industry—a feeling that they can cope with the challenges they encounter. However, if children experience more failure than success, they are likely to develop a sense of inferiority—a feeling that they are incapable of meeting the challenges of their world.

Parents can play an important role in determining whether their child feels industrious or inferior. Parents who teach their children to fish, swim, cook, sew, use carpentry tools, run farm equipment, or perform other tasks, and who do so with patience and admiration for what they are able to accomplish, tend to strengthen their children's sense of industry. But parents who belittle their child's efforts to repair a bicycle or build a model airplane and then show how they can do it better are likely to encourage a feeling of inferiority. Likewise, parents who snatch the sewing away from a child who drops the needle or who chase a child out of the kitchen for "making a mess" may foster feelings of inadequacy and inferiority.

After they enter school, children's feelings of industry or inferiority will also be affected by the level of their abilities in relation to those of other children and by their teachers' responses. Positive school experiences can outweigh negative home experiences, but the opposite is also possible—defeats and failures at school can undo the parents' efforts to foster feelings of competence and adequacy.

Influence of a Child's Abilities. In school children are ranked formally

The activities of elementary-school children show increasing *industriousness*, an interest in hobbies and projects through which they achieve some mastery of real-world challenges.

and informally according to their talents in various areas. In the classroom brighter children tend to get better grades, and it soon becomes clear to most children which ones will probably pass or fail a test, which ones will answer correctly or fumble when asked a question in class, and which ones will be the first and the last to fall out in a spelling bee. In gym class and on the playground children are ranked or rank themselves according to their athletic ability; in art and music classes it becomes clear who can draw or sing and who cannot.

These experiences confront children with a more or less objective appraisal of their abilities in relation to those of their peers. During the preschool years positive self-attitudes generally arise from the sense of accomplishment each child feels in mastering new skills, regardless of what other children are able to do. During middle childhood, however, *social comparison* becomes the main factor in determining what value children place on themselves. Feelings of competence and adequacy at this time depend less on what children are actually able to do than on their perceptions of themselves as more or less able than their peers (27–29).

Because elementary-school children are highly sensitive to social comparison, their feelings about their academic ability will depend upon the general intellectual level of their classmates. Children of average intelligence who are enrolled in a school with an intellectually average student body may experience gratifying academic success, whereas other average children who happen to be in a school with intellectually gifted youngsters may experience considerable embarrassment and failure in their classroom efforts. Children's self-attitudes are also influenced by how good they are at activities that are valued by their peers. Among a group of elementary-school boys who value sports, for example, being among the best or worst athletes can contribute substantially to having a positive or negative self-concept.

Children who have some talent will usually find a reward for it somewhere—with their parents, teachers, or peers. For those who are bright and gifted and for those who have at least some special skill, the school experience typically provides recognition. On the other hand, relatively dull youngsters who are also nonathletic and untalented will probably find it difficult to take pleasure in their efforts; consequently, they may develop an increasing sense of inferiority as a result of their school experience.

Influence of the Teacher. Teachers are in a unique position to maximize their students' achievement motivation, healthy competitiveness, and feelings of competence by encouraging and rewarding their efforts, stimulating their interest in learning, and minimizing their failures and limitations. A sensitive and committed teacher helps children discover and build up their assets while identifying and learning to live with their liabilities. A disinterested or insensitive teacher, on the other hand, can intensify a child's sense of ineptness and inferiority. Moreover, teachers serve as models that their students may copy in dealing with one another. Children who observe their teacher praising or encouraging a classmate tend to treat that child in the same way, thus reinforcing his or her industry; children who are scorned and ridiculed by their teacher, on the other hand, are likely to receive the same treatment from their peers (30, 31).

Other research confirms that teacher behavior can significantly affect the academic attitudes and performance of elementary-school children. In particular, the more teachers praise children or give them good grades for their academic work, the more children will expect to succeed intellectually and the more they will try to achieve. Conversely, less praise and lower grades lead to lower expectations and fewer achievement attempts (19, 32, 33).

It should be kept in mind that these are only generalizations. Some children, because of their own particular personality styles, may be spurred on to better performance more by being criticized for their mistakes than by being praised for their accomplishments. For the most part, however, children can be expected to demonstrate more positive attitudes toward themselves and to make more progress in school when their teachers have positive feelings toward them.

There is no question that teachers do form differing attitudes toward the children in their class. Silberman was able to identify four distinct attitudes simply by asking teachers a few brief questions about their pupils (34, 35):

Attachment ("Which student would you want to keep another year for the sheer joy of it?")

Indifference ("If a parent were to drop in unannounced for a conference, which child would you be least prepared to talk about?")

Concern ("If you could devote all your attention to a child who concerned you a great deal, whom would you pick?")

Rejection ("If your class were to be reduced in size, whom would you like to have removed?")

Silberman and other researchers have found that these attitudes are related to certain patterns of teacher-student interaction in the classroom, which are summarized in Table 12.1 (36–38). Although such teacher attitudes largely originate with the way in which children perform in the classroom, they in turn can affect how children feel about school and how well they do in their studies. For example, it has been found that certain acts on the part of teachers communicate to children a low expectation of doing well. These include calling on children infrequently; giving them only a short time to answer before calling on someone else; accepting or even praising poor work rather than encouraging better work; paying relatively little attention to what children are doing; and assigning them to seats in the corner or back row of the classroom (36).

Table 12.1   Relationships between Teachers' Attitudes and Patterns of
Teacher-Student Interaction.

Attitude toward the Student	Pattern of Classroom Interaction
Attached	Students tend to be high-achieving and well-behaved, they reward their teachers with desirable classroom behavior and in turn receive approval from the teacher
Indifference	Students pass quietly through the school year; they arouse neither the interest nor the concern of their teachers, who seldom call on them in class or give them individual attention
Concern	Students tend to be low achievers who nevertheless try hard and often ask for help; teachers devote considerable time and effort in trying to help them
Rejection	Students tend to be low achievers who arouse negative feelings in their teachers; teachers either ignore or are highly critical of them and spend more time trying to control their classroom behavior than in helping them with their studies

Source: Based on data reported by Good, T., & Brophy, J. Behavioral expressions of teacher attitudes. *Journal of Educational Psychology,* 1972, **63,** 617–624.

The impact that such expectations can have on how children actually do in school has been demonstrated in some important work by Rosenthal and Jacobsen on what has come to be known as the **pygmalion effect**. Pygmalion was a sculptor who, according to legend, breathed life into a statue he was carving and made her into exactly the kind of woman he wanted her to be. Rosenthal and Jacobsen told a number of elementary-school teachers at the beginning of a school year that certain students coming into their class were "intellectual bloomers who would show unusual intellectual gains." In fact, these children had been randomly chosen among their classmates. At the end of the year, however, it was found that "identified" children had made greater advances in reading and were rated more intellectually curious than those for whom the teachers had no special expectations (39–41).

Many people have wondered whether such a pygmalion effect really exists or whether it merely emerged because of the way Rosenthal and Jacobsen designed their research (42–45). Further studies must be done to determine how much teachers can raise or lower their students' achievements simply by having different expectations for them. Nevertheless, enough evidence exists in support of self-fulfilling prophecies in human behavior—that is, causing things to happen by expecting them to happen—to make this possibility a legitimate concern in classroom instruction.

**INCREASING
IMPORTANCE OF
THE PEER GROUP**

During the elementary-school years children's interactions with their peers become an increasingly important part of their life. As a result of these interactions they form new perceptions of themselves and become concerned about their popularity with their peer group; they develop flexible, conforming, or other ways of dealing with people; they experience a sense of social belonging or alienation; and they get caught up in rapidly changing patterns of peer-group organization. These interpersonal events make an indelible mark on the personality characteristics children carry with them into their adolescent and adult years.

**Self-Perceptions
and Popularity**

School-age children become keenly aware of one another's mental, physical, and personality characteristics, and the peer group is quick to identify its members according to their prominent traits. As an expression of the frank appraisals elementary-school children make of their classmates, nicknames and name-calling gain great vogue during middle childhood: "Fatty," "Red," "Four-eyes," "Freckles," "Snot," "Sissy," "Brain," "Teacher's pet," "Champ," and so forth. Because children of this age spend so much time together, they cannot help but see themselves (at least in part) through their peers' eyes. Research studies confirm a close relationship between grade-schoolers' concept of themselves and how they are perceived by their classmates (46).

In addition to serving as a mirror in which children come to see themselves more clearly than they have before, the peer group attaches certain values to the traits of its members and assigns status accordingly. Although the value of particular traits varies somewhat according to the age, sex, and social class of the peer group, some traits consistently lead to popularity (high status) or rejection (low status) among most elementary-school children.

First, a substantial body of research indicates that children who are popular among their peers tend to be friendly, sociable, and outgoing youngsters who participate in many group activities, comply with prevailing group standards, and treat others with kindness, acceptance, and sensitivity to their needs. In addition, popular children tend to be relatively well-adjusted psychologically and to come from homes where there is minimal tension and their parents are pleased with them. Unpopular children, on the other hand, tend to be shy and withdrawn; to avoid or be excluded from group activities; to treat others with indifference, insensitivity, hostility, and rejection; to have behavioral problems; and to be uncomfortable both at home and at school (47–55).

Second, school-age children who are bright and creative, perform well in their studies, and display various talents (especially athletic ability among boys) are generally more popular than those with less intelligence, fewer ideas, poorer grades, and little talent (54–58). Third, there is some

Children from 6 to 12 come in many different shapes and sizes. As early as the first grade, popularity among peers is related to physical appearance, with children of medium build preferred to those who are thin or chubby.

evidence that children's body build can affect their popularity. As early as the first grade children seem to prefer those who are of average or muscular build to those who are thin or chubby (59–61).

Yet we must be careful to recognize that there is a substantial interaction between what children are like and how popular they are. Not only do children's personality characteristics influence their popularity; their social status among their age-mates in turn affects how friendly, relaxed, considerate, and active they are in social situations. In other words, high social status can be the *cause* as well as the *result* of socially adaptive behavior. It is much easier for children to be relaxed and sociable when they feel accepted and well-liked in their peer group then when they feel that rejection may be just around the corner.

Individualism, Conformity, and Other Ways of Dealing with People

The ways in which children learn to deal with others in seeking peer acceptance often remain an integral part of their personality. Elementary-school children who have a solid sense of trust, autonomy, and self-worth usually move smoothly into interpersonal relationships. They tend to feel comfortable in social situations and to have a flexible

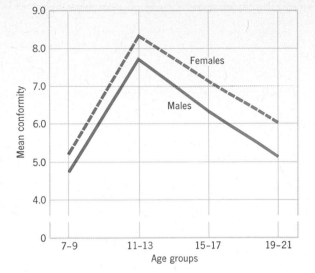

Figure 12.2 Conformity to peer influence as a function of age. (*Source.* Costanzo, P. R. & Shaw, M. E. Conformity as a function of age level. *Child Development,* 1966, **37,** 967–975. Copyright The Society for Research in Child Development, Inc., 1966. Used by permission.)

interpersonal style that allows them to get along well with many different kinds of people while retaining their own individuality.

Even while they are retaining their individuality, however, most school-age children begin to tailor their attitudes and actions to fit the prevailing trends in the peer group. Costanzo and Shaw, in an experimental study of conformity, found that children become increasingly likely to be influenced by the opinions of their peers from the first to the sixth grade; the impact of peer influence levels off during the junior high school years and then declines during high school (62; see Figure 12.2).

Although it is popularly believed that adolescence, rather than middle childhood, is the peak age of peer conformity, many other studies confirm the Costanzo and Shaw finding, namely, that the influence of the peer group reaches its height around the end of elementary school and begins to diminish soon thereafter (63–66). Such trappings as clothing and tastes in music sometimes give the impression that adolescents are rigid conformists to the norms of their group. With respect to their thoughts, feelings, and actions, however, adolescents are in fact much more individualistic than younger children, and they are also influenced much more by people and events beyond their own immediate group (67, 68).

The amount of influence exerted by children's peer groups depends upon several factors. First, the more time children spend with each other—in play groups or organized after-school activities as well as in the classroom—the more likely they are to influence each other. Second, the less actively involved children are with their parents, the more they tend to copy what they observe in their peer group. Third, children who are held in high esteem by the group have more influence on group attitudes and behavior than low-status children, and low-status children are, in turn, more susceptible to group influence than popular children. And finally, the more ambiguous a situation is, without a clear-cut way of dealing with it or a previously prescribed course of action to take, the more children will be influenced in their response by the consensus of their peer group (50, 69).

Most elementary-school children are able to combine flexible, individual ways of relating to others with certain elements of peer conformity. However, for those who have not been adequately prepared by nature or previous learning experiences to cope effectively with peer relationships, this period in their life is the time when certain inflexible interpersonal styles begin to appear. These styles develop as children try to compensate for anticipated peer rejection by sticking rigidly to some maladaptive social role, even when it results in self-defeating behavior. Four such maladaptive interpersonal styles are the *bully*, the *buffoon*, the *bootlicker*, and the *pseudo-adult*.

Children who feel inadequate sometimes resort to bullying smaller children to give themselves a sense of being powerful and looked up to.

Bullies seek out younger or smaller children whom they can dominate and browbeat, thereby relieving their own feelings of inadequacy when they are with children of their own age and size. *Buffoons* become clownish and play the fool in order to gain attention from their peers, whom they believe might otherwise ignore them completely. *Bootlickers* use flattery, servility, and outrageous bribes to try to buy "friendship" that they do not think they could obtain any other way. Both buffoons and bootlickers willingly endure humiliation and abuse as their price for escaping anonymity, and both come to wear indignities proudly as their badge of being noticed in the peer group.

Pseudo-adults spurn all of these techniques, seeking their comforts and rewards from grown-ups. These children typically get along better with their teachers and their parents' friends than with their own age-mates. Adults in turn are frequently impressed with their conscientiousness, diligence, respect for elders, and apparent emotional stability—all of which constitute a facade masking these children's emotional immaturity and basic inability to give and take in peer relationships. These four maladaptive styles can also be found in adults who bully, clown, wheedle, or remain aloof from others because they do not feel capable of being accepted and respected in a genuinely mutual relationship.

**Feelings of
Belonging or
Alienation**

The interpersonal experiences of childhood are an important factor in determining whether children develop a **sense of belonging** or a **sense of alienation.** The friendships of the elementary-school years enable children to feel that they belong to a society that extends beyond their own family.

Figure 12.3 Membership in four youth organizations in the United States, 1970. (*Source.* Based on data reported by White House Conference on Children. *Profiles of children.* Washington, D.C.: U.S. Department of Health, Education, and Welfare, 1970.)

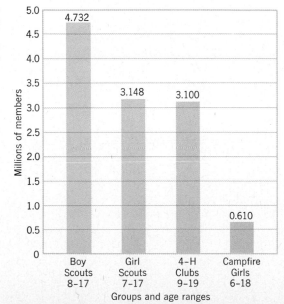

Usually this feeling expands as children begin to participate in various neighborhood and community activities, such as the corner gang, the settlement-house group, the Cub Scouts or Campfire Girls, the Sunday school, and the Little League. In 1970 membership in just four such groups (Boy Scouts, Girl Scouts, Campfire Girls, and 4-H Clubs) was over 11 million, which is approximately one-quarter of the total U.S. population of children in the age range they cover (see Figure 12.3). These groups help children to feel part of a broader society, and they can be especially useful in providing some sense of belonging to children who are experiencing rejection elsewhere.

On the other hand, children who are not accepted by their peers and have limited opportunities to participate in neighborhood and community groups often feel alienated from their society. Alienation is commonly described as a problem of adolescence rather than childhood, especially by personality theorists who are concerned about the difficulties of a complex technological society in providing meaningful roles for its teenage youth (70, 71). Yet alienation often begins during the lonely years of a middle childhood played out on a bare stage—without family, neighborhood, or community providing opportunities for participation in organized social and recreational activities. Whereas adolescent alienation is often due to young people's inability or reluctance to endorse the values of their society, the more basic alienation of young children is likely to stem from inadequate opportunities to learn what the values of the larger society are, or even that there is a larger community of which they could be a part.

Changes in the Structure of Peer-Group Relationships

Peer-group relationships during middle childhood become increasingly formal, cohesive, and organized. As 6- to 8-year-olds, children relate to each other in informal play groups with few if any rules and no fixed membership. The group forms by chance and consists of whoever happens to be on the sidewalk or street corner at a particular time. No one in the group has any special relationship with anyone else, and the amusements sought out by the group are whatever they happen to think of at the moment.

By the age of 10 or 11, however, the growing conformity among school-age children produces greater organization and cohesiveness in their peer groups, and their cognitive maturation leads to more focused and purposeful group activities (50, 72). Groups now gather around specific shared interests and planned events: they form into nature clubs, fan clubs, and secret societies with special rules, observances, passwords, and initiation rites; they make advance plans to build a fort, go to the movies, take a hike, or visit the candy store; and they develop a fixed membership, with each member expected to participate in the group's activities and nonmembers unwelcome.

During middle childhood children form larger and more organized play groups than before.

Adults contribute to the increasingly structured activities and organizations of elementary-school children by promoting such activities as 4-H Clubs, the Police Athletic League, and scouting. Besides giving children a sense of belonging, these groups are often valuable in teaching children special skills, helping them learn to work with others toward shared goals, and exposing them to adult models other than their parents and teachers. However, the adults who direct these activities need to avoid dominating or regulating them too strictly. For example, a Little League that is run primarily to give fathers a chance to play at being big-league managers and in which there is more emphasis on winning than on participating can do more harm than good. When adults take control of the activities they are supervising, children lose the opportunity to be childlike, to work out priorities and procedures among themselves, and to learn from making mistakes.

Chumships. Another significant change in the structure of interpersonal relationships during middle childhood is a shift shortly before adolescence from general friendships among several children to special **chumships** between two boys or two girls. The role of the "chum" in personality development was first elaborated by Harry Stack Sullivan, a distinguished psychiatrist who regarded the kind of interpersonal relationships people have as the most important determinant of how well adjusted they are (73). Preadolescent chums are always of the same sex and become inseparable best friends. They go to school together, play together, eat lunch together, sleep over at each other's homes, and share exclusively with each other their innermost hopes and fears.

Chumships are much more enduring then the small-group friendships of 10-year-olds. Membership in the latter groups may change fairly rapidly, as new members are accepted and old members move on to some other group they find more to their liking. Chumships, however, are likely to last for months at a time, and some children may have just one or two chums during the one- or two-year preadolescent period that bridges middle childhood and the teenage years. While it exists a chumship is an intense, exclusive, and highly meaningful relationship that provides important practice in the requirements for the more permanent and enduring intimate relationships of later life (74, 75).

Children who for one reason or another have not had chums may enter adolescence with a personality handicap. Not having experienced intimacy, they may not be prepared for the close and lasting friendships that people usually form during adolescence and adulthood. Without the experience of intimacy with a same-sexed peer, moreover, they may have difficulty later on with the more complex and challenging task of establishing intimacy with someone of the opposite sex, a topic to which we will turn in Chapter 16.

SEX-ROLE IDENTITY

Preschool boys and girls, although they dress differently and may show some differences in preferred activities, make relatively few distinctions among themselves and play together comfortably. However, beginning at about the age of 6 or 7, boys and girls tend to form separate play groups and to make numerous distinctions between how each other should behave. These changes reflect the fact that during the elementary-school years children start to form a psychological identity as members of one sex or the other.

The origins of sex-role identity are complex and not yet fully understood. Nevertheless, we can identify three factors that play a role in this developmental process. First, in their detailed review of research on sex differences, Maccoby and Jacklin conclude that there are some inborn differences between boys and girls that are found in all societies and are apparent early in life: as we have mentioned previously, males tend to be more aggressive than females and to have better quantitative and visual-spatial abilities, whereas females frequently excel in verbal ability (76). Such biological differences in mental abilities and personality style are likely to contribute to boys and girls forming a different sense of their sex-role identity.

However, biological factors provide only a limited explanation of this process. Constitutional differences that affect personality development exist primarily among individuals rather than between the sexes (77). For example, even though *average* aggressiveness may be greater among males than females, the variation in aggressiveness within both sexes is so great that there is considerable overlap between them—that is, many females will be more aggressive than many males. For the most part, then, we cannot rely on biology to account for the origin of sex-role identities but must examine the particular kinds of experiences children have in growing up.

Second, differences in how boys and girls are socialized by their parents may produce certain psychological differences between them. For example, parents tend to handle and play more roughly with their preschool sons than with their daughters, and they are more likely to punish their sons physically; this may result in boys being more physical than girls in their style of play (78–81). On the other hand, parents have been found to treat their sons and daughters alike in many important respects; for example, parents generally show the same amount of affection toward their sons as toward their daughters, and they encourage and permit both sexes to be independent (82–85).

Maccoby and Jacklin conclude, in fact, that parents tend to treat their children more according to what they perceive to be their individual temperament, interests, and abilities than according to any particular sexual stereotypes (76). Interestingly, however, there appears to be quite a discrepancy between parents' open-mindedness and the rigid sex-role definitions of school-age children. In a study by Looft 6- to 8-year-old boys and girls were asked what they would like to be when they grew up. Boys said that they would prefer to be, in order, football player, policeman, doctor, dentist, priest, scientist, pilot, and astronaut; girls said that they would prefer to be teacher, nurse, housewife, mother, stewardess, and salesgirl (86). Several other studies confirm that children of this age have stereotyped concepts of sex roles that limit the range of occupations regarded as appropriate for females (87–89).

Third, some aspects of sex-role identity tend to be acquired by means of the imitation and identification we discussed in Chapter 8. As children strive to be like their same-sexed parent, they develop a clearer sense of how males or females think, feel, and act. To examine this change, Masters and Wilkinson asked 4-year-olds, 7- and 8-year-olds, and adults to rate 52 toys according to whether they were more likely to be used by boys or girls. Most of the toys were consistently assigned to one sex or the other, indicating sex-role stereotypy in all three groups; however, the older children and the adults were the most stereotyped in their views and agreed almost perfectly, whereas the younger children had not yet formed as definite views about sex-appropriate behavior (90).

Research findings show that certain factors within the family promote identification and contribute to good psychological adjustment. Specifically, children are able to develop a relatively clear sex-role identity and make a relatively good adjustment in families where both parents are available, physically and psychologically; where both parents are reasonably well adjusted themselves; and where the parents maintain clearly differentiated, complementary, and stable roles in the family (91, 92).

Imitation and identification cannot explain certain aspects of sex-role identity in school-age children, however. In particular, children often define strict separation of their respective play groups as the way "real" boys and girls should act, even though they have undoubtedly seen their parents socializing with adults of both sexes. Similarly, they sometimes cling to rigid concepts of the proper roles for boys and girls despite contrary evidence from the models in their own family: Maccoby and Jacklin mention the case of a young girl who firmly believed that girls could become nurses but that only boys could become doctors—even though her own mother was a doctor.

It would therefore appear that children develop their sex-role identities partly in response to biological, socialization, and identification processes but also from their own oversimplified and exaggerated notions of what males and females can and should be like. As noted by Kohlberg and others, the immature judgment children display in holding such notions is consistent with the immaturity of their cognitive skills (93, 94).

Boy-girl separatism during middle childhood, with its opportunities for closeness within each sex group and the sharing of sex-role stereotypes, serves a useful function in the personality development of both boys and girls. Children who do not actively participate in the concerns of their same-sex peers or who spend large amounts of time with the opposite sex lose many opportunities to identify themselves as boys or girls. They are also likely to suffer some of the same lingering personality handicaps as children who have not had chums, because a well-developed sex-role identity helps prepare children for the heterosexual relationships of adolescence.

Elementary-school youngsters who have spent most of their time in play groups of the opposite sex may find it difficult to change the playmate relationships they have established with the opposite sex into dating relationships, and it may be equally hard for them to achieve closeness with young people of their own sex. At adolescence, when their peers begin partying and pairing off with members of the opposite sex, such boys and girls have trouble finding a place for themselves. Some of them continue to form friendly, brother-sister, platonic relationships with youngsters of the opposite sex, while others, uncomfortable with dating relationships and unaccustomed to being "one of the boys" (or girls), become social isolates.

Psychosexual
"Latency"

Because of the separation and apparent nonsexual orientation of elementary-school boys and girls, this period has sometimes been called the psychosexually **latent stage** (95, 96). Although this period does constitute a gap between the time when children begin to form their sex-role identity and the time when they begin to be openly interested in the opposite sex, much more goes on in the sexual life and attitudes of school-age children than meets the eye.

First, a sensitive observer can readily spot chinks in the armor of separatism that boys and girls wear so proudly. Despite their scorn for girls, boys take great pleasure in showing off in front of them and teasing them. Girls, in turn, no matter how much they pretend to ignore boys, pay attention to their antics and respond to teasing with tears, squeals, and retaliations that serve to encourage more teasing. Girls also do their share of showing off; for example, they may see to it that the boys know that most of the girls did better than most of them on a school achievement test. Such showing off and confrontations between the sexes enable elementary-school boys and girls to maintain their interest in each other while they are busy establishing their sex-role identities (97).

Second, school-age children think, wonder, and fantasize about sex a great deal. When boys reach the age of 10 or 11, they enter a period of intense curiosity about sexual anatomy and physiology, intercourse, contraception, and venereal disease. Because boys discuss these matters only

Although preadolescent boys and girls are generally not yet getting involved with each other on a boy-girl basis, there is nothing "latent" about their interest in sex and romance.

among themselves and no longer ask their parents frank and embarrassing questions, adults often do not notice thier upsurge of interest in sexual matters. However, anyone who has observed or can recall from his own experience elementary-school boys clustering with interest around a nude statue in a museum, looking up "dirty" words in the dictionary, poring over sex passages in novels, looking at the centerfold picture in *Playboy,* and using four-letter words or telling dirty jokes can have little doubt as to the insatiability of their sexual curiosity (98, 99).

During the later elementary-school years, girls develop an interest in romance. While not sharing boys' preoccupation with the physical aspects of sex, girls of this age dream of dashing, debonair men who may someday court them; they become ardent followers of magazine, movie, and television love stories; and they develop intense crushes on various national and local idols—pop singers, movie stars, football players—almost anyone other than one of their own age-mates. Often two girlfriends or a larger group of girls will have a crush on the same man; they will talk together for hours about their idol's virtues and endearing shortcomings, collect souvenirs of his activities, and flock to see or be close to him if they have the opportunity. For both sexes, then, the concept of psychosexual latency during middle childhood is accurate only with respect to pleasurable (as opposed to competitive) heterosexual *activities;* heterosexual *interest,* on the other hand, continues to grow steadily during the grade-school years.

FAMILY RELATIONS

The increasing importance of school and peer groups during middle childhood does not diminish the importance of family relationships. Home is still where children are fed and clothed, cared for when they are sick, and hopefully loved no matter what their teachers and peers think of them. Furthermore, many of the individual and peer-group activities of elementary-school children take place at home. They may play stoop-ball on the front steps, set up model trains and chemistry sets in the basement, sprawl on the floor in front of the television set, and occasionally just sit and read, make doll clothes, sort stamps, work on jigsaw puzzles, or play checkers, cards, or Monopoly.

Children who cannot enjoy being at home or around their families may be severely handicapped in their social development. For example, children who feel unloved or rejected by their parents are likely to develop feelings of alienation that only a fortunate combination of pleasurable peer-group and community activities can overcome. If children also feel unwelcome at home ("Play somewhere else; I can't stand the noise, and you make such a mess"), they may develop an acute sense of rootlessness, with no place to go for comfort and refuge. In other cases the home may be too chaotic or dilapidated for children to enjoy being there or inviting their friends over, even though they are free to do so. These children may feel that they are "second-class citizens" among their friends, because they are always playing at someone else's house and do not feel that they can invite anyone to their own home.

In a detailed study of adjustment among school-age children, Love and Kaswan have confirmed that children who are exposed to turmoil at home are more likely than their peers to have behavioral difficulties and be referred for psychological help (92). Fortunately, however, most families are fairly stable, so that the majority of school-age children and their parents remain psychologically close and mutually supportive of each other. Nevertheless, during middle childhood parents and children must do some readjusting to one another.

Parental Adjustment to a School-Age Child

Once children begin school, parents must come to grips with a drastic reduction in their dependency. Mothers in particular need to be aware that "loosening the apron strings" is necessary both for their children's personality development and for their own peace of mind. Most parents, however, although they are somewhat nostalgic about their children's babyhood, share their pride at being ready for school and their pleasure in advancing through the grades.

Those parents who find it difficult to accept the idea of their child arriving at school age and separating from them may sometimes be tempted to delay school ("She's so small and immature; maybe she should wait another year") or to discourage attendance ("You look a little pale today; I think you should stay home and rest"). Such parental actions, especially on the part of the mother, often contribute to *school phobia,* an abnormal development that we discuss in Chapter 14.

If parents can accept their children's increasing independence and absence from home, they will probably find the middle years of childhood as pleasurable for them as for their children (100). School-age children make relatively few demands on their parents; they do not need the close supervision of infants and preschoolers, and they are not agitating for adult status and privileges as adolescents do. Food and shelter, money for the movies, a baseball glove, an item of clothing that "all the kids are wearing," and not having ther parents bother them too much is about all that elementary-school children ask.

The second major adjustment parents must make at this time is deciding how much freedom their elementary-school children should have. Children need enough independence to encourage individuality and initiative on the one hand, but also enough supervision to protect them from real physical dangers and undesirable psychological influences on the other. Like preschoolers, children of this age who are rigidly and excessively controlled by their parents may become withdrawn, unhappy, unspontaneous, and overconformist, lacking in enthusiasm, creativity, and openness to new ideas; or they may become angry, aggressive, and rebellious, rejecting their parents' rules and values. On the other hand, children whose parents are almost totally permissive often fail to develop adequate internal controls and tend to become impulsive, inconsiderate, and potentially antisocial (101–104).

The simple and obvious dos and don'ts with which parents disciplined their preschoolers are replaced by more complicated questions during middle childhood. Parents must decide whether their child can sleep over at a friend's house, ride his or her bicycle in the street, or go swimming in the river. In making such decisions parents must weigh the freedoms they are willing to allow against their child's ability to handle these freedoms, insofar as they can make a determination. As a general rule, school-age children seem to profit most from being given as much freedom as seems warranted by the amount of responsibility and good judgment they have shown in the past.

Reassessment of
Parents by
School-Age
Children

Whereas preschool children view their parents as all-knowing and all-powerful paragons of virtue and better than anyone else's parents, school-age children realize that their parents are only human. They cannot answer all of their questions, and they cannot furnish them all the worldly goods their hearts desire. Parents do not completely control their own destiny, let alone that of the world. They have obligations to employers, customers, and clients; they are responsible to policemen, the Internal Revenue Service, and other civic officials and agencies; and they may even be dependent upon their friends or upon their own parents. At times parents become irrational and lose their temper over little or nothing; at other times they become tearful or depressed in response to apparently minor frustrations and disappointments; sometimes they fail to understand and appreciate the important things in life as seen by a grade-schooler.

As school-age children become aware of these facts of life, they may be temporarily disenchanted with their parents. No longer do parents seem to be supremely capable, informed, and just; rather, their image becomes somewhat tarnished. Their children may feel that they are so unsympathetic, old-fashioned, and out of touch that they become both an adversary and an embarrassment. At this age other children's parents may appear to be more tolerant or successful than their own ("Bob's parents let him have a dog, so why can't we have one?" "Why don't you ever get dressed up nice and go out to parties like Mary's and Jane's parents do?"). Some school-age children develop what is called the **family romance**; they imagine that they are really the offspring of noble or glamorous parents who will return some day to reclaim them from the dull and ordinary people who have only been posing as their mothers and fathers (105–108).

Common though it is, this middle-childhood disenchantment with parents rarely goes beneath the surface. Elementary-school children generally love and respect their parents; although they often criticize and complain about them, they will seldom permit anyone else to do so (109). School-age children are quick to take offense if anyone should say anything unkind about their parents; their loyalty and touchiness about their parents' good name demonstrate that there is a difference between what these youngsters may say and what they really feel about their parents.

Children's surface disenchantment with their parents and to some extent with adults in general carries over into adolescence and is often called the "generation gap." Yet most children's underlying love and respect for their parents also continues into adolescence, so that the generation gap is more of an apparent than a real phenomenon, as we elaborate in Chapter 16.

Essay

THE FEMINIZED CLASSROOM

In her book, *The Feminized Male: Classrooms, White Collars, and the Decline of Manliness,* Patrician Sexton criticized American schools for exerting a feminizing influence on elementary-school boys. Sexton held that the typical classroom rewards passive, conforming, and uncreative behavior while discouraging independence, assertiveness, or any form of disagreement with the teacher. As a result, she concluded, there is a basic conflict between healthy masculinity and academic achievement: boys who do well in school tend to be feminized, whereas those who maintain a firm sense of their masculine identity tend to be academic underachievers (110).

The feminization of elementary schools is frequently blamed on women teachers, who constitute more than 85 percent of all elementary-school teachers in the United States and more than 98 percent of those teaching at the third-grade level or below (111). It is widely believed that women teachers share fewer interests with the boys than with the girls in their classes and that they feel more comfortable relating to the girls because they presumably "understand" them better and because girls tend to be quieter and "better behaved" than boys (112). In support of this belief, numerous studies have found that schoolchildren of both sexes perceive women teachers as favoring girls over boys. There is also consistent evidence that women teachers scold or criticize boys more than girls and that they are more likely to reprimand boys in an angry rather than conversational tone of voice (113–118).

Such findings have led many people to plead for more men teachers in our elementary schools. However, a closer look at the classroom suggests that concern about the sex of the teacher may not be justified. Although women teachers may criticize boys more than girls, they also give them as much if not more praise than girls for performing well in the classroom.

Furthermore, most of a teacher's reprimands are usually aimed at a small group of problem children in the class, most of whom just happen to be boys; thus, a few disruptive boys are likely to account for a disproportionate share of the teacher's criticisms in a typical classroom, whereas boys who are not getting into difficulty are no more likely than girls to be criticized.

Also, even where teachers are observed to be "feminizing" boys, by consistently rewarding passivity, conformity, and other behaviors traditionally associated with the feminine sex role, their actions do not appear to have much impact. Boys exposed to "feminizing" teachers have not been found to become more feminine in their attitudes or behavior. Instead, available evidence suggests that the family and peer group exert more influence on sex-role identity than anything a teacher might say or do (34, 119, 120).

It has also been found that even where men are teaching in the elementary grades, they differ very little from women teachers in the way they treat their students. Men teachers also tend to approve of girls more often than boys and to criticize boys more frequently. Men teachers appear to allow more freedom in the class than do women teachers and to assign boys more often to positions of leadership. However, men teachers are as likely as women teachers to approve passive, dependent behavior in their students. In short, there is no conclusive evidence that a male teacher will improve boys' academic performance or that the sex of the teacher will make any difference in the achievement of either boys or girls (36, 111, 121, 122).

Thus, we see that women teachers do not really discriminate against boys as much as it is sometimes believed, their "feminizing" tendencies do not ordinarily interfere with masculine sex-role development, and they have about the same impact as men teachers on their students. In some cases it might be advantageous for fatherless boys to have a male teacher who can serve as an appropriate sex-role model for them (112). In general, however, incompatibilities between masculinity and academic achievement will not be resolved simply by increasing the number of male elementary-school teachers; what is needed is a change in how schools and the society define a good pupil, so that one can be a successful student and a full-fledged boy at the same time.

It should also be noted that girls, too, can be harmed by a feminized classroom. To the extent that an independent spirit and an inquiring mind are as important for girls as for boys in order to realize their personal and intellectual potential, any situation that encourages conformity, dependence, passivity, and uncritical thinking hampers optimal social and mental development. The challenge for our schools, then, is to impart knowledge, foster self-control, and stimulate creativity in boys and girls alike while also recognizing their need to become industrious, assertive, and self-reliant individuals.

Biography

Sigmund Freud

The twentieth century has sometimes been called "the Freudian Century" or the "Age of the Freudian Revolution." If these designations seem a bit extreme today, they nonetheless reflect the tremendous impact that Sigmund Freud's thinking has had on our conceptions of ourselves and the world. One reason why we hear less about Freud today than people did decades ago is that his ideas have become such an integral part of our thought and language that they seem to be part of our cultural heritage rather than the work of a particular man. People who dismiss Freud today fail to recognize that they have already assimilated much of his teaching as part of their cultural indoctrination.

What was at the heart of the Freudian revolution? Well, for one thing Freud posited the idea of *unconscious motivation,* the notion that we often carry out actions without any conscious awareness of intention. A guest who breaks his hostess's expensive vase may not be aware that his clumsiness is, in part, motivated by a rebuff given him by the hostess in another circumstance. The idea that we behave in nonrational ways struck at the heart of the cherished conception, widely held in the nineteenth century, that we are rational beings. Freud, in contrast, said that we are often under the regulation of motives of which we are not aware.

The position for which Freud was most vilified and which blocked, and still blocks, his acceptance in some quarters, was his insistence on the role of sexuality in neurotic behavior and in the formation of character and personality. Freud conceived of sexuality in the broad sense as an "instinct" with a pattern of gradual build-up and abrupt discharge. Hunger and thirst, as well as bowel and bladder tensions, also show this pattern and, from the Freudian view, have a sexual component. Freud believed that the sexual instinct developed and that it was first centered in the mouth (the oral stage) then in the anus (the anal stage) and finally in the genitals (the genital stage).

In Freud's view the human personality has three major components. One of these, the *id,* consists of the instincts, impulses, and wishes that are part of our biological heritage and are largely self-serving. The *ego,* in contrast, is a set of structures and processes (including intelligence and language) that, in effect, mediate between the id and the external world. For example, the id would urge a person to take what he or she wants whereas the ego would direct the individual to work to attain the desired goal. A third structure of the personality is what Freud called the *superego.* The superego represents the internalization of society's morals, values, and ethics and serves as a higher-order regulator of behavior.

According to Freud, many neurotic disturbances arise as a result of conflict among the id, ego, and superego. For example, most young children love the parent of the opposite sex and would like to be rid of the same-sexed parent (the so-called Oedipus and Electra complexes). A healthy resolution of this conflict is to identify with the same-sexed parent and to attain the opposite-sexed parent vicariously through this identification. A neurotic solution occurs if the child continues to use seductive behavior to attain the opposite-sexed parent while exhibiting hostile behavior to the same-sexed parent.

Freud also introduced the concept of *ego defense*. In order to adapt to reality, the ego has to combat id impulses that might interfere with this adaptation. The mechanisms at the ego's disposal include *denial* (the dieter who says he or she does not want the chocolate cake), *repression* (a kind of unconscious denial wherein the person is not even aware of the unacceptable impulse or desire), and *reaction formation* (or protesting too much, as seen in the child who has been told to refuse a sweet and protests vehemently that he or she does not want it.)

In addition to these and many other theoretical contributions, Freud also devised a technique of psychotherapy based on a process called "free association." In free association the patient says everything that comes to mind no matter how trivial, obscene, or perverted it appears to be. Freud also developed an elaborate theory of dream formation and used the analyses of dreams as part of his psychotherapeutic method.

Sigmund Freud was born in Austria in 1857. He was a bright, curious child who read broadly and voraciously. After some hesitation about what field to enter, he chose medicine, and his first research publications were physiological studies. He became interested, however, in certain disorders—called the neuroses—whose causation provoked some controversy. Some French psychiatrists were saying that certain neurotic conditions, such as hysterical paralysis, were induced by psychological causes and could be cured by hypnosis.

After visiting France, Freud returned to Vienna and began studying some of these "hysterical" subjects himself. Together with Joseph Breuer, Freud published *Studies in Hysteria*. This work gave intimations of his later thinking, but it was not until the publication of *The Interpretation of Dreams* in 1904 that Freud's sexual theory of the neuroses was clearly laid out. Although he had worked in isolation after a break with Breuer, Freud gradually attracted a number of younger psychiatrists, such as Alfred Adler and Carl Gustav Jung, and his work gradually came to be internationally known. Eventually journals devoted to psychoanalytic studies were published and psychoanalytic societies were founded in most of the advanced countries around the world.

After World War I, Freud's fame continued to grow and he attracted students from all over the world. In the early 1920s Freud suffered from a cancer of the jaw that eventually required surgery and a prosethetic device. This device was painful and marred Freud's appearance so that he curtailed his travel. (He visited the United States only once, in 1909, to give a series of lectures at Clark University in Worcester, Massachusetts). He continued his prolific writing and extended his concerns from psychopathology to broader issues such as religion and creativity. The Nazis made Freud's life in Vienna even more difficult and, with the help of friends, he and his family moved to England in 1938. Freud died there a year later.

Summary

Personality and social development in middle childhood is significantly influenced by the fact that children enter school and become increasingly involved in peer-group and community activities. The way in which children learn to cope with the many new academic and interpersonal demands of school will help shape their attitudes toward school and whether they develop a sense of industry or a sense of inferiority.

Children are usually enthusiastic about beginning school and advancing through the grades because it signifies growing up and provides them increasing opportunities to learn and do new things. Whether and how long this enthusiasm continues depends to a large extent upon the kind of school they attend and upon their parents' attitudes toward education. Generally speaking, the more opportunity children have to participate in the classroom and in extracurricular activities and the more the school curriculum is designed to make learning a lively, exciting, and meaningful adventure, the more children are likely to have positive feelings about their school experience. The most effective schools appear to be those that combine certain aspects of traditional, *learning-oriented* education (which aims to impart knowledge) and modern, *student-oriented* education (which aims to help children develop as people).

Children readily identify with their parents' feelings about school and education. Thus, parents who value and speak highly of school foster more positive attitudes about it than do parents whose words or actions show that they attach little importance to it. In general, relatively well-educated, middle-class parents tend to convey more positive attitudes toward school than do less well-educated, lower-class parents. However, there is considerable variation within social classes, and teachers should not assume that lower-class children are universally uninterested in or antagonistic toward school.

Most elementary-school children develop a motivation to achieve, an interest in competition, and feelings of competence. The more each of these is reinforced by success, the more children develop a *sense of industry*—a feeling that they are able to cope with the challenges they face in everyday life; the more they encounter failure, the more children are likely to develop a *sense of inferiority*—a feeling that they are inadequate to meet the challenges of their world.

The way in which parents respond to their children's efforts to learn and do things is the major influence determining whether they feel industrious or inferior. At school these feelings are also influenced by children's abilities and by how their teachers treat them. Being recognized in school for various skills and talents enhances a child's feelings of industry, whereas being ranked near the bottom—in the classroom, the gym class, the music class, and so forth—can reinforce feelings of inferiority. Teachers can encourage feelings of industry by helping their students receive recognition for their special assets and by sparing them embarrassment or humiliation about their limitations; on the other hand, they can make a child feel even more inferior by acting indifferent or insensitive to the child's needs and concerns.

During the elementary-school years children become increasingly involved in peer-group interactions that influence certain aspects of their personality and social development. Youngsters form new perceptions of themselves based on how their classmates see them, and they also assign popularity ratings to each other. Popular children at this age tend to be well-adjusted, friendly, sociable, and outgoing; they are kind and accepting toward others; and they accept the prevailing group standards. Unpopular children, on the other hand, tend to be shy, withdrawn, and not well adjusted; they do not participate in group activities and do not accept the group's standards of conduct; and they are hostile and rejecting toward others.

Although most children eventually become flexible in dealing with people and situations, middle childhood is a period of conformity to group standards. Peer-group influence on what children think, say, and do increases gradually during the elementary-school years, reaching a high point around the beginning of adolescence. Children who have difficulty either in maintaining a flexible interpersonal style or in conforming to certain common behaviors may develop individualistic but inflexible ways of relating to others that become maladaptive during adulthood.

Interpersonal experiences also determine whether elementary-school children develop a sense of *belonging* or of *alienation*. A sense of belonging—a feeling that one is an integral part of a larger society—emerges from enjoyable participation in neighborhood and community as well as peer-group activities. A sense of alienation—a feeling that one is an outsider in one's own society—arises when children are not accepted by their peer group and have no opportunity to participate in neighborhood and community activities.

Finally, the structure of the peer group changes gradually during middle childhood. Informal play groups are common at age 5 or 6, but these are gradually replaced by well-organized and highly structured friendship groups by age 10 or 11, which in turn are followed by "chumships"—a special kind of close relationship between just two boys or two girls. Sequential involvement in these peer relationships helps prepare children for more complex interpersonal relationships that begin during adolescence.

Elementary-school children begin to develop a psychological identity as members of either one sex or the other. Sex-role identity arises from a number of factors—from biological differences between the sexes, from differences in the way parents socialize their sons and daughters, and from children's identification with their same-sexed parent.

Because of school-age children's immature cognitive capacities, however, they tend to form more rigid and exaggerated concepts of sex role than they observe in their parents. As one result of this exaggeration boys and girls usually establish a strict separation in their play groups and in their notions of sex-appropriate activities. This separation has led some observers to suggest that middle childhood is a period of psychosexual "latency." However, boys and girls maintain considerable interest in the physical (the boys) or the romantic (the girls) aspects of relationships between the sexes.

As children mature, they and their parents must make new adjustments to each other. Parents must be able to loosen the apron strings in order for to each other. Parents must be able to loosen the apron strings for group activities, but they must also exert enough discipline and guidance to support their children's continuing to learn moral standards and self-control. Children must make some realistic reassessments of their parents, realizing that they are not the all-knowing, all-powerful individuals they once seemed to be. Although these readjustments may produce superficial tension and disaffection in the family, relations between elementary-school children and their parents usually remain firmly based on underlying feelings of love, trust, and loyalty.

References

1. Stendler, C. B., & Young, N. The impact of beginning first grade upon socialization as reported by mothers. *Child Development,* 1950, **21,** 241–260.
2. Stendler, C. B., & Young, N. Impact of first grade entrance upon the socialization of the child: Changes after eight months of school. *Child Development,* 1951, **22,** 113–152.
3. White House Conference on Children. *Profiles of children.* Washington, D.C.: U.S. Department of Health, Education and Welfare, 1970.
4. Barker, G. R., & Gump, P. V. *Big school, small school.* Stanford, Calif.: Stanford University Press, 1964.
5. Gump, P. V. Ecological psychology and children. In E. M. Hetherington (Ed.), *Review of child development research.* Vol. 5. Chicago: University of Chicago Press, 1975.
6. Baird, L. L. Big school, small school: A critical examination of the hypothesis. *Journal of Educational Psychology,* 1969, **60,** 253–260.
7. Wicker, A. W. Undermanning, performances, and students' subjective experiences in behavior settings of large and small high schools. *Journal of Personality and Social Psychology,* 1968, **10,** 255–261.
8. Willems, E. P. Sense of obligation to high school activities as related to school size and marginality of student. *Child Development,* 1967, **38,** 1247–1260.
9. Silberman, C. E. *Crisis in the classroom.* New York: Random House, 1970.
10. Blom, G. E., Waite, R. R., & Zimet, S. G. A motivational content analysis of children's primers. In P. H. Mussen, J. J. Conger, & J. Kagan (Eds.), *Readings in child development and personality.* New York: Harper, 1970.

11. Waite, R. R., Blom, G. E., Zimet, S. G., & Edge, S. First-grade reading textbooks. *Elementary School Journal,* 1967, **67,** 366–374.

12. Zimet, S. G. Children's interest and story preferences: A critical review of the literature. *Elementary School Journal,* 1966, **67,** 123–130.

13. Zimet, S. G. (Ed.) *What children read in school.* New York: Grune & Stratton, 1972.

14. Wiberg, J. L., & Trost, M. A comparison between the content of first grade primers and free choice library selections made by first grade students. *Elementary English,* 1970, **47,** 792–798.

15. Asher, S., & Markell, R. A. Sex differences on comprehension of high and low interest reading material. *Journal of Educational Psychology,* 1974, **66,** 680–687.

16. Minuchin, P., Biber, B., Shapiro, E., & Zimiles, H. *The psychological impact of school experience.* New York: Basic Books, 1969.

17. Katkovsky, W., Preston, A., & Crandall, V. J. Parents' attitudes toward their personal achievements and toward the achievement behaviors of their children. *Journal of Genetic Psychology,* 1964, **104,** 67–82.

18. Katkovsky, W., Preston, A., & Crandall, V. J. Parents' achievement attitudes and their behavior with their children in achievement situations. *Journal of Genetic Psychology,* 1964, **104,** 105–121.

19. Crandall, V. C. The Fels study: Some contributions to personality development and achievement in childhood and adulthood. *Seminars in Psychiatry,* 1972, **4,** 383–397.

20. Hess, R., & Shipman, V. Cognitive elements in maternal behavior. In J. Hill (Ed.), *Minnesota symposium on child psychology.* Minneapolis: University of Minnesota Press, 1967.

21. Katz, I. The socialization of academic motivation in minority group children. *Nebraska Symposium on Motivation,* 1967, **15,** 133–191.

22. Schultz, C. B., & Aurbach, H. A. The usefulness of cumulative deprivation as an explanation of educational deficiencies. *Merrill-Palmer Quarterly,* 1971, **17,** 27–39.

23. Richer, S. Middle-class bias of schools: Fact or fancy? *Sociology of Education,* 1974, **47,** 523–534.

24. Greenberg, J. W., & Davidson, H. H. Home background and school achievement of black urban ghetto children. *American Journal of Orthospychiatry,* 1972, **42,** 803–810.

25. Slaughter, D. T. Parental potency and the achievements of inner-city black children. *American Journal of Orthopsychiatry,* 1970, **40,** 433–440.

26. Erikson, E. H. *Childhood and society.* (2nd ed.) New York: Norton, 1963.

27. Coopersmith, S. *The antecedents of self-esteem.* San Francisco: W. H. Freeman, 1967.

28. Ruble, D. N., Feldman, N. S., & Boggiano, A. K. Social comparison between young children in achievement situations. *Developmental Psychology,* 1976, **12,** 192–197.

29. Veroff, J. Social comparison and the development of achievement motivation. In C. P. Smith (Ed.), *Achievement-related motives in children.* New York: Russell Sage, 1969.

30. Proshansky, H. M. The development of intergroup attitudes. In L. W. Hoffman & M. L. Hoffman (Eds.), *Review of child development research.* Vol. 2. New York: Russell Sage, 1966.

31. Glidewell, J. S., Kantor, M. B., Smith, L. M., & Stringer, L. A. Socialization and social structure in the classroom. In M. L. Hoffman & L. W. Hoffman (Eds.), *Review of child development research.* Vol. I. New York: Russell Sage, 1964.

32. Anderson, H. E., White, W. F., & Wash, J. A. Generalized effects of praise and reproof. *Journal of Educational Psychology,* 1966, **17,** 169–173.

33. Crandall, V. C., Katkovsky, W., & Preston, A. Motivational and ability determinants of young children's intellectual and achievement behaviors. *Child Development,* 1962, **33,** 643–661.

34. Silberman, M. Behavioral expression of teachers' attitudes and actions towards elementary school students. *Journal of Educational Psychology,* 1969, **60,** 402–407.

35. Silberman, M. Teachers' attitudes and actions toward their students. In M. Silberman (Ed.), *The experience of schooling.* New York: Holt, 1971.

36. Brophy, J. E., & Good, T. L. *Teacher-student relationships: Causes and consequences.* New York: Holt, 1974.

37. Everston, C., Brophy, J., & Good, T. Communication of teacher expectations: Second grade. Report No. 92, Research and Development Center for Teacher Education, University of Texas at Austin, 1973.

38. Good, T., & Brophy, J. Behavioral expression of teacher attitudes. *Journal of Educational Psychology,* 1972, **63,** 617–624.

39. Rosenthal, R., & Jacobsen, L. Teachers' expectancies: Determinants of pupils' IQ gains. *Psychological Reports,* 1966, **19,** 115–118.

40. Rosenthal, R., & Jacobsen, L. *Pygmalion in the classroom.* New York: Holt, 1968.

41. Rosenthal, R. The pygmalion effect lives. *Psychology Today,* 1973, 46–63.

42. Alpert, J. L. Teacher behavior and pupil performance: Reconsiderations of the mediation of Pygmalion effects. *Journal of Educational Research,* 1975, **69,** 53–57.

43. Elashoff, J. D., & Snow, R. E. *Pygmalion reconsidered.* Worthington, Ohio: Charles A. Jones, 1971.

44. Jensen, A. R. Review of Pygmalion in the classroom. *American Scientist,* 1969, **51,** 44–45.

45. Thorndike, R. L. Review of R. Rosenthal and L. Jacobsen, ''Pygmalion in the classroom.'' *American Educational Research Journal,* 1968, **5,** 708–711.

46. Bradley, F. O., & Newhouse, R. C. Sociometric choice and self perception of upper elementary school children. *Psychology in the Schools,* 1975, **12,** 219–222.

47. Campbell, J. D. Peer relations in childhood. In M. L. Hoffman & L. W. Hoffman (Eds.), *Review of child development research.* Vol. 1. New York: Russell Sage, 1964.

48. Campbell, J. D., & Yarrow, M. R. Perceptual and social correlates of social effectiveness. *Sociometry,* 1961, **24,** 1–20.

49. Commoss, H. H. Some characteristics related to social isolation of second grade children. *Journal of Educational Psychology,* 1962, **53,** 38–42.

50. Hartup, W. W. Peer interaction and social organization. In P. H. Mussen (Ed.), *Carmichael's manual of child psychology.* Vol. 2. New York: Wiley, 1970.

51. Horowitz, F. D. The relationship of anxiety, self-concept, and sociometric status among fourth, fifth, and sixth grade children. *Journal of Abnormal and Social Psychology,* 1962, **65,** 212–214.

52. Toigo, R. Social status and schoolroom aggression in third-grade children. *Genetic Psychology Monographs,* 1965, **71,** 221–268.

53. Winder, C. L., & Rau, L. Parental attitudes associated with social deviance in preadolescent boys. *Journal of Abnormal and Social Psychology,* 1962, **64,** 418–424.

54. Roff, M., Sells, S. B., & Golden, M. M. *Social adjustment and personality development in children.* Minneapolis: University of Minnesota Press, 1972.

55. Tuddenham, R. D. Studies in reputation. III. Correlates of popularity among elementary school children. *Journal of Educational Psychology,* 1951, **42,** 257–276.

56. Muma, J. R. Peer evaluation and academic performance. *Personnel Guidance Journal,* 1965, **44,** 405–409.

57. Northway, M. L., & Rooks, M. McC. Creativity and sociometric status in children. *Sociometry,* 1956, **18,** 450–457.

58. Yamamoto, L., Lembright, M. L., & Corrigan, A. M. Intelligence, creative thinking, and sociometric choice among fifth-grade children. *Journal of Experimental Education,* 1966, **34,** 83–89.

59. Lerner, R. M., & Gellert, E. Body build identification, preference, and aversion in children. *Developmental Psychology,* 1969, **1,** 456–462.

60. Lerner, R. M., & Schroeder, C. Physique identification, preference, and aversion in kindergarten children. *Developmental Psychology,* 1971, **5,** 538.

61. Staffieri, J. R. A study of social stereotype of body image in children. *Journal of Personality and Social Psychology,* 1967, **7,** 101–104.

62. Costanzo, P. R., & Shaw, M. E. Conformity as a function of age level. *Child Development,* 1966, **37,** 967–975.

63. Allen, V. L., & Newston, D. The development of conformity and independence. *Journal of Personality and Social Psychology,* 1972, **22,** 18–30.

64. Costanzo, P. R. Conformity development as a function of self-blame. *Journal of Personality and Social Psychology,* 1970, **14,** 366–374.

65. Harvey, O. J., & Rutherford, J. Status in the informal group: Influence and influencibility at differing age levels. *Child Development,* 1960, **31,** 377–385.

66. McConnell, T. R. Suggestibility in children as a function of chronological age. *Journal of Abnormal and Social Psychology,* 1963, **67,** 286–289.

67. Boyd, R. E. Conformity reduction in adolescence. *Adolescence,* 1975, **10,** 297–300.

68. Douvan, E., & Adelson, J. *The adolescent experience*. New York: Wiley, 1966.
69. Condry, J., & Siman, M. L. Characteristics of peer and adult-oriented children. *Journal of Marriage and the Family*, 1974, **36**, 543–554.
70. Keniston, K. *The uncommitted: Alienated youth in American society*. New York: Harcourt, 1965.
71. Mead, M. *Culture and commitment: A study of the generation gap*. New York: Doubleday, 1970.
72. Sherif, M., Harvey, O. J., White, B. J., Hood, W. R., & Sherif, C. W. *Intergroup conflict and cooperation: The Robbers Cave experiment*. Norman: University of Oklahoma Press, 1961.
73. Sullivan, H. S. *The interpersonal theory of psychiatry*. New York: Norton, 1953.
74. Hartup, W. W. The origins of friendships. In M. Lewis & L. A. Rosenblum (Eds.), *Friendship and peer relations*. New York: Wiley, 1975.
75. Maas, H. S. Preadolescent peer relations and adult intimacy. *Psychiatry*, 1968, **31**, 161–172.
76. Maccoby, E. E. & Jacklin, C. N. *The psychology of sex differences*. Stanford, Calif.: Stanford University Press, 1974.
77. Buss, A. H., & Plomin, R. *A temperament theory of personality development*. New York: Wiley, 1975.
78. Hoffman, M. L., & Saltzstein, H. D. Parent discipline and the child's moral development. *Journal of Personality and Social Psychology*, 1967, **5**, 45–57.
79. Minton, C., Kagan, J., & Levine, J. A. Maternal control and obedience in the two-year-old. *Child Development*, 1971, **42**, 1873–1894.
80. Moss, H. A. Sex, age, and state as determinants of mother-infant interaction. *Merrill-Palmer Quarterly*, 1967, **13**, 19–36.
81. Yarrow, L. J., Rubenstein, J. L., & Pedersen, F. A. Dimensions of early stimulation: *Merrill-Palmer Quarterly*, 1972, **18**, 205–218.
82. Allaman, J. D., Joyce, C. S., & Crandall, V. C. The antecedents of social desirability response tendencies of children and young adults. *Child Development*, 1972, **43**, 1135–1160.
83. Baumrind, D. Current patterns of parental authority. *Developmental Psychology Monographs*, 1971, **4**, Part 2, 1–103.
84. Hatfield, J. S., Ferguson, L. R., & Alpert, R. Mother-child interactions and the socialization process. *Child Development*, 1967, **38**, 365–414.
85. Sears, R. R., Maccoby, E. E., & Levin, H. *Patterns of child rearing*. Stanford, Calif.: Stanford University Press, 1957.
86. Looft, W. R. Sex differences in the expression of vocational aspirations by elementary school children. *Developmental Psychology*, 1971, **5**, 366.
87. Hewitt, L. S. Age and sex differences in the vocational aspirations of elementary school children. *Journal of Social Psychology*, 1975, **96**, 173–177.
88. Scheresky, R. The gender factor in six- to ten-year-old children's views of occupational roles. *Psychological Reports*, 1976, **38**, 1207–1210.
89. Williams, J. E., Bennett, S. M., & Best, D. L. Awareness and expression of sex stereotypes in young children. *Developmental Psychology*, 1975, **11**, 635–642.
90. Masters, J. C., & Wilkinson, A. Consensual and discriminative stereotypy of sex-type judgments by parents and children. *Child Development*, 1976, **47**, 208–217.
91. Block, J., von der Lippe, A., & Block, J. H. Sex-role and socialization patterns: Some personality concomitants and environmental antecedents. *Journal of Consulting and Clinical Psychology*, 1973, **41**, 321–341.
92. Love, L. R., & Kaswan, J. W. *Troubled children: Their families, schools and treatments*. New York: Wiley, 1974.
93. Guardo, C. J., & Bohan, J. B. Development of a sense of self-identity in children. *Child Development*, 1971, **42**, 1909–1921.
94. Kohlberg, L. A cognitive-developmental analysis of children's sex-role concepts and attitudes. In E. E. Maccoby (Ed.), *The development of sex differences*. Stanford, Calif.: Stanford University Press, 1966.
95. Freud, S. (1905) *Three essays on the theory of sexuality*. Standard Edition, Vol. VII. London: Hogarth, 1953.
96. Sarnoff, C. *Latency*. New York: Aronson, 1976.
97. Reese, H. W. Attitudes toward the opposite sex in late childhood. *Merrill-Palmer Quarterly*, 1966, **12**, 157–163.

98. Renshaw, D. C. Sexuality in children. *Medical Aspects of Human Sexuality,* 1971, **5,** 62–74.

99. Rutter, M. Normal psychosexual development. *Journal of Child Psychology and Psychiatry,* 1971, **11,** 259–283.

100. Kestenberg, J. S. The effect on parents of the child's transition into and out of latency. In E. J. Anthony (Ed.), *Parenthood.* Boston: Little, Brown, 1970.

101. Feshbach, S. Aggression. In P. H. Mussen (Ed.), *Carmichael's manual of child psychology.* Vol. 2. New York: Wiley, 1970.

102. Hoffman, M. L. Moral development. In P. H. Mussen (Ed.), *Carmichael's manual of child psychology.* Vol. 2. New York: Wiley, 1970.

103. MacDonald, A. P. Internal-external locus of control: Parental antecedents. *Journal of Consulting and Clinical Psychology,* 1971, **37,** 141–147.

104. Phares, E. J. *Locus of control in personality.* Morristown, N.J.: General Learning Press, 1976.

105. Davidson, A., & Fay, J. Fantasy in middle childhood. In M. R. Haworth (Ed.), *Child psychotherapy.* New York: Basic Books, 1964.

106. Freud, S. (1909) *Family romances.* Standard Edition, Vol. IX. London: Hogarth, 1959.

107. Kaplan, L. J. The concept of the family romance. *Psychoanalytic Review,* 1974, **61,** 169–202.

108. Lehrman, P. R. The fantasy of not belonging to one's family. *Archives of Neurology and Psychiatry,* 1927, **18,** 1015–1023.

109. Williams, J. W., & Stith, M. *Middle childhood: Behavior and development.* New York: Macmillan, 1974.

110. Sexton, P. C. *The feminized male: Classrooms, white collars, and the decline of manliness.* New York: Random House, 1969.

111. Lee, P. C., & Wolinsky, A. L. Male teachers of young children: A preliminary empirical study. *Young Children,* 1973, **28,** 342–352.

112. Biller, H. B. Paternal deprivation, cognitive functioning, and the feminized classroom. In A. Davids (Ed.), *Child personality and psychopathology.* New York: Wiley, 1974.

113. Brophy, J., & Good, T. Teachers' communication of differential expectation for children's classroom performance: Some behavioral data. *Journal of Educational Psychology,* 1970, **61,** 365–374.

114. Davis, O., & Slobodian, J. Teacher behavior towards boys and girls during first grade reading instruction. *American Educational Research Journal,* 1967, **4,** 261–269.

115. Everston, C., Brophy, J., & Good, T. Communication of teacher expectations: First grade. Report No. 91, Research and Development Center for Teacher Education, University of Texas at Austin, 1972.

116. Jackson, P., & Lahaderne, H. Inequalities of teacher-pupil contacts. *Psychology in the Schools,* 1967, **4,** 204–211.

117. Lippitt, R., & Gold, M. Classroom and social structure as a mental health problem. *Journal of Social Issues,* 1959, **15,** 40–49.

118. Meyer, W., & Thompson, G. Sex differences in the distribution of teacher approval and disapproval among sixth-grade children. *Journal of Educational Psychology,* 1956, **47,** 385–396.

119. Delefes, P., & Jackson, B. Teacher-pupil interaction as a function of location in the classroom. *Psychology in the Schools,* 1972, **9,** 119–123.

120. Fagot, B. I., & Patterson, G. An in vivo analysis of reinforcing contingencies for sex-role behaviors in pre-school child. *Developmental Psychology,* 1969, **1,** 563–568.

121. Peterson, J. Effects of sex of E and sex of S in the first and fifth grade children's paired-associate learning. *Journal of Educational Research,* 1972, **66,** 81–84.

122. Etaugh, C., & Hughes, V. Teacher's evaluations of sex typed behaviors in children: The role of teacher, sex, and school setting. *Developmental Psychology,* 1975, **11,** 394–395.

13 | Child Variations

COGNITIVE PROCESSES

School Achievement

Creativity

Cognitive Styles

SEX DIFFERENCES

Sex Differences in Academic Achievement

Sex Differences in Cognitive Styles

Sex-Role Stereotyping

FAMILY CONFIGURATION

Family Size, Intelligence, and Achievement

Maternal Employment

ETHNIC-GROUP DIFFERENCES

Academic Achievement in American Indian Children

Self-Esteem

CULTURAL DIFFERENCES

Conservation Behavior

Cognitive Style

Pictorial Depth Perception

ESSAY

Curriculum-Disabled Children

SUMMARY

REFERENCES

During the years of middle childhood individual differences in intelligence, verbal ability, and so forth become more prominent. In addition, as children begin school, new avenues for the expression of individual differences become available. Differences between boys and girls also become more varied at this time. Finally, the effects of family configuration, of socioeconomic level, and of cultural differences now appear not only in methods of child rearing but also in academic achievement.

COGNITIVE PROCESSES

In general, intelligence tends to be positively correlated with school achievement, although many bright children do poor schoolwork while some of average intelligence do extremely well in school. We will discuss some of the factors other than intelligence that are important for academic achievement. The relationship of creativity to intelligence is even more complex because a high IQ is not required for high creativity. We will examine some of the patterns of intelligence and creativity and some of the suggestions researchers have made for encouraging creativity at home and at school.

School Achievement

During elementary-school years it is important for children to learn how to read, write, and do arithmetic (1, 2) because these skills are required for all later academic achievement. As we suggested in earlier chapters, school success and school failure have to do with much more than sheer intellectual ability.

Achievement Motivation.   One important ingredient in school success is a child's motivation to achieve, to do well in whatever he or she undertakes, including schoolwork. This type of motivation has been extensively explored by David O. C. McClelland and his colleagues (3). To measure achievement they used a series of pictures and asked their subjects to tell a story about each one. The subjects who wrote or told stories emphasizing success were described as being high in need for achievement (*n*-achievement) while those whose stories did not show much interest in success were described as low in *n*-achievement.

Studies have shown that children of all ages who score high on achievement motivation do better on a variety of academic tasks than those who demonstrate low achievement motivation (4–6). For example, children who showed high *n*-achievement were more persistent and thus more likely to reach a solution on a problem-solving task than was true for those with low achievement motivation. The subjects with high *n*-achievement were also more likely than those with low *n*-achievement to continue to work at tasks even when there was no outside pressure or monitoring to do so (4).

It is generally assumed that achievement motivation is not inborn, but is learned from one's parents and family. A number of studies have suggested what parental actions and attitudes encourage high *n*-achievement in children. For example, middle-class mothers with small families tend to have children with high *n*-achievement (7). Apparently these mothers make demands on their sons for independence and mastery at an earlier age than do mothers who have larger families and smaller incomes (8).

Can achievement motivation be taught at school or elsewhere? Several studies suggest that it can. In one investigation, children from low-income black families competed in games and were taught to reflect upon their performance; they were helped to understand their own strengths and weaknesses in such competition, how to be more realistic in choosing their goals, how to decide what actions to take in order to reach their goals, and how to determine whether their goals were being reached. The children who received this training improved their achievement motivation and had a greater control over their environment. Their schoolwork also improved (9). In another, similar study, adolescents from different socioeconomic levels were given achievement motivation training. The effects of this training are shown in Figure 13.1 (147).

A less direct approach to teaching achievement motivation was taken in a study where children were allowed to evaluate themselves (10). The subjects for the study were two third-grade arithmetic classes that were using a programmed curriculum. As part of the program, the children usually took a test after completing each unit in their workbooks. Ordinarily, the teacher graded the tests, but for this experiment, the children were allowed to evaluate their own performance and to proceed to the next unit

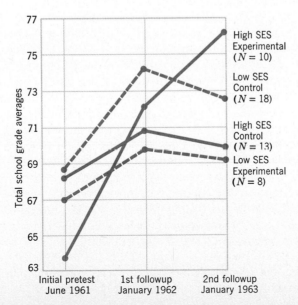

Figure 13.1 Effects of achievement-motivation training on average school grades for children at different S.E.S. levels. (*Source.* Kolb, D. A. Achievement motivation training for underachieving high-school boys. *Journal of Personality and Social Psychology,* 1965, **2,** 783–792, 301–304.)

High SES Experimental (*N* = 10)

Low SES Control (*N* = 18)

High SES Control (*N* = 13)

Low SES Experimental (*N* = 8)

Total school grade averages

Initial pretest June 1961   1st followup January 1962   2nd followup January 1963 if they had mastered the preceding one. It was found that children passed more tests and earned higher scores when they evaluated themselves than when the teacher did so. Apparently, allowing children to take some responsibility for their own learning enhances achievement motivation.

Level of Aspiration. Another factor that contributes to success in school is the child's level of aspiration—his or her expectation about success or failure. In general this level of aspiration depends upon the child's past experience, but the effects of past experience are not always simple and direct. As one might suspect, children who have consistently met with success in their schoolwork tend to aim just above the level of their past achievements (11, 12). However, children who have met consistent failure tend to set their goals either much too high or much too low. Possibly the fears and anxieties associated with failure make youngsters unrealistic about their abilities. Studies have shown that failure-oriented persons tend to choose either very high- or very low-risk tasks (13); these people tend to raise their level of aspiration after failure and to lower it after success (14).

Basically, the failure-oriented person comes to believe that he or she has no control over events—that success and failure are solely a matter of chance. This point of view is comforting in that the individual does not need to feel responsible for failure. It also makes the world appear to be a game of chance. When one bets on dice, roulette, or the horses, one feels that each failure is a prelude to success. And since success is arbitrary and improbable, when it occurs it means that the person's next efforts are likely to be met with failure. Thus, it is not surprising that poor people (who have low levels of aspiration about getting rich) buy lottery tickets and play the horses although their chances of winning are very small indeed.

Children who frequently fail in school are likely to take risks, such as offering to do the most difficult projects or problems, that seem far removed from their actual abilities. These actions are motivated by fear and anxiety and must be understood as defensive rather than as reality-oriented. They serve to protect the child in his or her belief that success is, after all, but a matter of chance and has nothing to do with ability or skill. Because repeated failure can be so permanently destructive, it would be desirable if every child could experience at least some success on a regular basis at home and at school.

Sociocultural Factors. Considerable evidence exists that children from low-income families do not perform as well academically as children from middle-income families (15, 16). We have already indicated in Chapter 12 that the reasons for this phenomenon are complex; it cannot be explained simply by saying that middle-income people are brighter than lower-income people. Even if this were true (and we are not convinced of this), it still would not explain the lower academic achievement of the poor. Success in school, as we have just seen, depends upon various factors such as motivation and level of achievement, as well as intelligence.

In the area of motivation, R. J. Havighurst (17) has suggested that lower-income families have different reward systems than do middle-income families, and these reward systems are not often used by middle-income teachers. For example, children from low-income families interpret punishment as a sign of love and affection; when they are not punished, they may lose respect for their teachers (18). Middle-class children tend to be more responsive to verbal rewards whereas lower-class children may be more responsive to concrete or tangible rewards (19).

Many low-income families in America are also from minority groups; some children from these groups are bilingual. This is true not only for Spanish American, Chinese American, and American Indian children, but for black children as well. Black children learn a complex dialect that differs substantially in its grammar, vocabulary, and syntax from standard English (20–22). The poor academic achievement of many low-income children could be due, at least in part, to their problems with standard English.

The importance of recognizing a child's native language was acknowledged at the national level by the Bilingual Education Act of 1968. This act calls for the teaching of curricula in both a child's native language and standard English. Although there are controversies about the value of bilingual education and about how it should be put into practice, there is at least a recognition now of the problems of bilingual children. Some bilingual programs in the United States and in Canada have been quite successful in teaching children to be proficient in speaking and reading English or French without discouraging the use of the children's first language (23, 24).

Creativity

Creativity is a difficult concept to define. It may mean the use of such processes as **divergent thinking**—thinking in unconventional directions. It may mean the ability to generate different ideas—to think of alternate uses for familiar objects and alternative solutions to problems. Creative processes, however, can only be understood by means of their end results—the actual ideas, products, and solutions that are developed. Whether a particular product is indeed "creative" or "original" requires social judgment, which is subject to error. The painter whose work is not appreciated until after his death is a case in point. Creativity thus always has a social, as well as an individual, dimension.

Psychologists have measured creativity in many different ways. Mednick (25), for example, has devised a Remote Associates Test (RAT) for measuring a person's creative potential. One item from this test is as follows:

(1) rat   blue   cottage

The subject is asked to find a fourth word that would modify each of the three given words and an associative link between them. In this instance the word "cheese" serves that purpose. Here are some other examples for you to try:

(2) surprise   line   birthday
(3) wheel   electric   high
(4) out   dog   cat
*(5) railroad   girl   class**

There are two 30-item forms for this test, and a subject's creativity score is the total number of correct answers on one or the other form (25).**

Wallach and Kogan (26) took a somewhat different approach to measuring creativity in children. They used a variety of techniques including story completion, asking children to find similarities among diverse objects, and asking children to describe various kinds of drawings. Figure 13.2 shows some of the figures employed by Wallach and Kogan as well as some of the more and less creative replies. In general Wallach and Kogan found (as have others [27, 28]) that creativity and intelligence are not highly correlated.

*The answers are: (2) party; (3) chair or wire; (4) house; and, (5) working.
**The items here are not from either form.

Albert Einstein did poorly in school. He provides a good example of the fact that school performance is not always a valid indication of intellectual ability and creativity. (New York Times)

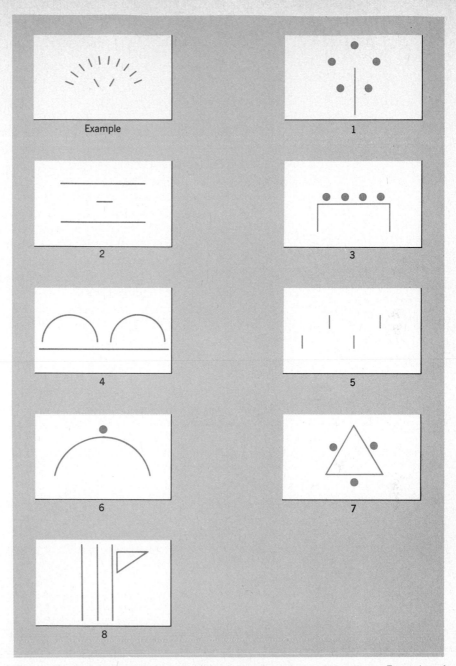

Figure 13.2 Figures used to assess children's creative response to patterns. Examples of creative and conventional responses are given below. (*Source.* Wallach, M. A. and Kogan, N. *Modes of thinking in young children.* New York: Holt, Rinehart and Winston, 1965.)

Item	Creative Response	Conventional Response
1	Lolipop bursting into pieces	Flower
3	Foot and toes	Table with things on top
4	Two haystacks on a flying carpet	Two igloos
5	Five worms hanging	Raindrops
7	Three mice eating a piece of cheese	Three people sitting around a table

Although the products of creative individuals are greatly valued by society, creative individuals are often discriminated against. Apparently such discrimination begins in elementary school. Teachers may be made very uncomfortable by a child who is constantly asking original and difficult questions. Creative children pose a challenge to teachers who, if they are insecure, see such children as a threat (29). In general, therefore, teachers prefer students who are highly intelligent to those who are highly creative.

And yet, teachers can learn to appreciate and to encourage creativity in their students. In an elaborate study, Olton and Crutchfield (30) taught a group of fifth-grade children certain productive thinking techniques. The children were given detective-mystery-type problems and then they were taught how to generate new ideas—particularly novel ones—how to evaluate solutions, how to look at problems in new ways, and so forth. The results of the program (shown in Table 13.1) were quite dramatic, and children who went through the training were more creative than those who had not. As this and other studies (31–33) indicate, certain aspects of creative thinking can be taught.

Cognitive Styles

In the past 20 or 30 years, psychologists have begun to look at differences in the way people process information and deal with their environment. These individual differences have come to be called "cognitive styles." The styles that have been studied the most include field independence/dependence, impulsivity/reflectivity, and locus of control (or internality/externality). Work on each of these styles has been done with elementary-school children.

Field Independence/Dependence. This cognitive style, which has been described by H. Witkin and his associates (34, 35), pertains to the way in which individuals orient themselves with respect to the environment. The "field independent" person tends to rely upon inner cues

Table 13.1 Productive Thinking Scores for Children Who Had and Did Not Have Instruction in Productive Thinking

Test Battery	Instruction Mean Scores	Control Mean Scores
Pretest	2.36	2.52
Posttest	7.12	4.76
Follow-up	5.20	3.40

Source: Olton, R. M., & Crutchfield, R. S. Developing the skills of productive thinking. In P. H. Mussen, J. Langer, & M. Covington, (Eds.), *Trends and issues in developmental psychology.* New York: Holt, 1969.

whereas the "field dependent" person looks for environmental cues for guidance. Witkin first became aware of this system when he was studying pilots during World War II. Some could fly literally by the "seat of their pants," while others required external cues, horizons, and so forth to orient themselves in space. In earlier Chapters (1, 9) we have discussed the Children's Embedded Figure Test, which assesses field dependency/independence in children.

Field independence has been related to several other factors. Field-independent children are more achievement-oriented and independent in the classroom than are field-dependent children (36). The mothers of field-independent children also have a greater tendency to encourage them to be independent and to strive for achievement than do mothers of field-dependent children (35). There is also a developmental dimension to field independence, most children become more field independent as they grow older (35).

Impulsivity/Reflectivity. When confronted with a problem, some children deal with it immediately without examination, whereas others think about it before they act. In other words, some children act impulsively, while others act reflectively. This dimension of cognitive functioning has been extensively explored by Jerome Kagan and his associates (38, 39). Other investigators have also studied the correlates of this dimension (for example, 40–43), and there is now an extensive body of literature on the behaviors and achievements that are associated with impulsivity/reflectivity.

The most common measure of impulsivity/reflectivity is the Matching Familiar Figures Test (MFFT); some of its examples are shown in Figure 13.3. The subject is asked to find a figure that is identical to a standard one from among a group of figures that closely resemble it. Clearly, to be successful, the subject must compare the figures carefully before making a judgment. Two measures are taken from children's responses. **Latency** is the time required by the child to complete the test. **Errors** are simply the number of mistakes the child makes. Impulsive children have short latencies and make many errors, whereas reflective children show the reverse pattern.

Studies using the MFFT have demonstrated that impulsive children make more mistakes than reflective children on serial-learning tasks (44), discrimination-learning tasks (45), and inductive-reasoning tasks (46). In a study of humor (47), reflective children showed greater understanding of the humorous situations, but impulsive children showed more spontaneous mirth. In solving problems reflective children can process information more efficiently than impulsive children (48). With appropriate training, however, children can become more reflective and less impulsive (for example, 49, 50).

Some investigators (51) have criticized the MFFT, saying that it measures only a very general dimension of human functioning. Others (52)

Figure 13.3 An item from the Matching Familiar Figures Test (MFFT). The top picture is the "standard" for which a correct match must be found. (*Source.* Kagan, J. Reflection-Impulsivity: The generality and dynamics of conceptual tempo. *Journal of Abnormal Psychology,* 1966, **71,** 17–24.)

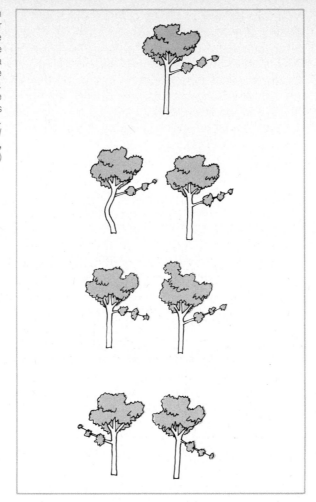

present evidence that the MFFT measures a very specific trait and not a general one. Still others demonstrate that there are statistical difficulties in using the MFFT (53). The only point on which everyone who has used the MFFT agrees is that it measures a fairly consistent individual difference even though no one is quite sure just how that difference should be interpreted.

Locus of Control. One of the cognitive styles that was described some 20 years ago by Julian Rotter (54) is only now receiving attention (55). **Locus of control**, which we mentioned in our earlier discussion of the effects of parental discipline, "refers to the degree to which individuals perceive the events in their lives as being a consequence of their own actions and thereby controllable (inner control), or as being unrelated to their own behaviors and therefore beyond personal control (external control)" (55, p. 2).

Locus of control is usually measured by a pencil-and-paper test called the Internal-External (I-E) Scale. There are, however, several different I-E scales, both for children and adults. The following items are taken from a scale for preschool and elementary-school children (56):

1. *Do you believe that you can stop yourself from catching cold?*
2. *Do you feel that getting the teacher to like you is very important?*
3. *Do you have a good luck charm?*
4. *Are you often blamed for things that are not your fault?*

As one might guess; the child who answers "yes" to the first two items and "no" to the last two has an internal orientation. By contrast, the child who answers "no" to the first two items and "yes" to the last two has an external orientation.

Among elementary-school children locus of control is related to a variety of behaviors. In one study (57), internal children showed a greater ability to delay gratification than did external children. The internal children chose a slightly larger reward (7 pennies as opposed to 5) that was presented after a somewhat longer period of time than the smaller reward. And a number of studies have shown that internality is generally associated with successful school achievement (for example, 58–60).

In a study to measure locus of control among black, white, and Spanish American children in grades 2, 4, and 6, there were age and group differences. Children became more internal as they grew older. Also, white children gave more internal responses than either black or Spanish American children, and children from well-to-do families were more internal than children from less well-to-do families (61). These findings may be related to culturally and socioeconomically linked child-rearing practices. In another investigation (62), it was found that boys who scored high in externality had parents who were highly directive; boys who scored high in internality usually had less directive parents. Interestingly, it was generally the mother who was the more directive parent.

Locus of control, then, like field independence/dependence and impulsivity/reflectivity, appears to be a fairly general dimension of behavior for both children and adults. But the close relationship between these cognitive styles and child-rearing practices, together with the fact that these styles can be taught, suggests that they may have more to do with social conditioning than with innate differences in personality.

SEX DIFFERENCES

During middle childhood, sex differences begin to appear in such areas as school achievement and cognitive style, and they become more prominent in such personality dimensions as assertiveness. We will also examine some of the ways in which these differences are encouraged, specifically the sex-role stereotyping by schools, parents, and the media.

Sex Differences in Academic Achievement

Not all investigators agree on the extent, if any, of sex differences in academic achievement. Furthermore, such factors as the women's liberation movement may be eliminating the differences that existed even a decade ago. Accordingly, the differences mentioned below should be viewed as pertaining to those of the past, and not necessarily to those that exist today or that will be found tomorrow.

Up until about the mid-1960s it was generally agreed that girls received higher grades in school than did boys, at least through high school (63–65). More recently, Maccoby and Jacklin (66) concluded that sex differences in academic achievement do not really become prominent until just before adolescence: "It is at about age 10 or 11 that girls begin to come into their own in verbal performance. From this age through the high school and college years we find them outscoring boys in a variety of verbal skills" (66, p. 84).

The opposite seems to hold true for quantitative skills. While earlier studies (63–65) showed that boys were superior to girls in mathematics in the early grades, later studies suggest that the differences do not become prominent until adolescence. Meaningful differences in mathematical ability begin to appear from ages 9 to 13 and become more consistent thereafter (4). Maccoby and Jacklin suggest that it is not simply a matter of the number of mathematics courses or the amount of training boys receive, but that boys and girls differ in interests and aptitude as well.

Some recent research suggests that boy-girl differences in verbal and mathematical ability may be more a matter of maturation than of sex per se. Boys and girls who matured early were found to do better in verbal skills and less well in spatial skills. The reverse held true for boys and girls who matured late. Because girls tend to mature earlier than boys, this could account for their tendency to do better than boys on verbal tasks. Conversely, because boys tend to mature later than girls, this could account for their tendency to do better than girls on spatial tasks. In short it may be rate of maturation, rather than sex per se, which accounts for some boy-girl differences in mental functioning in adolescence (129).

As we have already mentioned, achievement motivation is related to success in school. However, there are no significant boy-girl differences in academic achievement at the elementary-school level. Therefore, it is not surprising that no consistent boy-girl differences in n-achievement are found during those years (67, 68). It should be noted, though, that achievement motivation was studied by measuring such things as teacher ratings and self-imposed achievement standards, rather than by using projective techniques. In any event, it does not appear that boys differ significantly from girls in achievement motivation during the early school years.

Sex Differences in Cognitive Styles

Sex differences in cognitive style are not clear-cut during the elementary-school years; apparently consistent differences do not emerge until adolescence.

Field Independence/Dependence. As we mentioned in Chapter 9, Witkin and his colleagues have reported consistent sex differences between men and women on field independence/dependence measures (35). On the average, women appear to be more field-dependent than men. In their review of studies of field independence/dependence in children, however, Maccoby and Jacklin (66) report that many studies show no sex differences during the elementary-school years. In the few studies showing sex differences, boys were more field-independent: this trend continues and becomes more prominent during adolescence.

Maccoby and Jacklin (66) wonder whether boy-girl differences in field independence/dependence reflect differences in a specific personality trait. They suggest that this is not the case; they feel that tests of field independence/dependence assess spatial ability. Sex differences in spatial ability, like sex differences in field independence/dependence, become more prominent in adolescence. Therefore, one could say that field independence/dependence is simply a particular example of a general difference in spatial ability between men and women. On the other hand, *within* each sex, differences in field independence/dependence tests could reflect personality differences.

Impulsivity/Reflectivity. Earlier we pointed out that there is some controversy over how impulsivity/reflectivity should be defined. If it is defined narrowly—the ability to inhibit responses—then most of the research agrees with Kagan's (39) finding that there were no significant differences between boys and girls. In the mid-1970s some investigators used the Matching Familiar Figures Test (72) on more than 150 children in kindergarten and grades 2 and 5. Although there were a few sex differences, they were not consistent across grades or types of errors.

In reviewing sex differences in achievement and cognitive style, we have relied heavily on Maccoby and Jacklin's comprehensive summary. But this summary has been criticized on a number of points, which we listed in Chapter 8 (65). The problem is that sex differences in psychological characteristics is an enormously complex issue, both conceptually and empirically. An important lesson we have learned in the past decade is to be cautious in describing or interpreting such differences, particularly in childhood.

Sex-Role Stereotyping

One explanation for the fact that sex differences in achievement and cognitive style finally become noticeable and consistent in adolescence is that the social influences exerted on children do not manifest themselves until adolescence. In the preceding chapter we discussed factors that influence the development of sex-role identity; in this section we will look briefly at how some of these childhood social influences might contribute to sex differences in achievement and cognitive style that become prominent in adolescence.

Differential Parental Behavior. One factor affecting sex differences is the separate attitudes and expectations that parents hold for their sons and their daughters. Sometimes an attitude is conveyed directly and clearly, for example, "boys don't play with dolls" or "girls are not supposed to enjoy playing baseball." At other times, the parental influence is indirect; parental concepts of appropriate sex roles may be communicated in the way that relate to one another—the behavior that they model for their children.

Table 13.2 presents a summary of the findings of several studies (73), in which the parents of boys are compared with the parents of girls.

According to the author:

> *The leitmotiv of socialization practices for boys across the several age levels studied reflects an emphasis on the virtues of the Protestant ethic: an emphasis on achievement and competition, the insistence upon the control of feelings and expressions of affect and a concern for rule conformity. There is differential emphasis on enforcing the "Thou shalt nots" of child rearing; authority and control seem to pose the vital issues between parents, particularly fathers, and their sons at this age.*

> *For girls, on the other hand, emphasis is placed, particularly by their fathers, on developing and maintaining close interpersonal relationships: they are encouraged to talk about their troubles and to reflect upon life, are shown affection physically and are given comfort and reassurance. Where the issues between parent and son appear to be those of authority and control, the parent-daughter theme at the several age periods reflects an emphasis on relatedness, protection and support [73, p. 517].*

Most theorists (74–76) agree that much of a child's sex-role learning is due to the modeling behavior of the same-sex parent. Of course, children are exposed to other adults as well, especially when they enter school and when they begin to watch television. Although not too much is known about the effects of such modeling, we will present some of the findings.

Differential Teacher Behavior. In our essay on the "feminized" classroom in the preceding chapter, we indicated that both men and women elementary school teachers tend to reward children who are not aggressive, who are compliant and who do not challenge their authority (77–79). In our society, until recently, aggressiveness, independence, and rebelliousness were regarded as masculine traits and teacher behavior could thus be seen as a kind of "feminization" of male children. A possible explanation for such teacher behavior is that they must deal with groups of children rather than with individuals. When dealing with groups of children aggression on the part of some children is disruptive.

Hence, it may be the case that sex-role behavior that is reinforced on a one-to-one basis by parents may not be reinforced when children are dealt with as a group by teachers. This might account, in part, for the fact that boys show more behavior problems in school than girls (see Chapter 14).

If parents encourage boys to be aggressive on an individual level at home but to be submissive in the classroom, this inconsistency may cause them to have certain adjustment problems in school. Girls, who appear to be encouraged to act consistently (that is, with consideration and compliance) as individuals and in a group, have few behavior problems.

Differential Sex Roles on Television.   One of the uses made of television today is for persuasion. Although we have long been familiar with the overt persuasion of commercials, political advertisements, and editorials, we are only now beginning to appreciate the more subtle persuasion found in such programs as the "Mary Tyler Moore Show," "Maude," and "All in the Family." The "Mary Tyler Moore Show," for example, conveys the following messages: Puritan morality is okay in today's world; achievement and success are important values; sociability, external conformity, generosity, and consideration for others are appropriate modes of social interaction (80).

Today, girls are engaging in competitive team sports to a greater extent than ever before.

Table 13.2 Sex Differences in Child-Rearing Values of Mothers (M) and Fathers (F) from Four Samples

Items from Child-Rearing Practices Report*	Parents of Boys				Parents of Girls			
	Sample 1	Sample 2	Sample 3	Sample 4	Sample 1	Sample 2	Sample 3	Sample 4
I encourage my child always to do his best.	.01F**			.05M				
I feel a child should be given comfort when upset.					.10F		.05F	
I feel physical punishment is best method of discipline.	.10F	.10M .05F						
I express affection by holding, kissing, hugging my child.						.10M .05F	.01M .05F	.05F
I encourage my child to wonder and think about life.					.05F		.01M	
I take my child's preferences into account in making family plans.					.10F		.05M	
I find it difficult to punish my child.					.05M			.05F
I do not allow my child to say bad things about his teacher.	.10M .05F	.10M						
I am easygoing and relaxed with my child.						.10M	.10F	
My child and I have warm intimate times together.						.10M	.10F	
I have strict rules for my child.	.05F			.01F				
I expect my child to be grateful and appreciate his advantages.	.10F			.10F				
I believe praise gets better results than punishment.					.10M		.10M	
I make sure my child knows I appreciate his efforts.		.10M		.10M				
I encourage my child to talk about his troubles.	.05F				.05F		.10M .05F	

Item*				
I teach my child to control his feelings at all times.	.05M	.05M		.05M
I think a child should be encouraged to do better than others.		.05M	.05M .10F	
I believe scolding and criticism help a child improve.			.05M	.05F
I sometimes tease and make fun of my child.		.05F	.01F	
I do not allow my child to question my decisions.	.10M	.05F	.01F	.05F
I feel it is good for a child to play competitive games.	.05M .01F		.05M	
I make sure I know where my child is.				.05M .05F
I don't go out if I have to leave my child with a stranger.	.10M .01F		.10F	

*A self-report scale given to parents

**The numbers indicate the probability that a difference in the parents' response to boys or to girls was due to chance. The .01 figure indicates that the attained difference would be found by chance one in a hundred times. The letter next to the number shows which parent was making a differential response to boys and girls on that item.

Source: Block, J. H. Conceptions of sex role: Some cross cultural and longitudinal perspectives. American Psychologist, 1973, 28, 512–526.

Television programs are also persuasive in portraying sex roles. Although it is not clear whether this persuasion is effective, a number of studies have documented the messages pertaining to sex roles. Sometimes the message is subtle. For example, the proportion of women (as compared with men) who have major parts in television programs varies from about one-third to one-fourth (81–83). Not only do women play significantly fewer noteworthy parts than men, but they tend to appear in a more derogatory light, in a sexual context, or in romantic or family roles. Women are seldom portrayed as aggressors, and when they are they are usually punished (83).

A study of the sex roles shown in children's television programs provides similar results (84). Some of the most popular programs such as "Popeye," "Superman," "Bewitched," and "I Dream of Jeanie" were analyzed, and the results are given in Table 13.3. It seems clear that television for children, as for adults, portrays men and women in quite different ways. To the extent that television is a "hidden persuader," it can contribute to the perpetuation of outdated and derogatory sex-role stereotypes for *men* as well as women.

Table 13.3   Types of Behavior Portrayed by Male and Female Characters in Children's TV Programs

Behavior	Mean Frequency of Portrayal	
	Males	Females
Activity	14	9
Dominance	29	23
Aggression	25	13
Deference	25	37
Autonomy	8	5
Harm avoidance	16	17
Succorance	6	3
Nurturance	9	10
Magic	2	5
Recognition	5	3
Self-recognition	1	1
Construction	38	24
Total mean frequencies	178	150

Source: Sternglang, S. H., & Serbin, L. A. Sex role stereotyping in children's television programs. *Developmental Psychology,* 1974, **10,** 710–715.

FAMILY
CONFIGURATION

The family in America is undergoing rapid and dramatic changes. One change that appears to be continuing is that families are getting smaller as parents are deciding to have fewer children. Another change is that a large number of mothers hold full-time, paid jobs. We will discuss the effects of family size on children's intelligence and achievement and consider the

According to Zajonc, small families provide, on the average, a higher level of intellectual stimulation than do large families.

impact of employed mothers on child-rearing practices and child adjustment.

Since the mid-1960s, young people's scores on the Scholastic Aptitude Test (SAT) have generally been declining. This decline cannot be accounted for by the fact that different groups are now taking the test (statistical controls have been used), nor by changes in the difficulty of the test (at present the test has *easier* rather than more difficult items). One plausible explanation points to the amount of television children watch and another points to the quality of primary and secondary education provided by the schools.

In the mid-1970s, however, Zajonc and Marcus (85) offered a new and challenging explanation for the decline of SAT scores that they call the *confluence model*. This model assumes that each family member contributes something to the intellectual environment of the home. The more young children there are in the home, the lower the intellectual environment:

> *For the purpose of these examples consider the absolute intellectual levels of the parents to be 30 arbitrary units each, and of the newborn child to be zero. Thus the intellectual environment at the birth of the first child is $\frac{(30+30+0)}{3} = 20$. Suppose the second child is born when the intellectual level of the firstborn reaches 4. The second-born then enters an environment of $\frac{(30+30+4+0)}{4} = 16$. (Note that since the intellectual environment is an average of the absolute levels of all family members, the individual is included as part of his own environment) [86, p. 227].*

Zajonc and Marcus offer a great deal of evidence in support of their position, including a study (87) of some 800,000 young people who took the National Merit Scholarship Qualification Test (NMSQT). According to Table 13.4, students' achievement scores declined directly with their birth order. The relatively poor performance of twins can be accounted for with the confluence model since the presence of two young children of the same mental maturity lowers the intellectual environment of the home to a greater extent than would be true for siblings who were spaced several years apart. The authors account for the fact that only children do somewhat worse than first-born children by pointing out that they lack peer tutoring. First-borns tutor younger children and learn something thereby themselves, but this avenue is not open to only children.

The lower SAT scores could be the product of the "baby boom" and larger families after WWII. Now that families are getting smaller, one might predict that the SAT's will go up again when the children of these families

Table 13.4   Mean Scores on the National Merit Scholarship Qualification Test, 1965, by Birth Order and Number of Children in Family

Number of Children in the Family	Birth Order				
	1	2	3	4	5
1	103.76				
2	106.21	104.44			
3	106.14	103.89	102.71		
4	105.59	103.05	101.30	100.18	
5	104.39	101.71	99.37	97.69	96.87
Twins	98.04				

Source: Zajonc, R. B. Family configuration and intelligence. *Science,* 1976, **192,** 227–236.

reach college age. An important variable that affects the model is the spacing of the chidren. The model predicts that if the children are widely spaced, there will be a higher average intellectual environment in the home than if children are close in age. A large family with wide spacing may even provide the youngest child with a very rich intellectual environment conducive to superior achievement. Zajonc (86) offers data showing that children who are widely spaced perform better scholastically.

This theory is intriguing for many reasons. It suggests, for example, that children in single-parent homes may be penalized intellectually, if not emotionally. It may also help to explain some of the IQ differences between blacks and whites, since blacks tend to have larger families with the children spaced closely together. It should be remembered, however, that although the confluence model is interesting, it does not fully account for individual differences in academic achievement. It does, however, add a new and interesting dimension to the many variables that contribute to human performance.

Maternal Employment

In the mid-1970s, some 6 million children below 7 years of age had mothers who were employed on a full- or part-time basis. In an essay (Chapter 5), we discussed some of the daycare problems that arise for these children. But one can also ask about the quality of parental guidance these children receive and about other effects of the mother's employment.

Research on employed mothers has taken several different approaches (88). One approach has been to study the role-model effect of an employed mother on her children. Since we have already pointed out the importance of modeling for sex-role identity, is there a difference in this identity for girls whose mothers are employed as compared with girls whose mothers are not? Evidence suggests that there is a difference; for example, girls whose mothers are employed tend to have less-traditional sex-role concepts of themselves and others and to evaluate female competence more highly than do girls whose mothers are not employed (89–91).

Research has also been done on the emotional state of employed mothers. This aspect is important for her role as a mother. It was found that mothers who were working to fulfill some of their own personal needs—rather than simply to earn money—had daughters with a higher self-esteem and a more positive attitude toward their parents than did the mothers who were working only for financial reasons or the mothers who were not working outside the home (92–94).

Other studies have sought to determine how much control or supervision employed mothers are able to exercise over their children. The answer seems to depend upon the conditions or context of family life. If there is a stable family with positive relations between the parents, the children apparently get adequate supervision. If the family is not stable, maternal employment can make a difficult family situation worse (95, 96).

The role of social context was apparent in one study. The children who participated in the study made up the entire fifth grade in an elementary school. There were 142 children, of whom 108 had employed mothers. Using various tests, teacher's ratings, and other records, the researchers found that the children whose mothers were employed were either equally or better adjusted socially than the children whose mothers were not employed. In this case, where the majority of mothers in a community work outside the home, it is the norm rather than the exception (as once was the case) in children's lives (94).

In summary, the effects of maternal employment upon children vary according to the circumstances. One must consider why the mother is working, what the mother's attitude is toward herself and her family, the stability of the family, and the social context of the family. What can be conclusively stated is that maternal employment need not, and usually does not, have any negative effects upon the children.

ETHNIC-GROUP DIFFERENCES

Two areas of ethnic group differences during middle childhood that have received considerable attention are academic achievement and self-esteem.

Academic Achievement in American Indian Children

One minority group in America that is finally beginning to receive attention is the American Indian. Although there are significant differences among the various tribes, there are also many similarities. Indians have close-knit families and extended family ties, a fluid sense of time, very little competitiveness, and a generous sense of hospitality that extends to all visitors. Children growing up on a reservation thus are socialized quite differently from children growing up in a white, Anglo-American community.

Studies of the academic achievement of Indian children reveal a disheartening picture. In the mid-1970s American Indians were reaching only about half the educational level of the average American. The school dropout rate for Indians was twice the rate for the population at large. Finally, the illiteracy rate for Indians, regardless of tribe, was greater than for any other minority group in our country (97, 98). Even Indian children who are reared in foster homes with white parents seem to fail as often in school as those who live with their parents on the reservation (100).

What accounts for this poor achievement among American Indians? Certainly the isolation, economic deprivation, and prejudice Indians encounter in the larger white society are important factors. But so, too, is the Indian culture. One of the authors visited a Catholic mission school on the reservation in Pine Ridge, South Dakota. As he sat in a sixth-grade reading class, the teacher asked a question, but no child raised his or her hand. When the teacher called upon a particular young girl, she answered correctly. Since the Indian value system opposes competitiveness, children are reluctant to compete on tests or to try to do very well in school since that would set them apart from the group. And, for the Indian way of life, academic achievement is not really very important. It is not clear how Indians can be helped to retain their cultural values (cooperation) and yet learn how to survive economically (competitively) in contemporary America.

Self-
Esteem

An important factor in school achievement and successful interpersonal relations is *self-esteem,* which we defined in Chapter 8 as the value people place on themselves. Psychologists often measure self-esteem by means of a list of adjectives or statements, some of which are positive and some negative (101). The child is asked to check those adjectives or statements that are "true" and those that are "false" for him or her. Self-esteem is determined by the number of positive adjectives or statements that the child checks. Many such scales also contain "lie" statements. If a child checks these (for example, "I am the greatest," "I never do anything wrong"), it indicates that the child is either not paying attention or giving an exaggerated impression of self.

Self-esteem measures have been used extensively with black and white children to assess their feelings about themselves. Back in the 1930s some early investigators (102) found that black children had a rather low self-regard. In a biracial nursery school, black children rejected black dolls in favor of white dolls. In the 1950s it was found that black children in an all-black nursery school had a more substantial sense of self (103). These findings and others like them were interpreted to mean that black children in integrated situations had a lower self-esteem than white children (104–107).

But many changes have taken place in America during the past 20 years; the civil rights movement, the elimination of many stereotypical blacks from movies and television, the fact that blacks are increasingly able to enter many professions and occupations, the fact that many programs of black studies are now being offered at various universities and some high schools, and so forth. It is not surprising, therefore, that more recent studies are showing that black children have self-esteem as high as or higher than whites (109–111).

In one study made in the late 1960s black children described themselves as being popular with their peers, as being satisfied to be the kind of person they were, and as having a happier home life than that of the average child. In another study, investigators who tested 1900 children from grades 3 through 12 found that the black children had higher self-esteem than did the white children (110).

The latter study also found (and this has been confirmed by other investigators) that children in segregated schools tend to have a higher self-esteem than do children in desegregated schools. Some psychologists have pointed out that any group that finds itself in the minority suffers some loss of self-esteem, whether it be black children in a white school, Catholics in a predominantly Protestant school, or Jews in a school whose enrollment is largely Christian. Because a group feels itself in the minority, this fact by itself causes a loss of self-esteem.

But while this view may explain differences in segregated and desegregated schools, it does not account for the historical change in black children's self-esteem. While America has a long way to go in achieving full racial equality, we have made quite some progress since the time when blacks were depicted as menial laborers and clowns. The changing image of blacks in America seems to be reflected in the fact that many black children today have approximately the same self-esteem as do white children. On the other hand, a 1976 reinterpretation of past data on black self-esteem argues that the earlier data were misinterpreted and that it was *never* clearly demonstrated that black children had lower self-esteem than whites (130).

CULTURAL DIFFERENCES

Since the 1960s there has been a renewed interest in cross-cultural studies, particularly with elementary-school children. In part this renewed interest can be traced to the ease of air travel, which makes it possible for investigators to travel around the world. It also facilitates cooperation among investigators. And, as people throughout the world become more familiar with one another through television as well as travel, there is greater interest in other cultures. We will discuss some of the cross-cultural studies of conservation behavior (a field that has been researched most extensively), as well as cultural differences in depth perception.

Conservation
Behavior

The attainment of conservation—the idea that a quantity remains the same despite a change in its appearance—was first researched by Piaget in Switzerland; since then, investigators have wanted to know whether the norms found among Swiss children apply to children elsewhere. Cross-cultural studies might also be able to suggest some of the factors required for the attainment of conservation. For example, to what extent are schooling and living in an urban environment important for conservation? For these reasons, extensive cross-cultural research has been done in this field.

One of the difficulties in doing cross-cultural research is that children's performance on any given task may be due to various factors that are totally unrelated to the task but that, nonetheless, affect task performance. While one of the authors was on the Pine Ridge Reservation in South Dakota, giving a series of perceptual tests to Sioux Indian children, he noticed that they performed very poorly. Concerned because he felt they were not doing their best, he decided to speak with each child to try to get to know them all better. He discovered that the children felt embarrassed about their names—"White Mountain," "Running Cloud," and so forth—which often caused laughter among whites. The children were also unwilling to try very hard on the tests because of their cultural value about not being different from or better than their peers. After the children were allowed to talk and when they finally felt that they were accepted as persons and that their performance was only for the examiner and not a competition, they took the tests quite willingly and did as well as white urban youngsters. In cross-cultural research there is always the danger of confusing individual behavior with normative group behavior. Cole, Gay, Glick, and Sharp (113) present an interesting and extensive discussion of the problems of cross-cultural research based on their own experience with African children.

Much of the cross-cultural research on conservation has considered the age at which children acquire various concepts of conservation in different societies. Some studies report that there are no significant differences between children from technologically advanced and from technologically underdeveloped countries, while others do report differences. We will try to explain this discrepancy.

One of the early studies that found no differences between European and third-world children was made by Price-Williams (114). He went to West Africa to study the illiterate bush children who belonged to the Tiv tribe. To make sure that the children understood the conservaton tasks, Price-Williams used such materials as earth and nuts (for example, asking the children whether a row of nuts remained the same or changed in number when they were spread apart). When the tasks were presented to the Tiv children this way, they demonstrated conservation at about the same age as European children (115).

In an extensive study of conservation among Sioux Indian children in

South Dakota, other investigators found no differences in age between Sioux and Anglo-American children in attaining conservation (116). Likewise, it was found that concrete-operational children in Thailand attained conservation at about the same age as European children (117). And finally, few differences in conservation performance were found between European children living in Zambia and Zambian children (118).

In other investigations, however, differences have been observed between European and non-European children. In many cases the children who attained conservation at a later age came from rural areas and were relatively unschooled. This was true for unschooled Algerian children who were tested and found to understand the conservation of quantity at a later age than schooled European children (119).

Actually, one would expect some cross-cultural differences in this area. Piaget (112) argues that cognitive development depends upon both growth and experience so that the age at which children understand particular concepts will vary to some extent with the particular experiences they are exposed to. The experience factor is illustrated not only by the differences in conservation between schooled and unschooled children, but also by differences between children from cultures that emphasize particular skills.

As an illustration of this last point, Price-Williams and his colleagues (120) used a task demonstrating conservation of quantity (does a clay ball contain the same amount of clay when it is shaped as a sausage?) with Mexican children. Those who came from a pottery-making community did far better on this task than comparable children from a nonpottery-making community. On other conservation tasks, however, there was no difference between the groups. Similar results were found with pottery- and nonpottery-community children in Ghana (121).

In summary, conservation performance depends upon a child's general development, broad cultural conditioning and attitudes, and specific experiences. Although children all over the world attain concrete operations, the age at which they do so will depend upon these cultural and experiential factors as well as upon maturation.

Pictorial Depth Perception

In the 1960s investigations of black African children suggested that these youngsters were deficient in pictorial depth perception (123, 124), that is, they had difficulty using perspective cues to say what was near and what was far in a picture. These findings were attributed to the physical and social environment in which these children were reared.

Further research in the 1970s indicates that the earlier findings were incorrect. When nonverbal procedures were used to measure depth perception and when the number of depth cues in a picture was increased, young black African children were able to make adequate depth discriminations (125–127). These new findings point up the difficulties of cross-cultural research and the importance of not mistaking social or language misunderstandings for cognitive or perceptual inadequacies.

Essay

We hear a lot these days about learning-disabled children and the problems which they present to teachers and parents. It is our belief, however, that a good number of these children are mislabeled and should in fact be called *curriculum-disabled*. Such children suffer from being entered into school too early, from being introduced to formal instruction too soon, and from daily exposure to curriculum materials that are contradictory, confusing, and misleading. The failures of the curriculum-disabled child are attributable first and foremost to our educational system and to our societal values, not to some faulty wiring in the child's brain.

In practice, it is often difficult to distinguish between the curriculum-disabled child and the youngster who does indeed have a physical handicap (including minimal brain injury) that impairs learning. Some curriculum-disabled children are hyperactive, others are shy and withdrawn, while still others come on as aggressive bullies. The defensive patterns children assume to cope with the trauma of school failure are relatively independent of the causes of the failure and give no easy-to-read diagnostic clues. The symptoms of school failure are like fever: They tell you that something is wrong but not necessarily *what* is wrong.

The only sure way to distinguish a curriculum-disabled child from a physically handicapped child is by putting them in a nonpressured environment and exposing them to curriculum materials suited to their level of cognitive development and which are relatively devoid of ambiguity, contradictions, and confusions. In an environment such as this, curriculum-disabled children will flower to a much greater extent than handicapped children.

The foregoing diagnostic procedure is not just surmise on our part. For the past three years one of us (DE) has been running a school for curriculum-disabled children, the Mt. Hope School in Rochester, New York. The school is associated with the University of Rochester, but is not a laboratory school in the traditional sense. The children come from three inner-city schools and are referred by their parents. In age they range from 7 to 9 and they are selected because they have average intellectual ability but are a year or more behind in math or reading. Most of the children spend a year at the school and are then phased back into the neighborhood school.

We have already seen some dramatic transformations of child behavior. One youngster came to us as hyperactive and was constantly running, climbing on the tables, talking to or hitting other children while they were at work. Her mother complained bitterly that she could not do her work at home because of this child. Four months later this same mother complained about her daughter being too quiet—she was reading all the time! Most of our children not only got back to grade level, they also modulated their emotional responsiveness. In addition, a majority of the children have maintained their gains when back in the neighborhood schools.

On the other hand, some children did demonstrate their physical handicaps. About halfway through the program, once the children were turned on to learning and were working eagerly on their own, we began to see their handicaps in pure culture. One young man complained that the letters ran together on the page. Testing showed that he had a perceptual deficit, probably associated with minimal brain injury. While this perceptual deficit was easy to diagnose after the child was well into the program, it would have been difficult to diagnose at the beginning. Initially, the child's problems are so overlaid with emotion, with a sense of failure and inadequacy, that his or her performance on a diagnostic test battery is very unreliable.

This is not the place to describe our program in detail, but it may be appropriate to say something about the sorts of curriculum practices and materials we believe to be most conducive to curriculum disabilities. Perhaps the most culpable, and the most widespread, practice is too-early introduction to formal instruction in reading. Although we did not select on this basis, we discovered after the fact, that most of our children had October, November, or December birthdates. They tended to be the youngest children in their class. We believe that the importance of development has been neglected in our pressures to teach children early. In Russia and Scandinavia, formal instruction is not begun until children are 7. The number of reading failures is negligible. But in France, where reading instruction is begun at age 5, some 30 percent of the children experience school failure.

In addition to a too-early introduction to school subjects, the materials themselves can cause curriculum disabilities. Instructions that are too long and too cumbersome prevent children from demonstrating what they know. Exercises that are much too complicated to carry out produce frustration and anger. Illustrations and formats that do not relate to the task at hand defeat even the most well-intentioned and highly motivated child. Some children when confronted with the stupidities rampant in the curriculum materials believe, nonetheless, that it is they—not the materials—who are dumb. It is a gross injustice to label such a child, done in by curriculum, *learning*-disabled.

Although curriculum errors of the sorts described above can be found at all educational levels, they have their most devastating effects in the early elementary-school grades. It is during this period that children must learn the basic tool skills prerequisite to all later academic achievement. Children who are defeated by the curriculum in the first few grades can suffer lifelong deficiencies. The child who falls further and further behind because of deficits in tool skills such as reading is much too familiar to require comment.

But failure during the early school years can have other consequences as well. It is the period during which, according to Erik Erikson, children must acquire a sense of industry, a sense of competence in being able to do a job and to do it well. It is during this period that children establish lifelong attitudes toward work. Children whose sense of industry is not buttressed by their school experience have an enhanced sense of inferiority with respect to work competence. Clearly, children who fail because of the curriculum are handicapped not only with respect to academic achievement, but also with respect to any sort of work they seek to undertake.

Over the past 20 years we have witnessed many, many innovations in education, from open spaces to team teaching to back to "basics." And we have witnessed curriculum-reform movements that have given us innovative curricula in science, math, language arts, and social studies. Perhaps it is time to stop innovating—at least for a while. We have more curricula than we know what to do with and more alternatives than we can ever employ. What we need to do now is improve on what we have, consolidate our gains. Let us now direct our efforts toward modifying existing curriculum practices and materials to better fit the needs and the developmental levels of the children we teach. Let us work toward curricula which do not disable children but rather *enable* them to realize their abilities to the fullest.

Summary

As children enter school, individual differences in school achievement are apparent. These differences are due not only to a child's intelligence but to his or her achievement motivation, level of aspiration, and socioeconomic background. Children also differ in creativity—in their ability to think divergently. Since creativity is not innate, children can be be helped to become more creative.

Children also differ in their cognitive styles—in the ways in which they tend to view the world. Some children are impulsive, others are reflective; some are field-independent, others are field-dependent; and some view events as caused externally while others feel they have some measure of control over the events in their lives. Cognitive styles, like creativity, can be learned and are significantly influenced by the way in which children are reared.

In elementary school sex differences are evident in academic achievement and in cognitive styles but they are not as pronounced or as consistent as they will be in high school. Children learn how to act as males or females by observing their parents, teachers, other adults in the community, and people in the movies and television.

Family configuration in childhood can be related to both school achievement and adjustment. One theory suggests that intelligence and achievement are inversely related to the size of the family. This theory can account for both socioeconomic and birth-order differences in achievement. When both parents are living together, maternal employment can have either positive or negative effects upon the child, depending upon the mother's attitude, the stability of the family, and the family's social context.

Ethnic-group differences among school-age children appear in measures of intellectual abilities and self-esteem. Some 30 or 40 years ago it was found that black children had low self-esteem, but today the situation has changed and research shows that black children now have about the same self-regard as do white children.

Finally, cross-cultural studies have shown that while there are variations among different groups, the similarities in such achievements as conservation behavior and depth perception may be greater than the differences.

References

1. Bloom, B. S. *Stability and change in human characteristics*. New York: Wiley, 1964.
2. Hamachek, E. E. *Behavior dynamics in teaching, learning and growth*. Boston: Allyn & Bacon, 1975.
3. McClelland, D. O., Atkinson, J. W., & Clark, R. A. *The achievement motive*. New York: Appleton-Century-Crofts, 1953.
4. Wendt, H. W. Motivation, effort and performance. In D. C. McClelland (Ed.), *Studies in motivation*. New York: Appleton-Century-Crofts, 1955.
5. Evans, E. D. The effects of achievement motivation and ability upon discovery, learning and accompanying incidental learning under two conditions of incentive-set. *Journal of Educational Research*, 1967, **160**, 195–200.
6. Heckhausen, H. *The anatomy of achievement motivation*. New York: Academic Press, 1967.
7. Rosen, B. C. Family structure and achievement motivation. *American Sociological Review*, 1961, **26**, 574–585.
8. Winterbottom, M. R. The relation of need for achievement to learning experience in independence and mastery. In J. W. Atkinson (Ed.), *Motives in fantasy, action, and society*. Princeton, N.J.: Van Nostrand, 1958.
9. DeCharms, R. Motivation change in low income black children. Paper presented at the meetings of American Educational Research Association, Minneapolis, 1970.
10. Klein, R. D., & Schuler, C. F. Increasing academic performance through contingent use of self evaluation. Paper presented at the annual meeting of the American Educational Research Association, Chicago, April 1974.
11. Sears, P. S. Levels of aspiration in academically successful and unsuccessful children. *Journal of Abnormal Psychology*, 1940, 458–538.
12. Grune, E. W. Level of aspiration in relation to personality factors of adolescents. *Child Development*, 1945, **16**, 181–188.
13. Atkinson, J. W. Motivational alternatives or risk taking behavior. *Psychological Review*, 1957, **64**, 359–372.
14. Moulton, R. W. Effects of success and failure on level of aspiration as related to achievement motives. *Journal of Personality and Social Psychology*, 1965, 399–406.
15. Jencks, C., *et al*. *Inequality: A reassessment of family and schooling in America*. New York: Basic Books, 1972.

16. Coleman, J. S., *et al. Equality of educational opportunity.* Washington, D.C.: U.S. Government Printing Office, 1966. (Known as "The Coleman Report.")
17. Havighurst, R. J. Minority subcultures and the law of effect. *American Psychologist,* 1970, **25,** 313–322.
18. Elkind, D. Teacher child contracts. *The School Review,* 1971, **79,** 579–589.
19. Davis, A. Cultural factors in remediation. *Educational Horizons,* 1965, **43,** 231–251.
20. Taboo, W. Academic ignorance and black intelligence. *Atlantic Monthly,* 1972.
21. Marwit, S. J., Marwit, K. L., & Boswell, J. J. Negro children's use of non-standard grammar. *Journal of Educational Psychology,* 1972, **63,** 218–224.
22. Genshaft, J. L., & Hirst, M. Language differences between black children and white children. *Developmental Psychology,* 1974, **10,** 451–456.
23. Lambert, W. E. *Language, psychology and culture: Essays by Wallace E. Lambert* (A. S. Dil, Ed.) Stanford, Calif.: Stanford University Press, 1972.
24. Cohen, A. The Culver City Spanish Immersion Program: The first two years. *Modern Language Journal,* 1974, **58,** 95–103.
25. Mednick, S. The associative basis of the creative process. *Psychological Review,* 1962, **69,** 220–232.
26. Wallach, M. A., & Kogan, N. *Modes of thinking in young children.* New York: Holt, 1965.
27. Torrance, E. P. The Minnesota studies of creative behavior: National and international extensions. *Journal of Creative Behavior,* 1967, **1,** 137–154.
28. Getzels, J. W., & Jackson, P. W. *Creativity and intelligence.* New York: Wiley, 1962.
29. Marx, M. (Ed.), & Tombaugh, T. *Motivation.* San Francisco: Chandler, 1967.
30. Olton, R. M., & Crutchfield, R. S. Developing the skills of productive thinking. In P. H. Mussen, J. Langer, & M. Covington (Eds.), *Trends and issues in developmental psychology.* New York: Holt, 1969.
31. Covington, M. V., & Crutchfield, R. S. Facilitation of creative problem solving. *Programmed instruction,* 1965, 4, 3–5.
32. Crutchfield, R. S. Creative thinking in children: Its teaching and testing. In H. Brim, R. S. Crutchfield, & W. Holtzman (Eds.), *Intelligence: Perspective 1965.* New York: Harcourt, 1966.
33. Olton, R. M., *et al.* The development of productive thinking skills in fifth grade children. Technical report, Research and Development Center for Cognitive Learning. Madison: University of Wisconsin, 1967.
34. Witkin, H. A. Individual differences in the perception of embedded figures. *Journal of Personality,* 1950, **19,** 1–15.
35. Witkin, H. A., Dyk, R. B., Faterson, H. F., Goodenough, D. R., & Karp, S. A. *Psychological differentiation.* New York: Wiley, 1962.
36. Crandall, V. J., & Sinkeldam, C. Children's dependent and achievement behaviors in social situations and their perceptual field dependence. *Journal of Personality,* 1964, **32,** 1–22.
37. Kagan, S. Field dependence and conformity of rural Mexican and urban Anglo-American children. *Child Development,* 1974, **45,** 765–771.
38. Kagan, J., Rosman, B. L., Day, D., Albert, J., & Phillips, W. Information processing in the child: Significance of analytic and reflective attitudes. *Psychological Monographs,* 1964, **78** (1 Whole No. 578).
39. Kagan, J. Impulsive and reflective children: Significance of conceptual tempo. In J. D. Krumboltz (Ed.), *Learning and the educational process.* Chicago: Rand McNally, 1965.
40. Denney, D. R. Reflection impulsivity as determinants of conceptual strategy. *Child Development,* 1973, **44,** 657–660.
41. Eska, B., & Black, K. N. Conceptual tempo in young grade school children. *Child Development,* 1973, **44,** 657–660.
42. Messer, S. The effect of anxiety over intellectual performance on reflectivity-impulsivity in children. *Child Development,* 1970, **41,** 723–735.
43. Wagner, I., & Cimiotte, E. Impulsive und reflective kinder pruefen hypothesen: Strategiem beim problemloesen aufgezergt an blickervegungen. *Zeitschrift fuer entwicklungs psychologie und Paedagogische Psychologie,* 1975, **7,** 1–15.
44. Kagan, J. Reflection-impulsivity: The generality and dynamics of conceptual tempo. *Journal of Abnormal Psychology,* 1966, **71,** 17–24.

45. Massari, D. J., & Schack, M. Discrimination learning by reflective and impulsive children as a function of reinforcement schedule. *Developmental Psychology,* 1972, **6,** 183.

46. Kagan, J., Pearson, L., & Welch, L. Conceptual impulsivity and inductive reasoning. *Child Development,* 1966, **37,** 583–594.

47. Brodzinsky, D. M. The role of conceptual tempo and stimulus characteristics in children's humor development. *Developmental Psychology,* 1975, **11,** 843–850.

48. McKinney, J. D. Problem solving strategies in reflective and impulsive children. *Journal of Educational Psychology,* 1975, **67,** 807–820.

49. Egeland, B. Training impulsive children in the use of more effective scanning techniques. *Child Development,* 1974, **45,** 165–171.

50. Briggs, C., & Weinberg, R. Effects of reinforcement in training children's conceptual tempo. *Journal of Educational Psychology,* 1973, **65,** 383–394.

51. Block, J., Block, J. H., & Harrington, D. M. Some misgivings about the Matching Familiar Figures test as a measure of reflection-impulsivity. *Developmental Psychology,* 1974, **10,** 611–632.

52. Bentler, P. M., & McClain, J. A multitrait-multimethod analysis of reflection-impulsivity. *Child Development,* 1976, **47,** 218–226.

53. Ault, R. L., Mitchell, C., & Hartmann, D. P. Some methodological problems in reflection-impulsivity research. *Child Development,* 1976, **47,** 227–231.

54. Rotter, J. B. *Social learning and clinical psychology.* Englewood Cliffs, N.J.: Prentice-Hall, 1954.

55. Lefcourt, H. M. Recent developments in the study of focus of control. In *Recent progress in experimental personality research.* New York: Academic Press, 1972.

56. Nowicki, S. R., Jr., & Duke, M. P. A preschool and primary Internal External Control Scale. *Developmental Psychology,* 1974, **10,** 874–880.

57. Walls, R. T., & Smith, T. S. Development of preference for delayed reinforcement in disadvantaged children. *Journal of Educational Psychology,* 1970, **61,** 118–123.

58. Crandall, V. C., Kalkovsky, W., & Preston, A. Motivational and ability determinants of young children's intellectual-academic achievement behaviors. *Child Development,* 1962, **36,** 91–109.

59. McGhee, P. E., & Crandall, V. C. Beliefs in internal-external control of reinforcement and academic performance. *Child Development,* 1968, **39,** 91–102.

60. Chance, J. E. Internal control of reinforcements and the school learning process. Paper presented at the meeting of the Society for Research in Child Development, Minneapolis, March 1965.

61. Gruen, G. E., Korte, J. R., & Baum, J. F. Group measure of locus of control. *Developmental Psychology,* 1974, **5,** 683–686.

62. Loeb, R. C. Concomitants of boys' locus of control examined in parent-child interactions. *Developmental Psychology,* 1975, **11,** 353–358.

63. Tyler, L. E. *The psychology of human sex differences.* New York: Appelton-Century-Crofts, 1965.

64. Maccoby, E. *The development of sex differences.* Stanford, Calif.: Stanford University Press, 1966.

65. Block, J. Review of Maccoby and Jacklin's "The psychology of sex differences." *Contemporary Psychology,* 1976, **21,** 517.

66. Maccoby, E. E., & Jacklin, C. N. *The psychology of sex differences.* Stanford, Calif.: Stanford University Press, 1974.

67. Bandura, A., & Perloff, B. Relative efficacy of self monitored and externally imposed reinforcement systems. *Journal of Personality and Social Psychology,* 1968, **7,** 111–116.

68. Masters, J. C., & Christy, M. C. Achievement standards for contingent and non-contingent self reinforcements: Effects of task length and task difficulty. Paper read at the biannual meeting of the Society for Research in Child Development, Minneapolis, 1973.

69. Grusec, J. E. Waiting for reward and punishments: Effects of reinforcement value in choice. *Journal of Personality and Social Psychology,* 1968, **9,** 85–89.

70. Ault, R. L., Crawford, D. E., & Jeffrey, W. E. Visual scanning strategies of reflective, impulsive fast-accurate and slow-accurate children on the Matching Familiar Figures test. *Child Development,* 1973, **43,** 1412–1417.

71. Debus, R. L. Effects of brief observation of model behavior on conceptual tempo of impulsive children. *Developmental Psychology,* 1970, **2,** 22–32.

72. Egeland, B., & Weinberg, R. A. The Matching Familiar Figures Test: A look at its

psychometric credibility. *Child Development,* 1976, **47**, 483–491.

73. Block, J. H. Conceptions of sex role: Some cross cultural and longitudinal perspectives. *American Psychologist,* 1973, **28**, No. 6, 512–526.

74. Freud, S. *New introductory lectures in psycho-analysis.* New York: Norton, 1933.

75. Mischel, W. A social learning view of sex differences in behavior. In E. Maccoby (Ed.), *The development of sex differences.* Stanford, Calif.: Stanford University Press, 1966.

76. Kohlberg, L. A cognitive developmental analysis of children's sex role concepts and attitudes. In E. Maccoby (Ed.), *The development of sex differences.* Stanford, Calif.: Stanford University Press, 1966.

77. Fagot, B. I., & Patterson, G. R. An in vivo analysis of reinforcing contingencies for sex role behaviors in the preschool child. *Developmental Psychology,* 1969, **1**, 563–568.

78. Levitin, T. E., & Chananie, J. D. Responses of female primary school teachers to sex typed behaviors in male and female children. *Child Development,* 1972, **43**, 1309–1316.

79. Etaugh, C., & Hughes, V. Teacher's evaluations of sex typed behaviors in children: The role of teacher, sex, and school setting. *Developmental Psychology,* 1975, **3**, 394–395.

80. Chesebro, J. W., & Hamsher, C. D. Communication, values and popular television series. *Journal of Popular Culture,* Winter 1975, 589–602.

81. Clark, C. Race, identification, and television violence. In G. A. Comstock, E. A. Rubenstein, & J. P. Murray (Eds.), *Television and social behavior.* Vol. 5, *Television's effects: Further explorations.* Washington, D.C.: U.S. Government Printing Office, 1972.

82. DeFleur, M. Occupational roles as portrayed on television. *Public Opinion Quarterly,* 1964, **28**, 57–74.

83. Gerbner, G. Violence in television drama: Trends and symbolic functions. In G. A. Comstock & E. A. Rubenstein (Eds.), *Television and social behavior.* Vol. 1, *Media content and control.* Washington, D.C.: U.S. Government Printing Office, 1972.

84. Sternglang, S. H., & Serbin,, L. A. Sex role stereotyping in children's television programs. *Developmental Psychology,* 1974, **10**, 710–715.

85. Zajonc, R. B., & Markus, G. B. Birth order and intellectual development. *Psychological Review,* 1975, **82**, 74–88.

86. Zajonc, R. B. Family configuration and intelligence. *Science,* 1976, **192**, 227–236.

87. Breland, H. Birth order, family configuration, and verbal achievement. *Child Development,* 1974, **45**, 1011–1119.

88. Hoffman, L. W. Effects of maternal employment on the child: Review of Research. *Developmental Psychology,* 1974, **10**, 204–228.

89. Baruck, G. K. Maternal influences upon college women's attitudes toward women and work. *Developmental Psychology,* 1972, **6**, 32–37.

90. Meier, H. C. Mother-centeredness and college youths' attitudes towards social equality for women: Some empirical findings. *Journal of Marriage and the Family,* 1972, **34**, 115–121.

91. Koppel, B. E., & Labert, R. D. Self worth among children of working mothers. Unpublished manuscript. University of Waterloo, 1972.

92. Birnbaum, J. A. Life patterns, personality style and self esteem in gifted, family oriented and career committed women. Unpublished doctoral dissertation. University of Michigan, 1971.

93. Yarrow, M. R., Scott, P., deLeeuw, L., & Herning, C. Child rearing in families of working and non-working mothers. *Sociometry,* 1962, **25**, 122–140.

94. Woods, M. B. The unsupervised child of the working mother. *Developmental Psychology,* 1972, **6**, 14–25.

95. Glueck, S., & Glueck, E. Working mothers and delinquency. *Mental Hygiene,* 1957, **41**, 327–352.

96. McCord, J., McCord, J., & Thurber, E. Effects of maternal employment on lower class boys. *Journal of Abnormal and Social Psychology,* 1963, **67**, 177–182.

97. Edington, E. D. Academic achievement. *Journal of American Indian Education,* 1969, **8**, 10–15.

98. Erickson, D. A. Failure in Navajo schooling. *Parents Magazine,* 1970, **45**, 66–68.

99. Tunley, R. The 50,000,000 acre ghetto. *Seventeen,* 1970, **28**, 222–223.

100. Cundick, B. P., & Gottfredson, D. Changes in scholastic achievement and intelligence of Indian children enrolled in a foster placement program. *Developmental Psychology,* 1974, **10**, 815–820.

101. Coopersmith, S. *The antecedents of self-esteem.* San Francisco: W. H. Freeman, 1967.

102. Clark, K. B., & Clark, M. K. The development of consciousness of self and the emergence of racial identification in Negro preschool children. *Journal of Social Psychology,* 1939, **10,** 591–599.
103. Clark, K. B., & Clark, M. K. Racial identification and preference in Negro children. In E. Maccoby (Ed.), *Readings in social psychology,* New York: Holt, 1959.
104. Goodman, M. E. *Race awareness in young children.* Reading, Mass.: Addison-Wesley, 1952.
105. Moreland, J. K. Racial recognition by nursery school children in Lynchburg, Virginia. *Social Forces,* 1958, **37,** 132–137.
106. Moreland, J. K. A comparison of race awareness of Northern and Southern children. *American Journal of Orthopsychiatry,* 1966, **36,** 22–31.
107. Dreger, R. M., & Miller, K. S. Comparative psychological studies of Negroes and whites in the United States, 1959–1965. *Psychological Bulletin* monograph supplement, Vol. 70, No. 3, Part 2, 1968.
108. Powell, G. J. Self concept in black and white children. In G. J. Powell (Ed.), *Racism and mental health:* Pittsburgh: University of Pittsburgh Press, 1973.
109. Baugham, E. E., & Dahlstrom, W. G. *Negro and white children: A psychological study in the rural South.* New York: Academic Press, 1968.
110. Rosenberg, M., & Simmons, R. G. Black and white self-esteem: The urban school child. Arnold and Caroline Rose Monograph Series, *American Sociological Association Monograph Series,* 1972.
111. Soares, A. T., & Soares, L. M. Self perceptions of culturally disadvantaged children. *American Educational Research Journal,* 1969, **6,** 31–45.
112. Piaget, J. *The psychology of intelligence.* London: Routledge & Kegan Paul, 1950.
113. Cole, M., Gay, J., Glick, J., & Sharp, D. *The cultural context of learning and thinking: An exploration in experimental anthropology.* London: Methuen, 1971.
114. Price-Williams, D. A study concerning concepts of conservation of quantity among primitive children. *Acta Psychologica,* 1961, **18,** 297–305.
115. Price-Williams, D. Abstract and concrete modes of classification in a primitive society. *British Journal of Educational Psychology,* 1962, **32,** 50–61.
116. Voyat, G., & Silk, S. Cross-cultural study of cognitive development on the Pine Ridge Indian Reservation. *Pine Ridge Reservation Bulletin,* January 1970, **11,** 50–73.
117. Opper, S. A study of the intellectual development of Thai urban and rural children. Unpublished Ph.D. dissertation. Cornell University, 1971.
118. Heron, A., & Simonsson, M. Weight conservation in Zambian children. *International Journal of Psychology,* 1969, **4,** 281–292.
119. Bovet, M. Cognitive processes among illiterate children and adults. In J. Berry and P. Dasen (Eds.), *Culture and cognition: Readings in cross cultural psychology.* London: Methuen, 1974.
120. Price-Williams, D., Gordon, W., & Ramirez, M. Skill and conservation. *Developmental Psychology,* 1969, **1,** 769.
121. Adjei, E. A cross cultural investigation of Piaget's organism-environment interaction hypothesis. In P. Dasen & G. Seagrin (Eds.), *Inventory of cross cultural Piagetian research,* London: Methuen, 1973.
122. Kagan, S. Field dependence and conformity of rural Mexican and urban Anglo-American children. *Child Development,* 1974, **45,** 765–771.
123. Hudson, W. Pictorial depth perception in subcultural groups in Africa. *Journal of Social Psychology,* 1960, **52,** 183–208.
124. Hudson, W. Pictorial depth perception and educational adaptation in Africa. *Psychologica Africana,* 1962, **9,** 226–239.
125. Jahoda, G., & McGurk, H. Pictorial depth perception: A developmental study. *British Journal of Psychology,* 1974, **65,** 141–149.
126. McGurk, H., & Jahoda, G. The development of pictorial depth perception: The role of figural elevation. *British Journal of Psychology,* 1974, **65,** 367–376.
127. McGurk, H., & Jahoda, G. Pictorial depth perception by children in Scotland and Ghana. *Journal of Cross-Cultural Psychology,* 1975, **6,** 279–295.
128. Kolb, D. A. Achievement motivation training in underachieving high school boys. *Journal of Personality and Social Psychology,* 1965, 783–792, 301–304.
129. Waber, D. P. Sex differences in cognition: A function of maturation rate? *Science,* 1976, **192,** 572–573.
130. Banks, W. C. White preference in blacks: A paradigm in search of a phenomenon. *Psychological Bulletin,* 1976, **83,** 1179–1186.

14 Abnormal Development

LEARNING DISABILITIES

Effects of MBD on School Learning

Psychological Impact of Learning Disabilities

Treatment

SCHOOL PHOBIA

Origins of School Phobia

Recognizing the Seriousness of School Phobia

Treatment

OTHER NEUROSES

Conversion and Hypochondriasis

Depression

Habit Disturbances

Conduct Disorders

Treatment

ESSAY

Priorities in Mental Health Services for Children

SUMMARY

REFERENCES

As the three preceding chapters indicate, normal behavior patterns become increasingly complex and diversified during the elementary-school years. So, too, do abnormal developments. Mental retardation and childhood schizophrenia continue to be the two most significant forms of psychological impairment, and both are likely to become more apparent. As we have already pointed out, many retarded children are not identified until they enter school and begin to fall behind in their studies. Similarly, in the case of childhood schizophrenia, teachers and other adults may be the first to recognize psychological disorder that the parents have been unable or unwilling to see.

The entry into school also brings with it two important new forms of psychological disturbance. First, pre-existing patterns of minimal brain dysfunction may lead to various learning disabilities that interfere with school achievement. Second, children may develop school phobia, which is a psychological inability to attend school because of fears associated with being there.

School phobia is one of a number of neurotic disturbances that may emerge during middle childhood. Unlike most of the behavior problems of infancy and the preschool years, neurotic disturbances are caused mainly by children's psychosocial experiences and not by biological impairments. In addition to school phobia, the other primarily psychosocial disturbances we will discuss in this chapter are conversion, hypochondriasis, depression, habit disturbance, and conduct disorder.

LEARNING DISABILITIES

Although problems with learning in school are most likely to be due to limited intellectual endowment, an appreciable number of children with average or above-average intelligence fail to achieve grades commensurate with their intellectual capacity. It is estimated that as many as 25 percent of school children may be underachieving in this way (1). Among children seen in psychiatric clinics, moreover, one-third to one-half are there primarily because of school learning problems, and many others have secondary symptoms of such problems (2, 3).

Secondary symptoms of learning difficulty may arise from a physical illness that saps a child's energy or prevents him or her from attending class regularly; they can also be due to any serious psychological disturbance that impairs a child's ability to adapt to school, home, and social environments. When academic underachievement emerges as a primary problem in its own right, however, it can usually be traced to one of three causes: minimal brain dysfunction (MBD); sociocultural discontinuities between the school and the home or neighborhood; and specific neurotic conflicts about school learning, usually due to maladaptive patterns of family interaction.

Each of these factors may be a source of academic difficulty from the first grade on up into college. Since the sociocultural and neurotic determinants of underachievement become most apparent during adolescence, these will be discussed later. Here we will focus on learning problems that seem related to minimal brain dysfunction, since these are likely to appear early in a child's school career.

Before proceeding, however, it is important to note that the term **learning disabilities** does not refer to any single pattern of abnormal development. In schools that have special classes for "learning-disabled" children, and sometimes when the public's attention is being called to the needs of these children, the label "LD children" is used as if the group were homogeneous. Actually, this label applies to children with several kinds of academic underachievement. Since these children constitute a heterogeneous group, effective educational and treatment programs for them require adequate distinctions as to the source of their difficulties (4–6).

Particular care must be taken not to equate LD (learning disability) with MBD (minimal brain dysfunction). Learning disabilities can be due to emotional or sociocultural handicaps without any MBD, and some MBD children may never have learning difficulties (7). On the other hand, one-half to two-thirds of MBD is the single most common cause of school-learning problems in children of adequate intelligence (8–11).

Effects of MBD on School Learning

As we discussed in Chapter 12, the behavioral and perceptual-cognitive impairments associated with MBD interfere with school learning in two ways. First, because MBD children are restless and distractible, they have difficulty paying attention to their teacher and their assignments. They absorb less than other children from group discussions, they benefit less from individual study, they are slow to complete their homework and test papers, and they often fail to remember and follow directions (12–16).

Second, MBD usually impairs one or more specific intellectual functions that are necessary for mastering certain basic skills and subject matter. These include the ability to coordinate perceptual and motor functions (which, for example, is required for putting puzzles together or making drawings of geometric figures); a sense of spatial relations (which is required to distinguish left from right or north from south); the integration of various sensory modalities (which is required to be able to recognize that a spoken word is identical to the same word in print); the ability to understand the spoken word and to speak clearly; and adequate memory capacity (17–29). Because MBD children are impaired in these functions, they often fall behind their classmates in learning such basic language skills as reading and writing. Later on in elementary school and beyond, MBD children usually have difficulty with one or more specific subject areas.

Problems in Reading and Writing. Reading difficulties (**dyslexia**) are probably the most common and most severe kind of learning disability.

Table 14.1   Common Reading Errors of MBD Children with Dyslexia (Reading Disability)

Type of Error	Printed Word	What Child Reads
Reversal of word	"was"	"saw"
Transposition of letters within word	"sit"	"its"
Confusion of letters that are reversible	"*d*ig"	"*b*ig"
Confusion of letters that look alike	"*n*ow"	"*h*ow"
Confusion of letters that sound alike	"*t*own"	"*d*own"

Not all children who fail to read to their potential have MBD; poor reading can result from poor reading instruction in the school, and it may also reflect only a temporary lag in a child's cognitive maturation. However, the limited attention span of many MBD children makes them highly susceptible to dyslexia, since ability to pay attention to the printed page is one of the basic skills required in reading (30–32). In addition, the perceptual-cognitive impairments in MBD can handicap children in looking at written material with smooth left-to-right eye movements, in seeing letters accurately, and in combining letters to form words. As a result MBD children commonly make the kinds of reading errors listed in Table 14.1 (33, 34).

Dyslexia has a cumulative negative effect on almost all school learning. Most academic subjects require reading, and some measure achievement largely by how well a student can read and absorb large amounts of written material. Poor readers, therefore, have trouble in all of their courses, and without special remedial assistance they are likely to fall farther and farther behind their classmates each year.

Many of the same kinds of confusion, reversal, and substitution of letters that hinder MBD children in reading affect their writing (**dysgraphia**). If these children have problems with fine motor coordination as well (as many MBD children do), their compositions and other written work (arithmetic problems, map drawing, spelling tests) may be messy and illegible even when the children have managed to complete them.

Problems in Subject Areas. MBD children usually find that they are handicapped in one or more subject areas in the later years of elementary school and in high school. Those with serious and persistent reading problems are likely to receive relatively low grades in English and social studies. On the other hand, MBD children who have learned to read and write reasonably well may achieve at grade level or beyond in these subjects while doing poorly elsewhere. For example, their impaired capacity for conceptual thinking may prevent them from doing as well in science and mathematics as they do in social studies, where the course content is more closely tied to concrete, everyday experience. After reading, science and mathematics are in fact the two areas in which MBD children most commonly receive their lowest grades.

Psychological Impact of Learning Disabilities

Every learning disability puts a psychological strain on children and their parents. From the time they enter school, MBD children are handicapped in their efforts to achieve the skills and sense of mastery that normally promote initiative and self-confidence during middle childhood. In some cases these children may already have emotional problems if their parents have reacted negatively to their slow motor development and limited self-control. Other MBD children with understanding and supportive parents may have gotten along well as preschoolers but then encountered difficulties in elementary school, as they found themselves unable to compete with their classmates or realize their own potential.

This kind of self-awareness often leads learning-disabled children to develop a low opinion of themselves and to become easily discouraged. The way in which they are often treated by other children may make matters worse. MBD children are frequently the butt of jokes or jibes for errors they make, such as getting lost on the way to school (due to their poor sense of direction) or clumsily falling or dropping things (due to their poor coordination). Research by Bryan and others shows that learning-disabled children are unpopular with their classmates and frequently rejected (3, 35–37). For these reasons, learning-disabled children often become anxious or depressed about school, and they may resort to the kinds of aggressive, clownish, servile, or aloof behavior we described in Chapter 12 as efforts to deny or compensate for personal limitations.

Failure or poor performance in school is also difficult for most parents to accept, especially if they had not been aware of their child's handicap. Parents may also react to the problem in ways that make it worse. Some parents become angry and rejecting, as if the child were to blame for the learning handicap; some become overindulgent and overprotective, as if convinced that their child will never be able to take care of himself or herself; others deny the handicap and accuse the child of laziness or of not trying hard enough, or they accuse the school of picking on their child and of not doing a proper job of teaching.

The strong negative reaction of parents to a learning-disabled child can be attributed in part to what McCarthy and McCarthy call a "taste of honey" (38). Unlike retarded or severely emotionally disturbed children, learning-disabled MBD children often display essentially normal intelligence and many normal abilities (the "taste of honey"), which makes it difficult for parents to understand or accept the subnormal areas. Because they may expect more from their child than is realistically possible, these parents are often more disappointed and frustrated than the parents of children with more devastating handicaps, from whom less is expected.

Studies of learning-disabled children confirm that they have a less favorable emotional climate at home than do normal children or even their own normal siblings (22). The parents' negative attitudes make MBD children feel even less adequate and worthwhile than they would otherwise and discourage them even further from making constructive efforts to overcome their handicap. As would be expected, then, the degree to which these children can benefit from any treatment program depends in part on how supportive their families are; research findings indicate that the more accepting parents are and the more they become involved in the treatment program, the better the results (39–41).

Treatment

Before the 1960s it was widely believed that learning difficulties in physically healthy, normally intelligent children were due to "emotional blocks" (42). Psychoanalysts regarded these blocks as resulting from certain aggressive or sexual aspects of the learning process. For example, the taking in of information—as in looking at a page in a book—can be interpreted both as an active encounter with the environment and as an expression of curiosity. Learning problems can develop if this kind of activity makes children feel they are being too aggressive, or if their curiosity implies sexual curiosity that is taboo at home (for example, asking too many embarrassing questions or seeing things they are not supposed to see) (43–48).

When learning problems were interpreted largely in terms of such hypotheses, it was usually recommended that a learning-disabled child receive intensive psychotherapy. In the 1960s, however, some important scientific publications (49–51) and the efforts of the Association for Children with Learning Disabilities (ACLD) began to make both child specialists and the general public aware that MBD often causes learning difficulties. Now it is generally recognized that psychotherapy cannot be relied upon exclusively in working with learning-disabled children, since sexual and aggressive fantasies are rarely the sole cause of their academic underachievement (5, 52).

Research on the learning difficulties of MBD children has stimulated a number of new treatment approaches. As pointed out in Chapter 10, these children usually require a multifaceted program that combines psychotherapy, parent counseling, medication, and educational planning. Since the first three were discussed in the earlier chapter, we will now turn to educational planning.

Some special educators believe that the main reason MBD children have difficulty in school is because of their perceptual-motor handicaps. These educators accordingly emphasize training in basic visual and motor skills. Instead of being in a regular classroom, children receive this training in special facilities that resemble an exercise room. Numbers, letters, and geometrical shapes are painted on the floors or walls, and, instead of desks and chairs, there are walking rails and other pieces of equipment. The children are given walking and balancing exercises to improve their motor coordination; they trace designs to improve their visual organization; and they move rhythmically to music to help them better integrate their sensory experiences (53).

Other special educators believe that language is the MBD child's basic handicap in learning. Classrooms reflecting this philosophy utilize materials that encourage talking, listening, and reading—especially books and records (54, 55). Advocates of this approach believe that improved language skills will serve to reduce or eliminate the child's learning difficulties, just as those who favor perceptual-motor training believe that improvement in these skills will be sufficient to reverse an MBD child's backwardness in the classroom.

Despite the time and money that have been spent on developing these approaches, it appears that special skill training is not especially effective. In the first place, direct training in an academic task seems to produce much better results; for example, it has been found that children who have difficulty reading because they cannot scan well from left to right benefit more from ordinary reading instruction than from abstract exercises to improve their eye movements (20, 56, 57).

Second, MBD children may be learning-disabled for any one of a number of reasons. Some may be visually handicapped, others linguistically handicapped, and still others hyperactive without visual or linguistic handicaps. Clearly a treatment method designed to correct a specific handicap that a youngster does not have will do him or her little good; instead, a treatment method should be selected to meet the particular needs of an individual child (58, 59).

In the third place, because learning disabilities are cumulative, special skill training may be too little or too late to make much of a difference. Retarded readers who have fallen behind in several subject areas need help in catching up even if their reading improves. Moreover, improved skills do not necessarily change the learning-disabled child's typical negative self-attitudes and discouragement about school. Unless attention is paid to all aspects of a child's school adjustment—academically and emotionally—it is unlikely that his or her learning disability will be overcome.

For these reasons the current trend in working with learning-disabled children is toward what is called a "psychoeducational" approach. This approach begins with a careful diagnostic assessment of why children are having learning difficulties and what will best serve their needs. Subsequently these needs—for special skill training, tutoring in certain subject areas, programs to improve study habits or self-control, efforts to enhance self-esteem, or whatever—are met by consultants or specialists who work with the regular classroom teacher and spend a certain amount of time with the children but do not remove them completely from their regular classroom. This approach utilizes all available knowledge as to what may be helpful to individual children without imposing any particular treatment philosophy upon them (60–62).

The psychoeducational approach also utilizes several cognitive and behavioral treatment methods. Cognitive methods focus on teaching learning-disabled children certain ways of thinking or talking to themselves about academic tasks that help sustain their attention. One such technique developed by Douglas encourages hyperactive children to use self-directed verbal commands (''Stop!,'' ''Look!,'' ''Listen!'') to help themselves work deliberately on tasks, thereby avoiding hasty errors (63). Children also benefit from being given other strategies they can repeat to themselves (for example, ''Work on one problem at a time'') or being shown films of other children who are working on tasks in a careful, reflective manner (64–68).

Behavioral methods offer various kinds of rewards to learning-disabled children to encourage their attentiveness and discourage disruptive activity in the classroom. Even such simple procedures as giving children a piece of candy for performing well on a task has been found in experimental situations to be a potent way of getting them to perform even better (69). O'Leary and his colleagues have experimented with programs of total classroom management in which reinforcement principles are used to help learning-disabled children. In one of their studies a second-grade teacher awarded stars to her pupils in their afternoon session for ''appropriate'' behavior (as explicitly defined) and then gave a piece of candy at the end of each week to the child with the most stars.

During the time when stars and candy were being awarded, there was a marked reduction in the disruptive behavior of seven children who had been considered hyperactive. However, these children improved their behavior only during the afternoon sessions (when the reward program was in effect); they continued to be disruptive during the morning sessions. Thus, it would appear that such classroom management programs need to be integrated as a regular, ongoing feature of the classroom; a limited application cannot be expected to produce generalized or lasting results (70–72).

SCHOOL PHOBIA

School phobia is a reluctance or refusal to go to school because of intense anxiety experienced in the school setting. School-phobic children typically express this reluctance in the form of physical complaints that convince their parents to keep them home, especially headache, abdominal pain, nausea, or sore throat. Although such complaints are sometimes made up, these children usually suffer real physical distress, including pain, diarrhea, vomiting, and even fever. On occasion, either in addition to or instead of physical ailments, school-phobic children offer a number of criticisms of the school as their reason for not wanting to attend: the teacher is mean and unfair, the work is boring or too difficult, the bus ride is too long, the other children are unfriendly, and so forth.

Whether expressed as physical complaints or criticisms of the school, these children's apprehensions cannot be ignored or suppressed. The prospect of going to school fills them with such dread that, if they are compelled to go despite their complaints, they often become ill or panicky in class—vomiting, weeping, trembling, and pleading to be excused—and must be sent home.

Yet observations of school-phobic children make it clear that neither their physical discomfort nor their other complaints can be taken at face value. Their bodily symptoms usually appear in the morning when they wake up and disappear shortly after a decision has been made that they do not have to attend school that day. If it is then suggested that they go to school in the afternoon, their symptoms reappear within the hour; if they are permitted to stay home for a day, their symptoms return the next morning; if the parents then decide to forget about school for the rest of the week, their child is likely to remain in good health and spirits (especially if there are weekend activities to be enjoyed) until the following Monday, when the aches, pains, and complaints come back in full force.

As for the children's criticisms of the school, these invariably turn out to be rationalizations rather than their real reasons for not wanting to go. Attempts to deal with these complaints—by changing their teacher, putting them into a less advanced class, driving them to school, or even sending them to a different school—bring only temporary results. At first the children are happy and appreciative, and they approach the new school situation with enthusiasm. But a few days or weeks later they are back home again, physically ill or complaining about the new situation, and refusing to return. The true origin of a school phobia therefore lies not in any stated complaints, but rather in unstated and sometimes unconscious concerns these children have about attending school (73–77).

Before elaborating these concerns, it is important to distinguish school phobia from real fears about school and from truancy. A boy who has been threatened with a beating by the school bully or who faces an examination he expects to fail may be realistically apprehensive about going to school. If he learns that the bully has been expelled from school or that the examination has been canceled, he will quickly lose his fears. Phobic anxiety, on the other hand, is due to exaggerated concerns that go far beyond what is immediately apparent, and it can rarely be eliminated by making some superficial changes in the environment.

Truancy involves a conscious decision to skip school in order to do something else that is more fun. Some important ways in which truant children differ from school-phobic children are listed in Table 14.2 (78–80).

Table 14.2   Differences between School-Phobic and Truant Children

School-Phobic Children	Truant Children
1. Like school	1. Dislike school
2. Are doing average or above-average work in school	2. Are doing poorly in school
3. Are concerned about falling behind in their studies	3. Have little interest in their studies
4. Express eagerness to be able to return to school	4. Express wish that they didn't have to attend school
5. Have their parents' consent to be out of school	5. Are out of school without their parents' approval
6. Spend their time out of school at home	6. Spend their time out of school away from home

Origins of School Phobia

School phobia can appear at almost any time during the school years, and the specific concerns that produce it vary with age. Among children who display school-phobic tendencies in the elementary grades, their basic anxiety usually arises from concerns about being separated from their mother. Later on, particularly in junior and senior high school, school phobia is more likely to result from specific unpleasant experiences these children have had at school.

Separation from Mother. Young children who are reluctant to go to school have usually been overprotected by their mothers. Often they have not experienced a gradual separation from their mothers by attending nursery school, and their parents may have even been reluctant to leave them with a babysitter. These mothers frequently thrive on catering to their children's needs and wishes, especially in being solicitous to their children's physical ills, and they tend to feel lonely and unfulfilled when their children are not at home demanding attention.

This type of mothering during the early years sets the stage for children to balk at going to school and for their complaints to be promptly accepted as sufficient reason for them to stay home and be cared for (81–85). As we noted in Chapter 12, some mothers may even directly encourage nonattendance by finding their own reasons for keeping their child at home—bad weather, the child's slight cough, the child's need for rest before a family trip, and so forth.

Although the combination of an overprotective mother and an overdependent child does not invariably lead to school phobia, it does predispose a child to refuse to go to school in response to separation-related stress situations. Overdependent children often worry that something bad might happen to their parents when they (the children) are not home. If a parent should become ill or have an accident or if there should be a fire or

Intense anxiety about going to school (*school phobia*) is sometimes experienced in the early grades by children who have been overprotected by their mothers and cannot bear being separated from them.

burglary at home while they are at school, they may become extremely anxious about leaving their mother's side to attend school. Their anxiety thus becomes *displaced* from its real source (leaving home) to what was previously a neutral object (the school).

Unpleasant Experiences at School. School phobia in older children tends to be brought about by unpleasant school experiences that lead overdependent youngsters to prefer to remain safely at home (86–90). The actual nature of these experiences is seldom apparent in the reasons a youngster gives for not wanting to go to school; for example, there may have been some humiliation or embarrassment that is too painful for the youngster to talk or even think about. An athletically inept boy who is humiliated in his gym class may develop headaches or bouts of nausea that, significantly, appear only on the days when he has gym; similarly, a physically precocious 10- or 11-year-old girl who is embarrassed about her breast development may not be able to tolerate being stared at by her classmates, and therefore she may contrive a number of reasons why she must remain at home.

The Role of the Father. Whether a school phobia is due to separation anxiety or to unpleasant experiences at school, fathers as well as mothers play a role in them. In some cases the father is a carbon copy of the mother: he, too, overprotects the children and is easily convinced to let them stay home from school. In other cases the father is detached from the family and too absorbed in his own activities to pay much attention to what goes on at home. This detachment encourages an overprotective mother and an overdependent child to draw even closer together, and the child's staying at home may even become a secret that is kept from the father.

Recognizing the Seriousness of School Phobia

Despite the characteristic patterns of symptom formation and family interaction that prevail in school phobia, this disorder often goes unrecognized. The real physical distress of these children and their seemingly reasonable complaints about school frequently mask their actual pathological anxiety about going to school. Although the incidence of school phobia is therefore unclear, it is estimated at 1.5 percent of all school-aged children and up to 8 percent of those referred for professional help (87). It has also been found that whereas most learning and behavior problems of middle childhood occur more frequently among boys than girls, school phobia occurs about equally in boys and girls, with perhaps a slight preponderance among girls (2, 91, 92).

Why do girls equal or exceed boys in the incidence of school phobia when they are generally less susceptible to other psychological problems? It could be because girls are more likely than boys to have the kind of overprotective-overdependent mother-child relationship that contributes to school-phobic behavior. However, more research is required in order to be able to confirm this or any other hypothesis about sex differences in susceptibility to psychopathology.

Even when school phobia is recognized and properly identified, its potential seriousness is often overlooked. In its milder forms it may produce only slight discomfort, such as a slight stomachache, and come and go quickly, as on the days when gym is scheduled. Once a pattern of school nonattendance has become established, however, it tends to recur with increasing frequency and for longer and longer periods of time. Furthermore, once parents begin to accept minor physical ailments as adequate reason for children to stay home, it becomes very difficult for them to reverse themselves; the higher the standards they set for how sick their child must be to miss school, the more severe the symptoms the child is likely to develop.

For this reason most clinicians distinguish between *acute* (Type I) and *chronic* (Type II) school phobia (90, 93, 94). Acute school phobia usually occurs in a younger child who has not shown any previous behavior problems, and it does not interfere with his or her social development outside of school. Acute school phobics tend to be happy and industrious so long as they are allowed to remain at home. They continue to enjoy their friendships and peer-group activities, and they may even keep up with their studies if their teacher is willing to send home their assignments.

Chronic school phobia occurs in older children who have a history of behavior problems (including acute school phobia) and for whom staying out of school is just one of many adjustment difficulties. Chronic school phobics tend to withdraw from intellectual and social activities in general. They mope around the house without accomplishing anything (in contrast to those with acute school phobia, who may study hard or pursue hobbies), and they usually break off contact with their friends. Coolidge and his colleagues aptly call acute school phobia a "neurotic crisis" and chronic school phobia a "way of life" (95).

It is not difficult to see how repetitive and prolonged school phobia can interfere with normal personality development. Sheltered at home, school-phobic children lag behind their peers in learning self-reliance. Removed from day-to-day interaction with their classmates, they miss out on opportunities to improve their social skills and to develop a sense of belonging. Absent from school, they eventually fall behind in their studies and suffer academic failures that undercut their self-esteem.

Hence, persistent school phobia that goes unrecognized or untreated may have many unfortunate consequences. It is in fact more predictive of psychological problems in adulthood than are other youthful neurotic disturbances. For the most part, there is little relationship between childhood and adult neuroses; children with neurotic difficulties are somewhat more likely than normal children to have psychological problems as adults, but most of them do not (96–101). Chronic school phobia, on the other hand, often leads to poor adjustment in all work-related situations that demand a measure of independence and self-reliance (102).

Treatment Because of the far-reaching consequences of prolonged school absence, treatment usually aims at getting these children back to school as soon as possible (103). However, clinicians disagree as to what they mean by "soon." Some recommend that children undergo psychotherapy to help them uncover and resolve their anxiety about being in school before they try to return. In this approach, returning to school 6 to 12 months after beginning treatment is felt to be a successful outcome (77, 89, 104). However, other clinicians strongly believe that keeping a child out of school for psychotherapy only reinforces the symptom of nonattendance and delays recovery. From this point of view school phobia requires a "crisis" or "first aid" approach in which re-establishing at least minimal attendance is the first treatment priority and working to understand the separation or school-related anxiety comes later (74, 105, 106).

What is most important in treatment planning is to select the approach that best meets the needs of the individual child. If the school phobia has become chronic—that is, a "way of life," some psychotherapy will probably have to precede a return to school. Otherwise, a forced return is likely to cause the child to become more upset in school than before and to do poorly in his or her studies. On the other hand, if the school phobia is acute, children may benefit most from vigorous attempts to get them back to school before they become too accustomed to staying at home (75, 107–109).

Helping children with acute school phobia to stay in school and master their anxiety frequently taxes the ingenuity of therapists. Good results have been achieved with a variety of inventive behavioral methods, such as specific training exercises to help children feel less anxious in the classroom; reintroducing children to school gradually, as in having them attend for just an hour a day at first, then half a day, and finally a full day; asking children's mothers to go to school with them, perhaps even sitting for a while in their classroom, and then gradually leaving as the children begin to feel more comfortable, and educating parents to avoid the kinds of overprotective behavior that encourage nonattendance at school (110–112).

Treatment programs that combine helping children understand why they are anxious about school with keeping them in the classroom are generally very successful. Such programs can help more than 70 percent of school-phobic children to return to school comfortably in anywhere from a few days to a few months. However, consistent with the differences between acute and chronic school phobia, younger children generally have better prospects for improvement than older ones. More than 90 percent of children 10 years of age or younger have been found to recover from school phobia in various treatment studies, whereas the recovery rate for those 11 years of age or older is no greater than 50 percent (93, 94, 112–115).

OTHER NEUROSES

The formation of a **neurosis** is a complex process that requires a higer level of personality organization and differentiation than most preschoolers achieve. Hence it is not until the elementary-school years that children begin to display a variety of discrete neurotic disorders. The emergence of a neurotic reaction comprises the following two-step sequence: first, there is some internal psychological conflict or concern that causes intense, unbearable anxiety; and second, there are efforts to cope with the anxiety that diminish or disguise it, but in the process produce a maladaptive behavior pattern (91, 116–118).

The prelude to neurotic symptom formation sometimes appears in the behavior of preschool children who are unusually tense or anxious. The major indications of psychological tension in young children include irritability, constant crying, a refusal to eat or an inability keep food down, difficulty in going to sleep, frequent nightmares, and the kinds of transient phobias and rituals described in Chapter 10 (119). Preschoolers with such symptoms are usually apprehensive about their physical safety and about whether their basic needs are going to met; however, their cognitive capacities are not yet sufficiently developed for them to experience the types of internal conflict that generate a true neurotic reaction.

The clearest example of the true neurotic reactions that begin to appear during middle childhood is the school-phobic pattern we have just considered. In school phobia the internal conflict is between a wish to go to school (and thus continue with learning and peer-group activities) and a wish to stay home (thereby avoiding separation from the mother or some anxiety-provoking situation at school). These children's physical complaints keep them home and resolve their conflict: the matter is taken out of their hands, as it were, because they are too ill to go to school anyway. As a neurotic resolution of the conflict, however, the symptoms are maladaptive: they cause real physical distress, and they interfere with schoolwork and peer-group participation. In addition, school-phobic children are likely to suffer shame for not doing something they ought to do (that is, going to school) and guilt for doing something they should not do (that is, making their parents unhappy).

We discussed school phobia at length for two reasons: first, it is an excellent example of the process of neurotic symptom formation in school-age children; second, more than any other neurosis it directly and seriously interferes with the two major developmental tasks of middle childhood—entering school and shifting from primarily parent-oriented to primarily peer-oriented interpersonal relationships. We will next consider five other common neuroses of middle childhood: conversion, hypochondriasis, depression, habit disturbance, and conduct disorders.

Conversion and Hypochondriasis

Conversion and **hypochondriasis** are two closely related forms of neurotic behavior in which anxiety is "converted" into somatic symptoms or excessive concern about bodily functions. Conversion symptoms are sensory or motor impairments that arise without any organic cause, usually in the form of pain, numbness, or loss of muscle control in one or more parts of the body. Conversion reactions have been known to affect virtually every system of the body and even to produce blindness, fainting spells, or paralysis in people who are in perfect physical health (120–125).

One relatively common conversion symptom is **tics,** which are repetitive, involuntary muscle movements, usually of the face, head, and neck. Typical ticking movements include blinking the eyes, clearing the throat, yawning, stretching the neck, and shaking the head. In some cases ticking movements may be due to neurological disorders or to simple fidgeting or restlessness, and these must be carefully differentiated from tics that appear on a conversion-neurotic basis. Tics are observed in approximately 12 percent of all children of 6 to 12 years of age, most of whom manifest other signs of being tense and anxious. In most cases, these childhood tics disappear of their own accord by the time youngsters reach adolescence (126–129).

Hypochondriasis is a preoccupation with bodily functions with or without the formation of specific conversion symptoms. Hypochondriacal people tend to be very conscious of their heartbeat, breathing, digestion, and other physiological processes, and they quickly interpret any irregularity as certain evidence of illness. A slightly stuffy nose or a minor bout of diarrhea convinces hypochondriacs that they have the flu or worse; when they do in fact become ill, they exaggerate the severity of their symptoms and take longer than seems necessary to leave their sickbed. Even when they can find no symptoms to worry about—which is hardly ever—hypochondriacal people are sure that various ailments are just around the corner (130–132).

It is widely believed that conversion and hypochondriasis are primarily adult neuroses; reports from psychiatric clinics seldom list them among the primary symptoms of neurotic children. However, there is reason to think that these conditions are frequently overlooked or misdiagnosed in youngsters. In one study of a large sample of patients in a child psychiatry clinic, careful evaluation revealed that 13 percent of them had conversion reactions (133). Behaviorally oriented pediatricians likewise confirm that physical complaints and bodily concerns caused by anxiety are not at all rare among school-age children (116, 134, 135).

The Influence of Temperament and Family Environment. Although internalized psychological conflict always plays a role in neurotic symptom formation, the actual emergence of a neurosis and the kind of neurosis it is are determined largely by the child's basic temperament and the family environment. As we noted in Chapter 4, children differ from birth in many aspects of temperament; some are more active than others, some are more sensitive and responsive to stimulation, some adapt more readily to new situations, and some have more regular patterns of eating and sleeping. Research studies indicate that children who are temperamentally either extremely high or extremely low in activity level, sensitivity, adaptability, and regularity are the ones who are most likely to develop behavior disorders during childhood (136).

The family environment exerts considerable influence on the kind of behavior disorder children develop if their temperament and psychological conflicts combine to make them neurotic, especially in conversion and hypochondriasis. Children who develop these symptoms usually come from families that are very much concerned about health and illness. In such families the slightest physical complaint commands everybody's

Exaggerated concerns about health and illness, along with an overreliance on pills and potions, can be learned by children from observing parental models.

immediate attention and sympathy. Each member of the family has his or her own particular brand of aches, allergies, and infirmities and his or her own well-stocked shelf of medicines; family conversation frequently deals with the status of everyone's latest debility; and the "sick role" is learned as a way of life (118, 137).

In addition, most children who develop conversion and hypochondriasis usually model their symptoms after a real or imagined sickness of someone they are close to. Children with conversion headaches typically have a parent or relative who suffers head pain; those with abdominal complaints tend to have a parent who has ulcers, appendicitis, or poor digestion. Such a family pattern is so much a part of conversion symptom formation that clinicians usually hesitate to diagnose conversion unless they can identify the model for the child's symptoms.

Depression

Depression is a familiar and universal feature of human experience. Everyone has occasional moments of feeling sad, discouraged, or apathetic—the world looks grim, the future looks bleak, and nothing generates much interest or enthusiasm. Mild, transient depression is a common and normal reaction to failing at something important, being laid up with an illness or injury, or facing the breakup of a close personal relationship. In its more extreme forms depression is likely to involve constant moping or weeping, feelings of worthlessness and hopelessness, persistent thoughts about or attempts at suicide, an inability to sleep, the loss of one's appetite, and an overwhelming sense of inertia. Such symptoms, especially when they continue out of proportion to the situation that first caused them, constitute a pathological depressive reaction (138–143).

The common element in situations that cause people to feel depressed is *loss*. Depression in response to loss is most apparent when a loved one dies, moves away, or rejects a person's affections, leaving him or her to mourn the lost relationship. The earliest prototype of depression is the social isolation syndromes we discussed in Chapter 6, in which children fail to thrive when they are separated from their mothers or other primary caretakers. Other worries and discouragements that lead to depression similarly involve some kind of loss, such as the loss of a treasured toy, the loss of a desired promotion, or the loss of one's ability to function because of illness or physical handicap (144–146).

Because children seldom display the full range of depressive symptoms seen in depressed adults, it was believed at one time that young people do not develop depressive disorders (147). In the 1960s, however, clinicians began to recognize that children may express such disorders differently from adults. Because school-age children are experiencing an exciting period of rapidly expanding horizons, they generally tend to have considerable exuberance and optimism about the future. These positive developmental trends often counteract any overt feelings of sadness and discouragement even when children have suffered the kinds of losses that produce depression; instead, their depression emerges in a variety of "masked" forms (148–149).

Such **masked depression** is most likely to manifest itself in some form of aggressive, delinquent, or antisocial behavior in which the child's bad conduct is motivated by a need to compensate for a sense of loss. In particular, the sudden appearance of uncharacteristic temper tantrums, fighting, stealing, or truancy from school in children who had previously been well-behaved often signals the onset of an underlying depressive reaction (150–153). An increasing number of clinical reports also describe youngsters who, like depressed adults, are overtly sad, pessimistic, lethargic, and even contemplating suicide. These are children who look unhappy and express dissatisfaction with their lot in life; who are withdrawn and have little interest in any activities; and who have feelings of being rejected or of being unloved that cannot be relieved by efforts to comfort and reassure them (154–158).

Habit Disturbances

Habit disturbances are neurotic traits that, in common with other neurotic disorders, represent immature ways of behaving. Unlike other neuroses, however, habit disturbances do not necessarily originate in psychological conflict, even though they can and often do serve psychological needs. Rather, they arise simply as learned habits or as a result of delayed physical maturation. Two fairly common childhood behaviors that illustrate habit disturbance are enuresis (bed-wetting) and thumb-sucking.

Enuresis is normal in young children, who usually wet the bed at night from birth until a year or two after they have developed daytime control of

Figure 14.1 Incidence of enuresis (bed-wetting) and thumb-sucking at selected ages.

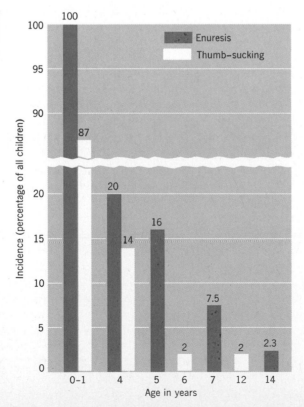

their bladder. Although by 4 years of age most children have stopped wetting the bed, a sizable number still continue to do so in middle childhood and even adolescence, as indicated in Figure 14.1 (159, 160).

Some clinicians have suggested that enuresis occurs among children who are angry at their mother and who express their feelings by symbolically urinating on her (the bedclothes), thereby giving her the extra work of changing and laundering their linen. Although such psychodynamic hypotheses are helpful in understanding some behavior problems—for example, the basic anxiety of school-phobic children about being separated from their mother—they do not go very far in explaining persistent enuresis. Available evidence seems to suggest that enuresis is most often caused by a delayed development of the neuromuscular control necessary to prevent urine from being discharged during sleep (161–164). As a result, enuresis often disappears with age as slower-maturing children gradually develop this control, which most of their peers have achieved by 4 or 5 years of age.

If it continues, enuresis can lead to a number of adjustment difficulties. Parents whose grade-school children are still wetting the bed may worry that their child is sick or disturbed, and they may also resent the laundering problems the child is causing. Either reaction can disrupt the parent-child relationship in ways that cause family problems. Persistent enuresis can also interfere with their peer relationships if, for example, it prevents children from going to summer camp or staying overnight at a friend's house. For these and similar reasons, children with enuresis are more likely than their peers to develop emotional problems (165). Hence, even though enuresis will probably disappear by itself in time—with the eventual maturation of bladder control—treatment should be undertaken to try to eliminate it early in middle childhood.

Many of the same considerations apply to thumb-sucking, which normally occurs in children up to about 3 or 4 years of age without any particular psychopathological causes or effects. However, thumb-sucking as a learned habit continues in about 2 percent of 6- to 12-year-old children, in whom it can lead to psychological problems. Thumb-sucking grade-schoolers are likely to be criticized by their parents, scolded by their teachers, and teased by their peers. Hence, efforts to help children get rid of this habit at an early age are desirable, especially since children who overcome thumb-sucking usually show an improved psychological adjustment (166).

Various conditioning procedures have proved to be the most effective means of eliminating habit disturbances. In the case of enuresis, for example, there is a specially designed mattress that is electrically sensitive to moisture, so that as soon as a sleeping child begins to urinate the mattress sets off an alarm that wakes the child up. In time the child becomes conditioned to wake up upon feeling the need to urinate, but

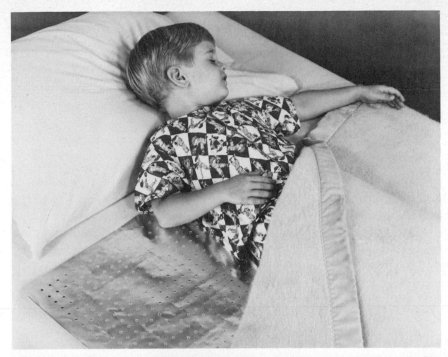

Methods developed by psychologists for training children to stop bedwetting are now being used in commercially available devices. The copy accompanying this advertisement, which appeared in a 1973 Sears, Roebuck catalog, says, "Buzzer alarm helps keep sleeper dry and more comfortable by conditioning him to stop bedwetting . . . alarm goes off to alert sleeper when first drops of moisture strike foil pads."

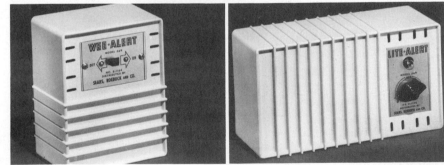

before actually doing so, so that he or she can get up and go to the bathroom. This simple procedure can help approximately 75 percent of enuretic children to learn bladder control in fairly short order (162, 167, 168).

Conduct Disorders The neurotic conflicts of middle childhood are often manifest in **conduct disorders,** including aggressive or rebellious behavior, stealing, vandalism, sadistic behavior, fire-setting, and truancy. In each of these conduct disorders children are expressing through action (''acting out'') some feeling or concern that they cannot talk about or otherwise resolve (169).

Elementary-school children who vandalize property and engage in other kinds of aggressive, destructive, and antisocial behavior are often suffering from underlying feelings of being weak and inadequate, alone and unloved.

For example, children who feel weak or powerless may try to obtain reassurance by bullying smaller children or torturing animals; youngsters with unspoken resentments against their parents may steal or vandalize in the hope that their parents will be taken to court and held liable for these acts.

Although many kinds of neurotic conflicts may lead to conduct disorders in middle childhood, all of them tend to include a feeling of inadequacy or loss. This helps to explain the close relationship we noted earlier between delinquent behavior and depression. For example, it is often found that elementary-school children who set fires or steal have suffered the loss of a parent due to death, divorce, or some form of rejection such as being sent off to a boarding school or to live with relatives (151).

Some characteristic features of conduct disorder are documented in an interesting report by Vandersall and Winer on 20 youthful fire-setters seen in a child psychiatry clinic (170). Nineteen of these children were boys and all of them were between 4 and 11 years of age. Most of these children had psychological problems related to aggression and impulse control. In addition, most of them appeared to feel inadequate, excluded, and lonely as a result of real or perceived losses of people on whom they had depended for affection and support. Similar depressive feelings have been observed in clinical work with fire-setting adolescents as well (171).

It should be stressed that even when their family lives together under one roof, children with conduct disorders are usually experiencing a distressing lack of parental attention or affection. Their neurotic behavior serves two purposes—to get back at their parents by causing them distress, and to recoup some of the attention and affection they feel deprived of. These neurotic ways of thinking appear from time to time in a great many children who never develop a conduct disorder, as in the fantasies of children who contemplate running away from home. Like Tom Sawyer, they think about how much their families will miss them when they are gone (thus getting their just deserts) and how ready their families will be to welcome them back with renewed love and devotion.

Like other neuroses, conduct disorders are the product not only of psychological conflict but also of a child's temperament and the family environment. Children who tend by nature to be physically active and impulsive are more inclined to channel their neurotic conflicts into conduct disorders than are relatively passive and ruminative children, who are more likely to develop conversion and phobic neuroses. As for the family, two types of behavior often lead to socially undesirable conduct in school-age children: role-modeling and implicit fostering.

In *role-modeling,* parents who are verbally or physically aggressive and disregard the feelings and rights of others serve as models that influence their neurotic children to act likewise. Convincing evidence exists that the best predictor of a child's engaging in antisocial behavior is having selfish, inconsiderate, irresponsible, and impulsive parents, especially fathers, who frequently get into trouble with the law (99, 172).

In *implicit fostering* (which is much less obvious), parents who are overtly altruistic and law-abiding unintentionally encourage and reinforce delinquent behavior in their children by anticipating and covertly sanctioning it. Typically such parents are inconsistent in their discipline, punishing their children on some occasions but not others for the same misconduct; they let their children know that they expect misbehavior, usually by accusing the youngsters of delinquent acts before they have committed any; and when their children do commit a delinquent act, their disapproval is focused on some detail ("Why did you take a radio when you have one at home?") rather than on the immorality of the act itself (173–175).

Treatment Like school phobia, most other neurotic disorders of middle childhood can usually be treated effectively with psychotherapy (176). Whether the treatment is on an individual, family, or group basis, most neurotic children can actively participate in and more readily benefit from psychotherapy than autistic, mentally retarded, schizophrenic, or MBD children. As one exception, we have already noted that children with a habit disturbance often profit from simple training procedures without psychotherapy.

Children with conduct disorders often constitute a second exception, in that persistent antisocial behavior is difficult to change. Child guidance clinics generally report that about two-thirds of their patients improve, and the remaining one-third tend to be either psychotic or seriously antisocial. Likewise, long-term follow-up studies indicate that neurotic behavior in children is generally *not* predictive of psychological disturbance in adulthood, but that serious antisocial behavior is highly likely to eventuate in adjustment difficulties later on (97, 100).

Essay

PRIORITIES IN MENTAL HEALTH SERVICES FOR CHILDREN

The Joint Commission on Mental Health of Children estimates that 1,400,000 children in the United States need professional mental health services, but that only about 400,000 of them are receiving such care (177). In some cases the schedules of mental health facilities and practitioners are already filled to capacity, and children in need of help languish on a waiting list. In other cases psychologically troubled children go undetected in the community, with no one reaching out to bring them into the network of mental health services available. In still other instances there is a mismatch between a child in need and the facilities available, so that no help is provided: there may be a center for retarded children that does not accept children who are also emotionally disturbed, or a child guidance clinic that does not work with youngsters who are retarded, or a residential treatment facility that is prohibitively expensive, and so forth.

These kinds of mismatch stem in part from past trends in assigning treatment priorities. The first child guidance clinic in the United States was founded by Lightner Witmer in 1896, and from that date until the 1960s child psychotherapists tended to focus their attention on nonretarded, nonpsychotic, nondelinquent children with neurotic difficulties. This focus was based on the fact that neurotic children, as compared with retarded, psychotic, and delinquent children, are easier to treat and profit more from psychotherapy; hence, on a simple cost/benefit basis, it was felt that the limited resources available should be concentrated on those with neurotic difficulties.

Beginning in the 1960s, however, two things happened that began to change this viewpoint. First, a number of professional and lay groups undertook programs of study and public information on children's problems that they felt were being overlooked. These programs, which were supported to a significant extent by federal and state legislation, led to additional research findings, new clinical approaches, and improved treatment facilities for meeting the needs of children with retardation, schizophrenia, and learning disabilities.

Second, the new fields of community psychology and community psychiatry began to call increasing attention to the mental health of communities rather than just individuals. The community mental health movement publicized the fact that treatment services for neurotic children reach only a small proportion of those who are psychologically impaired and ignore those who are most in need of help. Taken together, retarded, schizophrenic, and learning-disabled children are far more numerous than neurotic children, and the long-term consequences of their disturbances are much more serious. As a result of these two developments, present-day mental health planning is giving more attention to these previously neglected groups of disturbed children.

Now it may be that the pendulum is swinging too far in this direction. Because childhood neurosis is a relatively mild disorder that seldom leads directly into adult psychopathology, current interest in tackling more serious problems runs the risk of minimizing or overlooking it: "Leave the kid alone; he'll grow out of it." Such a casual attitude toward childhood neurosis can divert clinicians from situations in which the least amount of effort on their part could have the most impact in helping children overcome psychological disturbance. Furthermore, even if most neurotic children are likely to "outgrow" their problems sooner or later, why should they have to wait for later? Allowing children to struggle on with neuroses that could be promptly eliminated by appropriate treatment means burdening them with the psychological pain of their difficulties for longer than is necessary.

Ideally, then, there should be no priorities in deciding which children to treat; mental health professionals should only have to decide which treatment is most likely to help which children overcome or reduce their psychological difficulties. Open access to mental health services is an important goal to strive for; as much as possible, it should not be thwarted by administrative policies specifying who is an "acceptable" patient.

Summary

Just as normal behavior patterns become increasingly complex during the elementary-school years, abnormal developments occurring during middle childhood are more varied than those of the preschool period. The entry into school in particular brings with it two important new forms of psychological disturbance: a variety of *learning disabilities*, which involve school achievement that falls substantially below a child's intellectual capacity; and *school phobia*, which consists of a psychological inability to attend school because of intense anxiety experienced in the school setting. Numerous other *neurotic disturbances*, caused mainly by psychosocial experiences rather than constitutional factors, may first appear during the elementary-school years.

Learning disabilities, which are estimated to occur in as many as 25 percent of all school children, are most often caused by some form of minimal brain dysfunction (MBD). Because of restlessness and distractibility, MBD children cannot concentrate effectively on their studies, and their poor perceptual and motor coordination often hampers their performance in specific subject areas, especially those requiring reading and writing.

Learning-disabled children with MBD frequently suffer psychologically as a result of teasing or rejection by other children, lack of understanding or acceptance by their parents, and the frustration of not being able to learn and do things well. Hence, they usually require a *psychoeducational* treatment program that combines remedial work in school subjects with counseling for them and their parents around broader issues of psychological adjustment.

Children manifest school phobia either through physical complaints or complaints about the school that convince their parents to let them stay home. These complaints cannot be ignored, since school-phobic children do become acutely ill or panicky if they are forced to go to school; on the other hand, their physical complaints tend to disappear when they are allowed to stay home, and their complaints about the school continue no matter what is done to change or improve the situation they are complaining about.

Younger school-phobic children are typically anxious about being separated from their mother. Especially in cases where an overprotective mother has fostered overdependence in her son or daughter, the stage is set for the child to balk at going to school. Older school-phobic children are usually anxious about something that has happened at school. In both situations there is (a) a reluctance or inability to recognize the real source of the anxiety, (b) a displacement of the anxiety onto the school in general, and (c) a maladaptive flight from school as a way of reducing the anxiety—all of which define a phobic neurosis.

Treatment of school phobia utilizes various psychotherapeutic methods aimed at getting children back to school as soon as possible, even if only on a part-time basis. Treatment programs that try to help these children understand why they are anxious as well as attempts to keep them in the classroom have been successful in enabling more than 70 percent of school-phobic children to return to school within a short time. If school phobia has already become a chronic pattern, however, an extended period of psychotherapy and home tutoring may be necessary before the child can return to school.

As a form of neurosis, school phobia is a maladaptive effort to cope with anxiety that stems from psychological conflicts or concerns. Other common neuroses of middle childhood include *conversion, hypochondriasis, depression, habit disturbance,* and *conduct disorders.* Conversion and hypochondriasis involve physical symptoms and bodily concerns, respectively, that provide an acceptable excuse for avoiding situations that provoke anxiety. The family environment exerts considerable influence on the type of behavior disorder children develop if they become neurotic; this is especially clear in the case of conversion and hypochondriasis, which generally occur only in families that are very much concerned about health and illness and where certain family members provide "models" for the kind of bodily complaints or concerns a child develops.

Depression, which is characterized by feelings of sadness, pessimism, and apathy, is a response to a sense of loss. Because children have many positive experiences in growing up that counteract overt feelings of gloom and discouragement, their reactions to loss are often "masked." The most common manifestation of masked depression in school-age children is some form of aggressive, delinquent, or antisocial behavior by which the child is compensating for a sense of loss.

Habit disturbances can be viewed as neurotic traits, since they represent immature behavior, but they do not necessarily stem from psychological conflict. Rather, as illustrated by *enuresis* (bed-wetting) and *thumbsucking,* they arise as learned habits or as the result of delayed physical maturation. Although habit disturbances do not necessarily reflect psychopathology, they may become a source of anxiety and can lead to adjustment difficulties.

In conduct disorders a child acts out some feeling or concern that he or she cannot talk about or otherwise resolve. Previously well-behaved children may engage in fighting, stealing, vandalism, cruelty to animals, firesetting, and truancy in order to attract attention, achieve a sense of power, or cause problems for their parents. Children with neurotic conflicts are more likely to develop a conduct disorder if they have an active rather than a passive temperament and if they come from a family where antisocial attitudes are subtly modeled or encouraged.

Neurotic disorders of middle childhood generally do not lead to subsequent psychopathology, and they can usually be effectively treated with psychotherapy. However, this is not true for persistent antisocial conduct disorders; such disorders are very often a prelude to antisocial behavior in adolescence and adulthood. Children who are antisocial and psychotic account for most of the patients in children's mental health clinics who fail to improve.

References

1. Zigmond, N. K. Learning patterns in children with learning disabilities. *Seminars in Psychiatry,* 1969, **1,** 344–353.
2. Gardner, G. E., & Sperry, B. M. School problems: Learning disabilities and school phobia. In S. Arieti (Ed.), *American handbook of psychiatry.* Vol. II. New York: Basic Books, 1974.
3. Schechter, M. D. Psychiatric aspects of learning disabilities. *Child Psychiatry and Human Development,* 1974, **5,** 67–77.
4. Hartlage, L. C. Diagnostic profiles of four types of learning disabled children. *Journal of Clinical Psychology,* 1973, **29,** 458–463.
5. Heinicke, C. M. Learning disturbance in childhood. In B. B. Wolman (Ed.), *Manual of child psychopathology.* New York: McGraw-Hill, 1972.
6. Torgesen, J. Problems and prospects in the study of learning disabilities. In E. M. Hetherington (Ed.), *Review of child development research.* Vol. 5. Chicago: University of Chicago Press, 1975.
7. Wolff, P. H., & Hurwitz, I. Functional implications of the minimal brain damage syndrome. *Seminars in Psychiatry,* 1973, **1,** 105–115.
8. Galante, M. B., Flye, M. E., & Stephens, L. S. Cumulative minor deficits: A longitudinal study of the relation of physical factors to school achievement. *Journal of Learning Disabilities,* 1972, **5,** 19–24.
9. Wender, P. H. *Minimal brain dysfunction in children.* New York: Wiley, 1971.
10. Wender, P. H., & Eisenberg, L. Minimal brain dysfunction in children. In S. Arieti (Ed.), *American handbook of psychiatry.* Vol. II. New York: Basic Books, 1974.
11. Werry, J. S., & Sprague, R. L. Hyperactivity. In C. G. Costello (Ed.), *Symptoms of psychopathology: A handbook.* New York: Wiley, 1970.
12. Bryan, T. S. An observational analysis of classroom behaviors of children with learning disabilities. *Journal of Learning Disabilities,* 1974, **7,** 35–43.
13. Dykman, R. A., Ackerman, P. T., Clements, S. D., & Peters, J. E. Specific learning disabilities: An attentional deficit syndrome. In H. R. Myklebust (Ed.), *Progress in learning disabilities.* Vol. II. New York: Grune & Stratton, 1971.
14. Dykman, R. A., Walls, R. C., Suzuki, T., Ackerman, P. T., & Peters, J. E. Children with learning disabilities: Conditioning, differentiation, and the effect of distraction. *American Journal of Orthopsychiatry,* 1970, **40,** 766–782.
15. Keogh, B. K. Hyperactivity and learning disorders: Review and speculation. *Exceptional Children,* 1971, **38,** 101–109.
16. Lasky, E. Z., & Tobin, H. Linguistic and non-linguistic competing message effects. *Journal of Learning Disabilities,* 1973, **6,** 243–250.
17. Ackerman, P. T., Peters, J. E., & Dykman, R. A. Children with specific learning disabilities: Bender Gestalt test and other signs. *Journal of Learning Disabilities,* 1971, **4,** 437–446.
18. Adams, R. M., Koscis, J. J., & Estes, R. E. Soft neurological signs in learning-disabled children and controls. *American Journal of Diseases of Children,* 1974, **128,** 614–618.
19. Black, F. W. Cognitive, academic, and behavioral findings in children with suspected and documented neurological dysfunction. *Journal of Learning Disabilities,* 1976, **9,** 182–187.
20. Hallahan, D. P., & Cruickshank, W. M. *Psycho-educational foundations of learning disabilities.* Englewood Cliffs, N.J.: Prentice-Hall, 1973.
21. Kluever, R. Mental abilities and disorders of learning. In H. R. Myklebust (Ed.), *Progress in learning disabilities.* Vol. 2. New York: Grune & Stratton, 1971.

22. Owen, F. W., Adams, P. A., Forrest, T., Stolz, L. M., & Fisher, S. Learning disorders in children: Sibling studies. *Monographs of the Society for Research in Child Development,* 1971, **36,** No. 4.

23. Rourke, B. P. Brain-behavior relationships in children with learning disabilities: A research program. *American Psychologist,* 1975, **30,** 911–920.

24. Rourke, B. P., & Finlayson, M. J. Neuropsychological significance of variations in patterns of performance on the trail making test for older children with learning disorders. *Journal of Abnormal Psychology,* 1975, **84,** 412–421.

25. Rourke, B. P., Yanni, D. W., MacDonald, G. W., & Young, G. C. Neuropsychological significance of lateralized defects on the Grooved Pegboard Test for older children with learning disabilities. *Journal of Consulting and Clinical Psychology,* 1973, **41,** 128–134.

26. Rourke, B. P., Young G. C., & Flewelling, R. W. The relationships between WISC verbal-performance discrepancies and selected verbal, auditory-perceptual, visual-perceptual, and problem-solving abilities in children with learning disabilities. *Journal of Clinical Psychology,* 1971, **27,** 475–479.

27. Senf, G. M., & Freundl, P. C. Memory and attention factors in specific learning disabilities. *Journal of Learning Disabilities,* 1971, **4,** 94–106.

28. Vande Voort, L., & Senf, G. M. Audio visual intergration in retarded readers. *Journal of Learning Disabilities,* 1973, **6,** 49–58.

29. Vande Voort, L., Senf, G. M., & Benton, A. L. Development of audiovisual intergration in normal and retarded readers. *Child Development,* 1972, **4,** 1260–1272.

30. MacGinitie, W. H. Evaluating readiness for learning to read: A critical review and evaluation of research. *Reading Research Quarterly,* 1969, **4,** 396–410.

31. Wiener, M., & Cromer, W. Reading and reading difficulty: A conceptual analysis. *Harvard Educational Review,* 1967, **37,** 620–643.

32. Willows, D. M. Reading between the lines: Selective attention in good and poor readers. *Child Development,* 1974, **45,** 408–415.

33. Boder, E. A neuropediatric approach to the diagnosis and management of school behavioral and learning disorders. In J. Hellmuth (Ed.), *Learning disorders.* Vol. II. Seattle: Special Child Publications, 1966.

34. Heiman, J. R., & Ross, A. O. Saccadic eye movements and reading difficulties. *Journal of Abnormal Child Psychology,* 1974, **2,** 53–61.

35. Bryan, T. H. Peer popularity of learning disabled children. *Journal of Learning Disabilities,* 1974, **7,** 621–625.

36. Bryan, T. H. Peer popularity of learning disabled children. *Journal of Learning Disabilities,* 1976, **9,** 307–311.

37. Rubin, E. Z. Cognitive dysfunction and emotional disorders. In H. R. Myklebust (Ed.), *Progress in learning disabilities.* Vol. II. New York: Grune & Stratton, 1971.

38. McCarthy, J. J., & McCarthy, J. F. *Learning disabilities.* Boston: Allyn & Bacon, 1969.

39. Minde, K., Weiss, G., & Mendelson, N. A 5-year follow-up study of 91 hyperactive school children. *Journal of Child Psychiatry,* 1972, **11,** 595–611.

40. Philage, M. L., Kuna, D. J., & Becerril, G. A new family approach to therapy for the learning disabled child. *Journal of Learning Disabilities,* 1975, **8,** 490–499.

41. Peck, B. B. Reading disorders: Have we overlooked something? *Journal of School Psychology,* 1971, **9,** 182–191.

42. Harris, I. D. *Emotional blocks to learning: A study of the reasons for failure in school.* New York: Free Press, 1965.

43. Hellman, I. Some observations on mothers of children with intellectual inhibitions. *Psychoanalytic Study of the Child,* 1954, **9,** 259–273.

44. Jarvis, V. The visual problem in reading disability. *Psychoanalytic Study of the Child,* 1958, **13,** 451–470.

45. Liss, E. Motivations in learning. *Psychoanalytic Study of the Child,* 1955, **10,** 100–116.

46. Pearson, G. H. J. A survey of learning difficulties in children. *Psychoanalytic Study of the Child,* 1952, **7,** 322–386.

47. Sperry, B. M., Staver, N., & Mann, E. E. Destructive fantasies in certain learning difficulties. *American Journal of Orthopsychiatry,* 1952, **22,** 356–365.

48. Sperry, B. M., Staver, N., Reiner, B. S., & Ulrich, D. Renunciation and denial in learning difficulties. *American Journal of Orthopsychiatry,* 1958, **28,** 98–111.

49. Birch, H. G. (Ed.), *Brain damage in children.* Baltimore: Williams & Wilkins, 1964.

50. Clements, S. D. *Minimal brain dysfunction in children*. Washington, D.C.: National Institute of Neurological Diseases and Blindness, Monograph No. 3, 1966.
51. Clements, S. D., & Peters, J. E. Minimal brain dysfunctions in the school-age child. *Archives of General Psychiatry*, 1962, **6**, 185–197.
52. McCarthy, J. M. Learning disabilities: Where have we been? Where are we going? *Seminars in Psychiatry*, 1969, **1**, 354–361.
53. Barsch, R. H. *A movigenic curriculum*. Madison, Wis.: Bureau for Handicapped Children, 1965.
54. Bateman, B. D. Learning disorders. *Review of Educational Research*, 1966, **36**, 93–119.
55. Wiseman, D. A classroom procedure for identifying and remediating language problems. *Mental Retardation*, 1965, **3**, 20–24.
56. Mann, L. Perceptual training: Misdirections and redirections. *American Journal of Orthopsychiatry*, 1970, **40**, 30–38.
57. Quay, H. C. Special education: Assumptions, techniques, and evaluative criteria. *Exceptional Children*, 1973, **40**, 165–170.
58. Myers, P. I., & Hammill, D. D. *Methods for learning disorders*. New York: Wiley, 1969.
59. Ross, A. O. Learning difficulties of children: Dysfunctions, disorders, disabilities. *Journal of School Psychology*, 1967, **5**, 82–92.
60. Blom, G. E. The psychoeducational approach to learning disabilities. *Seminars in Psychiatry*, 1969, **1**, 318–329.
61. Frostig, M. Visual perception, integrative functions, and academic learning. *Journal of Learning Disabilities*, 1972, **5**, 5–15.
62. Frostig, M., & Horne, D. An approach to the treatment of children with learning difficulties. In J. Hellmuth (Ed.), *Learning disorders*. Vol. 1. Seattle: Special Child Publications, 1965.
63. Douglas, V. I. Stop, look and listen: The problem of sustained attention and impulse control in hyperactive and normal children. *Canadian Journal of Behavioral Science*, 1972, **4**, 259–281.
64. Palkes, H., Stewart, M. A., & Freedman, J. Improvement in maze performance of hyperactive boys as a function of verbal-training procedures. *Journal of Special Education*, 1971, **5**, 337–342.
65. Palkes, H., Stewart, M., Kahana, B. Porteus maze performance of hyperactive boys after training in self-directed verbal commands. *Child Development*, 1968, **39**, 817–829.
66. Egeland, B. Training impulsive children in the use of more efficient scanning techniques. *Child Development*, 1974, **45**, 165–171.
67. Meichenbaum, D. H., & Goodman, J. Training impulsive children to talk to themselves: A means of developing self-control. *Journal of Abnormal Psychology*, 1971, **77**, 115–126.
68. Ridberg, E. H., Parke, R. D., & Hetherington, E. M. Modification of impulsive and reflective cognitive style through observation of film-mediated models. *Developmental Psychology*, 1971, **5**, 369–377.
69. Patterson, G. R., Jones, R., Whittier, J., & Wright, M. A. A behavior modification technique for the hyperactive child. *Behavior Research and Therapy*, 1965, **2**, 217–226.
70. O'Leary, K. D., Becker, W. C., Evans, M. B., & Saudargas, R. A. A token reinforcement program in a public school: A replication and systematic analysis. *Journal of Applied Behavioral Analysis*, 1969, **2**, 3–13.
71. O'Leary, K. D., & Drabman, R. Token reinforcement programs in the classroom. *Psychological Bulletin*, 1971, **75**, 379–398.
72. O'Leary, K. D., Drabman, R., & Kass, R. E. Maintenance of appropriate behavior in a token program. *Journal of Abnormal Child Psychology*, 1973, **1**, 127–138.
73. Eisenberg, L. School phobia: A study in the communication of anxiety. *American Journal of Psychiatry*, 1958, **114**, 712–718.
74. Millar, T. P. The child who refuses to attend school. *American Journal of Psychiatry*, 1961, **118**, 398–404.
75. Sperling, M. School phobias: Classification, dynamics, and treatment. *Psychoanalytic Study of the Child*, 1967, **22**, 375–401.
76. Talbot, M. Panic in school phobia. *American Journal of Orthopsychiatry*, 1957, **27**, 286–295.
77. Waldfogel, S., Coolidge, J. C., & Hahn, P. B. The development, meaning, and management of school phobia. *American Journal of Orthopsychiatry*, 1957, **27**, 754–780.

78. Berg, I., Collins, T., McGuire, R., & O'Melia, J. Educational attainment in adolescent school phobia. *British Journal of Psychiatry,* 1975, **126,** 435–438.

79. Hersov, L. A. Persistent non-attendance at school. *Journal of Child Psychology and Psychiatry,* 1960, **1,** 130–136.

80. Hersov, L. A. Refusal to go to school. *Journal of Child Psychology and Psychiatry,* 1960, **1,** 137–145.

81. Berg, I., & McGuire, R. Are mothers of school-phobic adolescents overprotective? *British Journal of Psychiatry,* 1974, **124,** 10–13.

82. Clyne, M. B. *Absent: School refusal as an expression of disturbed family relationships.* London: Tavistock, 1966.

83. Coolidge, J. C., Tessman, E., Waldfogel, S., & Willer, M. L. Patterns of aggression in school phobia. *Psychoanalytic Study of the Child,* 1962, **17,** 319–333.

84. Estes, H. R., Haylett, C. H., & Johnson, A. M. Separation anxiety. *American Journal of Psychotherapy,* 1956, **10,** 682–695.

85. Malmquist, C. P. School phobia: A problem in family neurosis. *Journal of the American Academy of Child Psychiatry,* 1965, **4,** 293–319.

86. Hodgman, C. H., & Braiman, A. "College phobia": School refusal in university students. *American Journal of Psychiatry,* 1965, **121,** 801–805.

87. Kahn, J. H., & Nursten, J. P. School refusal: A comprehensive view of school phobia and other failures of school attendance. *American Journal of Orthopsychiatry,* 1962, **22,** 707–718.

88. Levenson, E. A. The treatment of school phobia in the young adult. *American Journal of Psychotherapy,* 1961, **15,** 539–552.

89. Leventhal, T., & Sills, M. Self-image in school phobia. *American Journal of Orthopsychiatry,* 1964, **34,** 685–695.

90. Weiner, I. B., *Psychological disturbance in adolescence.* New York: Wiley, 1970. Chap. 6. School Phobia.

91. Kessler, J. W. Neurosis in childhood. In B. B. Wolman (Ed.), *Manual of child psychopathology.* New York: McGraw-Hill, 1972.

92. Tyrer, P., & Tyrer, S. School refusal, truancy, and adult neurotic illness. *Psychological Medicine,* 1974, **4,** 416–421.

93. Kennedy, W. A. School phobia: Rapid treatment of fifty cases. *Journal of Abnormal Psychology,* 1965, **70,** 285–289.

94. Miller, L. C., Barrett, C. L., & Hampe, E. Phobias of childhood in a prescientific era. In A. Davids (Ed.), *Child personality and psychopathology: Current topics.* New York: Wiley, 1974.

95. Coolidge, J. C., Hahn, P. B., & Peck, A. L. School phobia: Neurotic crisis or way of life? *American Journal of Orthopsychiatry,* 1957, **27,** 296–306.

96. Cowen, E. L., Pederson, A., Babigian, H., Izzo, L. D., & Trost, M. A. Long-term follow-up of early detected vulnerable children. *Journal of Consulting and Clinical Psychology,* 1973, **41,** 438–446.

97. Kohlberg, L., LaCrosse, J., & Ricks, D. The predictability of adult mental health from childhood behavior. In B. B. Wolman (Ed.), *Manual of child psychopathology.* New York: McGraw-Hill, 1972.

98. Mellsop, G. W. Psychiatric patients seen as children and adults: Childhood predictors of adult illness. *Journal of Child Psychology and Psychiatry,* 1972, **13,** 91–101.

99. Robins, L. N. *Deviant children grown up.* Baltimore: Williams & Wilkins, 1966.

100. Robins, L. N. Follow-up studies of behavior disorders in children. In H. C. Quay & J. S. Werry (Eds.), *Psychopathological disorders of childhood.* New York: Wiley, 1972.

101. Rutter, M. L. Relationships between child and adult psychiatric disorders. *Acta Psychiatricia Scandinavica,* 1972, **48,** 3–21.

102. Pittman, F. S., Langsley, D. G., & DeYoung, C. D. Work and school phobias: A family approach to treatment. *American Journal of Psychiatry,* 1968, **124,** 1535–1541.

103. Lassers, E., Nordan, R., & Bladholm, S. Steps in the return to school of children with school phobia. *American Journal of Psychiatry,* 1973, **130,** 265–268.

104. Coolidge, J. C., Brodie, R. D., & Feeney, B. A ten-year follow-up study of sixty-six school-phobic children. *American Journal of Orthopsychiatry,* 1964, **34,** 675–684.

105. Leventhal, T., Weinberger, G., Stander, R. J., & Stearns, R. P. Therapeutic strategies with school phobia. *American Journal of Orthopsychiatry,* 1967, **37,** 64–70.

106. Sperling, M. Analytic first aid in school phobia. *Psychoanalytic Quarterly,* 1961, **30,** 504–518.

107. Barker, P. B. The in-patient treatment of school refusal. *British Journal of Medical Psychology,* 1968, **41,** 381–387.

108. Shapiro, T., & Jegede, R. O. School phobia: A babel of tongues. *Journal of Autism and Childhood Schizophrenia,* 1973, **3,** 168–186.

109. Veltkamp, L. J. School phobia. *Journal of Family Counseling,* 1975, **3,** 47–51.

110. Ayllon, T., Smith, D., & Rogers, M. Behavioral management of school phobia. *Journal of Behavior Therapy and Experimental Psychiatry,* 1970, **1,** 125–138.

111. Garvey, W. P., & Hegrenes, J. R. Desensitization techniques in the treatment of school phobia. *American Journal of Orthopsychiatry,* 1966, **36,** 147–152.

112. Hersen, M. The behavioral treatment of school phobia. *Journal of Nervous and Mental Disease,* 1971, **153,** 99–107.

113. Rodriguez, A., Rodriguez, M., & Eisenberg, L. The outcome of school phobia: A follow-up study based on 41 cases. *American Journal of Psychiatry,* 1959, **116,** 540–544.

114. Smith, S. L. School refusal with anxiety: A review of sixty-three cases. *Canadian Psychiatric Association Journal,* 1970, **15,** 257–264.

115. Weiss, M., & Burke, A. A five-to-ten-year follow-up of hospitalized school phobic children and adolescents. *American Journal of Orthopsychiatry,* 1970, **40,** 672–676.

116. Anthony, E. J. Neurotic disorders. In A. M. Freeman, H. I. Kaplan, & B. J. Sadock (Eds.), *Comprehensive textbook of psychiatry.* (2nd ed.) Baltimore: Williams & Wilkins, 1975.

117. Rexford, E. N., Van Amerongen, S. T., Psychological disorders of the grade school years. In S. Arieti (Ed.), *American handbook of psychiatry.* Vol. II. New York: Basic Books, 1974.

118. Shaw, C. R., & Lucas, A. R. *The psychiatric disorders of childhood.* (2nd ed.) New York: Appleton-Century-Crofts, 1970. Chap. 7, Psychoneurosis.

119. Sobel, R. Adjustment reactions in infancy and childhood. In A. M. Freedman, H. I. Kaplan, & B. J. Sadock (Eds.), *Comprehensive textbook of psychiatry.* (2nd ed.) Baltimore: Williams & Wilkins, 1975.

120. Chodoff, P. The diagnosis of hysteria: An overview. *American Journal of Psychiatry,* 1974, **131,**1073–1078.

121. Freud, S. (1910). *The psycho-analytic view of psychogenic disturbance of vision.* Standard Edition, Vol. XI. London: Hogarth, 1957.

122. Loof, D. H. Psychophysiologic and conversion reactions in children. *Journal of the American Academy of Child Psychiatry,* 1970, **9,** 318–331.

123. Nemiah, J. C. Hysterical neurosis, conversion type. In A. M. Freedman, H. I. Kaplan, & B. J. Sadock (Eds.), *Comprehensive textbook of psychiatry.* (2nd ed.) Baltimore: Williams & Wilkins, 1975.

124. Templer, D. I., & Lester, D. Conversion disorders: A review of research findings. *Comprehensive Psychiatry,* 1974, **15,** 285–294.

125. Woolsey, R. M. Hysteria, 1875–1975. *Diseases of the Nervous System,* 1976, **37,** 379–386.

126. Lapouse, R., & Monk, M. Behavior deviations in a representative sample of children: Variation by sex, age, race, social class, and family size. *American Journal of Orthopsychiatry,* 1964, **34,** 436–446.

127. Torup, E. A follow-up study of children with tics. *Acta Paediatrica,* 1962, **51,** 261–268.

128. Werry, J. S. Psychosomatic disorders. In H. C. Quay & J. S. Werry (Eds.), *Psychopathological disorders of childhood.* New York: Wiley, 1972.

129. Yates, A. J. Tics. In C. G. Costello (Ed.), *Symptoms of psychopathology.* New York: Wiley, 1970.

130. Dorfman, W. Hypochondriasis revisited: A dilemma and challenge to medicine and psychiatry. *Psychosomatics,* 1975, **16,** 14–16.

131. Nemiah, J. C. Hypochondriacal neurosis. In A. M. Freedman, H. I. Kaplan, & B. J. Sadock (Eds.), *Comprehensive textbook of psychiatry.* (2nd ed.) Baltimore: Williams & Wilkins, 1975.

132. Kenyon, F. E. Hypochondriacal states. *British Journal of Psychiatry,* 1976, **129,** 1–14.

133. Proctor, J. T. Hysteria in childhood. *American Journal of Orthopsychiatry,* 1958, **28,** 394–407.

134. Proctor, J. T. The treatment of hysteria in childhood. In M. Hammer & A. M. Kaplan (Eds.), *The practice of psychotherapy with children.* Homewood, Ill.: Dorsey Press, 1967.

135. Rock, N. L. Conversion reactions in childhood: A clinical study on childhood neuroses. *Journal of the American Academy of Child Psychiatry,* 1971, **10,** 65–93.

136. Thomas, A., & Chess, S. *Temperament and development in children.* New York: Brunner/Mazel, 1977.

137. Laybourne, P. C., & Churchill, S. W. Symptom discouragement in treating hysterical reactions of childhood. *International Journal of Child Psychotherapy,* 1972, **1,** 111–123.

138. Beck, A. T. *Depression: Causes and treatment.* Philadelphia: University of Pennsylvania Press, 1970.

139. Beck, A. T. Depressive neurosis. In S. Arieti (Ed.), *American handbook of psychiatry.* Vol. 3. New York: Basic Books, 1974.

140. Becker, J. *Depression: Theory and research.* New York: Halstead, 1974.

141. Grinker, R. R., Miller, J., Sabshin, M., & Nunn, R. *The phenomena of depression.* New York: Hoeber, 1961.

142. Mendelson, M. *Psychoanalytic concepts of depression.* (2nd ed.) New York; Spectrum, 1974.

143. Seligman, M. E. *Helplessness: On depression, development, and death.* San Francisco: W. H. Freeman, 1975.

144. Freud, S. (1917). *Mourning and melancholia.* Standard Edition, Vol. XIV. London: Hogarth, 1957.

145. Bibring, E. The mechanism of depression. In P. Greenacre (Ed.), *Affective disorders.* New York: International Universities Press, 1953.

146. Gaylin, W. (Ed.) *The meaning of despair: Psychoanalytic contributions to the understanding of depression.* New York: Science House, 1968.

147. Rie, H. E. Depression in childhood: A survey of some pertinent contributions. *American Journal of the Academy of Child Psychiatry,* 1966, **5,** 653–685.

148. Cytryn, L., & McKnew, D. H. Factors influencing the changing clinical expression of the depressive process in children. *American Journal of Psychiatry,* 1974, **131,** 879–881.

149. Malmquist, C. P. Depression in childhood. In F. F. Flach & S. C. Draghi (Eds.), *The nature and treatment of depression.* New York: Wiley, 1975.

150. Burks, H. L., & Harrison, S. I. Aggressive behavior as a means of avoiding depression. *American Journal of Orthopsychiatry,* 1962, **34,** 416–422.

151. Bonnard, A. Truancy and pilfering associated with bereavement. In S. Lorand & H. I. Schneer (Eds.), *Adolescents: Psychoanalytic approach to problems and therapy.* New York: Hoeber, 1961.

152. Glaser, K. Masked depression in children and adolescents. *American Journal of Psychotherapy,* 1967, **21,** 565–574.

153. Spiegel, R. Anger and acting out: Masks of depression. *American Journal of Psychotherapy,* 1967, **21,** 597–606.

154. Anthony, E. J. Childhood depression. In E. J. Anthony & T. Benedek (Eds.), *Depression and human existence.* Boston: Little, Brown, 1975.

155. Connell, H. M. Depression in childhood. *Child Psychiatry and Human Development,* 1972, **4,** 71–85.

156. Malmquist, C. P. Depressive phenomena in children. In B. B. Wolman (Ed.), *Manual of child psychopathology.* New York: McGraw-Hill, 1972.

157. Paulson, M. J., & Stone, D. Suicidal behavior of latency-age children. *Journal of Clinical Child Psychology,* 1974, **3,** 50–53.

158. Poznanski, E., & Zrull, J. P. Childhood depression: Clinical characteristics of overtly depressed children. *Archives of General Psychiatry,* 1970, **23,** 8–15.

159. Oppel, W. C., Harper, P. A., & Rider, R. V. The age of attaining bladder control. *Pediatrics,* 1968, **42,** 614–626.

160. Pierce, C. M. Enuresis and encopresis. In A. M. Freedman, H. I. Kaplan, & B. J. Sadock (Eds.), *Comprehensive textbook of psychiatry.* (2nd ed.) Baltimore: Williams & Wilkins, 1975.

161. Bindelglas, P. M. The enuretic child. *Journal of Family Practice,* 1975, **2,** 375–380.

162. Cohen, M. W. Enuresis. *Pediatric Clinics of North America,* 1975, **22,** 545–560.

163. Lovibond, S. H., & Coote, M. A. Enuresis. In C. G. Costello (Ed.), *Symptoms of psychopathology.* New York: Wiley, 1970.

164. Stehbens, J. A. Enuresis in school children. *Journal of School Psychology,* 1970, **8,** 145–151.

165. Werry, J. A., & Corrssen, J. Enuresis: An etiologic and therapeutic study. *Journal of Pediatrics,* 1965, **67,** 423–431.

166. Davidson, P. O. Thumbsucking. In C. G. Costello (Ed.), *Symptoms of psychopathology*. New York: Wiley, 1970.

167. Thorne, D. E. Instrumented behavior modification of bedwetting. *Behavioral Engineering*, 1975, **2,** 47–51.

168. Werry, J. S. The conditioning treatment of enuresis. *American Journal of Psychiatry*, 1966, **123,** 226–229.

169. Gold, M., & Mann, D. Delinquency as defense. *American Journal of Orthopsychiatry*, 1972, **42,** 463–479.

170. Vandersall, T. A., & Winer, J. M. Children who set fires. *Archives of General Psychiatry*, 1970, **22,** 63–71.

171. Macht, L. B., & Mack, J. E. The firesetter syndrome. *Psychiatry*, 1968, **31,** 277–288.

172. Wilson, H. Juvenile delinquency, parental criminality and social handicap. *British Journal of Criminology*, 1975, **15,** 241–250.

173. Carek, D. J., Hendrickson, W., & Holmes, D. J. Delinquency addiction in parents. *Archives of General Psychiatry*, 1961, **4,** 357–362.

174. Giffin, M. E., Johnson, A. M., & Litin, E. M. Specific factors determining anti-social acting out. *American Journal of Orthopsychiatry*, 1954, **24,** 668–684.

175. Singer, M. Delinquency and family disciplinary configurations: An elaboration of the superego lacunae concept. *Archives of General Psychiatry*, 1974, **31,** 795–798.

176. Kessler, J. W. *Psychopathology of childhood*. Englewood Cliffs, N.J.: Prentice-Hall, 1966. Chap. 10, Psychoneurosis in children.

177. Joint Commission on Mental Health of Children. *Crisis in child mental health: Challenge for the 1970s*. New York: Harper, 1970.

15 Physical and Mental Growth

PHYSICAL AND PHYSIOLOGICAL CHANGES

Changes in Body Size and Configuration

Development of Primary and Secondary Sex Characteristics

The Secular Trend

Body Image and Self-Satisfaction

MENTAL DEVELOPMENT

Test Intelligence

Formal Operational Thought and Its Manifestations

Issues in Formal Operational Thought

Affective Consequences of Formal Operational Thought

ESSAY

Implications of the Secular Trend

BIOGRAPHY

G. Stanley Hall

SUMMARY

REFERENCES

During early adolescence (from the age of about 11 to 14) marked physical, physiological, and mental changes take place that transform children into young adults. Middle adolescence (from about 14 to 18) is a period during which young people must adapt to the new physical and mental selves and to the social realities of adolescent life. Late adolescence or youth (from about 18 to 21) is a transition period during which the young person becomes a member of adult society.

In this chapter we will focus most of our attention on early adolescence because this is the period that has been most heavily researched, thereby giving us the most information. However, wherever it is appropriate and we have enough data, we will discuss the later phases of adolescence as well. What should be emphasized is that adolescence is a complex period of development with substages that differ as much from one another as do infancy, early childhood, and middle childhood.

PHYSICAL AND PHYSIOLOGICAL CHANGES

During most of the years of middle childhood, increases in height, weight, and body configuration tend to be rather gradual and continuous. All of this changes, however, during early adolescence, when there is a rapid increase in body size, changes in the body's proportions and composition, and swift development of the gonads (testes and ovaries) — the reproductive glands — and the physical characteristics that signal sexual maturity. Many of the changes that occur during adolescence are parallel for both boys and girls, while others are sex-specific. Boys, for example, undergo a significant increase in their muscle tissue and strength, whereas girls develop more fatty tissue, giving rise to their "rounded" body contours. Presumably these changes reflect evolutionary adaptations: the male's strength prepared him for hunting, fighting, and foraging; the female's contours attracted males and inclined them to mate, thereby insuring perpetuation of the species. In technological societies these differences are no longer of major significance.

Girls generally begin their adolescent growth about 2 years before boys of the same age, and they may have completed it before their male peers have even begun. This accounts for the fact that in the fifth, sixth, and seventh grades girls are often taller, heavier, and more sexually mature than boys. In the later grades boys begin to catch up and eventually become taller and heavier than girls.

The physical changes of adolescence are due to the action of **hormones** — discrete chemical substances produced mainly by the glands. Some of the hormones are being secreted for the first time during adolescence, whereas others are simply being secreted in larger amounts. Hormones work in different ways, but they generally stimulate receptors in one or more organs or tissues. According to Tanner, a single hormone can have a number of targets and effects. "**Testosterone** [the male hormone], for example, acts in many receptors, in the cells of the penis, the skin of the

face, the cartilages of the shoulder joints and certain parts of the brain''
(1). It is not clear precisely how hormones accomplish their task, although
contemporary endocrinology is making enormous strides in furthering our
understanding (2–4). We will limit our discussion here to the various
effects of increased hormone production that take place during adolescence.

Changes in Body Size and Configuration

While the over-all sequence of physical growth for boys and girls is comparable, there are important differences pertaining to the pacing, as well as the onset, velocity, and duration of the growth period.

Boys. Growth in body size and structure appears to go through several cycles during the first two decades of life. The first cycle begins shortly after conception and extends until about the end of the second year of life. During this time there is a rapid acceleration of body size and articulation which reaches a peak at midgestation and then declines slowly during the first and second years of infancy. A second growth cycle begins about the second year of life, reaches a peak and accelerates at about 2½ years of age, and then declines slowly until about age 7. The third cycle begins at about the age of 7 or 8 and accelerates gradually to a peak in the early teens, after which there is a gradual decline. During this peak, called the **adolescent growth spurt,** remarkable changes take place in body size and configuration.

In the case of boys (as well as girls) the age at which the growth spurt begins to accelerate, peak, and decline varies according to certain circumstances, including heredity, his family's socioeconomic status, and the culture in which he is growing up. Middle-class boys in the United States, Canada, and Great Britain reach the peak of acceleration in growth around 14 years of age. At this time a boy's height increases at the rate of about 10.5 centimeters (4.1 inches) a year. Because that peak velocity is not maintained throughout the year, however, his actual height for the year may increase anywhere from between 7 cm (2.76 inches) to 12 cm (4.72 inches) (1).

The adolescent growth spurt is controlled by different hormones than those that regulated growth during childhood. Consequently the relative size of some boys and girls vis-à-vis their peers will change significantly during adolescence. A boy who is about the same height as his friends during childhood may end up being considerably taller or shorter than they are in late adolescence and adulthood. About 30 percent of one's adult height is attained during the adolescent growth spurt. The velocity of growth in height for an average boy or girl is shown in Figure 15.1.

The various body parts also have their own sequence and velocity of growth. Growth tends to be most rapid at the periphery and to move toward the trunk. An adolescent's hands and feet become almost adult size before the legs and arms reach their full length or become fleshed out.

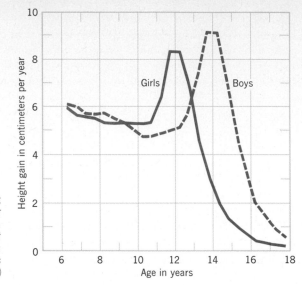

Figure 15.1 Adolescent spurt in height growth for boys and girls. (*Source.* Tanner, J. M. *Growth at adolescence.* Oxford: Blackwell Scientific Publications, 1962.)

While children appear to be "spindly," adolescents often appear to be "all hands and feet." After a young person's feet have become full size, then the calves and thighs attain their full length. A similar progression holds true for hands and arms. The peak velocity of forearm growth lags behind the peak velocity of hand growth, but it precedes upper-arm growth by about 6 months.

The heart and lungs, stomach, kidneys, musculature, and blood volume all increase and attain their final adult size and level of functioning during the adolescent growth spurt (roughly from about 11 to 15 years of age). The increased size and functional capacity of the respiratory, digestive, and circulatory systems are required by the young person's greater size and strength (5, 6).

It should be noted that some parts of the body do not participate in the growth spurt. The head and brain, for example, attain about 90 percent of their adult size by the age of 5. The lymphoid tissues of the tonsils, adenoids, and intestines increase gradually in size until early adolescence and then decrease progressively after that. Some children who suffer from allergies, sinus ailments, and tonsillitis may experience a spontaneous easing of symptoms as the tissues that are responsible decrease in size and perhaps sensitivity (5, 6). Facial growth also continues during this period, and the jaw and nose become larger, reaching a more mature relationship to the upper head, which had already attained its full size (6).

Girls. In North America and Great Britain, middle-class young women reach the peak velocity of their growth spurt at about the age of 12 — approximately 2 years ahead of boys.

Growth in girls also moves from the periphery toward the trunk. Girls, however, develop more subcutaneous fat on their arms and legs than do boys so that their veins and tendons usually do not show. With respect to trunk growth, girls' shoulders remain slender whereas their hips become broader and rounder; boys, on the other hand, develop wider and stronger shoulders while their hips remain slender.

The increase in girls' subcutaneous fat is not generally accompanied by a compensatory growth in muscle, as is true for boys. Consequently, girls have a higher percentage of body fat than do boys. They seldom attain the muscular strength of boys except in the case of girl athletes. In relation to their size, boys have "larger hearts and lungs, higher systolic blood pressure, a lower resting heart rate, and a greater capacity for carrying oxygen in the blood, and a greater power for neutralizing the chemical products of muscular exercise such as lactic acid" (1, p. 5). Again, these differences are probably the result of evolutionary differentiation of functions for men and women.

Development of Primary and Secondary Sex Characteristics

There are two types of changes in the reproductive system during early adolescence. The genitalia increase in size and eventually become functional in both boys and girls. That is, boys secrete live spermatozoa while girls ovulate fertile eggs. Changes in the genitalia and accessory organs (breasts) are described as changes in **primary sex characteristics**. Associated changes in body hair, sweat glands, sebaceous glands, and laryngeal muscles are described as changes in **secondary sex characteristics**. The period during which the primary and secondary sex characteristics develop is called puberty (*pubes* means hair). Although the sequence of events is about the same for boys and girls, the details differ significantly.

Boys. Among boys the first sign of puberty is usually a gradual enlargement of the scrotum and testes together with a darkening and wrinkling of the scrotum sac. Pubic hairs may begin to appear at about this time or somewhat later. There is an increase in height and in the size of the penis about a year after the enlargement of the scrotum and testes. Although the time varies substantially, a boy may have his first ejaculation of seminal fluid about a year after the onset of penis growth. The time ranges for the appearance of primary sex characteristics are shown in Figure 15.2 (1).

The development of secondary sex characteristics follows about the same sequence among all boys. Axillary (underarm) hair generally begins to grow about 2 years after pubic hair. Facial hair usually begins to appear at about the same time. The pattern of facial hair growth is generally as follows: Fine hairs first appear at the corners of the upper lip, and then all over the upper lip. Hair next appears on the cheeks and then begins to grow along the sides and lower border of the chin. The rest of the body hair (chest and legs) begins to grow at the same time as axillary hair, but it

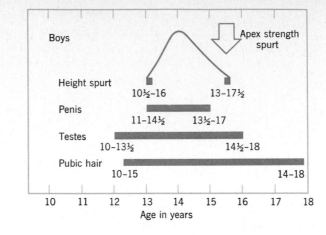

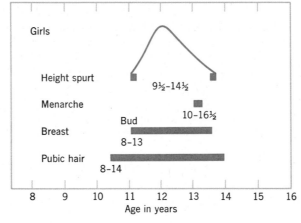

Figure 15.2 Sequence and age range of onset and conclusion of growth events in boys and girls at adolescence. The bars represent average boys and girls. The figures underneath them give the range of ages during which the events may begin and end. (*Source.* Tanner, J. M. *Growth at adolescence.* Oxford: Blackwell Scientific Publications, 1962.)

may continue into late adolescence. Individual differences in the amount of body hair that appears are largely due to heredity, but the reasons for the acceleration or retardation of body hair growth are still not known.

As the larynx enlarges and the vocal cords lengthen, there is a progressive lowering of voice pitch. This lowering is not always constant, however, and some boys are embarrassed to hear themselves uncontrollably shift from a high contralto to a low basso in the middle of a sentence. The final, adult pitch of the voice is usually not attained until late adolescence. Voice timbre — the quality that enables us to distinguish voices of the same pitch from one another — depends upon the size of the resonance chambers of the mouth and nose. Timbre changes as the mouth and nose increase in size during puberty (1).

Two skin changes take place during adolescence: the maturation of the sebaceous glands and: the maturation of the apocrine sweat glands (particularly in the axillary and genital areas). The sebaceous glands secrete a fatty substance that can accumulate in the pores, block them, and produce blackheads. The blocked pores may irritate the surrounding area and erupt onto the outer skin as acne. The apocrine sweat glands, which grow very rapidly during puberty, give rise to an odor that is considered unpleasant in our society. We will discuss how these skin changes affect adolescents' views about themselves in Chapter 18.

Girls. Among girls the first sign of puberty is usually the appearance of the "breast bud" — the second* of five stages (5) of breast development. In the case of some girls pubic hair appears before the breast bud, but among two-thirds of all girls pubic hair follows the breast bud. Enlargement of the uterus, vagina, labia, and clitoris generally occurs at the same time as breast development.

Certainly the most dramatic indication of the onset of puberty for girls is the menarche — the first menstruation. Undoubtedly there are different reasons for the variation in the age of menarche. About 50 percent of white American girls reach menarche between the ages of 12 and 14, and about 80 percent reach it between the ages of 11½ and 14½. Fewer than 2 percent of all girls reach menarche before the age of 10 or after the age of 16. Menstruation by itself, however, does not necessarily signal reproductive maturity; in some cases menstruation is anovulatory (an egg is not released), and there is a period of sterility that may last from 10 months to a year after the first menstruation (1).

Girls develop secondary sex characteristics in the same sequence as boys, but these are generally less marked. Thus, girls experience changes in the sebaceous glands and they have axillary and body hair, but to a lesser extent than boys. Of course there are wide individual differences, and some young women have more body hair than do young men at a comparable stage of development. Both boys and girls experience a roughening of the skin, particularly of the thighs and upper arms, but this is less prominent among girls. Figure 15.2 gives an over-all picture of pubertal development in girls and also suggests the range in age for the various body changes.

The Secular Trend   During the bicentennial celebration in 1976 many people visited such places as Williamsburg in Virginia and Mystic Seaport in Connecticut. In looking at buildings and boats that were constructed for people a century or more ago, it is quickly apparent that the beds were shorter and the headroom was lower than they are today. People in the 1970s are, on the average, taller and heavier than their counterparts hundreds of years ago.

---

*The stages are (a) preadolescence — the papillae alone are elevated, (b) the bud stage — the areola enlarges and the breast and papillae elevate, (c) the enlargement continues and the papillae and areola form a secondary mound, (d) the areola recesses and there is a final contouring of the breast, (e) there is a projection of the papillae (5).

Also, boys and girls are both reaching puberty at an earlier age than was true in the nineteenth century. This gradual change is known as the **secular trend**. To be more explicit, the average increase in height for white adults in the United States was about ½ inch per decade from 1915 to 1940 and about ⅛ inch per decade from 1940 to 1960. In other words, boys and girls in 1960 were about an inch taller and about 10 pounds heavier than their counterparts a quarter-century earlier (9).

The secular trend in the age of menarche is even more spectacular. Figure 15.3 shows the decrease in the age of menarche for girls from different coutries and for different periods in history. The beginning of the growth spurt has also declined over the years for both boys and girls. Young people in North America, Europe, Japan, and China are experiencing puberty and the growth spurt about 2 years earlier than they were a century ago (10).

There are probably a number of interrelated factors that can explain the secular trend, but two of them are believed to be better nutrition and medical care (1). However, it appears that there are physiological limits that cannot be exceeded. Once a population is meeting its maximum nutritional requirements, it is likely that the secular trend will end (6). Indeed, this seems to be what is happening among middle-class Americans and Britons today; between 1960 and 1970 there was no increase in their average height or decrease in their average age of menarche. However, in underdeveloped countries, where nutrition is not adequate and health standards are not too high, the secular trend will probably be continuing for many years to come (1, 11).

Figure 15.3 Decrease in age of menarche for girls from different countries and for different periods in history. (*Source.* Tanner, J. M. *Growth at adolescence.* Oxford: Blackwell Scientific Publications, 1962.)

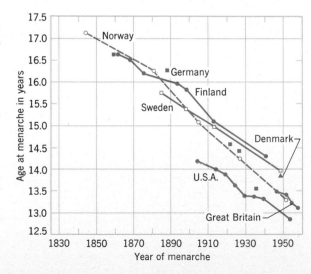

Body Image and Self-Satisfaction

Adolescents tend to evaluate themselves largely in terms of their physical characteristics. They do this, in part at least, because they have not yet had the opportunity to prove themselves vocationally. For example, in one study 20-year-old men could easily identify a photograph of their own body (excluding the face) from among a group of photographs ranging from high to low similarity. Men in their early forties, however, had difficulty making such an identification (12). One interpretation of this finding is that young men are more concerned about, and hence more familiar with, their physiques than are older men.

Most people in American society share an implicit concept of the ideal male or female body configuration against which they compare themselves to assess their relative attractiveness.

In evaluating their bodies, young people often compare themselves with certain ideal concepts that prevail in the society. According to one investigator (13, 14), certain stereotypes are held by all young people in America regardless of age, sex, race, ethnic background, or geographical location. Apparently American men (aged 10 to 20) and American women (aged 16 to 40) believe that the best leaders, athletes, and friends are muscular, well-proportioned men. Other studies show that Americans believe that hairiness, muscularity, and large genitals are a sign of virility among men (15, 16).

Since young people assess themselves according to the stereotypical ideal for either sex, their satisfaction with their own bodies depends upon the extent to which they approach that ideal. In America, for example, it is held to be ideal for a man to be 72 inches tall and to weigh between 171 and 180 pounds (17). Figure 15.4 shows how satisfaction about height among adolescent boys varies according to how close they come to the stereotypical ideal. In general, body image seems to be more important to girls than to boys, partly because society places much more emphasis on the female form than on the male form.

In the past, a woman's appearance was directly related to her chances of making a "good" marriage; hence great emphasis was placed upon her attractiveness. By age 16, if a girl did not have a 38-24-36 figure and a button nose she might consider herself ugly, a disappointment to her parents, and a useless commodity on the marriage market. Fortunately, these attitudes are changing (albeit slowly) and personal ability and achievements are becoming more salient than physical attractiveness in women's self-evaluations and in society's evaluations of women.

A number of studies have demonstrated that when adolescents are

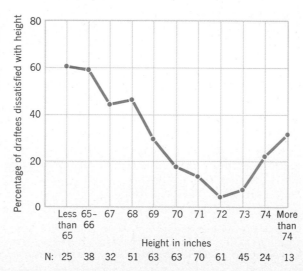

Figure 15.4 The relationship between an army draftee's height and his dissatisfaction with that height. (*Source.* Gunderson, E. K. E. Body size, self-evaluation, and military effectiveness. *Journal of Personality and Social Psychology,* 1965, **2,** 902–906.)

dissatisfied with their bodies, they often become anxious (18–21). It should be noted, however, that all of these studies show that more adolescents are *happy* with their bodies than are *unhappy* (22–23). As young people mature and begin to evaluate themselves in terms of personal qualities and achievement, they are less inclined to include their body image in their self-evaluation. Although body image continues to be an important part of one's self-concept throughout life, it is never again as prominent as it was during adolescence.

MENTAL DEVELOPMENT

The dramatic changes that occur in physical development during early adolescence often mask equally dramatic changes that are taking place in mental development. Thanks to the development of what Piaget (24) calls **formal operations,** young adolescents are able to deal with many variables at the same time, grasp metaphor and simile, construct ideals, and entertain — as well as reason about — contrary-to-fact propositions. They are able to understand historical time and different cultures. These changes in mental ability can be described quantitatively as well as qualitatively. Quantitatively, two issues seem to be of special importance: (a) the so-called age differentiation hypothesis and (b) the course of mental growth, which was long thought to reach a peak in adolescence and then to decline gradually thereafter.

Changes in the qualitative aspects of adolescent thinking have not been explored as extensively as those in childhood. Little experimental work has been done on the development of language, memory, and perception in adolescence. Much of the research that has been done on adolescent thinking has focued on adolescent reasoning and problem-solving. We will discuss some of this research as well as the issues pertaining to formal operational thinking, and then conclude by pointing out some of the affective consequences of attaining formal operational thinking.

Test Intelligence

For the most part, adolescents are experienced in taking tests and their performance tends to be quite stable over time. An adolescent's brightness can, however, sometimes cause a problem. A bright boy or girl may interpret test questions as more complex than they really are or use test items for the purpose of taking a political or social stand (25). When one of the authors was testing a young man on the Wechsler Adult Intelligence Scale (WAIS), one of the questions on the "comprehension" subscale was "Why should criminals be locked up?" and he answered, "I don't think they should be." When testing children, one must always try to determine "Does the child really understand the question?" When testing adolescents, on the other hands, the issue is: "Does he or she understand the question too well?"

With respect to mental growth, two questions are important: What is a young person's range of abilities during adolescence? And what is the course of growth in mental abilities during the adolescent period and after?

The Age Differentiation Hypothesis. One view of the nature of mental abilities is called the **age differentiation hypothesis** (26–28). It holds that in infancy mental abilities are rather separate and uncoordinated. During childhood, however, these abilities become progressively integrated and coordinated within a few higher-order abilities. Then, during adolescence, mental abilities become differentiated again so that there are more basic abilities than during childhood. Other investigators (29) believe that there is another stage of *dedifferentiation* in *late adulthood,* during which mental abilities coalesce somewhat into a less differentiated pattern.

This age differentiation hypothesis is of more than academic interest, since it is reflected in our school curricula. In elementary school children take a limited number of subjects such as arithmetic, reading, social studies, and science. But in high school the adolescent has a much wider range of choices, including foreign languages, biology, literature, business law, psychology, and home economics.

Some researchers believe that there is a differentiation during adolescence, while others believe that there is little or no change in one's basic abilities during that time (30–32). In part the differing views can be attributed to different methodologies and procedures. It would appear that the age differentiation hypothesis cannot be fully accepted or rejected. In our opinion there is probably some sort of differentiation, but not to the extent that its proponents suggest (35).

The Course of Mental Growth. When mental testing began, it was discovered that mental ability does not continue to increase throughout life. Rather, it appeared that mental ability reached a peak about the middle of adolescence and then declined after that (33). This view was based on the early standardization of the Stanford-Binet test, which showed that intelligence reached its height at about age 16. An even lower estimate of the height of intellectual performance was obtained from group tests given during World War I. In testing thousands of draftees, it was found that their average intelligence was that of a 13-year-old child (34).

Since that time many new studies have shown that intelligence not only does not decline with increasing age, but may even improve (35–43). One explanation for these discrepant findings is methodological. Those studies that have demonstrated an intellectual decline have often been based on cross-sectional research, wherein individuals at different age levels are tested at the same time. In such studies, adults might perform at a lower level than adolescents, not because they have failed to grow mentally but because they did not have the same education as today's adolescents. In contrast, those studies that have shown that intelligence continues to

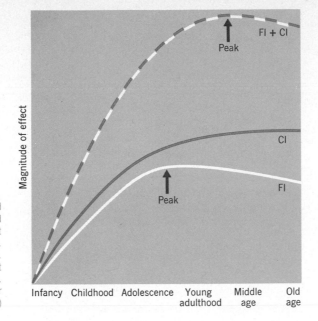

Figure 15.5 Fluid intelligence, crystallized intelligence, and the effect of the two combined. (*Source*. Horn, J. L. Intelligence — why it grows, why it declines. *Trans-action,* November 1967, 23–31.)

increase through maturity tend to be based on longitudinal research, in which the same individuals are tested repeatedly over time.

Another explanation for the discrepant findings is that intelligence tests measure *two* types of intelligence — one of which reaches a peak during adolescence while the other continues to increase with age (38, 40). The first type of intelligence has been called **fluid** intelligence; it is comprised of the underlying mental operations (such as those described by Piaget) that can be attributed to heredity and maturation as well as to experience. The other type of intelligence, known as **crystallized** intelligence, is comprised of the knowledge and skills that are acquired through socialization and acculturation.

One group of investigators (30, 38, 40, 41) argues that fluid intelligence reaches its highest point during adolescence and then tends to decline, while crystallized intelligence generally continues to increase. The way in which this hypothesis reconciles the two positions (that intelligence does or does not decline with age 19) is depicted in Figure 15.5.

Even these generalizations about fluid and crystallized intelligence must be qualified. The particular abilities and knowledge a person is able to maintain during maturity depends upon that person's original level of mental ability, his or her occupation, his or her general state of health, and so forth. It has been found that bright people retain a high-level intellectual functioning longer than those who are not so bright (44). And those whose careers are academically or intellectually oriented maintain their verbal skills longer than those who are in other fields. As Whitehead once said: "The imagination is most active between the ages of 19 and 35, and we mostly keep going thereafter on whatever fizz we experienced then" (quoted by Jones, 99). But it is also true — as shown by the creative work of men like Freud and Piaget — that many people have an abundance of intellectual fizz after the age of 35.

Formal Operational Thought and Its Manifestations

According to Piaget (45), thought emerges from the gradual internalization of actions; therefore, true thought (mental manipulation or experimentation of environmental givens) does not appear until 6 or 7 years of age, when actions become fully internalized. The system of thought of children (6 or 7 to about 10 or 11) — which, as we noted in Chapter 11, is called concrete operations — differs substantially from the system of thought that emerges during early adolescence (ages 11 to 14) — which is called formal operations.

We will describe the logic of formal operational thinking and then see how it manifests itself in the thinking and reasoning of adolescents. After discussing some of the issues of formal operational thought that are currently being debated in the research literature, we will examine some of the implications of formal operational thought on young people's social cognitions, their conceptions of themselves, and their views of other people.

The Logic of Formal Operational Thinking. It is useful to view formal operational thinking within the context of concrete operations. The concrete operational system is like a logical group since there is a set of elements (objects, attributes, relations) and operations (addition, subtraction, and so forth) together with a set of rules for combining elements and operations. One of these rules is **commutivity**: no matter how the elements of a set are combined, the results will be the same. For example, $A + (B + C) = (A + B) + C$. A second rule is **identity**: for every element in a set there is an identity element such that $A - A = 0$, or $A = A$. A third rule is **composition**: combining any two elements in a set will produce a third element which is also a member of the set, or $A + B = C$. The fourth rule is **reversibility**: for every operation in the set there is a second, inverse operation that can exactly cancel out the effects of the first. To illustrate, $A + B = C$, but $C - A = B$ and $C - B = A$.

It must be said that the child is not aware of the concrete operational system; it can only be inferred from his or her performance. The same is true for the formal operational system. Indeed, Piaget's idea of an intellectual "unconscious" is somewhat similar to Freud's concept of an affective unconscious. Freud found that each individual leads a rich life — of wishes, impulses, desires, and fantasies — of which he or she is only minimally aware. And Piaget found that each person has a very rich cognitive life, in which he or she uses complex systems of logical operations with virtually no awareness. When we are shown how much logic underlies our everyday behavior, we are like the Molière character who was surprised to discover that he had been speaking ''prose'' all of his life.

Once a child has attained concrete operations he or she can operate upon classes. For example, if a child knows that children equals boys plus girls, or $C = B + G$ (composition), then he or she automatically knows that $C - B = G$ (reversibility), that $B - B = 0$ (identity), and that $B + G = C$ is the same as $G + B = C$ (commutivity). The significance of this logical analysis of children's thinking is that it enables us to predict an entire set of related performances from a single performance.

When we move to the formal operational system, the logic becomes much more complex; indeed, it becomes **propositional logic**. This type of logic is a second-order logical system that operates on the first-order system providing much more range and flexibility of thought. Formal operational logic is to concrete operational logic what algebra is to arithmetic. Both concrete operational logic and arithmetic are tools that enable one to deal with objects in the real world. Formal operational logic and algebra, on the other hand, are tools that enable one to manipulate symbols — a step removed from the real world.

With formal operations one also acquires a new level of consciousness. Although adolescents are not aware of the logic behind their ongoing thought processes, they are now able to reflect upon and conceptualize their thoughts and thought processes — they can think about thinking. From a logical standpoint, what this means is that adolescents can now take the combinations that they were able to form at the concrete operational stage and operate upon them as if they were elementary classes, relations, or attributes. Thus, adolescents can conceive of many combinations that might not occur in fact. This means that a young person is able to construct ideals, possibilities, and contrary-to-fact statements that may be logically, but not factually, true (24).

To illustrate the potentialities of formal operational thinking, suppose you are at a restaurant and are given a menu that lists appetizers, entrées, desserts, and beverages. You have a number of alternative choices that might be represented as follows:

Order one thing

(1) order nothing   *(2) order just the appetizer*
(3) order just the entrée
(4) order just the dessert
(5) order just the beverage

Order two things
(6) order the appetizer and the entrée
(7) order the appetizer and the dessert
(8) order the appetizer and the beverage

(9) order the entrée and the dessert
(10) order the entrée and the beverage
(11) order the dessert and the beverage

Order three things
(12) order the appetizer, entrée, and beverage
(13) order the appetizer, entrée, and dessert
(14) order the appetizer, beverage, and dessert
(15) order the entrée, beverage, and dessert

Order four things
(16) order an appetizer, entrée, dessert, and beverage.

The ability to consider all of the above combinations (besides the actual food in each group) requires formal operational thought. One reason children have such difficulty in restaurants is that there are just too many choices to deal with. The rise of the fast food chains, such as McDonald's and Kentucky Fried Chicken, may be due in part to their appeal to children; the simple menu is easy for youngsters to cope with.

The adolescent is also able to use formal operations with verbal propositions that may or may not have real referents. The following set of propositions was suggested by Peel (46):

it is raining and cold (p. q)
or (v)* it is raining and not cold (p. q̄)
or (v) it is not raining and cold (p̄. q)
or (v) it is not raining and not cold (p̄. q̄).

These four propositions (p. q, p. q̄, p̄. q, p̄. q̄) can then be combined in a manner resembling the ways in which one can combine the four courses on the restaurant menu. Each combination will describe a different relationship between p and q. For example:

(a) *pq v p̄q (pq̄ v p̄q̄ false) is equivalent to* p implies q. *(When it rains it is cold.) This is the implicit logic we use to conclude that two events are causally connected.*
(b) *pq̄ v pq (p̄q and p̄q̄ false) is equivalent to* p is independent of q. *(It can rain whether or not it is cold.) This is the implicit logic we use to conclude that two events are not causally connected.*
(c) *pq̄ v p̄q (pq and p̄q̄ false) is equivalent to* p is incompatible with q. *(When it rains it is not cold and vice versa.) This is the implicit logic we use to decide that two events could not be connected.*
[46, p. 127]

The ability to combine propositions opens up enormous possibilities of thought; it is required for all scientific endeavors. Whether constructing a theory or conducting an experiment, the investigator must keep many

---

*(v) is the logical symbol for *or.*

variables in mind simultaneously and think about varying some while keeping others constant. This is the only way in which an investigator can formulate and test hypotheses experimentally.

Language and Memory. Not much systematic research has been done on the language development and memory capacities of adolescents. With respect to language, it can be assumed (from such tests as the Stanford-Binet and Wechsler Intelligence Scale for Children) that growth continues in vocabulary and in sentence and syntactical complexity, at least until middle adolescence. In addition, as a result of formal operations, young people can begin to understand the formal aspects of language and thus study grammar and syntax. Although these subjects are sometimes taught in elementary school, many teachers believe that children of this age do not really understand the parts of speech and the analysis of sentences. A recent study of language development in identical twins demonstrates that there is a dramatic increase in syntactical comprehension in early adolescence (47).

One aspect of adolescent language that has been studied is the understanding of metaphor and simile. A true metaphor, such as "Love's labour's lost," would seem to require formal operational thinking to be understood since a metaphor is a symbol for a symbol and, in a true metaphor, the relationship is conceptual or abstract. In the metaphor above, Shakespeare compares the endless hours spent thinking about a loved person as comparable, or proportionate, to physical labor. In this metaphor the connecting link is the idea that love and labor require a proportionate amount of effort.

There are, however, many metaphors in which the relationships are those of similarity rather than proportion. In one study (48) children and adolescents were asked to interpret similarity as well as proportionate metaphors. An example of a **similarity metaphor** was "He had a pickle for a nose," while a **proportionate metaphor** was "Morning roses were washed by dew." It was found that children could understand only the similarity metaphors. Adolescents, however, were able to interpret both kinds of metaphor. Furthermore, young people's ability to interpret proportionate metaphors correctly was highly correlated with their success on a measure of formal operational thinking. Other investigators have reported similar findings on metaphorical thinking (49–51).

Little research has been done on memory development in adolescence. It is clear, however, that as children get older they develop increasingly sophisticated and efficient mnemonic schemes (52–54). It seems reasonable to assume that this trend continues into adolescence and that formal operations are then used to develop mnemonic schemes that eliminate the need for tiresome memorization (55). Such schemes can vary from metaphorical associations to the "chunking" of information (such as the use of initials to designate federal agencies — FBI, NIH, and so forth). Apparently an individual's absolute memory span does not increase much beyond childhood, and the better memory of adolescents and adults (when and if they put their minds to it!) is due to their superior ability to classify and organize information (56–58).

Conservation Behavior. By and large, most conservations (of mass, number, length, quantity, distance, area, and so forth) are mastered in childhood at the concrete operational level of thought. But some conservation concepts (such as volume) seem to require formal operations. Originally Piaget and Inhelder (59) found that children did not understand the conservation of volume until about the age of 11 or 12; they would test for this by asking children whether a clay ball, rolled into a "sausage," still took up the same amount of space.

In several replications of Piaget and Inhelder's study, one of the authors found that a considerable proportion of adolescents and college students had never mastered the conservation of volume (60–62). Later research has supported these findings with other groups of adolescents and adults (63–65). Apparently the acquisition of formal operations, or at least their application to specific aspects of reality, is not as universal as the acquisition and application of concrete operations. It should be noted that the concept of volume has several levels of abstractness and that the studies made of adolescents and adults may have tapped the most abstract level. These studies dealt with **continuous volume** — the space filled by a continuous substance such as liquid or clay. But **discontinuous** volume — the space filled by a set of discontinuous objects — is easier to conserve. That is, it is easier for a subject to discover that a set of blocks takes up the same amount of space, no matter how they are arranged, than it is to discover that a clay ball that is rolled into a "sausage" still fills the same amount of space (66, 67). The concept of volume, like other concepts, can be understood at many levels; however, it is only in adolescence that continuous volume conservation tends to be fully understood.

Combinatorial Thinking. One of the new modes of thought that becomes possible with formal operational thought is combinatorial thinking (such as the restaurant menu example on page 539). To understand how such thinking actually develops in children, see Figure 15.6, which is an actual example from Piaget and Inhelder's original work.

The following are some of the quotations from children at two different ages who were presented with the problem depicted in Figure 15.6.

Ronald (7;1) mixes 4+g, then 2+g, 1+g, and 3+g: *"I think I did everything."*...*"I tried them all."* "What else could you have done?" "I don't know." We give him the glasses again: he again mixes 1+g, etc. "You took each bottle separately. What else could you have done?" — *"Take two bottles at the same time."* [He mixes 1+4+g, then 2+3+g, thus failing to cross over between the two sets of bottles, for example 1+2, 1+3, 2+4, and 3+4.] When we suggest that he had others, he puts 1+g in the glass already containing 2+3, which results in the appearance of the color: "Try to make the color again." — *"Do I put in two or three?"* [He

Figure 15.6 Materials used to assess combinatorial reasoning in children and adolescents. This diagram illustrates the problem of colored and colorless chemicals. Four similar flasks contain colorless, odorless liquids: (1) diluted sulphuric acid; (2) water; (3) oxygenated water; (4) thiosulphate. The smaller flask, labeled g, contains potassium iodide. Two glasses are presented to the subject; one contains 1 + 3, the other contains 2. While the subject watches, the experimenter adds several drops of g to each of these glasses. The liquid in the glass containing 1 + 3 turns yellow. The subject is then asked to reproduce the color, using all or any of the five flasks. (*Source.* Inhelder, B. & Piaget, J. *The growth of logical thinking from childhood to adolescence.* New York: Basic Books, 1958.)

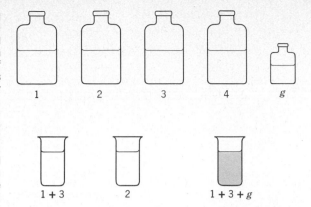

tries 2+4+g, then adds 3, then tries it with 1+4+2+g.] *"No, I don't remember any more"* (24, p. 111).

Inhelder and Piaget offer many examples of this kind showing that children have difficulty with multiple operations. They think of combining two things, but they do not spontaneously think of combining two or three different liquids at once with g. Even when this procedure is suggested to them, they have trouble dealing with multiple combinations in any systematic way. Compare this boy's response with that of an adolescent:

George (14;6) begins with 2+g; 1+g; 3+g; and 4+g: *"No, it doesn't turn yellow. So you have to mix them."* He goes on to the six two-by-two combinations and at last hits 1+3+g. *"This time I think it works."* "Why?" *"It's 1 and 3 and some water."* "You think it is water?" *"Yes, no difference in odor. I think it is water."* "Can you show me?" He replaces g with some water and mixes it with 1 + 3. *"No, it's not water. It's a chemical product: it combines with 1 and 3 and then it turns into a yellow liquid"* (24, p. 120).

Young people at the formal operational level, such as George, immediately understand that two or three liquids can be combined at one time. Formal operations thus provide methods of *discovering* or constructing hypotheses as well as methods of testing hypotheses. In adolescence, as compared with childhood, the methods of discovery and of verification become unified.

Inhelder and Piaget's findings have been supported by others. In one study (68) children and adolescents were asked to think up all of the possible combinations of four differently colored poker chips taken 0, 1, 2, 3, and 4 at a time. Although most adolescents ignored the "0" possibility, the majority came up with the remaining 15 possibilities. Piaget and Inhelder found that young people were able to generate combinations (order of elements unimportant) before they were able to generate permutations (order of elements important). This was also demonstrated by Neimark (69) in a longitudinal investigation. When her subjects were in

With the new mental abilities that make their appearance in adolescence (the formal operations described by Jean Piaget), young people are capable of engaging in scientific thinking, specifically, thinking of many different variables at the same time.

the fourth grade they could generate neither combinations nor permutations. In the sixth grade, half of the children could generate combinations but not permutations.

Conceptual Orientation Shifts. It seems reasonable to suppose that young people at the formal operational level of thought conceptualize their world somewhat differently than do children at the preoperational and concrete operational levels. Preoperational children tend to see things in terms of significant features — "A bike has wheels." Children at the concrete operational level tend to conceptualize things in terms of how they function — "A bike is to ride." Finally, adolescents tend to think about things in terms of general concepts — "A bike is a two-wheeled vehicle."

Obviously, we do not always think at the highest level of which we are capable. Adults who can think conceptually often think perceptually or functionally. Researchers have therefore wondered how easily children and adolescents can shift from their dominant mode of conceptualization to a lower or higher mode. Theoretically, young children should not be able to shift to a higher level because this requires abilities they do not have, but older children and adolescents should be able to think at a lower level. To study this issue, researchers used a concept-production task in which children and adolescents were asked to think up ideas related to pictures, words, and things — such as a real apple, a picture of an apple, and the word "apple." In general adolescents were able to think of as many ideas that were related to words as to pictures and things. Children, however, produced more concepts that pertained to pictures and things than to words. Thus, the research generally confirmed what had been hypothesized about conceptual orientation shifts (70–72).

Moral Development. According to Kohlberg (73), much of an individual's moral development occurs during adolescence and young adulthood. Several issues of moral development during adolescence have been explored: the relationship between moral development and actual behavior, the effects of training on moral thinking, and the mechanisms involved in moving from one stage of moral development to another.

The classic studies on the relationship between moral thinking and behavior were carried out by Hartshorne and May (74) in the late 1920s; morality was defined as a set of honorable traits such as honesty, trustfulness, and self-control. Essentially they found that there was very little consistency in children's moral behavior; a child might be honest in one situation but not in another. Similarly, a child's knowledge of what was right was no guide to his or her behavior. There was little or nor relationship between attending Sunday School or church, participating in Boy Scouts, and so forth and moral behavior.

Clearly, morality is not to be identified with any specific behaviors. From a developmental point of view, what determines a person's behavior in any given moral situation is his or her understanding of the situation; this will depend upon the individual's level of development and the nature of the situation. Thus, it is not so much what a person does, but *why* he or she does it, that is crucial to a moral evaluation of an action. For example, consider the college students at Berkeley who had to decide whether or not to participate in a sit-in demonstration to protest the administration's curtailment of political communication. Investigators gave Kohlberg's moral dilemmas to a random sample of Berkeley students. About 50 percent of the students who were at Kohlberg's Stage 5 (believed in obedience to rules which they evaluated and were accepted as valid by the individual) and about 80 percent who were at his Stage 6 (believed in universal ethical principles) participated in the demonstration. But about 60 percent of the students who were at Stage 2 (the proper action is that which satisfies the individual's own needs) also participated. Thus, sitting in for some students was an extremely important matter of conscience while for others it was a lark — a way of having a good time (75).

Another example of the relationship between moral understanding and moral action was provided by the famous Stanley Milgram experiments (76). In these investigations, the subjects were ordered to administer increasingly severe shocks to a middle-aged man (actually a stooge) as part of a "learning" experiment. Of the subjects who were at Kohlberg's Stage 6 (absolute moral principles), some 75 percent refused to continue administering severe shock in the experiment. Only about 13 percent of the subjects at the lower stages refused to continue.

In another study (77), seventh-grade students were tested for their level of moral development as well as for their conformity in social situations. The conformity test was as follows:

Subjects met in groups of six boys or girls who were acquainted prior to the experiment. The same group of six children was tested in both independent and interdependent conditions. In both conditions the subjects were instructed that a prize would be given for the most accurate performance. In the interdependent condition, *the prize would be awarded to the members of the most accurate* group, *each individual's correct judgment contributing one point towards his group's score. Competition was among all the groups tested. The instructions stated that "for each of you, winning a prize depends on how well the others on your team do, as well as what you do yourself." In the* independent condition, *how the others present in the room did had no bearing on winning a prize. Each individual was competing with all those members of other groups who had happened to sit in the same one of the six chairs. This stipulation was emphasized by having each chair labeled A . . . F, and referring to the subjects by letter names. It was pointed out that "For each of you, winning a prize depends only on how well you yourself do, and doesn't depend on what any of the other people in the room do. Each of you could win a prize or only some of you or more; whether you win is entirely up to you" [77, pp. 331–332].*

In both conditions the subjects had to decide which of the comparison strips of paper was the same length as a standard strip. The strips were presented on a page with the standard at the top and the comparison strips below. The subjects indicated their choice by pushing colored buttons that lit up colored lights, corresponding to the colors of the comparison strips. The subjects could not see each other's performance. Presumably they could learn about their partner's performance on a console board that indicated their own as well as their partner's choices. In fact, of course, the lights on the console were preprogrammed so that on 10 out of 20 trials the ostensible group choices were correct while on 8 trials the ostensible group choices were not correct. Conformity was thus measured by the extent to which the subject modified his or her choices in the direction of what appeared to be the group choice.

The results are shown in Table 15.1. As can be seen, conformity was greatest among the children at Kohlberg's Stage 3 ("good boy" or "good girl" morality is that which pleases and is approved by others) and least among students at the self-centered stages (1 and 2) and the more principled stages (4 and 5). It appears that when a young person's level of moral development is taken into account, reasonable predictions can be made about his or her moral action.

Issues in Formal Operational Thought

Inhelder and Piaget's (24) discussion of formal operational thought has led to a lot of research and has broadened our understanding of how adolescents think. At the same time, however, formal operational thinking has presented many problems. For example, researchers have wondered to what extent all adolescents attain formal operational thought. They have also wondered whether a given person functions on the same formal operational level in different situations. Other issues for research are whether formal operational thought can be affected by training and what its relationship is to other cognitive processes.

The Generality of Formal Operations. Earlier we noted that some adolescents and young adults have not attained the concept of volume conservation. Does this mean that these individuals have not attained formal operations or that they have simply not applied these operations in the area of volume? In part this question is methodological and implies

Table 15.1 Numbers of Students at Different Moral-Judgment Levels Who Conformed and Who Did Not Conform to Group Decisions

Moral Judgment Level	Boys		Girls		Combined	
	Con-formers	Non-conformers	Con-formers	Non-conformers	Con-formers	Non-conformers
1–2	6	13	2	4	8	17
3	2	1	8	6	10	7
4–5	3	12	0	6	3	18

Source: Saltzstein, H. D., Diamond, R. M. & Balenky, M. Moral judgment level and conformity behavior, *Developmental Psychology,* 1972, **7,** 327–336.

that there are tests that are universally accepted as measures of formal operations. In fact, no such tests exist, and failure on a particular test may mean either that the person does not have the necessary operations or that he or she has not applied them to a particular concept.

A number of investigators have replicated Piaget's experiments and found that adolescents did not succeed with them at the ages predicted by Inhelder and Piaget (24). For example, in a replication of a chemistry experiment (described on page 543), one investigator (78) found that substantially less than 75 percent of the 15-year-olds tested were successful (Inhelder and Piaget had found that more than 75 percent of young people that age could solve the problem). Likewise, in a replication of the pendulum experiment (79), less than 50 percent of the 13- to 15-year-olds solved the problem (more than 75 percent of Inhelder and Piaget's subjects of this age were successful).

In evaluating these results, as well as those of the volume conservation studies, Piaget (80) offered three possible explanations for the findings: (a) Some individuals mature at slower rates than others and therefore do not attain formal operations until middle or late adolescence; (b) The attainment of formal operations is not universal and represents but one of several alternative paths in the elaboration of mental abilities that occurs in adolescence; and (c) Most individuals attain formal operations but differ in the content areas in which they elaborate these operations. Piaget favors the last explanation and urges the development of new formal operational tasks to test the different content areas. But, as one of the authors noted (81), the construction of such tasks would require a Herculean effort. Nonetheless, it is possible that the failure of some investigators to find formal operations could be due to the tests and not to the subjects. On the other hand, it is clear that retarded children (those with an IQ of less than 75) never attain formal operations (82). Formal operations are thus related to intelligence and to maturation but in rather complex ways; age alone is no guarantee of attaining formal operations.

Individual Consistency in Formal Operational Thinking. It might be assumed that a person who shows formal operational thinking in one area would show it in other areas as well, but this is not the case. Once a person attains formal operations, he or she cannot immediately and automatically apply them to all conceptual areas. It takes time to learn to apply them to restaurant menus, chemistry experiments, poker games, and so forth.

One way in which to determine the extent of a person's formal operations is through factor analysis. In this procedure many tests purporting to measure formal operations are given to a group of subjects and the results are analyzed to see if there are several common dimensions. For example, do the various tests used by Inhelder and Piaget (24) to measure formal operations actually do just that? Several investigators have done a factor analysis of batteries of concrete and formal operational tasks (83–86). In general they have found that there is a common, logical operational factor that underlies the various Piagetian tasks. Although it appears that the Piagetian tasks do measure comparable logical abilities, a given individual might not perform equally well on all of these tasks.

Effects of Training on Formal Operational Thinking. To what extent can the use of formal operations be enhanced by training? One approach is to select groups with different experiential backgrounds; that is, to take groups that have varying amounts of formal education and to compare their performance on formal operational tasks. Apparently large differences in schooling do make a difference. It has been found that the more schooling (high school, college) the subjects had, the more likely they were to demonstrate formal operations (65, 87–89). Of course a person's level of education is also related to intelligence; the fact that there was a relationship between the amount of schooling and formal operations may only mean that brighter children are more likely than less-bright children to attain formal operations.

A more direct way to ascertain the effects of training is to try to teach young people how to think on a formal operational level. Apparently instruction in science has little effect upon success in formal operational thinking (78, 90). Some investigators have tried to train subjects directly with Piagetian measures, but, whereas some have noted a marked improvement on specific tasks (91), others have not. Thus, it would appear that training can help an individual on specific tasks, but it probably does not change underlying cognitive abilities.

Formal Operational Thought and Other Cognitive Processes. We have already noted that formal operational thought is related to general intelligence, but it has also been found to be related to cognitive style as well. Field-independent subjects, for example, tend to do better than field-dependent subjects on formal operational tasks (92, 93). Also, reflective subjects do better than subjects who are impulsive (93). Perhaps formal operations tend to free subjects from the press of environmental stimuli. In any case, it appears that formal operations are related to other aspects of intellectual functioning, including cognitive style.

Affective Consequences of Formal Operational Thought

Up until this point we have discussed cognitive development as if it were not related to the emotions of adolescents. However, typical adolescent emotions can only be fully understood within the context of formal operational thought because it is this thought that allows the young person to enter the world of ideals, theories, and possibilities. It is the adolescent's ability to compare the possible with the actual in many areas of his or her life that underlies, at least in part, the dissatisfaction that so often besieges these youngsters.

The Adolescent and His or Her World. Children, for the most part, live in the here and now. They are concerned with the world as they find it and with learning how to function in that world. Adolescents, however, are able to grasp things not only as they are but also as they might become — at home, at school, in the world at large, and with themselves. Awareness of discrepancies between the actual and the ideal feeds into adolescent dissatisfaction. It is only when they reach adolescence, for example, that adopted children feel compelled to seek out their real parents. Likewise, at this age previously happy, cheerful, and "gutty" handicapped and crippled children often experience their first real depression.

Adolescents are capable of conceiving contrary-to-fact situations and thus of ideals. They often are impatient with the world as they find it and are sensitive to injustice of all kinds.

icapped and crippled children often experience their first real depression.

Adolescents' awareness of the contrast between the ideal and the real often turns them into rebels. Not unlike children who find other children's toys more appealing than their own, adolescents find ideal situations enviable and their own real situation unbearable. Much of their rebellion is, however, purely verbal. They may verbally endorse humanitarian causes, but do little to implement them. Likewise, their acute dissatisfaction with their parents usually does not lead them to break away from their family and to go off on their own. Because there is a discrepancy between adolescents' ability to conceptualize ideals and their awareness of how to implement them in action, they are able to be quite adamant (and apparently hypocritical) in their demands. Toward the end of adolescence, when their ideals become tied to appropriate action, young people either become more tolerant of society in general and their parents in particular, or they take action to implement their ideals (work in a community action project, live in a commune, and so forth).

The Adolescent and the Self. Formal operational thought also affects adolescents' attitudes toward themselves. They become introspective and undertake self-analysis and criticism. They do this with a certain equanimity since they now understand that thought is private and that they do not have to share their thoughts with others. In contrast with children, adolescents can wear a facade that hides their real feelings from others.

Adolescents' new concern about themselves often amounts to an **intellectual egocentrism**, an inability to distinguish clearly between what they and other people are thinking about. In social situations, young adolescents feel as if they are on stage, and they assume that everyone else is watching and evaluating their performance. Thus, they are always performing for an **imaginary audience** that is, in part at least, of their own making. This feeling that others are watching and thinking about them accounts for the "self-consciousness" so characteristic of young adolescents. When young people stand before a mirror for hours on end they are imagining how the audience will react to them. When young adolescents get together they form an interesting group since each is an actor to himself or herself but an audience to everyone else (100).

A corollary to the "imaginary audience" is what one of the authors (100) has called the **personal fable**. Because of the adolescent's sense of always being at the center of attention, he or she begins to feel like a very special person. A young adolescent feels that his or her experiences are unique and that no one has ever experienced comparable feelings. "You don't know how it feels to be in love" or "You don't know how badly I want that car" are typical expressions of the adolescent's personal fable. It has other elements as well. Adolescents at this stage believe that other people will grow old and die but that it will never really happen to them. And it can get them into trouble too. A girl may believe that other girls will get pregnant but that it will never happen to her and she may fail

In adolescence young people often construct an imaginary audience, an audience of people who are looking at and admiring their appearance and behavior.

to take precautions. Or a boy or girl may feel that he or she will never get hooked on drugs but discover that he or she is not invulnerable after all.

There are several consequences of adolescent egocentrism: First, it accounts in part for the power of the peer group. Adolescents are so concerned about the reactions of others — particularly their peers — to themselves that they may do many things that contradict all of their previous training and their own best interests. Secondly, adolescents' feeling that they are always on stage may help to explain some of their attention-getting maneuvers, such as eccentric clothing and behavior. Another consequence of this egocentrism is that adolescents' interpersonal relations are often shallow and short-lived. The typical "crush" is often due to an adolescent's desire to idealize someone, and the fact that it lasts such a short time stems from the fact that no human being is ideal and the adolescent soon makes that discovery. But then he or she goes on to form new crushes. Friendships during this period are often based on self-definition and self-interest rather than on mutual interests and concerns. A pretty girl, for example, may befriend a plain-looking girl because the latter sets off her good looks; the plain-looking girl, on the other hand, may take pleasure in being associated with the pretty girl.

Toward the end of adolescence, this type of exploitative egocentrism gradually declines. The young person comes to realize that other people are thinking more about themselves and their own problems than about what he or she is doing. With the decline of adolescent egocentrism, there is a renewal of individuality and a new freedom from the conformity of the peer group. Interpersonal relations become based on mutual interests rather than self-interest and the personal fable is tempered by the discovery that friends share comparable feelings and fantasies. The young person also becomes more reconciled to society and to his or her own family; this is usually accomplished by beginning some type of productive work, which is a bridge between the ideal and the real. Productive work unites thought and action and enables a young person to look toward the future without despairing of the present. It also marks the passage from adolescence to adulthood; that is, from personal isolation to social integration.

Essay

IMPLICATIONS OF THE SECULAR TREND

As mentioned earlier, the secular trend is the tendency of young people today to grow taller and heavier and to reach puberty earlier than was true for those of the same age 100 years ago. Although the secular trend is at an end among some groups in America today, it is not among others. The secular trend thus has implications for education, child-rearing, and governmental action.

When young people enter puberty, not only do they acquire formal operations but they develop quite new attitudes, feelings, and interests. A number of studies have shown that adolescents today are more advanced in certain personal and social attitudes than those of about a generation earlier (94, 95). One study (94) found that ninth-graders in 1953 had the same interests and attitudes that eleventh-graders had a quarter of a century earlier. Another study reported that adolescents in 1957 were more socially oriented, more concerned with sex, and more interested in marriage and the family than were adolescents in 1935 (95). Although these studies are dated, they may demonstrate longterm trends.

One consequence of the secular trend, therefore, is that heterosexual interests are developing at a much earlier age than was true some years ago (96, 97). It used to be the rule that girls were an anathema to elementary-school boys. Now it appears that children who feel this way are in the minority. In one study of a fifth-grade class, it was found that 90 percent of the children had a ''sweetheart,'' 65 percent had already been kissed by the opposite sex, and 40 percent had already dated (96).

The educational implications of the secular trend are not clear-cut. On the one hand the school should recognize that some preadolescents have developed heterosexual interests, and for them it might be desirable to have certain places at school where they could congregate and socialize. The school might also arrange certain social projects that boys and girls could participate in together, such as hobby clubs, putting on a play, or putting out a school newspaper. The school, however, should not overlook the needs and interests of later-maturing boys and girls. These youngsters should not feel pressed to join in these activities or made to feel that they are peculiar or abnormal in any way.

Parents, too, need to take the secular trend into account. It makes little sense to abide by the age limitations that date back to an earlier generation. If young people have the social skill and maturity to start dating at age 14, it makes little sense for parents to insist that they wait until they are 16, the age at which the parents may have been allowed to date. The young person's readiness to engage in an activity — together with the parents' judgment of his or ability to handle the situation — should be the major consideration in deciding which activities the young person should be allowed to undertake.

The secular trend has already had certain effects on the larger society; for example, the voting age in federal elections has been lowered from 21 to 18. Also, some young people are getting married and having children at an earlier age. The secular trend may likewise be responsible for drug abuse among some adolescents (98). As the secular trend comes to an end in this country, the need for adjusting educational and child-rearing practices to earlier-maturing children will also end. So too will the demand for certain governmental policies to treat younger people as full-fledged adults. In the meantime, educators, parents, and government policymakers will need to remain sensitive to the implications of the secular trend for dealing with young people.

G. STANLEY HALL

Biography

To contemporary students of psychology and education, the name G. Stanley Hall probably rings few if any memory bells. Aside from his association with the child study movement, he is best recalled as the man who was responsible for bringing about Freud's one and only trip to America, and as the author of a classic two-volume work on adolescence. But Hall was also instrumental in getting experimental psychology established in America, in making Clark University an outstanding center for the training of developmental psychologists, and in spearheading many modern reforms in education. Hall was important not so much because of his substantive contributions, which were considerable, but rather because his openness, his breadth, and his inexhaustible intellectual enthusiasm were so stimulating to so many people. Even when he was wrong, as he often was, Hall nonetheless spurred his listeners and students to go out and make their case in the field, in the lab, or in the library.

Hall's parents were of old Yankee stock and of modest financial means. His father was a rather strict Puritan with a high moral sense and with some regrets about not having attained a higher station in life. When Hall's brilliance began to emerge and he went off to Williams College, his relations with his parents and his relatives—most of whom were untutored farm folk—became somewhat strained. As often happens in such cases, the insecurity of Hall's relatives in matters academic often came out in the form of teasing. When he was home on vacation, Hall was frequently treated to homilies about the limits of book learning and about the value of experience in practical matters.

Hall's estrangement from his Puritan background was gradual, however, and from Williams he went on to Union Theological Seminary. The ministry was one field where his parents and relatives could accept higher learning. But Hall became more interested in philosophy than in theology and wanted to study in Germany, the heartland of the major philosophical systems. Henry Ward Beecher, the clergyman and reformer, recognized Hall's talents and arranged financial support for him to make the trip. After three years in Germany, where Hall learned about love and beer as well as philosophy, he returned to New York. There he worked as a tutor for 18 months to get himself out of debt.

In 1872 Hall received an appointment at Antioch College where for four years he taught a variety of subjects including language, literature, and philosophy and engaged in a wide range of social, political, and religious activities. During this period Hall's talents as a gifted, articulate, and stentorian lecturer came into full maturity, and he was much in demand as a speaker. While Hall was at Antioch he began to read some of the new studies in physiological psychology being carried on in Germany by Wilhelm Wundt and his colleagues. Hall decided to return to Germany for further study, but got sidetracked by an offer to teach English at Harvard. Hall accepted in hopes that this might be a wedge to opening up an appointment in the Philosophy Department. The hope was ill-founded and Hall soon tired of grading English papers. During this same period Hall did work in the physiological laboratories and took his Ph.D. degree in psychology under William James. It was the first Ph.D. in psychology to be awarded in America.

After Harvard, Hall returned to Germany to study with Wundt, Helmholtz, and Fechner. As usual, Hall took courses and read in many different fields and became enthusiastic about the new biology that emanated from Darwin's evolutionary theories. When Hall returned to Boston after a second two-year stay in Europe, he was again very much in debt and without prospects of a job. One day C. W. Eliot, then president of

Harvard, rode up to Hall's door and, without dismounting, asked him if he would deliver a series of public lectures on pedagogy. Hall assented and the lectures were a great success. The success of the lectures was due in part to Hall's oratory, but also to his many references to educational institutions and practices Hall had observed abroad.

In 1881 Hall was given an appointment at Johns Hopkins University that eventually became a professorship in psychology and pedagogy. While at Johns Hopkins, Hall started a "formal" psychological laboratory in the sense that he called it by that name. William James had some equipment in a room at Harvard several years before the Johns Hopkins laboratory, but it was not officially designated a "laboratory." Ever since, there has been a continual debate about who established the first psychological laboratory in America. The students who studied under Hall while he was at Johns Hopkins were of some note and included men like Woodrow Wilson and John Dewey. But Hall was restless at Johns Hopkins and could not secure the support for the new psychology that he felt it needed and deserved.

It was this dissatisfaction, together with his own temperament (E. G. Boring called him a "founder"), that made him seriously consider and then accept the presidency of the to-be-founded Clark University in Worcester, Massachusetts. After accepting the presidency, Hall took an extended trip to Europe to visit many schools and get ideas for his own. Clark University opened in the fall of 1889 with great promise and with an excellent faculty. But the promise was not to be fulfilled, in part at least because Jonas Clark began to withdraw financial support from the University almost immediately after it opened. Hall remained as president until his retirement in 1921, after braving major and minor professional and personal tragedies. He died in 1924 just after having been elected for the second time to the presidency of the American Psychological Association, of which he had been the first president as well.

Summary

For girls, the adolescent growth spurt occurs about 2 years earlier than it does for boys; at this time there are increases in height and weight as well as changes in body composition and proportion. The primary and secondary sex characteristics also appear at this time. Among boys the primary characteristics include enlargement of the penis and scrotum, and among girls, menarche and breast development. The secondary sex characteristics include body hair and activation of the sweat glands.

The fact that young people today tend to be taller and heavier and to reach maturity at an earlier age than their counterparts did 100 years ago is called the secular trend. For American middle-class young people, however, this trend appears to be at an end. Among American young people there appear to be ideal body shapes and sizes; young people feel good about their bodies to the extent that they conform to these stereotypic ideals.

Although there is a differentiation of mental abilities in adolescence, this is confounded with the differentiation of interests so that the extent of differentiation is difficult to determine. With regard to the course of mental growth, the concept that intelligence reaches a peak in adolescence and then declines thereafter has been modified in recent decades. It is now believed that, although some aspects of intellectual functioning decline in adulthood, others continue to grow.

With respect to the qualitative aspects of mental growth, formal operations (as described by Inhelder and Piaget) enable adolescents to engage in combinatorial thinking, to grasp possibilities and ideals, to understand metaphor and simile, and to do scientific thinking. Formal operations enable young people to think about other people's thinking, to construct ideals, and to reflect upon their own mental processes. Sometimes their newfound intellectual abilities bring them into conflict with adults. However, as young people gain more social experience and engage in meaningful work, their idealism tends to be tempered by reality and they begin to accommodate themselves to the demands of adult society.

References

1. Tanner, J. M. Sequences, tempo, and individual variation in growth and development of boys and girls aged twelve to sixteen. In J. Kagan & R. Coles (Eds.), *12 to 16: Early adolescence*. New York: Norton, 1972.
2. Rosenfield, L. Role of androgens in growth and development of the fetus, child and adolescent. *Advances in Pediatrics,* 1972, **19,** 171–213.
3. Root, A. W. Endocrinology of puberty. *Journal of Pediatrics,* 1973, **83,** 1–19.
4. Grumbach, M. M., Grave, G. D., & Mayor, F. E. (Eds.) *The control of the onset of puberty.* New York: Wiley, 1974.
5. Tanner, J. M. *Growth at adolescence.* Oxford: Blackwell Scientific Publications, 1962.
6. Tanner, J. M. *Education and physical growth.* London: University of London Press, 1961.
7. Livson, M., & McNeil, D. The accuracy of recalled age of menarche. *Human Biology,* 1962, **34,** 218–221.
8. Meredith, H. V. A synopsis of pubertal changes in youth. *Journal of School Health,* 1967, **37,** 171–176.
9. Espenschade, A. S., & Meleney, H. E. Motor performances of adolescent boys and girls today in comparison with those of twenty years ago. *Research Quarterly,* 1961, **32,** 186–189.
10. Tanner, J. M. Earlier maturation in man. *Scientific American,* 1968, **218,** 21–26.
11. Muuss, R. E. Adolescent development and the secular trend. *Adolescence,* 1970, **5,** 267–284.
12. Arnhoff, F. N., & Damianopoulos, E. N. Self body recognition: An empirical approach to the body image. *Merill-Palmer Quarterly,* 1962, **8,** 143–148.
13. Lerner, R. M. The development of stereotyped·expectancies of body build relations. *Child Development,* 1969, **40,** 137–141.
14. Lerner, R. M. Some female stereotypes of male body build behavior relations. *Perceptual and Motor Skills,* 1969, **28,** 363–366.
15. Kurtz, R. M. Body image-male and female. *Trans-action,* 1968, **12,** 25–27.
16. Verinis, J. S. and Roll, S. Primary and secondary male characteristics: The hairiness and large penis stereotypes. *Psychological Reports,* 1970, **26,** 123–126.

17. Gunderson, E. K. E. Body size, self evaluation and military effectiveness. *Journal of Personality and Social Psychology,* 1965, **2,** 902–906.
18. Kurtz, R. M. Sex differences and variations in body attitudes. *Journal of Consulting and Clinical Psychology,* 1969, **33,** 625–629.
19. Jourard, S. M., & Secord, P. F. Body cathexis and the ideal female figure. *Journal of Abnormal and Social Psychology,* 1955, **50,** 243–246.
20. Secord, P. F., & Jowrard, S. M. The appraisal of body cathexis: Body and the self. *Journal of Consulting Psychology,* 1953, **17,** 343–347.
21. Stolz, H. R., & Stolz, L. M. Adolescent problems related to somatic variations. In N. B. Henry (Ed.), *The forty-third yearbook of the National Society for the Study of Education,* Chicago: University of Chicago Press, 1944. Part 1, Adolescence.
22. White, W. F., & Wash, J. A. Prediction of successful college academic performance from measures of body cathexis, self-cathesis and anxiety. *Perceptual and Motor Skills,* 1965, **20,** 431–432.
23. Clifford, E. Body satisfaction in adolescence. *Perceptual and Motor Skills,* 1971, **33,** 119–124.
24. Inhelder, B., & Piaget, J. *The growth of logical thinking from childhood to adolescence.* New York: Basic Books, 1958.
25. Elkind, D. Borderline retardation in low and middle income adolescents. In R. M. Allen, A. D. Cortazzo, & R. P. Toister (Eds.), *Theories of cognitive development.* Coral Gables: University of Miami Press, 1973.
26. Burt, C. The differentiation of intellectual abilities. *British Journal of Educational Psychology,* 1954, **25,** 159–177.
27. Burt, C. The evidence for the concept of intelligence. *British Journal of Educational Psychology,* 1955, **25,** 159–177.
28. Garrett, H. E. A developmental theory of intelligence. *American Psychologist,* 1946, **1,** 372–378.
29. Fitzgerald, J. M., Nesselroade, J. R., & Baltes, P. B. Emergence of adult intellectual structure prior to or during adolescence? *Developmental Psychology,* 1973, **9,** 114–119.
30. Horn, J. L. Human abilities: A review of research and theory in the early 1970's in M. R. Rosenzweig & L. W. Porter (Eds.): *Annual Review of Psychology,* Palo Alto, Calif.; 1976.
31. Anastasi, A. On the formation of psychological traits. *American Psychologist,* 1970, **25,** 899–910.
32. Reinert, G. Comparative factor analytic studies of intelligence throughout the whole life span. In L. R. Goulet & P. B. Baltes (Eds.), *Life span developmental psychology: Research and theory.* New York: Academic Press, 1970.
33. Terman, L. M. *The measurement of intelligence.* Boston: Houghton Mifflin, 1916.
34. Jones, H. E., & Conrad, H. S. The growth and decline of intelligence. *Genetic Psychology Monographs,* 1933, **13,** 223–298.
35. Baltes, P. B., & Labouvie, G. V. Adult development and intellectual performance: Description, explanation, modification. In C. Eisdorfer & M. P. Lawton (Eds.), *The psychology of adult development and aging.* Washington, D.C.: APA, 1973.
36. Baltes, P. B. Life span models of psychological aging: A white elephant. *Gerontologist,* 1973, **13,** 459–492.
37. Bromley, D. B. *The psychology of human aging.* (2nd ed.) Hammondsworth: Penguin, 1974.
38. Cattell, R. B. *Abilities and their structure, growth and action.* Boston: Houghton Mifflin, 1971.
39. Hooper, F. H., Fitzgerald, J., & Papalia, D. Piagetian theory and the aging process: Extensions and speculations. *Aging and Human Development,* 1971, **2,** 3–20.
40. Horn, J. L. Organization of data on life span development of human abilities. In L. R. Goulet & P. B. Baltes (Eds.), *Life span developmental psychology: Research and theory.* New York: Academic Press, 1970.
41. Horn, J. L. Psychometric studies of aging and intelligence. In S. Gershon & A. Raskin (Eds.), *Geriatric psychopharmacology: The scene today,* New York: Raven, 1975.
42. Matarazzo, J. D. *Wechsler's measurement and appraisal of adult intelligence,* (5th ed.) Baltimore; Williams & Wilkins, 1972.
43. Schaie, K. W. Translations in gerontology—from lab to life. *American Psychologist,* 1974, **29,** 802–807.

44. Horn, J. L. Intelligence—why it grows, why it declines. *Trans-action*, November 1967, 23–31.
45. Piaget, J. *The psychology of intelligence*. London: Routledge & Kegan Paul, 1950.
46. Peel, E. A. *The pupil's thinking*. London: Oldbourne Press, 1960.
47. Munsinger, H., & Douglass, A., II. The syntactic abilities of identical twins. *Child Development*, 1976, **47,** 40–50.
48. Bellow, P. M. A cognitive developmental study of metaphor comprehension. *Developmental Psychology*, 1975, **11,** 415–423.
49. Asch, S., & Nerlove, H. The development of double function terms in children. In B. Kaplan & S. Wapner (Eds.), *Perspectives in psychological theory*. New York: International Universities Press, 1960.
50. Gardner, H. Metaphors and modalities: How children project polar adjectives onto diverse domains. *Child Development*, 1974, **45,** 84–91.
51. Polio, M., & Polio, H. The development of figurative language in children. *Journal of Psycholinguistic Research*, 1974, **3,** 185–201.
52. Mandler, G., & Stephens, D. The development of free and constrained conceptualization and subsequent verbal memory. *Journal of Experimental Child Psychology*, 1967, **5,** 86–93.
53. Macey, B. M., Olson, F. A., Holmes, J. G., & Flavell, J. H. Production deficiency in young children's clustered recall. *Developmental Psychology*, 1969, **1,** 26–34.
54. Neimark, E. D., Slotnick, N. S., & Ulrich, T. Development of memorization strategies. *Developmental Psychology*, 1971, **5,** 427–432.
55. Neimark, E. D. An information processing approach to cognitive development. *Transactions, New York Academy of Sciences*, 1971, **33,** 516–528.
56. Belmont, J. M., & Butterfield, E. C. The relations of short-term memory to development and intelligence. In L. P. Lipsitt & H. W. Reese (Eds.), *Advances in Child Development and Behavior*. Vol. 4. New York: Academic Press, 1969.
57. Belmont, J. M., & Butterfield, E. C. What the development of short-term memory is. *Human Development*, 1971, **14,** 236–248.
58. Wapner, S., & Raud, S. Ontogenetic differences in the nature of organization underlying serial learning. *Human Development*, 1968, **11,** 249–259.
59. Piaget, J., & Inhelder, B. *Le developpement des quantites chez l'enfant*. Paris: Delachaux et Niestle, 1941.
60. Elkind, D. Children's discovery of mass, weight and volume conservation. *Journal of Genetic Psychology*, 1961, **98,** 219–227.
61. Elkind, D. Quantity conceptions in junior and senior high school students. *Child Development*, 1961, **32,** 551–560.
62. Elkind, D. Quantity conceptions in college students. *Journal of Social Psychology*, 1962, **57,** 459–465.
63. Hobbs, E. D. Adolescents concepts of physical quantity. *Developmental Psychology*, 1973, **9,** 431.
64. Tomlinson-Keasey, C. Formal operations in females from eleven to fifty-four years of age. *Developmental Psychology*, 1972, **6,** 364.
65. Graves, A. J. Attainment of mass weight and volume in minimally educated adults. *Developmental Psychology*, 1972, **7,** 223.
66. Piaget, J., Inhelder, B., & Szeminska, A. *The child's conception of geometry*. London: Routledge & Kegan Paul, 1960.
67. Lovell, K., & Ogilvie, E. The growth of the concept of volume in junior school children. *Journal of Child Psychology and Psychiatry*, 1961, **2,** 118–126.
68. Elkind, D., Barocas, R., & Rosenthal, H. Combinatorial thinking in adolescents from graded and ungraded classrooms. *Perceptual and Motor Skills*, 1968, **27,** 1015–1018.
69. Neimark, E. D. Longitudinal development of operational thought. Unpublished research report No. 16. Rutgers University, 1972.
70. Elkind, D. Conceptual orientation shifts in children and adolescents. *Child Development*, 1966, **37,** 493–498.
71. Elkind, D., Barocas, R., & Johnsen, P. Concept production in children and adolescents. *Human Development*, 1969, **12,** 10–21.
72. Elkind, D., Medvene, L., & Rockway, A. Representational level and concept production in children and adolescents. *Developmental Psychology*, 1969, **2,** 85–89.

73. Kohlberg, L. Moral development and the education of adolescents. In R. F. Purnell (Ed.), *Adolescents and the American high school*. New York: Holt, 1970.

74. Hartshorne, H., & May, M. A. *Studies in the nature of character*. Vol. 1, *Studies in deceit*. Vol. 2, *Studies in self control*. Vol. 3, Studies in the organization of character. New York: Macmillan, 1928–1930.

75. Hoan, N., Smith, M. B., & Block, J. Political, family and personality correlates of adolescent moral judgment. *Journal of Personality and Social Psychology*, 1968, **10**, 183–201.

76. Milgram, S. Behavioral study of obedience. *Journal of Abnormal and Social Psychology*, 1963, **67**, 371–378.

77. Saltzstein, H. D., Diamond, R. M., & Balensky, M. Moral judgment level and conformity behavior. *Developmental Psychology*, 1972, **7**, 327–336.

78. Dale, L. S. The growth of systematic thinking: Replication and analysis of Piaget's first chemical experiment. *Australian Journal of Psychology*, 1970, **22**, 277–286.

79. Jackson, S. The growth of logical thinking in normal and subnormal children. *British Journal of Educational Psychology*, 1965, **35**, 255–258.

80. Piaget, J. Intellectual evolution from adolescence to adulthood. *Human Development*, 1972, **15**, 1–12.

81. Elkind, D. Recent research on cognitive development in adolescence. In S. Dragastin (Ed.), *Adolescence in the Life Cycle*. Washington, D.C.: Hemisphere Publishing Corporation, 1975.

82. Inhelder, B. Some pathologic phenomena analyzed in the perspective of developmental psychology. In B. Inhelder & H. H. Chipman (Eds.), *Piaget and his school*. New York: Springer-Verlag, 1976.

83. Bart, W. M. The factor structure of formal operations. *British Journal of Educational Psychology*, 1971, **41**, 70–71.

84. Stephens, B., McLaughlin, J. A., Miller, C. K., & Miller, K. Factorial structure of the selected psycho-educational measures and Piagetian reasoning assessments. *Developmental Psychology*, 1972, **6**, 343–348.

85. Lee, L. C. The concomitant development of cognitive and moral modes of thought: A test of selected deductions from Piaget's theory. *Genetic Psychology Monographs*, 1971, 93–146.

86. Nassefat, M. *Étude quantitative sur l'evolution des operations intellectuelles*. Neuchâtel: Delachaux et Niestle, 1963.

87. Goodnow, J. Cross-cultural studies. In D. Elkind & J. H. Flavell (Eds.), *Studies in cognitive development*. New York: Oxford University Press, 1969.

88. Peluffo, N. Culture and cognitive problems. *International Journal of Psychology*, 1967, **2**, 187–198.

89. Papalia, D. E. The status of several conservation abilities across the life span. *Human Development*, 1972, **15**, 229–243.

90. Hall, J. W. Verbal behavior as a function of amount of schooling. *American Journal of Psychology*, 1972, **85**, 277–289.

91. Lathey, J. W. Training effects and conservation of volume. *Child Study Center Bulletin*. Buffalo, N.Y.: State University College, 1970.

92. Pascual-Leone, J. *Cognitive development and cognitive style*. Lexington, Mass.: Heath, 1973.

93. Neimark, E. D. Intellectual development during adolescence. In F. D. Horowitz (Ed.), *Review of Child Development Research*. Vol. 4. Chicago: University of Chicago Press, 1975.

94. Jones, M. C. A comparison of the attitudes and interests of ninth grade students over two decades. *Journal of Educational Research*, 1960, **51**, 175–186.

95. Harris, D. B. Sex differences in the life problems and interests of adolescents, 1935–1957. *Child Development*, 1959, **30**, 453–459.

96. Broderick, C. B., & Fowler, S. E. New patterns of relationships between the sexes among preadolescents. *Marriage and Family Living*, 1961, **23**, 27–30.

97. Kuhlen, R. G., & Houlehan, N. B. Adolescent heterosexual interest in 1942 and 1963. *Child Development*, 1965, **36**, 1949–1052.

98. Muuss, R. E. Adolescent development and the secular trend. *Adolescence*, 1970, **5**, 267–284.

99. Jones, H. E. Age changes in adult mental abilities. In H. S. Conrad (Ed.), *Studies in human development*. New York: Appleton-Century-Crofts, 1966.

100. Elkind, D. Egocentrism in adolescence. *Child Development*, 1967, **38**, 1025–1034.

16 | Personality and Social Development

STRIVING FOR INDEPENDENCE

Origins of Adolescent Independence-Striving

Ambivalent Feelings about Adolescent Independence

Patterns of Parental Authority

PROGRESS TOWARD MATURE SOCIAL RELATIONSHIPS

Peer-Group Belongingness

Heterosexual Interests and Dating

Sexuality, Security, and Intimacy

Attitudes toward Parents

INTEGRATION OF A PERSONAL IDENTITY

Identity Achievement and Identity Crisis

Continuity in Personality Development

SEX BEHAVIOR

Incidence of Premarital Intercourse

Permissiveness with Affection

DRUG USE

Incidence of Drug Use

Reasons for Using Drugs

Differences between Groups of Drug Users and Nonusers

ESSAY

Two Myths: Adolescent Rebellion and the Generation Gap

BIOGRAPHY

Harry Stack Sullivan

SUMMARY

REFERENCES

Adolescence recapitulates many of the developmental highlights of earlier years. Like infancy, adolescence is a period of rapid physical growth and major changes in bodily appearance. Like the preschool years, it is a time of expanding social horizons and emerging personality differences. Like middle childhood, it is marked by increasing liberation from the family and a continuing shift from home-centered to peer-group and community activities.

The landmarks of these developments vary during the adolescent's several-year odyssey between middle childhood and adulthood. Early adolescence, which coincides roughly with the junior-high-school years, is dominated by the adolescent growth spurt and physical sexual maturation. During middle adolescence, which coincides with the high-school years, young people are concerned primarily with achieving psychological independence from their parents and learning to handle dating and heterosexual relationships. Late adolescence usually begins around the last year of high school and continues until young people have formed a reasonably clear, consistent sense of their personal identity and have committed themselves to some fairly definite social roles, value systems, and life goals.

In Chapter 15 we described the accelerated physical growth of early adolescence, and in Chapter 17 we will consider the psychological implications of differences among teenagers in the nature and rate of their bodily changes. This chapter will focus on adolescents' striving for independence, their progress toward mature social relationships, and the integration of their personal identity. We will also cover changing patterns of sex behavior and drug abuse among young people and, in the essay, discuss the concepts of "adolescent rebellion" and the "generation gap."

STRIVING FOR INDEPENDENCE

In previous chapters we have traced children's developing independence—from their first struggles to sit up and stand by themselves, through their mastery of motor skills in the preschool years and their growing sense of industry and self-reliance during middle childhood. In midadolescence striving for independence is no longer just one aspect of a young person's activities; it becomes an end in itself. Adolescents strive for total psychological freedom from their parents—freedom to be their own person; to determine their own values; to plan their own future; to choose their own clothes, companions, and pastimes; and to preserve the privacy of their room, belongings, thoughts, and feelings.

Origins of Adolescent Independence-Striving

Adolescents' preoccupation with independence stems in part from their own mental and physical growth and in part from the expectations others have of them. By the age of 15 or 16 young people have attained most of their adult height, and they are nearing the peak of their intellectual capacities. They are capable of procreation, and they have accumulated

Privacy, a right to one's own thoughts and possessions, becomes a major concern of most adolescents.

considerable knowledge about the world around them. They feel qualified to run their own lives and be treated as adults, and they take great satisfaction in exercising their capabilities and trying on adult roles for size. Few things generate more resentment and humiliation in young people than having their maturity belittled or their freedom taken away.

Adults sometimes treat adolescents as being less capable and responsible than they are, for reasons we will discuss in a moment. However, adults generally foster independence-striving in adolescents by encouraging and expecting it. We do not specify the boundary between childhood and adulthood as clearly as do many primitive societies, some of which use puberty rites to mark the overnight passage of young people from child to adult roles (1). Yet we have a number of "mini-rites" by which we let young people know that we consider them ready for responsible self-determination.

For example, most states set 16 or 17 as the age at which adolescents can leave school, get working permits, be licensed to drive cars, and be tried in adult court for breaking the law. High-school students are also aware that they are nearing the age when they can vote, buy liquor, and marry without their parents' consent. In addition, most families provide a graduated series of ''mini-rites'' in the form of less restrictive rules and regulations. Parents usually set curfews that they relax a bit each year and eventually dispense with. They establish the age at which they will allow their adolescent children to date, use the family car, take out-of-town trips with their friends, and so forth. With each new permission parents are expressing confidence in the maturity of their children.

Ambivalent Feelings about Adolescent Independence

Even though adolescents press for independence and their parents encourage it, both groups experience some ambivalent feelings about it. This ambivalence occasionally leads to inconsistent behavior on both sides.

Adolescent Ambivalence. When they begin to enjoy new privileges, young people also regret some of the responsibilities that go with them. Being ''on their own'' means they can no longer expect their parents to provide all of their spending money, make difficult decisions for them, or shoulder the consequences of their mistakes in judgment. Emancipation also means that adolescents must deal with new situations in which they may feel awkward and inept—as when they are expected to apply for jobs, make their own arrangements for music lessons or doctors' appointments, and act as an adult in dealing with sales clerks, auto mechanics, and waiters in restaurants. Adolescents usually have to grope a bit until they can develop some confidence and facility in handling these situations; in the meantime, they may have to endure occasional painful moments of uncertainty and embarrassment. Hence, there are times when most young people yearn for the carefree days of childhood, when their parents took care of these practical matters for them.

As one consequence of this ambivalence about growing up, younger adolescents typically alternate between mature and childish behavior. One day they may take full responsibility for working out a difficult situation, and the next day they may turn helplessly to their parents for solutions to very simple problems. Sometimes they may show surprisingly good judgment and sensitivity, but on other occasions they may act impulsively and with little consideration for others. These abrupt swings in adolescents' maturity level do not reflect any moment-to-moment shifts in their basic capacities for independence; they merely signal the relative strength of the youngsters' wishes to become an adult and remain a child (2–4).

Parental Ambivalence. Parents typically enjoy seeing their children grow into adolescence, but not without some regrets. They pride themselves on the health, appearance, and accomplishments of their children, all of which reflect their own competence as parents. They may have the additional satisfaction of seeing that their children are more knowledgeable and mature than they were as youngsters and that they have good prospects for a rewarding adult life. Some parents view the progress of their children toward adulthood with welcome relief because it means that they are now free to do certain things that they felt they were unable to do while their children were young and dependent, such as spending more money on themselves, taking a trip, or moving to a farm or apartment.

On the other hand, their adolescent's increasing independence and exposure to possible dangers and disappointments causes many parents to be concerned. Most parents worry at least a little about how their youngsters will cope with social and academic frustrations; how they will handle sex, alcohol, tobacco, and drugs; whether they will drive safely;

Parents have to let their adolescent children grow up and experience new kinds of relationships, as in dating. For most parents this process is accompanied by some mixed feelings.

and whether their lives will be interrupted by some new war. Hence, parents may share with their adolescent sons and daughters some nostalgia for the earlier childhood years, when life was less complicated for them all.

Furthermore, adolescence may be a particularly difficult experience for parents (primarily mothers) who have thrived on their parental role and given child rearing top priority in their daily life. For such parents, the maturation of their children may signal the end of their most meaningful function in life. Even parents who have not been particularly child-oriented often feel some sadness as their youngsters approach the age when they will move out on their own, leaving behind a home that is a little emptier, a little quieter, and a little less caught up in the excitement of a younger generation. And, equally important, grown-up children are clear evidence to the parents that they too are growing older (5–10).

Because of such mixed feelings, parents also demonstrate an erratic approach to adolescent independence. Most alternate occasionally between treating their adolescent sons and daughters as incompetent children and as fully capable, self-reliant adults. Of course, adolescents are neither; they are no longer children but not yet adults. What they usually need is a graduated experience in autonomy in which their parents respect their capacities but stand ready to help and support them whenever they get into situations that they cannot handle.

Patterns of Parental Authority

Parents who are willing and able to impose reasonable controls on their adolescents, while making sure that they have opportunities for gradually increasing autonomy, contribute effectively to their children's self-confidence, self-control, self-reliance, and mature judgment. By contrast, parents who are overly controlling and restrictive are likely to undermine their child's self-confidence and capacity for autonomy, and parents who are too permissive or unable to maintain authority over their adolescent children make it difficult for them to learn responsibility and self-reliance.

These observations are based on extensive research concerned with parental styles of exercising power over adolescent children. In Chapter 8 we discussed Diana Baumrind's findings that parents who treat pre-schoolers in an *authoritative* manner are more likely to foster self-reliance in their children than are parents who are either *authoritarian* or *permissive*. Using the perceptions of adolescents, Glen Elder has similarly distinguished the following three patterns of parental power (11, 12):

Autocratic—*Parents do not allow adolescents to express their views on subjects regarding their behavior and do not permit them to regulate their own behavior in any way.*

Democratic—*Adolescents are encouraged to participate in discussing issues relevant to their behavior although the final decision is made or approved by the parents.*

*Permissive—Adolescents have more influence in making decisions
that concern them than do their parents.*

Working with data collected from several thousand junior- and senior-high-school students, Elder found three significant relationships between perceived parental style and adolescent attitudes. First, adolescents who saw their parents as democratic in exercising power were more likely to express confidence in and preference for governing themselves than those who saw their parents as autocratic or permissive. Second, democratically reared adolescents were more likely to want to be like their parents than those who were either autocratically or permissively reared. Third, those with democratic parents were less likely to feel rejected or unwanted than those with autocratic or permissive parents, especially when permissiveness took the form of leaving everything the adolescents did up to them.

Elder's work was extended by Lesser and Kandel in a detailed study of more than 2300 high-school students in the United States (13). They found that about 48 percent of American adolescents perceive their parents as autocratic or authoritarian, about 35 percent as democratic, and the remaining 17 percent as permissive. Fathers are more often viewed as authoritarian, while mothers are more commonly seen as democratic (see Table 16.1). This finding is consistent with other evidence showing that children tend to regard their fathers as stricter and more demanding and their mothers as more affectionate, supportive, protective, and child-centered (14, 15).

Lesser and Kandel also confirmed that parental permissiveness does not produce particularly strong feelings of being given independence, contrary to what some parents and adolescents may think. Rather, as indicated in Table 16.2, adolescents feel freer and are more satisfied with the adult status they are being granted when their parents are democratic, that is, when they neither dominate nor withdraw from decisions pertaining to their youngsters' activities.

Table 16.1 Adolescents' Perceptions of Parental Styles of Exercising Power

Parental Style	Percentage Who Saw Their Mother in This Style (n=983)	Percentage Who Saw Their Father in This Style (n=955)
Authoritarian	43	53
Democratic	40	29
Permissive	17	18

Source: Based on data reported by Lesser, G. S., & Kandel, D. Parent-adolescent relationships and adolescent independence in the United States and Denmark. *Journal of Marriage and the Family,* 1969, **31,** 348–358.

Table 16.2 Relationships between Feelings of Independence, Perceived Parental Authority, and Parental Explanations of Rules in American Adolescents

	Perceived Parental Authority			Frequency of Parental Explanations for Rules and Decisions		
Adolescents' Feelings	Authoritarian	Democratic	Permissive	Both Parents High	One High One Low	Both Parents Low
Percentage of Adolescents:						
Who feel both parents give them enough freedom	58	82	68	79	57	50
(n)	(239)	(164)	(76)	(300)	(293)	(224)
Who feel parents should treat them more as adults	63	44	64	47	51	68
(n)	(201)	(133)	(63)	(249)	(180)	(186)

Source: Based on data reported by Lesser, G. S., & Kandel, D. Parent-adolescent relationships and adolescent independence in the United States and Denmark. *Journal of Marriage and the Family,* 1969, **31,** 348–358.

Table 16.3   Attitudes toward Parents and Freedom from Parents

Adolescents' Reports	Freedom Allowed by Parents			
	Both Enough (n=520)	Mother Enough (n=99)	Father Enough (n=47)	Neither Enough (n=154)
Percentage of Adolescents:				
Who say it is harder to get along with parents than it used to be	29	32	55	53
Who feel that their parents are old-fashioned	17	33	32	55
Who mention one or more specific conflicts with mother during the past year	68	74	81	81
Who mention one or more specific conflicts with father during the past year	59	69	70	67

Source: Based on data reported by Lesser, G. S., & Kandel, D. Parent-adolescent relationships and adolescent independence in the United States and Denmark. *Journal of Marriage and the Family,* 1969, **31,** 348–358.

Of the adolescents who viewed their parents as democratic, 82 percent believed they were being given enough freedom and 44 percent felt they should be treated more as adults. By contrast, just 68 percent of the adolescents who viewed their parents as permissive and 58 percent of those who viewed their parents as authoritarian felt they were being given enough freedom, and 64 percent in the permissive group and 63 percent in the autocratic group believed they should be treated more as adults. As the table also shows, when both parents usually explained their decisions and rules, adolescents tended to feel that they were being given enough freedom and were being treated as adults.

As one further step Lesser and Kandel compared adolescents' feelings about having enough freedom with their attitudes toward their parents. As summarized in Table 16.3, those who thought they had enough freedom were generally less inclined to view their parents as old-fashioned, to have difficulties getting along with them, or to recall specific conflicts with them than was true for adolescents who wanted to have more freedom.

PROGRESS TOWARD MATURE SOCIAL RELATIONSHIPS

As part of their social maturation, adolescents give increased attention to peer-group belongingness and to their relationships with the opposite sex. Although these aspects of interpersonal relationships overlap considerably, each has separate implications for personality development. In addition, social maturation influences how adolescents deal with their needs for sexuality, security, and intimacy, and how they feel about their parents.

Peer-Group Belongingness

Teenagers typically react to being in a transitional period of development by seeking solidarity in their own ranks. No longer satisfied with being children but not yet accepted as adults, they concentrate on establishing groups or cultures of their own. Adolescent groups provide useful opportunities for young people to share responsibility for their own affairs, to experiment together with ways of handling new situations, and to learn from one another's mistakes. Even more important, having their own age group gives adolescents a reassuring reference group and a source of group-based identity while they are passing from childhood to adulthood (16, 17).

Adolescent cultures accordingly consist of unique values that young people subscribe to and that give them a sense of belonging to an identifiable group. For the most part, these values involve tastes in clothing, language, music, and leisure-time activities that are seldom shared or appreciated by adults. Many people believe that such superficial manifestations of adolescent individuality reflect a basic disaffection for adults ("Don't trust anyone over 30") and a rejection of societal codes of decency, propriety, and respect for authority. Although we will consider this issue in the essay at the end of this chapter, we should note here that the cultural trappings of adolescence may be due as much to adult opportunism as to the actions of young people themselves.

Adult opportunism enters the picture as a function of the teenager's new role as a consumer. Most adolescents have money to spend and freedom to decide how they will spend it. This makes them a substantial market for such items as clothes, records, and rock-music concerts; obviously, large profits can be made by entertainers, manufacturers, and promoters who create adolescent fads. To some extent, therefore, the way adolescents look, act, and spend their leisure time may have less to do with their own originality than with what is portrayed in movies, magazines, and television programs as being the fashion for their age group (17–19).

From middle childhood through midadolescence the mounting importance of peer-group belongingness is due to adolescents' needs for identification with a group and to their strivings for independence. Because adolescents want to be grown-up, they find it difficult to rely entirely on their parents for affection and esteem; since they do not want to feel overly dependent upon their parents, they look to their peer group for acceptance.

Important Factors in Popularity. In adolescence as in middle childhood, peer acceptance and popularity come most readily to those who are physically attractive, bright, talented, self-confident, energetic, and comfortable in interpersonal situations (20–25). Conversely, adolescents who are not too attractive or bright, who have doubts about their own self-worth, and who are afraid of rejection by their peers are likely to act in ways that make their fears come true. Such young people often invite

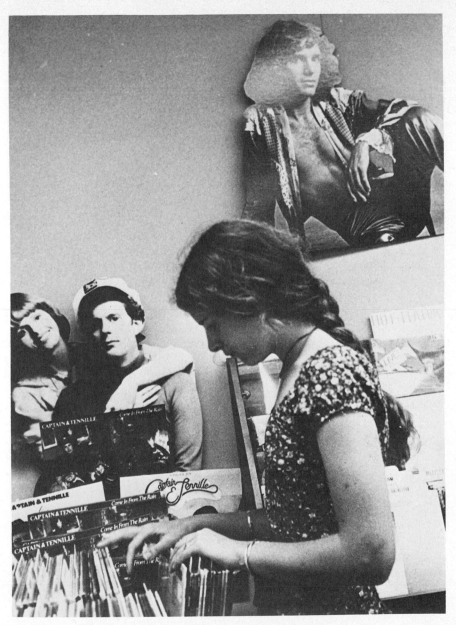

Most people are aware of distinctive adolescent tastes in music and other areas. What is less widely appreciated is that these tastes are often fostered by adults who promote fads for business purposes.

rejection and ridicule by withdrawing from peer-group activities; by being timid, nervous, and ill-at-ease with their peers; by seeking attention and acceptance through servility or silliness; or by trying to hide their feelings of inadequacy with sarcasm, bluster, and bravado.

There are discontinuities as well as continuities in peer acceptance between childhood and adolescence. A girl who had been a skinny ugly duckling with braces on her teeth may suddenly blossom into an attractive adolescent who is popular with boys and admired (and envied) by girls. Similarly, a boy who had been small and thin may emerge from his adolescent growth spurt as tall and muscular, thus bolstering his self-image and gaining new respect from others. At the same time, previously popular children who remain emotionally childish while their peers are learning to act in more mature ways may no longer be sought after as a friend and companion. Partly for these reasons, friendship choices are found to change a great deal during the early adolescent years (26).

Fortunately for many adolescents, their widening world gives them new opportunities to discover what they can do well and become known for. A boy who was too small to play well in the baseball and football games of middle childhood may become the star of his high-school wrestling team in the flyweight class. A girl with vocal or dramatic talent that remained untapped in elementary school may become a soloist or lead actress in the musical or dramatic programs put on in high school. Young people with limited intellectual abilities who had struggled through elementary school with little gratification may perform extremely well in the nonacademic curricula offered in high school, such as mechanical arts, home economics, or secretarial courses. With these opportunities adolescents may be able to develop feelings of self-worth and self-confidence that they never had before and at the same time enhance their peer-group status.

Stability of Friendships. Despite the shifting of friendship choices during early adolescence, there tends to be an increasing stability from middle childhood through young adulthood. Horrocks and his colleagues have studied fluctuations in friendship choice by asking children of different ages to name their three best friends and then repeating the question 2 weeks later (27–29). The extent to which the second list differs from the first provides a rough index of fickleness versus stability. Figure 16.1

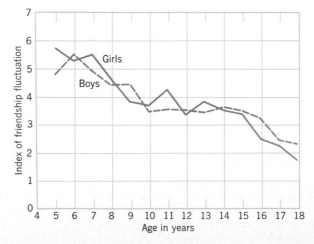

Figure 16.1 Relationship between chronological age and friendship fluctuation for urban boys and girls. (*Source.* Horrocks, J. E., & Buker, M. E. A study of friendship fluctuation of preadolescents. *Journal of Genetic Psychology*, 1951, **78**, 131–144.)

shows the average fluctuation index of boys and girls from the age of 5 to 18. The data clearly reflect a trend toward greater stability in friendship choice with increasing chronological age.

Heterosexual Interests and Dating

The most significant aspect of interpersonal relationships that emerges during adolescence is an interest in the opposite sex. Three factors contribute to the beginnings of heterosexual interest at this point: (a) the hormonal changes that take place during puberty produce sexual feelings that motivate boys and girls to seek each other's company; (b) adolescents view heterosexual relationships as an aspect of being grown-up and therefore value them; and (c) parents and peers expect adolescents to be interested in the opposite sex. Parents may have some reservations about when and whom their son or daughter should date, but they are likely to become even more concerned if their adolescent child shows no heterosexual interest.

When adolescents are asked why they enjoy dating, they consistently give one or more of the following reasons: to assert their independence, to gain status, to seek sexual gratification, to have companionship, to participate in dating activities, and—as they get older—to look for a "steady" and eventually to find a mate (30–32). Despite its attractiveness, however, dating develops slowly through several phases of adolescent group formation, and it brings with it numerous sources of conflict and concern.

Phases of Group Formation and Heterosexual Development. In a widely cited analysis of adolescent social structure, Dexter Dunphy has charted group formation as depicted in Figure 16.2 (33). At the beginning of adolescence, boys and girls stand apart from each other in the unisex groups that characterize middle childhood (Stage 1). Soon they begin to interact as boy-girl groups (Stage 2), after which they enter a transition period when some boys and girls pair off (Stage 3). Later on, adolescents get together largely in boy-girl pairs (Stage 4), and by late adolescence this pattern is replaced by couples whose closest relationship is with each other and who have only loose associations with other couples (Stage 5).

Specifically what this means is that boys and girls who before adolescence had little to do with one another begin during early adolescence to arrange parties in which they gingerly test the new sensations and feelings that are associated with emerging sexuality. They drink Cokes, listen to records, dance, chase one another, wrestle, and perhaps do some experimental necking in the corner, but strictly in the context of a group activity without any consistent pairing off. Later on they begin dating, which means that their social affairs are for couples who come as a pair and are not just groups of boys and girls. Over time, casual and occasional dating tends to become more frequent dating and then turn into "going steady" or at least narrowing the field to a few serious interests (31, 34, 35).

Although the sequence of these stages is fairly uniform, the age of

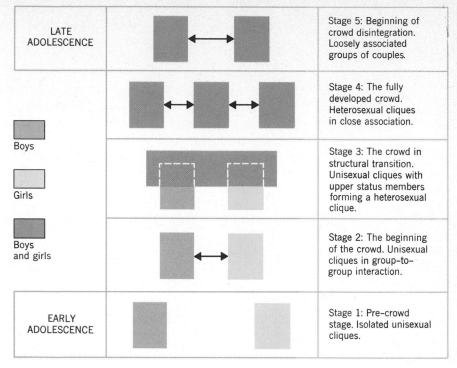

Figure 16.2 Stages of group development in adolescence. (*Source.* Dunphy, D. C. The social structure of urban adolescent peer groups. *Sociometry,* 1963, **26,** 230–246.)

transition from one stage to another varies. Most girls in the United States begin dating around the age of 14 and boys soon after, even though boys at this age may be a year or two behind girls in physical and emotional maturity (36). Since dating is primarily a social relationship defined by cultural norms and not by biological development, differences in physical maturation appear to have little effect on the age at which adolescents begin to date (37).

As a cultural phenomenon, however, dating patterns do differ. For example, adolescents in urban areas tend to start dating earlier than those in rural areas, and middle-class youngsters are likely to begin dating sooner than working-class adolescents (38). Although the latter group begins formal dating relatively late, they soon progress to going steady and getting married, whereas middle-class adolescents tend to do more casual dating before going steady and getting married.

Sources of Concern about Dating. Beginning to date confronts adolescents with many new concerns, mainly in the form of difficult decisions they must make. When a boy is deciding whether to ask a particular girl out, for example, he often weighs the possible rewards of getting the date against the risk of being turned down. The more attractive and popular the girl is, the happier he will be if she accepts the date, but the more likely he is to have the deflating experience of being refused. If she is neither attractive nor popular, he is less likely to be refused, but his pleasure at her acceptance will not be so great. A boy can avoid such an approach-avoidance conflict by not dating at all, but then he denies himself the opportunity for a heterosexual relationship—nothing ventured, nothing gained.

Girls face similar problems in being asked for dates and in deciding which invitations to accept. A girl who wants to go out with a particular boy has to find some middle course between being too coy and reserved (in which case he may not notice her) and being too obvious about her feelings (in which case she may get an unwanted reputation as a flirt or "boy chaser"). Furthermore, when a girl is asked out by a boy she doesn't like, she must decide whether to accept just in order to have some kind of a date, or to decline in the hope that she will hear from someone she likes better, even if it means that she winds up without a date at all (3, 39).

Surveys have found that most adolescents feel inadequate about dating, and at least in the beginning feel shy, self-conscious, and uneasy. The majority of adolescents are afraid of "doing something wrong" on the first date, and one study of 1500 high-school students found that one-fourth of the boys and one-third of the girls felt they were failures at dating (37, 40, 41).

From an adult point of view such concerns often seem silly and inconsequential. For adolescents, however, successful dating can be crucial to their feelings of self-esteem and peer-group belongingness. Young people who do not date or who do so awkwardly tend to feel inferior to their more socially competent peers. Moreover, the increasing popularity of heterosexual activities in the peer group may cause nondating adolescents to feel socially excluded.

Once adolescents begin to date, another problem they must confront is how to handle sex. In our society boys are usually expected to initiate kissing and petting, in which they have little or no prior experience and in which they risk being rebuffed or, worse yet, laughed at for a clumsy effort. Girls, who are expected to set limits on sexual activity, must decide how far to let things go in order to maintain a boy's interest, but not cause him to lose respect. For both boys and girls, sexual overtures and decisions are influenced by the expectations of their peer group (which they feel pressured to live up to) and the standards of their parents (which they feel a need to live within). The stricter the moral codes of adolescents, the more likely it is that their efforts to become sexually experienced will cause them anxiety (about being detected) and guilt (about doing something wrong) (16, 42, 43).

Turning to where young people learn about sexual matters, in 1975 Thornburg reported that about 40 percent of adolescents he surveyed

Table 16.4   Sources of Initial Sex Information (in Percentages)

Source	Males (n=180)	Females (n=271)	Total (n=451)
Mother	5.4	19.3	13.5
Father	3.0	1.0	1.8
Peers	45.2	35.3	39.4
School	17.2	21.1	19.5
Literature	20.3	19.7	20.0
Physician	.3	.5	.4
Minister	.6	.4	.4
Experience	7.9	2.7	5.0

Source: Thornburg, H. D., Adolescent sources of initial sex information. In R. E. Grinder (Ed.), Studies in adolescence. (3rd ed.) New York: Macmillan, 1975.

obtained their first information about sex from their peers and another 20 percent obtained it from reading (44). Table 16.4 lists these and other sources of initial sex information for both boys and girls. The reason girls receive much more of their first information from their mothers than do boys is that this information includes what mothers tell their daughters about menstruation. Thornburg notes that his findings do not differ very much from data compiled 20 or 30 years ago, which suggests that neither the present-day sex education in many schools nor today's presumed openness to family discussions of sexual matters has had much influence on adolescents' sources of initial information about sex.

Sexuality, Security, and Intimacy

The stresses and strains of adolescent heterosexuality have been beautifully described by Harry Stack Sullivan in his conception of the interacting needs for *sexuality,** security,* and *intimacy* (45). Sexuality refers to the expression of sexual urges; security refers to freedom from anxiety; and intimacy refers to close collaborative relationships between people. According to Sullivan, a significant part of growing up is learning to satisfy all three of these needs in interpersonal relationships, without letting any one need interfere or conflict with the others.

Sexuality versus Security.   According to Sullivan, the sexual uncer-

*Sullivan actually used "lust" as his term for sexuality. Because lust has many negative connotations that Sullivan did not mean to imply—one of the definitions in *The Random House Dictionary* is "illicit sexual desire"—we have decided to use the more neutral word "sexuality" instead.

Table 16.5 Frequency of Masturbation among High-School Students

	Twice a Month or More	Ever to Once a Month	Never	N
Male (percentage)	77	12	11	586
Female (percentage)	17	23	60	581

Source: Gagnon, J. H., Simon, W., & Berger, A. J. Some aspects of sexual adjustment in early and later adolescence. In J. Zubin & A. M. Freedman (Eds.), *Psychopathology of adolescence.* New York: Grune & Stratton, 1970.

tainties that begin in midadolescence represent conflicts between the need for sexuality and the need for security. Adolescents must learn to handle sex in ways that do not cause anxiety, which most of them do in the course of their dating experiences. However, young people who are excessively insecure in expressing sexual urges may either avoid the opposite sex or seek out platonic, brother-sister types of relationships. People in whom such conflicts between sexuality and security continue into adulthood often tend not to marry or to arrange marriages in which there is little or no sex.

One important aspect of sexuality that often causes anxiety among adolescents is masturbation. Masturbation is extremely common among high-school boys and not uncommon among girls, as indicated in Table 16.5 (46). The observation that masturbation is more frequent among boys than girls is usually attributed to the fact that they experience puberty in different ways. Specifically, adolescent boys are more inclined to think of their physical maturation in terms of specific sexual activity, whereas girls are more inclined to think of it in terms of romance, love, and marriage (36, 47). Although nearly 80 percent of boys surveyed said that they masturbated twice a week or more, it should be noted that no amount of masturbation is really excessive, with the very rare exception of a boy who becomes so preoccupied with it that he can scarcely do anything else.

This point needs to be emphasized, because masturbation has been and still is a topic of religious prohibition, a source of fear that the "unnatural" loss of semen might sap the body's vitality, and the subject of dire warnings about "self-abuse" leading to insanity. With these myths and warnings all around them, and with parents trying to prevent their youngsters from masturbating, many generations of adolescents have suffered guilt and anxiety about it (4). Religious issues aside, we can say that there is absolutely no evidence that masturbation causes any kind of physical or psychological harm, except for a person's feelings that it is a bad or wrong thing to do (42, 48, 49).

Intimacy versus Sexuality. Intimacy begins to be important in heterosexual relationships during late adolescence. Before this time, despite their increasing interest in the opposite sex, young people have usually been close friends and confidants primarily with members of their own sex. But now, as the larger peer group becomes less important and dating becomes more serious, boys and girls who are going together are likely to become good friends who visit in each other's homes, share with each other their hopes and fears, turn to each other for comfort and support, and contemplate the long-range future of their relationship. When a boy and girl can be one another's best friend, as well as steady dates and partners in sexual experiences, they have achieved a mature capacity for heterosexual intimacy.

In developing this capacity older adolescents go through a process of resolving conflicts between such intimacy and their needs for sexuality and security. Early in their heterosexual experience adolescents often make a distinction between sexual partners on one hand and those whom they respect and want to be close to on the other. As a reflection of this conflict, boys and girls sometimes let go sexually with partners they do not particularly admire, do not want to have as good friends, and frequently do not expect to have much future contact with (as in the weekend or summer romance). However, when a boy or girl is dating someone who is really looked up to and longed for as a "steady," the relationship is kept relatively "pure." The resolution of this conflict is, of course, affected by social values as well as personality development, in that the more the larger society views sex as something that "good" as well as "bad" people can and should enjoy, the more quickly adolescents outgrow their distinction between "sacred" (platonic) and "profane" (sexual) relationships.

Young people who do not mature enough to be able to combine sexuality and intimacy in a relationship with one person of the opposite sex enter adulthood with a psychological split in this respect. As adults they may have active sex lives but never marry; or they may marry and have a very limited sex life; or they may have chaste marriages together with an active extramarital life with partners they don't particularly respect.

Intimacy versus Security. To integrate heterosexual intimacy with their security needs, adolescents must redirect their earlier chumship attachments toward members of the opposite sex. Young people who have had few chumships may never feel comfortable in getting close to other people of either sex. Since intimacy threatens their security, they feel psychologically safer in distant, formal, or superficial relationships with large numbers of people then they do in close, intense relationships with just a few people or a single boyfriend or girlfriend.

Other young people may feel secure in close, collaborative relationships with members of their own sex but not in such relationships with members of the opposite sex. An adolescent who does not resolve this type of conflict may become an adult who, if he or she marries at all, cannot regard the spouse as a close friend and confidant. Such people usually limit the marital relationship to sexual, homemaking, and child-rearing roles, while relying on parents, siblings, and same-sexed friends for advice, shared confidences, and discussing personal matters.

Attitudes toward Parents

As adolescents become more independent and socially mature, their attitudes toward their parents often change. The increasing amount of interest, affection, and commitment young people are giving to peer-group and heterosexual activities—especially when they begin to date seriously—means that they have less for their parents. Parents have to learn to give up some of their children's affection, which always hurts a little—especially if there has been a close family bond. When adolescents realize that their parents have been hurt as a result of being replaced by other love objects, they frequently feel guilty and try to justify to themselves their growing attachments outside the family.

Adolescents sometimes think up plausible reasons for turning away from their parents, especially a conviction that their parents are unattractive. Some midadolescents become highly critical of the appearance of their opposite-sex parent: boys grumble about their mothers' hair styles, weight, makeup, and clothes, and girls complain about the fact that their fathers are losing their hair, developing a paunch, or wearing outdated clothing (3, 8, 50).

Adolescents may also find many things "wrong" with their parents' behavior: they smoke too much, they don't get enough exercise, they have boorish or uninteresting friends, they are old-fashioned or set in their ways, they lead dull lives, and so forth. Such criticisms do not necessarily mean a lessening of an adolescent's love for his or her parents. They simply help to remind the adolescent that his or her parents are of a different generation and have a different outlook, so that the young person does not have to feel guilty about seeking and enjoying romantic attachments in his or her own generation.

Furthermore, these superficial criticisms do not mean that adolescents' basic values are incompatible with those of their parents, or that the parents have any less influence over their adolescent children. As we noted in Chapter 13, adolescents conform most to the influence of their peers in early adolescence, but then this conformity gradually declines from about age 12 to 21. Thus, although midadolescents are spending more time with their peers, they are becoming less influenced by them. Also, adolescents who run counter to this general trend by continuing to be influenced by the group are usually doing so for one of two reasons: either they lack self-esteem and feel they must ingratiate themselves with their peers, or their parents are not providing enough guidance for them and so they are relying on their peers to fill the parental vacuum (51–54).

It should be noted that the source of influence to which adolescents are most responsive varies somewhat with the situation. For example, young people are more likely to listen to their parents than to their peers on such matters as their future educational and occupational plans, as well as how to handle interpersonal relationships other than those with their peers. On the other hand, adolescents are more likely to listen to their peers when it comes to how to dress, how to handle peer relationships, and how to spend leisure time (55–57).

As youngsters near the end of adolescence, neither their parents nor peers exercise much influence on them, since they are becoming confident in their own capacities for making decisions. While continuing to weigh the opinions offered by peers, parents, and other adults, older adolescents increasingly think for themselves and rely on their own good judgment (58–60). Such independence was expressed by a late adolescent boy as follows:

"Conformity is what you do to keep your parents from nagging at you while you make up your mind what you really want to do do" (61).

INTEGRATION OF A PERSONAL IDENTITY

In earlier chapters we traced the process of **identity formation** from infancy—when children learn to recognize themselves as persons who are distinct from other persons and things; through the preschool years—when boys and girls become aware of the physical differences between the sexes; and into middle childhood—when youngsters begin to adopt sex-differentiated roles and to recognize each other's individual abilities, talents, and interests. Developing a clear and consistent image of oneself becomes important during late adolescence, when it culminates in the integration of a sense of personal identity.

The role of identity formation in adolescent development was first spelled out by Erik Erikson. Erikson defined the end of adolescence as a time when people have become reasonably sure of what they believe in and what they want to do with their lives. A sense of personal identity is the product of everything young people have learned about themselves in their various roles as student, son or daughter, athlete, musician, boyfriend or girlfriend, church member, grocery clerk, and so forth. Once achieved, this integrated view of their roles, abilities, interests, attitudes, and impact on other people gives adolescents a feeling of continuity with their past and helps prepare them for their future. An integrated personal identity, in other words, should mean that young people know who they are, where they have been, and what possibilities they might want to consider for the future (62–64).

This is not to say that late adolescents make permanent and fixed commitments to various life goals and value systems. On the contrary, personal identity is an ongoing process that changes with age as people learn new things and experience different roles—spouse, parent, employee, boss, grandparent, widow, and so forth (65). But late adolescence is the time when people's sense of identity, no matter how much it may sub-

As part of consolidating
their sense of personal
identity, late adolescents
begin to think about future
commitments to
educational and
occupational goals.

sequently change, begins to take some consistent form that makes sense
to them and gives meaning and direction to their lives.

In the process of developing an integrated sense of identity, adolescents
spend several years considering and trying out a wide range of roles and

ideologies. They think about various job and career possibilities, they date and make friends with many different people, and they consider the merits of various social, political, economic, and religious philosophies. Because adolescents are actively sorting out the types of work, friends, potential mates, and philosophy of life to which they may want to make a meaningful commitment, they frequently change their minds about what they like to do, the people they like to be with, and their responses to different situations. Adolescents are therefore less predictable than they were as children, and they themselves have to tolerate uncertainty as they search for a consistent life style.

The fact that adolescents spend several years developing an integrated identity has led to two widely believed but inaccurate generalizations about adolescent development: first, that normal adolescents go through an **identity crisis** during which their attempts to achieve identity produce psychological storm and stress; and second, that because of this presumed psychological turmoil there is little continuity between what people are like as adolescents and what they are like as adults.

Erikson and numerous other psychoanalytic writers have held that adolescents *must* experience great inner turmoil in order to become well-adjusted and mature adults (66–69). However, these views are based almost entirely on clinical experience with troubled adolescents who sought therapy because of psychological problems. Research studies of adolescents who have been chosen at random from those enrolled in school (rather than from those who are in psychiatric treatment) show a different picture. These studies demonstrate that most adolescents proceed smoothly toward an identity integration without experiencing a tumultuous crisis and that there is substantial continuity between their adolescent and adult personalities.

Identity
Achievement and
Identity Crisis

In describing and measuring four *identity statuses,* James Marcia and his colleagues have helped to explain the process of identity formation (70–72). Identity status describes where a person is with respect to making a meaningful commitment to an occupation and/or value system or ideology, as follows:

Identity achievement—commitment to an occupation that has been chosen from among several previously considered possibilities; commitment to an ideology after re-evaluating and resolving past beliefs in such a way that the person is now truly free to act.

Identity foreclosure—premature commitment to goals and beliefs that have been suggested by others (usually parents) without the person's having considered alternative possibilities on his or her own terms.

Identity moratorium—an ongoing effort to consider possibilities and make commitments that has not yet resulted in a clear and satisfying self-definition.

Identity diffusion—lack of commitment and a lack of interest in working to sort out values and future possibilities.

Studies of college freshmen show that these four statuses are fairly equally distributed among them, and also that they relate to some differences in personality functioning. Identity achievement students tend to perform better on intellectual tasks, are more self-confident and less anxious, and have a greater capacity for intimate interpersonal relationships than the other three groups. Identity foreclosure students tend to be more rigid than the other groups; to set unrealistically high goals for themselves and then work least effectively on intellectual tasks; to display an inflated self-esteem that quickly crumbles when it is challenged; and to become involved in stereotyped and superficial relations with others. Identity moratorium and identity diffusion students tend to fall between the others on most of these dimensions; however, the identity moratorium students are inclined to be the most anxious of all four groups, and identity diffusion students somewhat resemble the foreclosure group in having poor self-esteem and superficial interpersonal relationships (73–77).

Although these identity statuses help to explain late adolescent behavior at a given point in time, they are only phases in a young person's development and not permanent traits. For example, an adolescent can demonstrate identity achievement with respect to a future occupation and identity moratorium with respect to general belief systems. Young people may also change their identity status during college, although identity achievement is a fairly stable status that adolescents tend to move toward rather than away from (78).

Table 16.6 illustrates the changes in identity status that took place for 47 college engineering students followed by Waterman and his colleagues from their freshman to their senior years (79). The most significant changes as shown in the table are movement out of the foreclosure and moratorium statuses and into the achievement status. The frequency of identity diffusion remains the same, with about equal numbers moving in and out. In a similar study of students in a liberal arts college, Waterman and Goldman found the same kind of progressive developmental change: students tended to move through the moratorium status to become identity achievers, and the majority left college with their sense of identity relatively well established (80).

Despite such variations in identity status, numerous other studies of high-school and college students indicate that most adolescents progress toward maturity fairly smoothly, without going through any tumultuous crisis. No more than 20 percent are likely to suffer significant psychological distress, and instances of mild distress (such as heightened self-consciousness, lowered self-esteem, and instability of the self-image) are more likely to occur in early adolescence, when young people are coping with major physical changes, than in later adolescence, when they are working to integrate their personal identity (81–89).

Table 16.6 College Students in Each Occupational and Ideological Identity Status and the Number Who Moved out of and into Each Status from the End of the Freshman Year to the Senior Year ($n=47$)

Status	Freshmen	Seniors	Freshmen Moving out of Status by Senior Year	Freshmen Moving into Status by Senior Year
Occupation:				
Identity achievement	7	19	2	14
Identity moratorium	8	0	8	0
Identity foreclosure	17	14	5	2
Identity diffusion	15	14	8	7
Ideology:				
Identity achievement	5	20	0	15
Identity moratorium	4	1	4	1
Identity foreclosure	19	7	13	1
Identity diffusion	17	17	5	5

Source: From Waterman, A. S., Geary, P. S., & Waterman, C. K. Longitudinal study of changes in ego identity status from the freshman to the senior year at college. *Developmental Psychology*, 1974, **10,** 387–392.

Continuity in Personality Development

Longitudinal studies have also demonstrated considerable continuity in personality development from adolescence to adulthood. Although people do change as they get older—they learn more, fill new roles, and seek new means of coping with the changing circumstances of their life—they remain basically the same in the way in which they think, handle interpersonal relationships, and are perceived by others.

The most extensive longitudinal studies of personality development were started by the Institute of Human Development of the University of California at Berkeley in 1928 (90). Haan and Day have summarized the data from tests, interviews, ratings, and other sources that were collected at regular intervals for two samples in the study: one group that was followed from age 12 to 50 (from the Oakland Growth Study) and another group that was followed from age 12 to 40 (from the Guidance Study) (91). Table 16.7 lists 34 traits grouped into the following categories: ways of approaching and processing information, forms of interpersonal reactions, responses to socialization influences, and manner of self-presentation. All of the correlation ratios larger than .50 indicate statistically significant consistency over the time period studied. The findings strongly suggest that these traits are established by early adolescence and are not significantly affected by the process of adolescent development or by subsequent adult experience. Numerous other studies confirm that

Table 16.7 Trait Consistencies from Adolescence to Adulthood in the Oakland Growth Study (OGS; ages 12-50) and the Guidance Study (GS; ages 12-40)*

Items	Females		Males	
	OGS	GS	OGS	GS
Ways of approaching and processing information:				
esthetically reactive	.85	.60	.76	.80
verbally fluent	.66	.69	.79	.81
wide interests	.72	.69	.79	.84
prides self on objectivity	.65	.51	.79	.60
introspective	.57	.70	(.49)	.66
thinks unconventionally	.66	.71	(.27)	.65
ruminative	.54	.66	(.18)	.51
has concern about body	(.38)	.54	.51	.51
Forms of interpersonal reactions:				
arouses liking	.60	.68	.71	.63
assertive	.69	.76	(.47)	.68
socially poised	.76	.72	.67	(.49)
values independence	.69	.63	.50	.52
aloof	.74	.59	.60	.58
distrustful	.57	(.49)	.55	.56
Responses to socialization influences:				
fastidious	.69	.70	.71	.63
sex-typed behavior	.59	.67	.52	.77
rebellious	.70	.75	.61	.73
overcontrolled	.64	.72	.61	.79
undercontrolled	.70	.66	.72	.73
pushes limits	.67	.69	.77	.64
feels victimized	(.47)	.52	.74	.65

Table 16.7 Trait Consistencies from Adolescence to Adulthood in the Oakland Growth Study (OGS; ages 12-50) and the Guidance Study (GS; ages 12-40)* (cont.)

Items	Females		Males	
	OGS	GS	OGS	GS
Manner of self-presentation:				
interesting	.74	.77	.62	.65
cheerful	.69	.70	.62	.67
satisfied with self	.57	.70	.57	.67
satisfied with appearance	.67	.55	(.48)	.56
talkative	.72	.63	.65	.68
intellectual level	.80	.78	.87	.86
rapid tempo	.64	.72	(.44)	.62
physically attractive	.73	.69	.60	.67
basic hostility	.62	.66	.63	.56
self-dramatizing	.69	.71	.71	.69
self-defeating	.61	.57	.75	.81
fearful	.73	.57	.61	.58
reluctant to act	.63	.55	(.40)	.67

*Correlation ratios ≥ .50 indicate significant consistency.
Source: Haan, N., & Day, D. A longitudinal study of change and sameness in personality development: Adolescence to later adulthood. *International Journal of Aging and Human Development,* 1974, **5,** 11–39.

personality development is usually not disrupted by adolescence, but rather proceeds with considerable continuity through adolescence into adulthood (92–98).

SEX BEHAVIOR Since the 1960s Americans' attitudes toward sex have become increasingly liberal. Some people have become concerned that this liberalization may be leading to the moral decay of our society, especially that young people are becoming sexually amoral and promiscuous. The popular media frequently dramatize sexual "swingers" as if they were the typical young people of today. Even professional journals in the mid-1960s published assertions that adolescents no longer have any regard for virginity (99) and that "adolescent premarital intercourse . . . has become a perfunctory aspect of the dating system" (100).

During the 1960s many social scientists tried to determine the actual extent of adolescent sex behavior to see whether it was more extensive than in past generations. Two important books emerged from these efforts—*The Sexual Behavior of Young People,* by Michael Schofield, and *The Social Context of Premarital Sexual Permissiveness,* by Ira Reiss (101, 102). Both authors made a large-scale study of representative adolescents and came to the same conclusion, namely, that there is not nearly as much sexual activity among adolescents as is commonly believed and that—as of 1967—there had been no significant increase since the 1920s in the proportion of unmarried young people who had had sexual intercourse.

From the Reiss and Schofield data, it was argued well into the 1970s that adolescents today are not much more likely than in the past to engage in premarital intercourse (19, 103–105). However, research undertaken in the 1970s indicates that, even though there has been no "sexual revolution" in this country, there has been a gradual change in the sexual behavior of the young. We now know that adolescents are more sexually active than in the past and more likely to have intercourse; we also know, however, that this greater permissiveness is closely tied to affection so that there has been no increase in promiscuity.

Incidence of
Premarital
Intercourse

Information on the incidence of premarital intercourse can be summarized for three age groups—16-year-olds, 19-year-olds, and college students—as depicted in Figure 16.3. The data for the frequency of adolescents reporting having had intercourse by age 16 come from three sources: the famous Kinsey studies of the late 1940s and early 1950s; a 1970 study of 4220 high-school students by Vener and his colleagues and a repetition of this study in 1973; and a nationally representative sample of adolescents published by Sorenson in 1973 (106–110). The information on intercourse by age 19 comes from the Kinsey and Sorenson reports, and the findings among groups of college students (who overlap somewhat in age with the 19-year-olds) is drawn from the work of several other investigators (111–119).

Taken together, these data indicate that the frequency of premarital intercourse among adolescent males has either remained the same or increased slightly, whereas among females it has increased substantially. Thus, it appears that young people are more likely today than in the past to have premarital intercourse, but that the biggest change has taken place among females—college women today are about as likely as college men to have premarital intercourse.

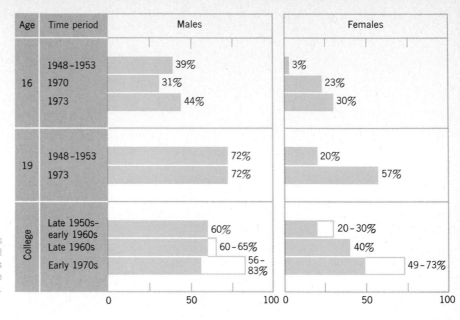

Age	Time period	Males	Females
16	1948–1953	39%	3%
	1970	31%	23%
	1973	44%	30%
19	1948–1953	72%	20%
	1973	72%	57%
College	Late 1950s–early 1960s	60%	20–30%
	Late 1960s	60–65%	40%
	Early 1970s	56–83%	49–73%

Figure 16.3 Adolescents reporting premarital intercourse (percentages at various ages, and time periods).

Permissiveness with Affection

Contrary to common opinion, the increased sexual permissiveness of young people is still closely linked to love and affection. Today's youth are more likely than the preceding generation to consider sexual intercourse within the context of a close, trusting, exclusive, and relatively enduring relationship, but they continue to reject casual, indiscriminate, or promiscuous sexuality. The prevailing code of permissiveness with affection among young people has been found consistently in studies of adolescent sex behavior from the 1960s to the mid-1970s (120–123). Data from one of these studies—a nationwide sampling of adolescents and young adults—are reported in Table 16.8. As can be seen, 93.5 percent of the 14- to 17-year-olds felt that a couple should at least be going steady before they should consider having intercourse, and 78.3 percent felt that they should be engaged or married. Although the older subjects showed somewhat more liberal attitudes, only 15.7 percent of the 18- to 20-year-olds and 26.5 percent of the 21- to 23-year-olds believed that intercourse would be appropriate for a couple who were just good friends or casually attracted to each other.

Among adolescents who are sexually experienced, most have relatively inactive rather than "swinging" sex lives. In one national survey of unmarried 15- to 19-year-old girls, for example, 60 percent of those who reported sexual experience had had intercourse with just one partner, and 70 percent had had sexual relations just once or twice in the month preceding the interview. Only 10 percent had had six or more sex partners, and only 10 percent had had intercourse six or more times in the previous

Table 16.8 Percent of American Youth Who View Different Types of Relationships as Appropriate for Considering Coitus

Type of Relationship	Males by Age			Females by Age		
	14-17 (n=469)	18-20 (n=540)	21-23 (n=566)	14-17 (n=530)	18-20 (n=580)	21-23 (n−624)
Only if married	67.6	33.5	23.5	86.5	58.6	46.0
Officially engaged	10.7	14.8	15.0	7.7	16.7	19.2
Tentatively engaged	6.7	15.5	16.1	2.1	11.7	15.4
Going steady	8.5	20.5	19.0	2.5	9.7	13.6
Good friends	2.1	8.1	14.3	0.8	1.2	3.2
Casually attracted	4.4	7.6	12.2	0.4	2.1	2.6

Source: Based on data reported by Luckey, E. B., & Nass, G. D. A comparison of sexual attitudes and behavior in an international sample. *Journal of Marriage and the Family,* 1969, **31**, 364–379.

month (120). This and other evidence suggests that promiscuity is rare among adolescents and that when it occurs it is usually a sign of psychological maladjustment (124–127).

DRUG USE   There has definitely been a revolution in the use of drugs by young people from 1965 to 1975. In the early and mid-1960s few adolescents used drugs (other than alcohol), with the possible exception of those living in disadvantaged ghetto areas. Then, during the late 1960s, illegal drugs became more available and more widely publicized, due in part to such phenomena as the "hippie" movement and the preachings of Timothy Leary, a once-famous advocate of LSD ("acid") who predicted in 1966 that 10 million Americans would be "turning on" within the next few years (128, 129).

The National Commission on Marijuana and Drug Abuse reported that in 1967 15 percent of all high-school students and 22 percent of all college students had had some experience with marijuana, but that by 1972 these figures had increased to 22 percent for high-school and 50 percent for college students (130). Unfortunately, the increasing use of this and other drugs among adolescents since 1965 has led many people to believe that it is very common. One can read in the professional literature that "drug use has become an integral part of current youth culture" (131) and that "the overwhelming majority of high school students use marijuana" (132); the newspapers tell us that on the college campus "marijuana is the common denominator among all groups" (133). However, these statements do not accurately reflect the findings of research studies. We will summarize some of these studies and then discuss why young people use drugs and what differences there are between groups that use and do not use them.

Incidence of Drug Use

Literally hundreds of surveys on adolescent drug use have been conducted since 1965. Many of these studies are hard to compare with each other because they were conducted at different times in various parts of the country and because they asked totally different questions (for example, "Have you *ever tried* marijuana?" versus "Do you *use* marijuana?"). On the other hand, several analyses of self-report questionnaires about drug use indicate that they can and do provide valid information (134, 135). Table 16.9 presents findings from a representative sample of large-scale studies in which high-school and college students in different parts of the country were asked whether they had *ever used* alcohol, marijuana, amphetamines ("speed"), LSD, and heroin (136–152).

These data indicate that alcohol is by far the most common drug used by young people, followed by marijuana, and then by amphetamines, LSD, and heroin. Drug use is more common among college students than among high-school students, and there is some tendency for the more recent studies to report higher rates of use. However, the rate of increase seems to have dropped off sharply since the early 1970s, and other evidence in these studies suggests that by the mid-1970s the use of marijuana had pretty much leveled off and the use of other illegal drugs was either remaining the same or decreasing.

Additional information from these studies indicates that the percentage of young people who have ever used a drug far exceeds the percentage of those who become regular users. For example, the reports from Dallas; Alleghcny County, Pennsylvania; and Massachusetts show that the percentage of high-school students who have ever used alcohol ranges from 60 to 92.7, but the percentage in these same samples who use alcohol once a week or more is only 26. Similarly, the percentage of high-school students who have ever used marijuana ranges from 14 to 38.9, but the percentage range for weekly use is only 6 to 15. The percentage range for those who have ever used amphetamines is 8 to 13.4, but only 3 to 4.5 for weekly use; for those who have ever used LSD 6 to 11, but only 1.4 to 2 for weekly use; and for those who have ever used heroin 2 to 3, but only 0.4 to 2 for weekly use. Thus although the use of drugs among adolescents has obviously increased from 1965 to 1975, it cannot be said that the majority of high-school students regularly use drugs or that "drug use has become an integral part of the youth culture."

Table 16.9 also shows some regional differences in the use of drugs. The percentage of adolescents who have ever tried drugs tends to be higher on the East and West coasts than in the Midwest or South. Such regional differences in the use of marijuana, as well as the percentage of

Table 16.9   Percent of High-School and College Students Who Reported That They Had Ever Used Various Drugs

Location and Date of Report	Number of Students	Alcohol	Marijuana	Ampheta-mines	LSD	Heroin
High-School Students						
Utah, 1969 (136)	47,182	—*	12.2	10.0	4.9	—
Madison, Wis., 1969 (137)	781	—	22.6	5.4	4.8	1.9
Dallas, 1970 (138)	25,587	71	14	8	6	3
Montgomery Co., Md., 1970 (139)	1348	—	18.7	7.8	5.9	1.9
San Mateo Co., Calif., 1970 (140)	25,756	—	42.9	20.0	14.4	—
Suburban New York City, 1971 (141)	1704	—	24.0	12.0	10.0	1.0
Michigan, 1971 (142)	4220	—	12.3	6.8	6.6	—
National Merit Scholars, 1971 (143)	23,000	—	24	10	7	4
Collier Co., Fla., 1972 (144)	2974	—	23	—	9	—
Kentucky, 1972 (145)	19,929	55	—	—	—	—
Allegheny Co., Pa., 1973 (146)	1600	69	23	13	7	2
Massachusetts, 1973 (147)	14,127	92.7	38.9	13.4	11.9	2.0
New England, 1974 (148)	4500	—	35	12	9	2
College Students:						
National samples, late 1960s (19)	41,630	—	25	12	5	—
Five universities, 1971 (149)	931	78-92	28-49	6-32	2-11	1-2
Illinois, 1973 (150)	1629	—	49.3	23.9	14.5	1.6
Georgia, 1973 (151)	24,475	34.8	23.6	—	8.0	—
Maryland, 1974 (152)	1385	87	63	20	10	—

*This drug was not asked about in the particular study.

adolescents who have tried it, are presented in Table 16.10 (153).

Kandel has noted a regular progression from smoking and drinking to using marijuana and then harder drugs. In her samples 27 percent of the high-school students who smoked or drank subsequently used marijuana, but only 2 percent of those who neither smoked nor drank did so; similarly, 26 percent of the marijuana users went on to try LSD, amphetamines, or heroin, but only 1 percent of those who had never used marijuana did so. Thus, although only about 25 percent of those who try

Table 16.10   Adolescent Marijuana Users and Nonusers by Region (in percentage)

	Region											
	South			North Central			Northeast			West		
Level of use	1971	1972	1973	1971	1972	1973	1971	1972	1973	1971	1972	1973
Nonusers (not interested in trying)	84	86	79	77	83	80	68	80	70	63	63	72
Nonusers (interested in trying)	5	3	8	10	4	5	12	7	7	14	4	1
Experimenters*	9	5	8	7	5	8	13	8	15	10	12	18
Occasional users*	2	3	2	3	6	3	3	4	4	6	11	3
Frequent users*	**	3	3	3	2	4	4	1	4	7	10	6
Total	100	100	100	100	100	100	100	100	100	100	100	100

*Experimenters were those who had used marijuana 1-9 times; occasional users were those who had used it 10-59 times; and frequent users were those who had used it 60 times or more.
**Less than 1 percent.
Source: Josephson, E. Trends in adolescent marijuana use. In E. Josephson & E. E. Carroll (Eds.), *Drug use: Epidemiological and sociological approaches.* New York: Hemisphere, 1974.

one drug go on to a stronger one, the stronger drugs are hardly ever used except by those who have already experimented with the milder ones (154). Work by other researchers tends to confirm this ''stepping-stone'' hypothesis—that strong drug use evolves from mild drug use (155).

Reasons for Using Drugs

Almost as many surveys have been made of the reasons young people give for using drugs as of the prevalence of drug use. Although drug users can be classified in many ways, we find it most useful to speak about *experimental, social, medicinal,* and *addictive* patterns of drug use.

Young people who *experiment* with drugs try them one or perhaps a few times out of curiosity to see what they are like, and then stop using them. *Social* users take drugs as a way of participating in a social event. Although groups may get together primarily or solely to share drug experiences on a regular basis, social drug use is largely limited to parties and other special occasions.

Medicinal drug use is the taking of a drug to relieve anxiety or tension or to enjoy a drug experience for its own sake. In contrast to social use, medicinal drug use is an individual experience; although two or more people may take drugs together for medicinal purposes, they are likely to focus on their own experiences rather than to interact in any way. *Addictive* drug use, which is also an individual expeience, is the habituation to a certain drug. Since addictive drug users suffer real physical or psychological distress (withdrawal symptoms) when they are deprived of drugs, they are likely to use drugs regularly and frequently.

These patterns of drug use help to clarify an important distinction between drug *use* and drug *abuse*. From a psychological point of view, using a drug is not necesarily an abuse; people can take small amounts of mild drugs (alcohol or marijuana) occasionally without doing themselves any harm. Legal issues aside, then, it is the heavy use of drugs and the taking of strong drugs that are most likely to *abuse* a person's physical and psychosocial functioning. Experimental and social drug use seldom result in such abuse, whereas medicinal use may have this result and addiction to a drug always constitutes drug abuse.

Despite the increase in adolescent drug use from 1965 to 1975, there is relatively little drug *abuse*. For example, of 2004 junior- and senior-high-school students in a Southern city who were surveyed in 1974, 22.5 percent reported that they had used some drug other than alcohol; however, only 9.8 percent had used any drug during the month preceding the survey, and only 5 percent reported that they had used drugs more than five times during that month (156). In the 1971 survey of five universities (presented in Table 16.9), 76 to 86 percent of the students who drank said that they did so only on weekends and at parties, and another 6 to 20 percent said that they had had a drink 10 times or less in their lives; 47 to 57 percent of the students who said that they had used marijuana reported using it 10 times or less, and another 25 to 41 percent reported using it only on weekends and at parties (145). From these and many other studies, it can be seen that most adolescents who have tried drugs do so experimentally and socially, with only a very small minority using drugs medicinally or addictively.

Differences between Groups of Drug Users and Nonusers

The fact that most adolescents do not take drugs, or certainly not on a regular basis, does not mean that one should ignore the psychological difficulties of medicinal or addictive users. Generally speaking, the heavier the use of alcohol and other drugs by young people, the more likely it is that they will do poorly in school, withdraw from peer-group activities, and have emotional problems (157–165). The research that has been done so far does not indicate whether heavy drug use has led to these psychosocial difficulties or whether these difficulties have led to heavy drug use. There is little doubt, however, that heavy drug use and problems in living go together.

On the other hand, few differences have been found between those who do not use drugs and occasional marijuana users. For example, college students who smoke marijuana once in a while are about as well adjusted as those who do not, and they do not appear to have the emotional disturbances of those who use harder drugs (166–168). Numerous investigators have said that college marijuana users are more open to experience, more venturesome, and less conventional than nonusers—but this comes as no surprise, since trying marijuana itself is doing something new and unconventional (169–171).

Some interesting research has been done on the influence the family may have on adolescent drug use. After surveying several thousand high-school students in Toronto, Smart and Fejer concluded that drug use of all kinds by adolescents is directly related to their parents' reported use of alcohol, tobacco, and such drugs as tranquilizers and sedatives. Parents who rarely, if ever, used drugs themselves seldom had children who did so (172). From their findings Smart and Fejer argue that the way to get adolescents to stop using drugs is to persuade the adult generation to do so.

It has also been found that adolescents who use drugs heavily tend to have permissive or rejecting parents and a generally negative emotional climate at home (173–178). Hence it may be that drug-using parents have drug-using offspring not only because of the example they set, but also because they are neglectful parents who foster many kinds of problem behavior in their children, including drug abuse (179). If this view is correct, parents need to do more than simply curb their own use of drugs in order to influence their children's drug behavior.

Essay

TWO MYTHS:
ADOLESCENT
REBELLION AND
THE GENERATION
GAP

According to some writers, the modern American adolescent belongs to a youth culture that is cut off from and at odds with the adult world. The typical characteristics of this youth culture are held to be laziness, sloppiness, sexual promiscuity, drug abuse, insistence on immediate gratification, bad manners, disrespect for authority, and rejection of traditional values. This youthful alienation is attributed to such causes as parental pampering and permissiveness; a rapidly changing world that exposes adolescents to experiences their parents never had and cannot understand; the long apprenticeship between childhood and adulthood that exists in a complex technological society; and adolescents' disaffection for what they see as a materialistic and hypocritical adult generation that has done little to eliminate war, injustice, and human misery.

These notions of widespread adolescent rebellion and a "gap" between the generations are discussed in numerous books that were published between 1961 and 1975, including Coleman's *The Adolescent Society*, Keniston's *The Uncommitted: Alienated Youth in American Society*, Feuer's *The Conflict of Generations*, Mead's *Culture and Commitment: A Study of the Generation Gap*, Friedenberg's *The Anti-American Generation*, and Hendin's *The Age of Sensation* (180–185). Coleman feels that we need to "bring adolescents back into the home [and] reduce the pervasiveness of the adolescent society." Feuer and Mead both believe that adults must find some way of communicating across the "generation gap" before young people take over and tear down the institutions on which our society is based. And Friedenberg comments:

The young are more likely to look upon their feelings as a guide to what is good . . . and to view the demands of society . . . as a problem that cannot and should not be approached by rational means [p. 123].

In assessing these views, it should be emphasized that we really do not have a homogeneous "youth culture" in this country. Instead, our adolescent population comprises many dissimilar cultures. Young people of different age and sex, from diverse ethnic and social-class backgrounds, and representing various parts of the country are likely to think and act as differently from one another as they do from adults. For example, there are obviously few similarities in the values or behavior of a group of 17-year-old black boys in New York's Harlem, a group of 13-year-old girls in suburban Detroit's Grosse Point Shores, a group of adolescent 4-H Club members in rural Kansas, and a group of adolescent Chicanos in southern California. Comparative studies consistently point out gaps *within* the adolescent generation that are due to such differences in their background (18, 186–188).

Moreover, there are differences in orientation even within groups of adolescents from the same background. In a study of 151 adolescent girls from similar backgrounds, Kovar identified five different attitudes toward parental and social values, which she called *peer-oriented, adult-oriented, delinquent, anarchic Bohemian,* and *autonomous* (189). In research with white working-class boys, Simon, Gagnon, and Buff found four distinct types: *collegiates*—boys who are academically oriented and upwardly mobile; *hippies*—boys who tend to "turn on and drop out"; *greasers*—boys who hang out on the corner and ride motorcycles; and *family-oriented youth*—those who confine themselves primarily to family values and activities (190).

With respect to individual young people, there is very little evidence to support the view that today's adolescents are in rebellion against the values of their family and society; in fact, there is considerable data showing that most young people get along well with their parents and uphold adult values. Both Offer and Offer (85) and Douvan and Adelson (36) report finding that most adolescents respect their parents, want to be like them, and maintain basically harmonious relations with them as well as with other adults. The majority of young people are satisfied with their homes and tend to view their fathers as reliable and knowledgeable and their mothers as understanding and sympathetic. Adolescents and their parents often disagree on a variety of trivial issues, such as styles of clothing and grooming, curfews, and use of the family car; however, these disagreements seldom undermine the bonds of love within the family or split parents and children into warring camps.

Surveying 13- to 18-year-old boys, Meissner found that 89 percent said that they were happy in their homes, 84 percent spent half or more of their leisure time at home, and 74 percent felt proud of their parents and enjoyed having them meet their friends (191). Lesser and Kandel found that only 11 percent of the adolescents they studied felt removed from their mothers and only 23 percent felt removed from their fathers, whereas the rest felt at least moderately close to their parents (13). In a national survey of candidates for National Merit Scholarships, only 16 percent felt that their parents rarely understood them and their problems, whereas 51 percent indicated that their parents understood them half of the time and 31 percent indicated that their parents almost always understood them. When asked whether the lines of communication were open between them and their parents, 46 percent of these young people said "almost always," 36 percent said "about half the time," and only 17 percent said "hardly ever or never" (143). These data certainly do not indicate that American adolescents feel alienated from their parents or unable to communicate with them.

With respect to values, the evidence overwhelmingly shows that high-school and college students feel a keen sense of social and ethical responsibility (rather than a desire for immediate gratification), and that the majority support rather than reject the values of their parents. Beneath superficial appearances to the contrary, young people generally share the same standards of conduct and decency as their parents. Even among the few adolescents who hold unconventional views, most are found to do so in agreement with their parents and not out of rebellion against them (86, 192–197).

This predominant continuity in values between adolescents and their parents was found to exist even among the campus activists who, although representing no more than 15 percent of college students, received enormous publicity during the late 1960s. Rather than being "alienated youth," as frequently charged, most of these students were closely identified with their parents, who themselves held liberal attitudes and tended to be politically active (198–200). Those activists who were truly alienated from their families, together with young people who have no feelings of closeness toward their parents and do not share their parents' standards of conduct, represent a small minority of young people in whom alienation is a symptom of psychological disorder. For these and other reasons many social scientists have pointed out why "adolescent rebellion" and the "generation gap" are myths, at least with respect to the overwhelming majority of young people (201–206). Yet these notions persist; possibly it is because the adolescents who are causing trouble make good stories for newspapers and magazines as well as television and movies. We are certainly much more likely to hear and read about the bad than the good in adolescent behavior, which may give us a distorted impression of the number of adolescents who are at odds with their parents and society.

We are also more likely to remember vivid events and people than bland ones. Seeing a few scraggly, unwashed, boorish adolescents loitering on the street corner can make us forget the thousands of ordinary-looking young people who may be sitting in a classroom, practicing with a football team, working at a part-time job, taking a music lesson, or helping with some chore at home. Taken together, then, conceptions of adolescent rebellion and the generation gap are probably being nourished by newspapers, magazines, television, and movies that focus on the spectacular and the sensational in adolescent behavior, as well as our own memories of what is shocking and repugnant rather than what is commonplace.

Biography

Harry Stack Sullivan

Harry Stack Sullivan is generally regarded as America's most original psychiatrist. He constructed what he called an "interpersonal" theory of human behavior and always stressed the interrelateness of human beings. He believed that mental disturbance is not like a physical illness, a part of the individual who contracts it, but rather an interpersonal process, a product of the relations between people. Even when alone, the troubled person is still dealing with social relationships. For Sullivan, emotional disturbances always were to be described as interpersonal processes rather than as disturbances encapsulated within the person.

At the heart of Sullivan's system was the concept of the *self*. This concept is socially derived from the way others react to us and much of our day-to-day behavior is concerned with enhancing, defending or maintaining self-esteem. Sullivan believed that the self is developmental in nature and that it grows and changes with the different types of social interactions young people engage in as they mature. The adult self is a composite of the reflected appraisals that others have made of a person while growing up.

During infancy a child has an undifferentialed sense of self but nonetheless reacts to parental ministrations with feelings of "Good me" or of "Bad me." If parents are accepting, meet the baby's needs when they are made known, and are warm and affectionate, the infant gets a sense of "Good me." On the other hand, if parents are rejecting and do not heed the infant's cries for attention or cuddle the baby, the baby may develop a sense of "Bad me."

During early childhood, when children acquire many new skills including language, the self becomes symbolically elaborated. Whereas the infant self responded to the parents' actions, the preschool child responds to the parents' words. The child who hears "no no stop that," or "you are so clumsy," or "you are so messy" soon acquires a symbolic sense of "Bad me." On the contrary, a child who receives a preponderance of positive appraisals is likely to develop a symbolic sense of "Good me." It should be said, however, that Sullivan felt that some negative appraisals are useful for keeping the positive self-conception from becoming "inflated."

During childhood proper, the child's self is further elaborated, thanks to interactions with nonfamilial adults and children. Now the child's self-concept begins to include the appraisals of peers and of teachers. Such appraisals can balance, in part, negative appraisals received at home. But negative appraisals received at school ("you are so dumb") can also undo, at least in part, the effects of positive appraisals received at home. The self, in Sullivan's system, is never static, and it changes with development and with circumstances.

In early adolescence young people often enter into a special interpersonal relationship that Sullivan calls a *chumship*. This chumship usually enables the young person to share his or her innermost feelings and to become concerned with another person at a deep level by being the only one to know the chum's inner feelings and thoughts. In Sullivan's view, chumship is essential to the attainment of true *intimacy,* which he conceived as a lifelong commitment to another person. For Sullivan, true intimacy is never casual but always demanding—it means giving, taking, and above all communicating, even when it is not convenient to do so.

Starting in early adolescence, Sullivan believed, a dichotomy develops between sexuality (which he called lust) and intimacy. Young people seek to satisfy their sexual needs with persons other than those with whom they are friends. In later adolescence, however, the gap between sexuality and intimacy is closed and young people can now be friends with girls or boys with whom they are in love. Of course, this healthy development presupposes a positive self-concept and a successful chumship. Individuals who have not been fortunate in these regards may become emotionally troubled.

Sullivan was born in Norwich, New York in 1892. He grew up on a farm where, as a Catholic, he had few friends in the predominantly Protestant community. His interests drew him to medicine and thereafter to psychiatry. His first work was in a mental hospital (St. Elizabeth's in Washington, D.C.) with schizophrenics, with whom he was extraordinarily successful. Later he moved to New York and private practice. He was a superb clinician to whom other psychiatrists often came when they were having trouble with their patients. Sullivan could be tough on professionals, but he was always kind and thoughtful with patients.

After about ten years in New York Sullivan moved to Maryland, where he continued his practice and extensive consulting. He had trouble writing, however, and most of his books were produced by his students working from tapes. After World War II Sullivan was concerned about atomic proliferation and worked hard for world peace. He died in Paris in 1949 on his way home from meetings of the World Federation for Mental Health.

Summary

The main aspects of personality development that take place during adolescence are achieving psychological independence from one's parents, learning to handle dating and heterosexual relationships, and integrating a sense of personal identity. Adolescents want to establish their independence partly because they have reached most of their adult physical and mental growth and partly because it is expected by others. Yet both adolescents and their parents have mixed feelings about independence. Adolescents like being treated as adults, but they also miss the freedom from responsibility they enjoyed as children; parents like seeing their children grow up, but they also regret that they themselves are growing older and nearing the end of their child-rearing role.

Parents differ in their attempts to exert authority over their adolescent children. Some are *autocratic,* imposing their own views on their children; some are *democratic,* discussing with their youngsters those issues in which the latter have a stake; and some are *permissive,* allowing their children to make all of their own decisions. Democratically reared adolescents generally have more positive feelings about their parents and about their own capacity to be independent than those who have autocratic or permissive parents. In other words, parents who are able and willing to exert reasonable control over their adolescent children, while making sure that they have opportunities for increased autonomy, make the largest contribution to their children's self-confidence, self-control, self-reliance, and mature judgment.

Because adolescents are no longer children but not yet adults, they rely heavily on peer-group acceptance for a sense of belongingness. Popularity comes most readily to young people who are physically attractive, bright, talented, self-confident, energetic, and comfortable in interpersonal situations; some of these qualities are both the result and the cause of peer acceptance.

There are distinct phases in heterosexual relationships during adolescence. First there are separate groups of boys and girls who have little to do with each other; then young people move toward mixed boy-girl social functions, and then they pair off into dating couples who eventually start to go steady and become seriously interested in one another. Dating brings with it many new sources of concern, since boys and girls must learn how to cope with heterosexual relationships and must make decisions about how they should act.

Learning to handle heterosexuality means trying to satisfy certain kinds of needs without having them conflict. There are needs for *sexuality* (the expression of sexual urges), for *security* (freedom from anxiety), and for *intimacy* (close collaborative relationships with others). When a boy and girl can be very close friends as well as steady dates and partners in sexual experiences, without feeling anxious or threatened, they have achieved a mature capacity for heterosexual intimacy.

Adolescents also need to form a clear and consistent image of themselves. This *sense of identity* gives young people an integrated view of what they are like as individuals, what they believe in, and what possibilities might lie open for them in the future. While consolidating their personal identity, adolescents spend several years considering and trying out various roles and value systems. Adolescent behavior, therefore, is more changeable and less predictable than that of younger children, but this does not mean that adolescents normally have an *identity crisis*. Most adolescents pass through this period fairly smoothly, and no more than 20 percent are likely to suffer significant psychological distress. In general, personality development is continuous from adolescence to adulthood, so that what a person is like as an adolescent generally indicates what he or she will be like as an adult.

Two aspects of adolescent behavior that have changed considerably during the past generation are sexual permissiveness and drug use. Although there has been no "sexual revolution" (as is often claimed), there has been a gradual increase in sexual permissiveness. This permissiveness, however, has been closely linked to affection and commitment. Thus, young people today are more likely now than in the past to consider premarital intercourse, but largely within the context of a close, trusting, exclusive, and relatively enduring relationship. Most adolescents would reject casual, indiscriminate, or promiscuous sexuality.

The use of such drugs as marijuana, amphetamines, LSD, and heroin by young people increased substantially in the late 1960s and early 1970s. However, any alarm that American adolescents were developing a "drug culture" appeared to be premature and unjustified. By the mid-1970s the number of young people who were using marijuana seemed to have leveled off, and the number who were using other, more potent drugs appeared to be declining. It should be noted that most adolescents who have used drugs are either *experimenters,* who try a drug a few times to see what it is like, or *social users,* who drink alcohol or smoke marijuana occasionally at parties or other social gatherings. Relatively few young people abuse drugs to the point of becoming regular or addicted users whose consumption leads to psychosocial problems.

Many social critics believe that today's adolescents are in rebellion against the values of their family and society and that there is a dangerous gap between their generation and the adult world. Although catchy and dramatic, these notions of "adolescent rebellion" and the "generation gap" are not substantiated by social science research data. Although most families have disputes about trivial matters, American adolescents and their parents generally love and respect each other and share the same standards of conduct and decency. Beneath the superficial trappings of adolescent tastes and preferences, most young people identify with the values of their parents and of the subculture in which they are growing up. Rather than constituting a distinct and homogeneous generation that is cut off and alienated from adults, adolescents from different ethnic and cultural backgrounds probably differ as much from each other as they do from adults.

References

1. Brown, J. K. Adolescent initiation rites: Recent interpretations. In R. E. Grinder (Ed.), *Studies in adolescence.* (3rd ed.) New York: Macmillan, 1975.
2. Beres, D. Character formation. In S. Lorand & H. I. Schneer (Eds.), *Adolescents: Psychoanalytic approach to problems and therapy.* New York: Hoeber, 1961.
3. Josselyn, I. M. *Adolescence.* New York: Harper, 1971.
4. Kiell, N. *The universal experience of adolescence.* New York: International Universities Press, 1964.
5. Anthony, E. J. The reaction of parents to adolescents and their behavior. In E. J. Anthony & T. Benedek (Eds.), *Parenthood.* Boston: Little, Brown, 1970.
6. Chilman, C. S. Families in development at mid-stage of the family life cycle. *Family Life Coordinator,* 1968, **17,** 297–331.

7. Cohen, R. S., & Balikov, H. On the impact of adolescence upon parents. In S. C. Feinstein & P. Giovacchini (Eds.), *Adolescent psychiatry*. Vol. III. New York: Basic Books, 1974.

8. Lidz, T. The adolescent and his family. In G. Caplan & S. Lebovici (Eds.), *Adolescence: Psychosicial perspectives*. New York: Basic Books, 1969.

9. Newman, M. B., & San Martino, M. R. Adolescence and the relationship between generations. In S. C. Feinstein & P. Giovacchini (Eds.), *Adolescent psychiatry*. Vol. IV. New York: Aronson, 1976.

10. Ravenscroft, K. Normal family regression at adolescence. *American Journal of Psychiatry,* 1974, **131,** 31–35.

11. Elder, G. H. Structural variations in the child rearing relationship. *Sociometry,* 1962, **25,** 241–262.

12. Elder, G. H. Parental power legitimation and its effects on the adolescent. *Sociometry,* 1963, **26,** 50–65.

13. Lesser, G. S., & Kandel, D. Parent-adolescent relationships and adolescent independence in the United States and Denmark. *Journal of Marriage and the Family,* 1969, **31,** 348–358.

14. Dahlem, N. W. Young Americans' reported perceptions of their parents. *Journal of Psychology,* 1970, **74,** 187–194.

15. Gulo, E. V. Attitudes of rural school children toward their parents. *Journal of Educational Research,* 1966, **59,** 450–452.

16. Seiden, A. M. Sex roles, sexuality, and the adolescent peer group. In S. C. Feinstein & P. Giovacchini (Eds.), *Adolescent psychiatry*. Vol. IV. New York: Aronson, 1976.

17. Mays, J. B. The adolescent as a social being. In J. G. Howells (Ed.), *Modern perspectives in adolescent psychiatry*. New York: Brunner/Mazel, 1971.

18. Gottlieb, D., & Ramsey, C. E. *The American adolescent*. Homewood, Ill.: Dorsey, 1964.

19. Weiner, I. B. Perspectives on the modern adolescent. *Psychiatry,* 1972, **35,** 20–31.

20. Allen, C. D., & Eicher, J. B. Adolescent girls' acceptance and rejection based on appearance. *Adolescence,* 1973, **8,** 125–137.

21. Cavior, N., & Dokecki, P. R. Physical attractiveness, perceived attitude similarity, and academic achievement as contributors to interpersonal attraction among adolescents. *Developmental Psychology,* 1973, **9,** 44–54.

22. Hartup, W. W. Peer interaction and social organization. In P. H. Mussen (Ed.), *Carmichael's manual of child psychology*. Vol. 2. (3rd ed.) New York: Wiley, 1970.

23. Horowitz, H. Prediction of adolescent popularity and rejection from achievement and interest tests. *Journal of Educational Psychology,* 1967, **58,** 170–174.

24. Stroebe, W., Insko, C. A., Thompson, V. D., & Layton, B. D. Effects of physical attractiveness, attitude similarity, and sex on various aspects of interpersonal attraction. *Journal of Personality and Social Psychology,* 1971, **19,** 79–91.

25. Walster, E., Aronson, V., Abrahams, D., & Rottman, L. Importance of physical attractiveness in dating behavior. *Journal of Personality and Social Psychology,* 1966, **4,** 508–516.

26. Horrocks, J. E., & Benimoff, M. Stability of adolescent's nominee status, over a one-year period, as a friend by their peers. *Adolescence,* 1966, **1,** 224–229.

27. Horrocks, J. E., & Buker, M. E. A study of friendship fluctuation of preadolescents. *Journal of Genetic Psychology,* 1951, **78,** 131–144.

28. Horrocks, J. E., & Thompson, G. G. A study of friendship fluctuations of rural boys and girls. *Journal of Genetic Psychology,* 1946, **69,** 189–198.

29. Thompson, G. G., & Horrocks, J. E. A study of friendship fluctuations of urban boys and girls. *Journal of Genetic Psychology,* 1947, **70,** 53–63.

30. Grinder, R. E. Relations of social dating attractions to academic orientation and peer relations. *Journal of Educational Psychology,* 1966, **57,** 27–34.

31. McDaniel, C. O. Dating roles and reasons for dating. *Journal of Marriage and the Family,* 1969, **31,** 97–107.

32. Skipper, J. K., & Nass, G. Dating behavior: A framework for analysis and an illustration. *Journal of Marriage and the Family,* 1966, **28,** 412–420.

33. Dunphy, D. C. The social structure of urban adolescent peer groups. *Sociometry,* 1963, **26,** 230–246.

34. Broderick, C. B. Socio-sexual development in a suburban community. *Journal of Sex Research,* 1966, **2,** 1–24.
35. Broderick, C. B., & Weaver, J. The perceptual context of boy-girl communication. *Journal of Marriage and the Family,* 1968, **30,** 618–627.
36. Douvan, E., & Adelson, J. *The adolescent experience.* New York: Wiley, 1966.
37. Burchinal, L. G. Adolescent dating attitudes and behavior. In M. Gold & E. Douvan (Eds.), *Adolescent development.* Boston: Allyn & Bacon, 1969.
38. Lowrie, S. H. Early and late dating: Some conditions associated with them. *Journal of Marriage and the Family,* 1961, **23,** 284–291.
39. Place, D. M. The dating experience for adolescent girls. *Adolescence,* 1975, **10,** 157–174.
40. Breed, W. Sex, class and socialization in dating. *Marriage and Family Living,* 1956, **18,** 137–144.
41. Crist, J. R. High school dating as a behavior system. *Marriage and Family Living,* 1953, **15,** 23–28.
42. Berger, A. S., & Simon, W. Sexual behavior in adolescent males. In S. C. Feinstein & P. Giovacchini (Eds.), *Adolescent psychiatry.* Vol. IV. New York: Aronson, 1976.
43. Juhasz, A. M. Sexual decision-making: The crux of the adolescent problem. In R. E. Grinder (Ed.), *Studies in adolescence.* (3rd ed.) New York: Macmillan, 1975.
44. Thornburg, H. D. Adolescent sources of initial sex information. In R. E. Grinder (Ed.), *Studies in adolescence.* (3rd ed.) New York: Macmillan, 1975.
45. Sullivan, H. S. *The interpersonal theory of psychiatry.* New York: Norton, 1953.
46. Gagnon, J. H., Simon, W., & Berger, A. J. Some aspects of sexual adjustment in early and later adolescence. In J. Zubin & A. M. Freedman (Eds.), *Psychopathology of adolescence.* New York: Grune & Stratton, 1970.
47. Gagnon, J. H., & Simon, W. *Sexual conduct.* Chicago: Aldine, 1973.
48. Dranoff, S. M. Masturbation and the male adolescent. *Adolescence,* 1974, **9,** 169–176.
49. Reevy, W. R. Adolescent sexuality. In A. Ellis & A. Abarbanel (Eds.), *The encyclopedia of sexual behavior.* Vol. 1. New York: Hawthorn, 1961.
50. Joseph, T. P. Adolescents: From the views of the members of an informal adolescent group. *Genetic Psychology Monographs,* 1969, **79,** 3–38.
51. Bronfenbrenner, U. *Two worlds of childhood: U.S. and U.S.S.R.* New York: Russell Sage, 1970.
52. Feshbach, N. D. Nonconformity to experimentally induced group norms of high-status versus low-status members. *Journal of Personality and Social Psychology,* 1967, **6,** 55–63.
53. Landsbaum, J. B., & Willis, R. H. Conformity in early and late adolescence. *Developmental Psychology,* 1971, **4,** 334–337.
54. McGhee, P. E., & Teevan, R. C. Conformity behavior and need for affiliation. *Journal of Social Psychology,* 1967, **72,** 117–121.
55. Brittain, C. V. Adolescent choices and parent-peer cross-preferences. *American Sociological Review,* 1963, **28,** 385–391.
56. Kandel, D. B., & Lesser, G. S. Parental and peer influences on educational plans of adolescents. *American Sociological Review,* 1969, **34,** 213–223.
57. Won, G. Y., Yamamura, D. S., & Ikeda, K. The relation of communication with parents and peers to deviant behavior of youth. *Journal of Marriage and the Family,* 1969, **31,** 43–47.
58. Larson, L. E. The influence of parents and peers during adolescence: The situation hypothesis revised. *Journal of Marriage and the Family,* 1972, **34,** 67–74.
59. Purnell, R. F. Socioeconomic status and sex differences in adolescent reference-group orientation. *Journal of Genetic Psychology,* 1970, **116,** 233–239.
60. Query, J. M. The influence of group pressures on the judgments of children and adolescents: A comparative study. *Adolescence,* 1968, **3,** 153–160.
61. Douvan, E. Commitment and social contract in adolescence. *Psychiatry,* 1974, **37,** 22–36.
62. Erikson, E. H. The problem of ego identity. *Journal of the American Psychoanalytic Association,* 1956, **4,** 56–121.
63. Erikson, E. H. *Childhood and society.* (2nd ed.) New York: Norton, 1963.
64. Erikson, E. H. *Identity: Youth and crisis.* New York: Norton, 1968.
65. Erikson, E. H. Identity and the life cycle. *Psychological Issues,* 1959, **1,** 1–171.
66. Freud, A. Adolescence as a developmental disturbance. In G. Caplan & S. Lebovici (Eds.), *Adolescence: Psychosocial perspectives.* New York: Basic Books, 1969.

67. Geleerd, E. R. Some aspects of ego vicissitudes in adolescence. *Journal of the American Psychoanalytic Association,* 1961, **9,** 394–405.

68. Spiegel, L. A. Disorder and consolidation in adolescence. *Journal of the American Psychoanalytic Association,* 1961, **9,** 406–417.

69. White, R. B. Adolescent identity crisis. In J. C. Schoolar (Ed.), *Current issues in adolescent psychiatry.* New York: Brunner/Mazel, 1973.

70. Marcia, J. E. Development and validation of ego-identity status. *Journal of Personality and Social Psychology,* 1966, **3,** 551–558.

71. Marcia, J. E. Ego identity status: Relationship to change in self-esteem, "general maladjustment," and authoritarianism. *Journal of Personality,* 1967, **35,** 119–133.

72. Marcia, J. E., & Friedman, M. L. Ego identity status in college women. *Journal of Personality,* 1970, **38,** 249–263.

73. Cross, J. J., & Allen, J. G. Ego identity status, adjustment, and academic achievement. *Journal of Consulting and Clinical Psychology,* 1970, **34,** 288.

74. Orlofsky, J. L., Marcia, J. E., & Lesser, I. M. Ego identity status and the intimacy vs. isolation crisis in young adulthood. *Journal of Personality and Social Psychology,* 1973, **27,** 211–219.

75. Oshman, H., & Manosevitz, M. The impact of the identity crisis on the adjustment of late adolescent males. *Journal of Youth and Adolescence,* 1974, **3,** 207–216.

76. Stark, P. A., & Traxler, A. J. Empirical validation of Erikson's theory of identity crises in late adolescence. *Journal of Psychology,* 1974, **86,** 25–33.

77. Waterman, A. S., & Waterman, C. K. Relationship between freshman ego identity status and subsequent academic behavior: A test of the predictive validity of Marcia's categorization system for identity status. *Developmental Psychology,* 1972, **6,** 179.

78. Waterman, A. S., & Waterman, C. K. A longitudinal study of changes in ego identity status during the freshman year of college. *Developmental Psychology,* 1971, **5,** 167–173.

79. Waterman, A. S., Geary, P. S., & Waterman, C. K. Longitudinal study of changes in ego identity status from the freshman to the senior year at college. *Developmental Psychology,* 1974, **10,** 387–392.

80. Waterman, A. S., & Goldman, J. A. A longitudinal study of ego identity at a liberal arts college. *Journal of Youth and Adolescence,* 1976, **5,** 361–369.

81. Grinker, R. R. "Mentally healthy" young males (homoclites). *Archives of General Psychiatry,* 1962, **6,** 405–453.

82. King, S. H. Coping and growth in adolescence. *Seminars in Psychiatry,* 1972, **4,** 355–366.

83. Kysar, J. E., Zaks, M. S., Schuchman, H. P., Schon, G. L., & Rogers, J. Range of psychological functioning in "normal" late adolescents. *Archives of General Psychiatry,* 1969, **21,** 515–528.

84. Masterson, J. F. The psychiatric significance of adolescent turmoil. *American Journal of Psychiatry,* 1968, **124,** 1549–1554.

85. Offer, D., & Offer, J. B. *The psychological world of the teenager.* New York: Basic Books, 1969.

86. Offer, D., & Offer, J. B. *From teenage to young manhood: A psychological study.* New York: Basic Books, 1975.

87. Rutter, M., Graham, P., Chadwick, O. F. D., & Yule, W. Adolescent turmoil: Fact or fiction? *Journal of Child Psychology and Psychiatry,* 1976, **17,** 35–56.

88. Silber, E., Hamburg, D. A., Coelho, G. V., Murphey, E. B., Rosenberg, M., & Pearlin, L. I. Adaptive behavior in competent adolescents: Coping with the anticipation of college. *Archives of General Psychiatry,* 1961, **5,** 354–365.

89. Simmons, R. G., Rosenberg, F., & Rosenberg, M. Disturbance in the self-image at adolescence. *American Sociological Review,* 1973, **38,** 553–568.

90. Eichorn, D. H. The Berkeley longitudinal studies: Continuities and correlates of behaviour. *Canadian Journal of Behavioral Science,* 1973, **5,** 297–320.

91. Haan, N., & Day, D. A longitudinal study of change and sameness in personality development: Adolescence to later adulthood. *International Journal of Aging and Human Development,* 1974, **5,** 11–39.

92. Bronson, W. The role of enduring orientations to the environment in personality development. *Genetic Psychology Monographs,* 1972, **87,** 3–80.

93. Cox, R. D. *Youth into maturity.* New York: Mental Health Materials Center, 1970.

94. Kagan, J., & Moss, H. A. *Birth to maturity: A study in psychological development.* New York: Wiley, 1962.

95. Monge, R. H. Developmental trends in factors of adolescent self-concept. *Developmental Psychology,* 1973, **8,** 382–393.

96. Monge, R. H. Structure of the self-concept from adolescence through old age. *Experimental Aging Research,* 1975, **1,** 281–291.

97. Symonds, P. M., & Jensen, A. R. *From adolescent to adult.* New York: Columbia University Press, 1961.

98. Woodruff, D. S., & Birren, J. E. Age changes and cohort differences in personality. *Developmental Psychology,* 1972, **6,** 252–259.

99. Hurlock, E. B. American adolescents today—A new species. *Adolescence,* 1966, **1,** 17–21.

100. Glassberg, B. Y. Sexual behavior patterns in contemporary youth culture: Implications for later marriage. *Journal of Marriage and the Family,* 1965, **27,** 190–192.

101. Schofield, M. *The sexual behavior of young people.* Boston: Little, Brown, 1965.

102. Reiss, I. L. *The social context of premarital sexual permissiveness.* New York: Holt, 1967.

103. Godenne, G. D. Sex and today's youth. *Adolescence,* 1974, **9,** 67–72.

104. Maddock, J. W. Sex in adolescence: Its meaning and its future. *Adolescence,* 1973, **8,** 325–342.

105. Offer, D. Attitudes toward sexuality in a group of 1500 middle class teenagers. *Journal of Youth and Adolescence,* 1972, **1,** 81–90.

106. Kinsey, A. C., Pomeroy, W. B., & Martin, C. E. *Sexual behavior in the human male.* Philadelphia: Saunders, 1948.

107. Kinsey, A. C., Pomeroy, W. B., Martin, C. E., & Gebhard, P. H. *Sexual behavior in the human female.* Philadelphia: Saunders, 1953.

108. Vener, A. M., Stewart, C. S., & Hager, D. L. The sexual behavior of adolescents in middle America: Generational and American-British comparisons. *Journal of Marriage and the Family,* 1972, **34,** 696–705.

109. Vener, A. M., & Stewart, C. S. Adolescent sexual behavior in middle America revisited: 1970–1973. *Journal of Marriage and the Family,* 1974, **36,** 728–735.

110. Sorenson, R. C. *Adolescent sexuality in contemporary America: Personal values and sexual behavior ages 13–19.* New York: World, 1973.

111. Ehrmann, W. *Premarital dating behavior.* New York: Holt, 1959.

112. Freedman, M. B. The sexual behavior of American college women. *Merrill-Palmer Quarterly,* 1965, **11,** 33–48.

113. Grinder, R. E., & Schmitt, S. S. Coeds and contraceptive information. *Journal of Marriage and the Family,* 1966, **28,** 471–279.

114. Bell, R. R., & Chaskes, J. B. Premarital sexual experience among coeds, 1958 and 1968. *Journal of Marriage and the Family,* 1970, **32,** 81–84.

115. Kaats, G. R., & Davis, K. E. The dynamics of sexual behavior of college students. *Journal of Marriage and the Family,* 1970, **32,** 390–399.

116. Robinson, K. E., King, K., & Balswick, J. O. The premarital sexual revolution among college females. *The Family Coordinator,* 1972, **21,** 189–194.

117. Arafat, I., & Yorburg, B. Drug use and the sexual behavior of college women. *Journal of Sex Research,* 1973, **9,** 21–29.

118. Bauman, K. E., & Wilson, R. R. Sexual behavior of unmarried university students in 1968 and 1972. *Journal of Sex Research,* 1974, **4,** 327–333.

119. King, M., & Sobel, D. Sex on the college campus: Current attitudes and behavior. *Journal of College Student Personnel,* 1975, **16,** 205–209.

120. Luckey, E. B., & Nass, G. D. A comparison of sexual attitudes and behavior in an international sample. *Journal of Marriage and the Family,* 1969, **31,** 364–379.

121. Conger, J. J. Sexual attitudes and behavior of contemporary adolescents. In J. J. Conger (Ed.), *Contemporary issues in adolescent development.* New York: Harper, 1975.

122. Kantner, J. F., & Zelnik, M. Sexual experience of young unmarried women in the United States. *Family Planning Perspectives,* 1972, **4,** 9–18.

123. Lewis, R. A., & Burr, W. R. Premarital coitus and commitment among college students. *Archives of Sexual Behavior,* 1975, **4,** 73–79.

124. Dreyer, P. H. Changes in the meaning of marriage among youth: The impact of the "revolution" in sex and sex role behavior. In R. E. Grinder (Ed.), *Studies in adolescence.* (3rd ed.) New York: Macmillan, 1975.

125. Halleck, S. L. Sex and mental health on the campus. *Journal of the American Medical Association,* 1967, **200,** 684–690.

126. Rainwater, L. Sex in the culture of poverty. In C. B. Broderick & J. Bernard (Eds.), *The individual, sex, and society*. Baltimore: Johns Hopkins Press, 1969.

127. Schofield, M. Normal sexuality in adolescence. In J. G. Howells (Ed.), *Modern perspectives in adolescent psychiatry*. New York: Brunner/Mazel, 1971.

128. McGlothlin, W. H. Drug use and abuse. *Annual Review of Psychology*, 1975, **26**, 45–64.

129. Schachter, B. Psychedelic drug use by adolescents. *Social Work*, 1968, **13**, 33–39.

130. National Commission on Marijuana and Drug Abuse. *Drug use in America: Problem in perspective*. Washington, D.C.: U.S. Government Printing Office, 1973.

131. Proskauer, S., & Rolland, R. S. Youth who use drugs: Psychodynamic diagnosis and treatment planning. *Journal of the American Academy of Child Psychiatry*, 1973, **12**, 32–47.

132. Millman, R. B., & Khuri, E. T. Drug abuse and the need for alternatives. In J. C. Schoolar (Ed.), *Current issues in adolescent psychiatry*. New York: Brunner/Mazel, 1973.

133. Darnton, J. Many on campus shifting to softer drugs and alcohol. *The New York Times*, Jan. 17, 1971. Salt Lake City, Utah.

134. Single, E., Kandel, D., & Johnson, B. D. The reliability and validity of drug use responses in a large scale longitudinal survey. *Journal of Drug Issues*, 1975, **5**, 426–443.

135. Smart, R. G. Recent studies of the validity and reliability of self-reported drug use, 1970–1974. *Canadian Journal of Criminology and Corrections*, 1975, **17**, 326–333.

136. Governor's Citizen Advisory Committee on Drugs, State of Utah. *Drug use among high school students in the state of Utah*, 1969.

137. Udell, J. G., & Smith, R. S. *Attitudes, usage, and availability of drugs among Madison high school students*. Madison, Wis., University of Wisconsin Bureau of Business Research and Service, 1969.

138. Dallas Independent School District. *Report of ad hoc committee on drug abuse*, 1970.

139. Joint Committee on Drug Abuse, Montgomery County, Md. *A survey of secondary school students' perceptions of and attitudes toward use of drugs by teenagers*, 1970.

140. San Mateo County Department of Public Health and Welfare. *Five mind-altering drugs* (plus one). Research and Statistics Section, 1970.

141. Tec, N. Drugs among suburban teenagers: Basic findings. *Social Science and Medicine*, 1970, **5**, 77–84.

142. Hager, D. L., Vener, A. M., & Stewart, C. S. Patterns of adolescent drug use in middle America. *Journal of Counseling Psychology*, 1971, **18**, 292–297.

143. Merit Publishing Company. *Who's who among American high school students: Second annual national opinion survey*, 1971, Northfield, Ill.

144. Lombillo, J. R., & Hain, J. D. Patterns of drug use in a high school population. *American Journal of Psychiatry*, 1972, **128**, 836–841.

145. Kane, R. L., & Patterson, E. Drinking attitudes and behavior in high-school students in Kentucky. *Quarterly Journal of Studies on Alcohol*, 1972, **33**, 635–646.

146. Adler, P. T., & Lotecka, L. Drug use among high school students. *International Journal of the Addictions*, 1973, **8**, 537–548.

147. Gelineau, V. A., Johnson, M., & Pearsall, D. A survey of adolescent drug use patterns. *Massachusetts Journal of Mental Health*, 1973, **3**, 30–40.

148. Rosenberg, J. S., Kasl, S. V., & Berberian, R. M. Sex differences in adolescent drug use: Recent trends. *Addictive Diseases*, 1974, **1**, 73–96.

149. Toohey, J. V. An analysis of drug use behavior at five American universities. *Journal of School Health*, 1971, **41**, 464–468.

150. Levy, L. Drug use on campus: Prevalence and social characteristics of collegiate drug users on campuses of the University of Illinois. *Drug Forum*, 1973, **2**, 141–171.

151. Strimbu, J. L., Schoenfeldt, L. F., & Sims, O. S. Drug usage in college students as a function of racial classification and minority group status. *Research in Higher Education*, 1973, **1**, 263–272.

152. Girdano, D. A., & Girdano, D. D. Drug usage trends among college students. *College Student Journal*, 1974, **8**, 94–96.

153. Josephson, E. Trends in adolescent marijuana use. In E. Josephson & E. E. Carroll (Eds.), *Drug use: Epidemiological and sociological approaches*. New York: Hemisphere, 1974.

154. Kandel, D. Stages in adolescent involvement in drug use. *Science,* 1975, **190,** 912–914.
155. Whitehead, P. C., & Cabral, R. M. Scaling the sequence of drug-using behavior: A test of the stepping-stone hypothesis. *Drug Forum,* 1975–1976, **5,** 45–54.
156. Frenkel, S. I., Robinson, J. A., & Finman, B. G. Drug use: Demography and attitudes in a junior and senior high school population. *Journal of Drug Education,* 1974, **4,** 179–186.
157. Annis, H. M., & Watson, C. Drug use and school dropout: A longitudinal study. *Canadian Counsellor,* 1975, **9,** 155–162.
158. Gossett, J. T., Lewis, J. M., & Phillips, V. A. Psychological characteristics of adolescent drug users and abstainers. *Bulletin of the Menninger Clinic,* 1972, **36,** 425–435.
159. Holroyd, K., & Kahn, M. Personality factors in student drug use. *Journal of Consulting and Clinical Psychology,* 1974, **42,** 236–243.
160. McKillip, J., Johnson, J. E., & Pretzel, T. P. Patterns and correlates of drug use among urban high school students. *Journal of Drug Education,* 1973, **3,** 1–12.
161. Millman, D. R., & Su, W. Patterns of illicit drug and alcohol use among secondary school students. *Journal of Pediatrics,* 1973, **83,** 314–320.
162. Smart, R. G., & Fejer, D. Recent trends in illicit drug use among adolescents. *Canada's Mental Health,* Suppl. No. 68, 1971.
163. Smith, G. M., & Fogg, C. P. Teenage drug use: A search for causes and consequences. *Personality and Social Psychology Bulletin,* 1974, **1,** 426–429.
164. Stein, K. B., Soskin, W. F., & Korchin, S. J. Drug use among disaffected high school youth. *Journal of Drug Education,* 1975, **5,** 193–203.
165. Wechsler, H., & Thum, D. Teen-age drinking, drug use, and social correlates. *Quarterly Journal of Studies on Alcohol,* 1973, **34,** 1220–1227.
166. Hochman, J. S., & Brill, N. Q. Chronic marijuana use and psychosocial adaptation. *American Journal of Psychiatry,* 1973, **130,** 132–140.
167. McAree, C. P., Steffenhagen, R. A., & Zheutlin, L. S. Personality factors and patterns of drug usage in college students. *American Journal of Psychiatry,* 1972, **128,** 890–893.
168. Walters, P. A., Goethals, G. W., & Pope, H. G. Drug use and lifestyle among 500 college undergraduates. *Archives of General Psychiatry,* 1972, **26,** 92–96.
169. Crain, W. C., Ertel, D., & Gorman, B. S. Personality correlates of drug preference among college undergraduates. *International Journal of the Addictions,* 1975, **10,** 849–856.
170. Cunningham, W. H., Cunningham, I., & English, W. D. Sociopsychological characteristics of undergraduate marijuana users. *Journal of Genetic Psychology,* 1974, **125,** 3–12.
171. Hogan, R., Mankin, D., Conway, J., & Fox, S. Personality correlates of undergraduate marijuana use. *Journal of Consulting and Clinical Psychology,* 1970, **35,** 58–63.
172. Smart, R. G., & Fejer, S. Drug use among adolescents and their parents: Closing the generation gap in mood modification. *Journal of Abnormal Psychology,* 1972, **79,** 153–160.
173. Gorsuch, R. L., & Butler, M. C. Initial drug abuse: A review of predisposing social psychological factors. *Psychological Bulletin,* 1976, **83,** 120–137.
174. Krug, S. E., & Henry, T. J. Personality, motivation, and adolescent drug use patterns. *Journal of Counseling Psychology,* 1974, **21,** 440–445.
175. Jessor, R., Jessor, S. L., & Finney, J. A social psychology of marijuana use: Longitudinal studies of high school and college youth. *Journal of Personality and Social Psychology,* 1973, **26,** 1–15.
176. Prendergrast, T. J., & Schaefer, E. S. Correlates of drinking and drunkenness among high-school students. *Quarterly Journal of Studies on Alcohol,* 1974, **35,** 232–242.
177. Streit, F., & Oliver, H. G. The child's perception of his family and its relationship to drug use. *Drug Forum,* 1972, **1,** 283–289.
178. Tolone, W. L., & Dermott, D. Some correlates of drug use among high school youth in a midwestern rural community. *International Journal of the Addictions,* 1975, **10,** 761–777.
179. Tec, N. Parent-child drug abuse: Generational continuity or adolescent deviancy. *Adolescence,* 1974, **9,** 351–364.
180. Coleman, J. C. *The adolescent society.* Glencoe, Ill.: Free Press, 1961.
181. Keniston, K. *The uncommitted: Alienated youth in American society.* New York: Harcourt, 1965.

182. Feuer, L. S. *The conflict of generations.* New York: Basic Books, 1969.

183. Mead, M. *Culture and commitment: A study of the generation gap.* New York: Doubleday, 1970.

184. Friedenberg, D. Z. (Ed.) *The anti-American generation.* Chicago: Aldine, 1971.

185. Hendin, H. *The age of sensation.* New York: Norton, 1975.

186. Boyd, R. E., Mockaitis, J. P., & Hedges, N. A. Socio-political liberalism in three adolescent samples. *Adolescence,* 1973, **8,** 455–462.

187. Friesen, D. Value orientations of modern youth: A comparative study. *Adolescence,* 1972, **7,** 265–275.

188. Lipset, S. M., & Raab, E. The non-generation gap. *Commentary,* 1970, **50,** 35–39.

189. Kovar, L. C. *Faces of the adolescent girl.* Englewood Cliffs, N.J.: Prentice-Hall, 1968.

190. Simon, W., Gagnon, J. H., & Buff, S. A. Son of Joe: Continuity and change among white working class adolescents. *Journal of Youth and Adolescence,* 1972, **1,** 13–34.

191. Meissner, W. W. Parental interaction of the adolescent boy. *Journal of Genetic Psychology,* 1965, **107,** 225–233.

192. Eve, R. A. "Adolescent culture," convenient myth or reality? *Sociology of Education,* 1975, **48,** 152–167.

193. Frederickson, L. C. Value structure of college students. *Journal of Youth and Adolescence,* 1972, **1,** 155–163.

194. Jessor, S. L., & Jessor, R. Maternal ideology and adolescent problem behavior. *Developmental Psychology,* 1974, **10,** 246–254.

195. Lerner, R. M., Schroeder, C., Rewitzer, M., & Weinstock, A. Attitudes of high school students and their parents toward contemporary issues. *Psychological Reports,* 1972, **31,** 255–258.

196. Thomas, L. E. Generational discontinuity in belief: An exploration of the generation gap. *Journal of Social Issues,* 1974, **30,** 1–22.

197. Tolor, A. The generation gap: Fact or fiction? *Genetic Psychology Monographs,* 1976, **94,** 35–130.

198. Block, J. H. Generational continuity and discontinuity in the understanding of societal rejection. *Journal of Personality and Social Psychology,* 1972, **22,** 333–345.

199. Horn, J. L., & Knott, P. D. Activist youth of the 1960's: Summary and prognosis. *Science,* 1971, **171,** 979–985.

200. Thomas, L. E. Family correlates of student political activism. *Developmental Psychology,* 1971, **4,** 206–214.

201. Adelson, J. What generation gap? *The New York Times Magazine,* Jan. 18, 1970, 10–45.

202. Bandura, A. The stormy decade: Fact or fiction? *Psychology in the School,* 1964, **1,** 224–231.

203. Blos, P. The generation gap: Fact and fiction. In S. C. Feinstein, P. L. Giovacchini, & A. A. Miller (Eds.), *Adolescent psychiatry.* Vol. I. New York: Basic Books, 1971.

204. Schwartz, G., & Merten, D. The language of adolescence: An anthopological approach to the youth culture. *American Journal of Sociology,* 1967, **72,** 453–468.

205. Weiner, I. B. The generation gap—fact and fancy. *Adolescence,* 1971, **6,** 155–166.

206. Weiner, I. B. The adolescent and his society. In J. R. Gallagher, F. P. Heald, & D. C. Garell (Eds.), *Medical care of the adolescent.* (3rd ed.) New York: Appleton-Century-Crofts, 1976.

17 Adolescent Variations

PHYSICAL DIFFERENCES

Early and Late Maturation

Physique, Temperament, and Interpersonal
Attractiveness

SCHOOL-RELATED DIFFERENCES

Sex-Role Stereotyping in Secondary School

Creativity in High School

The High-School Dropout

SEX DIFFERENCES

Academic Achievement and Mental Ability

Self-Concept and Self-Esteem

THE FAMILY

Varying Patterns of Adolescent Development

Father Absence and Adolescent Girls

RACIAL AND CULTURAL DIFFERENCES

Self-Concept among Black and White Adolescents

Self-Concept Development in Other Cultures

ESSAY

From Ghetto School to College Campus

Discontinuities

Continuities

SUMMARY

REFERENCES

During adolescence, individual variations become especially prominent. First of all, young people reach puberty at different ages, experiencing the psychological effects of either early or late maturity. Then there are differences in body build, which appear to be related to temperament. In school young people differ with respect to sex-role stereotyping, creativity, and "dropping out"; and at home young people have different experiences due to their family pattern and whether or not there has been a death or divorce. Members of different ethnic groups vary in their self-concepts and degree of self-esteem, and in various cultures there are different adolescent self-systems.

PHYSICAL DIFFERENCES

During adolescence young people become quite self-conscious and concerned about their appearance. In general, they are pleased if their own body type matches the culturally stereotyped ideal, and they are unhappy if it does not. Most young people want to have a "sex appropriate" appearance. In the short range, a late-maturing boy may have such "feminine" traits as a high-pitched voice and a fair amount of fatty tissue. These temporary aspects of appearance will be discussed as a problem of early and late maturation. The longer-range problem of a permanent body configuration and its conformity to the ideal body type will be dealt with as an aspect of body type and temperament.

Early and Late Maturation

As we noted in Chapter 15, the start of the adolescent growth spurt is quite variable and can occur anywhere from about the age of 8 to 14 for girls and from about the age of 9 to 15 for boys. Young people who begin their growth spurt relatively early are called **early maturers** and those who begin it relatively late are called **late maturers.** A number of studies have shown that there are characteristic problems and attitudes associated with early and late maturation (1–13), but these differ for boys and girls.

Early-maturing Boys. In America, early maturation for boys usually has more positive than negative consequences. In general, the early-maturing boy has three advantages: Because of his larger size and greater strength he is better in many competitive sports. In football, for example, the larger, heavier boy has an advantage, especially if he is playing on the line. The advantage of a taller boy in basketball is obvious. Early-maturing boys also have an asset in social relationships with girls; they tend to be as tall as or taller than girls and to have developed a heterosexual interest. Finally, because they are taller and heavier than their peers, early maturers often assume, or are chosen for, leadership positions (7–9).

However, there are also certain disadvantages as well. One problem of the early-maturing boy is that, while physically he may be a man, psychologically he is still a boy. Physical growth sometimes badly outpaces psychological growth. A young man, for example, may still want the physical attention from his parents that he had been accustomed to (being kissed, being tucked in at night), and yet feel that he is too large, his voice too deep, his beard too rough to ask for such things. Parents, in turn, feel awkward about fondling an adolescent the way they might a child.

The early-maturing boy, thus, may look like a man but think and feel as a boy. Discrepancies between social expectations based on his size and his actual behavior can at times be upsetting to all concerned. A case in point is the nearly 6-foot-tall 12-year-old who still wants to go out "trick or treating" on Halloween. Imagine the shock of a homemaker when she sees a 6-foot apparition, covered in a sheet, at her door asking for candy. On the other hand, there is also the opposite situation in which a young man who has matured psychologically tries to assert his independence but is still treated as a child by his parents.

In general, though, the advantages of early maturation for boys in our society outweigh the disadvantages. And some of the advantages seem to last well beyond adolescence. Longitudinal follow-up studies of early- and late-maturing boys have looked at their personality when they reached their thirties. In the matter of height and weight, late maturers generally caught up with the early maturers. But the late maturers seemed to be less stable and to have personalities that were less well integrated than the early maturers.

Early-maturing Girls. For early-maturing girls in America, there may be more disadvantages than advantages. Early-maturing girls are conspicuous among their peers—both boys and girls—and seem out of place. The physically mature sixth-grader with a well-developed bust who is interested in dating is physically and socially different from her classmates. Not surprisingly, early-maturing girls are often embarrassed about their conspicuousness, bigness, tallness, complexion, and menstruation (11–13).

Although early-maturing girls may date older boys, they seldom make friends among older girls, who sometimes view them as competitors or as being psychologically immature. Early-maturing girls may also be exposed to social situations for which they are not fully prepared. The stares and knowing looks of men of all ages may be disturbing to a 12-year-old who may not know how to handle or interpret such attentions.

Coupled with these problems, an early-maturing girl (like an early-maturing boy) needs to be a child at times. When a mature young woman suddenly decides to play hopscotch, or to get into a swing, adults may be a little taken aback. Of course, early maturation has certain advantages. Early-maturing girls, particularly if they are attractive, may be admired by their age-mates and may assume leadership roles. And these girls' early introduction to heterosexual relations—to which they have to adapt on their own—may give them a lasting superiority in social skills.

Late-maturing Boys. Boys whose growth spurt comes late (that is,

In early adolescence young people of roughly the same age vary widely in size and physical maturity.

after the age of 13 or 14) are confronted with a number of problems. Their friends (or former friends) are taller and heavier, have masculine voices, and have begun to shave; they are also interested in girls. This makes the late-maturing boy socially and physically different from his classmates. He is also missing out on learning social skills at a time when others are learning them, and he cannot complete athletically. In fact, he may even be teased for his high voice and rounded body contours.

On the other hand, the late-maturing boy does not have some of the social pressures that are faced by the early maturer. And the late maturer can compete with his peers academically and in such specialized areas as music. Late-maturing boys can also find a place for themselves in the school's athletic program by managing the equipment for the interscholastic team or by becoming skilled at such activities as badminton, Ping-Pong, swimming, or running.

For the late-maturing boy, the early adolescent years are usually not too pleasant. Besides his immediate feelings of being inadequate are fears that he will never reach adult height and weight. When the young man's growth spurt does occur, it may be too late to change the self-concepts he has already developed. Perhaps that is why when they are in their thirties, late maturers are described as more rebellious, touchy, impulsive, assertive, insightful, and self-indulgent than their early-maturing peers (3).

Late-maturing Girls. In some ways, late-maturing girls have advantages. Since being tall is not as important to girls as it is to boys (12, 13), a girl who is shorter than her peers does not feel particularly handicapped (as a short boy would). Then, too, the late-maturing girl is not pressed into social situations for which she is not prepared. And her lack of interest in boys forestalls conflicts with parents about dating, parties, and so forth.

And yet there are certain disadvantages as well. One study found that late-maturing girls were regarded by their peers as being more quarrelsome, more demanding, and more argumentative than early-maturing girls (12, 13). Another study also suggests that late-maturing girls behave in a less socially adequate fashion than do early-maturing girls (5). The findings of these studies are, however, not entirely clear-cut since the late-maturing girls were probably chronologically older than the early-maturing girls, and age was not controlled for in these investigations. But it is possible that the negative personality traits reported for the late-maturing girls arose from the fact that they resented not being able to compete socially with the early-maturing girls at a younger age. Unfortunately these studies were done decades ago and comparable studies have not been done recently. Accordingly, some of the findings may be less true today, when girls are broadening their roles, than they were decades ago.

Physique, Temperament, and Interpersonal Attractiveness

Since ancient times naïve or intuitive psychology has suggested a connection between physique and temperament. In plays and stories fat men are depicted as being good-humored and sensuous; lean men as being reserved and calculating (Shakespeare wrote, "Cassius has a lean and hungry look"); short men are thought to be aggressive; and strong men, self-confident leaders. These associations between physique and temperament are still with us. Consider the roles played by Humphrey Bogart, Sidney

In this, as in many other motion pictures, the characters portrayed by the actors fit their body types. Humphrey Bogart is a lean and tough mesomorph, Peter Lorre is a thin, nervous ectomorph, and Sidney Greenstreet is a fat, jolly, if sinister, endomorph.

Greenstreet, and Peter Lorre in the old Humphrey Bogart movies. In contemporary films contrast the physiques and parts played by Charlton Heston, the late Zero Mostel, and Anthony Perkins. These associations between physique and temperament can also be found on television; for example, the aggressive role played by the 5-foot-6½-inch ''Fonzie'' in ''Happy Days.''

Sheldon (14) tried to establish a scientific relationship between physique and temperament. He developed a method by which he believed he could reliably measure the extent to which an individual fit within the three body types: lean **ectomorph,** muscular **mesomorph,** or fat **endomorph.** One advantage of Sheldon's system was that it recognized that no one person fits entirely within any one body type and that it is the relative proportions of endomorphy, ectomorphy, and mesomorphy that determine a person's category. In Sheldon's system each individual receives a score on all three body types and the largest score determines that person's somatotype.

Sheldon's work, however, has been criticized by other researchers. Although he did find a correlation between physique and temperament in the predicted directions, his methods were faulty. Among other things, he rated both the somatotype and the personality traits himself. It is quite possible, therefore, that he contaminated his personality ratings by his knowledge of the subjects' somatotypes. In the 1950s Parnell (15) used more objective methods for somatotyping individuals; he determined endomorphy (or fatness) by measuring the depth of subcutaneous fat in three parts of the body. He assessed mesomorphy (or muscularity) by measuring the thickness of the bones and muscles in the arms and legs. Ectomorphy (or leanness) was measured by dividing an individual's height by the cube root of his or her weight. This measurement gives an estimate of over-all body mass or density. When a person is measured in this way, and when age is taken into account, the person's somatotype can be determined by referring to certain tables that were established by Parnell (15).

When Sheldon described temperament, he relied on activities and functions that are related to the body. For example, he claimed that fat people

Table 17.1   Basic Temperamental Traits

Endomorphy	Mesomorphy	Ectomorphy
1. Dependent	Dominant	Detached
2. Relaxed	Assertive	Tense
3. Calm	Confident	Anxious
4. Kind	Aggressive	Considerate
5. Love of comfort	Love of risk	Love of privacy
6. Extrovert of affect*	Extrovert of action**	Introvert
7. Extensive rapport	Enduring rapport	Intensive rapport
8. Cheerful-depressed	Even-explosive†	Hypersensitive-apathetic
9. Self-satisfied	Self-assured	Self-centered
10. Soft-tempered	Quick-tempered	Gentle-tempered
11. Complacent	Irascible	Reflective
12. Amiable	Talkative	Reserved
13. Warm	Active	Cool
14. Affected	Reckless	Suspicious
15. Tolerant	Energetic	Inhibited
16. Generous	Enterprising	Restrained
17. Forgiving	Outgoing	Precise
18. Needs people when disturbed	Needs action when disturbed	Needs solitude when disturbed
19. Stress on being	Stress on doing	Stress on perceiving
20. Lets things happen	Makes things happen	Watches things happen

*Shows feelings openly.
**Is physically active and animated.
†Shows sporadic bursts of temper.
Source: Cortés, J. B., & Gatti, F. M. Physique and self description of temperament. *Journal of Consulting Psychology*, 1965, **29**, 432–439.

showed a "love of eating," "pleasure in digestion," and a "love of physical comfort." Likewise, muscular individuals (or mesomorphs) were described as showing a "need and enjoyment of exercise" and "physical courage for combat." In a more recent attempt to quantify personality traits in relation to temperament, Cortés and Gatti (16) established the traits that are listed in Table 17.1. They arrived at these traits by reviewing the descriptions of temperament made by many other investigators.

In their study, Cortés and Gatti somatotyped 100 17½-year-old boys according to the Parnell method described above. Only the young men who could clearly be categorized as belonging to one of the somatotypes participated in the temperament assessment part of the study. The boys' temperament was determined by asking each of them to select, from among groups of adjectives, those that they believed best described themselves. The adjectives were chosen from the lists shown in Table 17.1.

The results of the study were quite positive. In general, the young men chose adjectives that were believed to be linked to their somatotype.

Endomorphs rated themselves significantly more often as kind, relaxed, warm, and soft-hearted. Mesomorphs rated themselves significantly more often as confident, energetic, adventurous, and enterprising. Ectomorphs described themselves as detached, shy, tense, and reserved. [16, p. 437]

For 90 percent of the subjects the largest number of adjectives they checked corresponded to the given somatotype.

In a second study, Cortés and Gatti used the same procedures with girls. While boys generally tend to be more mesomorphic, girls are inclined to be more endomorphic. However, the fact that there are variations among girls makes it possible to somatotype them. There appeared to be a closer relationship between physique and temperament in girls than had been found for boys. This may have been due, at least in part, to the fact that the girls were a few years older than the boys. Their personality traits could have become more integrated than those of the boys. It is also possible, though, that physique plays a greater role in determining girls' temperaments than it does for boys.

Why are temperamental traits so closely associated with physique? On the one hand, it might be argued that temperament, like physique, is largely inherited—that physique and temperament are sex-linked characteristics. On the other hand, some persons believe that the relationship is cultural; that is, that people develop the temperament that society expects of them—a self-fulfilling prophecy.

Our own belief is that temperament is associated with the emotions, which are closely related to physiology. It is conceivable—indeed probable—that differences in physiology that are closely linked to differences in physique could be related to temperament. Of course, one's environment may play an important role in fostering and reinforcing (or in some cases inhibiting) physiologically related propensities. That is to say, it is possible that sociocultural stereotyping together with one's own biological makeup bring about the observed correlation between physique and temperament.

In this connection, a study of 7-year-old children was quite interesting (17). Children of this age clearly have had less cultural conditioning than adolescents and their physical types are not yet well delineated. In this study, 37 girls and 33 boys were somatotyped and the results were related to their personality characteristics as determined by rating scales. A strong correlation was found between their physiques and temperaments in the expected directions. For example, 7-year-old ectomorphs showed greater anxiety, submissiveness, and meticulousness than did the endomorphs or mesomorphs.

These data could mean simply that sociocultural shaping begins quite early in life, which we know it does, but they could also mean that there is a potentiality for shaping. It is entirely possible that some children can be shaped more easily into certain temperamental traits than can others. Without the potentiality or the actual shaping, the traits might not appear. As we have said before, we believe that nature interacts with nurture, thus producing the observed correlations between physique and temperament.

Closely related to the association between physique and temperament is the well-established association between physical attractiveness and social popularity (18–21). In this case, however, the cause is almost entirely social, for physical attractiveness must be perceived and evaluated by others in order for the relationship with popularity to exist. As we have seen, in our society there are "ideal" looks against which people judge themselves as well as others. But there is still the question of whether popularity may not sometimes depend upon other factors such as personality and school achievement.

One study (22) that attempted to answer this question included boys and girls at two different grade levels (5th and 11th). The students in both groups had been classmates for years and knew one another quite well. Black-and-white photographs were taken of all of the participants. In individual sessions each subject was asked to rate the photographs of the young people in his or her grade by assigning them to one of the following categories: handsome (or pretty), average, or ugly. The subjects were also asked to rank the pictures from the most to the least attractive. There was a good correlation between the rating and the ranking of the pictures, and individual subjects were quite consistent in their assessments of attractiveness. Each subject also rated and ranked his or her classmates with repect to liking and disliking them and filled out a questionnaire evaluating the similarity or dissimilarity in attitudes between the subject and each classmate.

Table 17.2 Correlates of Popularity Rankings

Grade Level	Sex of Judges	Sex of Subjects	Correlation between Popularity Rankings and				Correlation between PA and ATT
			PA	ATT	CGA	NATS	
5	Boys	Boys	.96	.92	.15	.35	.88
		Girls	.94	.84	.36	.32	.71
	Girls	Boys	.89	.76	.10	.37	.75
		Girls	.67	.74	.23	.23	.83
11	Boys	Boys	.64	.90	.12	.06	.45
		Girls	.87	.83	.31	.15	.75
	Girls	Boys	.74	.96	.03	.20	.66
		Girls	.47	.92	.09	−.08	.63

PA — Physical attractiveness
ATT — Perceived attitude similarity
CGA — Cumulative grade averages
NATS — National Achievement Test scores
Source: Cavior, N., & Dokecki, P. R. Physical attractiveness, perceived attitude similarity and academic achievement as contributors to interpersonal attraction among adolescents. *Developmental Psychology,* 1973, **ix,** 44–54.

Some of the results of this study are presented in Table 17.2. As can be seen, there was a very high correlation in both age groups between popularity and physical attractiveness. But there were also high correlations between popularity and similar attitudes and between physical attractiveness and similar attitudes. In general, it appeared that for fifth-graders (with the exception of girls judging girls) physical attractiveness was more important than similarity of attitudes or academic achievement in determining popularity. But for eleventh-graders (with the exception of boys ranking girls) popularity depended more upon having similar attitudes than upon being physically attractive.

These results seem to have a common-sense explanation. Among children, who do not have too many differentiated interests and attitudes, physical appearance is more important than attitudes in deciding popularity. But among adolescents, the reverse is true. One's attitudes (or personality) are more important than one's physical attractiveness in order to be popular. Among eleventh-grade boys, however, young women are more popular because of their appearance than because of their personality—a well-known phenomenon.

What, then, of the well-established correlation between appearance and popularity cited earlier? It should be noted that in all of those studies the subjects did not know one another. It may well be the case that when adolescents (or even adults, for that matter) do not know one another, popularity (or interpersonal attractiveness) ratings are made on the basis of physical attractiveness. Among young people who do know one another, however, physical attractiveness (with the exceptions noted above) may be less important than personality in determining popularity.

SCHOOL-RELATED DIFFERENCES

The American high school is a society in miniature. Many of them are large, with from 1000 to 4000 students, often from different socioeconomic levels and ethnic backgrounds. Most large high schools offer opportunities to participate in sports, music, debating, the school newspaper, and so forth. In this regard, the high school reflects the many interests and abilities that characterize the intellectual development of adolescents. In our discussion of the high school, we will focus on sex-role stereotyping, creativity, and the high-school dropout.

Sex-Role Stereotyping in the Secondary School

Since the mid-1960's, it has become apparent that the schools are promoting a considerable amount of sex-role stereotyping. Although co-education appears to provide equal education for boys and girls, this is really not the case at all. One of the obvious forms of sex bias is that a disproportionate share of money, facilities, and equipment are earmarked for boys' athletics. Also, boys are offered more courses in vocational preparation such as shop, science, and mechanics than are girls. Although girls are now enrolled in some of these courses, they were designed for boys.

Some of the more subtle forms of sex bias appear in textbooks (23). History books consistently refer to "men" and use such phrases as "our revolutionary forefathers," or "the men who conquered the West," or "the men who built our nation." Sometimes demeaning terms are used for women, or they are portrayed as weak and timid. In science and mathematics books at both the junior and senior high-school level, little mention is made of women scientists and mathematicians of note. And mathematics problems often depict women performing housewifely chores (23). For example, a typical problem might be: "Ruth is braiding strips of material for a rug. How many strips, each ¾-inch wide, can she cut from 54 inches of material?"

Another form of sex-role stereotyping is the establishment of special vocational or academic schools in large metropolitan areas. These schools are usually for boys only and are often based on the same sex stereotypes that prevail in the high school, where it is assumed that boys alone are interested in science, shop, and mechanics (24). Although there is some evidence of change, the change is small and gradual. In the United States in 1970 no high-school girls were enrolled in agricultural science, but in 1972, 5 percent of the students were girls. In 1965 only about 5 percent of

High schools today are providing many more opportunities than before for young women to engage in competitive sports.

the high-school students enrolled in health courses were male, but by 1971 this figure had risen to more than 12 percent (25). Although there is a long way to go in eliminating sex stereotypes, it seems encouraging that males are beginning to enter fields that had been considered ''female,'' and that women are beginning to enter formerly ''male'' ones.

At the college level, however, almost all students enrolled in technical courses (metallurgy, engineering, oceanography, and so forth) are men while almost all students enrolled in consumer and homemaking courses are women (25). In general, school policies only reflect the sex-role stereotyping that is found in American society at large. According to one group of writers:

"The average woman" is a statistical creation, a fiction. She has been used to defend the status quo of the labor market, on the assumption that knowing the sex of an employee reliably predicts her

job aptitudes. This assumption is false. Knowing that a worker is female allows us to predict that she will hold a job in a "woman's field" and that she will be substantially underpaid for a woman of her qualifications. But knowing that a worker is a woman does not help us much to predict what she wants from her job [26, p. 96].

To reduce or eliminate sex-role stereotyping in the society at large—but more specifically in the schools—will not be easy (27). It will mean providing more role models in the form of women in leadership positions in many occupations, including that of high-school principal. It will also mean getting rid of the stereotyped idea that successful women hate men and are aggressive. Employers' attitudes toward women also need to be changed. Women today can and do make long-range commitments to their jobs and they are often very well qualified for promotions and advancement. Many women must work on a regular basis in order to provide or supplement the family income, and many women feel that a career is an essential part of their life.

It should be emphasized that abolishing sex-role stereotypes and the opening up of more job opportunities will help men as well as women. Men are almost as burdened by sex-role stereotypes as are women; by getting rid of them, American men can hope to express their full human potential rather than just a culturally sanctioned part of it. Men will also benefit by having more job fields available to choose from.

Creativity in High School

The creative person is generally thought to be a little strange, outspoken, nonconforming, and independent of mind. Indeed, some of the early studies of adolescent creativity have found such traits (28, 29). Highly creative young people did not conform either intellectually or socially to the extent that highly intelligent (but not too creative) young people did. Not surprisingly, as we indicated in our discussion of creativity in children, teachers preferred more intelligent (and conforming) students to those who were more creative (and nonconforming).

These early findings may have given an incorrect impression of how well a creative adolescent adjusts in high school. In two related studies, Walberg (30, 31) has shown that creative adolescents are well integrated socially within the high school. The subjects (2225 boys and 741 girls) were chosen from a national sample of high-school physics classes. Creative adolescents were identified by their responses to biographical questions dealing with leadership, art, science, performing arts (dancing, acting), music, and writing. A subject was classified as creative if he or she indicated that one or more descriptions (such as the following) held true for him or her. *"Musician – How good are you in music?* I have a great deal of interest in music. I have entered competitions and have won one or more prizes, either for my own performances or for the production of

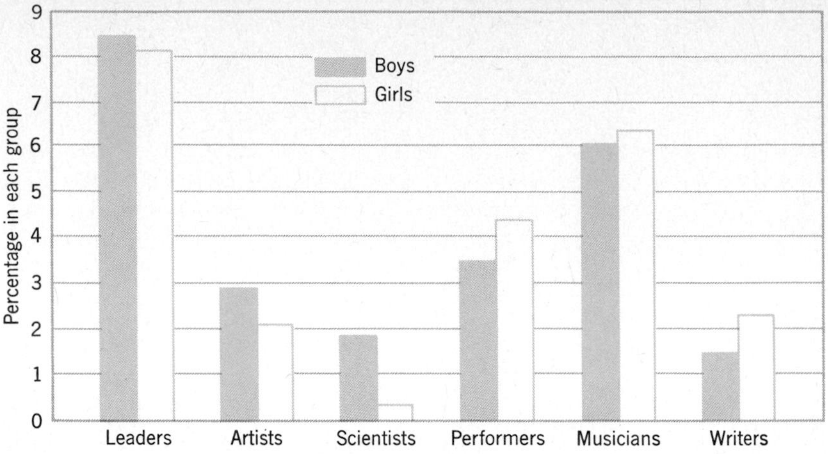

Figure 17.1 Percentage of boys and girls who had achieved distinction in various areas. (*Source.* Walberg, H. J., Varieties of adolescent creativity and the high school environment. *Exceptional Children*, 1969, **36**, 5–12.)

original pieces of music.'' Figure 17.1 shows what percentage of the young people were considered to be creative in various fields based upon their responses.

With respect to adapting to school, it was found that:

In contrast to other students, the creative students more often report themselves as more creative and imaginative and as having more creative opportunities. They more often like school, get high marks and question their teachers. Also they more often think it is important to be intelligent, have at least two cases of books in the home, study and read outside of school, and talk to adults about future occupations. Lastly, they more often follow through work despite difficulties and distractions [30, p. 130].

The pattern for creative boys and girls was quite similar.

How can we account for the fact that some investigators believe that creative adolescents are well adjusted in high school (30, 31), while others (28, 29) believe that they are socially alienated? In part, this discrepancy may depend upon one's perspective. The data suggesting that creative young people are well adjusted comes from their own ratings of school, schoolwork, and school activities, while the data suggesting that they are alienated comes from teacher ratings in which highly intelligent students are preferred over the highly creative. Possibly many creative young people have found a place for themselves in the high school even if they are not particularly valued by all of their teachers.

The High-School Dropout

In today's highly technological and competitive job market, dropping out of high school is generally not thought to be desirable, even by young people themselves. Whereas, in the 1940s, almost half of the young people who started high school did not complete it, today only 20 percent of our

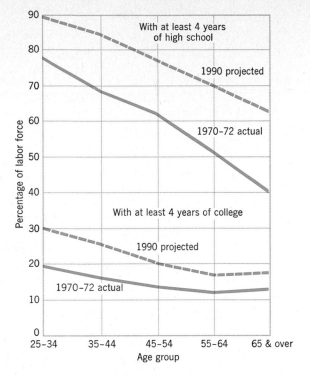

Figure 17.2 Percentage of civilian labor force, by age, with at least four years of high school and at least four years of college, 1970-1972 actual and 1990 projected. (*Source. Monthly Labor Review,* 1973, **96,** 27.)

youth do not finish high school. These figures apply to both men and women and to whites and non-whites. The fact that more adolescents are staying in school longer has meant that there are fewer of them in the labor force. It appears that these trends will continue throughout the 1970s and beyond (32).

Despite the decline in the percentage of high-school dropouts, even the present 20 percent is not desirable. Among other things, high-school dropouts are less likely than high-school graduates to qualify for and get jobs, and this is especially true for girls. But there are group differences as well. The unemployment rate for white male dropouts is substantially higher than that of white male graduates. For blacks, however, the unemployment rate is about the same for dropouts and for graduates (33). Of course, some of the factors that lead young people to drop out of school also make it difficult for them to get or keep jobs.

Dropping out of school correlates highly with such deviant behavior as delinquency, drug addiction, early and illegitimate pregnancy, and alcoholism. Dropouts tend to have a low self-esteem and to be alienated from society at large. In effect, they do not develop their potentialities, and thus they often become a problem to the larger society. In many cases an adolescent has personal problems that lead him or her to drop out of school, and these same problems lead to deviant behavior as well. Dropping out of school is as much a symptom as it is a cause of personal difficulties. Not having a high-school diploma only compounds the dropout's personal problems; it does not cause them (34).

School Performance. Cervantes (35) cites patterns of school performance that can predict whether a young person will drop out of school. By seventh grade potential dropouts are about 2 years behind in mathematics and reading and have long received poor marks in school. The potential dropout has usually failed one or more grades and generally has a poor attendance record. Many of these young people have changed schools often, and they frequently present management problems in the classroom. A later study (34) generally confirmed Cervantes's conclusions:

> *The majority of students who did poorly in their high school careers could have been identified early in the elementary school. By the second grade 50% had already experienced their first failure, 75% by the fourth grade, and 90% by the seventh grade. The critical areas of initial difficulty were English and mathematics [34, p. 143.].*

The Family. When young people have become physically mature enough and old enough to work, low-income families may encourage them to do so (35–38). But the family's income itself is not as important as the parents' attitudes. Most low-income families in America can afford to send their children to high school. But these parents may have blue-collar jobs that require little formal education. They may communicate, directly or indirectly, that they have made it "without an education" and that their children can, too. Survey research shows that parents who have themselves completed some high school or college work have proportionately more children who finish high school (39). Of course, many low-income families, particularly upwardly mobile immigrant families who want to make the most of every opportunity for themselves and their children, succeed in sending their children to high school and often to college.

But attitudes toward school are only part of the picture. Low-income adolescents may find it difficult to compete academically and socially with those from the middle class. Low-income adolescents may have to work part time or help at home with housework and caring for younger siblings. Opportunities for educational enrichment (particularly travel) are also probably quite limited (40).

Besides these factors, there is the nature of family life itself. Among both low- and middle-income adolescents who drop out of school, there are often family quarrels and conflicts. Some young people leave home (with its constant bickering) and school, since it seems to be the only way to escape from an impossible situation. In these homes there is little real communication among family members and little real caring and sharing with one another (38). Marital problems are also more common among the parents of young people who drop out of school than they are among the parents of those who finish school (35–38).

Peers. Not surprisingly, school dropouts report that they do not feel that they have ever been accepted by their peer group. Many young people who feel alienated from their peers attribute it to money. They do not think they can afford to date and to dress in such a way that would make them acceptable to their peers. Consequently, they feel poorly treated. Both boys and girls may drop out of school in order to escape from a painful situation. Some girls who drop out of school marry soon thereafter, partly to compensate for the rejection they experienced at school (39–41).

The High School. It is generally recognized today that many aspects of the high school itself can lead adolescents to drop out. These include the heavy emphasis on academic subjects and college preparation as well as the lack of vocational courses. Many young people leave school simply because it does not meet any of their vocational or recreational needs. It has been found that most dropouts are enrolled in a "general curriculum" before they leave school. To remedy this situation, many school systems are beginning to offer more meaningful vocational courses (such as computer programming), and they are arranging work-study programs where young people can work part time as apprentices for school credit. Although there are many reasons why young people drop out of school, making changes in the school curriculum may help to some extent in keeping them there.

SEX DIFFERENCES

During adolescence, sex differences become especially prominent, not only in the area of physical development, but also in academic achievement (even though this does not represent differences in aptitude), in self-concepts, and in sex-role satisfaction.

Academic Achievement and Mental Ability

As we have said in earlier chapters, girls tend to score higher on tests of verbal ability while boys tend to do better on tests of spatial ability (42). But there are wide individual variations in these regards. Moreover, achievement tests and school grades bear little relationship to one's later job or vocational choice. For example, one study showed that girls were superior to boys on measures of IQ, scientific processes, and understanding science (43). Occupationally, however, very few women enter the fields of science and engineering.

Table 17.3 shows how boys do in relationship to girls on achievement tests. Why, then, do women's occupational choices differ so much from their aptitudes? It would seem to be largely a matter of sociocultural conditioning. Hopefully, young women will begin to broaden their vocational horizons. For example, "housewife" and "actress" are the two most popular occupations for freshman high-school girls (44).

A somewhat different perspective on this issue comes from longitudinal

Table 17.3 Mean Scores for Boys and Girls on Various Psychological Measures

Measures by Group	Girls	Boys
Cognitive		
IQ	118.1	113.3
Science Processes	105.5	102.9
Understanding Science	34.4	32.9
Physics Achievement	16.5	18.6
Science Activities		
Applied Life	1.1	.9
Nature Study	1.6	1.3
Academic	1.5	1.5
Tinkering	.8	1.5
Cosmos	1.9	2.0
Values		
Social	41.4	35.0
Aesthetic	42.8	36.6
Religious	41.9	35.5
Economic	36.1	43.6
Political	39.2	44.6
Theoretical	38.6	44.6
Personality		
Affiliation	3.4	3.0
Change	3.2	2.9
Order	2.6	2.5
Rigidity	2.1	2.1
Achievement	3.1	3.1
Dogmatism	1.9	2.1
Authoritarianism	2.0	2.0

Source: Walberg, H. Physics, femininity and creativity. *Developmental Psychology,* 1969, **1,** 47–54.

studies of aptitude and achievement. A nationwide program of testing to identify gifted students—Project Talent—has worked with about 1000 high schools since 1960 (45, 46). Repeated testing of the young people in these schools over the years has revealed some interesting trends. Ac-

Table 17. Results of Various Achievement Tests for 10th-Grade Boys and Girls in 1960 and 1975

Achievement Tests	Males (n^{1975} = 871)			Females (n^{1975} = 926)		
	Raw Score		Percentile* Difference	Raw Score		Percentile Difference
	1960	1975		1960	1975	
Vocabulary	18.5	15.7	−17%	17.3	15.5	−11%
English	77.3	73.4	−12%	84.5	79.7	−16%
Reading comprehension	28.8	28.4	− 1%	29.8	29.1	− 2%
Creativity	9.1	10.0	8%	8.4	10.1	16%
Mechanical reasoning	12.4	12.2	− 2%	8.5	9.2	7%
Visualization	8.9	8.8	− 1%	7.8	8.1	4%
Abstract reasoning	8.7	9.5	11%	8.7	9.4	8%
Quantitative reasoning	8.5	7.8	− 8%	8.0	7.2	− 8%
Mathematics	10.5	10.7	2%	9.9	10.3	3%
Computation	25.7	18.7	−17%	30.8	26.9	−11%

*Percentiles result when scores are transformed into percentages for easier comparability.
Source: Flanagan, J. C. Changes in school levels of achievement Project TALENT ten and fifteen year retests. *Educational Researcher,* 1976, **5,** 6–8.

cording to Table 17.4, there have been some rather dramatic declines in achievement from 1960 to 1975. But there have been some gains as well, and girls seem to have improved more than boys in creativity and in mechanical reasoning. These changes cannot be attributed to different populations of young people, to more difficult tests, and so forth, since these and other factors have been statistically controlled.

What do these findings mean? There are no simple answers. Vocabulary, for example, is related to reading, and the decline in vocabulary scores might be attributed to less reading among adolescents—perhaps because of television. But this is a hypothesis that needs to be tested. It is also possible that the schools are requiring less written work than they did before, and this may help to explain the decline. One of the authors of this text has suggested a different explanation (83). In the late 1950s and 1960s new curricula that were quite difficult (such as the new math) came to the schools. Declining SAT scores in some areas could mirror the effects of these more difficult curricula. Gains made by girls may mirror, in part, effects of the women's movement.

Because women have been in some respects regarded as second-class citizens in America, they have demonstrated a lower self-esteem and poorer self-concepts than have men. Many studies, for example, have found that girls were more unhappy about their sex than were boys (47–49), and other studies show that girls have more difficulty with their self-image and with their body image than do boys (50–54). However, still other investigations suggest that girls and boys have about the same amount of self-esteem (55, 56). To better understand these discrepant findings, we will discuss three aspects of the self: self-consciousness, self-image stability, and self-esteem.

Adolescent Self-Consciousness. When an individual is consciously concerned about the impression he or she is making on other people, the situation can be rather awkward. Several investigators (57–60) have tried to measure adolescent self-consciousness to determine whether young men or women are more self-conscious in social situations. They used the following type of question: "If a teacher asked you to get up in front of the class and talk a little bit about your summer, would you be very nervous, a little nervous, or not at all nervous?" (60).

The results showed that self-consciousness increased a great deal from childhood to early adolescence and that this increase was greater for girls than it was for boys. The subjects in this sample were white children living in urban areas (we will discuss racial and ethnic differences later). These findings seem to reflect the fact that in our society, a female's physical appearance is more closely related to popularity and upward marital mobility than it is for males. Since girls have more at stake with their appearance than do boys, it seems clear that they would be more concerned with, and self-conscious about, their appearance than would boys.

Self-Image Stability. To measure self-image stability (that is, how sure or unsure the individual is about himself or herself) the investigators (60) constructed a scale that included such items as: "A kid told me 'Some days I like the way I am. Some days I do not like the way I am.' Do your feelings change like this?" The scale was administered to a large group of elementary-school pupils. The results showed that there was an increase in self-*in*stability during early adolescence, with girls showing more instability than boys (60). Again, these results make a certain amount of sense if it is recognized that girls generally feel less positive about themselves than do boys. It should be emphasized, though, that this is a matter of cultural conditioning and not something inherent in "femaleness."

However, this instability does not apply to other areas. In a study to measure choice stability over time, boys and girls were asked to list such things as favorite colors, television programs, animals, and so forth. Two weeks later they were asked the same questions again. The results showed that choice stability increased with age, and at all grade levels, girls were more consistent and stable in their choices than were boys (61).

Self-Esteem. One of the measures of self-esteem (as we have noted earlier, an individual's negative or positive attitudes toward the self) used such items as the following: "Everybody has some things about him which are good and some things about him which are bad. Are most of the things about you good, bad, or are both about the same?" (60). Again, the results showed that for white adolescents, girls had a somewhat lower self-esteem than did boys.

In part these results may be due to the close relationship between girls' appearances and their self-concepts. In a recent study, for example, adolescent boys and girls were asked to rate themselves and their peers against a scale of ideal appearance (61). The young people were also given a personality test that measured personal adjustment, self-reliance, a sense of personal worth, a sense of personal freedom, feelings of belonging, withdrawal tendencies, and nervous symptoms. From these data a component measure "Sense of Personal Worth" was abstracted and used in the analysis.

It was found that both boys and girls tended to rate themselves as equal or superior to their peers in appearance. However, more boys than girls rated their own appearance as above that of their peers. Similarly, some 43.7 percent of the boys did not want to change anything about their appearance, but only 12.2 percent of the girls felt this way. Among the girls (but not the boys) there was a positive correlation between their personal-appearance ratings and their adjustment. The girls also scored lower than the boys on the measure of personal adjustment.

These results are consistent with the trends we have already noted. In a society where a woman is valued—even in today's liberalized climate—by her looks, appearance plays a large part in a woman's self-conception. Apparently, we are still quite far from a social milieu in which women, as well as men, can be evaluated according to their abilities and achievements rather than their appearance.

THE FAMILY

During adolescence, as young people try to discover who they are and achieve greater independence from their parents, they often come into conflict with their parents and siblings. Here we will discuss the relationship between family life and varying patterns of adolescent development, as well as the effect of father absence upon girls. Although we have discussed father absence in earlier chapters, the emphasis in those discussions was largely upon boys.

Varying Patterns of Adolescent Development

Over the years a husband-and-wife team, Daniel and Judith Baskin Offer, have engaged in a longitudinal study of a group of white, middle-class males from the Midwest (65). Seventy-three subjects participated in the study during their school years. One purpose of this study was to describe various "normal" routes of adolescent growth into adulthood. Therefore, data were collected from such sources as interviews with teachers and parents and tests given to the boys themselves. Data collection began in 1962 and was continued through 1970, when most of the subjects had either been out of school for 4 years or had completed college.

As a group these boys were quite typical of the mainstream of American life. Most of them came from intact families. In growing up these young men showed the usual conflict between wanting to be accepted by their parents and also wanting to be free from parental control. Politically the families were middle-of-the-road, and there was considerable consistency in views between the parents and offspring. Although opposed to the war in Vietnam, the young men said that they would serve if they were called. Their attitudes toward blacks ranged from "they should be shipped back to Africa" to praise for radical black groups such as the Black Panthers.

In evaluating the enormous amount of data they collected, the Offers discerned what appeared to be three different developmental routes toward adulthood: **continuous growth** (23 percent of the total group); **surgent growth** (35 percent of the total group); and **tumultuous growth** (21 percent of the total group). The remaining young men showed some mixture of the main patterns.

Continuous Growth.

The subjects described within the continuous growth grouping progressed throughout adolescence and young manhood with a smoothness of purpose and self-assurance of their progression toward a meaningful and fulfilling adult life. These subjects were favored by circumstances. Their genetic and environmental background was excellent. Their childhood had been unmarked by death or serious illness of a parent or a sibling. The nuclear family remained a stable unit throughout their childhood and adolescence. The continuous growth subjects had mastered previous developmental stages without setbacks. They were able to cope with internal and external stimuli through an adaptive combination of reason and emotional expression. These subjects accepted general cultural and societal norms and felt comfortable within this context. They had a capacity to integrate experiences and to use them as a stimulus for growth [65, p. 40].

In general, the young men in this group appeared to be very "well adjusted" with respect to themselves and to the larger society. Compared with the young men in the other groups, they seemed to be relatively happy. They were not smug or condescending; rather they seemed to feel a certain continuity and stability with the past which was projected into the future. In a very real sense, the stability of their earlier life gave them confidence in dealing with the future; they seemed to know what was to come and how to cope with it.

Surgent Growth.

Developmental spurts are illustrative of the pattern of growth of the surgent growth group. These subjects differed in the amount of emo-

tional conflict experienced and in their patterns of resolving conflicts. There was more concentrated energy directed towards mastering developmental tasks than was obvious for members of the continuous growth group. At times these subjects would be adjusting very well, integrating their experiences and moving ahead, and at other times, they seemed to be stuck at an almost "premature closure" and unable to move forward. A cycle of progression and regression is more typical of this group than of the first group. The defenses they used, anger and projection, represent more psychopathology than the defenses used by the first group [65, p. 43].

The boys in this group experienced more family trauma (death, divorce, and serious illness) than was true for those in the continuous growth group. These boys came into conflict with their parents more often about basic viewpoints and values than was true for those in the continuous group. Likewise they experienced more mood swings from brash self-confidence to depression. Although the young men in this group established strong friendships, they had to work hard to make and keep these friends.

The over-all pattern of adjustment of these young men was adequate in that they established long-range goals and worked toward them. But these boys were less introspective about their goals, and they had to work harder to maintain their equilibrium than was true for the continuous group.

Tumultuous Growth. The young men in this group exemplify what is usually described in the literature as the "stormy decade" of adolescence; they have problems at home and at school and sometimes get into trouble with the law.

The subjects demonstrating a tumultuous growth pattern came from less stable backgrounds than did those in the other two groups. Some of the parents in the group had overt marital conflicts, and others had a history of mental illness in the family. Hence, the genetic and environmental backgrounds of the subjects in the tumultuous growth group were decidedly different from those of the other groups. Also present was a social class difference. Our study population was primarily middle class, but this group contained many subjects who belonged to the lower middle class. For them, functioning in a middle and upper-middle class environment might have been a cause for additional stresses [65, p. 45].

In their early lives, these young men seem to have experienced more unhappy than happy events. Their relationships with their parents were full of conflicts, and many of these young men had overt clinical symptoms. The men in this group did, however, have strong family attachments that were better than could be found among psychiatric patients. Nevertheless, these young men were more subject to anxiety and emotional turmoil than was true for the young men in the other groups. Not surprisingly, as a group, these young men did not do as well academically as the other two groups (which has no bearing on their future occupational success). In short, this group experienced the most painful adolescence of all.

These three patterns are of interest because they demonstrate the close relationship between family life and adolescent development. Although a stable, continuous home life does not guarantee a conflict-free adolescence, it helps. The Offers' study suggests that the adolescent who is in conflict with his or her family and society may be an overworked stereotype. As the Offers demonstrate, a large percentage of young people move through adolescence without much storm and stress. What we do not know, and what studies such as the Offers' may eventually reveal, is what effect these patterns of adolescent development may have on the young men's later careers. It would also be helpful to have comparable profiles for young women.

Father Absence and
Adolescent Girls

As we have said in earlier discussions, father absence can occur by death or by divorce and at different points in a child's development. The effects of father absence will depend upon these and other factors. For example, many studies (66–68, 84) show that father absence has a significant effect upon preadolescent boys, but that the same does not appear to hold true for young girls. These findings are inconsistent with certain social psychological theories suggesting that sex-role learning and effective heterosexual relations require a good relationship with the parent of the opposite sex (69–71).

As we observed in Chapter 9, however, this apparent discrepancy in the effect of father absence upon girls may be due to a delayed or "sleeper" effect. From this perspective, father absence during childhood may very well influence a daughter's behavior, but not until adolescence or young adulthood. Such a sleeper effect might account at least in part for the fact that young boys are seen much more often than young girls in mental health clinics. But during adolescence and later the reverse holds true, and many more young women than young men seek psychological help for their problems.

In a carefully controlled and well-designed study, Mavis Hetherington (72) tested the sleeper effect hypothesis. Her subjects were three groups of girls, 24 in each group, who were attending a community recreational center. One group of girls came from intact families, another group had parents who were divorced, and the third group had lost their fathers through death. All of the girls ranged in age from 13 to 17. They were extremely well matched, since all of them were first-born children and none had any brothers. Six girls in two of the groups and five in another were only children. For the two groups of father-absent girls, there were no males living in the home after the separation had occurred. And there were no differences between the groups on such factors as the mean age of the mothers, religious affiliation, fathers' and mothers' employment, or number of siblings.

Various measures were used to assess the girls' personalities and behavior. Some of the most interesting measures were observational—what areas of the recreation hall the girls spent their time in, what chair they sat in for an interview, and how they behaved at dances. In addition, the girls' mothers were interviewed about their daughters and about their lives in general.

The results confirmed the hypothesis of a **sleeper effect** in that the father-absent adolescent girls differed significantly from the father-present girls in many ways. There were also marked differences in the behavior of the girls whose fathers were absent because of divorce as compared with those whose fathers were absent because of death. In general, the girls of divorced parents gravitated more toward boys than did those from intact homes. In contrast, the girls whose fathers had died were more inhibited in their behavior toward boys than were the other two groups.

Table 17.5   Mean Frequency with Which Early and Late* Separated Father-Absent Girls Engaged in Various Behaviors at a Recreational Center

Observational Variable	Father Absent			
	Divorced Early	Divorced Late	Death Early	Death Late
Playful aggression	5.14	2.60	2.15	3.54
Seeking praise, encouragement, & attention from male adults	3.14	1.60	1.46	.82
Seeking praise, encouragement, & attention from female adults	2.14	.80	2.31	1.27
S-initiated physical contact & nearness with male adults	2.28	1.50	2.69	.91
S-initiated physical contact & nearness with male peers	2.93	3.30	2.31	1.00
S-initiated physical contact & nearness with female peers	3.21	1.50	3.38	1.73
Male areas	9.14	5.80	3.23	1.09
Female areas	11.64	11.70	16.54	18.45
Female activities	12.78	18.00	15.38	16.91

*Divorce or death occurring before the child was five was considered early, when it occurred thereafter it was considered late.

Source: Heatherington, E. M. Effects of father absence on personality development in adolescent daughters. *Developmental Psychology*, 1972, **7,** 313–326.

Some of the data are presented in Table 17.5. The girls with divorced parents spent a lot of time in the "male" areas of the recreation center, whereas the girls whose fathers had died spent most of their time in the "female" areas. At dances, the former group tended to linger near the stag line, whereas the latter group tended to stay with other girls or even hide in the bathroom. This had nothing to do with their attractiveness, since both groups of girls were asked to dance equally often.

The following descriptions of their daughters given by mothers emphasize this difference in orientation: the first description was provided by a widowed mother and the second by a divorced mother:

She is almost too good. She has lot of girl friends, but doesn't date much. When she's with girls, she's gay and bouncy–quite a clown but she clams up when a man comes in. Even around my brother she never says much. When boys do phone she often puts them off even though she has nothing else to do. She says she has lots of time for that later, but she's sixteen now and very pretty, and all her friends have boy friends.

The kid is going to drive me over the hill. I'm at my wit's end. She was so good until the last few years. Then POW!, at eleven she really turned on. I came home early and found her in bed with a young hood and she's been bouncing from bed to bed ever since. She doesn't seem to care who it is; she can't keep her hands off men. It isn't just boys her own age; when I have men friends here she kisses them when they come in the door and sits on their knees all in a playful fashion but it happens to them all. Her uncle is a sixty-year-old priest and she even made a "ha ha" type pass at him. It almost scared him to death! I sometimes get so frantic I think I should turn her in to the cops, but I remember what a good kid she used to be and I do love her. We still have a good time together when we're alone and I'm not nagging about her being a tramp. We both like to cook and we get a lot of good laughs when we are puttering around in the kitchen. She's smart and good-looking–she should know she doesn't have to act like that [72, p. 322].

In discussing the results of her study, Hetherington concludes that the effects of father absence in girls manifest themselves largely "as an inability to act appropriately with males rather than in other deviations from appropriate sex typing or interactions with other females." Why the absence of a father should have these effects upon adolescent girls is not clear, and many explanations are possible. Perhaps, for example, the mother's ambivalence toward men after a divorce is communicated to her daughter. Perhaps the disruption of family life due to divorce (73) leads young women to seek out the attention of males as compensation for attention they are not receiving at home. And when father absence is due to death, the girl may fear becoming attached to males for fear of being hurt again.

Young women whose fathers are absent as a result of divorce are often unusually flirtatious.

RACIAL AND
CULTURAL
DIFFERENCES

Most of the research that has been done on racial and cultural differences among adolescents pertains to differences in self-concept and in self-esteem. Accordingly, these are the differences we will discuss here.

Self-Concept among Black and White Adolescents

Self-concept and self-esteem, at least as they are usually measured, depend very much upon the social context. For example, as we wrote earlier, there is a lot of evidence showing that any group in the minority will have a lower self-esteem than the majority group. In a high school, this holds true whether the minority is Catholic and the majority Protestant, or whether the minority is white and the majority black, and so forth. It is the fact of being in a minority group, and not the racial or ethnic status itself, that leads to lowered self-esteem (74–76).

In one study (77), twelve 15-year-olds in a Southern city and in a Northern city were given a self-concept scale. In the Southern city white students had an over-all positive mean score of 332 (30th percentile) on the scale, whereas black students had a mean score of 348 (50th percentile), which was significantly higher. In the Northern city, however, the blacks scored slightly lower than the whites on the self-concept scale—321.9 as opposed to 327.4 for the whites.

To explain these results, the investigator, Gloria Johnson Powell, points out that the social context is extremely important. The adolescents who were surveyed in the North lived in a conservative university town whose residents were largely white and middle-class. But blacks, who comprised only about 6 percent of the population, generally had low incomes and lived in substandard housing. Hence, for the Northern sample, the blacks were the minority group and were also economically disadvantaged vis-à-vis the whites.

In contrast, the adolescents who were surveyed in the South lived in a city that had several black colleges and where many black professionals were prominent in the community. Blacks comprised about 35 percent of the population. The black high-school students were active in the civil rights movement, and the community itself was regarded as being in the vanguard of that movement. Furthermore, the schools became progressively desegregated starting in 1956. Dr. Powell concludes: "A cohesive black community with strong black adult models could in part contribute to the total positive self-concept seen among the southern black students."

Other studies also show that in the mid-1970s black young people were demonstrating a more positive self-image and a more enhanced self-esteem than was true in the early 1960s (78). It appears, therefore, that as America moves, however haltingly, toward greater integration of blacks, their own feelings of self-esteem will increase. What is surprising in Powell's data is the relatively low self-esteem of the white students in the South. Perhaps the pressures of growing up in a competitive milieu can reduce one's self-esteem as much as being in a minority group.

Self-Concept Development in Other Cultures

The field of cognitive psychology is not well defined, especially when it comes to considering the self-concept. To the extent that one views the self-concept as a concept, it clearly falls within cognitive psychology. But if it is viewed as an affective scheme whose measurement reveals facets of personality, the boundaries between affective and cognitive psychology become blurred. Many of the studies of self-concept are found in that blurry area.

Two extensive studies on adolescents' self-concept have been undertaken in Europe and reported in two books. In *Le moi et l'autre dans la conscience de l'adolescent,* Rodriguez Tome (79) presents a theoretically oriented questionnaire study of French-speaking adolescents' conceptions of themselves and others. Tome distinguished three dimensions of adolescents' self-conceptions: *egotism* (such as the tendency to feel superior), *self-control* (such as the ability to solve problems without help), and *sociability* (such as one's confidence in oneself). He found that these factors were statistically almost completely independent of one another.

Tome also distinguished between the individual's own self-image and his or her social self-image. The subjects were asked to describe themselves as they saw themselves (self-image proper) and as they thought others saw them (social self-image). The same three personality factors appeared in both descriptions and were as uncorrelated for descriptions of the self-image proper as they were for the social self-image. There was almost no change with age (from 12 to 18 years for boys and from 12 to 21 years for girls) in the relative weights that were given to egotism, self-control, and sociability. At all age levels, French-speaking adolescents ranked themselves highest on sociability and lowest on egotism.

In addition, Tome compared the adolescent's self-image with those given by the parents. He found that French-speaking parents generally viewed their offspring as more egotistical and less self-controlled than did the offspring themselves. Parents and their offspring generally disagreed on the adolescent's sociability, but mothers and fathers generally agreed in their appraisal of their adolescent children. Tome also asked the young people to judge themselves as they believed their parents would and asked the parents to judge their children as they thought their children would. The children were closer to the mark than their parents were. Apparently the young people had a better idea of what their parents thought of them than the parents did of what the young people thought of themselves.

In *Le moi ideal de l'adolescent,* Gerard Lutte (80) examines the development of the **ego-ideal*** in children between the ages of 10 and 11 and 16 and 17 in several countries. Here are some of the more striking results: First, the ego-ideal seems to develop differently in different cultures. In America, a child's ego-ideal is the parents, but then it changes during adolescence. In Germany and Portugal, however, parents remain an important ego-ideal for young people from 10 through 17 years of age. Girls and boys have different models for their ego-ideal between the ages of 10 and 13. Girls often have a friend as their model, whereas boys tend to have a celebrity as theirs. Lutte argues that it is hard to defend the position that the ego-ideal develops in regular stages because it is affected by so many different factors.

One of the things that influences an adolescent's self-concept is his social class. Lutte found that young people from both the middle and the working class hoped to achieve better positions in life. But those from the working class really aspired too high; given the realities of life, they would

---

*The sort of person one would like to be.

have to surmount some very difficult obstacles to reach their goals. Comparable findings have been made about American adolescents from lower-income families (81, 82). However, adolescents from the middle class were more realistic about their limitations and gave more weight to such factors as intelligence and willpower in reaching their goals.

Essay

FROM GHETTO SCHOOL TO COLLEGE CAMPUS

The provision of a college education for disadvantaged black students is a multifaceted problem. The side of the problem that most interests us, as psychologists, is its sociopsychological aspect. More concretely, the ghetto school is a different sociopsychological milieu from the college campus, whereas the suburban school, particularly at the high-school level, has already taken on many of the modes, practices, and styles of the college domain. So, while there is considerable continuity between suburban high school and college campus, this is not the case for the ghetto high school. Indeed, the continuities that do exist between the ghetto school and the predominantly white college campus are largely negative in their implications. Accordingly, it might be instructive to consider some of the discontinuities and continuities between the ghetto school and the college campus as well as some of the implications these transitions have for the feelings and attitudes of black students.

Discontinuities

One of the fundamental discontinuities the black student encounters in the transition from ghetto school to college campus resides in the disparity between the attitudes of school and college teachers towards academic success and academic failure. The resulting discontinuity for the black student might be summarized as follows. The schoolteacher is likely to blame himself or herself if the failing child is white but to blame the youngster if he or she is black. But the college teacher is likely to lay the blame for failure on the white college student but to blame materials, preparation, or himself when a black student fails. For the black student, the college teacher's attitude will either reinforce his or her anger at the ghetto schoolteacher, or produce resentment of the college teacher for treatment according to different criteria from those applied to the white student, or both.

A second discontinuity experienced by black students derives from the different ways academic success and failure are handled by college and ghetto school. In ghetto schools, promotion is to a large extent independent of academic achievement. Since most children are failing anyway, it is necessary to promote them to make way for the new youngsters coming in. It is not unusual, for example, to find ghetto high school students purportedly in the tenth grade who are reading at fourth-grade level. In the suburban school the same child would be in a special class or remedial program.

At the college level, however, a very different scene emerges. College students who fail, like advantaged children, repeat the course or take remedial work. Academic success at the college level is a prerequisite to promotion and degrees as it was not in the ghetto school. This discrepancy between criteria for promotion can cause difficulty for disadvantaged youth, who were accustomed to automatic promotion. If, after 12 years of social promotions, they confront a college program where academic success is the only road to promotion, they may well feel frustrated and cheated, and that they are treated with duplicity.

A final discontinuity encountered by the disadvantaged black student moving from the ghetto school to the college campus is of a somewhat different order. In ghetto schools black children are usually in the majority; in most colleges and universities they are in the minority. The ghetto school provides, therefore, a feeling of community and strength in numbers. Put differently, black culture dominates the ghetto school. When the disadvantaged black student enters the college or the university, he or she is (unless entering a black school) clearly in the minority. What usually happens is that black students band together in self-defense and adopt certain group strategies that were seldom needed in the ghetto school.

Continuities

The black student who moves to the white college discovers that the white college teachers are as unprepared for him or her as the white schoolteachers were. Most teachers of ghetto children have little understanding, or respect for, the family structure, language habits, and mores of black children. At the college level, unfortunately, the same lack of preparation is likely to obtain. To be sure, the college teacher generally prides himself or herself on having liberal attitudes and feels enlightened and unprejudiced. He or she may, nonetheless, still bear the burden of a middle-class history and bear the residual traces of the black stereotypes so current until only a few years ago. Moreover, if he or she tries to treat black students in the same way as white students, he or she finds that the black students will *not* be treated as if the teacher were colorblind. The black student wants his or her blackness recognized and respected. Hence the college teacher, like the ghetto-school teacher, often feels at a loss with respect to just what stance to take *vis-à-vis* black students.

A second continuity experienced by black students entering predominantly white colleges is a persistent confusion between educational goals and social ends. This confusion is as common among college teachers as it is among instructors in the ghetto schools. Indeed, it is a confusion which permeates the thinking of the white community generally. What the black student encounters in school as well as in college is the belief, on the part of whites, that the provision of good education for blacks will resolve the problem of racial prejudice in America. The fact that there are a good many well-educated blacks in America who are still subjected to restricted housing and job discrimination (although perhaps a little less today than heretofore) has not served to quell the idea that if blacks are provided with quality education our racial problems will be solved.

The final continuity between the ghetto school and the white college is the relative absence of black male teachers at all levels of schooling. It is true that increasing numbers of black teachers are working in ghetto schools, but they are almost all females. At the college level, the dearth of black teachers and the new demand for them have made black college teachers the most sought-after faculty in the college community. Despite this rush to hire black teachers, however, their number on predominantly white campuses is ridiculously small.

The lack of black male teachers has particular consequences for black male students. White males who are taught by females in the grade schools have fathers who provide a male role model at home, someone concrete after whom they can model their behavior. This is much less true in the ghetto family. To continue the contrast, when the white male enters the university, he finds an abundance of white male teachers with whom he can identify in order to establish his professional identity. But for the black student, establishing a professional identity means in part that he must identify with and model himself after an adult male who is white—a male towards whom he has strong antipathies. The black male in the predominantly white university thus has built-in resistances to acquiring a professional identity that have nothing at all to do with his intelligence or talent.

Many colleges and universities around the country are currently trying to provide liberal arts and professional training for disadvantaged black students. But such programs confront the student and the university with sociopsychological problems such as those described above. Both the students and the schools will be best served if these problems are dealt with openly and honestly.

Summary

Individual differences become more prominent during adolescence. Young people reach puberty at different ages, and it is believed that early-maturing boys and late-maturing girls have fewer adjustment problems than do late-maturing boys and early-maturing girls. During adolescence, body types become clear and different body types become associated with particular temperamental traits. Although thin people are not always introverted nor fat people always outgoing and jolly, it occurs much more often than would be expected by chance. Physical attractiveness is related to popularity but so too is attitude similarity, particularly among older adolescents.

In the junior and senior high schools sex-role stereotyping is still found in the curriculum that is offered, in the use of funds and facilities for athletics, and in the content of textbooks. Creative adolescents are also stereotyped. Although they are happy and see themselves as well-integrated in the school, they are not liked as much as intelligent but uncreative young people—at least by their teachers. At the other extreme are the high-school dropouts. Although their numbers have been decreasing, some 20 percent of all young people do not finish high school. There are usually many reasons for this, including a history of poor schoolwork, conflicts and problems within the family, and difficulty in dealing with peers.

Sex differences in adolescence are reflected in such findings as girls' superiority in verbal ability and boys' superiority in spatial tasks. Although girls are as bright as or brighter than boys, and do not differ from them in vocational aptitude, girls enter a more limited range of occupations than do boys. Sex differences also appear in the fact that girls are more self-conscious and have a lower self-esteem than do boys. This is undoubtedly due to our cultural attitudes toward women.

Family life influences the pattern of adolescent development. Some adolescents mature "continuously," others mature in "surges," and still others have a "tumultuous" experience. Another family influence on adolescents is whether or not the father is absent. Usually, a father's absence does not clearly affect girls until adolescence. Those girls who do not have a father living at home because of divorce tend to gravitate toward males, whereas those girls who have lost their father through death tend to gravitate away from males.

Finally, recent research suggests that there has been an increase in the self-esteem of black adolescents, particularly in social contexts where blacks are prominent as successful role models. Cross-culturally, it appears that American and Western European adolescents differ in how they view themselves, their parents, and their ego-ideals.

References

1. Tanner, J. M. Sequence, tempo and individual variation in the growth and development of boys and girls aged twelve to sixteen. *Daedalus,* 1971, 907–930.
2. Dwyer, J., & Mayer, J. Psychological effects of variations in physical appearance during adolescence. *Adolescence,* 1968–1969, 353–368.
3. Jones, M. C. The later careers of boys who were early- or late-maturing. *Child Development,* 1957, **28,** 113–128.
4. Latham, A. J. The relationship between pubertal status and leadership in junior high school boys. *Journal of Genetic Psychology,* 1951, **78,** 185–194.
5. More, D. M. Developmental concordance and discordance during puberty and early adolescence, *Child Development Monographs,* 1953, **18** (56).
6. Mussen, P. H., & Jones M. C. Self conceptions, motivations and interpersonal attitudes of late and early maturing boys. *Child Development,* 1957, **28,** 243–256.
7. Mussen, P. H., & Jones, M. C. The behavior-inferred motivations of late- and early-maturing boys. *Child Development,* 1958, **29,** 61–67.

8. Mussen, P. H., & Boutourline-Young, H. Relationships between rate of physical maturing and personality among boys of Italian descent. *Vita Humana,* 1964, **7,** 186–200.

9. Jones, M. C., & Bayley, N. Physical maturing among boys as related to behavior. *Journal of Educational Psychology,* 1950, **51,** 129–148.

10. Weatherly, D. Self perceived rate of physical maturation and personality in late adolescence. *Child Development,* 1964, **35,** 1197–1210.

11. Stolz, H. R., & Stolz, L. M. Adolescent problems related to somatic variations. In N. B. Henry (Ed.), *Adolescence: 43rd Yearbook of the National Committee for the Study of Education.* Chicago: University of Chicago Press, 1944.

12. Stone, S. P., & Barber, R. Attitudes and interests of pre- and post-menstrual females of the same chronological age. *Journal of Comparative and Physiological Psychology,* 1937, **23,** 439–455.

13. Stone, S. P., & Barber, R. Attitudes and interests of pre and post menstrual females. *Journal of Genetic Psychology,* 1939, **54,** 27–71.

14. Sheldon, W. *The varieties of temperament.* New York: Harper, 1942.

15. Parnell, R. W. *Behavior and physique: An introduction to practical and applied sociometry.* London: Edward Arnold, 1958.

16. Cortés, J. B., & Gatti, F. M. Physique and self description of temperament. *Journal of Consulting Psychology,* 1965, **29,** 432–439.

17. Davidson, M., McInnes, R., & Parnell, R. The distribution of personality traits in seven year old children: A combined psychological, psychiatric and somatotype study. *British Journal of Educational Psychology,* 1957, **27,** 48–61.

18. Roff, M., & Brody, D. S. Appearance and choice status during adolescence. *Journal of Psychology,* 1953, **36,** 347–356.

19. Stroebe, W., Insko, C. A., Thompson, V. D., & Layton, B. D. Effects of physical attractiveness, attitude similarity and sex on various aspects of interpersonal attraction. *Journal of Personality and Social Psychology,* 1971, **1,** 79–91.

20. Walster, E., Aronson, E., Abrahams, D., & Rottman, L. Importance of physical attractiveness in dating behavior. *Journal of Personality and Social Psychology,* 1966, **4,** 508–516.

21. Byrne, D., London, O., & Reeves, K. The effects of physical attractiveness, sex, and attitude similarity on interpersonal attraction. *Journal of Personality,* 1968, **36,** 259–271.

22. Cavior, N., & Dokecki, P. R. Physical attractiveness, perceived attitude similarity, and academic achievement as contributors to interpersonal attraction among adolescents. *Developmental Psychology,* 1973, **9,** 44–54.

23. Trecker, J. L. Sex stereotyping in the secondary school curriculum. *Phi Delta Kappan,* 1973, **55,** 110–112.

24. Saario, T. N., Jacklin, C. N., & Tittle, C. K. Sex role stereotyping in the public schools. *Harvard Educational Review,* 1973, **43,** 386–314.

25. U.S. Department of H.E.W., Office of Education, Bureau of Adult, Vocational and Technical Information. *Trends in Vocational Education.* Washington, D.C.: General Services Administration, 1972.

26. Leviten, T. E., Quinn, R. P., & Staines, G. L. A woman is fifty eight per cent of a man. *Psychology Today,* 1973, **6,** 89–101.

27. Shafer, S. M. Adolescent girls and future career mobility. In R. E. Grinder (Ed.). *Studies in adolescence,* New York: Macmillan, 1975.

28. Getzels, J. W., & Jackson, P. W. The meaning of "giftedness": An examination of an expanding concept. *Phi Delta Kappan,* 1958, **40,** 75–77.

29. Getzels, J. W., & Jackson, P. W. The highly intelligent and highly creative adolescent: A summary of some research findings. In C. W. Taylor & F. Barron (Eds.), *Scientific creativity: Its recognition and development.* New York: Wiley, 1963.

30. Walberg, H. J. Varieties of adolescent creativity and the high school environment. *Exceptional Children,* 1971, **38,** 111–116.

31. Walberg, H. J. A portrait of the artist and scientist as young men. *Exceptional Children,* 1969, **36,** 5–12.

32. Havighurst, R. J., Graham, R. A., & Eberly, D. American youth in the mid-seventies. *The Bulletin of the National Association of Secondary School Principals,* 1972, **56,** 1–13.

33. Young, A. M. The high school class of 1972: More at work, fewer in college. *Monthly Labor Review,* 1973, **96,** 26–32.

34. Fitzsimmons, S. J., Cheever, J., Leonard, E., & Macunovica, D. School failures: Now and tomorrow. *Developmental Psychology,* 1969, **1,** 134–146.

35. Cervantes, L. F. *The dropout: Causes and cures.* Ann Arbor: Univ. of Michigan Press, 1965.
36. Cervantes, L. F. Family background, primary relationships and the high school dropout. *Journal of Marriage and the Family,* 1965, **27,** 218–223.
37. Cervantes, L. F. The isolated nuclear family and the dropout. *The Sociological Quarterly,* 1965, **6,** 103–118.
38. Tuel, J. K. Dropout dynamics. *California Journal of Educational Research,* 1966, **17,** 5–11.
39. Andure, C. E. Identifying potential dropouts. *California Education,* 1965, **3,** 31.
40. Campbell, G. V. A review of the dropout problem. *Peabody Journal of Education,* 1966, **44,** 102–109.
41. Williams, R. L., & Pickens, J. W. Contributing factors to school departures in Georgia. *Psychological Reports,* 1967, **20,** 693–694.
42. Maccoby, E. E., & Jacklin, C. N. *The psychology of sex differences.* Stanford, Calif.: Stanford Univ. Press, 1974.
43. Walberg, H. J. Physics, femininity and creativity. *Developmental Psychology,* 1969, **1,** 47–54.
44. Harmon, L. W. The childhood and adolescent career plans of college women. *Journal of Verbal Behavior,* 1971, **1,** 45–56.
45. Flanagan, J. C., & Jung, S. M. *Progress in education: A sample survey (1960–1970).* Palo Alto, Calif.: American Institutes for Research, 1971.
46. Flanagan, J. C. Changes in school levels of achievement: Project TALENT ten and fifteen year retests. *Educational Researcher,* 1976, **5,** 6–8.
47. Hathaway, S. R., & Monachesi, E. D. *Adolescent personality and behavior, MMPI patterns of normal, delinquent, dropout, and other outcomes.* Minneapolis: University of Minnesota Press, 1963.
48. McKee, J. P., & Seriffs, A. C. The differential evaluation of males and females. *Journal of Personality,* 1957, **25,** 356–371.
49. McKee, J. P., & Sheriffs, A. C. Men's and women's beliefs, ideals and self concepts. *American Journal of Sociology,* 1959, **64,** 356–363.
50. Kohlberg, L. A cognitive developmental analysis of children's sex role concepts and attitudes. In E. E. Maccoby (Ed.), *The development of sex differences.* Stanford, Calif.: Stanford University Press, 1966.
51. Offer, D., & Howard, K. I. An empirical analysis of the Offer self-image questionnaire for adolescents. *Archives of General Psychiatry,* 1972, **27,** 529–533.
52. Watson, G., & Johnson, D. *Social psychology: Issues and insights.* Lincoln; University of Nebraska Press, 1972.
53. Bem, S. L., & Bem, D. J. Training the woman to know her place: The power of a nonconscious ideology. In D. W. Johnson (Ed.), *Contemporary social psychology.* Philadelphia: Lippincott, 1973.
54. Bohan, J. S. Age and sex differences in self concept. *Adolescence,* 1973, **31,** 379–384.
55. Rosenberg, M. *Society and the adolescent self image.* Princeton, N.J.: Princeton University Press, 1965.
56. Piers, E. V., & Harris, D. B. Age and other correlates of self concept in children. *Journal of Educational Psychology,* 1964, **55,** 91–95.
57. Rosenberg, F. R., & Simmons, R. G. Sex differences in the self concept at adolescence. *Sex Roles,* 1975, **1,** 147–159.
58. Rosenberg, M. Psychological selectivity in self esteem formation. In Sherif, C. W., & Sherif, M. (Eds.), *Attitude, ego involvement and change.* New York: Wiley, 1967.
59. Simmons, R. G., Rosenberg, F., & Rosenberg, M. Disturbance in self image at adolescence. *American Sociological Review,* 1973, **38,** 553–568.
60. Simmons, R. G., & Rosenberg, F. Sex, sex roles and self image. *Journal of Youth and Adolescence,* 1975, **4,** 229–258.
61. Musa, K. E., & Roach, M. E. Adolescent appearance and self concept. *Adolescence,* 1973, **8,** 385–393.
62. Baittle, B., & Offer, D. On the nature of male adolescent rebellion. In S. C. Feinstein, P. Giovacchini, & A. A. Miller (Eds.), *Annals of Adolescent Psychiatry.* New York: Basic Books, 1971.
63. Offer, D. *The psychological world of the teenager.* New York: Basic Books, 1969.
64. Offer, D., & Sabshin, M. The psychiatrist and the normal adolescent. *American Medical Association Archives of General Psychiatry 9,* 1963, 427–432.

65. Offer, D., & Offer, J. B. *From teenage to young manhood: A psychological study.* New York: Basic Books, 1975.

66. Biller, H. B., & Balnom, R. M. Father absence, perceived maternal behavior and masculinity of self concept among junior high school boys. *Developmental Psychology,* 1971, **4,** 178–181.

67. Hetherington, E. M. Effects of paternal absence on sex-typed behaviors of Negro and White pre-adolescent males. *Journal of Personality and Social Psychology,* 1966, **4,** 87–91.

68. Lynn, D. B. *The father: His role in child development.* Monterey, Calif.: Brooks, Cole, 1974.

69. Mussen, P., & Rutherford, E. Parent-child relations and parental personality in relation to young children's sex role preference. *Child Development,* 1963, **34,** 489–607.

70. Biller, H. B., & Weiss, S. D. The father-daughter relationship and the personality development of the female. *Journal of Genetic Psychology,* 1970, **116,** 79–93.

71. Santrock, J. W. Paternal absence, sex typing and identification. *Developmental Psychology,* 1970, **2,** 264–272.

72. Hetherington, E. M. Effects of father absence on personality development in adolescent daughters. *Developmental Psychology,* 1972, **7,** 313–323.

73. Hetherington, E. M., Cox, M., & Cox, R. Beyond father absence: Conceptualization of effects of divorce. *Paper presented at the meetings of the Society for Research in Child Development,* Denver, April 1975.

74. Rosenberg, M. *Society and the adolescent self image.* Princeton, N.J.: Princeton Univ. Press, 1965.

75. Sherwood, J. J. Self identity and referent others. *Sociometry,* 1965, **27,** 66–81.

76. Rosenberg, M., & Simmons, R. G. Black and white self esteem: the urban school child. *Rose Monograph Series, American Sociological Association,* 1972.

77. Powell, G. J. Self concept in black and white children. In S. J. Powell (Ed.), *Racism and mental health,* Pittsburgh: University of Pittsburgh Press, 1973.

78. Reese, C. Black self-concept, *Children Today,* March–April 1974, 24–26.

79. Tome, H. R. *Le moi et l'autre dans la conscience de l'adolescent.* Paris: Delachaux et Niestle, 1972.

80. Lutte, G. *Le moi ideal de l'adolescent.* Brussels: Dessart, 1971.

81. Kuvlesky, W. P., & Upham, W. K. Social ambitions of teen-age boys living in an economically depressed area of the south: a racial comparison. Paper read at the annual meeting of the Southern Sociological Society, Atlanta, 1967.

82. Kuvlesky, W. P., & Thomas, K. A. Social ambitions of Negro boys and girls from a metropolitan ghetto. *Journal of Vocational Behavior,* 1971, **1,** 177–187.

83. Elkind, D. Humanizing the curriculum. *Childhood Education,* 1977, **53,** 179–182.

84. Santrock, J. W. Effects of father absence on sex-typed behaviors in male children: Reason for the absence and age of onset of the absence. *The Journal of Genetic Psychology,* 1977, **130,** 3–10.

18 Abnormal Development

SCHIZOPHRENIA

Indications of Adolescent Schizophrenia

Outcome of Adolescent Schizophrenia

DEPRESSION AND SUICIDAL BEHAVIOR

Basic Facts about Adolescent Suicidal Behavior

Origins of Adolescent Suicidal Behavior

ACADEMIC UNDERACHIEVEMENT

Sociocultural Reasons for Academic Underachievement

Psychological Reasons for Academic Underachievement

Treatment

DELINQUENT BEHAVIOR

Incidence of Delinquency

Causes of Delinquency

Intervention

ESSAY

On the Continuity of Normal and Abnormal Behavior

SUMMARY

REFERENCES

The notions of adolescent turmoil we have discussed in the preceding chapters have three widely believed corollaries with respect to abnormal development:

1. All adolescents are a little crazy or at least neurotic—"One of the unique characteristics of adolescence . . . is the recurrent alternation of episodes of disturbed behavior with periods of quiescence" (1, p. 61).

2. It is difficult if not impossible to distinguish normal from abnormal development during these years—"The momentous biological and psychological changes are so great in this transition from childhood to young adulthood that the lines between normal and pathological are never more blurred or indistinct" (2, p. 693).

3. Most instances of seemingly deviant behavior in adolescents are short-lived disturbances that will disappear of their own accord—"The cure for adolescence belongs to the passage of time and the gradual maturation processes" (3, pp. 40–41).

Contrary to these beliefs, research findings show that only about 20 percent of adolescents have psychological problems that prevent them from functioning well at school or in social situations; another 60 percent feel mildly anxious or depressed on occasion, but without any major disruption in their daily life; and the remaining 20 percent show no signs of psychological disorder (4). These are the same percentages that are found among adults: approximately 20 percent suffer from moderate or severe psychological problems, 60 percent have mild or fleeting problems, and 20 percent have few or no problems (5).

Furthermore, clinicians who are knowledgeable about adolescent development are usually able to distinguish between normal and disturbed young people. Even though the usual variability of adolescents makes it difficult at times to determine exactly what kind of psychopathology they may have, it is seldom difficult for experienced professionals to tell what is normal from what is abnormal behavior (4, 6–8).

Moreover, data reported by Weiner and Del Gaudio indicate that serious disturbances among adolescents are just about as stable and likely to persist as among adults (9). Utilizing a countywide case register in Rochester, New York, they collected information on all 12- to 18-year-olds who had visited a psychiatric clinic, hospital, or office practitioner during a 2-year period. Then they kept track of each time any of their 1334 subjects returned for psychiatric help during the following 10 years.

Table 18.1 shows the percentage of patients in four diagnostic categories who displayed diagnostic stability—that is, their diagnosis remained about the same whenever they returned for further help. Information from a similar study with adult patients is also included for comparison (10). It can be seen that adolescents show less over-all diagnostic stability than do adults (60.0 percent versus 75.8 percent) but that for the most serious of these conditions, schizophrenia, an adult degree of stability has pretty well been established in adolescence (72.2 percent versus

Table 18.1 Adolescent and Adult Psychiatric Patients Who Demonstrated
Diagnostic Stability over Time

Diagnostic category	Adolescents		Adults	
	n	Stability (in Percentage)	n	Stability (in Percentage)
Schizophrenia	90	72.2	179	82.1
Other	495*	52.7	254**	71.3
Total	585	60.0	433	75.8

*Includes neurosis, personality disorder, and situational disorder
**Includes neurosis, personality disorder, situational disorder, acute brain syndrome, and
  psychophysiological reaction
Source: Based on data reported by Babigian, H., *et al.* Diagnostic consistency and change in a follow-up study of 1215 patients. *American Journal of Psychiatry,* 1965, **121,** 895-901. Weiner, I. B., & Del Gaudio, A. C. Psychopathology in adolescence: An epidemiological study. *Archives of General Psychiatry,* 1976, **33,** 187–193.

82.1 percent). Other followup studies of adolescent patients confirm that, despite the idea of "normative turmoil," their patterns of disturbance are sufficiently stable to be clearly distinguished from normal behavior (11–15).

There is also ample evidence demonstrating that adolescents who manifest obvious symptoms of behavior disorder rarely outgrow them. Those who *appear* disturbed are likely to *be* disturbed and to *remain* disturbed unless they receive adequate treatment (16, 17). In the Weiner and Del Gaudio study, for example, 54.2 percent of the adolescents returned for further psychiatric care after their first course of treatment had been finished, which is far beyond what would be expected if their disturbances had simply been maturational phenomena that should pass in time.

Studies of college students who have psychological problems that are serious enough to require professional help lead to the same conclusion. Most of these students are found to have had academic or social problems earlier in life that were not treated adequately and have become worse. Likewise, only a minority of college freshmen with behavior problems are passing through a temporary "adjustment reaction." Without adequate treatment, these young people continue to have adjustment problems 4 or 5 years later (18–20).

Psychological disturbance beginning in adolescence is largely accounted for by five conditions, each of which we have touched on in earlier chapters: schizophrenia, depression and suicidal behavior, school phobia, academic underachievement, and delinquent behavior. School phobia as it appears in adolescents was discussed in Chapter 15, and the other four conditions will be considered here.

SCHIZOPHRENIA

Approximately 25 to 30 percent of the adolescents admitted to psychiatric clinics and private offices are diagnosed as schizophrenic (8, 9). Because clinicians hesitate to attach a label to severe disorders in young people unless the symptoms are extremely clear-cut, these figures probably underestimate the frequency of schizophrenia among adolescents brought for professional help. Whatever the incidence of schizophrenia is among young people, it is generally agreed that most forms of schizophrenic disturbance begin during the adolescent and early adult years (21).

Given this fact, and in view of the potential severity and grave consequences of a schizophrenic disorder, the possibility of schizophrenia is usually considered when an adolescent begins to act in a peculiar or atypical manner. In Chapter 10 we discussed the incidence, symptoms, and origins of schizophrenia; here we will focus on certain indications and the outcome of schizophrenia that begins in adolescence.

Indications of
Adolescent
Schizophrenia

It is usually difficult to recognize and diagnose schizophrenia when it begins in adolescence. No more than 30 to 40 percent of schizophrenic young people initially show the disordered thinking, poor contact with reality, and inappropriate emotional responses that characterize this disturbance. The rest display a mixed picture in which these features of schizophrenia are secondary to or obscured by other kinds of symptom. For example, many young people in the early phases of a schizophrenic breakdown suffer mainly from symptoms of depression, including feelings of hopelessness, lack of interest in people or activities, and thoughts about suicide. Others seems to have a conduct disorder, with complaints of restlessness and difficulty concentrating and a history of family conflict, stealing, fighting, running away, truancy, and school failure (4, 22–24).

Evidence from studies by Watt and others suggests that boys and girls who are developing schizophrenia change in different ways during their high-school years. As children, preschizophrenic boys tend to have been less happy and cheerful than other boys, and as adolescents they tend to become more irritable, aggressive, negativistic, and defiant of authority. Preschizophrenic girls tend to have been emotionally immature and more outgoing than other girls as children, and as adolescents they tend to become increasingly shy and inhibited and to withdraw from peer-group activities (25–28). These and other characteristics that distinguish preschizophrenic adolescents from their peers, as described by their teachers, are listed in Table 18.2.

In another interesting piece of research, Barthell and Holmes looked back at how many pictures of adults who became schizophrenic had been included in their high-school yearbooks (29). There were significantly fewer pictures of these preschizophrenic youngsters than of a comparison group of their classmates, which may be taken as an index of their lack of

Table 18.2 Significant Differences between Preschizophrenic High-School Students and Controls as Described by Their Teachers

Boys		Girls	
Controls	Preschizophrenic	Controls	Preschizophrenic
Achieving	Underachieving	Secure	Insecure
Dependable	Undependable	Mature	Immature
Self-controlled	Emotional	Adjusted	Maladjusted
Cheerful	Depressed	Sociable	Unsociable
Adjusted	Maladjusted	Talkative	Quiet
Pleasant	Unpleasant	Considerate	Egocentric
Cooperative	Negativistic		
Considerate	Egocentric		
Well-behaved	Antisocial		

Source: Based on data reported by Watt, N. F., & Lubensky, A. W. Childhood roots of schizophrenia. *Journal of Consulting and Clinical Psychology,* 1976, **44,** 363–375.

participation in peer-group activities (at least in school) prior to their becoming overtly disturbed.

Generally speaking, then, young people who become schizophrenic during or soon after adolescence tend to have passed through childhood without having been successful in making friends. They either kept to themselves and avoided other children, or they served as an exploiter or a flunky with their peers, rather than as a mutual partner in genuine friendships (30, 31). Hard-pressed to cope with the interpersonal demands of adolescence, preschizophrenics either become more withdrawn and depressed or they become antisocial and delinquent. Later, as their disorder becomes entrenched, these young people begin to show the characteristic schizophrenic impairments of thinking, reality testing, and emotional integration.

Outcome of Adolescent Schizophrenia

Among adults who are hospitalized for the first time because of a schizophrenic breakdown, approximately one-third recover, another one-third improve sufficiently to be discharged from the hospital but suffer occasional relapses that require rehospitalization, and the remaining one-third fail to improve and remain permanently hospitalized. Modern methods in treating schizophrenia appear to be increasing somewhat the percentage of hospitalized patients who can return home. However, this increased discharge rate has been accompanied by an increased rate of rehospitalization; only about 15 to 40 percent of adult schizophrenics living in the community are able to achieve what most people would regard as an average level of adjustment (32).

The course of adolescent schizophrenia closely resembles this adult pattern, although those who develop schizophrenia before the age of 30 have somewhat less favorable prospects than those who develop it later

(33). Data collected from five follow-up studies conducted at different times in different parts of the world indicate that 23 percent of adolescents who have been hospitalized for schizophrenia recover, 25 percent improve but suffer lingering symptoms or occasional relapses, and the remaining 52 percent make little or no progress and require continuing residential care (34–38). Unfortunately, there is little information of this type on schizophrenic adolescents who do not require hospitalization. It is possible that these young people have a better chance to improve or recover than those who have been hospitalized.

Besides the severity of schizophrenia, six other factors influence its outcome in adolescents. In general, young people have better prospects for early improvement or complete recovery if (a) they are older when schizophrenia first appears, (b) their previous school and social adjustment has been adequate, (c) their disturbance begins suddenly, (d) they respond quickly to initial treatment, (e) their family is able to accept their disturbance, and (f) their future treatment, school, work, and living arrangements can be adequately planned (8, 39–42).

Treatment of schizophrenic adolescents concentrates on helping them develop or re-establish effective ties with reality and with other people. Many kinds of psychotherapy are used to achieve these ends, including both individual therapy and therapy with groups and families. Antipsychotic drugs may be included in the treatment program to reduce particularly disruptive symptoms and facilitate progress in psychotherapy. For those requiring residential care, a *milieu* program is often helpful, in which a series of structured activities involving schoolwork, recreation, and socializing among the patients are incorporated as regular parts of the treatment plan (43–45).

DEPRESSION AND SUICIDAL BEHAVIOR

In adolescents as in younger children, depressive disorders are not diagnosed very often, even though depression is fairly common at this age. Between 35 and 40 percent of junior high school, senior high school, and college students report having some feelings of sadness, worthlessness, or pessimism about the future, although not to the extent that their schoolwork or social activities are substantially impaired (4, 46, 47). Among adolescents who are seen in psychiatric clinics and hospitals, fewer than 10 percent are diagnosed as being primarily depressed (4 percent of 10- to 14-year-olds, 7 percent of 15- to 17-year-olds, and 11 percent of 18- to 19-year-olds); yet half of these youngsters are likely to exhibit such depressive symptoms as melancholia, self-depreciation, crying spells, and suicidal thoughts or attempts (48).

Of all mental disorders, depression is the one that poses the greatest risk of suicide (49, 50); as noted by Silverman, "Suicide is the mortality of depressive illness" (51, p. 157). Feelings of depression are thus important in the study of adolescent psychopathology both because of their frequency and because of their relationship to suicidal behavior.

Basic Facts about Adolescent Suicidal Behavior

Actual suicide is rare among children and adolescents. In 1971 young people below the age of 20 accounted for less than 6 percent of the 24,092 known suicides in the United States, and 90 percent of these suicidal youths were between 15 and 19 (52). Thus, the suicide rate increases sharply from early to later adolescence—from 0.7 per 100,000 young people aged 10 to 14 to 6.6 per 100,000 15- to 19-year-olds. Among adults the suicide rate climbs steadily from 13.7 per 100,000 at age 25 to 34 to 21.6 per 100,000 at age 55 to 64, and it remains at about this level to the age of 85 (see Figure 18.1).

Although suicide occurs less often among adolescents than among adults, it is more likely to be a cause of death during the late teen years than at any other time in life. This is due in part to the fact that adolescents as a group enjoy relatively good physical health: they are no longer afflicted with various childhood diseases, and they are not yet susceptible to many of the chronic illnesses that plague older people. As shown in Table 18.3, suicide is the eleventh leading cause of death among the general population in the United States but the fourth leading cause for those between 15 and 19.

Figure 18.1 Suicide rates in the United States by age groups. (*Source:* Based on data from *Vital Statistics of the United States,* 1971, **2,** *Mortality.* Rockville, Md.: U.S. Department of Health, Education, and Welfare, 1975.)

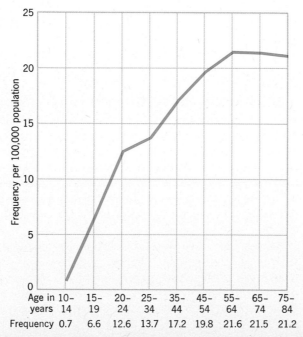

Age in years	10–14	15–19	20–24	25–34	35–44	45–54	55–64	65–74	75–84
Frequency	0.7	6.6	12.6	13.7	17.2	19.8	21.6	21.5	21.2

Table 18.3 Leading Causes of Death among Adolescents in the United States

Cause	Age 15-19		General Population	
	Rate per 100,000	Rank	Rate per 100,000	Rank
Accidents	63.8	1	54.9	4
Homicide	8.5	2	9.1	12
Cancer	6.9	3	163.2	2
Suicide	6.6	4	11.7	11
Heart disease	4.0	5	359.5	1

Based on data from *Vital statistics of the United States, 1971.* Vol. II, *Mortality.* Rockville, Md.: U.S. Department of Health, Education, and Welfare, 1975.

Even though adolescents are much less likely to commit suicide than are adults, they are equally likely to make suicide attempts. Approximately one out of every 1000 adolescents in the United States attempts suicide each year, which is the same 0.1 percent yearly rate as estimated for adults (50). Although adolescents account for less than 6 percent of the actual suicides in this country each year, they account for 12 percent of the known attempts (53). As in the case of most deviant behavior, however, these figures are probably underestimates, especially among young people (54). Parents often try to deny or hide the suicide attempts of their youngsters, and well-meaning professionals sometimes record them as accidents.

Among adolescents who consider suicide, boys are far more likely than girls to kill themselves—by a ratio of more than three to one (52); on the other hand, girls account for 80 to 90 percent of the adolescent suicide attempts (53, 55). The same sex difference holds for adults: men are three times more likely to commit suicide, whereas women are three times more likely to attempt it. Since 1970, however, there has been a slight decrease in these sex differences in suicidal behavior, which may be one reflection of the general trend in our society toward less distinct sex-role differences (54, 56).

Adolescents also differ by sex in the methods they use to commit suicide. As can be seen in Figure 18.2, most boys who kill themselves use firearms or explosives, whereas most girls take poison (52). For those who only attempt suicide, poison is the most common method—used by about 80 percent of the boys and 90 percent of the girls (57, 58).

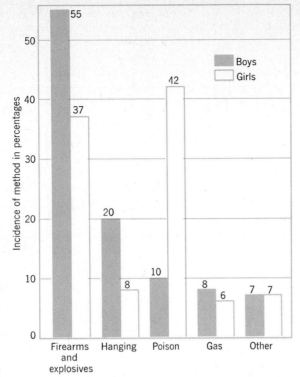

Figure 18.2 Suicide methods used by adolescents. (*Source: Based on data from Vital Statistics of the United States, 1971, **2,** Mortality.* Rockville, Md.: U.S. Department of Health, Education, and Welfare, 1975.)

Origins of Adolescent Suicidal Behavior

Adolescent suicidal behavior has sometimes been viewed as a sudden, impulsive reponse to some immediate disappointment or frustration, such as failing a test, being jilted by a boyfriend or girlfriend, or losing an argument with one's parents. However, in-depth studies of suicidal adolescents indicate that their behavior has much more complex origins than these. Young people who attempt suicide have usually experienced increasing family instability and discord, which has led them to feel alienated from their parents and unable to turn to them for support. These adolescents have often been desperately seeking closeness and emotional support from other people, only to have the relationships they value most collapse for one reason or another. Faced with mounting family conflict, dissolving social relationships, and an increasing sense of isolation and helplessness, they have gradually come to the conclusion that suicide is the only alternative left (59–64).

Lonely, alienated young people from disrupted or disorganized homes thus constitute a high-risk group for suicidal behavior. As to whether this risk will become a reality, the most clear-cut factor that appears to influence the decision of a depressed adolescent to attempt suicide is the presence of a suicidal model. In one study of suicidal adolescents, 44 percent knew about the suicide or attempted suicide of a close friend or relative, and 25 percent had had a parent make a suicide attempt (65).

It is also important to recognize that adolescent suicide attempts are nearly always efforts by troubled youngsters to communicate their distress, particularly to their parents, and to bring about a change in how they are being treated by others. For this reason, attempted suicide is often called "a cry for help" (66, 67). Furthermore, since these attempts among young people are usually intended to make an impact on their parents, the vast majority of attempts are made at home, often while the parents are there.

What follows adolescent suicide attempts largely depends upon their impact. If a suicide attempt startles an adolescent's parents into recognizing his or her difficulties, and if the parents begin to offer some help with or at least talk more acceptingly about these difficulties, there is a good chance of forestalling another attempt. On the other hand, if the parents show little reaction to a suicide attempt, if they fail to see it as a reason for changing their behavior, or—even worse—if they treat it with anger or ridicule rather than with sympathetic understanding, there is considerable risk that their offspring will make further and more serious suicide attempts (8, Chap. 5).

Research reports bear grim testimony to the aftermath of suicide attempts that fail to achieve their purpose. Of adults who kill themselves, 75 percent have previously made suicide attempts or gestures, and more than 20 percent of adults who make a suicide attempt eventually die by their own hand (68, 69). Among adolescents who attempt suicide, as many as 46 percent have been found to have previously threatened or attempted suicide, which far exceeds the 0.1 percent yearly rate among adolescents at large (70).

ACADEMIC
UNDER-
ACHIEVEMENT

Academic underachievement appearing in adolescence usually has a long history. In a study of equally bright achieving and underachieving high-school students who had gone through school together, Shaw and Mc-Cuen found that the underachieving boys had tended to receive lower grades than the achieving boys beginning in the very first grade. By the third grade, the underachievers had dropped to a significantly lower performance level, and they declined in achievement each year up to the tenth grade. A similar but somewhat delayed pattern was found for under-achieving girls; they began to receive lower grades than the achieving girls in the sixth grade and by the ninth grade they had a significantly lower performance level (71). Whereas minimal brain dysfunction is the most common reason for school failure among elementary-school children with adequate intelligence, among adolescents such failure is more commonly due to sociocultural and psychological factors.

Sociocultural factors lead to academic underachievement by providing young people with little *motivation* or *opportunity* to learn. Students who are motivated to work hard in school tend to be interested in learning. Doing well in school gives them a sense of satisfaction, and they see a definite relationship between their school achievement and realizing some long-range goals, such as getting a certain kind of job or getting into college. Students who are content to get by in school without applying themselves usually do not have this kind of motivation. More often than not they dislike school and do not see any relationship between what they learn there and what they will be doing in the future (72–74).

Lack of motivation has also proved to be a significant reason for leaving school. Contrary to what might be expected, fewer than 10 percent of those who quit school do so because of failing grades or lack of money. Rather, the most common reason why boys leave school is "lack of interest" and for girls it is marriage or pregnancy (75).

Young people generally acquire their attitudes toward school from their families. It has been found consistently that parents of underachieving adolescents place less emphasis on education than do parents of achieving adolescents; these parents, therefore, are not likely to encourage either intellectual interests or positive attitudes toward teachers and the school (76, 77). As we have noted earlier, parents who doubt the usefulness of formal education as a way of getting ahead in life pay little attention to how their children are doing in school. The rewards and punishments they employ in child rearing seldom have anything to do with whether their youngsters are doing their homework or receiving good grades. As a consequence, their children are not likely to develop much motivation to achieve academically.

The responsibility for such indifference to formal education, especially among lower-class and some minority youths, does not lie entirely on the parents' shoulders, however. For many of these young people, as well as for many first-generation Americans, the schools are too out of touch with their way of life to be able to understand their needs and give them a meaningful education. Moreover, as also mentioned previously, the schools have often given these youngsters' parents good reason to regard them as hostile, uncaring, patronizing, middle-class institutions, and as a result the parents have deliberately directed their children's energies elsewhere (78).

The peer group can also contribute to low motivation to achieve in school. If adolescents belong to a clique that belittles academic achievement as not only unimportant but "unmanly" or "unfeminine," their needs for peer-group acceptance may override any academic motivation they might otherwise have had (73, 79, 80). In a study of young people from an inner-city neighborhood who dropped out or remained in school, Cervantes reports an interesting confirmation of this peer-group influence. When asked about trends in their neighborhood, those who remained in school said they believed that the majority of high-school students in their neighborhood were planning to continue in school, whereas the dropouts said that most of their neighborhood group were planning to leave school. In other words, these groups of young people from the *same neighborhood* perceived the neighborhood differently, to fit with their own actions (81).

Disadvantaged adolescents' motivation to stay in school may also be undermined by role-models whose success or failure in life has no relationship to formal education. Inner-city youth may see many adults who owe whatever success they achieve to shrewdness rather than to formal education, and this does little to establish the value of school in these children's eyes. However, when black, Puerto Rican, and other disadvantaged minority-group adults who have benefited from formal education become visible to their own young people—as is beginning to happen in banks, department stores, and numerous skilled trades and professions—then these young people will come to regard school as a means of success-

Being part of a peer group that places some value on school learning helps adolescents achieve at the level of their abilities. When the peer group penalizes members who do well in school, on the other hand, underachievement may result.

ful adaptation to the adult world. Without such visible role-models, adolescents may find it easy to discount whatever their parents or teachers say about the importance of school.

With respect to opportunity, adolescents need an adequate educational background in order to be able to realize their academic potential in high school and beyond. One of the most important sociocultural reasons for high-school underachievement is the lack of good elementary-school preparation. Children who attend underequipped and understaffed schools and who sit in crowded classrooms listening to bored or inept teachers may never acquire the basic academic skills and study habits that are necessary for handling high-school work. The inequality of educational opportunity is most obvious in certain inner-city schools and those in depressed rural areas, where money and facilities are in shortest supply. On the other hand, it should not be overlooked that there are many good schools operating in economically poor areas and many fine, underpaid teachers working in these schools.

Psychological Reasons for Academic Underachievement

The psychological reasons for academic underachievement usually involve maladaptive patterns of family interaction that include (a) some underlying hostility of an adolescent toward his or her parents that cannot be expressed directly; (b) some concerns about rivalry with one or more family members that lead to a fear of failure or a fear of success; and (c) a passive-aggressive style of behavior. These three neurotic patterns often occur together to constitute a specific psychological disturbance that is called **passive-aggressive underachievement** (82–84).

Hostility toward Parents. Passive-aggressive underachievers tend to have considerable resentment toward their parents, usually because of parental authoritarianism that has included heavy academic pressure (76, 85, 86). These parents typically expect or demand high grades from their children, often higher than they could earn even if they were working to capacity. In addition, they often try to impose on their youngster certain long-term academic goals (such as getting into an Ivy League school) or career directions (such as becoming a lawyer or physician) that are important to them but that do not particularly interest their son or daughter.

Because passive-aggressive underachievers have difficulty expressing their resentment directly, they cannot complain openly about their parents' demands and expectations (87). Instead, they express it indirectly through poor school performance. This is an effective means of retaliation, since poor grades distress these youngsters' parents and frustrate their aspirations. However, underachievement is often a self-defeating maneuver, since it may also prevent a young person from realizing his or her own educational and career goals.

Concerns about Rivalry. Passive-aggressive underachievers typically suffer from fears of failing or fears of succeeding that inhibit their

Some adolescents do poorly in school as an indirect way of expressing anger or resentment toward their parents. (Drawing by Lorenz; © 1970 The New Yorker Magazine, Inc.)

"Do you realize, young man, what C-minus can mean in terms of lifetime earnings?"

academic efforts. Those who fear failure have a low opinion of their abilities and believe that there is no way in which they can rival the accomplishments of their parents and siblings. They are discouraged by the slightest criticism, and the more their family expresses disappointment in them ("Why can't you get the marks your brother does?"), the less they try to achieve anything in school.

To maintain some self-respect, adolescents who fear failure often set unrealistically high goals for themselves and then work only halfheartedly to attain them. In this way they try to deny their limitations and escape any feeling of having been a failure: their ambitious goals give them a ready-made excuse for not succeeding, and their lackadaisical effort provides the often-heard rationalization "I could have done better if I had wanted to, but I really didn't feel like working hard." Thus, these adolescents carefully hedge their bets. They rarely risk making a mistake, they consistently deny having exerted themselves even when they have, and they pride themselves on what they have been able to accomplish with minimal effort ("I got a C without even cracking a book").

By contrast, adolescents who fear success are concerned that if they do well in school, the less able members of their family will be envious or resentful. Since these young people do not want to be criticized or rejected for their accomplishments, they make light of their own abilities. They set limited goals that are easily within their grasp, and having achieved them, they neither announce nor work toward anything more ambitious ("I was lucky to do as well as I did"). By taking this approach to their studies, adolescents who fear success do not achieve anything that they think might threaten other people or diminish their affection (88, 89).

Passive-aggressive underachievement that is due to a fear of success usually arises at a time when young people are on the verge of surpassing their parents. This neurotic reaction is responsible in part for the disproportionately large number of high-school dropouts among children whose parents did not complete high school; it also accounts for many cases in which children of high-school-educated parents begin to do poorly in their final years of high school, thereby reducing their chances of getting into college—the so-called **senior neurosis** (90). This situation may develop if parents are *overtly* enthusiastic about college but communicate a different *covert* message, such as: "We've had a good life without a college education; now you're going to go away, and it will cost us a lot of money, and you'll get all kinds of new ideas, and we'll never be close as a family again."

Passive-aggressive Style of Behavior. A passive-aggressive behavioral style is a means of problem-solving by purposeful inactivity. Passive-aggressive underachievers take pains to make sure that they do *not* do the kinds of things that would earn them good grades. More than anything else, they can be distinguished from achieving students by their lack of effort and by the almost unbelievable inefficiency of their study habits when they do make an effort (73, 91, 92).

Thus, it is not unusual for bright underachievers to read widely but not to read material that has been assigned as homework, and to keep themselves informed about almost everything except what is to be discussed in class or asked on examinations. If passive-aggressive underachievers should happen to absorb information related to their schoolwork, they use other techniques to prevent their knowledge from improving their grades: they remain silent during class discussions, or they "forget" to write down or turn in assignments, or they "misunderstand" or "overlook" a section of an examination. It is important to stress that these techniques are indirect, neurotic efforts to express anger and avoid rivalry; there is usually no conscious awareness of their origin and purpose, or even that they are responsible for poor achievement.

Treatment   Ways of treating underachievement and the results that can be expected depend upon its specific cause. Underachievement that is due to sociocultural factors often proves difficult to change, since it is so closely related to the environmental variables that have been influencing the young person for many years. To be successful, any treatment must promote a value system that differs from the one that has led to the problem; that is, a system in which academic success is seen as rewarding and useful for the future. Despite many obstacles in attempting to modify long-standing value systems, a number of behavioral methods are proving to be useful in helping young people change their viewpoint about school learning and thus reverse their previous underachievement (73).

As in the case of most neurotic disturbances in young people, on the other hand, psychologically determined underachievement is relatively easy to modify. Psychotherapy aimed at helping passive-aggressive underachievers recognize their underlying resentment toward their parents and expressing it more directly can fairly quickly reduce or eliminate the need to express it indirectly through poor grades. Work with parents to help them understand and curtail the pressure they are putting on their offspring can also contribute to a fairly rapid reversal of this pattern of underachievement (8, Chap. 7).

DELINQUENT BEHAVIOR   Delinquent behavior consists of acts that violate the law. Despite the apparent clarity of this statement, delinquency among young people is difficult to define and measure. It covers an enormous range of crimes, from felonies (assault, robbery) and misdemeanors (loitering, drunkenness) to behavior that is illegal only because of the person's age (purchasing liquor, running away from home). Among young people who commit illegal acts, furthermore, only some are caught; of those who are caught only some are arrested; and of those who are arrested only some come to trial in juvenile court (93–95).

For these reasons it is almost impossible to know how much delinquency there is, who should be called a "delinquent," or which kinds of young people should be studied in order to learn more about the nature and origins of delinquent behavior. Indeed, any general statement about "delinquents" or "delinquency" that does not take these complexities into account should be taken with a grain of salt, whether it appears in the popular media or in the professional literature.

Incidence of
Delinquency

Although the exact extent of delinquency is not known, statistical reports
from the U.S. Children's Bureau and the Department of Justice indicate
that it is a major and steadily increasing problem. Each year approximately 3 percent of American children between the age of 10 and 17
appear in juvenile court for offenses other than traffic violations, and the
rate of juvenile court cases has increased more rapidly than the population
of young people almost every year since 1961 (see Figure 18.3) (96). It is
estimated that one out of every nine young people will make a court
appearance before his or her eighteenth birthday (97). Boys outnumber
girls among those arrested by a ratio of 3.4 to one, and three times as
many urban as rural adolescents appear in juvenile courts (97, 98).

In assessing these figures, one must take into consideration the fact that
the existence of a juvenile court in a community appears to increase the
likelihood that an adolescent will be arrested, perhaps because the police
are more willing to arrest juveniles when they know that there are special
facilities for dealing with them (99). Hence the establishment of juvenile
and family courts in our cities and towns may have had the paradoxical
effect of increasing the number of adolescents who are arrested, perhaps
faster than actual increases in the teenage crime rate.

Similarly, the sex and social-class characteristics of juveniles who appear in court may have less to do with who commits crimes than with who
gets arrested for them. Specifically, it is known that boys and lower-class
youngsters are more likely to be arrested than girls and middle-class adolescents who have committed the same offenses (100). On the other hand,
data collected by Gold from a representative sample of adolescents in a
medium-sized community points to some real sex- and social-class differences in the number and seriousness of offenses committed, whether or
not the acts were discovered. The boys in Gold's sample were much more
likely than the girls to have committed delinquent acts, and the lower-

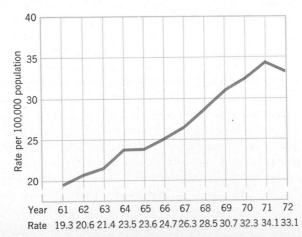

Figure 18.3 Rates of
juvenile court cases per
100,000 population of
10- to 17-year-olds.
(*Source:* Based on data
from U.S. Children's
Bureau, *Juvenile court
statistics.* Washington,
D.C.: Department of
Health, Education, and
Welfare, 1974.)

Year 61 62 63 64 65 66 67 68 69 70 71 72
Rate 19.3 20.6 21.4 23.5 23.6 24.7 26.3 28.5 30.7 32.3 34.1 33.1

class boys reported more delinquency than the middle-class boys; however, there were no social-class differences among the girls (95).

The significance of juvenile crimes must also be assessed in light of the adult crime rate and the nature of the offenses committed. Young people below the age of 18 account for 25.6 percent of the total arrests in the United States (excluding traffic violations), but adolescents also constitute about 25 percent of the population (98). Thus, contrary to common belief, adolescents are not responsible for a disproportionate share of the lawbreaking in this country. On the other hand, it is hardly reassuring to think that our young people already have the same arrest rate as do adults.

As for the type of offenses committed, in 1974 42 percent of the total arrests of youngsters under 18 were on charges of running away, loitering, curfew violation, disorderly conduct, drunkenness, violation of liquor laws, and the like (98). In a discussion of abnormal behavior it is important to distinguish between these minor infractions of the law, especially when they occur for the first time or only once, and serious crimes and repetitive delinquency. Any and all violations of the law can be a source of public concern, but it is the serious and repetitive violations that demand special attention from mental health professionals. Long-term followup studies indicate that those who display prominent antisocial behavior during their school years are likely as adults to have a high frequency of arrests, alcoholism, divorce, unemployment, child neglect, dependency on social agencies, and psychiatric hospitalization (101).

Causes of Delinquency

Delinquent behavior stems from three types of cause. As one cause, antisocial conduct may be a secondary symptom of psychotic, organic, or neurotic disturbances. Adolescents with schizophrenia or brain dysfunction sometimes commit crimes because they lack the judgment to tell right from wrong or because they cannot control their impulses (8, Chap. 8). Some forms of epilepsy, in particular, may lead to youthful outbursts of angry, assaultive, antisocial behavior (102–104). Neuroses contribute to delinquent behavior primarily in the form of reactions to depression, which we discussed in Chapter 14 in relation to the conduct disorders of middle childhood. An example would be children who steal or vandalize property after the death of a parent.

In most cases, however, repetitive delinquency is due to either antisocial cultural influences or an antisocial personality style. These other two major causes of juvenile delinquency produce two kinds of delinquent youngster—the *sociological* and the *characterological*.

Sociological Delinquency. **Sociological delinquents** are usually well-adjusted members of a subculture that holds antisocial values. These delinquents generally collaborate with other adolescents to commit crimes that earn them status and recognition in their peer group. Subcultures that foster sociological delinquency grant prestige to successful law-breakers and reject those who refuse to participate in antisocial activities. In such a context, then, delinquent youths experience a sense of self-esteem and belongingness, while nondelinquents feel outcast and unworthy (105–108).

Consistent with the fact that they are psychologically well-adjusted members of their group, sociological delinquents have usually enjoyed good family relationships during their early life. As infants and preschoolers, they have had attentive parents and siblings who helped them develop their basic capacities for judgment, self-control, and interpersonal relatedness. Later on, however, as elementary-school children and adolescents, they have usually received little parental supervision, and they have been influenced less by their family than by antisocial models outside the home. Thus, sociological delinquency tends to be associated with unsupervised development in a disorganized home that is located in a deteriorated, high-delinquency neighborhood (109–111).

However, it would be mistaken to conclude that sociological delinquency occurs uniquely as a product of lower-class neighborhoods and values. In the first place, delinquent adolescent groups are considered deviant in all social classes. The actions of delinquent gangs are usually as disturbing and unacceptable to lower-class as to middle-class adults. Second, even though delinquent groups are found more often in lower-class neighborhoods, delinquency is very much a middle-class as well as lower-class phenomenon, including the formation of troublemaking gangs (112–116). Third, middle-class adolescents commit just about the same kinds of delinquent acts as lower-class youths (116, 117).

Characterological Delinquency. In contrast to sociological delinquents, **characterological delinquents** are usually loners who have no group membership or loyalties. They commit their crimes alone or perhaps in temporary alliance with one or two other delinquents, whom they seldom regard as friends. The offenses of these delinquents represent a direct translation of aggressive, acquisitive, and pleasure-seeking impulses into immediate action: they break the law simply to express anger, satisfy a whim, or obtain something they want, and not because they are trying to impress their peers or qualify for peer-group acceptance (99).

A characterological delinquent's self-centeredness and lack of interest in social-group membership typify a character disorder called **psychopathic** or **sociopathic personality.** Disorders of character do not begin to take shape until late adolescence or early adulthood, at the point when identity becomes integrated and one's individual personality style is fairly crystallized. The unique thing about a **character disorder,** as opposed to a neurotic disturbance, is that its symptoms are not "alien" or disturbing to the person who has them; rather, they are simply part of his or her nature and a comfortable way of being. In this respect the difference between *character* and *character disorder* is not always obvious. In fact, the difference between them is often defined externally—an individual's personality style becomes labeled a "character disorder" when other people see his or her behavior as markedly offensive, self-defeating, or antisocial.

Psychopathic personality is the major character disorder that emerges during adolescence. It is most often seen in characterologically delinquent youngsters, although psychopaths do not necessarily commit criminal acts. The two major features of a psychopathic personality are an underdeveloped conscience and an inability to identify with other people. Because they lack conscience, psychopaths feel little guilt about harming other people; they can trample on others' rights and feelings without the slightest remorse. Because they cannot identify with other people, psychopaths are essentially loveless individuals. Their emotional relationships are shallow and fleeting, and they have little capacity for loyalty and devotion to anyone but themselves (118–120).

A psychopathic personality style emerges primarily in people who have experienced severe parental rejection during their early life, especially when this rejection has been manifest in arbitrary, inconsistent, or nonexistent discipline. Rejected children form deep reservoirs of anger, resentment, suspicion, and distrust. Reared without parental affection, they rarely become capable of compassion and interpersonal warmth. They have learned not to expect consideration or nurturance from others, and they see little reason for not exploiting to the full a world that they have found to be hostile and uncaring (101, 121–123).

Intervention   Sociological and characterological delinquency pose enormous obstacles to any form of corrective intervention. Sociological delinquents are well-integrated members of a group they value, and they have little reason to change; characterological delinquents suffer from long-standing personality impairments that are extremely difficult to modify.

What little success there has been in combating sociological delinquency has been due mainly to social action programs, such as job-upgrading projects and the Police Athletic League (93, 124, 125). The goal of such neighborhood-based programs is to convince delinquent youths that there are ways of having fun and making money that can be as rewarding as criminal behavior without the risk of going to jail. Some progress has also been made with these young people through individual counseling to help them identify, prepare for, and obtain jobs they will like (126, 127).

Characterological delinquents need prolonged and intensive psychotherapy to modify their long-standing psychological problems, and the success rate even in the most ambitious of these programs is limited (128, 129). Considerable ingenuity has been used to apply new treatment methods in these programs, especially behavioral and family-oriented

Table 18.4   Major Differences between Sociological and Characterological Delinquents

Sociological Delinquents	Characterological Delinquents
1. Are psychologically well-adjusted	1. Are maladjusted; have psychopathic personality
2. Are accepted members of their delinquent group	2. Have no group membership; have little sense of loyalty to others
3. Commit crimes in collaboration with friends	3. Commit crimes alone; rarely seek or make friends
4. Have good family relationship in early life, followed by inadequate parental supervision in middle childhood and adolescence	4. Have experienced severe parental rejection since early life

methods (130, 131). However, there is as yet no basis for optimism about being able to modify delinquent behavior that is rooted in long-standing character pathology.

Essay

ON THE CONTINUITY OF NORMAL AND ABNORMAL BEHAVIOR

Throughout this book we have placed chapters on normal and abnormal development side by side, because we believe firmly in the continuity of normality and abnormality in human behavior. From this point of view the differences between disturbed and well-adjusted persons are *quantitative* (a matter of degree) rather than *qualitative* (a matter of kind).

According to the continuity (or quantitative) perspective, the same personality factors account for both normal and abnormal behavior; maladjusted individuals simply have more or less than the optimum amount of a particular trait. For example, a moderate amount of self-control contributes to good adjustment, whereas too little self-control can lead to pathological impulsivity and too much self-control to pathological inhibition and rigidity. Likewise, a moderate capacity to reflect upon one's experience tends to promote good adjustment, whereas not enough reflection can lead to poor planning and judgment and too much reflection to paralyzing indecision and self-consciousness.

The continuity approach sees the boundary between normality and abnormality as a two-way street: every aspect of a disturbed person's behavior can be understood as an exaggeration of a normal way of thinking, feeling, or acting; and every normal person can occasionally think, feel, or act as neurotic or even psychotic people do. The difference between them is one of degree—normal people behave less often in an exaggerated fashion and can more effectively stop themselves from doing so than people whom clinicians would consider psychologically disturbed.

There is no way to provide conclusive evidence that this quantitative perspective is more accurate than viewing normality and abnormality as qualitatively different, that is, as representing different kinds or dimensions of personality functioning. All quantitative differences can be looked at qualitatively as well. For example, in the case of two men, one of whom is 5′8″ tall and the other 5′11″, an observer could say that they are both of medium height, but that one is taller than the other. This would be a quantitative distinction emphasizing continuity between them. Another observer could simply describe them as "the tall one" and "the short one." This would be a qualitative distinction emphasizing discontinuity. Since both observers would be technically correct, you could choose whichever point of view you preferred.

With respect to normal and abnormal behavior, we prefer the continuity viewpoint for two reasons. First, this approach discourages us from regarding psychologically disturbed persons as "different" from the rest of us. If we can think of these people as having "more of" or "less of" something that we all have, rather than as being in a completely different dimension, the chances are that we will do a better job of trying to understand them and of meeting their psychological needs. A discontinuity perspective, on the other hand, encourages us to regard those who are psychologically disturbed as foreign and unfathomable, and thus to relegate them to places where they will be out of sight and out of mind.

Second, there are greater possibilities for research in human development and behavior if normality and abnormality are seen as involving the same dimensions of personality. If researchers focus on dimensions of personality wherever they are found, rather than choosing to study either normal or abnormal behavior as such, there will be greater possibilities for joint efforts and interrelated investigations among students of normal and abnormal development.

Clearly this essay has not given equal time to arguments that could be made in favor of the discontinuity approach. However, our purpose has not been to present both sides of this issue, but rather to close our discussion with some indication of our reasons for having presented normal and abnormal child development as closely intertwined phenomena.

Summary

Although the variability of adolescent behavior makes it difficult at times to determine exactly what kind of psychopathology is present in a disturbed youngster, experienced professionals can readily distinguish normal from abnormal development during the teenage years. Contrary to common belief, adolescents who manifest disturbed behavior seldom grow out of it; they tend to remain disturbed unless they receive adequate treatment.

This chapter has dealt with four conditions that frequently reflect psychological disturbance beginning in adolescence: *schizophrenia, depression* and *suicidal behavior, academic underachievement,* and *delinquent behavior.* Schizophrenia is diagnosed in 25 to 30 percent of the adolescents who are admitted to psychiatric hospital units and in 6 to 8 percent of those who are seen in psychiatric clinics and private offices. In the case of most schizophrenic adolescents, the primary features of this disorder are obscured by other, more apparent difficulties. During the early phases of a schizophrenic breakdown, young people often become withdrawn and depressed or they display antisocial attitudes and delinquent behavior; only later do they begin to exhibit clear-cut signs of schizophrenia.

Among adolescents who are hospitalized for schizophrenia, approximately 25 percent recover, 25 percent improve but suffer relapses from time to time, and the remaining 50 percent require continuing residential care. In general, there is a more favorable long-range outcome for schizophrenic adolescents if they were fairly well adjusted before the onset of their disturbance, if they receive adequate treatment, and if they respond quickly to initial treatment.

About 35 to 40 percent of all adolescents report depressive symptoms, including feelings of sadness, worthlessness, or pessimism about the future. These feelings are important not only because of how often they occur, but also because of their relationship to suicidal behavior. Actual suicide occurs less often among adolescents than among adults; however, suicide is more likely to be a cause of death during the late teen years than at any other time in life, and adolescents make proportionately the same number of suicide attempts as do adults.

Adolescents who attempt suicide tend to be alienated young people from disrupted or disorganized homes who are struggling with mounting family conflict, dissolving social relationships, and an increasing sense of isolation and helplessness. A suicide attempt often represents a "cry for help," and whether it will be repeated may depend upon how effectively it has communicated a young person's distress and brought about changes in how he or she is being treated by others.

Academic underachievement among adolescents occurs primarily because of *sociocultural* or *psychological* factors. Sociocultural factors include the values and influence of a subcultural or peer group that do not encourage learning. Unmotivated students do not enjoy school and do not see any relationship between school and their long-range goals; this lack of interest, rather than an inability to do the work, is the main reason why adolescents drop out of school. Young people generally acquire their attitudes toward school from their families. Disadvantaged minority-group adolescents often do not have families or adult role-models in their neighborhood who have done well in life because of formal education. Another sociocultural factor that may lead to adolescent underachievement is an inadequate elementary-school education, that is, one that fails to teach the basic academic skills and study habits that are necessary for handling high-school work.

The psychological reasons for underachievement usually involve three maladaptive patterns of family interaction. First, these adolescents tend to resent academic pressure being put on them by their parents and to use poor or failing grades as an indirect way of retaliating. Second, they often have concerns about rivalry with their parents and siblings that make them fearful of failure or success. Third, they typically employ methods of purposeful inactivity—neglecting or "forgetting" to do things they should—as a way of accomplishing such goals as academic grades below their capacity.

Taken together, these three patterns constitute a specific form of psychological disturbance called *passive-aggressive underachievement*. Underachievement that is due to sociocultural factors is difficult to modify, but psychologically determined underachievement can usually be reduced or eliminated by means of short-term individual or family therapy.

Delinquent behavior consists of acts that violate the law. Although a certain amount of youthful delinquency is not detected or reported, approximately 3 percent of all 10-to-17-year-olds appear in juvenile court for offenses other than traffic violations each year. Delinquency rates have increased steadily since 1961, and it appears that more illegal acts are committed by boys than by girls and by lower-class young people than by middle-class youth. On the other hand, 42 percent of the total arrests of adolescents are for relatively minor infractions such as running away, loitering, and disorderly conduct.

Delinquent behavior can result from a psychotic, neurotic, or organic disturbance that impairs a young person's judgment or self-control. However, most repetitive delinquency is due either to antisocial cultural influences or to an antisocial personality style—called, respectively, *sociological* and *characterological* delinquency.

Sociological delinquents are generally well-adjusted members of a subculture that holds antisocial values, and they commit crimes together to earn and maintain prestige in their peer group. By contrast, characterological delinquents are usually loners who have no group membership or loyalties. They commit crimes because of a *psychopathic personality disorder,* which is characterized by an underdeveloped conscience and an inability to identify with other people. Since they are highly self-centered and have no regard for the rights and feelings of others, they translate their acquisitive, aggressive, or pleasure-seeking impulses into immediate action, thereby frequently breaking the law. Both sociological and characterological delinquency are extremely difficult to modify through psychological methods of intervention.

References

1. Group for the Advancement of Psychiatry. *Normal adolescence: Its dynamics and impact.* New York: Scribner, 1968.
2. Redlich, F. C., & Freedman, D. X. *The theory and practice of psychiatry.* New York: Basic Books, 1966.
3. Winnicott, D. W. Adolescence: Struggling through the doldrums. In S. C. Feinstein, P. L. Giovacchini, & A. A. Miller (Eds.), *Adolescent psychiatry.* Vol. I. New York: Basic Books, 1971.
4. Masterson, J. F. *The psychiatric dilemma of adolescence.* Boston: Little, Brown, 1967.
5. Srole, L., Langner, T. S., Michael, S. T., Opler, M. D., & Rennie, T. A. *Mental health in the metropolis: The midtown Manhattan study.* New York: McGraw-Hill, 1962.
6. Gallemore, J. I., & Wilson, W. P. Adolescent maladjustment or affective disorder. *American Journal of Psychiatry,* 1972, **129,** 608–612.
7. Meeks, J. E. Nosology in adolescent psychiatry: An enigma wrapped in a whirlwind. In J. C. Schoolar (Ed.), *Current issues in adolescent psychiatry.* New York: Brunner/Mazel, 1973.
8. Weiner, I. B. *Psychological disturbance in adolescence.* New York: Wiley, 1970.
9. Weiner, I. B., & Del Gaudio, A. C. Psychopathology in adolescence: An epidemiological study. *Archives of General Psychiatry,* 1976, **33,** 187–193.
10. Babigian, H. M., Gardner, E. A., Miles, H. C., & Romano, J. Diagnostic consistency and change in a follow-up study of 1215 patients. *American Journal of Psychiatry,* 1965, **121,** 895–901.
11. Garber, B. *Follow-up study of hospitalized adolescents.* New York: Brunner/Mazel, 1972.
12. Hartmann, E., Glaser, B. A., Greenblatt, M., Solomon, M. H., & Levinson, D. J. *Adolescents in a mental hospital.* New York: Grune & Stratton, 1968.
13. King, L. J., & Pittman, G. D. A six-year follow-up study of 65 adolescent patients. *Archives of General Psychiatry,* 1970, **22,** 230–236.
14. Kivovitz, J., Forgotson, J., Goldstein, G., & Gottlieb, F. A follow-up study of hospitalized adolescents. *Comprehensive Psychiatry,* 1974, **15,** 35–42.
15. Pichel, J. I. A long-term follow-up study of 60 adolescent psychiatric outpatients. *American Journal of Psychiatry,* 1974, **131,** 140–144.
16. Jones, F. H. A 4-year follow-up of vulnerable adolescents. *Journal of Nervous and Mental Disease,* 1974, **159,** 20–39.
17. Masterson, J. F. The symptomatic adolescent five years later: He didn't grow out of it. *American Journal of Psychiatry,* 1967, **123,** 1338–1345.
18. Deutsch, A., & Ellenberg, J. Transience vs. continuance of disturbance in college freshmen. *Archives of General Psychiatry,* 1973, **28,** 412–417.
19. Selzer, M. L. The happy college student myth. *Archives of General Psychiatry,* 1960, **2,** 131–136.
20. Taube, J., & Vreeland, R. The prediction of ego functioning in college. *Archives of General Psychiatry,* 1972, **27,** 224–229.
21. Holzman, P. S., & Grinker, R. R. Schizophrenia in adolescence. *Journal of Youth and Adolescence,* 1974, **3,** 267–279.
22. Arieti, S. *Interpretation of schizophrenia.* (2nd ed.) New York: Basic Books, 1974.
23. Offord, D. R., & Cross, L. A. Behavioral antecedents of adult schizophrenia. *Archives of General Psychiatry,* 1969, **21,** 267–283.
24. Symonds, A., & Herman, M. The patterns of schizophrenia in adolescence. *Psychiatric Quarterly,* 1957, **31,** 521–530.
25. Watt, N. F., Stolorow, R. D., Lubensky, A. W., & McCelland, D. C. School adjustment and behavior of children hospitalized for schizophrenia as adults. *American Journal of Orthopsychiatry,* 1970, **40,** 637–657.
26. Watt, N. F. Longitudinal changes in the social behavior of children hospitalized for schizophrenia as adults. *Journal of Nervous and Mental Disease,* 1972, **155,** 42–54.
27. Watt, N. F., & Lubensky, A. W. Childhood roots of schizophrenia. *Journal of Consulting and Clinical Psychology,* 1976, **44,** 363–375.
28. Woerner, M. G., Pollack, M., Rogalski, C., Pollack, Y., & Klein, D. F. A comparison of the school records of personality disorders, schizophrenics, and their sibs. In M. Roff, L. N. Robins, & M. Pollack (Eds.), *Life history research in psychopathology.* Vol. 2. Minneapolis: University of Minnesota Press, 1972.

29. Barthell, C. N., & Holmes, D. S. High school yearbooks: A nonreactive measure of social isolation in graduates who later became schizophrenic. *Journal of Abnormal Psychology,* 1968, **73,** 313–316.

30. Kreisman, D. Social interaction and intimacy in preschizophrenic adolescence. In J. Zubin & A. M. Freedman (Eds.), *The psychopathology of adolescence.* New York: Grune & Stratton, 1970.

31. Pitt, R., Kornfeld, D. S., & Kolb, L. C. Adolescent friendship patterns as prognostic indicators for schizophrenic adults. *Psychiatric Quarterly,* 1963, **37,** 499–508.

32. Mosher, L. R. Schizophrenia: Recent trends. In A. M. Freedman, H. I. Kaplan, & B. J. Sadock (Eds.), *Comprehensive textbook of psychiatry.* (2nd ed.) Baltimore: Williams & Wilkins, 1975.

33. Pollack, M., Levenstein, S., & Klein, D. F. A three-year posthospital follow-up adolescent and adult schizophrenics. *American Journal of Orthopsychiatry,* 1968, **38,** 94–109.

34. Annesley, P. T. Psychiatric illness in adolescence: Presentation and prognosis. *Journal of Mental Science,* 1961, **107,** 268–278.

35. Carter, A. B. Prognostic factors of adolescent psychoses. *Journal of Mental Science,* 1942, **88,** 31–81.

36. Errera, P. A sixteen-year follow-up of schizophrenic patients seen in an outpatient clinic. *Archives of Neurology and Psychiatry,* 1957, **78,** 84–87.

37. Masterson, J. F. Prognosis in adolescent disorders—schizophrenia. *Journal of Nervous and Mental Disease,* 1957, **125,** 219–232.

38. Warren, W. A study of adolescent psychiatric in-patients and the outcome six or more years later: II. The follow-up study. *Journal of Child Psychology and Psychiatry,* 1965, **6,** 141–160.

39. Gittelman-Klein, R., & Klein, D. F. Premorbid asocial adjustment and prognosis in schizophrenia. *Journal of Psychiatric Research,* 1969, **7,** 35–53.

40. Roff, J. D. Adolescent schizophrenia: Variables related to differences in long-term adult outcome. *Journal of Consulting and Clinical Psychology,* 1974, **42,** 180–183.

41. Stephens, J. H., Astrup, C., & Mangrum, J. C. Prognosis in schizophrenia: Prognostic scales cross-validated in American and Norwegian patients. *Archives of General Psychiatry,* 1967, **16,** 693–698.

42. Vaillant, G. E. Positive prediction of schizophrenic remissions. *Archives of General Psychiatry,* 1964, **11,** 509–518.

43. Easson, W. M. *The severely disturbed adolescent: Inpatient, residential, and hospital treatment.* New York: International Universities Press, 1969.

44. May, P. R. Schizophrenia: Overview of treatment methods. In A. M. Freedman, H. I. Kaplan, & B. J. Sadock (Eds.), *Comprehensive textbook of psychiatry.* (2nd ed.) Baltimore: Williams & Wilkins, 1975. Pp. 923–938.

45. Rinsley, D. B. Residential treatment of adolescents. *American handbook of psychiatry.* Vol. II. New York: Basic Books, 1974. Pp. 353–366.

46. Albert, N., & Beck, A. T. Incidence of depression in early adolescnce: A preliminary study. *Journal of Youth and Adolescence,* 1975, **4,** 301–308.

47. Murray, D. C. Suicidal and depressive feelings among college students. *Psychological Reports,* 1973, **33,** 175–181.

48. Weiner, I. B. Depression in adolescence. In F. F. Flach & S. C. Draghi (Eds.), *The nature and treatment of depression.* New York: Wiley, 1975.

49. Silver, M. A., Bohnert, M., Beck, A. T., & Marcus, D. Relation of depression to attempted suicide and seriousness of intent. *Archives of General Psychiatry,* 1971, **25,** 573–576.

50. Stengel, E. *Suicide and attempted suicide.* Baltimore: Penguin, 1964.

51. Silverman, C. The epidemiology of depression: A review. *American Journal of Psychiatry,* 1968, **124,** 883–891.

52. *Vital Statistics of the United States,* 1971. Vol. II, *Mortality.* Rockville, Md.: U.S. Department of Health, Education, and Welfare, 1975.

53. Seiden, R. H. *Suicide among youth.* Washington, D.C.: U.S. Department of Health, Education, and Welfare, Public Health Service Publication No. 1971, 1969.

54. Weissman, M. M. The epidemiology of suicide attempts, 1960–1971. *Archives of General Psychiatry,* 1974, **30,** 737–746.

55. Jacobinzer, H. Attempted suicides in children. *Journal of Pediatrics,* 1960, **56,** 519–525.

56. Shneideman, E. S. Suicide. In A. M. Freedman, H. I. Kaplan, & B. J. Sadock (Eds.), *Comprehensive textbook of psychiatry.* (2nd ed.) Baltimore: Williams & Wilkins, 1975.

57. Toolan, J. M. Suicide and suicidal attempts in children and adolescents. *American Journal of Psychiatry*, 1962, **118**, 719–724.

58. Tuckman, J., & Connon, H. E. Attempted suicide in adolescents. *American Journal of Psychiatry*, 1962, **119**, 228–232.

59. Corder, B. F., Page, P. V., & Corder, R. F. Parental history, family communication and interaction patterns in adolescent suicide. *Family Therapy*, 1974, **1**, 285–290.

60. Jacobs, J. *Adolescent suicide*. New York: Wiley, 1971.

61. Jacobs, J., & Teicher, J. D. Broken homes and social isolation in attempted suicides of adolescents. *International Journal of Social Psychiatry*, 1967, **13**, 139–149.

62. Levenson, M., & Neuringer, C. Problem-solving behavior in suicidal adolescents. *Journal of Consulting and Clinical Psychology*, 1971, **37**, 433–436.

63. Perlstein, A. P. Suicide in adolescence. *New York State Journal of Medicine*, 1966, **66**, 3017–3020.

64. Yusin, A. S. Attempted suicide in an adolescent: The resolution of an anxiety state. *Adolescence*, 1973, **8**, 17–28.

65. Teicher, J. D., & Jacobs, J. Adolescents who attempt suicide: Preliminary findings. *American Journal of Psychiatry*, 1966, **122**, 1248–1257.

66. Darbonne, A. R. Study of psychological content in the communications of suicidal individuals. *Journal of Consulting and Clinical Psychology*, 1969, **33**, 590–596.

67. Farberow, N. L., & Shneidman, E. S. (Eds.). *The cry for help*. New York: McGraw-Hill, 1961.

68. Dorpat, T. L., & Ripley, H. S. The relationship between attempted suicide and committed suicide. *Comprehensive Psychiatry*, 1967, **8**, 74–79.

69. Shneidman, E. S., & Farberow, N. L. (Eds.), *Clues to suicide*. New York: McGraw-Hill, 1957.

70. Shaffer, D. Suicide in childhood and early adolescence. *Journal of Child Psychology and Psychiatry*, 1974, **15**, 275–291.

71. Shaw, M. C., & McCuen, J. T. The onset of academic underachievement in bright children. *Journal of Educational Psychology*, 1960, **51**, 103–108.

72. Hummel, R., & Sprinthall, N. Underachievement related to interests, attitudes, and values. *Personnel and Guidance Journal*, 1965, **44**, 388–395.

73. Morrow, W. R. Academic underachievement. In C. G. Costello (Ed.), *Symptoms of psychopathology*. New York: Wiley, 1970.

74. Pierce, J. V., & Bowman, P. H. *Motivation patterns of superior high school students. The gifted student*. Washington, D.C.: Cooperative Research Monograph No. 2, U.S. Dept. of Health, Education, and Welfare, 1960.

75. Hathaway, S. R., & Monachesi, E. D. *Adolescent personality and behavior*. Minneapolis; University of Minnesota Press, 1963.

76. Morrow, W. R., & Wilson, R. C. Family relations of bright high-achieving and underachieving high school boys. *Child Development*, 1961, **32**, 501–510.

77. Wilson, R. C., & Morrow, W. R. School and career adjustment of bright high-achieving and under-achieving high school boys. *Journal of Genetic Psychology*, 1962, **101**, 91–103.

78. Katz, I. The socialization of academic motivation in minority group children. *Nebraska Symposium on Motivation*, 1967, **15**, 133–191.

79. Braham, M. Peer group deterrents to intellectual development during adolescence. *Educational Theory*, 1965, **15**, 248–258.

80. Dalsimer, K. Fear of academic success in adolescent girls. *Journal of the American Academy of Child Psychiatry*, 1975, **18**, 719–730.

81. Cervantes, L. F. *The dropout: Causes and cures*. Ann Arbor: University of Michigan Press, 1965.

82. McIntyre, P. M. Dynamics and treatment of the passive-aggressive underachiever. *American Journal of Psychotherapy*, 1964, **18**, 95–108.

83. Marcus, I. F. Family interaction in adolescents with learning difficulties. *Adolescence*, 1966, **1**, 261–271.

84. Weiner, I. B. Psychodynamic aspects of learning disability: The passive-aggressive underachiever. *Journal of School Psychology*, 1971, **9**, 246–251.

85. Davids, A., & Hainsworth, P. K. Maternal attitudes about family life and child rearing as avowed by mothers and perceived by their under-achieving and high-achieving sons. *Journal of Consulting Psychology*, 1967, **31**, 29–37.

86. Sutherland, B. K. Case studies in educational failure during adolescence. *American Journal of Orthopsychiatry*, 1953, **23**, 406–415.

87. Shaw, M. C., & Grubb, J. Hostility and able high school underachievers. *Journal of Counseling Psychology,* 1958, **5,** 263–266.

88. Brown, M. The motive to avoid success: A further examination. *Journal of Research in Personality,* 1974, **8,** 172–176.

89. Romer, N. The motive to avoid success and its effects on performance in school-age males and females. *Developmental Psychology,* 1975, **11,** 689–699.

90. Hogenson, D. L. Senior neurosis: Cause-effect or derivative. *School Psychologist,* 1974, **28,** 12–13.

91. Frankel, E. A comparative study of achieving and underachieving high school boys of high intellectual ability. *Journal of Educational Research,* 1960, **53,** 172–180.

92. Mondani, M. S., & Tutko, T. A. Relationship of academic underachievement to incidental learning. *Journal of Consulting and Clinical Psychology,* 1969, **33,** 558–560.

93. Eldefonso, E. *Law enforcement and the youthful offender.* (2nd ed.) New York: Wiley, 1973.

94. Erikson, M. L., & Empey, L. T. Court records, undetected delinquency and decision-making. In D. R. Cressey & D. A. Ward (Eds.), *Delinquency, crime, and social process.* New York: Harper, 1969.

95. Gold, M. *Delinquent behavior in an American city.* Belmont, Calif.: Brooks/Cole, 1970.

96. U.S. Children's Bureau. *Juvenile court statistics.* Washington, D.C.: Department of Health, Education, & Welfare, 1974.

97. *Profiles of children: 1970 White House conference on children.* Washington, D.C.: U.S. Government Printing Office, 1970.

98. U.S. Department of Justice. *Sourcebook of criminal justice statistics–1974.* Washington, D.C.: U.S. Government Printing Office, 1975.

99. Weiner, I. B. Juvenile delinquency. *Pediatric Clinics of North America,* 1975, **22,** 673–684.

100. Wirt, R. D., & Briggs, P. F. The meaning of delinquency. In H. C. Quay (Ed.), *Juvenile delinquency: Research and theory.* Princeton, N.J.: Van Nostrand, 1965.

101. Robins, L. N. *Deviant children grown up.* Baltimore: Williams & Wilkins, 1966.

102. Berman, A., & Siegal, A. A neuropsychological approach to the etiology, prevention, and treatment of juvenile delinquency. In A. Davids (Ed.), *Child personality and psychopathology: Current topics.* Vol. 3. New York: Wiley, 1976.

103. Livingston, S., & Paul, L. L. Neurological evaluation in child psychiatry. In A. M. Freedman, H. I. Kaplan, & B. J. Sadock (Eds.), *Comprehensive textbook of psychiatry.* (2nd ed.) Baltimore: Williams & Wilkins, 1975.

104. Stevens, J. R. Psychiatric implications of psychomotor epilepsy. *Archives of General Psychiatry,* 1966, **14,** 461–471.

105. Empey, L. T. Delinquent subcultures: Theory and recent research. In D. R. Cressey & D. A. Ward (Eds.), *Delinquency, crime, and social process.* New York: Harper, 1969.

106. Glaser, D. Social disorganization and delinquent subcultures. In H. C. Quay (Ed.), *Juvenile delinquency: Research and theory.* Princeton, N.J.: Van Nostrand, 1965.

107. Quay, H. C. Personality and delinquency. In H. C. Quay (Ed.), *Juvenile delinquency: Research and theory.* Princeton, N.J.: Van Nostrand, 1965.

108. Short, J. F. Youth, gangs and society: Micro- and macrosociological processes. *Sociological Quarterly,* 1974, **15,** 3–19.

109. Duncan, P. Parental attitudes and interactions in delinquency. *Child Development,* 1971, **42,** 1751–1765.

110. Jenkins, R. L., & Boyer, A. Types of delinquent behavior and background factors. *International Journal of Social Psychiatry,* 1968, **14,** 65–76.

111. Jenkins, R. L., NurEddin, E., & Shapiro, I. Children's behavior syndromes and parental responses. *Genetic Psychology Monographs,* 1966, **74,** 261–329.

112. Elkind, D. Middle-class delinquency. *Mental Hygiene,* 1967, **51,** 80–84.

113. Marwell, G. Adolescent powerlessness and delinquent behavior. *Social Problems,* 1966, **14,** 35–47.

114. Miller, J. G. Research and theory in middle-class delinquency. *British Journal of Criminology,* 1970, **10,** 33–51.

115. Tobian, J. J. The affluent suburban male delinquent. *Crime and Delinquency,* 1960, **16,** 273–279.

116. Vaz, E. W. Juvenile delinquency in the middle-class youth culture. In D. R. Cressey & D. A. Ward (Eds.), *Delinquency, crime, and social process.* New York: Harper, 1969.

117. Frease, D. E. Delinquency, social class, and the schools. *Sociology and Social Research,* 1973, **57,** 443–459.
118. Cleckley, H. M. *The mask of sanity.* (5th ed.) St. Louis: Mosby, 1976.
119. Jenkins, R. L. The psychopathic or antisocial personality. *Journal of Nervous and Mental Disease,* 1960, **131,** 528–537.
120. McCord, W., & McCord, J. *The psychopath: An essay on the criminal mind.* Princeton, N.J.: Van Nostrand, 1964.
121. Anderson, R. E. Where's Dad? Paternal deprivation and delinquency. *Archives of General Psychiatry,* 1968, **18,** 641–649.
122. Bandura, A., & Walters, R. H. *Adolescent aggression: A study of the influence of child-training practices and family interrelationships.* New York: Ronald Press, 1959.
123. Fodor, E. M. Moral development and parent behavior antecedents in adolescent psychopaths. *Journal of Genetic Psychology,* 1973, **122,** 37–43.
124. Amos, W. E., Manella, R. L., & Southwell, M. A. *Action programs for delinquency prevention.* Springfield, Ill.: Thomas, 1965.
125. Rhodes, W. C. Delinquency and community action. In H. C. Quay (Ed.), *Juvenile delinquency: Theory and research.* Princeton, N.J.: Van Nostrand, 1965.
126. Massimo, J. L., & Shore, M. F. The effectiveness of a comprehensive vocationally-oriented psychotherapeutic program for adolescent delinquent boys. *American Journal of Orthopsychiatry.* 1963, **33,** 634–642.
127. Shore, M. F., & Massimo, J. L. After ten years: A follow-up study of comprehensive vocationally oriented psychotherapy. *American Journal of Orthopsychiatry,* 1973, **43,** 128–132.
128. Berman, S. Techniques of treatment of a form of juvenile delinquency, the antisocial character disorder. *Journal of the American Academy of Child Psychiatry,* 1964, **3,** 24–52.
129. Unwin, J. R. Stages in the therapy of hospitalized acting-out adolescents. *Canadian Psychiatric Assocation Journal,* 1968, **13,** 115–119.
130. Davidson, W. S., & Seidman, E. Studies of behavior modification and juvenile delinquency: A review, methodological critique, and social perspective. *Psychological Bulletin,* 1974, **81,** 998–1011.
131. Stuart, R. B. Behavioral contracting within the families of delinquents. *Journal of Behavior Therapy and Experimental Psychiatry,* 1971, **2,** 1–11.

Glossary

Accommodation   Term used by Piaget to convey changes the person makes in his or her behavior in order to adapt to the constraints of the real world.

Achievement motivation   An inclination to strive for success and an accompanying capacity to experience pleasure in being successful.

Achievement tests   Tests that measure the knowledge an individual has acquired as a result of instruction.

Acrosome   A caplike structure on the head of the sperm.

Acuity   The ability to discriminate between visual stimuli.

Adherences   Ideas and conceptions appropriate to earlier stages of development that are carried over to later stages.

Adolescent growth spurt   The period (usually age 12 for girls and age 14 for boys) when rate of growth in height is the most rapid.

Age differentiation hypothesis   The hypothesis that mental ability becomes differentiated into more abilities in adolescence than were present in childhood.

Albinism   A genetic trait in which the skin pigment called melanin is lacking.

Alleles   Genes at the same loci on paired chromosomes.

Altrusim   Behavior that is kind, considerate, generous, and helpful to others.

Amniocentesis   A procedure, involving extraction of amniotic fluid from a pregnant woman and analyzing the fluid, that allows the prediction of genetic abnormalities of a fetus while still in utero.

Amnion   The membrane that surrounds the fetus.

Amnionic cavity   Fluid-filled sac that protects the embryo.

Animism   Characteristic of the young child's thinking, the belief that inanimate objects are alive.

Answers at random   Responses during a semi-clinical interview that are guesses and unrelated to the child's system of thought.

Anticipations   Ideas and concepts that are appropriate to later stages but appear at earlier stages.

Aptitude tests   Tests that measure knowledge an individual has presumably acquired spontaneously and without special tutelage.

Attachments   Special kinds of close relationships to selected people that begin at about 6–8 months of age and include both love and dependence.

Attention   A selective response to a stimulus.

Babbling   Repetitive vocalizations by the infant; thought to be a stage in the development of speech production.

Basal age   In intelligence testing, the item age level at which the child passes all of the items.

Behavior therapy   The systematic use of rewards and punishments to alter maladaptive behavior.

Blastocyst   The early embryo when it is still a hollow sphere of cells.

Blending   The situation in which two unlike genes for a given trait give expression to a phenotype midway between the phenotypes for each gene's own expression.

Body image   The image an individual holds of his or her own body, its components, and their relations one to the other.

Breech delivery   Delivery of a baby whose buttocks or feet rather than head are so oriented as to emerge first.

Canalization   Term used to describe the fact that genetic potentials are channeled by a variety of factors during development.

Castration anxiety   A term used by psychoanalysts to refer to presumed fears among boys of having their penises removed. This kind of anxiety reaches its peak during the preschool years and may contribute to the generally heightened concern about bodily injury observed among boys at this age.

Catharsis hypothesis   A belief that opportunities to express or discharge feelings and behavior reduce the subsequent frequency or intensity of these feelings and behavior. As applied to aggressive behavior in children — specifically, that fantasy outlets for aggression through television viewing will reduce aggressive behavior — this hypothesis appears to be erroneous.

Ceiling In intelligence testing, the item age level at which the child fails all of the items.

Character disorder A form of psychological disturbance in which the symptoms are not disturbing to the person but are rather part of his or her nature and a comfortable way of being. There is often a fine line between "character" and "character disorder"; the difference between them may be defined by whether others like or don't like a person's style of behavior.

Characterological delinquents Socially isolated, self-centered young people who commit crimes to express anger, satisfy a whim, or obtain something they want. These youngsters direct translation of aggressive, acquisitive, and pleasure-seeking impulses into immediate action; indicative of a psychopathic character or personality disorder.

Childhood schizophrenia A rare but severely disabling form of schizophrenia that appears in children between 2 and 12 years of age.

Chromosomes Strings of genes which come in pairs. Each species has its own number of chromosome pairs. Humans have 46 chromosomes or 23 chromosome pairs.

Chumships A special kind of close relationship that often develops in the preadolescent years between two boys or two girls.

Circular reactions Term used by Piaget to describe a repetitive self-stimulating activity such as thumb sucking.

Classical conditioning An experimental procedure by which a response comes to be elicited by a stimulus that did not elicit it spontaneously. Involves presenting stimuli together with responses in such a way that a previously neutral stimulus comes to elicit the response in question.

Clustering Tendency to group conceptually related items in memory.

Cognitive environment The environmental cues that facilitate memory.

Cognitive styles Consistent individual patterns of response on a variety of related tasks, e.g., field independence–field dependence.

Commutativity In logic, the rule that no matter in what order elements are grouped, the results of the operations upon them will be the same: $A + (B + C) = (A + B) + C$.

Compensation One of the processes said by Piaget to underly conservation. It involves the recognition that, in a transformation of form, what is lost in one dimension is gained in another.

Composition In logic, the rule that combining any two elements of the set will produce a third element also in the set: $A + B = C$.

Concepts Ideas that represent the similarities in diverse events, people, and things.

Concrete operations Piagetian term for the new mental abilities that appear at about the age of 6 or 7 and permit syllogistic reasoning and the learning of rules.

Conditioned response   A response that, through classical conditioning, comes to be elicited by the conditioned stimulus.

Conditioned stimulus   That stimulus which, through classical conditioning, comes to elicit the unconditioned response.

Conduct disorders   Neurotic disturbances in which children "act out" some feeling or concern that they cannot talk about or otherwise resolve. Conduct disorders most commonly involve uncharacteristic aggressive or rebellious behavior, stealing, vandalism, sadistic behavior, fire-setting, and truancy.

Confluence model   A model suggested by Zajonc to explain the relation between family size and intelligence. In general the model predicts that a child's intelligence is inversely related to the size of his or her family.

Connotative learning   Learning that involves a "search for meaning," an attempt to symbolize an experience or to experience a symbol.

Conscience   An internal sense of right and wrong. A person's conscience tells him or her what he should do, and violating the dictates of one's conscience results in feelings of guilt.

Conservation tasks   Piagetian tasks that confront the child with a situation wherein he or she must make a judgment on the basis of perception or reason. A judgment on the basis of reason is said to be evidence the child has conservation.

Contingent response   A response to some behavior that comes directly after it. Contingent responses are much more likely to influence behavior than responses that, because of some lapse of time, seem unrelated to the behavior — that is, are noncontingent.

Continuous growth   A pattern of growth during adolescence in which the young person moves toward adulthood smoothly and without major disruptions.

Continuous volume   The space filled by a continuous quantity such as a liquid or clay.

Control variables   The variables in an experiment that are kept constant so as not to affect the relationship between the independent and dependent variables.

Controlled scribble   Stage in the development of drawing.

Conversion   A neurotic disturbance in which anxiety is "converted" into somatic symptoms; these symptoms consist of sensory or motor impairments that arise without any organic cause, usually in the form of pain, numbness, or loss of muscle control in one or more parts of the body.

Correlative methods   Those methods used primarily to answer the question What goes with what? for example, What behavior goes with what age?

Creode   The particular path, of the several alternatives, taken by an embryo in the course of fetal development.

Criterion referenced tests   Tests on which an individual is assessed according to an absolute standard; for instance, passing 80 percent of the items might be considered success, anything less a failure.

Cross-fostering method   A research strategy for distinguishing between genetic and environmental determinants of behavior; offspring born to and reared by parents having some condition are compared with children born to parents having the condition but reared by adoptive or foster parents not having it.

Crystallized intelligence   The body of knowledge and skills an individual has acquired.

Cultural drift hypothesis   A view that the higher incidence of mental retardation (and other serious psychological handicaps) in lower than in middle or upper socioeconomic classes is a result of the tendency of families with a history of such handicaps to drift toward a lower socioeconomic class because of their limited social and vocational capacities.

Custodial retardates   Severely retarded (IQ 25–39) and profoundly retarded (IQ below 25) persons who are largely incapable of learning to take care of themselves and require institutionalization, usually early in life.

Decentering   In perception, the process of attending to other than the dominant aspects of the perceptual configuration.

Decision time   The time between successive movements.

Deductive reasoning   Reasoning that moves from the general to the specific.

Deep structure   In Noam Chomsky's terminology, the deep structure of a sentence pertains to its true, unambiguous meaning.

Delayed conditioning   Procedure in classical conditioning wherein the conditioned stimulus is presented after the unconditioned stimulus is terminated.

Deoxyribonucleic acid (DNA)   The chemical that makes up the gene and that carries the genetic code in a double helix arrangement.

Dependent variable   The variable(s) the experimenter measures to assess the effects of the independent variable.

Detachment   The process by which children around age 2 begin to separate themselves from their parents, thereby outgrowing their infant attachments and dependecies.

Diasthesis-stress model   A way of conceptualizing disorders as resulting from a combination of an inherited or constitutional predisposition toward the disorder (diasthesis) with disturbing developmental and psychosocial experiences that precipitate it (stress).

Differentiated crying The crying of an infant that communicates to the parents what the infant wants — to be fed, to be held, and so on.

Differentiation One of the processes by which growth occurs; involves the separation into two or more components of what was once one.

Discontinuous volume The space filled by discrete objects such as square blocks.

Displacement The process of transferring a feeling or attitude from its real source to an inappropriate or previously neutral object. Displacement is especially apparent in the formation of phobias.

Divergent thinking Thinking that moves in nonconventional directions.

Dominant Applied to a gene or gene complex that, paired with an unalike gene or gene complex, has its trait expressed in the phenotype.

Down's syndrome A syndrome of malformation associated with the possession of an extra chromosome. Afflicted individuals are mentally retarded and physically handicapped.

Dysgraphia Inability to write at a level consistent with one's other language skills.

Dyslexia Impaired capacity to read at the level of one's intellectual ability. Dyslexia is the most common kind of learning disability that appears in school-age children.

Early maturers Young adolescents who mature a year or two before the majority of their age mates.

Echolalia A speech abnormality that consists of automatically repeating the words spoken by other people.

Ectoderm Type of cell which forms the inner layers of organs and the body.

Ectomorph Body type characterized by thinness and sometimes associated with personality traits of shyness, nervousness, and social isolation.

Educable retardates Mildly retarded persons who have a Wechsler IQ between 55 and 69, reach between a third- and six-grade education in school, and as adults can usually do unskilled or semiskilled work and meet the routine demands of social living.

Ego-ideal An internal sense of aspiration and of what one ought to do; failure to live up to one's ego-ideal results in feelings of shame.

Egocentric speech In Piagetian terms, speech that does not take the listener's perspective into account.

Elaborated code Term used by sociolinguist Bernstein for the language of the upper classes, where most of the meaning is communicated by the words and grammar.

Encoding In memory research, the process or processes involved in receiving and recording information to be retained.

Endoderm Type of cell which forms the outer layers of body organs and of the body.

Endomorph Body type characterized by fatness and sometimes associated with personality traits of jolliness and sociability.

Enuresis Bed-wetting. Normal in children up to age 4, it constitutes a habit disturbance when it persists into middle childhood.

Episiotomy A small incision made by a physician during the delivery of a baby to prevent uncontrolled tearing of the vaginal opening.

Equilibration The Piagetian term for the general process of learning which involves a conflict (say, between perceptual and rational judgments) and its resolution by a higher order construction.

Errors In cognitive style research, the number of mistakes the child makes on the test.

Expression The way in which a particular phenotype appears.

External locus of control An inclination to guide one's behavior according to what the external situation appears to call for or will allow; associated with weak morality and a belief that one's destiny is in the hands of fate or of those who wield power.

Extinction Procedure in operant conditioning whereby a response is weakened by not being followed by reinforcement.

Extradimensional shift In concept learning, switching from one dimension to another, as from color to form.

Factor analysis A statistical procedure used to determine whether performance on a number of different measures has some underlying commonalities.

Familial retardation Mild to moderate mental retardation (Wechsler IQ 50–69) in persons without identifiable biological defects but with a family history of retardation. Between 65 and 75 percent of retardates have familial retardation, and there is considerable controversy concerning whether this condition is inherited or caused by psychosocial factors.

Family romance A fantasy of some elementary-school children that they are the offspring of noble or glamorous parents who will return some day to reclaim them from the dull and ordinary people who have been posing as their mother and father.

Field dependent Applied to a cognitive style in which the individual uses external cues to a greater extent than internal cues in orienting his or her behavior.

Field independent Applied to a cognitive style whereby the individual uses internal cues to a greater extent than external cues in orienting his or her behavior.

Fluid intelligence The underlying mental abilities and processes involved in acquiring knowledge.

Fontanelle "Soft spot" on the head of an infant where the skull bones have not yet grown together.

Formal discipline Educational concept which holds that learning one subject, such as Latin, improves the mind and makes it easier to learn other subjects.

Formal operations In Piagetian terminology, the system of mental abilities that appears in early adolescence and makes possible the understanding of such things as propositional logic, simile and metaphor, ideals, and contrary-to-fact conditions.

Fovea That part of the eye (the retina) concerned with central vision, the area of greatest acuity.

Gametes The cells of reproduction: sperm and ova.

Generative grammar A grammar described by Noam Chomsky that involves a set of rules from which a great number of different sentences can be generated from a fixed number of words.

Genes The basic units of heredity, which carry the blueprints for the final form and function of the individual.

Genotype The actual genetic composition for any given trait.

Global concept of number The concept of a young child who understands number as a kind of name.

Graphic collection In concept-formation research, the grouping of items as figures (houses, etc.) rather than on the basis of their properties.

Habit disturbances Neurotic traits that represent immature ways of behaving. These disturbances do not necessarily stem from psychological conflict, but arise as learned habits or as the result of delayed maturation.

Habituation The diminution of a response to a stimulus as a consequence of continued attention to it.

Heritability Term used in genetics to indicate the extent to which a given trait is determined by the genes as opposed to the environment.

Heterozygous Paired genes (alleles) not alike in their genetic codes.

Holophrastic Applied to the first words produced by an infant to express complex meanings — one word is used to convey what an adult might convey by a phrase.

Homozygous Paired genes (alleles) alike in their genetic codes.

Hormones Chemical substances that regulate growth and other physiological processes.

Horizontal dècalage The Piagetian term for the phenomenon that concepts which are equally difficult logically are not so empirically. Consequently concepts (such as mass and weight) which are of comparable logical difficulty are nonetheless attained at different age levels.

Hostile aggression Aggressive behavior aimed at people and accompanied by angry feelings toward them.

Hyperactive child syndrome Essentially a synonym for minimal brain dysfunction, but the preferred term among child specialists who wish to emphasize the prominence of hyperactivity in this condition and who are unconvinced of its necessary relationship to neurological impairment.

Hypochondriasis A neurotic disturbance consisting of preoccupation with bodily functions and excessive concerns about becoming ill.

Identification A process in which people respond to the feelings, attitudes, and actions of others by adopting them as their own.

Identity In logic, the rule that for every element in a set there is another element to which it is identical, so that $A - A = 0$ and $A = A$.

Identity achievement A successful endpoint in the process of identity formation consisting of commitments to goals and beliefs that have been carefully chosen by the person and are consistent with his or her needs, interests, and abilities.

Identity crisis Significant psychological distress experienced by adolescents who are having difficulty integrating their sense of personal identity. Contrary to common belief that identity crises are a normal and expectable aspect of adolescent development, they are in fact a pathological reaction to developmental stress and occur in fewer than 20 percent of young people.

Identity diffusion A stalemate in the process of identity formation in which late adolescents have not yet made any meaningful commitments to goals or beliefs and are not currently interested in working to sort out their values and future possibilities.

Identity foreclosure A premature termination of the process of identity formation involving commitment to the goals and beliefs of others, without the person's having considered alternative possibilities on his or her own terms.

Identity formation The process by which people by the end of adolescence develop a clear and consistent image of themselves that gives them an integrated sense of what they are like as individuals, what they believe in, and what future directions their lives are likely to take.

Identity moratorium An ongoing process of identity formation in late adolescence in which the person is considering and beginning to make commitments to goals and beliefs but has not yet achieved a clear and satisfying self-definition.

Imaginary audience A mental constructon by the young adolescent out of the belief that other people are as concerned with his or her behavior and appearance as he or she is.

Imitation The process by which the infant repeats some action or sound he or she has seen or heard.

Imminent justice Belief held by young children that transgressions will be immediately punished.

Impulsivity   A cognitive style characterized by a tendency to act before thinking.

Independent variable   The variable(s) in an experiment that are directly under the experimenter's control.

Individuation   The process by which children begin at around age 2 to establish a separate identity and to assert independence from their parents.

Inductive reasoning   Reasoning that moves from the specific to the general.

Infantile autism   A rare but extremely serious psychotic disorder that begins at or soon after birth and is characterized by failure to develop normal attachments to people, intolerance for changes in the environment, and speech peculiarities.

Insight   A mode of problem solving wherein the solution is found by a sudden integration of experience — the "Aha" reaction.

Instrumental aggression   Aggressive behavior that is aimed at attaining or retrieving some object, territory, or privilege. Instrumental aggression is largely impersonal, although others may suffer as a result of it.

Instrumental competence   The inclination and capacity to cope with experience in a self-reliant and socially responsible manner.

Integration   One of the processes of growth that involves the bringing together of one or more previously separate elements.

Intellectual egocentrism   The failure to distinguish between what other people are thinking about and the focus of one's own concerns.

Intelligence quotient   Measure of an individual's relative brightness arrived at by dividing his or her mental age (attained on an IQ test) by his or her chronological age and then multiplying by 100: $IQ = \frac{MA}{CA} \times 100$.

Internal locus of control   An inclination to guide one's behavior according to internal standards of right and wrong; associated with strong morality and a belief in being able to control one's destiny.

Intuitive concept of number   The concept of a young child who understands number in terms of a dimension such as length, width, or numerosity.

Kibbutzim   Collective settlements in Israel in which children are reared communally.

Klinefelter's syndrome   A condition produced by possession of three sex chromosomes (XXY) that results in a sterile, feminized male.

Language acquisition device   A system whereby the child can acquire typical ways of understanding and producing sentences.

Late maturers   Adolescents who mature one or more years after the majority of their age mates.

Latency   In cognitive style research, the time required by the child to take the test.

Latent stage   The period during middle childhood when boys and girls keep to their own sex and show little apparent interest in the opposite sex. Although psychosexual development is often presumed to be "latent" during these years, careful observation of elementary-school children reveal that their lack of heterosexual activities is nevertheless accompanied by a steady growth of interest in the physical and romantic aspects of sex.

Learning disabilities   School achievement that falls substantially below a student's intellectual capacity. Learning disabilities may result from several different causes, including minimal brain dysfunction, sociocultural discontinuities between the school and the home or neighborhood, and specific neurotic conflicts about school learning.

Level of aspiration   The level of success to which an individual aspires.

Leveling   A process in memory whereby certain information is "rounded off": a week and a half becomes a week, and so on.

Liberal education   Greek concept of education which involved promoting the growth of the whole person, improving the body as well as the mind.

Liberated conviction   A response during a semi-clinical interview reflecting a newly discovered concept on the part of the child.

Locus   The position on a chromosome of a particular gene.

Locus of control   A cognitive style that deals with whether individuals believe their behavior is predominantly controlled from within (internal locus of control) or from without (external locus of control).

Logical multiplication   The mental process by which the individual combines two classes to form a third which contains members of both. Americans × Protestants = American Protestants.

Long term memory   Memory of meaningful events, places, and things retained over a long period of time.

Mainstreaming   An approach to the education of retarded and other learning-handicapped children that stresses meeting their needs as much as possible through the regular classroom rather than segregating them in special classes.

Masked depression   The indirect expression of depression through behavior other than the overt sadness and discouragement that usually characterize this condition. The most common manifestation of masked depression in school-age children is some form of aggressive, antisocial, or delinquent behavior by which the child is attempting to compensate for a sense of loss.

Maternal deprivation   A term previously used to describe social isolation syndromes (which see). Research indicating that many persons other than an infant's mother can become important attachment figures has resulted in replacing "maternal deprivation" with the broader designation "social isolation."

Mediation deficiency   In research on learning and memory, an inability to use verbal mediation.

Meiosis   A form of cell division in which each daughter cell receives only half the number of chromosomes in the parent cell.

Mental age   The score attained by an individual on an intelligence test wherein items passed are counted in months and years.

Mental contents   The products of mental activity — ideas, concepts, memories, and so forth.

Mental experiments   Trying a solution out in one's head before attempting it in fact.

Mental processes   The acts of thinking, such as reasoning, problem solving, and concept formation.

Mental retardation   Significantly subaverage general intellectual functioning beginning very early in life and existing concurrently with deficits in adaptive behavior.

Mesoderm   Type of cell involved in the composition of muscle and bone.

Mesomorph   Body type characterized by muscularity and sometimes associated with personality traits of assertiveness and leadership.

Metapalet   In Israeli kibbutzim, the person in charge of the young children.

Minimal brain dysfunction (MBD)   A disorder of behavioral and cognitive functioning that is presumed to involve some impairment of the central nervous system; its primary symptoms are hyperactivity, distractibility, impulsivity, and excitability, and its secondary consequences include learning disabilities, antisocial behavior, and chronic low self-esteem.

Mitosis   A form of cell division in which each daughter cell ends up with the same number of chromosomes as the parent cell.

Moro reflex   A reflex shown by the newborn infant that involves a symmetrical moving of the arms away from the body, after which the arms are returned to the midline; forerunner of adult startle response.

Movement time   The time required to perform a specific movement.

Myelinization   The process by which nerve cells are coated with a myelin sheath, which makes them more efficient conductors of nerve impulses.

n-achievement   A measure of an individual's achievement motivation.

Named scribble stage   Stage in the development of drawing at which children give names to their productions.

Neural tube   The forerunner of the spinal column and brain stem during early fetal development.

Neurosis   A maladaptive effort to cope with anxiety that stems from psychological conflicts or concerns.

Neurotic behavior   Repetitively immature, inappropriate, and maladaptive ways of responding to people and situations.

Norm group Population whose scores on a test are used as a standard against which to measure a given individual's performance.

Norm referenced tests Tests wherein an individual's score is interpreted with reference to the performance of a group of comparable age and schooling.

Object permanence The understanding by an infant, demonstrated by behavior, that he or she believes that an object continues to exist when it is no longer present to the senses.

Observational research Studies in which the data consist of records made of events while they are happening.

Operant learning Mode of learning in which the eliciting stimulus is unknown and the response is strengthened or weakened by reinforcement.

Orienting reflex Movement of the head in the direction of an intruding stimulus.

Ossicles The small bones of the middle ear which transfer the mechanical action of the eardrum to inner ear, where it is transformed into nerve impulses.

Part-whole confusion A speech peculiarity in which only a part of something is used to refer to the whole thing, as in calling one's dinner "ketchup."

Partial reinforcement Rewarding behavior some but not all of the times that it occurs. Behavior that is partially reinforced becomes more firmly entrenched and more resistant to change than behavior that is always rewarded.

Passive-aggressive underachievement A neurotic disturbance in which performance below capacity emerges as an indirect, nonactive, and maladaptive way of expressing anger and coping with concerns about rivalry.

Personal fable A mental construction by the young adolescent to the effect that he or she is special and unique (will not die, grow old, and so on).

Phenomenalistic causality The belief that events which happen together cause one another, characteristic of the young child's thinking.

Phenotype A genetic trait as it actually appears or is realized.

Phenylketonuria A genetic defect of metabolism that can, if not corrected by a special diet, produce mental retardation.

Phobia Exaggerated, unrealistic, and disruptive fears of relatively harmless objects or situations.

Phonemes The constituent sounds of any spoken language.

Placenta Structure, formed during pregnancy, that attaches to the uterine wall and provides nourishment to the fetus.

Primary sex characteristics   The genitalia and accessory organs (breasts).

Problem solving   The mental processes involved in finding ways to overcome or to remove barriers to a desired goal.

Production deficiency   In learning and memory research, a failure to use verbal mediation effectively.

Pronomial reversal   A speech peculiarity in which pronouns are reversed, as in a person referring to himself or herself as "you" rather than as "I" or "me."

Proportionate metaphor   A metaphor in which the relationship is one of proportion. "How wide is the ocean, how deep is the sea, that is how much you mean to me" is a proportionate metaphor.

Propositional logic   Logic that deals with statements which can be true or false rather than with classes and relations.

Psychopathic personality   A character disorder marked by an underdeveloped conscience and an inability to identify with other people. Because they feel little guilt about trampling on others' rights and feelings, and because they have little capacity for loyalty and devotion to anyone but themselves, psychopaths are more likely than most people to break the law.

Purposivism   The belief that everything has a purpose, characteristic of the young child's thinking.

Pygmalion effect   Based on the legend of a sculptor named Pygmalion, this term is sometimes used to describe situations in which a person's behavior appears to have been determined by what others have expected of him or her. In schools the Pygmalion effect refers to the influence that teachers' expectations may have on their students' performance.

Range of reaction   The many possible genotypes that could be produced by a single genotype.

Reaction time   The time between the onset of the stimulus and the response.

Recapitulation   The doctrine that each individual in his or her development passes through the same evolutionary stages as did the human race.

Recessive   Applied to a gene or gene complex that, paired with an unlike gene or gene complex, does not have its trait expressed in the phenotype.

Reflectivity   A cognitive style characterized by a tendency to think before acting.

Reinforcement   Whatever stimuli serve to weaken or to strengthen a response.

Restricted code   Term used by Bernstein for the language of lower-class people that depends upon gesture, intonation, and context for much of its meaning.

Retrieval   In memory research, the process or processes involved in eliciting information that has been stored.

Retrospective research   Studies in which the data consist of records or recollections of past events; such data tend to be less reliable and less useful than data from ongoing events.

Reversal shift   In concept learning, switching from one value of a dimension to another, as from black to white.

Reversibility   In Piagetian terminology, the child's ability to return to the starting point of a procedure analogous to reversing addition by subtraction.

Reversible sentences   Sentences in which it makes sense to reverse subject and object: "The boy kissed the girl" is reversible whereas "The dog bit the man" is not really reversible.

Risk research   A research strategy for separating aspects of a condition that have caused it from aspects of the condition that have resulted from it; subjects are selected on the basis of their being likely to develop a condition (at risk) and are studied in advance of their beginning to manifest it.

Rituals   Exaggerated attention to certain routines that individuals must perform in order to avoid feeling anxious.

Romancing   Response in a semi-clinical interview that is a fanciful construction and does not reflect the child's true level of understanding.

Rubella   A form of measles that, contracted by pregnant woman early in the pregnancy, can cause abnormalities in the fetus.

Scheme   A basic pattern of behavior or thought that can be generalized to many different stimuli and can be joined with other schemes to form more elaborate patterns.

Schizophrenia   A serious breakdown in the cognitive, interpersonal, and integrative aspects of personality functioning; its major manifestations include disconnected thinking, illogical reasoning, peculiar concept formation, distorted perceptions, poor social skills, withdrawal from people, inappropriate emotional reactions, and inadequate controls over ideas, affects, and impulses.

School phobia   A reluctance or refusal to go to school because of intense anxiety experienced in the school setting.

Secondary circular reactions   Term used by Piaget to describe a repetitive action involving some object. An infant who touches a mobile again and again to see it move shows a secondary circular reaction.

Secondary sex characteristics   Body hair, the sweat and sebaceous glands, and changes in the laryngeal muscles.

Secular trend   The tendency for later generations to mature at an earlier age and to be taller and heavier than earlier generations.

Self-concept   The conception an individual has of himself or herself.

Self-esteem   The value people place on themselves and the extent to which they anticipate success in what they do.

Semi-clinical interview   A correlative method devised by Jean Piaget to assess cognitive development; combines features of the mental test and the psychiatric interview.

Senior neurosis A pattern of declining school performance in the last year of high school sometimes observed in children of high school educated parents; they have underlying concerns about qualifying for college and thereby surpassing their parents' achievements.

Sense of alienation A feeling of being an outsider in one's own society, without meaningful ties to groups or institutions in the community. This feeling may arise in elementary-school children who have limited opportunities for participation in organized social and recreational activities and for learning what the values of their larger society are.

Sense of autonomy A feeling that one can exert some control over himself or herself and over his or her environment. This feeling is fostered during the preschool years by parents who encourage their children to do as much for themselves as possible and to take pride in their accomplishments.

Sense of belonging A feeling that one is an integral part of a larger society extending beyond one's family. This feeing usually emerges in middle childhood from enjoyable participation in peer-group, neighborhood, and community activities.

Sense of industry A feeling of being able to cope with challenge. This feeling is shaped during middle childhood by the degree to which success in their efforts reinforces children's achievement motivation, competitiveness, and sense of competence.

Sense of inferiority A feeling of being incapable of meeting the challenges of one's world. This feeling emerges in middle childhood among children who experience more failure than success in their efforts to learn, do, and compete.

Sense of shame and doubt A negative view of one's capacities and of one's abilities to influence his or her own destiny. This feeling is fostered during the preschool years by parents who prevent their children from doing things on their own or demand more from them than they are capable of.

Sense of trust A general feeling that one's needs will be met and that the world is a safe place. This feeling of security is fostered during the first 2 years of life by affectionate, responsible, and stimulating parental care.

Separation anxiety Marked distress that occurs in most infants between approximately 8 and 24 months of age in response to even brief separation from their parents or other people to whom they have become attached.

Sharpening A process that occurs in memory by which striking features are not only recalled by elaborated.

Short term memory Memories of such things as numbers or names that are learned for a short time interval only.

Similarity metaphor A metaphor in which the relationship is one of similarity — ''cauliflower ear'' is a similarity metaphor.

Simultaneous conditioning   Procedure in classical conditioning wherein the conditioned and unconditioned stimuli are presented at the same time.

Situation sampling   A corrective method involving repeated observations of children in a given situation.

Sleeper effect   Usually refers to the fact that effects of family disruption (death or divorce) may not appear immediately in the children but only years after the event.

Social desirability   The motivation for giving socially acceptable rather than true responses on a self-report questionnaire.

Social isolation syndromes   A serious abnormality that occurs in infancy and consists of retarded physical and mental growth and a total lack of interest in people, objects, or play. This syndrome appears in children who are deprived of adequate sensory stimulation and devoted parental care.

Socialization   The process through which children acquire the social judgment and self-control necessary for them to become responsible adult members of their society. The content of socialization is transmitted to children by their parents and consists of the sociocultural attitudes, traditions, and values to which they subscribe.

Sociological delinquents   Psychologically well-adjusted members of a subculture that holds antisocial values who commit crimes together to earn and maintain prestige in their peer group.

Sondage   French word for "sounding," used by Piaget and his co-workers to describe the preliminary exploration that precedes a formal research investigation.

Spontaneous conviction   A response given during a semi-clinical interview reflecting the child's true mode of thinking.

Storage   In memory research, the process or processes involved in the retention of information received.

Stranger anxiety   A marked wariness of unfamiliar people that often appears in infants at 6 to 8 months of age, after they have begun to form selective attachments; this kind of anxiety usually peaks at around 1 year of age and then gradually diminishes.

Strategies   Specific techniques or patterns used by different subjects in problem-solving situations.

Suggested conviction   A response given during a semi-clinical interview reflecting the examiner's suggested answer rather than the child's own conviction.

Surface structure   In Noam Chomsky's terminology, the surface structure of a sentence pertains to its apparent meaning.

Surgent growth   A pattern of growth in adolescence characterized by many spurts ahead but also by occasional regressions.

Symbiotic mother-child relationship   The abnormal persistence beyond age 2 of a child's infant dependence on his or her mother, so that little progress is made toward establishing a separate and distinct identity.

Teknonym Term used in anthropology to designate the family member who will represent the parents after their deaths.

Telgraphic speech Speech used by the young child in which some grammatical components, such as articles, are left out.

Temperament Inborn differences among people that affect how they respond to their experiences, especially with regard to such general traits as activity level, emotionality, and sensitivity to stimulation.

Tertiary circular reactions Repetitive actions in which the child uses one object to attain or manipulate another. Pulling a string to make a mobile move would be a tirtiary circular reaction.

Testosterone The male hormone which regulates, among other things, the appearance of primary and secondary sex characteristics in the male.

Therapeutic milieu A type of residential or daycare treatment in which every member of the staff, every feature of the environment, and every aspect of the daily routine is utilized to help disturbed people overcome their personality handicaps.

Tic A conversion symptom involving repetitive, involuntary muscle movements, usually of the face, hand, and neck.

Time sampling A correlative method involving repeated observations of children at fixed time intervals.

Trainable retardates Moderately retarded persons who have a Wechsler IQ between 40 and 54, cannot progress beyond second-grade level in academic subjects, and as adults usually require a protected setting such as an institution or sheltered workshop.

Transductive reasoning Reasoning from the particular to the particular rather than from the general to the specific or vice versa; characteristic of the young child's thinking.

Transposition In learning research, the ability to transfer a relational response from one set of stimuli to another.

Trisomies Physical and mental abnormalities associated with the possession of an extra chromosome.

Trophoblast The outer layer of cells of the blastocyst which attaches to the uterine wall and will become the placenta.

True concept of number Concept of number which involves the notion of a unit.

Tumultuous growth A pattern of growth during adolescence that is marked by emotional conflict and trauma both at home and at school.

Validity Evidence that a test measures what it purports to measure.

Unconditioned response That response which in classical conditioning is naturally elicited by the unconditioned stimulus.

Unconditioned stimulus That stimulus in classical conditioning which naturally elicits the unconditioned response.

Undifferentiated crying   The crying of an infant that does not communicate to the parents what the infant wants.

Untrainable retardates   See Custodial retardates.

Visual cliff   An experimental arrangement for testing depth perception in infants; it involves encouraging the infant to crawl across a glass panel several feet above the ground.

Visual pursuit   Movements made by the eye when following a moving object.

Yolke sac   Part of the developing embryo; largely a relic of our evolutionary past that serves no major function.

Zygote   The fertilized ovum.

Photo Credits

Chapter 1
Opener: Library of Congress. Page 13: Smithsonian Institute. Page 19: Alice Kandell/Photo Researchers. Page 21: Yves de Braine/Black Star. Page 23: Susan Kuklin/Photo Researchers.

Chapter 2
Opener: Richard Frieman/Photo Researchers. Page 37: Courtesy Division of Human Genetics, N.Y.U. Medical Center. Page 42: Reprinted from May, 1967 *Psychology Today Magazine.* Copyright © 1967 Ziff-Davis Publishing Company. All rights reserved. Page 44: From I. Michael Lerner and William J. Libby, *Heredity, Evolution and Society,* 2nd ed., W. H. Freeman and Company, 1968. Photos by G. W. Bartelmez. Page 57: Sam Sweezy/Stock, Boston. Page 60: Joel Gordon.

Chapter 3
Opener: T. C. Abell/Stock, Boston. Page 72: Monkmeyer. Page 73: Lew Merrim/Monkmeyer. Page 75: Mimi Forsyth/Monkmeyer. Page 76: Suzanne Szasz. Page 78: Courtesy Nigel Cox. Page 81: David Linton, From *Scientific American,* May 1961, p. 66. Page 84: William Vandivert. Page 103: Courtesy Piaget Society.

Chapter 4
Opener: Hella Hammid/Rapho-Photo Researchers. Page 116: Lynn Mahon/Monkmeyer. Page 121: Dr. Harry F. Harlow, University of Wisconsin Regional Primate Research Center. Page 124: Andrew Lewis Botwick/Monkmeyer. Page 128: Dr. Harry F. Harlow, University of Wisconsin Regional Primate Research Center.

Chapter 5
Opener: Ingeborg Lippmann/Magnum. Page 154: Leonard Freed/Magnum. Page 156: Courtesy WHO. Photo by A. Isaza. Page 158: Marc Riboud/Magnum. Page 171: David Mangurian.

Chapter 6
Opener: Bruce Roberts/Rapho-Photo Researchers. Page 189: Courtesy Halbert B. Robinson, from *The Mentally Retarded Child* by Halbert B. Robinson and Nancy M. Robinson, McGraw-Hill, 1965. Page 191: Courtesy Irene A. Uchida. Page 194: Marlis Muller.

Chapter 7
Opener: Sybil Shelton/Monkmeyer. Page 212 to 217: Joel Gordon. Page 218: Courtesy Rhoda Kellogg Gitlin. Page 220: From *Introduction to Psychology,* 3rd ed., by Norman L. Munn, L. Dodge Fernald, and Peter S. Fernald. Copyright © 1974 by Houghton Mifflin Company. Used by permission. Photo by Sheila A. Farr. Page 226: Courtesy H. N. Switzky. Page 228: Courtesy G. M. Solley. Page 241: Lew Merrim/Monkmeyer. Page 246: Courtesy Italian Cultural Institute.

Chapter 8
Opener: Burk Uzzle/Magnum. Page 257: Mimi Forsyth/Monkmeyer. Page 261: Burk Uzzle/Magnum. Page 267: Alice Kandell/Photo Researchers. Page 277: (left) Hella Hammid/Rapho-Photo Researchers; (right) Leo de Wys. Page 280: (top) David S. Strickler/Monkmeyer; (bottom) Ray Ellis/Rapho-Photo Researchers. Page 281: Courtesy Albert Bandura, Stanford University. Page 287: Courtesy Harvard University News Office.

Chapter 9
Opener: Marion Bernstein. Page 309: Reproduced by special permission from Preschool Embedded Figures Test by Susan W. Coates © copyright 1972 by Consulting Psychologists Press, Inc., Palo Alto, California. Page 310: (left) Irene Bayer/Monkmeyer; (right) Cary Wolinsky/Stock, Boston. Page 319: Novosti from Sovfoto. Page 320: Paolo Koch/Rapho-Photo Researchers. Page 321: Audrey Topping/Rapho-Photo Researchers. Page 323: Louis Goldman/Rapho-Photo Researchers. Page 324: Sybil Shelton/Monkmeyer. Page 325: Photo by Meryle Joseph.

Chapter 10

Opener: Arthur Tress/Photo Researchers. Page 342: Hanna W. Schreiber/Photo Researchers. Page 359: Sybil Shelton/Monkmeyer.

Chapter 11

Opener: Rita Freed/Nancy Palmer. Page 374: (left) Perry Ruben/Monkmeyer; (right) Susan Kuklin/Photo Researchers. Page 380: Marion Bernstein. Page 381: Julie O'Neil/Stock, Boston. Page 394: Sam Falk/New York Times Pictures. Page 404: The Bettmann Archive.

Chapter 12

Opener: Alice Kandell/Photo Researchers. Page 416: Falk/Monkmeyer. Page 417: Hugh Rogers/Monkmeyer. Page 423: Bob Burdick/Leo de Wys. Page 428: Susan Kuklin/Photo Researchers. Page 430: Laurence Fink/Nancy Palmer. Page 433: Alex Webb/Magnum. Page 437: (left) Joel Gordon; (right) John Ioan Gotman. Page 443: Brown Brothers.

Chapter 13

Opener: Ray Ellis/Photo Researchers. Page 467: Lawrence Frank/Photo Researchers. Page 471: (top) Paolo Koch/Photo Researchers; (bottom) Ray Ellis/Photo Researchers.

Chapter 14

Opener: Arthur Tress/Photo Researchers. Page 499: Elizabeth Wilnox/Photo Researchers. Page 505: Joel Gordon. Page 509: Courtesy of Sears Roebuck and Company. Page 510: Hugh Rogers/Monkmeyer.

Chapter 15

Opener: Dan S. Nelkin/Photo Trends. Page 533: Ed Lettau/Photo Researchers. Page 544: (top) Peter Vandermark/Stock, Boston; (bottom) Van Bucher/Photo Researchers. Page 550: Charles Harbutt/Magnum. Page 552: David S. Strickler/Monkmeyer. Page 555: Courtesy New York Public Library Picture Collection.

Chapter 16

Opener: Mimi Forsyth/Monkmeyer. Page 565: Hugh Rogers/Monkmeyer. Page 567 and 573: Suzanne Anderson/Photo Researchers. Page 583: (top) Sybil Shackman/Monkmeyer; (bottom) Susan Kuklin/Photo Researchers. Page 600: Wide World.

Chapter 17

Opener: (top) Richard Frear/Photo Researchers; (bottom) Bettye Lane. Page 616: Alice Kandell/Photo Researchers. Page 618: The Bettmann Archive. Page 624: David Strickler/Monkmeyer. Page 639: Rick Smolan/Stock, Boston.

Chapter 18

Opener: Hans Namuth/Photo Researchers. Page 662: Michal Heron/Monkmeyer.

Name Index

Abate, F., 345, 365
Abbot, J., 13, 14, 32
Abelson, W. D., 316, 335
Ables, B. S., 349, 367
Abrahams, D., 572, 604, 621, 646
Abramowicz, H. K., 190, 203
Achenbach, T. M., 47, 62
Ackerman, P. T., 343, 364, 491, 516
Adams, G., 85, 107
Adams, P., 491, 494, 517
Adams, R. M., 491, 516
Adelson, J., 429, 450, 576, 598, 599,
    605, 610
Adler, P. T., 592, 608
Agras, W. S., 358, 369
Ainsworth, M. D. S., 88, 109, 114, 115, 120,
    122, 123, 126, 131, 134, 136, 139,
    141-144, 172, 181, 198, 206
Ajuriaguerra, J., 378, 407
Alanen, Y. O., 349, 367
Albert, N., 656, 676
Albrink, M. J., 159, 179
Alcott, B., 10, 32
Alexander, B. K., 121, 141
Allaman, J. D., 435, 450
Allen, C. D., 572, 604
Allen, J., 196, 205
Allen, J. G., 585, 606
Allen, R. P., 340, 341, 361, 364, 370
Allen, V. L., 313, 335, 429, 449
Allinsmith, W., 275, 294
Allyon, T., 346, 366
Aloia, G. F., 200, 207
Alpert, J. L., 426, 449
Alpert, R., 278, 295, 435, 450
Alter, E., 397, 410
Altmeyer, R., 231, 250
Amatruda, C. S., 169, 180, 256, 292
Ambrose, J. A., 117, 140
Ambuel, J. P., 361, 370
Ames, L. B., 256, 292, 328, 336, 370, 407
Amos, W. E., 670, 679
Anagoslopoulou, I., 386, 408
Anastasi, A., 536, 556
Anderson, D., 400, 411
Anderson, E. P., 126, 129, 142, 278, 295
Anderson, H. E., 425, 448

Anderson, R. E., 670, 679
Anderson, V. E., 302, 307, 332, 333
Andure, C. E., 628, 629, 647
Annesley, P. T., 656, 676
Annis, H. M., 596, 609
Anthony, E. J., 352, 355, 357, 368, 369, 502,
    504, 507, 520, 521, 568, 603
Anthony, S., 328, 329, 330, 336
Apgar, V., 190, 203
Appel, L. F., 230, 250, 390, 409
Appelbaum, M. I., 164, 180
Applefield, J. M., 285, 296
Appleton, T., 71, 73, 84, 85, 106, 258, 292
Arafat, I., 589, 607
Arajarvi, T., 349, 367
Arber, S., 263, 293
Arieti, S., 349, 351, 367, 368, 654, 675
Aristotle, 4
Arlen, M., 393, 410
Armington, J. C., 81, 107
Arnhoff, F. N., 533, 557
Aron, A. M., 341, 364
Aronfreed, J., 272, 294
Aronson, V., 572, 604, 621, 646
Asch, S., 541, 559
Ashenden, B., 196, 205
Asher, S., 418, 448
Astrup, C., 656, 676
Atkinson, J. W., 259, 292
Aug, R. G., 349, 367
Aurbach, H. A., 422, 448
Ayllon, T., 502, 520

Babigian, H., 347, 366, 501, 519, 652,
    653, 675
Baer, D. M., 129, 143
Baertl, J. M., 158, 179
Baird, L. L., 416, 447
Baker, L., 195, 196, 204, 205
Bakwin, H., 197, 206
Baldwin, J. M., 10, 32
Balenky, M., 546, 547, 560
Balikov, H., 568, 604
Balint, A., 258, 292
Ball, G. G., 232, 250
Baller, W. R., 186, 202, 213, 248

Balnom, R. M., 636, 648
Balow, B., 344, 365
Balswick, J. O., 589, 607
Baltes, P. B., 536, 558
Bandura, A., 29, 32, 276, 277, 281, 282, 295, 358, 369, 599, 610, 670, 679
Bane, M. J., 302, 333
Baratz, J. C., 315, 335
Barber, R., 614, 615, 617, 646
Barcai, A., 345, 365
Bardet, C., 172, 181
Bardwick, J. M., 262, 284, 293
Bark, E. A., 170, 180
Barker, G. R., 416, 447
Barker, P. B., 502, 520
Barnet, A. B., 81, 107
Barocas, R., 543, 545, 559
Baroff, G. S., 192, 204
Barr, E., 361, 370
Barrett, C. L., 355, 358, 369, 502, 519
Barsch, R. H., 495, 518
Bart, W. M., 548, 560
Bartak, L., 195, 196, 204, 205
Barteleme, P. F., 68, 106
Barthell, C. N., 654, 676
Bartko, J. J., 351, 368
Bartlett, F., 230
Barton, S., 196, 205
Bateman, B. D., 495, 518
Bauman, K. E., 589, 607
Baumeister, A. A., 188, 202
Baumrind, D., 259, 260, 282, 292, 435, 450
Bayley, N. A., 70, 78, 106, 169, 180, 213, 214, 248, 300, 332, 614, 646
Beach, D. R., 233, 251
Bear, R. R., 245, 253
Bearison, D. J., 398, 411
Becerril, G., 494, 517
Beck, A. T., 506, 521, 656, 676
Beck, L., 361, 370
Becker, J., 506, 521
Becker, W. C., 496, 518
Beckwith, L., 123, 141
Beilin, H., 236, 252, 396, 398, 410
Bell, R. Q., 82, 108, 115, 132, 139, 143, 144
Bell, R. R., 589, 607
Bell, S. M., 88, 109, 114, 115, 122, 123, 126, 131, 136, 139, 142-144
Bellak, L., 349, 367
Beller, E. K., 127, 143
Bellow, P. M., 541, 559
Belmont, J. M., 190, 203, 542, 559

Belmont, L., 227, 249
Belmont, T., 311, 334
Bem, D. J., 632, 647
Bem, S. L., 632, 647
Benda, C. E., 190, 203
Bender, E. P., 311, 334
Bender, L., 347-349, 350, 352-354, 367
Benedek, T., 49, 62, 130, 143
Benimoff, M., 574, 604
Bennett, S., 348, 367
Bennett, S. M., 435, 450
Bentler, P. M., 358, 369
Benton, A. L., 491, 517
Berberian, R. M., 592, 608
Berecz, J. M., 356, 369
Bereiter, C., 302, 325, 333, 336, 402, 403, 411
Berens, A. E., 262, 293
Beres, D., 566, 603
Berg, I., 497, 498, 519
Berger, A. J., 579, 605
Berger, A. S., 577, 605
Bergman, A., 130, 143
Bergman, T., 82, 108
Berkowitz, B. T., 346, 366
Berkowitz, L., 286, 296
Berlin, I., 354, 369
Berliner, D. C., 381, 407
Berlyne, D., 226, 249
Berman, A., 668, 678
Berman, S., 670, 679
Bernal, J., 115, 139
Berney, K., 231, 250
Bernstein, B., 314, 315, 324, 335
Berry, J. W., 309, 334
Best, D. L., 435, 450
Bettelheim, B., 195, 196, 205, 323, 336, 347, 367
Bever, T. G., 236, 239, 252, 253
Biber, B., 419, 448
Bibring, E., 506, 521
Bibring, G. L., 49, 62
Bieri, J., 308, 334
Bijou, S. W., 129, 143
Biller, H. B., 264-266, 293, 444, 451, 636, 648
Bindelglas, P. M., 508, 521
Binet, A., 14, 220, 221, 248, 404-406
Birch, H. G., 55, 63, 83, 107, 132, 144, 190, 192, 203, 204, 227, 249, 350, 367, 494, 504, 517, 520
Birns, B., 152, 153-157, 162, 170, 172, 179-181
Birren, J. E., 588, 607
Black, F. W., 379, 407, 491, 516

Blackman, L. S., 200, 207
Bladholm, S., 501, 519
Blank, M. S., 227, 249
Blau, A., 54, 63
Blizzard, R. M., 198, 206
Block, J., 436, 450, 546, 560
Block, J. H., 262, 293, 436, 450, 599, 610
Block, M. B., 194, 204
Blom, G. E., 418, 447, 448, 496, 518
Bloom, K., 120, 140
Bloom, L., 87-90, 108, 109, 238, 240, 252
Blos, P., 599, 610
Blumenthal, R. S., 265, 293
Boder, E., 492, 517
Boersma, F., 398, 411
Boggiano, A. K., 424, 448
Bohan, J. B., 436, 450
Bohan, J. S., 632, 647
Bohnert, M., 656, 676
Bomberg, D., 349, 367
Bonnard, A., 507, 511, 521
Bornstein, M. H., 82, 107
Bosack, T. N., 93, 110
Boskowitz, E. P., 172, 181
Botkin, P. T., 242, 253, 389, 390, 409
Bouquet, F., 313, 335
Boutourline-Young, H., 614, 646
Bovet, M., 234, 251, 396, 398, 410
Bower, T. G. R., 83, 95, 107, 110
Bower, W. B., 375, 407
Bowerman, M., 87, 108
Bowes, A. E., 352, 368
Bowlby, J., 118, 119, 126, 127, 129, 136, 137, 142, 197, 206
Bowman, P. H., 661, 677
Boyd, R. E., 429, 449, 598, 610
Boyer, A., 669, 678
Brackbill, Y., 85, 88, 92-94, 107, 109, 110, 119, 140
Bradburn, W., 308, 334
Bradley, F. O., 427, 449
Bradley, R. H., 163, 164, 180
Bradway, K. P., 300, 332
Bragge, B. W. E., 313, 335
Braham, M., 661, 677
Braiman, A., 499, 519
Braine, M. D. S., 87, 90, 108, 109, 240, 253
Brainerd, C. J., 235, 237, 252, 396, 410
Branche, C. F., 325, 336
Brasel, J. A., 198, 206
Brazelton, T. B., 170, 172, 181
Breed, W., 577, 605

Breland, H. M., 311, 312, 374
Brenton, M., 200, 207
Bridger, W. H., 227, 249
Briggs, C., 403, 411
Briggs, P. F., 667, 678
Brill, N. Q., 596, 609
Brindley, C., 311, 334
Brittain, C. V., 582, 605
Broderick, C. B., 553, 560, 575, 605
Brodie, R. D., 501, 519
Brody, B., 393, 410
Brody, D. S., 621, 649
Bromley, D. B., 536, 558
Bronfenbrenner, U., 276, 294, 318, 323, 336, 581, 605
Bronson, G. W., 124, 125, 141, 142, 160, 161, 180
Bronson, W. C., 258, 269, 292, 293, 588, 606
Brookshire, K. H., 232, 250
Brophy, J. E., 425, 426, 441, 442, 448, 449, 451
Brossard, L. M., 119, 140
Brown, A. L., 229, 249, 250
Brown, B. R., 315, 324, 335
Brown, D. G., 310, 334
Brown, J. L., 152, 178
Brown, J. K., 565, 603
Brown, J. V., 161, 179
Brown, M., 665, 678
Brown, R., 10, 32, 87, 108, 238, 240, 252
Bruininks, R. H., 200, 207
Bruner, J. S., 70, 106, 218, 248
Brunskill, A., 95, 110
Bryan, J. H., 282, 283, 295-297
Bryan, T. H., 493, 517
Bryan, T. S., 491, 516
Bryant, P. E., 227, 235, 249, 252
Bryson, C. Q., 196, 205
Bucher, B., 396, 410
Buchsbaum, S., 348, 367
Budoff, M., 200, 207
Buff, S. A., 598, 610
Bugner, M., 127, 142
Buker, M. E., 574, 604
Bullard, D. M., 198, 206
Bullis, G. O., 81, 107
Burchinal, L. G., 576, 605
Burke, A., 502, 520
Burke, H. L., 507, 521
Burlingham, D. T., 197, 198, 206, 263, 293
Burr, W. R., 590, 607
Burt, C., 192, 204, 536, 558
Buss, A. H., 133, 144, 284, 296,

435, 450
Busses, A. M., 383, 408
Butler, M. C., 596, 609
Butterfield, E. C., 188, 202, 224, 249, 542, 559
Byrne, D., 621, 646

Cabral, R. M., 595, 609
Cadoret, R. J., 352, 368
Caldwell, B. M., 123, 134, 141, 144, 163-165, 180, 198, 206
Caldwell, M. B., 307, 333
Caldwell, R., 82, 108
Calhoun, L. G., 236, 252
Campbell, D., 126, 142
Campbell, G. V., 628, 629, 647
Campbell, J. D., 427, 449
Campbell, S. B., 344, 364
Campione, J. C., 229, 232, 249, 251
Cancelli, A., 392, 409
Candell, W., 173, 181
Cantwell, D. P., 195, 196, 204, 205, 340, 343-345, 364, 365
Carek, D. J., 512, 522
Carey, R. L., 397, 410
Caron, A., 82, 108
Caron, R., 82, 108
Carpenter, A., 376, 407
Carpenter, G. C., 115, 116, 139, 140
Carroll, A. W., 200, 207
Carter, A., 392, 409
Carter, A. B., 656, 676
Carver, R. C., 382, 407
Casler, L., 197, 198, 206
Cassady, V. M., 200, 207
Castle, P., 70, 106, 116, 140
Castner, B. M., 256, 292
Cato, 4
Cattell, P., 70, 78, 106
Cattell, R. B., 536, 537, 558
Cavalli-Sforza, L. L., 39, 62
Cavior, N., 572, 604, 621, 622, 646
Cazden, C. B., 389, 409
Cervantes, L. F., 628, 647, 661, 662, 677
Cesa-Bianchi, M., 313, 335
Chadwick, O. F. D., 585, 606
Chalfant, J. G., 341, 364
Chan, C., 198, 206
Chandler, M. J., 50, 62
Chapin, H. N., 358, 369
Charles, D. C., 186, 202
Charlesworth, R., 269, 270, 294
Chaskes, J. B., 589, 607

Cheever, J., 628, 646
Cherry-Persach, E., 315, 324, 335
Chess, S., 132, 144, 153, 154, 179, 190, 203, 323, 336, 504, 521
Chillen, T. W., 396, 410
Chilman, C. S., 568, 603
Chinsky, J. M., 233, 251
Chittenden, E. A., 383, 408
Chodoff, P., 503, 520
Chomsky, C., 388, 409
Chomsky, N., 17, 32, 87, 89, 108, 240, 242, 253, 389
Christie, D. J., 229, 250
Christie, J. F., 398, 411
Christy, M. D., 383, 408
Churchill, S. W., 505, 521
Chzhi-Tsin, V., 390, 409
Cincona, L., 313, 335
Cisin, I. H., 286, 296
Clancy, H., 198, 206
Clarey, S., 240, 253
Clark, D. H., 305, 307, 333
Clark, E., 239, 253
Clark, R. A., 259, 292
Clarke, A. D. B., 134, 135, 144, 166, 180, 198, 199, 206, 207
Clarke, A. M., 134, 135, 144, 166, 180, 198, 199, 206, 207
Clarke-Stewart, K. A., 131, 132, 143
Clayton, B. E., 192, 204
Cleckley, H. M., 670, 679
Clements, S. D., 341, 364, 491, 494, 516, 518
Clifford, E., 535, 558
Clifton, R. K., 71, 73, 84, 85, 92, 106, 109, 258, 292
Clover, P., 311, 334
Clyne, M. B., 498, 519
Coates, B., 126, 129, 142, 276, 283, 286, 295-297
Coates, S., 309, 334
Coder, R., 400, 411
Coelho, G. V., 585, 606
Coffin, T. E., 286, 296
Cohen, B. D., 390, 409
Cohen, J., 54, 63
Cohen, L. B., 92, 109
Cohen, M. W., 508, 521
Cohen, R. S., 568, 604
Cohen, R. Y., 86, 108
Cohrssen, J., 508, 521
Coleman, J. C., 597, 609
Coleman, J. S., 302, 332
Collard, R. R., 322, 336
Collier, G., 170, 172, 181
Collins, T., 497, 519

Comenius, J. A., 6
Comly, H. H., 346, 366
Commoss, H. H., 427, 449
Condon, W. S., 85, 108
Condry, J., 430, 450
Conger, J. J., 590, 609
Conn, J. H., 258, 292
Connell, H. M., 507, 521
Conners, C. K., 340, 341, 345, 360, 363-365
Connolly, K., 378, 407
Connon, H. E., 658, 677
Conrad, H. S., 536, 558
Conrad, R., 391, 409
Constantini, A. F., 387, 407
Conway, J., 596, 609
Cook, J. W., 200, 207
Cookson, D., 311, 334
Coolidge, J. C., 497, 498, 501, 518, 519
Cooper, D., 400, 411
Cooper, R. B., 230, 250, 390, 409
Coopersmith, S., 28, 32, 260, 292, 379, 407, 424, 448
Coote, M. A., 508, 521
Cordano, A., 158, 179
Corder, B. F., 659, 677
Corder, R. F., 659, 677
Corman, H. H., 134, 144
Corrigan, A. M., 427, 449
Corsini, D. A., 229, 249
Cortés, J. B., 619, 620, 646
Coss, R. G., 194, 204
Costanzo, P. R., 429, 449
Costello, C. G., 358, 369
Courtney, R. G., 236, 252
Cowen, E. L., 501, 519
Cowles, M., 325, 336
Cox, A., 195, 205
Cox, F. N., 126, 142
Cox, M., 638, 648
Cox, R., 638, 648
Cox, R. D., 588, 606
Craft, M., 191, 203
Crain, W. C., 596, 609
Cramer, P., 310, 334
Crandall, V. C., 259, 292, 421, 425, 435, 448, 450
Crandall, V. J., 421, 448
Cratty, B. J., 76, 77, 106, 213, 214, 248, 375, 376, 378, 407
Cravioto, J., 155, 156, 170, 172, 180, 181
Crawford, D. G., 230, 250

Crist, J. R., 577, 605
Cromer, W., 492, 517
Cross, A., DeP., 263, 293
Cross, H. A., 121, 141
Cross, J. J., 585, 606
Cross, L. A., 654, 675
Crowell, D. H., 85, 107
Cruickshank, R. M., 83, 107
Cruickshank, W. M., 491, 516, 495
Crumley, F. E., 265, 293
Cunningham, I., 596, 609
Cunningham, L., 352, 368
Cunningham, W. H., 596, 609
Curcio, F., 397, 410
Cushna, B., 313, 335
Cury, C. P., 172, 181
Cytryn, L., 506, 521
Czajka, J. L., 263, 293

Dabek, R., 401, 411
Dablem, N., 231, 250
Dahlem, N. W., 509, 604
Dale, L. S., 548, 549, 560
Dalsimer, K., 661, 677
Damianopoulos, E. N., 533, 557
Damon, A., 212, 248
D'Andrade, R., 259, 292
Danielson, U., 361, 370
Darbonne, A. R., 660, 677
Darnton, J., 591, 608
Darwin, C., 8-10, 32
Davids, A., 663, 677
Davidson, A., 440, 451
Davidson, E. S., 286, 296, 297
Davidson, H. H., 422, 448
Davidson, M., 621, 646
Davidson, P. O., 508, 522
Davidson, W. S., 671, 679
Davis, K. E., 282, 296, 589, 607
Davis, O., 441, 451
Dawes, H. C., 279, 295
Day, D., 586, 588, 606
Dayton, G. O., 81, 107
Dean, R. F. A., 172, 181
deBorgson-Bardies, B., 236, 252
Decarie, T. G., 119, 125, 140, 142
DeFries, J. C., 305, 333
de la Cruz, F. F., 190, 203
Delefes, P., 442, 451
Del Gaudio, A. C., 652-654, 675
Delicardie, E., 170, 172, 181
DeLucia, C. A., 93, 110
DeMyer, M. K., 195, 196, 204, 205,

354, 369
DeMyer, W. E., 196, 205
Denhoff, E., 344, 364
Dennis, M. G., 68, 106
Dennis, W., 68, 106, 169, 180, 198, 206
Denson, R., 344, 365
Dermott, D., 596, 609
Des Lauriers, A. M., 354, 369
Despert, J. L., 349, 350, 367
Deur, J. L., 265, 266, 272, 293, 294
Deutsch, A., 653, 675
Deutsch, H., 315, 324, 335
Devor, G., 316, 336
DeVries, R., 224, 249
DeYoung, C. D., 501, 519
Diamond, R. M., 546, 547, 560
Dickens, C., 8
Dickerson, D. J., 232, 251
Dickerson, J. W. T., 155, 179
Dobbing, J., 155, 179
Dogan, K., 341, 364
Dokecki, P. R., 572, 604, 621, 622, 646
Doleys, D. N., 275, 294
Donaldson, M., 239, 240, 252
Dorfman, W., 504, 520
Dorpat, T. L., 660, 677
Douglas, J. W. B., 68, 106
Douglas, V. I., 341, 343, 344, 346, 366, 496, 518
Douglass, A., 541, 559
Douvan, E., 429, 450, 576, 579, 598, 605
Downing, J., 403, 441
Drabman, R. S., 286, 297, 346, 366, 496, 518
Dranoff, S. M., 579, 605
Drash, P. W., 341, 364
Dreyer, P. H., 591, 607
Drillien, C. M., 54, 63, 68, 106, 190, 203
Dunn, L. M., 200, 207
Dubey, D. R., 345, 365
Dubin, E. R., 284, 296
Duncan, P., 669, 678
Dunn, L. M., 222, 248
Dunphy, D. C., 575, 604
DuPan, R. M., 198, 206
Durkin, D., 403, 411
Dwyer, J., 614, 645
Dwyer, T. F., 49, 62
Dye, H., 198, 199, 207
Dyer, J. L., 325, 336

Dykman, R., 343, 364
Dykman, R. A., 491, 516

Easson, W. M., 656, 676
Easton, E., 54, 63
Eberly, D., 627, 646
Eckerman, C. O., 125, 129, 142, 143, 268, 293
Eckert, H. M., 219, 248
Edgcumbe, R., 127, 142
Edge, S., 418, 448
Edwards, C. P., 284, 296
Edwards, J., 12, 14
Edwards, J. E., 352, 368
Edwards, J. H., 331, 334
Egeland, B., 496, 518
Ehrenfreund, D., 233, 251
Ehrmann, W., 589, 607
Eichenwold, H. F., 155, 179
Eicher, J. B., 572, 604
Eichler, A. W., 198, 206
Eichorn, D. H., 219, 248, 586, 606
Eimas, P. D., 85, 108
Eisenberg, L., 193, 196, 204, 205, 340, 343, 345, 348, 353, 361, 364, 365, 367, 369, 491, 497, 502, 516, 518, 520
Eisenberg, P. B., 85, 108
Ekstein, R., 195, 205, 354, 369
Elardo, R., 163, 180
Elashoff, J. D., 426, 449
Eldefonso, E., 666, 670, 678
Elder, G. H., 568, 604, 569
Elkind, D., 7, 27, 31, 32, 79, 91, 107, 109, 224, 226, 236, 249, 252, 378, 385, 386, 395, 401, 403, 407, 408, 410, 411, 535, 542, 543, 545, 548, 551, 558-560, 631, 648, 669, 678
Ellenberg, J., 653, 675
Elman, M., 361, 370
Elmer, E., 352, 368
Emerson, P. E., 122, 123, 132, 141, 144, 152, 179, 263, 293
Empey, L. T., 666, 669, 678
Endsley, R. C., 240, 253
Engelhardt, D. M., 345, 365
Engelmann, S., 245, 253, 325, 336, 402, 403, 411
Engelmann, T., 151, 178
Engelmann, Z., 151, 178
English, W. D., 596, 609
Eriksen, B. A., 227, 249
Eriksen, C. W., 227, 249
Erikson, E. H., 30, 32, 49, 62, 131,

143, 262, 288-290, 293, 309, 310, 334, 442, 448, 582, 584, 605
Erikson, M. L., 666, 678
Erlenmeyer-Kimling, L., 192, 204, 301, 332
Ernhart, C. B., 191, 203
Eron, L. D., 286, 297
Errera, P., 656, 676
Ertel, D., 596, 609
Escalona, S. K., 134, 135, 144
Espenschade, A. S., 532, 557
Esterson, A., 351, 368
Estes, R. E., 491, 498, 516, 519
Etaugh, C., 123, 141, 442, 451
Etemad, J., 349, 367
Evans, M. B., 496, 518
Eve, R. A., 599, 610
Everston, C., 425, 441, 448, 451
Eyman, R. K., 187, 188, 202
Eysenck, H. J., 311, 334

Fabian, A. A., 192, 203
Fagan, J. F., 115, 139
Fagot, B. I., 442, 451
Fairbairn, W. R. D., 129, 143
Falade, S., 172, 181
Falender, C. A., 165, 180, 193, 204
Fantz, R. L., 80, 81, 83, 107, 115, 139
Farberow, N. L., 660, 677
Fay, J., 440, 451
Feeney, B., 501, 519
Feighner, A., 346, 366
Feingold, B. F., 340, 344, 364, 365
Fejer, D., 596, 609
Fejer, S., 596, 609
Feldman, D., 305, 333
Feldman, N. S., 424, 448
Feldman, S. S., 122, 123, 129, 141
Ferenczi, S., 127, 142
Ferguson, L. R., 435, 450
Fernandez, P. B., 190, 203
Ferreira, A. J., 54, 63
Ferster, C., 354, 369
Feshbach, N. D., 274, 279, 294, 316, 317, 335, 336, 581, 605
Feshbach, S., 274, 279, 285, 286, 294-296, 440, 451
Feuer, L. S., 597, 610
Fifer, G., 305, 307, 333
Finlayson, M. J., 491, 517
Finman, B. G., 595, 609
Finney, J., 596, 609
Fischer, L. K., 68, 106, 190, 197, 203, 206

Fish, B., 345, 360, 365
Fishbein, H. D., 389, 409
Fisher, S., 491, 494, 517
Fitzgerald, H. E., 93, 109
Fitzgerald, J., 536, 558
Fitzgerald, J. M., 536, 558
Fitzgibbon, W. C., 200, 207
Fitzpatrick, L. J., 278, 295
Fitzsimmons, S. J., 628, 646
Flaherty, D., 126, 142
Flanagan, J. C., 630, 631, 647
Flavell, J. H., 230, 233, 242, 250, 251, 253, 277, 295, 389-391, 409, 541, 559
Flershman, A. E., 218, 248
Flewelling, R. W., 491, 517
Flye, M. E., 491, 516
Fodor, E. M., 670, 679
Fogg, C. P., 596, 609
Forehand, R., 275, 294
Forgotson, J., 653, 675
Formby, D., 115, 139
Forness, S., 347, 366
Forrest, T., 491, 494, 517
Fowler, S. E., 553, 560
Fowler, W., 151, 178, 245, 253
Fox, S., 596, 609
Foy, J. L., 50-52, 62
Fraiberg, S., 197, 206, 256, 292
Francis-Williams, J., 172, 181
Frank, L. K., 11
Frankel, E., 665, 678
Frankel, G. W., 383, 385, 408
Frankie, G., 278, 295
Frease, D. E., 669, 679
Frederichs, A. G., 230, 250, 391, 409
Frederickson, L. C., 599, 610
Freedheim, D. K., 191, 203
Freedman, D. A., 197, 206
Freedman, D. G., 133, 144
Freedman, D. X., 359, 361, 370, 652, 675
Freedman, J., 496, 518
Freedman, M. B., 589, 607
Freeman, B. J., 194, 196, 204, 205
Freitag, G., 194, 204
Frenkel, S. I., 595, 609
Freud, A., 197, 198, 206, 584, 605
Freud, S., 14, 32, 127, 143, 230, 250, 276, 357, 369, 443-445, 437, 450, 503, 506, 520, 521, 538
Freundl, P. C., 491, 517
Friedenberg, E. Z., 597, 610
Friedlander, B. Z., 91, 109

Friedman, M. L., 584, 606
Friedman, S., 116, 140
Friedrich, L. K., 285, 286, 296, 297
Friesen, D., 598, 610
Froebel, F. H., 8, 12, 245
Frostig, M., 496, 518
Fry, C. L., 242, 253, 389, 390, 409
Fry, P. G., 155, 179
Fulton, D., 231, 250
Furth, H., 7, 31, 231, 250

Gage, N. L., 381, 407
Gagne, E., 390, 391, 409
Gagnon, J. H., 579, 598, 605, 610
Galante, M. B., 491, 516
Gallagher, C. C., 359, 370
Gallemore, J. L., 652, 675
Gampel, D. H., 200, 207
Garai, J. E., 260, 292
Garber, B., 653, 675
Garber, H., 193, 204
Gardner, E. A., 652, 653, 675
Gardner, E. B., 218, 248
Gardner, G. E., 490, 500, 516
Gardner, H., 541, 559
Gardner, L. I., 198, 206
Gardner, R. A., 346, 366
Garguilo, R., 390, 391, 409
Garmezy, N., 352, 368
Garrett, H. E., 536, 558
Garvey, W. P., 502, 520
Gatti, F. M., 619, 620, 646
Gaylin, W., 506, 521
Geary, P. S., 585, 586, 606
Geber, M., 172, 173, 181
Gebhard, P. H., 589, 607
Gediman, H. K., 349, 367
Geleerd, E. R., 584, 606
Gelineau, V. A., 592, 608
Gellert, E., 428, 449
Gelman, R., 237, 242, 252, 253, 396, 397, 410
Geringer, E., 397, 410
Gesell, A., 11, 15, 74, 81, 106, 107, 169, 180, 213, 248, 256, 292, 328, 336
Getzels, J. W., 625, 626, 646
Gewirtz, J. L., 93, 110, 117, 119, 127, 129, 140, 143, 276, 295, 313, 335
Gibbs, F. A., 192, 203
Gibson, E. J., 83, 107, 385, 408
Gibson, J., 85, 108, 227, 249
Gibson, L. J., 227, 249
Giffin, M. E., 512, 522
Gilkeson, M. R., 190, 203

Gimseth, E., 314, 335
Ginott, H., 276, 294
Girardeau, F. L., 192, 204
Girdano, D. A., 592, 608
Girdano, D. D., 592, 608
Gittelman-Klein, R., 656, 676
Glaser, B. A., 653, 675
Glaser, D., 669, 678
Glaser, H. H., 198, 206
Glaser, K., 507, 521
Glaser, R., 382, 383, 407, 408
Glasman, L. D., 232, 251
Glassberg, B. Y., 589, 607
Glazer, J. A., 270, 294
Glick, B. S., 358, 369
Glidewell, J. S., 425, 448
Glucksberg, S., 242, 253, 389, 409
Go, E., 226, 249, 385, 408
Goddard, K. E., 93, 110, 152, 179
Godenne, G. D., 589, 607
Goethals, G. W., 596, 609
Golbeck, S., 226, 249, 385, 408
Gold, M., 441, 451, 509, 522, 666, 668, 678
Goldberg, S., 71, 73, 84, 85, 106, 160, 180, 258, 292, 311, 334
Golden, M., 162, 180
Golden, M. M., 427, 449
Goldfarb, W., 199, 207, 348, 350, 352, 354, 367, 369
Goldstein, G., 653, 675
Goldstein, H., 200, 207
Goldstein, M. J., 351, 353, 368
Good, T. L., 425, 426, 441, 442, 448, 449, 451
Goodman, H., 200, 207
Goodman, I., 286, 297
Goodman, J., 346, 366, 496, 518
Goodman, J. F., 200, 207
Goodnow, J., 227, 234, 249, 251, 549, 560
Goodson, B. D., 219, 248
Goodwin, M. S., 127, 142
Gordon, I. J., 101, 110, 165, 180
Gordon, N. J., 286, 297
Gordon, M., 54, 63
Gorman, B. S., 596, 609
Gorsuch, R. L., 596, 609
Gossett, J. T., 596, 609
Gottesman, I. I., 353, 369
Gottfried, A. W., 191, 203
Gottlieb, D., 572, 598, 604
Gottlieb, F., 653, 675
Gottlieb, J., 200, 207
Gove, W. R., 348, 367

Graham, F. K., 85, 108, 191, 203
Graham, G. G., 157, 158, 179
Graham, P., 585, 606
Graham, R. A., 627, 646
Graliker, B. V., 187, 202
Granthan-McGregor, S. M., 170, 180
Grave, G. D., 527, 557
Graves, A. J., 395, 410, 542, 549, 559
Graves, S. B., 286, 297
Gray, M. L., 85, 107
Gray, S. W., 325, 336
Graziano, A. M., 346, 366
Green, D. R., 381, 407
Greenfield, P. M., 219, 248
Gregor, A. J., 301, 332
Greenberg, J. W., 422, 448
Greenblatt, M., 653, 675
Grief, E. B., 400, 411
Grinder, R. E., 575, 589, 604, 607
Grinker, R. R., 506, 521, 585, 606, 654, 675
Grinspoon, L., 360, 370
Gross, J. C., 200, 207
Gross, M. B., 346, 366
Grossman, H. J., 185, 202
Gruenberg, E. M., 185, 202
Grubb, J., 663, 678
Grugett, A., 348, 352, 367
Grumbach, M. M., 527, 557
Grusec, J. E., 358, 369
Guardo, C. J., 436, 450
Gulo, E. V., 569, 604
Gump, P. V., 416, 447
Gunderson, E. K. E., 534, 558
Gunderson, J. G., 347, 348, 366, 367
Gunter, L., 54, 63
Guntrip, H. J. S., 129, 143
Guskin, S. L., 200, 207
Gussow, J. D., 190, 203
Guzman, A., 341, 364

Haaf, R. A., 115, 139
Haan, N., 586, 588, 606
Haber, A., 68, 106
Haetn, M. M., 383, 408
Hagen, J. W., 228, 249
Hager, D. L., 589, 692, 697, 698
Hahn, P. B., 497, 501, 518, 519
Haigh, G., 227, 249
Hain, J. D., 592, 608
Hainsworth, P. K., 663, 677
Haith, M. M., 82, 83, 107, 108, 168, 180
Hale, S. A., 228, 249
Hall, G. S., 10, 14, 32, 554-556

Hall, J. W., 549, 560
Hall, V. C., 20, 33
Hallahan, D. P., 491, 495, 516
Halliday, M. A. K., 90, 109
Halperin, M. S., 393, 409
Halverson, H. M., 135, 144, 256, 270, 292, 294
Hamburg, D. A., 585, 606
Hammar, S. L., 343, 364
Hammill, D. D., 495, 518
Hampe, E., 355, 358, 369, 501, 502, 519
Hansen, E., 126, 142
Hanson, R. A., 164, 180
Hardy, J. B., 56, 63
Harig, P. T., 353, 369
Harlow, H. F., 121, 126, 129, 140-143
Harlow, M. K., 121, 129, 140, 143
Harmon, L. W., 629, 647
Harner, L., 239, 253
Harper, L. V., 132, 144
Harper, P. A., 68, 106, 190, 203, 508, 521
Harris, D. B., 553, 560, 632, 647
Harris, I. D., 494, 517
Harris, Z., 87, 108
Harrison, R. H., 200, 207
Harrison, S. I., 507, 521
Harter, M. R., 83, 107
Hartlage, L. C., 491, 516
Hartmann, E., 653, 675
Hartshorne, H., 545, 560
Hartup, W. W., 126, 129, 142, 269, 270, 276, 279, 283, 294-296, 427, 430, 432, 434, 449, 450, 572, 604
Harvey, O. J., 429, 432, 449, 450
Harway, V., 352, 368
Hatfield, J. S., 435, 450
Hathaway, S. R., 632, 647, 661, 677
Hatton, H., 85, 108
Haugan, G. M., 119, 140
Havighurst, R. J., 627, 646
Hay, D. F., 282, 295
Haylett, C. H., 498, 519
Haywood, H. C., 226, 249
Heagarty, M. C., 198, 206
Healy, W., 15
Heaton, C., 126, 142
Heber, R., 101, 110, 150, 165, 178, 180, 186, 193, 202, 204
Hecaen, H., 378, 407
Hedges, N. A., 598, 610
Hegrenes, J. R., 502, 520
Hegron, A. G., 230, 250

Heider, G. M., 135, 144
Heilbrun, A. B., 351, 368
Heiman, J. R., 492, 517
Heinecke, C. M., 126, 142, 491, 494, 516
Held, R., 70, 106, 116, 140
Hellman, I., 494, 517
Henderson, R. A., 187, 202
Hendin, H., 597, 610
Hendrickson, W., 512, 522
Henker, B., 82, 108
Henry, T. J., 596, 609
Hen-Tow, A., 82, 108
Herb, T. S., 348, 367
Herman, M., 654, 675
Herrnstein, R. J., 192, 204
Hersen, M., 502, 520
Hersov, L. A., 497, 519
Hertzig, M. E., 132, 144, 156, 157, 179, 192, 204
Herzog, E., 265, 266, 293, 313, 335
Hess, J., 68, 106
Hess, R. D., 245, 253, 315, 324, 335, 421, 448
Heston, L. L., 352, 368
Hetherington, E. M., 265, 266, 278, 293, 295, 311, 334, 496, 518, 636-638, 648
Hewitt, L. S., 435, 450
Hicks, D. J., 282, 295
Higgins, E. T., 389, 409
Higgins, J., 272, 294
Hilgard, J. R., 69, 106
Hills, C. B., 11
Hilton, I., 313, 335
Hindley, C. B., 172, 181
Hingten, J. N., 196, 205
Hirsch, S. R., 352, 368
Hoaf, R. A., 82, 108
Hoan, N., 546, 560
Hobbs, E. D., 395, 410, 542, 559
Hobbs, M. T., 187, 202
Hobbs, S. A., 275, 294
Hochman, J. S., 596, 609
Hodgman, C. H., 499, 519
Hoffman, H. R., 284, 296
Hoffman, L. W., 260, 262, 292
Hoffman, M. L., 274-276, 282, 283, 294-296, 400, 411, 435, 440, 450, 451
Hoffman, S. P., 345, 365
Hogan, J. C., 218, 248
Hogan, K. A., 310, 334
Hogan, R., 136, 144, 218, 248, 596, 609

Hogarty, P. S., 164, 180
Hogenson, D. L., 665, 678
Hohle, R. H., 80, 107
Hohman, L. B., 191, 203
Hollien, H., 115, 139
Holmes, D. J., 512, 522
Holmes, D. S., 654, 676
Holmes, J. G., 541, 559
Holroyd, K., 596, 609
Holzman, P. S., 654, 675
Honig, R., 123, 141
Hood, L., 240, 252
Hood, W. R., 432, 450
Hooper, F. H., 536, 558
Horn, J. L., 150, 178, 536, 537, 558, 559, 610
Horne, D., 496, 518
Horowitz, A. B., 92, 109
Horowitz, F. D., 427, 449
Horowitz, H., 572, 604
Horrocks, J. E., 574, 604
Houlehan, N. B., 553, 560
Hoving, K. L., 387, 407
Howard, K. I., 632, 647
Howland, A., 25, 33
Hoy, E., 341, 364
Hoyt, J. D., 230, 250, 391, 409
Hsu, F. L. K., 322, 336
Huesmann, L. R., 286, 297
Huessy, H. R., 340, 364
Hughes, V., 442, 451
Hull, C., 226, 249
Huller, M. W., 85, 108
Hummel, R., 661, 677
Humphreys, L. S., 305, 333
Hunt, J., McV., 162, 180
Hunter, I. M. L., 233, 251
Huntington, D., 101, 110, 165, 180
Huntington, D. S., 49, 62
Huppertz, J. W., 20, 33
Hurlock, E. B., 589, 607
Hurvich, M., 349, 367
Hurwitz, I., 491, 516
Husek, T. R., 383, 407
Hutt, C., 83, 85, 107, 108, 194, 204, 311, 334
Hutt, S. S., 85, 108
Hyman, L., 232, 251
Hymes, J. L., Jr., 326, 336

Ikeda, K., 582, 605
Ilg, F. L., 81, 107, 256, 292, 328, 336, 378, 407
Ingram, T. T. S., 54, 63

Inhelder, B., 230, 231, 234, 237, 238, 250-252, 392, 396, 398, 409, 410, 535, 539, 542, 543, 547, 558-560
Insko, C. A., 572, 604, 621, 646
Ipsen, J., 152, 179
Iscoe, I., 305, 307, 330
Isett, R., 226, 249
Izzo, L. D., 501, 519

Jacklin, C. N., 262, 293, 308, 334, 434, 435, 436, 450, 623, 629, 646, 647
Jackson, B., 442, 451
Jackson, J. C., 85, 108
Jackson, P., 441, 451
Jackson, P. W., 625, 626, 646
Jackson, R. L., 155, 179
Jackson, S., 548, 560
Jacobinzer, H., 658, 676
Jacobs, J., 659, 660, 677
Jacobsen, L., 426, 449
Jacobus, K. A., 229, 249
Jacoby, S., 318-320, 336
Janis, I. L., 286, 296
Jarvik, L. F., 192, 204, 301, 332
Jarvis, P. E., 242, 253, 389, 390, 409
Jarvis, V., 494, 517
Javert, C. T., 54, 63
Jeffrey, W. E., 92, 109
Jegede, R. O., 502, 520
Jencks, C., 301, 302, 327, 332, 333
Jenkins, D. D., 375, 407
Jenkins, J., 392, 409
Jenkins, R. L., 669, 670, 678, 679
Jensen, A. R., 150, 178, 188, 192, 203, 204, 301-304, 332, 333, 426, 449, 558, 607
Jessner, T., 50-52, 62
Jessor, R., 596, 599, 609, 610
Jessor, S. L., 596, 599, 609, 610
Jester, R., 101, 110
Joffe, J. M., 54, 63
Johnsen, P., 545, 559
Johnson, A. M., 498, 512, 519, 522
Johnson, B. D., 592, 608
Johnson, D., 632, 647
Johnson, J., 344, 364
Johnson, J. E., 596, 609
Johnson, K. G., 190, 203
Johnson, M., 592, 608
Johnson, N. E., 344, 364
Johnson, P. J., 232, 251
Johnson, R. C., 233, 251
Joiner, L. M., 200, 207

Jones, F. H., 653, 755
Jones, H. E., 536, 538, 558, 560
Jones, H. R., 229, 249
Jones, K. L., 344, 365
Jones, M. C., 553, 560, 614, 617, 645, 646
Jones, M. H., 81, 107
Jones, R., 346, 366, 496, 518
Jones, R. L., 200, 207, 233, 251
Jordan, K., 350, 367
Joseph, T. P., 581, 605
Josephson, E., 593, 594, 608
Josselyn, I. M., 566, 577, 581, 603
Jourard, S. M., 535, 558
Joyce, C. S., 435, 450
Juhasz, A. M., 577, 605
Jung, S. M., 630, 647
Jusczyk, P., 85, 108
Justice, R. S., 187, 202

Kaats, G. R., 589, 607
Kaffman, M., 323, 336
Kagan, J., 82, 108, 127, 134, 135, 142, 144, 159, 168, 179, 180, 278, 283, 295, 296, 435, 588, 606
Kahana, B., 346, 366, 496, 518
Kahn, J. H., 499, 500, 519
Kahn, M., 596, 609
Kamin, L. J., 150, 178, 192, 204, 301, 332
Kandel, D., 569-571, 582, 595, 598, 604, 605, 609
Kandel, H. J., 346, 366
Kane, R. L., 592, 596, 608
Kane, S. H., 191, 203
Kannel, W. B., 159, 179
Kanner, L., 193, 196, 204, 205, 258, 292
Kantner, J. F., 590, 607
Kantor, M. B., 425, 448
Kantowitz, S. R., 85, 108
Kaplan, L. J., 440, 451
Karmel, B. Z., 83, 107
Karp, S. A., 29, 33
Kasatkin, N. I., 93, 110
Kasl, S. V., 592, 608
Kass, R. E., 496, 518
Kaswan, J. W., 436, 439, 450
Katkovsky, W., 421, 425, 448
Katlef, E., 397, 410
Katz, I., 421, 448, 661, 677
Kaufman, I. C., 126, 142
Kavanaugh, R. D., 308, 334
Kaye, H., 93, 110

Keeran, C. V., 188, 202
Keith, S. J., 348, 367
Kendler, H. H., 232, 235, 250-252
Kendler, T. S., 235, 250-252
Keniston, K., 432, 450, 597, 609
Kennedy, W. A., 501, 502, 519
Kenyon, F. E., 504, 520
Keogh, B. K., 219, 248, 491, 516
Keogh, J. F., 214, 248
Keogh, J. J., 375, 376, 407
Kessen, W., 82, 83, 107, 226, 249
Kessler, J. W., 185, 202, 357, 369, 500, 502, 512, 519, 522
Kestenberg, J. S., 439, 451
Kety, S. S., 352, 368
Khuri, E. T., 591, 608
Kiell, N., 566, 579, 603
King, K., 589, 607
King, M., 589, 607
King, L. J., 653, 675
King, S. H., 585, 606
Kinsey, A. C., 589, 607
Kivovitz, J., 653, 675
Klapper, J. T., 286, 296
Klauss, R. A., 325, 336
Klein, D. F., 654, 656, 675, 676
Klein, H. R., 348, 367
Klein, R. E., 168, 180
Kluever, R., 491, 516
Knight, J., 390, 409
Kniveton, B. H., 282, 295
Knobloch, H., 79, 107
Knott, P. D., 599, 610
Kobasigawa, A., 392, 409
Koch, H. L., 313, 335
Koch, R., 187, 190, 202, 203
Koegel, R. L., 196, 205
Koegler, R. R., 226, 249, 348, 367, 385, 408
Koffka, K., 386, 408
Kogan, K. L., 133, 144
Kohen-Raz, R., 123, 141, 174, 181
Kohlberg, L., 135, 144, 400, 401, 411, 436, 450, 501, 512, 519, 545, 560
Kohler, W., 97, 110, 386, 408
Kokcncs, B., 379, 407
Kolansky, H., 358, 369
Kolb, L. C., 655, 676
Koluchova, J., 166, 168, 180, 198, 206, 207
Kolvin, I., 196, 205
Konstadt, L., 29, 33
Korchin, S. J., 596, 609
Korman, T. A., 229, 250

Korn, S. J., 132, 144, 190, 203
Korner, A. F., 133, 144
Kornfeld, D. S., 655, 676
Koscis, J. J., 491, 516
Koslowski, B., 95, 110
Kotelchuck, M., 127, 142, 263, 293
Koumides, O. P., 192, 204
Kovar, L. C., 598, 610
Krager, J. M., 360, 370
Kramer, M., 347, 366
Krause, R. M., 242, 253
Krauss, R. M., 315, 324, 335, 389, 409
Krebs, D. L., 282, 295
Kreisman, D., 655, 676
Kreitler, H., 256, 292
Kreitler, S., 256, 292
Kreutzer, M. A., 230, 250
Kron, R. E., 93, 110, 152, 179
Krug, S. E., 596, 609
Kruger, E., 361, 370
Kuenne, M. R., 233, 251
Kugelmass, S., 385, 408
Kuhlen, R. G., 553, 560
Kuhn, D., 166, 180, 237, 252
Kuna, D. J., 494, 517
Kunen, S., 390, 391, 409
Kurtines, W., 400, 411
Kurtz, R. M., 534, 535, 557, 558
Kutz, S. L., 268, 293
Kuvlesky, W. P., 642, 648
Kysar, J. E., 585, 606

Labouvie, G. V., 536, 558
Labov, W., 315, 335
LaCrosse, J., 135, 144, 501, 512, 519
LaFranchi, S., 195, 204
Lahaderne, H., 441, 451
Laing, R. D., 351, 368
Lamb, M. E., 263, 265, 273
Lambert, B., 216, 217, 248
Lampl, E. E., 124, 125, 141
Landsbaum, J. B., 581, 605
Langford, W. S., 361, 370
Langner, T. S., 652, 675
Langsley, D. G., 501, 519
Lapouse, R., 355, 369, 504, 520
Larson, L. E., 582, 605
Lasko, J. K., 313, 335
Lasky, E. Z., 491, 516
Lassers, E., 501, 519
Latham, A. J., 614, 645
Lathey, J. W., 549, 560
Latif, I., 88, 109

Laufer, M. W., 346, 366
Lavigueur, H., 344, 364
Lawson, D., 192, 204
Laybourne, P. C., 505, 521
Layman, D., 346, 366
Layton, B. D., 572, 604, 621, 646
Layzer, D., 302, 333
Leary, T., 591
Leboyer, F., 61, 63
Lee, L. C., 548, 560
Lee, P. C., 441, 442, 451
Lefcourt, H. M., 273, 294
Leff, J. P., 352, 368
Leff, R., 354, 369
Lefford, A., 227, 249
Lefkowitz, M. M., 286, 297
Legg, C., 266, 293
Lehrman, P. R., 440, 451
Leiblich, A., 385, 408
Leiderman, P. H., 161, 179
Leifer, A. D., 285, 286, 296, 297, 305, 333
Lembright, M. L., 427, 449
Lenard, H. G., 85, 108
Lennenberg, E. H., 88, 109
Leonard, C., 230, 250
Leonard, E., 628, 646
Leonard, S. D., 229, 249
Leopold, W. F., 90, 109
Lerner, M. I., 57, 63
Lerner, R. M., 428, 449, 534, 557, 599, 610
Lesser, G. S., 305, 307, 333, 569-571, 582, 598, 604, 605
Lesser, I. M., 585, 606
Lester, B. M., 92, 109
Lester, D., 503, 520
Levenson, E. A., 499, 519
Levenson, M., 659, 677
Levenstein, S., 656, 676
Leventhal, T., 499, 501, 502, 519
Levi, A., 20, 33
Levin, H., 275, 294, 435, 450
Levine, D., 397, 410
Levine, J., 82, 108
Levine, J. A., 435, 450
Levine, M., 382, 407
Levinson, D. J., 653, 675
Levitan, M., 36-38, 62
Leviten, T. E., 625, 646
Levy, L., 592, 608
Lewin, D., 344, 364
Lewin, K., 18, 32
Lewis, A., 52, 63

Lewis, J. M., 596, 609
Lewis, M., 79, 82, 106, 108, 160, 180, 311, 334
Lewis, R. A., 590, 607
Lewontin, R. C., 150, 178, 302-304, 333
Liben, L., 231, 250
Liddicoat, R., 172, 181
Lidz, T., 351, 368, 568, 581, 604
Liebert, R. M., 284, 286, 287, 296, 297, 398, 411
Liem, J. H., 352, 368
Lightbown, P., 240, 252
Lindzey, G., 192, 204, 301-303, 307, 332
Lintz, L. M., 93, 110
Lippitt, R., 441, 451
Lipset, S. M., 598, 610
Lipsett, L. P., 93, 110
Lipton, R. C., 198, 206
Liss, E., 494, 517
Liss, P. H., 383, 408
Litin, E. M., 512, 522
Little, B. C., 345, 365
Livingston, S., 668, 678
Locke, J., 6
Lockyer, L., 195, 205
Lodge, A., 81, 107
Loehlin, J. C., 192, 204, 301-303, 307, 332
Loew, L. H., 195, 204
Loftus, R., 352, 368
Lombillo, J. R., 592, 608
London, O., 621, 646
London, P., 282, 295
Loney, J., 346, 366
Loof, D. H., 503, 520
Looft, W. R., 435, 450
Lord, E., 322, 336
Lotecka, L., 592, 608
Lotter, V., 193, 195, 196, 204, 205
Lovaas, O. I., 196, 205
Love, L. R., 436, 439, 450
Lovell, K., 542, 559
Lovibond, S. H., 508, 521
Lowe, R. C., 25, 26, 33, 236, 252, 396, 410
Lowell, E. L., 259, 292
Lowenfeld, V., 216, 217, 248
Lowrey, G. H., 69, 71-74, 84, 106
Lowrie, S. H., 576, 605
Lowry, G. G., 374, 407
Lubensky, A. W., 654, 655, 675
Lucas, A. R., 502, 505, 520

Luckey, E. B., 590, 591, 607
Lully, J., 165, 180
Lutte, G., 641, 648
Lyle, J., 284, 296
Lynn, D. B., 263, 264, 266, 283, 293, 310, 334, 636, 648
Lytton, H., 275, 294

Maas, H. S., 434, 450
McAree, C. P., 596, 609
McBride, G., 198, 206
McCall, R. B., 163, 164, 180
McCance, R. A., 155, 179
McCarrell, N., 230, 250, 390, 409
McCarthy, D., 82, 86, 108, 307, 333
McCarthy, J. F., 493, 517
McCarthy, J. J., 493, 517
McCarthy, J. M., 494, 518
McCarver, R. B., 391, 409
Maccoby, E. E., 122, 123, 129, 141, 224, 249, 262, 275, 293, 294, 307, 308, 333, 334, 434-436, 450, 629, 647
McClelland, D. C., 224, 249, 259, 292, 654, 655
McConnell, T. R., 429, 449
McConville, M., 308, 334
McCord, J., 670, 679
McCord, W., 670, 679
McCorkel, R. J., Jr., 52, 53, 63
McCuen, J. T., 660, 677
McDaniel, C. O., 575, 604
MacDonald, A. P., 273, 276, 294, 440, 451
MacDonald, G. W., 491, 517
McDonald, R. I., 54, 63
Macey, B. M., 541, 559
McFarland, R. A., 212, 248
McGhee, P. E., 581, 605
MacGinitie, W. H., 492, 517
McGlothlin, W. H., 591, 608
McGraw, M. B., 69, 86, 106, 108
McGuire, R., 497, 498, 519
McGurk, H., 79, 106
Macht, L. B., 511, 522
Maciel, W., 172, 181
McInnes, R., 621, 646
McIntire, R. W., 119, 140
McIntyre, P. M., 663, 677
Mack, J. E., 511, 522
MacKay, M., 361, 370
McKee, J. P., 233, 251, 632, 647
McKeon, R., 4, 31

McKeown, T., 311, 334
McKillip, J., 596, 609
McKinney, W. T., 121, 141
McKnew, D. H., 506, 521
McLagen, M., 115, 139
McLaughlin, J. A., 548, 560
McManus, T., 25, 33
MacMillan, D. L., 200, 207
Macmillan, M. B., 195, 204
Macnamara, J., 89, 109
McNamara, P. M., 159, 179
McNeil, D., 88, 109, 117, 140, 240, 253
Macunovica, D., 628, 646
McWatters, M. A., 344, 365
Maddock, J. W., 589, 607
Mahler, M. S., 130, 143
Malmquist, C. P., 498, 506, 507, 519, 521
Malone, S., 386, 408
Manella, R. L., 670, 679
Mandler, G., 541, 559
Mangrum, J. C., 656, 676
Mankin, D., 596, 609
Mann, D., 509, 522
Mann, E. E., 494, 517
Mann, I., 80, 107
Mann, L., 82, 108, 347, 366, 495, 518
Mann, N. A., 195, 204
Manosevitz, M., 266, 293, 585, 606
Maratsos, M. P., 239, 242, 253
Marcia, J. E., 584, 585, 606
Marcus, D., 656, 676
Marcus, I. F., 663, 677
Marcus, J., 323, 336
Margolis, R. A., 345, 365
Markell, R. A., 418, 448
Marks, I. M., 355, 358, 369
Markus, G. B., 192, 204
Marland, S. P., 403, 411
Marolla, F. A., 311, 334
Marsh, J. G., 233, 251
Marsh, L., 216, 248
Martin, B., 122, 141, 259, 272, 276, 292
Martin, C. E., 589, 607
Martin, M. M., 213, 214, 248, 375, 376, 378, 407
Marwell, G., 669, 678
Masanz, J., 400, 411
Mason, K. O., 263, 293
Masse, G., 172, 181
Massimo, J. L., 670, 679

Masters, J. C., 278, 295, 436, 450
Masterson, J. F., 585, 606, 652-654, 656, 675, 676
Matarazzo, J. D., 536, 558
Matas, L., 124, 141
Matheny, A. P., Jr., 308, 333
May, M. A., 545, 560
May, P. R., 656, 676
Mayer, J., 614, 645
Mayor, F. E., 527, 557
Mays, J. B., 572, 604
Mead, G. H., 378, 407
Mead, M., 432, 450, 597, 610
Medawar, P. B., 149, 178
Mednick, S. A., 350, 352, 367, 368
Medvene, L., 545, 559
Meeks, J. E., 652, 675
Mehler, J., 236, 252
Meichenbaum, D. H., 346, 366, 496, 518
Meissner, W. W., 598, 610
Melear, J. D., 328, 336
Meleney, H. E., 532, 557
Melhuish, E., 117, 140
Mellsop, G. W., 501, 519
Mendelsohn, H., 286, 296
Mendelson, M., 344, 364, 506, 521
Mendelson, N., 494, 517
Mendelson, W. B., 344, 364
Menkes, J., 344, 364
Menkes, M., 344, 364
Menlove, F. L., 358, 369
Menolascino, F. J., 190, 203
Menyuk, P., 386, 408
Meredith, H. V., 172, 181
Merrill, M. A., 220, 248
Merten, D., 599, 610
Metcalfe, M., 192, 204
Meyer, W., 441, 451
Meyers, C. E., 200, 207, 302, 307, 332
Michael, S. T., 652, 675
Midlarsky, E., 283, 296
Miles, H. C., 652, 653, 675
Milgram, S., 546, 560
Millar, T. P., 497, 518
Miller, C. K., 548, 560
Miller, D. J., 92, 109
Miller, E. L., 186, 202
Miller, J., 506, 521
Miller, J. G., 669, 678
Miller, K., 548, 560
Miller, L., 123, 141
Miller, L. B., 325, 336

Miller, L. C., 355, 358, 369, 501, 502, 519
Miller, L. K., 383, 408
Miller, P. H., 398, 411
Miller, R. G., 340, 364
Miller, R. T., 349, 354, 367
Miller, S. A., 402, 411
Millichap, J. G., 345, 365
Millman, D. R., 596, 609
Millman, R. B., 591, 608
Mills, M., 117, 140
Minde, K., 341, 343, 344, 364, 494, 517
Minton, C., 435, 450
Minuchin, P., 419, 420, 448
Miranda, S. B., 83, 107, 115, 139
Mischel, W., 283, 296, 310, 334
Miser, A. L., 230, 250
Mishler, E. G., 352, 368
Mockaitis, J. P., 598, 610
Moffitt, A., 85, 107
Mohr, G., 68, 106
Molfese, D., 386, 388, 408
Monachesi, E. D., 632, 647, 661, 677
Moncrieff, A. A., 192, 204
Mondani, M. S., 665, 678
Money, J., 48, 62
Monge, R. H., 588, 607
Monk, M. A., 355, 369, 504, 520
Montagu, A., 36-38, 62
Montessori, M., 218, 245, 246, 326, 336
Montgomery, J., 194, 204
Moore, D. N., 245, 253
Moore, R. S., 245, 253
Moore, S. G., 270, 294
Moore, T. W., 123, 127, 141
Morales, E., 158, 179
More, D. M., 614, 617, 645
Moreign, F., 172, 181
Morf, M. E., 308, 334
Morgan, G. A., 124, 141
Morgan, H. S., 191, 203
Morris, L. A., 196, 205
Morrison, F. J., 168, 180
Morrison, J. R., 344, 365
Morrow, W. R., 661, 663, 665-667
Mosher, L. R., 347, 348, 366, 367, 655, 676
Moss, H. A., 116, 125, 132, 134, 139, 142, 144, 160, 180, 435, 450, 588, 606
Moss, J., 402, 411

Mulhern, J., 4-6, 31
Muller, E., 115, 139
Muma, J. R., 427, 449
Munsinger, H., 192, 204, 226, 249, 541, 559
Murphey, E. B., 585, 606
Murphy, L. B., 71, 106, 159, 179
Murray, D. C., 656, 676
Murray, J. P., 284, 296, 397, 410
Murray, T., 115, 139
Musa, K. E., 632, 633, 647
Mussen, P. H., 614, 636, 645, 646, 648
Muuss, R. E., 532, 554, 557, 560
Myers, N. A., 229, 250
Myers, P. I., 495, 518
Myrianthopolous, N. C., 344, 365

Nagy, M., 328, 336
Najarian, P., 198, 206
Nakazema, S., 88, 89, 109
Nanson, J. L., 344, 365
Nass, G. D., 575, 590, 591, 604, 607
Nassefat, M., 548, 560
Neale, J. M., 286, 296
Needleman, H. I., 344, 365
Neimark, E. D., 230, 250, 541, 543, 549, 559, 560
Nelson, A. K., 86, 108
Nelson, K. B., 190, 203
Nemeth, E., 343, 364
Nemiah, J. C., 503, 504, 520
Nerlove, H., 541, 559
Nesselroade, J. R., 536, 558
Neuringer, C., 659, 677
Nevis, S., 115, 139
Newhouse, R. C., 427, 449
Newman, M. B., 568, 604
Newston, D., 429, 449
Nichols, P. L., 301, 302, 305, 307, 332, 333
Niem, T. C., 321, 336
Niswander, K. R., 54, 63
Nitko, A. J., 383, 408
Noble, H., 355, 358, 359
Nordan, R., 501, 519
Northway, M. L., 427, 449
Norton, J. A., 196, 205
Nowlis, V., 127, 143
Numark, E., 391, 409
Nunn, R., 506, 521
NurEddin, E., 669, 678
Nursten, J. P., 499, 500, 519

O'Connell, E. J., 133, 144
O'Conner, G. O., 187, 202
Offer, D., 184, 202, 585, 589, 598, 599, 606, 607, 632-636, 647, 648
Offer, J. B., 585, 598, 599, 606, 633-636, 648
Offord, D. R., 350, 368, 654, 675
Ogilvie, E., 542, 559
Oldfield, S., 313, 335
Olds, S. W., 340, 364
O'Leary, K. D., 346, 366, 496, 518
Oliveau, D. C., 358, 369
Oliver, H. G., 596, 609
Olson, D. R., 389, 409
Olson, F. A., 541, 559
Olson, J. P., 161, 179
O'Malley, J., 341, 364
O'Media, J., 497, 519
Omenn, G., 344, 365
Omori, Y., 190, 203
Omwake, E., 286, 296
Opie, I., 402, 411
Opie, P., 402, 411
Opler, M. D., 652, 675
Oppel, W. C., 68, 106, 190, 203, 508, 521
Ordy, J. M., 81, 107
Orlofsky, J. L., 585, 606
Ornitz, E. M., 195, 204
O'Rogan, K., 236, 252
Osborne, M., 389, 409
Osborne, R. T., 301, 307, 332, 333
Oshman, H. P., 266, 293, 585, 606
Osofsky, J. D., 133, 144, 315, 335
Osser, H., 227, 249
Ounsted, C., 194, 204
Overly, N. V., 325, 336
Owen, D., 283, 296
Owen, F. W., 491, 494, 517

Page, P. V., 659, 677
Paine, R. S., 341, 364
Palermo, D. S., 239, 252, 386, 388, 408
Palkes, H. S., 340, 346, 361, 364, 366, 370, 496, 518
Palmer, B., 119, 140
Pamalee, A. A., 68, 106
Pampiglione, G., 192, 204
Papalia, D. E., 536, 549, 558, 560
Papousek, H., 94, 110
Paris, S. G., 392, 409
Parke, R. D., 272, 276, 294, 496, 518

Parker, R., 101, 110
Parnell, R. W., 619, 621, 646
Parton, D. A., 118, 140
Pasamanick, B., 79, 107
Pascual-Leone, J., 549, 560
Pathwardan, V. N., 155, 179
Patterson, E., 592, 596, 608
Patterson, G. R., 346, 366, 442, 451, 496, 518
Patton, R. G., 198, 206
Paul, L. L., 668, 678
Paulson, M. J., 507, 521
Pearlin, L. I., 585, 606
Pearsall, D., 592, 608
Pearson, G., 159, 179
Pearson, G. H., 494, 517
Peck, A. L., 501, 519
Peck, B. B., 494, 517
Pedersen, F. A., 120, 125, 131, 134, 136, 140, 142, 143, 263, 293, 435, 450
Pederson, A., 501, 519
Pederson, L. J., 93, 110
Peel, E. A., 540, 559
Pelled, N., 123, 141
Peluffo, N., 235, 252, 549, 560
Perlmutter, M., 229, 250
Perlstein, A. P., 659, 677
Persach, E., 397, 410
Pestalozzi, J. H., 7, 8, 245
Peters, J., 343, 364
Peters, J. E., 491, 494, 516, 518
Peterson, J., 442, 451
Petzel, T. P., 596, 609
Phares, E. J., 440, 451
Phatak, P., 173, 181
Philage, M. L., 494, 517
Phillips, V. A., 596, 609
Phoenix, M. D., 93, 110
Piaget, J., 7, 10, 16-18, 21-25, 31-33, 74, 87, 89, 95-100, 102-104, 106, 108, 110, 224, 230-238, 241-243, 249, 250-253, 328-330, 337, 378, 380, 382, 385-387, 390, 392, 393, 396-401, 407-410, 535, 537-539, 542, 543, 547, 548, 558, 560
Pichel, J. I., 653, 675
Pick, A. D., 227, 249, 383, 385, 408
Pickens, J. W., 629, 647
Pierce, C. M., 508, 521
Pierce, J. V., 661, 677
Piers, E. V., 632, 647
Piers, G., 271, 294
Pine, F., 130, 143
Pitt, R., 655, 676

Pittman, F. S., 501, 519
Pittman, G. D., 653, 675
Pivchik, E. C., 198, 206
Place, D. M., 577, 605
Plato, 4
Plomin, R., 133, 144, 284, 296, 344, 365, 435, 440
Poag, K., 385, 408
Polio, H., 541, 559
Polio, M., 541, 559
Polizos, P., 345, 365
Pollack, M., 654, 656, 675, 676
Pollack, Y., 654, 675
Pollitt, E., 198, 206
Pomerleau-Malcuit, A., 92, 109
Pomeroy, W. B., 589, 607
Pontius, W., 196, 205
Poole, E., 172, 181
Pope, H. G., 596, 609
Popham, W. J., 383, 407
Post, B., 311, 334
Poulos, R. W., 284, 286, 287, 296, 297
Powell, G. F., 198, 206
Powell, G. J., 639, 640, 648
Poznanski, E. O., 355, 356, 369, 507, 521
Pratt, K. C., 86, 108
Prawatt, R. S., 392, 409
Prechtl, H. F., 85, 108
Preisman, R., 352, 368
Prendergrast, T. J., 596, 609
Preston, A., 259, 292, 421, 425, 448
Preyer, W., 9, 32
Prior, M., 195, 204
Proctor, J. T., 504, 520
Proshansky, H. M., 425, 448
Proskauer, S., 591, 608
Provence, S., 101, 110, 198, 199, 206, 207
Prugh, D. G., 350, 367
Purnell, R. F., 582, 605
Pusser, H. E., 286, 297

Quay, H. C., 341, 364, 495, 518, 669, 678
Quay, L. C., 200, 207
Query, J. M., 582, 605
Quinn, R. P., 625, 646

Raab, E., 598, 610
Rabson, A., 259, 263, 292, 293
Rachman, S., 358, 369
Rader, N., 385, 408
Radin, N., 264, 293

Rafferty, J. Y., 260, 292
Ragins, N., 352, 368
Rainwater, L., 591, 608
Ramsey, C. E., 572, 588, 604
Rao, K. S., 155, 179
Rau, L., 278, 295, 427, 449
Raud, S., 542, 559
Ravenscroft, K., 568, 604
Rayner, R., 356, 369
Raz, I., 227, 249
Record, R. G., 311, 334
Redlich, F. C., 652, 675
Rees, F., 198, 206
Rees, J., 198, 206
Reese, C., 640, 648
Reese, H. W., 233, 251, 437, 450
Reeves, K., 621, 646
Reevy, W. R., 579, 605
Reichler, R. J., 196, 205
Reider, R. O., 348, 367
Reifman, A., 348, 367
Reiner, B. S., 494, 517
Reinert, G., 536, 558
Reiss, I. L., 589, 607
Rennie, T. A., 652, 675
Renshaw, D. C., 438, 451
Resick, P. A., 275, 294
Rest, J. R., 400, 411
Rewitzer, M., 599, 610
Rexford, E. N., 502, 520
Rheingold, H. L., 93, 110, 119, 125, 126, 129, 140, 142, 143, 197, 198, 206, 282, 295
Rheingold, J. C., 51, 63
Rhodes, W. C., 670, 679
Ricciuti, H. N., 124, 141
Richardson, S. A., 157, 179, 190, 192, 203, 204
Richer, J. M., 194, 204
Richer, S., 422, 448
Richmond, J., 165, 180
Ricks, D., 135, 144, 501, 512, 519
Ridberg, E. H., 496, 518
Rider, R. V., 68, 106, 190, 203, 508, 521
Rie, E. D., 361, 370
Rie, H. E., 361, 370, 506, 521
Riley, D. A., 233, 251
Rimland, B., 194, 195, 204, 205
Rinsley, D. B., 656, 676
Ripley, H. S., 660, 677
Ritchey, G., 126, 142
Ritter, K., 230, 250
Ritvo, E. R., 195, 196, 204, 205
Ritvo, S., 199, 207

Roach, M. E., 632, 633, 647
Robbins, O., 397, 410
Roberts, D., 285, 296
Roberts, M. W., 275, 294
Robertson, J., 127, 142
Robey, J. S., 170, 172, 181
Robins, L. N., 501, 512, 519, 668, 670, 678
Robinson, H. B., 49, 62, 123, 141, 192, 204
Robinson, I., 311, 334
Robinson, I. E., 586, 607
Robinson, J. A., 595, 609
Robinson, N. M., 49, 62, 123, 141, 192, 204
Robles, B., 155, 156, 179
Robson, K. S., 116, 125, 132, 139, 142
Rock, N. L., 504, 521
Rockefeller, L. S., 11
Rockway, A., 545, 559
Rodnick, E. H., 351, 353, 368
Rodriguez, A., 196, 205, 502, 520
Rodriguez, M., 502, 520
Roff, J. D., 656, 676
Roff, M., 427, 449, 621, 646
Rogalski, C., 654, 675
Rogers, J., 585, 606
Rogers, M., 502, 520
Rohwer, W. D., 245, 253
Rolf, J. E., 353, 369
Roll, S., 397, 410, 523, 557
Rolland, R. S., 591, 608
Romano, J., 652, 653, 675
Romer, N., 660, 678
Rommetvert, R., 388, 408
Rooks, M. McC., 427, 449
Root, A. W., 527, 557
Rosales, L., 170, 172, 181
Rose, M., 81, 107
Rose, S. A., 227, 249
Rose, S. N., 115, 139
Rosen, R., 259, 262
Rosenberg, B. G., 313, 335
Rosenberg, D., 88, 109
Rosenberg, F., 585, 606
Rosenberg, F. R., 632, 633, 647
Rosenberg, J. S., 592, 608
Rosenberg, M., 585, 606, 632, 639, 647, 648
Rosenberg, S., 172, 181, 390, 409
Rosenblatt, C., 344, 365
Rosenblatt, P. C., 313, 334
Rosenblith, J. F., 160, 179
Rosenblum, L. A., 126, 142
Rosenfeld, R., 345, 365

Rosenfield, L., 527, 557
Rosenthal, D., 350, 352, 353, 367-369
Rosenthal, H., 543, 559
Rosenthal, R., 426, 449
Rosenthal, T. L., 398, 411
Ross, A. O., 492, 495, 517, 518
Ross, B., 231, 250
Ross, D. M., 281, 295, 340, 363
Ross, G., 127, 142
Ross, H. S., 125, 142
Ross, H. W., 93, 110, 119, 140
Ross, R., 361, 370
Ross, S. A., 281, 295, 340, 363
Roth, S., 198, 206
Rothenberg, B. B., 236, 252
Rotter, G. C., 389, 409
Rotter, G. S., 315, 324, 335
Rotter, J. B., 273, 294
Rottman, L., 572, 604, 621, 646
Rourke, B. P., 491, 517
Rousseau, J. J., 6, 7, 12, 31
Routh, D. K., 88, 108, 119, 140
Rovee, C. K., 86, 108
Rowe, J., 344, 364
Rubenstein, J. L., 120, 125, 134, 136, 140, 142, 435, 450
Rubin, E. Z., 493, 517
Rubin, R., 344, 365
Ruble, D. N., 424, 448
Ruff, H. A., 83, 107
Rule, B. G., 279, 295
Rushton, J. P., 282, 283, 295, 296
Rutherford, E., 636, 648
Rutherford, J., 429, 449
Ruttenberg, B. A., 196, 206
Rutter, M., 195-198, 204-206, 256, 292, 348-350, 367, 368, 438, 451, 501, 519, 585, 606
Ryan, S. M., 230, 250
Rynders, J. E., 200, 207

Saario, T. N., 623, 646
Sabshin, M., 184, 202, 506, 521
Sackett, G. P., 121, 141
Safer, D. J., 340, 341, 344, 345, 360, 361, 364, 365, 370
Salapatek, P., 82, 83, 107
Salinsky, M., 308, 334
Saltz, R., 198, 206
Saltzstein, H. D., 275, 294, 435, 450, 546, 547, 560
Sameroff, A. J., 50, 54, 62, 63, 93, 110, 134, 144
Sampson, E. E., 313, 335
Sander, L. W., 85, 108

San Martino, M. R., 568, 604
Santrock, J. W., 265, 293, 636, 648
Santwik, J. W., 229, 240
Sarnoff, C., 437, 450
Sarver, G. S., 25, 33
Satterfield, B. T., 345, 346, 365, 366
Saudargas, R. A., 496, 518
Scarr-Salapatek, S., 80, 107, 150, 151, 178, 192, 204, 301, 305, 307, 332
Schachter, B., 591, 608
Schachter, J., 352, 368
Schachter, S., 313, 335
Schaefer, E. S., 596, 609
Schaefer, G., 50, 62
Schaefer, J. W., 361, 370
Schafer, R., 276, 295
Schaffer, H. R., 95, 110, 122, 123, 132, 141, 144, 152, 179, 263, 293
Schaie, K. W., 536, 558
Schechter, M. D., 490, 493, 516
Scheerenberger, R. C., 185, 202
Scheffelin, M. A., 341, 364
Scheinfeld, A., 260, 292
Scheresky, R., 435, 450
Schmidt, B. J., 172, 181
Schmitt, S. S., 589, 607
Schnall, M., 397, 410
Schneider, R. E., 396, 410
Schoenfeldt, L. F., 592, 608
Schofield, M., 589, 591, 607, 608
Schon, G. L., 585, 606
Schooler, C., 311, 334
Schopler, E., 196, 205
Schreibman, L., 196, 205
Schroeder, C., 428, 449, 599, 610
Schuchman, H. P., 585, 606
Schuham, A. I., 351, 368
Schulsinger, F., 352, 368
Schulsinger, H., 352, 368
Schultz, C. B., 422, 448
Schurr, K. T., 200, 207
Schwartz, G., 599, 610
Schwarz, C., 386, 408
Schwentzer, T., 397, 410
Scott, P. M., 132, 144, 283, 296
Scrimshaw, N. S., 55, 63
Sears, P. S., 127, 143
Sears, R. R., 9, 11, 14, 32, 127, 129, 143, 275, 278, 294, 295, 435, 450
Seay, W., 121, 126, 141, 142
Secord, P. F., 535, 558
Seiden, A. M., 572, 577, 604
Seiden, R. H., 658, 676
Seidman, E., 671, 679

Seitz, V., 316, 335
Seligman, M. E., 506, 521
Sells, S. B., 427, 449
Selman, R. L., 277, 295
Selzer, M. L., 653, 675
Semler, I. J., 305, 307, 333
Senecol, M. J., 172, 181
Senf, G. M., 491, 517
Seriffs, A. C., 632, 647
Sever, J. L., 190, 203
Severy, L. J., 282, 296
Sexton, P. C., 441, 451
Schacter, H. S., 375, 407
Shafer, S. M., 625, 646
Shaffer, D., 660, 677
Shantz, M., 242, 253
Shapiro, E., 419, 448
Shapiro, I., 669, 678
Shapiro, T., 502, 520
Sharan (Singer), S., 308, 333
Shaw, C. R., 502, 505, 520
Shaw, M. C., 660, 663, 677, 678
Shaw, M. E., 429, 449
Sheldon, W., 618, 619, 646
Sheppard, T. L., 397, 398, 410
Sherick, I., 266, 293
Sherif, C. W., 432, 450
Sherif, M., 432, 450
Sherman, M., 233, 251
Sherwood, J. J., 639, 648
Shetty, T., 346, 366
Shields, J., 353, 369
Shinn, M. W., 10, 32
Shipman, V. C., 308, 315, 324, 333, 335, 421, 448
Shlapack, W., 86, 108
Shneidman, E. S., 658, 660, 676, 677
Shore, M. F., 670, 679
Short, J. F., 669, 678
Shumacher, G., 229, 250
Shwartz, A., 88, 109
Siegal, A., 668, 678
Siegler, R. S., 398, 411
Silber, E., 585, 606
Silberman, C. E., 418, 447
Silberman, M., 425, 442, 448
Sills, M., 499, 501, 519
Silver, M. A., 656, 676
Silverman, C., 656, 676
Silverman, I. W., 397, 410
Siman, M. L., 430, 450
Simmer, M. L., 88, 108
Simmons, R. G., 585, 606, 632, 633, 639, 647, 648

Simon, B., 346, 366
Simon, N., 195, 205
Simon, T., 221, 248
Simon, W., 577, 579, 598, 605, 610
Sims, O. S., 592, 608
Sims-Knight, J., 230, 250
Sinclair, H. J., 89, 109, 396, 398, 410
Sinclair-deZwart, H., 387, 408
Singer, M., 512, 522
Singer, M. T., 271, 294, 351, 368
Singer, R., 285, 286, 296
Singer, S. B., 360, 370
Single, E., 592, 608
Siqueland, E. R., 85, 108
Sitkei, E. G., 302, 307, 332
Skeels, H. M., 80, 107, 150, 178, 198, 199, 207, 300, 332
Skinner, B. F., 17, 32, 93, 110, 240, 253, 382, 407
Skipper, J. K., 575, 604
Skodak, M., 300, 332
Skoogberg, E. L., 313, 374
Slaff, B., 54, 63
Slaughter, D. T., 422, 448
Slobin, D. I., 89, 109, 240, 253, 388, 408
Slobodian, J., 441, 451
Slotnick, N. S., 230, 250, 391, 409, 542, 559
Smart, R. G., 592, 596, 608, 609
Smedslund, J., 235, 252, 396, 410
Smith, C. P., 259, 292
Smith, D., 502, 520
Smith, D. W., 344, 365
Smith, G. M., 596, 609
Smith, H. T., 71, 106
Smith, L. E., 123, 126, 141, 142
Smith, L. M., 425, 448
Smith, M. B., 546, 560
Smith, M. D., 89, 109
Smith, R., 285, 296
Smith, R. F., 242, 253
Smith, R. S., 592, 608
Smith, S. L., 502, 520
Smith, S. W., 190, 203
Smith, T. A., 307, 333
Smothergill, D. W., 398, 411
Smythe, P. M., 157, 179
Snow, R. E., 426, 449
Sobel, D., 589, 607
Sobel, R., 503, 520
Sobol, M. P., 286, 297
Sollenberger, R. T., 322, 336
Solley, C. M., 227, 249

Solomon, M. H., 653, 675
Sorenson, R. C., 589, 607
Soskin, W. F., 596, 609
Southwell, M. A., 670, 679
Sparks, H. L., 200, 207
Spears, W. C., 80, 107
Sperling, M., 358, 370, 497, 502, 518, 520
Sperry, B. M., 490, 494, 500, 516, 517
Spicker, H. H., 200, 207
Spiegel, L. A., 584, 606
Spiegel, R., 507, 521
Spitz, R. A., 117, 140, 196, 197, 206
Sprafkin, J. N., 286, 287, 297
Sprague, R. L., 491, 516
Sprinthall, N., 661, 677
Spuhler, J. N., 192, 204, 301-303, 307, 332
Srole, L., 652, 675
Sroufe, L. A., 124, 141, 258, 292, 345, 360, 365
Staffieri, J. R., 428, 449
Staines, G. L., 625, 646
Stambak, M., 227, 249
Stander, R. J., 502, 519
Stanton, J. E., 200, 207
Stark, P. A., 585, 606
Stark, R. E., 115, 139
Staver, N., 494, 517
Stayton, D. J., 122, 123, 131, 141, 143, 144, 146
Stearns, R. P., 502, 519
Stechler, G., 116, 140
Stedman, D., 166, 180
Steele, B., 81, 107
Steele, R., 196, 205
Steffe, L. P., 397, 410
Steffenhagen, R. A., 596, 609
Stehbens, J. A., 508, 521
Stein, A. H., 285, 286, 296, 297
Stein, K. B., 596, 609
Stein, M., 93, 110
Steinberg, G. G., 345, 360, 365
Steinberg, H. R., 345, 360, 365
Stendler, C. B., 415, 447
Stengel, E., 656, 658, 676
Stephen, E., 191, 203
Stephens, B., 548, 560
Stephens, J. H., 656, 676
Stephens, L. S., 491, 516
Stephers, D., 541, 559
Stern, D. N., 116, 140, 311, 334
Steuer, F. B., 285, 296
Stevens, J. R., 668, 678

Stevens-Long, J., 196, 205, 343, 364
Stevenson, H. L., 234, 251
Stewart, C. S., 589, 592, 607, 608
Stewart, M. A., 340, 344, 361, 364-366, 370, 496, 518
Stewart, S., 361, 370
Stewart, W. A., 315, 335
Stingle, K. G., 276, 295
Stith, M., 441, 451
Stoats. A., 240, 253
Stock, M. B., 157, 179
Stodolsky, S. S., 305, 307, 333
Stolorow, R. D., 654, 675
Stolz, H. R., 535, 558, 614, 615, 646
Stolz, L. M., 491, 494, 517, 535, 558, 614, 615, 646
Stone, D., 507, 521
Stone, J. L., 71, 106
Stone, J. M., 397, 410
Stone, S. P., 614, 615, 617, 646
Stott, D. H., 54, 63
Stoudt, H. W., 212, 248
Streissguth, A. P., 344, 365
Streit, F., 596, 609
Strimbu, J. L., 592, 608
Stringer, L. A., 425, 448
Stroebe, W., 572, 604, 621, 646
Stuart, R. B., 671, 679
Stuckland, S. P., 150, 165, 178
Stunk, J., 233, 251
Su, W., 596, 609
Sudia, C. E., 265, 266, 293, 313, 335
Sullivan, H. S., 434, 450, 578, 579, 599-601, 605
Sully, J., 10, 32
Sum, G., 361, 370
Sun, K. H., 86, 108
Suomi, S., 121, 141
Surwillo, W. W., 377, 407
Sussevein, B. J., 242, 253
Sutherland, B. K., 633, 677
Sutton-Smith, B., 313, 335
Suzuki, T., 491, 516
Swaminathan, N. C., 155, 179
Swanlund, T., 397, 410
Swanson, H. D., 38, 40, 41, 45-47, 62, 152, 178
Switt, C. D., 83, 107
Switzkey, H. N., 226, 249
Sykes, E., 344, 364
Symonds, A., 654, 675
Symonds, P. M., 588, 607
Szeminska, A., 234, 251, 252, 395, 410, 542, 559

Szurek, S., 349, 354, 367, 369

Taber, T., 303, 333
Talbot, M., 497, 518
Tannenbaum, J., 123, 141
Tanner, J. M., 374, 407, 527-529, 530-532, 557, 614, 645
Tarakanov, V. V., 309, 409
Tarjan, G., 187, 188, 202
Taube, J., 653, 675
Tayzer, D., 301, 332
Tec, N., 592, 596, 608, 609
Tecce, J. J., 116, 140
Teevan, R. C., 581, 605
Teicher, J. D., 659, 660, 677
Templer, D. I., 503, 520
Tennes, K. H., 124, 125, 141
Tenney, Y. J., 385, 408
Terman, L. M., 14, 15, 220, 248, 536, 558
Tessman, E., 498, 519
Thiele, R. L., 188, 203
Thoday, J. M., 302, 333
Thomas, E. B., 132, 144, 161, 179
Thomas, A., 132, 144, 153, 154, 179, 323, 336, 504, 521
Thomas, K. A., 641, 648
Thomas, L. E., 599, 610
Thomas, M. H., 286, 297
Thompson, G., 441, 451
Thompson, G. G., 574, 604
Thompson, H., 256, 292
Thompson, S. K., 311, 334
Thompson, V. D., 572, 604, 621, 646
Thornburg, H. D., 577, 578, 605
Thorndike, R. L., 426, 449
Thorne, D. E., 509, 522
Thum, D., 596, 609
Thurman, S. K., 188, 203
Thurston, D., 191, 203
Tiller, P. O., 313, 314, 335
Tilton, J. R., 195, 204
Tittle, C. K., 623, 646
Tizard, B., 125, 142
Tizard, J., 125, 142, 157, 179, 190, 192, 198, 203, 204, 206
Toban, W., 386, 408
Tobian, J. J., 669, 678
Tobin, H., 491, 516
Todd, G. A., 119, 140
Toigo, R., 427, 449
Tolone, W. L., 596, 609
Tolor, A., 599, 610
Tome, H. R., 640, 641, 648

Tomlinson-Keasey, C., 230, 250, 542, 559
Toohey, J. V., 592, 608
Toohey, M. L., 351, 368
Toolan, J. M., 658, 677
Torgesen, J., 491, 516
Torup, E., 504, 520
Towbin, A., 344, 365
Towne, R. C., 200, 207
Trabasso, T., 235, 252
Traxler, A. J., 585, 606
Trecker, J. L., 623, 646
Treffert, D. A., 193, 195, 204, 205
Troshinsky, C., 345, 360, 365
Trost, M. A., 418, 448, 501, 519
Tuckman, J., 658, 677
Tuddenham, R. D., 427, 449
Tuel, J. K., 628, 647
Tulkin, S. R., 302, 332, 333
Tulving, E., 392, 409
Turiel, E., 400, 411
Turner, E. A., 388, 408
Turnure, J. E., 347, 366
Tutko, T. A., 665, 678
Tyler, B. B., 260, 292
Tyler, F. B., 260, 292
Tyler, R. W., 382, 407
Tyrer, P., 500, 519
Tyrer, S., 500, 519

Udelf, M. S., 81, 107
Udell, J. G., 592, 608
Ulrich, D., 494, 517
Ulrich, T., 230, 250, 391, 409, 541, 559
Unwin, J. R., 670, 679
Upham, W. K., 642, 648
Uzgiris, I. C., 162, 180

Vaillant, G. E., 656, 676
Valenstein, A. F., 49, 62
Van Amerongen, S. T., 502, 520
Vandersall, T. A., 511, 522
Vande Voort, L., 491, 517
Van Doorninck, W., 386, 408
Vaught, S. M., 308, 334
Vaz, E. W., 669, 678
Vega, L., 170, 172, 181
Veltkamp, L. J., 502, 520
Vener, A. M., 589, 592, 607, 608
Verinis, J. S., 534, 557
Vernon, P. E., 235, 252
Veroff, J., 259, 292, 424, 448
Vetter, H. J., 117, 140

Vigorito, J., 85, 108
Von Bernuh, H., 85, 108
von der Lippe, A., 436, 450
Voulloux, P., 172, 181
Vreeland, R., 653, 675
Vurpillot, E., 383, 408

Wachs, T. D., 162, 180
Waddington, C. H., 148, 178
Wadland, W., 266, 293
Waite, R. R., 418, 447, 448
Waizer, J., 345, 365
Walbek, N. H., 283, 296
Walberg, H. J., 625, 626, 629, 630, 646, 647
Walder, L. O., 286, 297
Waldfogel, S., 497, 498, 501, 518, 519
Waldrop, M. F., 135, 144, 270, 294
Wales, R., 239, 240, 252
Walk, R. D., 83, 107
Walkowitz, J., 54, 63
Wallon, H., 328, 337
Walls, R. C., 491, 516
Wallston, B., 123, 141
Walster, E., 572, 604, 621, 646
Walters, P. A., 596, 609
Walters, R. H., 276, 277, 294, 295, 670, 679
Wapner, S., 542, 559
Ward, J. W., 232, 251
Warren, J. M., 232, 250
Warren, W., 656, 678
Wash, J. A., 425, 448, 535, 558
Washburne, C. W., 403, 411
Waterman, A. S., 585, 586, 606
Waterman, C. K., 585, 586, 606
Waters, E., 124, 141
Watrous, B., 322, 336
Watson, C., 596, 609
Watson, E. H., 374, 407
Watson, G., 632, 647
Watson, J. B., 135, 144, 356, 369
Watson, J. S., 258, 292
Watt, N. F., 654, 655, 675
Watts, J. C., 95, 101, 110
Waxler, C. Z., 132, 144, 282, 283, 295, 296
Waxler, N. E., 352, 368
Weatherly, D., 614, 646
Weaver, J., 575, 605
Wechsler, D., 221, 222, 248
Wechsler, H., 596, 609
Weenstein, H., 173, 181

Weigert, E., 50-52, 62
Weinberg, D. H., 397, 410
Weinberg, R. A., 151, 179
Weinberger, G., 502, 519
Weiner, I. B., 349, 367, 499, 501, 519, 572, 589, 599, 604, 610, 652-654, 656, 660, 663, 666-669, 675-678
Weiner, S. L., 239, 252
Weinstock, A., 599, 610
Weisberg, P., 93, 110, 119, 140
Weisberg, R., 242, 253
Weiss, G., 341, 343, 344, 361, 364, 494, 517
Weiss, J., 385, 408
Weiss, M., 502, 520
Weiss, S. D., 82, 108, 265, 293, 636, 648
Weissman, M. M., 658, 676
Weisz, J. R., 235, 252
Weithorn, C. J., 361, 370
Weller, T., 308, 333
Wellman, A. M., 230, 250
Wellman, B. L., 213, 214, 248
Welner, J., 352, 368
Welsh, C. A., 89, 109
Wenar, C., 196, 206
Wender, P. H., 340, 341, 343, 345, 352, 360, 361, 363-365, 368, 491, 516
Werner, E. E., 174, 181
Werry, J. S., 341, 343, 347, 350, 354, 364, 366, 491, 504, 508, 509, 516, 520, 522
West, M. J., 282, 295
Westheimer, I., 126, 142
Wetherford, M. J., 92, 109
Wethle, E., 311, 334
Whatley, J. L., 268, 293
White, B. J., 432, 450
White, B. L., 70, 95, 101, 106, 110, 116, 140, 245, 253, 258, 292
White, L., 350, 368
White, R. B., 584, 606
White, R. M., Jr., 232, 251
White, R. W., 259, 292
White, S. H., 231, 250
White, W. F., 425, 448, 535, 558
Whitehead, A. N., 538
Whitehead, P. C., 595, 609
Whiteman, M., 315, 324, 335, 397, 410
Whiteside, J., 226, 249, 385, 408
Whiting, B., 284, 296
Whiting, J. W. M., 127, 143
Whittier, J., 346, 366, 496, 518

Wiberg, J. L., 418, 448
Wickelgren, L., 81, 107
Wicker, A. W., 416, 447
Widdowson, E. M., 155, 179
Wiener, G., 68, 106, 190, 203
Wiener, J., 282, 295
Wiener, M., 492, 517
Wilkinson, A., 436, 450
Wilkinson, E. M., 54, 63
Willems, E. P., 417, 447
Willemsen, E., 126, 142
Willer, M. L., 498, 519
Willerman, L., 344, 365
Williams, H. G., 376, 407
Williams, J. E., 435, 450
Williams, J. W., 441, 451
Williams, R. L., 629, 647
Willis, R. H., 581, 605
Willows, D. M., 492, 517
Wilson, A. A., 190, 203
Wilson, A. B., 302, 333
Wilson, H., 511, 522
Wilson, R. C., 661, 663, 677
Wilson, R. R., 589, 607
Wilson, R. S., 148, 178
Wilson, W. C., 346, 366
Wilson, W. P., 652, 675
Wilton, K. M., 398, 411
Winder, C. L., 427, 449
Winer, J. M., 511, 522
Wing, J. K., 195, 199, 205, 207
Winick, M., 192, 204
Winnicott, D. W., 129, 143, 652, 675
Wirt, R. D., 667, 678
Wiseman, D., 495, 518
Wishy, B., 12, 32
Witkin, H. A., 308, 334
Witmer, L., 14, 512
Wittig, B. A., 126, 142
Woerner, M. G., 654, 675
Wohlwill, J. F., 17, 25, 26, 32, 33, 236, 252, 396, 410
Wolf, K. M., 196, 206
Wolf, K. W., 117, 140
Wolf, R. M., 382, 407
Wolfensberger, W., 188, 203
Wolff, P. H., 73, 95, 98, 106, 110, 114-117, 139, 491, 516
Wolff, W. M., 196, 205
Wolinsky, A. L., 441, 442, 451
Wollersheim, J. P., 200, 207
Woltmann, A. G., 358, 370
Won, G. Y., 582, 605
Wood, J. W., 190, 203

Woodruff, D. S., 588, 607
Woolsey, R. M., 503, 520
Worden, P., 391, 393, 409, 410
Wright, C., 123, 141
Wright, J. C., 242, 253, 389, 390, 409
Wright, M. A., 346, 366, 496, 518
Wright, S. W., 188, 202
Wunsch, J. A., 258, 292
Wynne, L. C., 351, 368

Yamamoto, L., 427, 449
Yamamura, D. S., 582, 605
Yannet, H., 191, 203
Yanni, D. W., 491, 517
Yarrow, L. J., 119, 120, 122, 124,
   125, 127, 131, 134, 136, 140-143,
   198, 206, 435, 450
Yarrow, M. R., 132, 144, 282, 283,

295, 296, 427, 449
Yates, A. J., 504, 520
Yerushalmy, J., 54, 63
Yolles, S. F., 347, 366
Yorburg, B., 589, 607
Youness, J., 231, 250
Young, A. M., 627, 641
Young, G. C., 491, 517
Young, N., 415, 447
Yule, W., 172, 181, 585, 606
Yusin, A. S., 659, 677
Yussen, S. R., 229, 230, 249, 390,
   391, 409

Zahn, T. P., 345, 365
Zajonc, R. B., 192, 204
Zaks, M. S., 585, 606
Zara, R. C., 233, 251

Zaslow, M., 385, 408
Zax, M., 54, 63
Zeaman, D., 232, 251
Zeiler, M. D., 234, 251
Zelazo, P., 127, 142
Zelnik, M., 590, 607
Zerbin-Rudin, E., 350, 367
Zheutlin, L. S., 596, 609
Zigler, E., 188, 193, 203, 204, 224,
   249, 316, 335
Zigmond, N. K., 490, 516
Zimet, S. G., 418, 447, 448
Zimiles, H., 419, 448
Zimmerman, B. J., 398, 411
Zimmerman, R. R., 121, 129, 140
Zinchenko, V. P., 390, 409
Zrull, J. P., 507, 521
Zwirner, W., 275, 294

Subject Index

Academic achievement: in American Indians, 474-422
  and family size, 472-473
  and intelligence, 454
  and level of aspiration, 456
  and motivation, 259, 454-456
  parental influences on, 420-422
  and school drop-out, 628
  sex differences in, 464
  social class influences on, 421-422, 456-457
  teachers' influences on, 425-426
  see also Learning disability
Academic underachievement: concerns about rivalry in, 663-666
  fear of failure in, 663-665
  fear of success in, 665
  hostility in, 663-666
  motivation in, 661-663
  passive-aggressive behavior in, 665-666
  psychological reasons for, 663-666
  sociocultural reasons for, 661-663
  treatment of, 666
  see also Learning disability
Accommodation, 95
Achievement motivation, see Academic achievement
Achievement tests, 381-383
Acrosome, 36
Adherences, in interviews, 24
Adolescent growth spurt, 527
  early, 614-615
  late, 616-617
Adolescent rebellion, myth of, 597-599
Adolescent schizophrenia:
  indications of, 654-655
  outcome of, 655-656
  see also Childhood schizophrenia; Schizophrenia
Adolescent turmoil, 584, 652-653
Age differentiation hypothesis, 536
Aggresssion: development of, 279-282
  hostile versus instrumental, 279-281
  impact of television on, 284-286
  sex differences in, 310-311
Albinism, 49
Alcohol, see drug use

Alienation, sense of, 431-432
Alleles, 40
Altruism: development of, 282-283
  impact of television on, 286-287
Amniocentesis, 49
Amniotic cavity, 44-45
Amphetamines, see Drug use
Animism, 243-244
Anoxia, 190-191, 344
Anthropomorphism, 328-329
Anticipation, in interviews, 24
Aptitude tests, 381-383
Assimilation, 95
Attachments to people: behaviors that foster, 122-123
  nature of, 121-122
  origins of, 127-129
  and separation anxiety, 125-127
  and stranger anxiety, 123-125
Attention, in infancy, 91-92
Audition, in infancy, 83-85
Authoritarian control, 259, 568-571
Authoritative control, 259
Autonomy, sense of, 262

Babbling, 88, 117-118
  sex differences in, 159-160
Baby biographies, 9-10
Basal age, 221
Bayley Scales of Infant Development, 169
Behavior-directed discipline, 276
Behavior therapy, 93-94
  in childhood schizophrenia, 354
  in delinquent behavior, 670-671
  in habit disturbances, 508-509
  in infantile autism, 196
  in learning disabilities, 496
  in minimal brain dysfunction, 346
  in phobic reactions, 358
  in school phobia, 562
Belonging, sense of, 431-432, 572
Bereiter-Engelmann program, 325
Bilingual Education Act, 457
Birth hazards, 58-59
Birth order effects: in infancy, 162-163
  in preschool years, 311-313
Birth process, 57-58

Body awareness, *see* Body image
Body build, *see* Physique
Body image: in adolescence, 533-535, 614
in middle childhood, 378-380
in preschool years, 256-258
Breech delivery, 58

Canalization, 148
Castration anxiety, 258
Catharsis hypothesis, 285-286
Causality, sense of, 99-101, 243
Causative methods, 24-26
Cerebral palsy, 191
Cesarean section, 58
Characterological delinquency, 669-670
Character disorder, nature of, 669-670
Child guidance movement, 14-15
Childhood fears, 354-355
Childhood rituals, 357
Childhood schizophrenia: as distinguished from infantile autism, 347-348
incidence of, 347
neurological dysfunction in, 350
origin of, 350-353
prognosis in, 353-354
sex differences in, 348
symptoms of, 349-350
treatment of, 354
see also Schizophrenia
Children's Embedded Figure Test (CEFT), 29, 461
Child study institutes, 11-12
Child study movement, 10-11
"Chitling Test," 28
Chorion, 43, 45
Chromosomes, 38, 39, 40, 41
Chumships, 433-434
Circular reactions, 96
Class, concepts of, 237-238
Classical conditioning, 92-93
Clustering, 391
Cognitive styles, 29, 460-463
sex differences, in, 464-465
Color blindness, 41
Colostrum, 59
Combinatorial thinking, 542-544
Communal farms, *see* Kibbutz
Compensation training, 397
Concept formation: in adolescence, 544-545

in infancy, 98-101
in middle childhood, 401-402
in preschool years, 242-244
Conceptual orientation shifts, 544-545
Concrete operations, 380
rules of, 538-539
Conditioned response, 92-93
Conditioned stimulus, 92-93
Conduct disorders, 509-512. *See also* Delinquent behavior
Confluence model, 472
Conformity, 429-430
in adolescence, 581-582
and morality, 546-547
Conscience, 271, 274. *See also* Morality
Conservation behavior: in adolescence, 542
compensation in, 397
cultural differences in, 477-478
equilibration in, 397-398
horizontal decalage in, 395
in middle childhood, 393-399
and number conservation, 235-236
in preschool years, 233-238
reversibility in, 396-397
training in, 396-399
transitive inferences in, 234-235
types of, 393-396
Construction standard theory, 219
Contingent response, 120
Continuity: of normal and abnormal behavior, 671-672
in personality development, 134-135, 586-588
Continuous growth, in adolescence, 634
Controlled observation, 19-22
Control variable, 24-25
Conversion reaction, 503-506
Correlative methods, 18-24
Creativity, 457-460, 625-626
Creode, 148
Criterion-referenced tests, 382-383
Cross-cultural studies: of adolescence development, 639-641
in Africa, 172-173, 477-479
of American Indians, 474-475, 477
in China, 320-322
in Europe, 172, 478
in India, 173
of infant development, 169-174

in Israel, 123, 173-174, 322-324
in Japan, 173
in Latin America, 170-172
of middle childhood development, 476-479
of preschool development, 314-324
in Soviet Union, 318-320
Cross-fostering method, 352
Cross-modal transfer, 226-227
Crying, 88, 114-115
Crystallized intelligence, 537-538
"Cuddlers," 132, 152
Cultural differences: in academic achievement, 474-475
in adolescence, 639-641
in conservation behavior, 477-478
in infancy, 169-174
in middle childhood, 476-479
in parental reinforcement style, 316-318
in pictorial depth perception, 478-479
in preschool years, 314-324
Cultural drift hypothesis, 192
Custodial retardates, 188

Dating, 575-578
Daycare, 174-178
Death: children's concepts of, 244, 328-330
talking with children about, 330-331
Decentering, 386
Decision time, 376
Deductive reasoning, 95
Delayed conditioning, 92-93
Delinquent behavior:
and depression, 506-507, 510-511
causes of, 668-670
characterological, 669-670
implicit fostering of, 511-512
incidence of, 667-668
intervention in, 670-671
nature of, 666
role-modeling in, 511
sociological, 668-669
Deoxyribonucleic acid (DNA), 41-43
Dependent variable, 24-25
Depression: in adolescence, 656-657
and delinquent behavior, 506-507, 510-511
masked, 506-507
in middle childhood, 506-507
nature of, 506

Detachment, in infancy, 129-131
Dexedrine, 345
Diasthesis-stress model, 353
Diet, *see* Nutrition
Differential methods, 26-30
Differentiated crying, 88
Differentiation, in physical growth, 69-70
"Difficult" children, 132-133
Discipline: in adolescence, 568-571
 behavior-directed versus person-directed, 276
 consistent versus inconsistent, 272-274
 instructive versus punitive, 274-276
 in middle childhood, 439-440
 and morality, 273-276
Discrimination learning, in preschool years, 231-233
Displacement: in phobic reactions, 357
 in school phobia, 499
Divergent thinking, 457
Doubt, sense of, 262
Down's syndrome, 47, 189-190
Drinking, *see* Drug use
Drop-outs, school, 626-629
Drug therapy: in childhood schizophrenia, 354
 in minimal brain dysfunction, 345-346, 359-362
Drug use: as distinguished from drug abuse, 595-596
 effects of, 596
 incidence of, 591-595
 patterns of, 595
 reasons for, 595-596
 regional differences in, 592-593
 stepping-stone hypothesis of, 593-595
Dysgraphia, 492-493
Dyslexia, 491-492

Early childhood education, 245, 324-328
Early maturation, 614-615
"Easy" children, 132
Echolalia, 195
Ectoderm, 43
Ectomorphy, 618-621
Educable retardates, 185-186
Education: early childhood, 245, 324-328
 historical approaches to, 4-9

sociocultural discontinuities in, 642-644
 see also Academic achievement; School
Educational planning: in learning disabilities, 494-496
 in minimal brain dysfunction, 347
Egocentric speech, 242
Egocentrism, in adolescence, 551-553
Ego-ideal, 271, 641
Embryonic development: abnormalities in, 47-49
 blastocyst period in, 43-45
 embryonic period in, 45-47
 fetal period in, 47
Embryonic period, 45-47
Endoderm, 44
Endomorphy, 618-621
Enuresis, 507-508
Epistomy, 58
Equilibration training, 397-398
External locus of control, 273-275
Extinction, 94

Factor analysis, 304-305
Familial retardation, 188, 192-193
Family constellation: and adolescent behavior, 633-638
 and infant behavior, 162-163
 and middle childhood behavior, 471-474
 and preschool behavior, 311-314
Family romance, 440
Family size: and academic achievement, 472-473
 and intelligence, 472-473
Father absence, 265-266, 313-314, 636-638
Fear of failure, 663-665
Fear of success, 665
Fears, childhood, 354-355
Feminized classroom, 441, 442
Fatal period, 47
Field independence/dependence, 29, 460-461
 and formal operations, 549
 sex differences in, 308-309, 465
Fire-setting, 511
Fontanelle, 71
Formal discipline, doctrine of, 4
Formal operations, 535, 538-553
 and adolescent attitudes, 549-553
 and combinatorial thinking, 542-544

and conceptual orientation shifts, 544-545
 and conservation behavior, 542
 and field independence/dependence, 549
 generality of, 547-548
 and impulsivity-reflectivity, 549
 individual consistency in, 548-549
 and language usage, 541
 logic of, 538-541
 and memory, 541-542
 training, effects of, 549
Friendships, *see* Peer relationships

Gametes, 36-38
Gazing, in infancy, 115-116
Generation gap, myth of, 597-599
Generative grammar, theory of, 86-87
Generosity, *see* Altrusim
Genes, in prenatal growth, 38-43
Genetic endowment: and intelligence, 150-151, 300-302
 nature of, 148-150
 and temperament, 152-155
Genotype, 40, 148-149
Gesell Developmental Scale, 169
Group formation: in adolescence, 575-576
 in middle childhood, 432-434
Growth rates, in infancy, 68-69

Habit disturbances, 507-509
Habituation, in infancy, 91-92
Head start programs, 16, 245, 324-328
Hearing, 83-85
Heritability, concept of, 300. *See also* Genetic endowment
Heroin, *see* Drug use
Holophrastic speech, 89-90
Home environment: deprived, 166-169
 and infant behavior, 163-169
 and intelligence, 163-164, 166-169
 intervention programs for, 164-166
Home Inventory Scale, 163
Home visitor programs, 164-165
Horizontal decalage, 395
Hormones, 526-527
Hostile aggression, 279-281
Hyperactive achild syndrome, 340. *See also* Minimal brain dysfunction
Hypochondriasis, 504-506

Identification: in academic underachievement, 661
and aggression, 279-282
and altruism, 282-283
and attitudes toward school, 420
in conduct disorders, 511
in conversion reactions, 505-506
as differentiated from imitation in drug use, 596
factors influencing, 278-279
and morality, 279
in phobic reactions, 356
and sex-role identity, 435-436
in suicidal behavior, 659-660
Identity formation: achievement in, 584-585
in adolescence, 582-585
and continuity in personality development, 586-588
crisis in, 584
diffusion in, 584-585
foreclosure in, 584-585
in infancy, 130
in middle childhood, 434-348
moratorium in, 584-585
nature of, 582-584
in preschool years, 526-258, 283,284
status, 584-585
see also Sex-role identity; Sexual identification
Imaginary audience, 551
Imitation: and aggression, 281-282
and altruism, 283
as differentiated from identification, 276-278
in infancy, 118
in preschool years, 281-283
Imminent justice, 399-400
Implicit fostering, 511-512
Impulsivity/reflectivity, 461-462
and formal operations, 549
sex differences in, 465
Independence:
adolescent strivings for, 564-566
ambivalent feelings about, 566-568
parental adjustment to, 439
Independent variable, 24-25
Individuation, in infancy, 129-131
Inductive reasoning, 95
Industry, sense of: influence of child's abilities on, 423-424
parents' influence on, 422-423
teachers' influence on, 424-426

Infantile autism: biogenetic theory of, 195
characteristics of, 193-195
as distinguished from childhood schizophrenia, 347-348
incidence of, 193
interpersonal isolation in, 193-194
language abnormalities in, 195
origins of, 195-196
outcome of, 196
preservation of sameness in, 194-195
psychogenetic theory of, 195
treatment of, 196
Inferiority, sense of: influence of child's abilities on, 423-424
parents' influence on, 422-423
teachers' influence on, 424-426
Instructive discipline, 274-276
Instrumental aggression, 279-281
Instrumental competence, 259-260
Integration, in physical growth, 69-70
Intelligence: and academic achievement, 454
and early deprivation, 166-169
and family size, 472-473
and home environment, 162-164, 166-169
and nutrition, 156-157
crystallized, 537-538
environmental contribution to, 192-193, 300-302
ethnic differences in, 302-307
fluid, 537-538
genetic contribution to, 150-151, 192-193, 300-302
group differences in, 302-307
growth and decline of, 536-538
heritability of, 301
racial differences in, 302-307
social class differences in, 302
see also Mental abilities
Intelligence quotient (IQ), 79, 221-222
Intelligence testing: in adolescence, 535-536
in infancy, 77-80
in preschool years, 220-224
Intelligence tests, standardization of, 27-28
Internal-External (I-E) Scale, 463
Internal locus of control, 273
Interpersonal isolation, in infantile autism, 193-194
Intimacy, needs for, 578-581

Klinefelter's syndrome, 48
Kibbutz, 123, 129, 173-174, 322-324

Lallation, 88
Language abnormalities, in infantile autism, 195
Language acquisition: in adolescence, 541
early speech in, 89-91
generative grammar in, 86-87
holophrastic speech in, 89-90
in infancy, 86-91
in middle childhood, 386-390
language utilization in, 386-387
and perceptual development, 227-229
pivot grammar in, 87
in preschool years, 238-242
referential communication skills in, 241-242, 389-390
stages of vocalization in, 88-89
syntactic knowledge in, 387-389
telegraphic speech in, 90
theories of, 239-241
Language acquisition device, 240
Language usage: growth of, 387
social class differences in, 314-316
Late maturation, 616-617
Latent stage, 437-438
Lead poisoning, 192
Learning: in infancy, 92-94
in preschool years, 231-233, 238-242
Learning disability: behavior therapy in, 496
causes of, 490-491
educational planning in, 494-496
incidence of, 490
kinds of, 491-493
and minimal brain dysfunction, 342-343, 491-493
parental reactions to, 494-
psychoeducational approach in, 495-496
psychological impact of, 493-494
treatment of, 494-496
see also Academic underachievement
Level of aspiration, 456
Liberated conviction, in interviews, 22-24
Locus of control, 273-274
measurement of, 462-463
variations in, 463

see also Morality
Logical manipulation, 385
Long-term memory, 229
LSD, *see* Drug use

Mainstreaming, 199-200
Malnourishment, *see* Nutrition
Marijuana, *see* Drug use
Masked depression, 506-507
Mastery, feelings of, 258-262
  and achievement motivation, 259
  and instrumental competence,
    259-260
  and self-esteem, 260-262
  sex differences in, 260-262
Masturbation, 579
Matching Familiar Figures Test
    (MFFT), 461-462
Maternal deprivation, 197. *See also*
    Social isolation syndromes
Maternal employment, 473-474
Medication, *see* Drug therapy
Meiosis, 38, 39
Memory: in adolescence, 541-542
  for early childhood experiences,
    231
  information processing in, 390-391
  information retrieval in, 392-393
  information storage in, 391-392
  long-term, 229
  in middle childhood, 390-393
  in preschool years, 229-231
  short-term, 229
Menarche, 531-532
Mental abilities: age differentiation
    hypothesis of, 536
  ethnic differences in, 304-307
  racial differences in, 304-307
  sex differences in, 307-308, 629-631
  see also Intelligence
Mental age, 79, 121
Mental growth:
  in adolescence, 535-553
  in infancy, 77-101
  in middle childhood, 380-402
  in preschool years, 219-244
  qualitative aspects of, 80-101,
    224-244, 383-402, 538-553
  quantitative aspects of, 77-80,
    220-224, 381-383, 535-538
Mental health services, priorities in,
    512-513
Mental hygiene movement, 14-15
Mental retardation:

biological causes of, 189-192
categories of, 185-188
causes of, 188-193
definition of, 185
educational planning in, 199-201
incidence of, 185
and institutional care, 187-188
mild, 185-186
moderate, 187-188
profound, 188
severe, 188
Mental tests, *see* Intelligence testing
Mesoderm, 45
Mesomorphy, 618-621
Metapelet, 123
Minimal brain dysfunction: age
    variations in, 343-344
  antisocial behavior in, 343
  behavioral impairments in, 340-341
  behavior therapy in, 346
  causes of, 344-345
  and diet, 344
  drug therapy in, 345-346, 359-362
  educational planning in, 347
  genetic contribution to, 344
  incidence of, 340
  and learning disability, 342-343,
    491-493
  maladaptive consequences of,
    342-344
  manifestations of, 340-341
  neurological signs in, 341
  parent counseling in, 346
  perceptual-cognitive impairments
    in, 341
  psychotherapy in, 346
  self-esteem in, 343
  sex differences in, 340
  treatment of, 345-347
Mitosis, 38, 39
Modern educational approaches,
    419-420
Mongolism, *see* Down's syndrome
Montessori method, 246, 326
Moral development, *see* Morality
Morality: adolescent development of,
    545-547
  age-related changes in, 399-401
  and conformity, 546-547
  and imminent justice, 399-400
  internalized standards of, 274-276,
    279
  locus of control in, 273-274
  preschool development of, 273-276

role of understanding in, 545-546
stages of development of, 400
Moro reflex, 72
Motor development: in infancy, 73-77
  in middle childhood, 375-378
  in preschool years, 213-219
Movement time, 376
Myelinization, 71

Natural childbirth, 61
Neural tube, 46
Neurosis, nature of, 502-503. *See
    also specific neuroses*
"Noncuddlers," 132-152
Normality, definitions of, 184-185
Norm group, 26-28
Norm-referenced tests, 382
Number, concepts of, 237
Number conservation, 235-236
Nutrition: and infant development,
    155-158
  and intelligence, 156-157
  and minimal brain dysfunction, 344

Obesity, 158-159
Observational research, 134
Operant conditioning, 93-94
Operant learning, 93-94
Orientation, in infancy, 91-92
Orienting behavior, in infancy,
    114-121
Orienting response, 91
Ossicles, 83-84

Parental authority, patterns of,
    568-571
Parent counseling: in infantile autism,
    196
  in minimal brain dysfunction, 346
Parent education, and infant
    stimulation, 101-106
Partial reinforcement, 272
Part-whole confusion, 195
Passive-aggressive
    underachievement, 663-666
Paternal deprivation, 265-266,
    636-638
Peabody Picture Vocabulary Test
    (PPVT), 222
Peer relationships: in adolescence,
    572-581
  and alienation, 431-432
  and belonging, 431-432, 572
  chumships in, 433-434

Peer relationships (*continued*)
conflicting needs in, 578-581
conformity in, 429-430, 581-582
and dating, 575-578
developmental changes in structure of, 432-434, 575-576
in middle childhood, 427-434
in preschool years, 268-271
and school drop-out, 629
stability of, 574-575
Perceptual development:
cross-modal transfer in, 226-227
decentering in, 386
in infancy, 80-86
and language acquisition, 227-229
logical organization in, 385-386
in middle childhood, 383-386
in preschool years, 224-229
search strategies in, 383-385
Permissiveness, parental, 260, 568-571
Person-directed discipline, 276
Phenomenalistic causality, 243
Phenotype, 40, 148-149
Phenylketonuria (PKU), 48-49
Phobias: disposition to, 355-356
nature of, 355
origin of focus in, 356-357
outcome of, 358
treatment of, 358
see also School phobia
Phonemes, 88
Physical development, secular trend in, 531-532, 553-554
Physical growth: in adolescence, 526-535
differentiation in, 69-70
direction of, 69
in infancy, 71-77
integration in, 69-70
in middle childhood, 374-380
in preschool years, 212-219
principles of, 68-71
rate of, 68-69
sequence of development in, 71, 527-529
sex differences in, 527-529
Physique: and popularity, 621-623
and temperament, 617-621
Pictorial depth perception, cultural differences in, 478-479
Pivot grammar, 87
Placenta, 43
Play, sex differences in, 309-310

Play observations, 29
Play therapy, 358
Popularity: in adolescence, 572-574
in middle childhood, 427-428
and physical attractiveness, 621-623
in preschool years, 270
Pregnancy, 49-61
fathers' reactions to, 50, 52-53
labor and delivery in, 57-61
as life crisis, 59-53
maternal emotions in, 53-54
maternal-fetal interactions in, 53-57
maternal habits in, 54-55
maternal illness in, 55-56
mothers' reactions to, 50-52
Rh incompatibility in, 56-57
Prenatal growth, 36-43
gametes in, 36-38
genes in, 38-43
Preschool Embedded Figures Test, 309
Preservation of sameness, in infantile autism, 194-195
Problem-solving, in infancy, 94-95
Projective methods, 28-29
Project Talent, 630
Promiscuity, *see* Sex behavior
Pronomial reversal, 195
Propositional logic, 539
Psychoeducational approach, in learning disability, 495-496
Psychopathic personality, 669-670
Psychosexual latency, 437-438
Psychotherapy: in academic underachievement, 666
in delinquent behavior, 670-671
in infantile autism, 196
in learning disabilities, 494
in minimal brain dysfunction, 346
in neuroses, 512
in phobic reactions, 538
in school phobia, 501-502
Puberty, 529. *See also* Sex characteristics, development of
Punitive discipline, 274-276
Purposivism, 244
Pygmalion effect, 426

Racial differences: in educational experience, 642-644
in intelligence, 302-307
in self-esteem, 639-640
Random answers, in interviews,

22-24
Range of reaction, 148
Reaction time, 376
Reading: instruction in, 403
learning of, 402-404
materials used for teaching of, 418
sex differences in, 418
Reasoning, in infancy, 95-98
Rebozo, 170
Recapitulation, doctrine of, 10
Referential communication skills, 241-242, 389-390
Reflexive smiling, 117
Remote Associates Test, 457-458
Research methods: causative, 24-26
correlative, 18-24
cross-fostering, 352
differential, 26-30
factor analytic, 304-305
interview, 21-24
observational, 19-22, 134
retrospective, 134
risk, 352
situation sampling, 20
self-report, 28
time sampling, 20
Retrospective research, 134
Reversibility training, 396-397
Reversal shift problem, 231-232
Rh incompatability, 56-57
Risk research, 352
Ritalin, 345
Rituals, in early childhood, 357
Role modeling, *see* Identification
Romancing, in interviews, 22-24
Rorschach Test, 28-29
Rubella, 55-56, 190

Sacks Sentence Completion Test, 103
Scheme, in interviews, 23
Schemes, 96
Schizophrenia: in adolescence, 654-656
biogenetic theory of, 350
characteristics of, 349
diasthesis-stress model of, 353
incidence of, 347
origin of, 350-353
psychosocial theory of, 350-352
see also Childhood schizophrenia
School: achievement in, *see* Academic achievement
children's attitudes toward, 415-422

drop-outs from, 626-629
educational policies in, 417-420
feminized classroom in, 441-442
influence of size of, 415-417
parents' attitudes toward, 420-422
sex-role influence of, 441-442, 623-625
traditional versus modern approaches in, 419-420
School phobia: acute, 501
behavior therapy in, 502
chronic, 501
consequences of, 501
displacement in, 499
as distinguished from truancy, 497-498
incidence of, 500
nature of, 496-497
origins of, 498-500
outcome of, 502
psychotherapy in, 501-502
separation anxiety in, 498-499
seriousness of, 500-501
sex differences in, 500
treatment of, 501-502
Scribble stage, 216-217
Search strategies, 383-385
Secondary circular reactions, 96
Secular trend, 531-532, 553-554
Security, needs for, 578-581
Selective smiling, 117
Self-concept: in adolescence, 632-633
cross-cultural studies of, 640-642
in middle childhood, 424
nature of, 378-380
in preschool years, 256-262
Self-esteem, 260-262
in black children, 475-476
in minimal brain dysfunction, 343
racial differences in, 639-640
sex differences in, 632-633
Self-report techniques, 28
Semi-clinical interview, 21-24
Senior neurosis, 665
Senorimotor period, 95-98
Sensory deprivation, 166-169, 197-198. *See also* Social isolation syndromes
Separation anxiety, 125-127
in school phobia, 498-499
Sex behavior: attitudes toward, 590-591
changes in, 588-589
incidence of, 598

and morality, 577
sex differences in, 577-589
Sex characteristics, development of, 529-531
Sex differences: in academic achievement, 464
in achievement-related behavior, 260-262
in adolescent maturation, 614-617
in aggression, 310-311
in babbling, 159-160
in childhood schizophrenia, 348
in cognitive style, 464-465
in dating, 576-577
in delinquent behavior, 667-668
in development of sex characteristics, 529-531
in field independence/dependence, 308-309, 465
in impulsivity/reflectivity, 465
in infancy, 159-161
in mental abilities, 307-308, 629-631
in minimal brain dysfunction, 340
in motor skills, 375-376
in physical growth, 374, 526
in play behavior, 160, 309-310
in reading, 418
in school phobia, 500
in self-awareness, 632
in self-esteem, 632-633
in sex behavior, 577, 589
in somatotype, 620
in sources of sex information, 577-578
in suicidal behavior, 658
in susceptibility to psychological disorder, 348
in preschool years, 307-311
in toilet training, 213
Sex information, sources of, 577-578
Sex role, school's influence on, 623-625
Sex-role identity: and attitudes toward school, 421
development of, 434-436
parental influences on, 435-438, 465-466
teachers' influence on, 441-442, 466-467
television's influence on, 467-470
see also Sexual identification
Sexual identification, development of, 283-284. *See also* Sex-role identity

Sexual identity, in the preschool years, 256-258
Sexuality, needs for, 578-581
Shame, sense of, 262
Short-term memory, 229
Sibling rivalry, 266-268
Sickle cell anemia, 49
Signaling behaviors, in infancy, 114-121
Simultaneous conditioning, 92-93
Situation sampling, 20
Sleeder effect, 636-637
"Slow-to-warm-up" children, 133
Smell, sense of, 85-86
Smiling, 117
Social class differences: in academic achievement, 456-457
in attitudes toward school, 421-422, 662
in delinquent behavior, 667-668
in infant behavior, 161-162
in intelligence, 302
in language usage, 314-316
in parental reinforcement style, 316-318
in preschool behavior
in school drop-out
Social comparison, 424
Social desirability, 28
Social isolation, in animals, 121
Social isolation syndromes: as distinguised from infantile autism, 199
and maternal deprivation, 197
and minimal brain dysfunction
nature of, 196-198
recovery from, 198-199
and sensory deprivation, 197-198
Socialization: nature of, 271
in preschool years, 271-284
role of discipline in, 272-276
role of identification in, 276-284
Social smiling, 117
Sociological delinquency, 668-669
Sociopathic personality, 669-670
Somatotypes, 618-621
Sondage, in interviews, 22
Space, sense of, 99-101
Special classes, 199-201
Spoiling, of infants, 135-136
Spontaneous conviction, in interviews, 22-24
Stanford-Binet, 27, 220-221, 307
Stepping-stone hypothesis, 593-595

Stranger anxiety, 123-125
Suicidal behavior: basic facts about, 657-658
  origins of, 659-660
  sex differences in, 658
Suggested conviction, in interviews, 22-24
Surgent growth, in adolescence, 634-635
Symbiotic mother-child relationship, 130
Syntactic knowledge, growth of, 387-389

Taste, sense of, 85-86
Telegraphic speech, 90
Television viewing: and aggression, 284-286
  and altruism, 286-287
  and sex-role identity, 467-470
Temperament: and child-rearing practices, 133-134
  genetic contribution to, 152-155
  and infant care, 132-133
  and phobic reactions, 356
  and physique, 617-621

in infancy, 132-134
  role of in conduct disorders, 511
  role of in neurosis, 504
Tertiary circular reactions, 97
Testosterone, 527
Thalidomide, 55
Thematic Apperception Test, 28-29
Therapeutic milieu, 354
Thumbsucking, 508
Tics, 503-504
Time, concepts of, 239
  sense of, 100-101
Time sampling, 20
Toilet training, 213
TRAD enrichment program, 326
Traditional educational approaches, 419-420
Trainable retardates, 187-188
Transductive reasoning, 243
Transitive inferences, 234-235
Transposition problem, 233
Trisomies, 47
Trophoblast, 43
Truancy, 497-498
Trust, sense of, 131
Tumultuous growth, in adolescence,

635-636. *See also* Adolescent turmoil
Turmoil, in adolescence, 584

Unconditioned response, 92-93
Unconditioned stimulus, 92-93
Underachievement, *see* Academic underachievement
Undifferentiated crying, 88
Unselective smiling, 117
Untrainable retardates, 188

Vision, in infancy, 80-83
Visual acuity, 80-81
Visual cliff, 83

Wechsler Intelligence Scale for Children (WISC), 27, 304, 307
Wechsler scales, 221-222, 535

Yolk sac, 45
Youth cultures, 572, 597-598

Zygote, 38, 43